THE PAPERS OF ALEXANDER HAMILTON

Museum of the City of New York

Alexander Hamilton
Engraving by William Rollinson, after wash drawing by
Archibald Robertson, *circa* 1794–1804

THE PAPERS OF
Alexander Hamilton

VOLUME XX
JANUARY 1796–MARCH 1797

HAROLD C. SYRETT, EDITOR

Associate Editors

BRIGID ALLEN

BARBARA A. CHERNOW PATRICIA SYRETT

 COLUMBIA UNIVERSITY PRESS

NEW YORK AND LONDON, 1974

FROM THE PUBLISHER

The preparation of this edition of the papers of Alexander Hamilton has been made possible by the support received for the work of the editorial and research staff from the generous grants of the Rockefeller Foundation, Time Inc., and the Ford Foundation, and by the far-sighted cooperation of the National Historical Publications Commission. To these organizations, the publisher expresses gratitude on behalf of all who are concerned about making available the record of the founding of the United States.

The Charles E. Merrill Trust, through a generous grant, has enabled the Press to publish this volume and three other volumes.

Copyright © 1974 Columbia University Press
International Standard Book Number: 0-231-08919-8
Library of Congress Catalog Card Number: 61-15593
Printed in the United States of America

ACKNOWLEDGMENTS

SINCE THE PUBLICATION in 1973 of Volumes XVIII and XIX of *The Papers of Alexander Hamilton* the editors have incurred new obligations which they wish to take this opportunity to acknowledge. Of the many individuals who generously shared their specialized information or provided assistance, the editors are especially indebted to

Mr. Roger Bruns, National Historical Publications Commission

Miss Doris E. Cook, Manuscript Cataloguer, Connecticut Historical Society, Hartford

Miss Joyce L. Eakin, Assistant Director, Libraries, United States Army Military History Research Collection, Carlisle Barracks, Pennsylvania

Mrs. Phebe R. Jacobsen, Assistant Archivist, Hall of Records, Annapolis, Maryland

Miss Mary-Jo Kline, Boston, Massachusetts

Mr. John Knowlton, Washington, D.C.

Professor Richard Kohn, Rutgers University, The State University of New Jersey

Miss Anne McCabe, Columbia University Libraries

Professor Joseph H. Smith, School of Law, Columbia University

Miss Sara M. Solberg, New York City

Miss Anne Stern, New York City

Mr. Samuel Streit, New York City

Professor David Syrett, Queens College, City University of New York

Professor A. P. Whitaker, Pitman, New Jersey

PREFACE

THIS EDITION of Alexander Hamilton's papers contains letters and other documents written by Hamilton, letters to Hamilton, and some documents (commissions, certificates, etc.) that directly concern Hamilton but were written neither by him nor to him. All letters and other documents have been printed in chronological order. Two volumes of Hamilton's legal papers, entitled *The Law Practice of Alexander Hamilton,* have been published by the Columbia University Press under the editorial direction of the late Julius Goebel, Jr. The third and last volume of this distinguished work is being completed by Professor Joseph H. Smith, George Welwood Murray Professor of Legal History of the School of Law, Columbia University.

Many letters and documents have been calendared. Such calendared items include routine letters and documents by Hamilton, routine letters to Hamilton, some of the letters or documents written by Hamilton for someone else, letters or documents which have not been found but which are known to have existed, letters or documents which have been erroneously attributed to Hamilton, and letters to or by Hamilton that deal exclusively with his legal practice.

Because all of Hamilton's significant legal opinions appear in *The Law Practice of Alexander Hamilton* they have been omitted from these volumes.

The notes in these volumes are designed to provide information concerning the nature and location of each document, to identify Hamilton's correspondents and the individuals mentioned in the text, to explain events or ideas referred to in the text, and to point out textual variations or mistakes. Occasional departures from these standards can be attributed to a variety of reasons. In many cases the desired information has been supplied in an earlier note and can be found through the use of the index. Notes have not been added when in the opinion of the editors the material in the text was either self-explanatory or common knowledge. The editors, moreover, have not thought it desirable or necessary to provide full annotation for Hamilton's legal correspondence. Finally, the editors on some occasions have been unable to find the desired information, and on other occasions the editors have been remiss.

GUIDE TO EDITORIAL APPARATUS

I. SYMBOLS USED TO DESCRIBE MANUSCRIPTS

AD	Autograph Document
ADS	Autograph Document Signed
ADf	Autograph Draft
ADfS	Autograph Draft Signed
AL	Autograph Letter
ALS	Autograph Letter Signed
D	Document
DS	Document Signed
Df	Draft
DfS	Draft Signed
LS	Letter Signed
LC	Letter Book Copy
[S]	[S] is used with other symbols (AD[S], ADf[S], AL[S], D[S], Df[S], L[S]) to indicate that the signature on the document has been cropped or clipped.

II. MONETARY SYMBOLS AND ABBREVIATIONS

bf	Banco florin
V	Ecu
f	Florin
₶	Livre Tournois
d.	Maravedis (also md and mde)
medes	Penny or denier
ps	Piece of eight

£	Pound sterling or livre
Ry	Real
rs vn	Reals de vellon
rdr	Rix daller
s	Shilling, sou or sol (also expressed as /)
sti	Stiver

III. SHORT TITLES AND ABBREVIATIONS

Annals of Congress — *The Debates and Proceedings in the Congress of the United States: with an Appendix, Containing Important State Papers and Public Documents, and All the Laws of a Public Nature* (Washington, 1834–1849).

ASP — *American State Papers, Documents, Legislative and Executive, of the Congress of the United States* (Washington, 1832–1861).

Carter, *Territorial Papers* — Clarence E. Carter, ed., *The Territorial Papers of the United States* (Washington, 1934–).

3 Dallas, *U.S. Reports* — A. J. Dallas, *Reports of Cases Ruled and Adjudged in the Several Courts of the United States and of Pennsylvania, Held at the Seat of the Federal Government. Vol. III, Second Edition. Edited, With Notes and References to Later Decisions, by Frederick C. Brightly* (New York and Albany, 1882).

Debrett, *A Collection of State Papers* — John Debrett, *A Collection of State Papers, Relative to the War against France Now carrying on by Great-Britain and the several other European Powers, Containing Authentic Copies of Treaties, Conventions, Proclamations, Manifestoes, Declarations, Memorials, Remonstrances, Official*

	Letters, Parliamentary Papers, London Gazette Accounts of the War, &c. &c. &c. Many of which have never before been published in England (London: Printed for J. Debrett, opposite Burlington House, Piccadilly, 1794–1797).
Dropmore Papers	*The Manuscripts of J. B. Fortescue, Esq., Preserved at Dropmore* (Historical Manuscripts Commission, Vol. 30), III (London, 1899).
Duvergier, *Lois*	J. B. Duvergier, *Collection Complète des Lois, Décrets, Ordonnances, Réglemens, et Avis du Conseil-d'Etat, Publiée sur les Editions Officielles du Louvre; de L'Imprimerie Nationale, Par Baudouin; et Du Bulletin des Lois* (Paris, 1824–1825).
Evans, *Holland Land Company*	Paul Demund Evans, *The Holland Land Company* (Buffalo, 1924).
Executive Journal, I	*Journal of the Executive Proceedings of the Senate* (Washington, 1828), I.
Goebel, *Law Practice*	Julius Goebel, Jr., ed., *The Law Practice of Alexander Hamilton: Documents and Commentary* (New York and London, 1964–).
GW	John C. Fitzpatrick, ed., *The Writings of George Washington* (Washington, 1931–1944).
Hamilton, *History*	John C. Hamilton, *Life of Alexander Hamilton, a History of the Republic of the United States* (Boston, 1879).
Hamilton, *Intimate Life*	Allan McLane Hamilton, *The Intimate Life of Alexander Hamilton* (New York, 1910).
Hamilton, *James Monroe*	Stanislaus Murray Hamilton, ed., *The Writings of James Monroe Including a Collection of His Public and Private Papers and*

Hamilton, *Reminiscences*	*Correspondence Now for the First Time Printed* (New York, 1898–1903). James A. Hamilton, *Reminiscences of James A. Hamilton* (New York, 1869).
HCLW	Henry Cabot Lodge, ed., *The Works of Alexander Hamilton* (New York, 1904).
JCC	*Journals of the Continental Congress, 1774–1789* (Washington, 1904–1937).
JCH Transcripts	John C. Hamilton Transcripts, Columbia University Libraries.
JCHW	John C. Hamilton, ed., *The Works of Alexander Hamilton* (New York, 1851–1856).
Journal of the Assembly of the State of New-York. At Their Nineteenth Session	*Journal of the Assembly of the State of New-York. At Their Nineteenth Session, Begun and Held at the City-Hall, of the City of New-York, on Wednesday, the Sixth of January, One Thousand Seven Hundred and Ninety-Six* (New York, 1796).
Journal of the Assembly of the State of New-York. At Their Twentieth Session	*Journal of the Assembly of the State of New York; At their Twentieth Session, the first Meeting begun and held at the City of New-York the first day of November, 1796; and the second at the City of Albany, the third Day of January, 1797* (Albany, n.d.).
Journal of the House, I, II, III	*Journal of the House of Representatives of the United States* (Washington, 1826), I, II, III.
Journal of the Senate of the State of New-York. At Their Nineteenth Session	*Journal of the Senate of the State of New-York. At Their Nineteenth Session, Begun and Held at the City-Hall, of the City of New-York, on Wednesday, the Sixth of January, One Thousand Seven Hundred and Ninety-Six* (New York, 1796).

King, *The Life and Correspondence of Rufus King* — Charles R. King, ed., *The Life and Correspondence of Rufus King* (New York, 1894–1900).

Martens, *Recûeil*, VI — Georg Friedrich von Martens, *Recûeil des principaux Traités d'Alliance, de Paix, de Trêve, de Neutralité, de Commerce, de Limites, d'Echange etc. conclus par les puissances de l'Europe tant entre elles qu'avec les puissances et etats dans d'autres parties du monde depuis 1761 jusqu'à présent*, 2nd edition (Göttingen, 1829), VI.

Miller, *Treaties*, II — Hunter Miller, ed., *Treaties and Other International Acts of the United States of America* (Washington, 1931), II.

"Minutes of the S.U.M." — MS minutes of the Society for Establishing Useful Manufactures, City of Paterson, New Jersey, Plant Management Commission, Successors to the Society for Establishing Useful Manufactures.

Monroe, *A View of the Conduct of the Executive* — James Monroe, *A View of the Conduct of the Executive, in the Foreign Affairs of the United States, Connected with the Mission to the French Republic, During the Years 1794, 5 & 6* (Philadelphia: Printed by and for Benjamin Franklin Bache, 1797).

Moore, *International Adjudications* — John Bassett Moore, ed., *International Adjudications: Ancient and Modern, History and Documents, Together with Mediatorial Reports, Advisory Opinions, and the Decisions of Domestic Commissions, on International Claims* (New York, 1929–1936).

Morris, *In the Account of Property* — Robert Morris, *In the Account of Property* (King & Baird, Printers, No. 9 Sansom Street [Philadelphia], n.d.).

Paltsits, *Farewell Address* — Victor Hugo Paltsits, ed., *Wash-*

	ington's Farewell Address (New York: Published by the New York Public Library, 1935).
Parliamentary History	*The Parliamentary History of England, From the Earliest Period to the Year 1803. From Which Last-Mentioned Epoch It is Continued Downwards in the Work Entitled, "The Parliamentary Debates"* (London, 1806–1820).
Parliamentary Register	*The Parliamentary Register; Or, History of the Proceedings and Debates of the House of Commons; Containing an Account of the most interesting Speeches and Motions; accurate Copies of the most remarkable Letters and Papers; of the most material Evidence, Petitions, &c. laid before and offered to the House* (London, 1775–).
PRO: F.O. (Great Britain)	Public Record Office of Great Britain.
1 Stat.	*The Public Statutes at Large of the United States of America* (Boston, 1845).
2 Stat.	*The Public Statutes at Large of the United States of America* (Boston, 1850).
6 Stat.	*The Public Statutes at Large of the United States of America* [Private Statutes] (Boston, 1846).
9 Stat.	*The Statutes at Large and Treaties of the United States of America* (Boston, 1851).
Steiner, *James McHenry*	Bernard C. Steiner, *The Life and Correspondence of James McHenry* (Cleveland, 1907).
Wharton,*Revolutionary Diplomatic Correspondence*	Frederick J. Turner, ed., "Correspondence of the French Ministers to the United States, 1791–1797," *Annual Report of the American Historical Association for the Year 1903* (Washington, 1904), II.

Wharton, *Revolutionary Diplomatic Correspondence* — Francis Wharton, ed., *The Revolutionary Diplomatic Correspondence of the United States* (Washington, 1889).

IV. INDECIPHERABLE WORDS

Words or parts of words which could not be deciphered because of the illegibility of the writing or the mutilation of the manuscript have been indicated as follows:
1. ⟨-----⟩ indicates illegible words with the number of dashes indicating the estimated number of illegible words.
2. Words or letters in broken brackets indicate a guess as to what the words or letters in question may be. If the source of the words or letters within the broken brackets is known, it has been given a note.

V. CROSSED-OUT MATERIAL IN MANUSCRIPTS

Words or sentences crossed out by a writer in a manuscript have been handled in one of the three following ways:
1. They have been ignored, and the document or letter has been printed in its final version.
2. Crossed-out words and insertions for the crossed-out words have been described in the notes.
3. When the significance of a manuscript seems to warrant it, the crossed-out words have been retained, and the document has been printed as it was written.

VI. TEXTUAL CHANGES AND INSERTIONS

The following changes or insertions have been made in the letters and documents printed in these volumes:
1. Words or letters written above the line of print (for example, 9th) have been made even with the line of print (9th).
2. Punctuation and capitalization have been changed in those instances where it seemed necesary to make clear the sense of the

writer. A special effort has been made to eliminate the dash, which was such a popular eighteenth-century device.

3. When the place or date, or both, of a letter or document does not appear at the head of that letter or document, it has been inserted in the text in brackets. If either the place or date at the head of a letter or document is incomplete, the necessary additional material has been added in the text in brackets. For all but the best known localities or places, the name of the colony, state, or territory has been added in brackets at the head of a document or letter.

4. In calendared documents, place and date have been uniformly written out in full without the use of brackets. Thus "N. York, Octr. 8, '99" becomes "New York, October 8, 1799." If, however, substantive material is added to the place or date in a calendared document, such material is placed in brackets. Thus "Oxford, Jan. 6" becomes "Oxford [Massachusetts] January 6 [1788]."

5. When a writer made an unintentional slip comparable to a typographical error, one of the four following devices has been used:
    a. It has been allowed to stand as written.
    b. It has been corrected by inserting either one or more letters in brackets.
    c. It has been corrected without indicating the change.
    d. It has been explained in a note.

6. Because the symbol for the thorn was archaic even in Hamilton's day, the editors have used the letter "y" to represent it. In doing this they are conforming to eighteenth-century manuscript usage.

THE PAPERS OF ALEXANDER HAMILTON

1796

Petition of Merchants and Masters of Vessels Trading from the City of Albany to the City of New York [1]

[New York, January 1–19, 1796]

To the Congress of the United States

The Memorial & Petition of the Subscribers respectfully sheweth

That Your Memorialists are Owners or Masters or both of coasting vessels employed ordinarily and exclusively in transporting articles between the Cities of New York and Albany.

That by a late Act of Congress constituting the City of Hudson a Port of Entry [2] the Port of Albany has been annexed to it as part of the same district and consequently severed from the District of New York.

That this arrangement subjects Your Memorialists to all the regulations of Vessels trading between different districts and to a variety of embarrassments and expences, in carrying on their business, very prejudicial to it, to which they were not before subject and which as they humbly apprehend can tend in no wise to the security or advantage of the United States their Revenue or Trade.

That while your Memorialists are disposed to see with pleasure any arrangement which accommodates their fellow Citizens of Hudson, they must unavoidably feel regret, if it must necessarily be at their expence—and if no expedient can be devised by which the evil to them can be remedied.

For though from Geographical position their annexation to Hudson may appear most natural; yet no connection can be more unnatural, when considered with reference to the Commercial relations of the two places. New York is at once the Market as well for the produce carried from Albany as for the supply to Albany & the Country connected with it of all the foreign and other articles of which they stand in need.

If it can appear expedient to Congress to reannex the port of Albany to the District of New York the inconvenie⟨nce⟩ under which Your Memorialists suffer will be removed—their business will return to its former situation—The City of Hudson will retain the convenience of being a port of Entry—all parties will be accommodated and no detriment as they with great deference conceive will ensue to the U States. In such an arrangement it will be of course necessary that the intermediate Waters should be common to the two Districts.

With this view Yr. Memoria[li]sts respectfully submit their case to the favourable consideration of Congress & pray that an Act may be passed accordingly.[3]

ADf, Hamilton Papers, Library of Congress.

1. On January 20, 1796, this petition was laid before the House and "referred to the Committee of Commerce and Manufactures; that they do examine the matter thereof, and report the same, with their opinion thereupon, to the House" (*Journal of the House*, II, 424). On March 24, 1796, the committee's report was referred to a Committee of the Whole House (*Journal of the House*, II, 480).

2. This is a reference to Section 4 of "An Act supplementary to the act, intituled 'An act to provide more effectually for the collection of the Duties on goods, wares and merchandise imported into the United States, and on the tonnage of ships or vessels.'" This section reads in part: "That from and after the last day of May next, there shall be established the following new districts and ports of delivery, to wit: In the state of New York, a district to be called the district of Hudson; which shall include the city of Hudson, and all the waters and shores northward of the said city on Hudson river, and the town of Catskill below the said city; and the said city of Hudson shall be the sole port of entry for the said district; to which shall be annexed the towns or landing-places of Catskill, Kinderhook and Albany, as ports of delivery only; and the collector for the said district shall reside at Hudson, and a surveyor to reside at Hudson, and another, at Albany, as is now by law established . . ." (1 *Stat.* 421 [February 26, 1795]).

3. Section 2 of "An Act in addition to an act intituled 'An act supplementary to the act, intituled An act to provide more effectually for the Collection of the Duties on Goods, Wares and Merchandise imported into the United States, and on the Tonnage of Ships or Vessels'" reads in part: "That from and after the last day of June next, the district of Hudson, in the state of New York, shall be confined to the limits of the city of Hudson; and all other places, which were, by the act, intituled 'An act supplementary to the act, intituled An act to provide more effectually for the collection of the duties on goods, wares and merchandise imported into the United States, and on the tonnage of ships or vessels,' included in the said district of Hudson, shall be annexed to the district of New York" (1 *Stat.* 476 [May 27, 1796]).

The Defence No. XXXVI [1]

[New York, January 2, 1796]

It is now time to fulfil my promise of an examination of the constitutionality of the Treaty.[2] Of all the objections which have been contrived against this instrument, those relating to this point are the most futile. If there be a political problem capable of complete demonstration, the constitutionality of the Treaty in all its parts is of this sort. It is even difficult to believe that any man in either House of Congress who values his reputation for discernment or sincerity will publicly hazard it by a serious attempt to controvert the position.

It is nevertheless too much a fashion with some politicians, when hard pressed on the expediency of a measure to entrench themselves behind objections to its constitutionality. Aware that there is naturally in the public mind a jealous sensibility to objections of that nature, which may predispose against a thing otherwise acceptable if even a doubt in this respect can be raised, they have been too forward to take advantage of this propensity without weighing the real mischief of the example. For, however it may serve a temporary purpose, its ultimate tendency is, by accustoming the people to observe that alarms of this kind are repeated with levity and without cause, to prepare them for distrusting the cry of danger, when it may be real. Yet the imprudence has been such, that there has scarcely been an important public question which has not involved more or less of this species of controversy.

In the present case, the motives of those, who may incline to defeat the Treaty are unusually strong for creating if possible a doubt concerning its constitutionality. The Treaty having been ratified on both sides, the Dilemma plainly is between a violation of the constitution by the Treaty and a violation of the constitution by obstructing the execution of the Treaty.

ADf, Hamilton Papers, Library of Congress; *The* [New York] *Herald; A Gazette for the Country,* January 2, 1796.
1. For background to this document, see the introductory note to "The Defence No. I," July 22, 1795.
2. See "The Defence No. XVII," September 22, 1795.

The VI Article of the Constitution of the U States declares that "that Constitution and the laws of the U States made in pursuance thereof, and *all Treaties made or which shall be made under the authority of the U States*, shall be the *Supreme law of the land*, any thing in the constitution or laws of any State to the contrary notwithstanding." A law of the land till revoked or annulled by the competent authority is binding not less on each branch or department of the Government than on each Individual of the Society. Each house of Congress collectively as well as the members of it separately are under a constitutional obligation to observe the injunctions of a preexisting law and to give it effect. If they act otherwise they infringe the constitution; the theory of which knows in such case no discretion on their part. To resort to first principles for their justification in assuming such a discretion is to go out of the constitution for an authority which they cannot find in it—it is to usurp the original character of the people themselves—it is in principle to prostrate the Government.

The cases must be very extraordinary that can excuse so violent an assumption of discretion. They must be of a kind, to authorise a revolution in government; for every resort to original principles in derogation from the established constitution partakes of this character.

Recalling to view, that all but the first ten articles of the Treaty are liable to expire at the termination of two years after the present War; if the objection to it in point of constitutionality cannot be supported, let me ask who is the man hardy enough to maintain that the instrument is of such a nature as to justify a revolution in Government?

If this can be answered in the affirmative, adieu to all the securities which nations expect to deri⟨ve⟩ from Constitutions of Government. They become mere bubbles subject to be blown away by every breath of party. The precedent would be a fatal one. Our Government from being fixed and limited would become revolutionary and arbitrary. All the provisions, which our Constitution with so much solemnity ordains "for forming a more perfect union, establishing justice, insuring domestic tranquillity, providing for the common defence, promoting the general welfare and securing the blessings of liberty to ourselves and our Posterity", evaporate and disappear.

Equally will this be the case if the rage of party spirit can meditate, if the momentary ascendancy of party in a particular branch of the Govt. can effect and if the people can be so deceived as to tolerate, that the pretence of a violation of the constitution shall be made the instrument of its actual violation.

This, however, cannot be. There are already convincing indications, on the very subject before us, that the good sense of the people will triumph over prejudice and the arts of party, that they will finally decide according to their true interest and that any transient or partial superiority which may exist, if abused for the purpose of infracting the constitution, will consign the perpetrators of the infraction to ruin and disgrace. But alas what consolation would there be in the ruin of a party for the ruin of the Constitution!

It is time to enter upon the momentous discussion. The question shall be examined under the four following views: 1 in relation to the theory of the constitution 2 in relation to the manner in which it was understood by the convention who framed it & by the people who adopted it 3 in relation to the practice upon a similar power in the Confederation 4 in relation to the practice under our present constitution prior to the Treaty with G B. In all these relations the constitutionality of that Treaty can be vindicated beyond the possibility of a serious doubt.

I   As to the theory of the Constitution. The constitution of the U States distributes its powers into three Departments—Legislative —Executive Judiciary. The 1. Article defines the structure and specifies various powers of the Legislative Department. The second article establishes the organisation and powers of the Executive Department. The third article does the same with regard to the Judiciary Department. The 4 & 5 & the 6 article, which is the last, are a miscellany of particular provisions.

The 1st article declares that "all *legislative powers* granted by the Constitution shall be vested in a Congress of the U States which shall consist of a senate & House of Representatives."

The 2d article, which organises and regulates the Executive

Department, declares that "the EXECUTIVE POWER shall be vested in a President of the U States of America" and, proceeding to detail particular authorities of the Executive, it declares that "The President shall have power, by and with the advice and consent of the Senate, TO MAKE TREATIES, provided two thirds of the Senators present concur." There is in no part of the Constitution an explanation of this power to make Treaties, any definition of its objects or delineation of its bounds. The only other provision in the constitution respecting it is in the 6th article, which provides, as already noticed, that all Treaties made or which shall be made under the authority of the UStates shall be the supreme law of the land; and this, notwithstanding any thing in the constitution or laws of any state to the contrary.

It was impossible for words more comprehensive to be used than those which grant the power to make treaties. They are such as would naturally be employed to confer a *plenipotentiary* authority. A power "to make Treaties," granted in these indefinite terms, extends to all kinds of treaties and with all the latitude which such a power under any form of Government can possess. The power *"to make,"* implies a power to act *authoritatively* and *conclusively;* independent of the after clause which expressly places treaties among the Supreme Laws of the land. The thing to be made is a Treaty; With regard to the objects of the Treaty, there being no specification, there is of course a *charte blanche*. The general proposition must therefore be that whatever is a proper subject of compact between Nation & Nation may be embraced by a Treaty between the President of the U States, with the advice and consent of the Senate, and the correspondent Organ of a foreign state.

The authority being general it comprises of course whatever cannot be shewn to be, necessarily, an exception to it.

The only constitutional exception to the power of making Treaties is that it shall not change the constitution; which results from this fundamental maxim that a delegated authority cannot rightfully transcend the constituting act unless so expressly authorised by the constituting Power.[3] A treaty for example cannot transfer the legislative power to the Executive Department nor the power of

3. At this point in the newspaper the following sentence has been inserted: "An Agent cannot new modled his own commission."

this last Department to the Judiciary; in other words it can not stipulate that the President and not Congress shall make laws for the U States; that the Judges and not the President shall command the national forces &c.

Again there is also a *natural* exception to the power of making treaties, as there is to every other delegated power; which respects abuses of authority in palpable and extreme cases. On natural principles, a Treaty which should manifestly betray or sacrifice primary interests of the State would be null. But this presents a question foreign from that of the modification or distribution of constitutional powers. It applies to the case of the pernicious exercise of a power, where there is legal competency. Thus the power of Treaty, though extending to the right of making alliances offensive and defensive, may yet [4] be exercised in making an alliance so obviously repugnant to the safety of the State as to justify the non observance of the Contract.[5]

Beyond these exceptions to the Power, none occurs that can be supported.

Those which have been insisted upon towards invalidating the Treaty with Great Britain are not even plausible. They amount to this, that a treaty can establish nothing between the U States and a foreign nation which it is the province of the legislative authority to regulate in reference to the U States alone. It cannot for instance establish a particular rule of commercial intercourse between the U States & G Britain because it is provided in the constitution, that Congress shall "have power *to regulate commerce with foreign nations.*" This is equivalent to affirming that all the objects upon which the legislative power may act in relation to our own Country are excepted out of the power to make Treaties.

Two obvious considerations refute this doctrine. One that the power to make Treaties and the power to make laws are different things, operating by different means, upon different subjects, the other, that the construction resulting from such a doctrine would defeat the power to make Treaties; while its opposite reconciles this power with the power of making laws.

4. In the newspaper, "might not" is substituted for "may yet."
5. At this point in the draft H wrote and crossed out: "But what are truly cases of this kind we may learn from the following passages from Vatel."

The power to make laws is "the power of pronouncing authoritatively the will of the Nation as to all persons and things over which it has jurisdiction"; or it may be defined to be "the power of prescribing rules binding upon all persons and things over which the nation has jurisdiction." It acts compulsively upon all persons, whether foreigners or Citizens, and upon all things, within its territory, and it acts in like manner upon its own citizens and their property without its territory in certain cases and under certain limitations. But it can have no obligatory action whatsoever upon a foreign nation or any person or thing within the jurisdiction of such foreign Nation.

The power of Treaty on the other hand is the power by *agreement, convention* or *compact* to establish rules binding upon *two* or *more* nations their respective citizens and property. The rule established derives its reciprocal obligation from promise, from the faith which the contracting parties pledge to each other, not from the power of either to prescribe a rule for the other. Tis not here the will of a SUPERIOR that commands, tis the consent of two independent parties that contract.

The means which the power of legislation employs are *laws* which it enacts, or rules which it enjoins, the subject upon which it acts is *the Nation of whom it is*, the persons and property within the jurisdiction of that Nation. The means, which the Power of Treaty employs, are *contracts* with other nations, who may or may not enter into them, the subject upon which it acts is the *nations contracting* and those persons and things *of each* to which the contract relates. Though a Treaty may effect what a law can, yet a law cannot effect what a Treaty may. These discriminations are obvious and decisive; and however the operation of a Treaty may in some things resemble that of a law no two ideas are more distinct than that of *legislating* and that of *contracting*.

It follows that there is no ground for the inference pretended to be drawn, that the legislative powers of Congress are excepted out of the power of making Treaties. It is the province of the latter to do what the former cannot do. Congress (to pursue still the case of regulating Trade) may regulate by law our own Trade and that which foreigners *come* to carry on with us, but they cannot regulate the Trade which we may *go* to carry on in foreign countries, they can give to us no rights no privileges there. This must depend on the will and regulation of those countries; and consequently it is the province of the power of Treaty to establish the rule of commercial intercourse *between* foreign nations and the U States. The Legislature may regulate our own Trade but Treaty only can regulate the mutual Trade between our own and another Country.

The constitution accordingly considers the Power of Treaty as different from that of Legislation. This is proved in two ways 1 that while the Constitution declares that all the *legislative* powers which it grants shall be vested *in Congress*, it vests the power of making Treaties in *The President* with consent of the Senate 2 that the same article by which it is declared that the EXECUTIVE Power shall be vested in a President and in which sundry executive powers are detailed, gives the Power to make Treaties to the President with the auxiliary agency of the Senate. Thus the power of making Treaties is placed in the class of Executive authorities;[6] while the force of law is annexed to its results. This agrees with the distribution commonly made by theoretical write[r]s—though perhaps the power of Treaty from its peculiar nature ought to form a class by itself.

When it is said that Congress shall have power to regulate Commerce with foreign nations this has reference to the distribution of the general legislative power of regulating Trade between the National and the particular Governments, and serves merely to distinguish the right of regulating our external Trade as far as it can be done by law, which is vested in Congress, from that of regulating the trade of a state within itself which is left to each state.[7]

This will the better appear from the intire Clause—"The Congress shall have power to regulate Commerce with foreign Nations and among the several States and with the Indian Tribes" which is the same as if it had been said "The whole power of regulating trade *by law* shall reside in Congress, except as to the Trade within a

6. In MS, "authorises."
7. At this point in the draft H wrote and crossed out: "This will be foreign to the regulation of the mutual trade between a foreign country and the U States, because this is not an object of law but of Treaty. It can only be done by mutual consent.
"The very turn of expression concurs with the reason of the thing to shew the sense of the provision The Congress shall have power to regulate Trade with foreign."

State, the power to regulate which shall remain with such state." But it is clearly foreign to that mutual regulation of Trade between the U States and other nations which from the necessity of mutual consent can only be performed by Treaty. Tis indeed an absurdity to say that the power of regulating Trade by law is incompatible with the power of regulating it by Treaty; since the former can by no means do what the latter can alone accomplish. Consequently tis an absurdity to say that the *legislative* power of regulating trade is an exception to the power of making Treaties.

Laws are the acts of legislation of a particular Nation for itself. Treaties are the acts of the legislation of several nations for themselves jointly & reciprocally. The Legislative power of one State cannot reach the cases which depend on the joint legislation of two or more States. For this, resort must be had to the *pactitious* power or the power of Treaty. This is another attitude of the subject displaying the fallacy of the proposition that the legislative powers of Congress are exceptions to or limitations of The Power of The President, with the aid of the Senate, to make Treaties.   Camillus

From William Duer [1]

New York, January 2, 179[6.] [2] "Will you pardon me, my dear Sir, in requesting of you if you can make it Convenient, a second Loan of Fifty Dollars in the Course Ten Days. I shall be able to return it to you, and first Fifty you was kind Enough lend me." [3]

ALS, Hamilton Papers, Library of Congress.

1. Duer, a prominent New York City businessman and speculator, had served as Assistant Secretary of the Treasury from September, 1789, to late March or early April, 1790. He was governor of the Society for Establishing Useful Manufactures from its inception in 1791 until the collapse of his financial affairs in 1792. On March 23, 1792, Duer was imprisoned for debt, and except for a short period in 1797 when he was released at H's intercession, he remained in prison until his death on May 7, 1799.

2. Duer mistakenly dated this letter "1795." At the bottom of the letter H wrote: "ought to be 1796 sent a Check upon Off of D & Deposit AH."

3. The following entry for January 2, 1796, appears in H's Cash Book, 1795–1804: "William Duer Dr. to Cash for this sum lent him some time since 50— for this sum lent this day ₱ note of this day 50—" (AD, Hamilton Papers, Library of Congress).

To Jonathan Dayton [1]

[New York, January 4, 1796. On January 15, 1796, Dayton wrote to Hamilton: "Your letter of the 4th is before me." *Letter not found.*]

1. Dayton, a veteran of the American Revolution, had served in the New Jersey Assembly in 1786, 1787, and 1790 and was a Federalist member of the House of Representatives from 1791 to 1799. Dayton was Speaker of the House from March 4, 1795, to March 3, 1799.

To Jedidiah Morse [1]

[New York, January 4, 1796] [2]

Sir

You will confer a favour upon me by permitting me to render you the little service which may be in my power on the present occasion & without compensation. Be assured it will give real pleasure & let that be my recompence.

Mr. Kent & I have conferred on your affair.[3] It is necessary for us to see the book in question in order to a safe opinion. Can one be had?

With respect & esteem   Sir   Your obed serv   A Hamilton
Jany. 4. 1795

ALS, Free Library of Philadelphia; copy, New-York Historical Society, New York City.
1. Morse, the famous geographer, was minister of the First Congregational Church, Charlestown, Massachusetts.
2. H mistakenly dated this letter "1795."
3. Morse had requested H's aid in a case of plagiarism. William Winterbotham, in *An Historical, Geographical, Commercial and Philosophical View of the United States of America and of the European Settlements in the West Indies* (4 Vols., New York: Printed by Tiebout and O'Brien, 1796; and London: Printed by J. Ridgway, 1795), had copied from one of the several editions of Morse's *The American Geography; or, A View of the Present Situation of the United States of America* (1st ed., Elizabethtown, 1789). Morse described the plagiarism in the following letter which he wrote to James Kent on January 21–25, 1796: "Agreeably to my engagement I forward to you & Mr Hamilton, 21 numbers of Winterbotham's History of America,

being all that have yet been printed in this country. I have marked with a pencil, what he has taken from my Work, referring to the pages from whh he has copied, so that in a short-time you can now examine for yourselves— by one taking the copy of Winterbotham whh I send & the other a copy of the last Editn. of the Geogy. Vol. I.—& I should be glad you wd. compare them that you might see the nature of the work & how artfully, in many instances, he has transposed paragraphs & sentences, apparently with a view to deceive the reader. In some instances the transposition of the matter of the Work has benefitted it—in more, it has in my opinion been altogether immaterial, & in not a few, it has injured the Work.

"You will easily perceive by a comparison of the titles & plans of the two works that they very nearly resemble each other. Winterbotham's title is a nearer imitation of the title of the *first* than of the *last* editn. of the Geogy. Wish you wd. have at hand the Old Editn when you make the comparison. You told me I think yt. you had it. It appears to me that Winterboth(am's) Work may not improperly be styled 'an ⟨en⟩largement of mine, on the same plan.' We both begin our Works with a 'history of the Discovery of America.' Instead of my *summary* he has given it at length—by inserting in connection, & *verbatim* 165 pages (the whole of Ch. 2d.) from the first Vol. of Robertson's America. We next proceed to give a 'General description of America.' Mine is pretty lengthy but his varied in matter, (though similar in arrangement,) by copious extracts from Clavigero, Franklin, &c. &c. We next give a Summary account of the Discovery & settlement of N. America; there we perfectly agree, as you will see, he having copied from me verbatim the whole of this Article & also the two next, viz. the general Description & Divisions of N. America. Then, instead of proceeding (as I have thought) in natural order, he passes over the particular Descriptions of the British Dominions & proceeds to the General Acct. of the U. States & leaves the forementioned Dominions to be described *after* the U.S. where he introduces my acc't of the British Dominions almost verbatim. In our general Acct of the U.S. you will see we also *exactly* agree for a great number of pages. He leaves out however, the *Natural history*, in what I conceive to be its proper place, but he inserts it verbatim in future numbers not yet printed in N. York. It is proper that you shd. know that I have the English Editn. of this Work complete, & that the N.Y. edit. has hitherto been taken p. for p. from it. You will notice his various enlargements on the Constitution, trade manufactures &c. of the U.S.—particularly that he has taken the whole of Mr. Hamilton's report on Manufactures, instead of an Abstract as I have done. In the history of the Revolution he has greatly enlarged having taken about 170 pages from Dr. Ramsay, in addition to what he has copied from mine. We then travel together through all the States & you will see that we very well agree. He has indeed, inserted the Constitutions, (two or three instances excepted) at large & also the census of the several states, where I have only given Abstracts. He has also made some additions to the History & many transpositions. And the Descriptions of N. Hamp Virginia & Kentuckey, he has almost entirely copied, from Belknap, Jefferson, & Imlay & Filson—from the former he has taken, in different parts of the Work about 230 pages & whh is nearly the Whole of his 3d. Vol. But I need not add the work will speak for itself. I have sd. thus much, merely to save you the trouble of a critical examination of the Work—or rather to assist you in it.

"After going over the Work with care & a great deal of labour, I have estimated that nearly a third part of the whole of Winterbothams work, has been copied verbatim from my work, or about 600 pages out of about 2000. In the 21 Nos. I send you, I make, of what is marked as from my Work, about 485 pages—& from the other 12, not yet printed about 114. The 4 Vols of Winterbotham contains 2023 pages. The first vol of my Geogy. contains 696 pages exclusive of yr Introduction, whh makes 62 pages—somewhat larger indeed than Winterbotham's, so that Winterbotham was not far from the Truth when he sd. that the whole of M's Geogy. was contained in his Work.

"Jany. 25th On running over this rough sketch of a Letter I find it contains some things not mentioned in the other—mixed with some that are. It may be of some use & I enclose it." (ADfS, Yale University Library.)

The books to which Morse is referring are: William Robertson, *The History of America* (London: Printed for W. Strahan; T. Cadell, in the Strand; and J. Balfour, at Edinburgh, 1777); Abbé D. Francesco Saverio Clavigero, *The History of Mexico* (trans. [from Italian] by Charles Cullen, 2 Vols., London: G. G. J. & J. Robinson, 1787); Benjamin Franklin, *Two Tracts: Information to those who would remove to America. And, Remarks concerning the Savages of North America* (London: John Stockdale, 1784); David Ramsay, *The History of the American Revolution* (2 Vols., Philadelphia: R. Atken & Son, 1789); Jeremy Belknap, *The History of New-Hampshire* (3 Vols.: Vol. 1, Philadelphia: Printed for the Author by Robert Atkin, 1784; Vol. 2, Boston: Isaiah Thomas and Ebenezer T. Andrews, 1791; Vol. 3, Boston: Belknap and Young, 1792); Thomas Jefferson, *Notes on the State of Virginia* (Philadelphia: Prichard and Hall, 1788); Gilbert Imlay, *A Topographical description of the Western Territory of North America; containing a succinct account of its Climate, Natural History, Population, Agriculture, Manners and Customs* (New York: Samuel Campbell, 1793); John Filson, *The Discovery, Settlement And present state of Kentucke: and An Essay towards the Topography, and Natural History of that important Country . . .* (Wilmington: Printed by James Adams, 1784).

The Defence No. XXXVII [1]

[New York, January 6, 1796]

It shall now be shewn, that the objections to the Treaty founded on its pretended interference with the powers of Congress tend to render the Power of making Treaties in a very great degree if not altogether nominal. This will be best seen by an enumeration of the cases of pretended interference.[2]

I The power of Congress to lay taxes is said to be impaired by those stipulations which prevent the laying of duties on particular articles, which also prevent the laying of higher or other duties on British commodities than on the commodities of other countries and

ADf, Hamilton Papers, Library of Congress; *The* [New York] *Herald, A Gazette for the Country,* January 6, 1796.

1. For background to this document, see the introductory note to "The Defence No. I," July 22, 1795.

2. The objections to the Jay Treaty which follow were made by Alexander J. Dallas in "Features of Jay's Treaty" (*Dunlap and Claypoole's* [Philadelphia] *American Daily Advertiser,* July 31, 1795.

which restrict the power of increasing the difference of duties on British Tonnage and on goods imported in British Bottoms.

II The power of Congress to regulate Trade is said to be impaired by the same restrictions respecting duties, inasmuch as they are intended & operate as regulations of Trade—by the stipulations against prohibitions in certain cases and in general by all the rights privileges immunities, and restrictions in Trade which are contained in the Treaty, all which are so many regulations of commerce, which are said to encroach upon the legislative authority.

III The power of Congress to establish a uniform rule of naturalization is said to be interfered with by those provisions of the Treaty which secure to the settlers within the precints of the British Posts the right of becoming citizens of the U States, and those which in certain cases remove the disability of alienism as to property.

IV The power of Congress "to define and punish piracies and felonies committed on the high seas and offences against the law of Nations" is said to be contravened by those parts of the Treaty which declare that certain acts shall be deemed piracy which constitute certain other things offences & stipulate the reciprocal punishment of them by each.

V It is also said that the constitution is violated in relation to that provision which declares that "no money shall be drawn from the Treasury but in consequence of appropriations made by law"—by those parts of the Treaty which stipulate compensations to certain Commissioners and indemnifications to G Britain in certain cases to be adjusted and pronounced by the commissioners, and generally by all those parts which may involve an expenditure of money.

[VI] [3] The constitution is said to be violated in that part which requires the establishment of *Officers* of the U States by law—by those stipulations of the Treaty which without the intervention of law provide for the appointment of Commissioners.

[VII] The Constitution is said to be violated in that part, which empowers Congress to dispose of and make all needful rules and regulations respecting the *territory* or other property of the U States, by those provisions of the Treaty which respect the adjustment boundary in the cases of the Rivers St Croix & Mississippi.

---

3. This number and those that follow have been taken from the newspaper rather than the MS, in which H made several mistakes.

[Lastly,] The Constitution is said[4] to be violated in its provisions concerning the Judiciary Department by those parts of the Treaty which contemplate the confiding to the determination of Commissioners certain questions between the two Nations.

A careful inspection of the Treaty with these objections in view will discover that of the 28 articles which compose it at least seventeenth are involved in the charge of unconstitutionality and these seventeen comprise all the provisions which adjust past controversies or establish rules of Commercial Intercourse between the Parties. The other eleven, whch are the 1st 10th 17th 18th 19th 20th 22d. 23d and 24,[5] except the first, are made up of provisions which have reference to War; the first merely declaring that there shall be peace between the parties. And it is a question even with respect to all of these, except the 1st & 10th, whether they also are not implicated in the charge; inasmuch as some of their dispositions have commercial relations. Is not this alone sufficient to bring under strong suspicion the validity of the principles which impeach the constitutionality of the instrument?

It must have been observed, that the argument in the last number is applicable to all the legislative powers of Congress, as well as to that of regulating trade which was selected by way of illustration, the ground of it being common to all. Indeed the instance of the regulation of Trade is that which is most favourable to the opposite doctrine—since foreign nations are named in the clause; the true intent of which however has been explained.[6]

The same reasoning too would extend the power of Treaties to those objects which are consigned to the legislation of individual states; but here the constitution has announced its meaning in express terms, by declaring that the treaties which have been and shall be made under the authority of the U States shall be the supreme law of the land *any thing in the constitution or laws of any state to the contrary notwithstanding.* This manifestly recognises the

---

4. H's first draft of the remainder of this sentence, which he crossed out, reads: ". . . to be violated in those parts which regard the Judiciary Tribunals and the modes of Trial to be observed—by those articles of the Treaty which refer to Commissioners the liquidation of mutual claims."
5. For the text of these articles of the Jay Treaty, see "Remarks on the Treaty . . . between the United States and Great Britain," July 9–11, 1795, notes 2, 48, 59, 63, 67, 71, 72, and 74.
6. See "The Defence No. XXXVI," January 2, 1796.

supremacy of the power of treaties over the laws of particular states and goes even a step farther.

The obvious reason for this special provision in regard to the laws of individual states is that there might otherwise have been room for question whether a Treaty of the Union could embrace objects the internal regulation of which belonged to the separate authorities of the States. But with regard to the U States there was no room for a similar question. The power of Treaty could not but be supposed commensurate with all those objects to which the legislative power of the Union extended.[7]

It is a question among some theoretical Writers—whether a Treaty can repeal *preexisting* laws? This question must always be answered by the particular form of Government of each Nation. In our constitution, which gives *ipso facto* the force of law to Treaties, making them equally with the Acts of Congress, the supreme law of the land, a Treaty must necessarily repeal an antecedent law contrary to it; according to the legal maxim that "*leges posteriores priores contrarias abrogant*" *[8]

But even in those forms of government in which there may be room for such a question, it is not understood that a Treaty containing stipulations which require the repeal of antecedent laws is on that account unconstitutional and null. The true meaning is that the antecedent laws are not *ipso facto* abrogated by the Treaty. But the Legislature is nevertheless bound in good faith under the general limitation stated in another place [9] to lend its authority to remove obstacles which previous laws might oppose to the fair execution of a Treaty.

---

* Posterior laws abrogate those which are prior to them if contradictory.

7. In the newspaper the following clause was added to this sentence: "which are the proper subjects of compacts with foreign nations."

8. See Blackstone, who wrote: "Where the common law and a statute differ, the common law gives place to the statute; and an old statute gives place to a new one. And this upon a general principal of universal law, that, '*leges posteriores priores contrarias abrogant:*' consonant to which it was laid down by a law of the twelve tables at Rome, that '*quod populus postremum jussit, id jus ratum esto*' " (*Commentaries on the Laws of England. In Four Books. By Sir William Blackstone, Knt. One of the Justices of His Majesty's Court of Common Pleas. The Tenth Edition, With the Last Corrections of the Author; Additions by Richard Burn, LL.D. And Continued to the Present Time, By John Williams, Esq.* [London: Printed for A. Strahan; T. Cadell, in the Strand; and D. Prince, Oxford, 1787], I, 89).

9. See "The Defence No. XXXVI," January 2, 1796.

One instance of the inconsistency prevailing in the arguments against the Treaty negotiated by Mr. Jay [is] observable on this point. To get rid of the infractions of our Treaty of peace with G Britain by certain laws of particular States, it is strenuously maintained that Treaties controul the laws of states. To impeach the constitutionality of the Treaty under consideration it is objected that in some points it interferes with the objects of state-legislation. The express provision of the constitution in this particular quoted above has not been sufficient to check the rage for objection.

The absurdity of the alleged interferences will fully appear by shewing how they would operate upon the several kinds of Treaties usual among nations. These may be classed under three principal heads 1 Treaties of Commerce 2 Treaties of Alliance 3 Treaties of Peace.

Treaties of Commerce are of course excluded, for every Treaty of Commerce is a system of rules devised to regulate and govern the Trade between Contracting Nations; invading directly the *exclusive* power of regulating Trade which is attributed to Congress.

Treaties of Alliance whether defensive or offensive are equally excluded, and this on two grounds—1 because it is their immediate object to define a case or cases in which one nation shall take part with another in war, contrary, in the sense of the objection, to that clause of the constitution which gives to Congress the power of declaring war, and 2 because the succours stipulated in whatever shape they may be must involve an expenditure of money—not to say that it is common to stipulate succours in money either in the first instance or by way of alternative. It will be pertinent to observe incidentally in this place, that even the humane and laudable provision in the XXII article,[10] which all have approved, is within the spirit of the objection; for the effect of this is to restrain the power and discretion of Congress to grant reprisals till there has been an unsuccessful demand of Justice.[11]

3 Treaties of peace are also excluded or at the least are so narrowed as to be in the greatest number of cases impracticable. The

---

10. In the newspaper this is incorrectly printed as "the seventeenth article."
11. In the newspaper the following sentence has been added to this paragraph: "Nothing can better illustrate the unreasonable tendency of the principle."

most common conditions of these Treaties are restitutions or cessions of territory on one side or on the other, frequently on both sides, regulations of boundary, restitutions & confirmations of property—pecuniary indemnifications for injuries or expences. It will probably not be easy to find a precedent of a Treaty of Peace which does not contain one or more of these provisions as the basis of the cessation of hostilities, and they are all of them naturally to be looked for in an agreement which is to put an end to the state of War between conflicting nations. Yet they are all precluded by the objections which have been enumerated—pecuniary indemnifications, by that which respects the appropriation of money; restitutions or cessions of territory or property, regulations of boundary, by that which respects the right of Congress to dispose of and make all needful rules and regulations concerning the territory and property of the U States. It is to be observed likewise that cessions of territory are almost always accompanied with stipulations in favour of those who inhabit the ceded territory securing personal privileges and private rights of property; neither of which could be acceded to on the principle of that objection, which relates to the power of naturalization; for this power has reference to two species of rights, those of privilege and those of property. An act allowing a foreigner to hold real estate is so far an act of naturalization; since it is one of the consequences of alienism not to be able to hold real estate.

It follows that if the objections which are taken to the Treaty on the point of constitutionality are valid, The President with the advice and consent of the senate, can make neither a Treaty of Commerce nor Alliance, and rarely, if at all, a Treaty of Peace. It is probable that on a minute analysis, there is scarcely any species of treaty which would not clash, in some particular, with the principle of those objections; and thus, as was before observed, the power to make treaties granted in such comprehensive and indefinite terms and guarded with so much precaution would become essentially nugatory.

This is so obviously against the principles of sound construction, it at the same time exposes the Government to so much impotence in one great branch of political power, in opposition to a main intent of the Constitution—and it tends so directly to frustrate one principal object of the institution of a General Government—the convenient management of our external concerns—that it cannot but be rejected by every discerning man who will examine and pronounce with sincerity.

It is against the principles of sound construction; because these teach us that every instrument is so to be interpreted, that all the parts may if possible consist with each other and have effect. But the construction which is combated would cause the legislative power to destroy the power of making Treaties. Moreover, If the power of the Executive Department be inadequate to the making of the several kinds of Treaties which have been mentioned, there is then no power in the Government to make them; for there is not a syllable in the constitution which authorises either the Legislative or Judiciary Department to make a Treaty with a foreign Nation. And our Constitution would then exhibit the ridiculous spectacle of a Government without a power to make Treaties with foreign nations: a result as inadmissible as it is absurd, since in fact our Constitution grants the power of making Treaties in the most explicit and ample Terms to the President with the advice and consent of the Senate.

On the contrary, all difficulty is avoided by distinguishing the provinces of the two powers according to ideas which have been always familiar to us and which were never exposed to any question till the Treaty with G Britain gave exercise to the subtilties of party-spirit.

By confining the power to make laws within its proper sphere & restricting its action to the establishment of rules for our own nation and those foreigners who come within our jurisdiction, and by assigning to the power of Treaty the office of concerting those rules of mutual intercourse and connection between us and foreign nations which require their consent as well as our own; allowing to it the latitude necessary for this purpose, a harmonious agreement is preserved between the different powers of the Government that to make laws and that to make treaties between the authority of the Legislative & the authority of the Executive department.

Hence Though Congress by the Constitution have power to lay taxes, yet a Treaty may restrain the exercise of it in particular cases: for a Nation like an individual may abrige its moral power by agreement and the organ charged with the legislative power of a nation may be restrained in its operation by the agreements of the Organ of its *Fœderative* Power or power to contract. Let it be remembered that the Nation is the CONSTITUENT; & that the Executive within its sphere is no less the organ of its will than the Legislature.

Though Congress are empowered to make regulations of Trade; yet they are not exclusively so empowered, but regulations of Trade may also be made by Treaty, and where other nations are to be bound by them must be made by Treaty.

Though Congress are authorised to establish a uniform rule of naturalization, yet this contemplates only the ordinary cases of internal administration. In particular & extraordinary cases, those in which the pretensions of a foregin Government are to be managed —a Treaty may also confer the rights and privileges of Citizens. Thus the absolute cession and plenary dominion of a province or district possessed by our arms in War may be accepted by the Treaty of Peace on the condition that its inhabitants shall in their persons and property enjoy the privileges of citizens.

The same reasoning applies to all the other instances of supposed infraction of the legislative authority; with regard to piracies and offences against the laws of Nations; with regard to expenditures of money; with regard to the appointment of officers; with regard to the judiciary tribunals; with regard to the disposal and regulation of national territory & property. In all these cases the power to make laws and the power to make treaties are concurrent and coordinate. The latter and not the former must act where the cooperation of other Nations is requisite.

As to what respects the Commissioners agreed to be appointed, they are not in a strict sense OFFICERS. They are *arbitrators* between the two Countries. Though in the Constitutions, both of the U States and of most of the Individual states, a particular mode of appointing officers is designated, yet in practice it has not been deemed a violation of the provision to appoint Commissioners or special Agents for special purposes in a different mode.

As to the provision, which restricts the issuing of money from the Treasury to cases of appropriation by law, and which from its intrinsic nature may be considered as applicable to the exercise of every power of the Government, it is in no sort touched by the

Treaty. The constant practice of the Government, the cause of an expenditure or the contract which incurs it, is a distinct thing from the appropriation for satisfying it. Thus the salary of a public officer is fixed by one law, the appropriation for its payment by another. So, the Treaty only stipulates what may be a cause of Expenditure. An appropriation by law will still be requisite for actual payment.

As to the disposal & regulation of the territory and property of the U States, this will be naturally understood of dispositions and regulations purely domestic and where the title is not disputed by a foreign power. Where there are interfering claims of foreign powers, as neither will acknowlege the right of the other to decide, TREATY must directly or indirectly adjust the dispute.

So far then is it from being true that the Power of Treaty can extend to nothing upon which, in relation to ourselves, the Legislative Power may act—that it may rather be laid down as a general rule that a Treaty may do between different Nations whatever the legislative Power of each may do with regard to itself. The exceptions to this rule are to be deduced from the unfitness & inconvenience of its application to particular cases and are of the nature of abuses of a general principle.

In considering the power of Legislation, in its relations to the Power of Treaty, instead of saying that the objects of the former are excepted out of the latter, it will be more correct, indeed it will be intirely correct to invert the rule and to say that the Power of Treaty is the power of making exceptions in particular cases to the power of Legislation. The stipulations of Treaty are in good faith restraints upon the exercise of the last mentioned power. Where there is no Treaty it is completely free to act. Where there is a Treaty, it is still free to act in all the cases not specially excepted by the Treaty. Thus Congress is free to regulate Trade with a foreign nation with whom we have no Treaty of Commerce in such manner as they judge for the interest of the U States, and they are also free so to regulate it with a foreign nation with whom we have a Treaty, in all the points which that Treaty does not specifically except. There is always therefore great latitude for the exercise of the legislative power of regulating Trade with foreign Nations notwithstanding any Treaties of Commerce which may be formed.

The effect of a Treaty to impose restraints upon the legislative power may in some degree be exemplified by the case of the compacts which the legislative Power itself makes, as with regard to the Public Debt. Its own compacts are in good faith exceptions to its power of action. Treaties with foreign powers for obvious reasons are much stronger exceptions. CAMILLUS

The Defence No. XXXVIII [1]

[New York, January 9, 1796]

The manner in which the power of Treaty as it exists in the Constitution was understood by the Convention, in framing it, and by the people in adopting it, is the point next to be considered.

As to the sense of the Convention, the secrecy with which their deliberations were conducted does not permit any formal proof of the opinions and views which prevailed in digesting the power of Treaty. But from the *best opportunity of knowing the fact,* I aver, that it was understood *by all* to be the intent of the provision to give to that power the most ample latitude to render it competent to all the stipulations, which the exigencies of National Affairs might require—competent to the making of Treaties of Alliance, Treaties of Commerce, Treaties of Peace and every other species of Convention usual among nations and competent in the course of its exercise to controul & bind the legislative power of Congress. And it was emphatically for this reason that it was so carefully guarded; the cooperation of two thirds of the Senate with the President being required to make a Treaty. I appeal for this with confidence to every member of the Convention—particularly to those in the two houses of Congress. Two of these, are in the House of Representatives, Mr. Madison & Mr. Baldwin.[2] It is expected by the adversaries of the Treaty that these Gentlemen will in their places obstruct its

ADf, Hamilton Papers, Library of Congress; *The* [New York] *Herald; A Gazette for the Country,* January 9, 1796.

1. For background to this document, see the introductory note to "The Defence No. I," July 22, 1795. The material within brackets in this essay has been taken from the newspaper.

2. Abraham Baldwin, member of the House of Representatives from Georgia.

execution. However this may be, I feel a confidence that neither of them will deny the assertion I have made. To suppose them capable of such a denial were to suppose them utterly regardless of truth.

But though direct proof of the views of the Convention on the point cannot be produced—yet we are not wholly without proof on this head. Three Members of the Convention dissented from the Constitution, Mr. Mason, Mr. Gerry & Mr. Randolph.[3] Among the reasons for his dissent published by Mr. Mason,[4] we find this clause "By declaring all Treaties supreme laws of the land, the Executive and the Senate have, *in many cases*, an *exclusive* power of *legislation*, which might have been avoided by proper distinctions with respect to Treaties, and *requiring the assent of the House of Representatives* where it could be done with safety." This shews the great extent of the power in the conception of Mr. Mason—that in many cases it amounted to an *exclusive power of legislation;* nor did he object to the extent, but only desired that it should have been further guarded, by certain distinctions and by requiring in certain cases the assent of the House of Representatives.

Among the objections to the constitution addressed by Mr Gerry to the legislature of Massachusettes[5] we find one to have been "that Treaties of the *highest importance* might be formed by the President with the advice of two thirds of a *quorum* of the Senate." This shews his idea of the magnitude of the power; and impliedly admitting as well as Mr Mason the propriety of this, he seems only to have desired that the concurrence of the senate should have embraced two thirds of the *whole body* instead of two thirds of a *quorum*. But how small and how insignificant would the power of Treaty be, according to the doctrine lately advanced with regard to its constitutional limit?

As to the sense of the Community, in the adoption of the Consti-

---

3. George Mason, Elbridge Gerry, and Edmund Randolph.
4. This is a reference to George Mason's "Objections to This Constitution of Government," dated September, 1787, and later printed in pamphlet form and in various Virginia newspapers. It is published and annotated in Robert A. Rutland, ed., *The Papers of George Mason, 1725-1792* (Chapel Hill, 1970), III, 991-94.
5. Gerry's letter to the Massachusetts General Court, October 18, 1787, is printed in *Debates and Proceedings in the Convention of the Commonwealth of Massachusetts, Held in the Year 1788, and Which Finally Ratified the Constitution of the United States* (Boston, 1856), 24-26.

tution ⁶ this can only be ascertained from two sources, the writings for and against the Constitution and the debates in the several state Conventions.⁷

I possess not at this moment materials for an investigation which would enable me to present the evidence they afford. But I refer to them, with confidence, for proof of the fact, that the organisation of the power of Treaty in the Constitution was attacked and defended, with an admission on both sides of its being of the character which I have assigned to it. Its great extent & importance—its effect to controul by its stipulations the legislative authority were mutually taken for granted—and, upon this basis, it was insisted by way of objection—that there were not adequate guards for the safe exercise of so vast a power—that there ought to have been reservations of certain rights, a better disposition of the power to impeach, and a participation, general or special, of the House of Representatives. The reply to these objections, acknowleging the delicacy and magnitude of the power, was directed to shew that its organisation was a proper one and that it was sufficiently guarded.*

* FŒDERALIST Vol II No ⁸ XLII has these passages "the power to make treaties and to receive and send ambassadors speak their own propriety. Both of them are comprised in the articles of confederation *with the difference only* that the former is *disembarrassed* by the plan of the convention of an exception by which treaties might be substantially frustrated by regulations of the states." This plainly alludes to the *proviso* which has been cited and commented upon. "It is true that when treaties of commerce stipulate for the appointment of articles the admission of foreign consuls may fall within the power of making commercial treaties" and in No. LXIV are these passages "the power of making treaties is an important one, especially *as it relates to War Peace and commerce;* and it should not be delegated but in such a mode and with such precautions as will afford the *highest security* that it will be exercised by men the best qualified for the purpose and in the manner most condusive to the public good." "There are few who will not admit that the affair of *Trade* and *Navigation* should be regulated by a system cautiously formed and steadily pursued and that both our treaties and our laws should correspond with and be made to promote it." "Some are displeased with it (that is the power of treaty) not on account of any errors or defects in it, but because as the treaties when made are to have the force of laws they should be made only by men invested with legislative authority"—"others though content that treaties should be made in the mode proposed are averse to their being the *supreme laws* of the land."

It is generally understood that two persons were concerned in the writings of these papers who from having been members of the convention had a good opportunity of knowing its views—and were under no temptation at that time, in this particular, to misrepresent them.

In the ADDRESS and reasons of dissent of the Minority of the convention of Pennsylvania to their constituents they state that they had suggested the fol-

The manner of exercising a similar power under the CONFEDERATION shall now be examined.

---

lowing proposition among others for an *amendment* to the constitution "That no treaty which shall be directly opposed to the existing laws of the United States in Congress assembled shall be valid *until* such laws shall be repealed or made conformable to such treaty." [9] This shews that it was understood that the power of treaty in the constitution extended to abrogating even *pr[e]existing* laws of the United States which was thought exception[a]ble; while no objection was made to the idea of its controuling future exercises of the legislative power. The same address states in another place that the President and Senate "may form Treaties with foreign Nations that may controul and abrogate the constitution and laws of the several states."

In the 2d volume of the debates of the convention of Virginia which is the only part I possess—there are many passages that shew the great extent of the power of treaty in the opinion of the speakers on both sides. As quotation would be tedious I will content myself with refering to the papers where they will be found (viz) 91, 99, 131, 137, 143, 147, 150, 186.[10] It will in particular appear that while the opposers of the constitution denied the power of the house of Representatives to break in upon or controul the power of treaties, the friends of the constitution did not affirm the contrary but merely contended that the House of Representatives might check by its *influence* the President and Senate on the subject of treaties.

6. In the draft H mistakenly wrote "Treaty." In the newspaper the word appears correctly as "Constitution."

7. At this point in the draft H wrote and crossed out the following: "I have not leisure at this time for a research into these; but I trust my memory with assurance, when I assert, that upon examination it will be found that the *manner of depositing* the Power of Treaty was attacked and defended, until mutual admission of its being of the character which I have ascribed to it as in the view of the General Convention. Its great extent, its effect to controul by its stipulations the legislative power were urged, not by way of objection to the quantum of the power, but by way of argument for further guards, by reservations of particular rights, by a better organization of the power to impeach by letting the House of Representatives into a participation in the authority to make Treaties. The reply to the objection acknowleging the magnitude of the Power, was directed to shew that its deposit was properly made and adequately guarded.

"Without going into detail on this part of the subject, I may refer to the   numbers of the Fœderalist and to the debates of the several conventions particularly that of Virginia. In the latter, the assailants of the constitution dwelt particularly on the danger that the power of Treaty might be exercised to alienate our right to the navigation of the Mississippi and insisted that some special provision ought to have been inserted for its security."

8. In the draft H omitted the remainder of this footnote, and it appears only in the newspaper.

9. *The Address and Reasons of Dissent of the Minority of the Convention of the State of Pennsylvania, to their Constituents . . . December 12, 1787* (Philadelphia: Printed by E. Oswald, at the Coffee-House, 1787). This "proposition," which is the thirteenth, continues with the following statement: ". . . neither shall any treaties be valid which are in contradiction of the constitution of the United States, or the constitutions of the several states."

10. *Debates and Other Proceedings of the Convention of Virginia, Convened at Richmond, on Monday the 2d day of June, 1788, for the purpose of de-*

To judge of the similarity of the provision it will be useful to quote the terms in which it is made. They are these "The U States in Congress assembled shall have the sole and exclusive right & power of *entering into Treaties and Alliances, provided that no Treaty of Commerce* shall be made whereby the legislative power of the respective states shall be restrained from imposing such imposts and duties on foreigners as their own people are subjected to or from prohibiting the importation or exportation of any species of commodities whatsoever." (Article IX)

It will not be disputed that the words "Treaties and alliances" are of equivalent import and of no greater force than the single word TREATIES. An alliance is only a species of Treaty, a *particular* of a *general*. And the power of *"entering into Treaties,"* which terms confer the authority under which the former Government acted, will not be pretended to be stronger than the power *"to make* Treaties," which are the terms constituting the authority under which the present Government acts. It follows that the power respecting treaties under the former and that under the present Governt. are similar.

But though similar, that under the present Government is more comprehensive; for it is divested of the restriction in the proviso cited above—and is fortified by the express declaration that its acts shall be valid notwithstanding the constitution or laws of any state. This is evidence, (as was the fact) of a disposition in the Convention to disembarrass and reinforce the power of making Treaties.

It ought not to pass unnoticed, that an important argument results from the *proviso* which accompanies the power granted by the Confederation as to the natural extent of this power. The declaration, that no Treaty of Commerce shall be made restraining the legislative power of a state from &c [imposing such duties and imposts on foreigners as their own people are subject to, or from prohibiting the importation or exportation of any species of commodities whatsoever] [11] is an admission 1 that the general power of entering into Treaties includes that of making Treaties of Com-

---

liberating on the Constitution recommended by the Grand Federal Convention to Which is prefixed, the Federal Constitution (Petersburg: Printed by William Prentis, 1789), II. H is referring to page numbers.

11. Space left blank in MS. The words in brackets have been taken from the newspaper.

merce, and 2 that without the limitation in the proviso, a Treaty of Commerce might have been made which would restrain the legislative authority of the State in the points interdicted by that proviso.

Let it not be said that the proviso by implication granted the power to make Treaties of Commerce; for besides that this is inconsistent with the more obvious meaning of the clause—the first article of the Confederation leaves to the States individually every power not *expressly* delegated to the U States in Congress assembled. The power of Congress therefore to make a Treaty of Commerce and every other Treaty they did make—must be vindicated on the ground that the express grant of power to enter into Treaties & alliances is a *general*, which necessarily includes as *particulars*, the various treaties they have made & the various stipulations of those Treaties.

Under this power thus granted & defined, the alliance with France was contracted; guaranteeing in the case of a defensive War her West India possessions, and when the *casus fœderis* occurs obliging the U States to make War for the defence of those possessions and consequently to incur the expences of War.[12]

Under the same power, Treaties of Commerce were made with France, the U Netherlands, Sweden and Prussia.[13] Besides that every Treaty of Commerce is necessarily a *regulation* of Commerce between the parties—it has been shewn in the antecedent comparison[14] of those Treaties[15] with the one lately negotiated, that they

12. This is a reference to the Treaty of Alliance between the United States and France, signed at Paris on February 6, 1778. Articles 1 and 7 of this treaty read: "Art. 1. If War should break out betwan france and Great Britain, during the continuence of the present War betwan the United States and England, his Majesty and the said united States, shall make it a common cause, and aid each other mutually with their good Offices, their Counsels, and their forces, according to the exigence of Conjunctures as becomes good & faithful Allies. . . .

"Art. 7. If his Most Christian Majesty shall think proper to attack any of the Islands situated in the Gulph of Mexico, or near that Gulph, which are at present under the Power of Great Britain, all the said Isles, in case of success, shall appertain to the Crown of france." (Miller, *Treaties*, II, 36, 38.)

13. For these treaties, see Miller, *Treaties*, II, 3–29, 59–95, 123–49, 169–83.

14. H is referring to "The Defence No. XXVII," November 28, 1795, which Rufus King wrote.

15. At this point in the newspaper the following note appears: "Articles 2d, 3, and 4th of treaty with France 2d, 3d, and 20th of treaty with Russia 2d, and 3d, of treaty with Holland 3d, and 4th of Treaty with Sweaden." See note 13.

produce the specific effects of restraining the legislative power from imposing higher or other duties on the articles of those nations than on the like articles of other nations and from extending prohibitions to them which shall not equally extend to other nations the most favoured; and thus abrige the exercise of the legislative power to tax, and the exercise of the legislative power to regulate Trade. These Treaties likewise define & establish the same case of piracy which is defined in the Treaty with G Britain.[16] Moreover the Treaty with France [17] as has been elsewhere [18] shewn with regard to rights of property *naturalizes* the whole French Nation.

The Consular Convention with France,[19] negotiated likewise under the same power grants to the Consuls of that Country various authorities and jurisdictions, some of the *judicial* nature, which are actual transfers to them of portions of the internal jurisdiction and ordinary judiciary power of the Country the exercise of which our Government is bound to aid with its whole strength. It also grants exemptions to French Consuls from certain kinds of taxes & to them and French Citizens from all personal services; all which are very delicate interferences with our internal police and ordinary jurisdiction.

Under the same Power the Treaty with *Morrocco* [20] was formed, which besides various other regulations relative to War and several relative to Trade, contains the rule that neither party shall make

16. See Article 16 (originally 18) and Article 21 (originally 23) of the Treaty of Amity and Commerce between the United States and France, February 6, 1778 (Miller, *Treaties*, II, 16, 19); Articles 15 and 19 of the Treaty of Amity and Commerce between the United States and the Netherlands, October 8, 1782 (Miller, *Treaties*, II, 72–73, 76–77); Articles 17 and 23 of the Treaty of Amity and Commerce between the United States and Sweden, April 3, 1783 (Miller, *Treaties*, II, 136–37, 142); Articles 17 and 20 of the Treaty of Amity and Commerce between the United States and Prussia, September 10, 1785 (Miller, *Treaties*, II, 174–77); Articles 20 and 21 of the Treaty of Amity, Commerce, and Navigation between the United States and Great Britain, November 19, 1794 (Miller, *Treaties*, II, 260–61). See also "Remarks on the Treaty . . . between the United States and Great Britain," July 9–11, 1795, note 70.

17. This is a reference to the Treaty of Amity and Commerce between the United States and France, February 6, 1778 (Miller, *Treaties*, II, 3–29).

18. See "The Defence No. XVII," September 22, 1795.

19. The consular convention with France was signed at Versailles on November 14, 1788. For the text, see Miller, *Treaties*, II, 228–44.

20. The Treaty of Peace and Friendship between Morocco and the United States was signed on June 28 and July 15, 1786. For the text, see Miller, *Treaties*, II, 185–227.

War, without a previous demand of reparation, in restraint of the general discretionary power of Congress to declare war.

Under the same power, the Treaty of Peace with Great Britain [21] was made. This treaty contains the establishment of a boundary line between the parties which, in part, is arbitrary and could not have been predicated upon precise antecedent right. It prohibits the future confiscation of the property of adherents to G Britain, declares that no person shall on account of the part he took in the war suffer any future loss or damage in his person liberty or property and provides for the release of such persons from confinement & the discontinuance of prosecutions against them. It is difficult to conceive a higher act of controul both of the legislative & judiciary authority than by this article. These provisions are analogous in principle to those stipulations which in the [second and ninth] [22] articles of the Treaty under examination have given occasion to a constitutional objection.

Under the same power, various Treaties with Indians inhabiting the Territory of the U States have been made establishing arbitrary lines of boundary with them; which determine the right of soil on the one side and on the other. Some of these Treaties proceed on the principle of the U States having conquered the Indian Country and profess to make gratuitous concessions to them of the lands which are left to their occupation. There is, also, a feature of importance common to these Treaties, which is the withdrawing of the protection of the U States from those of their Citizens who intrude on Indian lands [23] leaving them to be punished at the pleasure of the Indians.

Hence it appears, that except as to the stipulation for appointing Commissioners, the Treaties made under the confederation contain all the features identically or by analogy which are topics of Constitutional objection to the Treaty before us. They restrain in certain instances the legislative power to lay taxes. They make numerous and equivalent regulations of Trade—they confer the benefits

21. This is a reference to the definitive treaty of peace, signed at Paris on September 3, 1783.
22. Space left blank in the draft. For Articles 2 and 7 of the Jay Treaty, see "Remarks on the Treaty . . . between the United States and Great Britain," July 9–11, 1795, notes 3 and 39.
23. In the newspaper this word is "laws."

of naturalization as to property. They define cases of piracy—They create causes of Expenditure. They direct and modify the power of war. They erect *within the country* tribunals unknown to our Constitutions & laws in cases to which they are competent, whereas the Treaty with G B only provides for the appointment of arbitrators in cases to which our Tribunals & laws are incompetent. And They make dispositions concerning the Territory & property of the U States.

It is true, that some of the Treaties made under the former Government, though subsequent to the proposing of the articles of Confederation to the States, were prior to the final adoption of these Articles; but still it is presumeable that the Treaties were negotiated with an eye to the powers of the *pending* National Compact. Those with Great Britain Sweden Prussia & Morrocco & the convention with France were posterior to the completion of that Compact.

It may perhaps be argued that a more extensive construction of the power of Treaty in the confederation than in our present constitution was countenanced by the Union in the same body of legislative powers, with the power of Treaty. But this argument can have no force when it is considered that the principal legislative powers with regard to the objects embraced by the Treaties of Congress were not vested in that body but remained with the individual states. Such are the power of *specific* taxation, the power of regulating Trade, the power of naturalization &c.

If in theory, the objects of legislative power are excepted out of the power of Treaty, this must have been equally, at least, the case with the legislative powers of the state Governments, as with those of the U States. Indeed the argument was much stronger for the exception, where distinct Governments were the depositories of the legislative power than where the same Government was the depository of that power and of the power of Treaty. Nothing but the intrinsic force of the power of Treaty could have enabled it to penetrate the separate spheres of the State Governments. The practice under the confederation, for so many years acquiesced in by all the states is therefore a conclusive illustration of the Power of Treaty and an irresistible refutation of the novel and preposterous doctrine which impeaches the Constitutionality of that lately negotiated. If the natural import of the terms used in the Constitution were less clear and decisive, than they are, that practice is a commentary upon them and fixes their sense. For the sense, in which certain terms were practiced upon a prior Constitution of Government, must be presumed to have been intended in using the like terms in a subsequent Constitution of Government for the same Nation.

Accordingly, the practice under the present Govt. before the late Treaty has corresponded with that sense.

Our treaties with several Indian Nations regulate and change the boundaries between them & the U States—and in addition to compensations in Gross they stipulate the payment of certain specific & pepetual annuities.[24] Thus a Treaty in August 1790 with the Creeks [25] (Article 4th) [26] promises them the yearly sum of One thousand five hundred Dollars. And similar features are found in subsequent Treaties with the Six Nations,[27] the Cherookees [28] and the North Western Indians. This last has *just* been ratified by the *unanimous voice* of the Senate.[29] It stipulates an annuity of 9500 Dollars, and relinquishes to the Indians a large tract of land which they had by preceding treaties ceded to the U States.

Hence we find that our former Treaties under the present Government as well as one subsequent to that under consideration contradict the doctrine set up against its constitutionality—in the important particulars of making dispositions concerning the Territory and property of the U States—and binding them to raise and pay money. These Treaties have not only been made by the President and ratified by the Senate, without any impeachment of their constitutionality but the House of Representatives has heretofore con-

---

24. In the margin opposite this sentence H wrote and crossed out: "unconstitutional appoint of Mr. Jay."

25. The treaty of peace and friendship between the United States and the Creeks was signed on August 7, 1790. For the text, see *ASP, Indian Affairs*, I, 81–82.

26. In the newspaper this is incorrectly cited as "Article 5th."

27. The Senate agreed to this article of agreement with the Iroquois League on March 26, 1792 (*Executive Journal*, I, 116).

28. For the treaty of peace and friendship with the Cherokees, dated July 2, 1791, see *ASP, Indian Affairs*, I, 124–25.

29. On August 3, 1795, Major General Anthony Wayne concluded a treaty with the Indians in the Northwest Territory at Greenville. It was approved by the Senate on December 22, 1795 (*Executive Journal*, I, 197). For the text, see Carter, *Territorial Papers*, II, 525–35.

curred and without objection in carrying them into effect by the requisite appropriation of money.

[The consular *convention* with France stands in a peculiar predicament. It was negotiated under the former government, and ratified under the present; and so may be regarded as a treaty of both governments, illustrative of the extent of the power of Treaty in both. The delicate and even the extraordinary nature of the provisions it contains have been adverted to. Though all reflecting men have thought ill of the propriety of some of them, as inconveniently breaking in upon our interior administration, legislative, executive and judiciary; only acquiesing in them from the difficulty of getting rid of stipulations entered into by our public agents under competent powers, yet no question has been heard about their constitutionality. And Congress have by law assisted their execution by making our judicial tribunals and the public force of the country auxiliary to the decrees of the foreign tribunals which they authorize within our territory.

If it should be said, that our constitution by making all former treaties and engagements as obligatory upon the United States under that constitution, as they were under the confederation, rendered the ratification of the convention a matter of necessity—the answer is that either the engagements which it contracted were already conclusive or they were not—if the former, there was no need of a ratification, of the latter, there was no absolute obligation to it. And in every supposition, a ratification by the President with the consent of the Senate could have been predicated only upon the power given in the present constitution in relation to treaties; and to have any validity must have been within the limit of that power.

But it has been heretofore seen that the inference from this instrument is no less strong, if referred to the power under the confederation, than if referred to the power under the present Constitution.] [30]

How happens it that all these Invasions of the Constitution if they were such were never discovered, and that the departments of the Government & all parties in the public councils should have cooperated in giving them a sanction. Does it not prove that ALL were convinced that the power of Treaty applied in our exterior relations

30. The three preceding paragraphs do not appear in the draft and have been taken from the newspaper.

to objects which in the ordinary course of internal administration & in reference to ourselves were of the cognizance of the legislative power? and particularly that the former was competent to bind the latter in the delicate points of raising and appropriating money? If competent to this, what legislative power can be more sacred, more out its reach?

Let me now ask (and a very solemn question it is, especially for those who are bound by oath to support the Constitution)— Has it not been demonstrated that the provisions in the Treaty are justified by the true & manifest interpretation of the Constitution sanctioned by the practice upon a similar power under the Confederation, and by the practice in other instances under the present government? [31]

If this has been demonstrated, what shall we think of the candor & sincerity of the objections which have been erected on the basis of a contrary supposition? Do they not unequivocally prove that the adversaries of the Treaty have been resolved to discredit it by every artifice they could invent? That they have not had truth for their guide & consequently are very unfit guides for the public Opinion, very unsafe guardians of the public weal?

It is really painful & disgusting to observe sophisms so miserable as those which question the constitutionality of the Treaty retailed to an enlightened people and insisted upon with so much seeming fervency & earnestness. It is impossible not to bestow on sensible men who act this part—the imputation of hypochrisy. The absurdity of the doctrine is too glaring to permit even Charity itself to suppose it sincere. If it were possible to imagine that a majority in any branch of our Government could betray the Constitution and trifle with the Nation so far as to adopt and act upon such a doctrine—it would be time to despair of the Republic.[32]

There would be no security at home, no respectability abroad. Our Constitutional Charter would become a dead letter & The

---

31. In the margin opposite the end of this paragraph H wrote and crossed out: "Note Treaty with France &ca. made prior to final ratification of Confed."

At this point in the draft H wrote and crossed out: "It is certain also that they are conformable with the sense of the Convention who digested the plan of that Government and that they are supported by the sense of the Nation for the long period of Eighteen years."

32. In the margin opposite this paragraph H wrote and crossed out "Algerines."

Organ of our Government for foreign Affairs would be treated with derision whenever he should hereafter talk of negotiation or Treaty. May the Great Ruler of Nations avert from our Country so greivous a calamity! * *Camillus*

* It is very probable that a Treaty with Algiers is now on its way to the U States which may be expected to contain similar stipulations with that with Morocco.³³ This Treaty which will have cost the U States no trifling sum & will [be] of very great value to our Trade must fall equally on the doctrine which I oppose.

33. See note 20. The Treaty of Peace and Amity between the United States and Algiers had been signed on September 5, 1795. It was submitted to the Senate on February 16, 1796, and consented to by the Senate on March 2, 1796 (Miller, *Treaties*, II, 275). Article 22 of the treaty reads: "Should any disturbance take place between the Citizens of ye United States & the Subjects of this Regency or break any Article of this Treaty War shall not be Declared immediately but every thing shall be Searched into regularly. the Party Injured shall be made Repairation. . . ." A similar provision was made in Article 24 of the Treaty of Peace and Friendship between the United States and Morocco (Miller, *Treaties*, II, 217).

Certificate on Robert Lenox ¹

[New York, January 11, 1796]

I certify, that I have an impression on my memory as strong as a circumstance so remote, and of such a nature admits, of my having towards the close of our late war with Great Britain, understood from some of the officers charged on the part of the United States, with the affair of prisoners and from officers of our army, who had been prisoners with the British, that Robert Lenox, now of this city, merchant, then having some connections with some of the British commissaries' of prisoners, had repeatedly manifested a kind and accommodating disposition towards our prisoners; an impression, which upon our regaining possession of New York, and my becoming acquainted with Mr. Lenox, induced me to shew him marks of cordiality and esteem.

ALEXANDER HAMILTON.
New York, Jan. 11, 1796.

[New York] *American Citizen and General Advertiser*, March 5, 1802.

1. Lenox, a native of Scotland, had migrated to New York City, where he became a prominent merchant and investor in real estate. He remained in New York City during part of the American Revolution and served the British as a clerk in the office of commissary of naval prisoners.

Lenox requested the above testimonial from H because his conduct during the American Revolution had recently been criticized. On December 25, 1795, in an article signed "One of the People," the following charge was made against Lenox: "It is not so remarkable, that Lenox should sport with the liberty of an American citizen, whose employment in this city in the American Revolution, as I have been informed, was to embitter the miseries of the unfortunate American prisoners on board the memorable prison-ship, called the Old Jersey, that eternal disgrace to British humanity, and instrument of *tory* barbarities and murders. The way I came to know such a political paricide resided in this city (if I may be allowed the expression) as Robert Lenox, was a person's mentioning in the country, to his great surprize, that he heard Robert Lenox was chosen an Alderman in the city of New-York. A person replied, he was sorry to hear of such an appointment, being impolitic and derogatory to the government, remarking that in consequence of refusing Lenox to inlist in the British army, he suffered three weeks longer confinement on board said prison-ship, suffering additional cruelties, and threatened with death if he would not comply; at which time, as he stated, there were from twenty to thirty dying daily with starvation, &c. to compel the prisoners to inlist, but with that firmness Americans possessed at that period, inspired with an enthusiastic zeal to establish the liberties of their country, the patriot informed Lenox, that he would not forsake his country, if he sacrificed his life; but happily for this virtuous freeman he was exchanged in three weeks after this base overture of the said Lenox, to force him to inlist. This tried patriot further observed, that he had once preferred death, rather than submit to this open enemy of his country under British tyranny, a diminution of which fortitude should never happen, by submitting to any exercise of power by Lenox over him in a free government, if it cost him his life, as a test of his unimpaired attachment to his country, base in gratitude to appoint such a character to an office in the government, to tyrannize over freemen of this description" (*The* [New York] *Argus, or Greenleaf's New Daily Advertiser*, December 25, 1795). According to Alfred F. Young, *The Democratic Republicans of New York: The Origins, 1763–1797* (Chapel Hill, 1967), 476, note 43, William Keteltas was the author of the article signed "One of the People." Lenox answered the charge in the same newspaper on December 28, 1795. See also *The* [New York] *Argus, or Greenleaf's New Daily Advertiser*, December 23, 30, 1795.

The attack on Lenox by "One of the People" occurred at this time because Lenox, a New York City alderman and director of the New York branch of the Bank of the United States, had been recently involved in convicting two Brooklyn ferrymen, charged with insulting Gabriel Furman, a merchant and alderman in New York City, and threatening the life of high constable James Culbertson. Thomas Burk and Timothy Crady, both Irish immigrants, had operated a ferry, which was owned by John Hicks, between lower Manhattan and Brooklyn. In November, 1795, following their arrest on the order of Furman for insulting him in a quarrel over their refusal to operate the ferry for him outside the scheduled hours, they had been committed to jail. Their trial, without a jury and with Furman as the sole witness, was held before Federalist magistrates in the Court of General Sessions. The court consisted of Mayor Richard Varick and four aldermen, one of whom was Lenox. Convicted on two formal charges, Burk and Crady were each sentenced to two months' hard labor, and Crady was also sentenced to twenty-five lashes. A month later both men escaped from jail and fled to Pennsylvania.

The case was then taken up by William Keteltas, a young Republican lawyer, who used it as a reason for attacking the "tyranny and partiality" of the court. In February, 1796, he criticized the New York Assembly, which had refused his petition that the magistrates be impeached, and he was charged by the Assembly with slander. By April, 1796, the case had become a major political issue. Keteltas, released from jail, where he had been committed for contempt of the Assembly, ran for that body. In the ensuing election Keteltas lost, but the Federalists won by the fairly narrow margin of 2,250 votes to 1,775. Later in the year H served as co-counsel with Keteltas in a damage suit which the latter had filed against the magistrates on behalf of Burk (Crady having died) in the New York Supreme Court. H achieved a compromise by arranging for the magistrates to settle with Burk out of court. In December, 1797, H served as chief counsel in the Circuit Court to William North, the former speaker of the Assembly, against whom Keteltas had brought a suit for arrest by improper procedures. The case was tried before a Federalist judge, John Sloss Hobart, without a jury and with Keteltas acting as his own advocate. Largely at H's instigation, the suit was dismissed. See *The* [New York] *Argus, or Greenleaf's New Daily Advertiser,* December 23, 25, 28, 30, 1795; *The* [New York] *Time Piece,* December 22, 1797. For a full account of these cases and their political repercussions, see Young, *The Democratic Republicans of New York,* 476–92; Sidney I. Pomerantz, *New York, an American City, 1783–1803: A Study of Urban Life* (Port Washington, New York, 1965 [2nd ed.]), 264–67.

Although H's testimonial for Lenox was written in 1796, Lenox did not use it until six years later. On March 1, 1802, the [New York] *American Citizen and General Advertiser,* which was a continuation of *The* [New York] *Argus, or Greenleaf's New Daily Advertiser,* revived the charge that Lenox had been guilty of cruelty to American prisoners during the Revolution. In answer to the charge, Lenox published a number of testimonials, among them the certificate by H printed above. Lenox's letter, addressed "To the Editors of the American Citizen," which enclosed the testimonials, reads: "In order to refute an attack made in some of your late papers on my name, and renewed in your paper of this morning with much violence, I request you to publish the inclosed papers.

"They were collected at the time they bear date, and some of them sent without application from me, for the purpose of being laid before the public on a similar occasion; but were then with-held.

"To them I will add my own declaration—that I never was in New York but a few weeks previous to the summer of 1779—that I never held a commission under his Britannic majesty—or any office or employment on board the prison ship Jersey—or any agency in victualling prisoners—or of any kind whatever, other than as a clerk in the commissary's office, and occasionally going with flags of truce: But, that a great part of my time was taken up about my own concerns, having been nearly one half the period from the year 1779 to 1783 in the West Indies, at Charleston, and elsewhere." ([New York] *American Citizen and General Advertiser,* March 5, 1802.)

From William Heth[1]

Virginia 11th January 1796

My dear Sir

I should have written to you long since, but from some doubts that a packet to *you* might excite curiosity, in your *Post Office,* not knowing of *what kidney*, your post-master & his clerks may be.

Capt Stratton² who now takes charge of this, promises to deliver it in person, and tho it is without Signature, you will be at no loss to guess from whom it comes, as it serves to enclose the piece mentioned to you last Winter, written by ——— you know who.³ Had it been forwarded to you when in Office, *even* Coll Hamilton, might for a moment have attributed it to views, & motives, by which the Author is incapable of being actuated. But admit that he *then had* motives for flattering you, he can have none now, and therefore he does not blush to say, that he loves you as a private friend; admires you as an able & most faithful public servant; and venerates you as a Man of most superior talents.⁴

A single line from you, informing of the same recd of this, will be very pleasing. The author will send you some other things lately written by him in the same stile.

Do you expect to be in Phila in the course of the Winter, or ensuing spring? I asked the Question, because public-business may oblige me there and I should be pleased to meet with you.

Mention me most respectfully to Mrs. Hamilton, and believe me to be most
    faithfully & affectionately   Yrs

Coll A Hamilton
New-Yorke

AL, Hamilton Papers, Library of Congress.
  1. Heth, a Federalist and veteran of the American Revolution, was collector of customs at Bermuda Hundred, Virginia.
  2. Henry Stratton, like Heth, was a resident of Chesterfield County, Virginia (*Heads of Families at the First Census of the United States Taken in the Year 1790 . . . Virginia* [Washington, 1908], 49). He was apparently the same Henry Stratton who commanded the Virginia state schooner *Alliance* in 1779 and 1780 (William P. Palmer and Sherwin McRae, eds., *Calendar of Virginia State Papers and Other Manuscripts, from July 2, 1790, to August 10, 1792. . .* , V [Richmond, 1885], 219).
  3. The author of the "piece" was Heth. See Heth to H, October 14, 1796. The piece may have been the article entitled "Philo-Jay," which appeared in *The* [Richmond] *Virginia Gazette, and General Advertiser,* December 10, 1794. Although primarily a defense of John Jay, this article contains the following reference to H: "I have been led into these observations by the conduct of a certain description of persons who, for several years past, have been extremely liberal of their abuse, and even wanton in their vilifications of some of our most meritorious citizens. Last year and the year before, Mr. Hamilton was the chief object of their vengeance. But since his character has been

rescued from the fangs of malicious falsehood, and due credit has been given by Congress to his talents and virtues, the tongue of slander has been, to a certain degree, gagged. . . ."

4. Heth had consistently supported H's financial and foreign policies while H was Secretary of the Treasury. See, for example, Heth to H, June 14, 1793; July 6, 1794.

From John Patterson [1]

Lansingburgh [New York] January 12, 1796. "A Journey to Kinderhook on particular business prevented my receiving the pleasure of your letter [2] untill my return two days ago. . . . I enclose this to my oldest son [3] who will wait upon you with it and receive your commands for his Brother John.[4] Having said so much I must beg to add a few words more as to your intended Pupil. . . . I must request you will please to order Indentures to be drawn and he will forward them to me to perfect and at the same time send you my Bond for the money. . . ."

ALS, Hamilton Papers, Library of Congress.
1. Patterson was married to Catharine Livingston, the fourth daughter of Robert Livingston, third lord of Livingston Manor. In 1795 and 1796 he was involved in litigation over the estate of his deceased father-in-law.
2. Letter not found.
3. Robert Patterson.
4. John W. Patterson. A note in H's Law Register, 1795–1804, states that on January 22, 1796, "John W Patterson commenced his Clerkship" (D, partially in H's handwriting, New York Law Institute, New York City).
On January 22, 1799, the New York Supreme Court read and filed "the certificate of Alexander Hamilton Esqr. of the Clerkship and moral character of John W. Patterson," and the Court "Ordered that the said John W. Patterson be examined as to his Learning and Ability to practice as an Attorney of this Court." Patterson was admitted to practice in the Supreme Court on January 26 (MS Minutes of the New York Supreme Court, 1797–1802 [Court of Appeals, Albany]).

To Angelica Church [1]

[*New York, January 13, 1796.* On February 19, 1796, Angelica Church wrote to Hamilton: "Your letters of January the 13th are received." *Letters not found.*]

1. Angelica Church was Elizabeth Hamilton's sister and the wife of John B. Church, an Englishman. H managed Church's business affairs in the United States.

From Jonathan Dayton

Philadelphia, January 15, 1796. "Your letter of the 4th [1] is before me. . . . There cannot, I presume, exist a doubt as to my right to a portion of the Certificates alluded to in your letter. . . .[2] Mr Stevens the elder [3] declared before his death to my father [4] that he would transfer them to me. . . . The short Interrogatory respecting our political prospect with which you conclude your letter, cannot be answered in a few words. Our session has hitherto been remarkably tranquil, but we can have no security that it will continue so, much longer. *That Instrument,* the cause of so much pleasure to some & of displeasure to others, *that Compact* which has already drawn forth so many pens & occasioned so much warmth—*The treaty* (as ratified) has for some time past been impatiently expected,[5] and will, when it arrives & is laid before the House, produce, or I err exceedingly, agitations, collisions & oppositions, the extent of which cannot be foreseen or calculated."

ALS, Hamilton Papers, Library of Congress.
1. Letter not found.
2. See H to John Stevens, October 26, 1795.
3. John Stevens, Sr., a shipowner and merchant, had been treasurer of the state of New Jersey and president of the New Jersey Ratifying Convention. Stevens had died in 1792.
4. Elias Dayton.
5. The Jay Treaty, which had been ratified by the United States on August 14, 1795, and by Great Britain on October 28, 1795 (Miller, *Treaties,* II, 245), arrived in the United States in January, 1796. On February 27, 1796, Secretary of State Timothy Pickering wrote to William A. Deas, United States chargé d'affaires at London: ". . . To add to our mortification we find that a copy of the treaty arrived a month since at Charleston South Carolina, with the ratifications of the King of Great Britain and of the President, and the ratifications together with the full powers of the Plenipotentiaries who negotiated the treaty, have there been published in the newspapers" (copy, Massachusetts Historical Society, Boston). Without waiting for official notice of the exchange of ratifications, George Washington proclaimed the treaty in effect on February 29, 1796, and submitted it to the Senate on March 1 (*Annals of Congress* V, 48).

From Robert Morris [1]

Alexander Hamilton Esqre Phila 15 Janry 1796

Dear Sir

I wrote to you on the 16 Novr & on the 18th Decemr. You have not acknowledged the receipt of either of those letters, but as they were sent by Post I must suppose they got to your hand. Should that be the Case and any part of the Contents are not satisfactory, explain yourself freely, for I am entirely disposed to act in conformity with your desires in the business depending between us. I expect soon to hear of Mr. Marshalls [2] Arrival in London & perhaps Mr Church [3] and he may adjust the business for us.

I am very Sincerely Dr Sir Yours RM

LC, Robert Morris Papers, Library of Congress.

1. Morris, who had been a partner in the Philadelphia mercantile firm of Willing, Morris, and Company, had served in the Continental Congress from 1775 to 1778, in the Provincial Assembly from 1775 to 1776, in the Pennsylvania legislature from 1778 to 1779, 1780 to 1781, and 1785 to 1787. From July, 1781, to November, 1784, he held the office of Superintendent of Finance. He was a delegate to the Constitutional Convention in 1787 and a United States Senator from 1789 to 1795. By 1795 he was involved in numerous and complicated land speculations which led to his imprisonment for debt in February, 1798.

2. For James Marshall's trip to Europe, see Morris to H, June 7, 1795, note 10, October 8, 1795.

3. This is a reference to a debt which Morris owed to John B. Church. See the introductory note to Morris to H, June 7, 1795. See also Morris to H, July 20, November 16, December 18, 1795.

From Oliver Wolcott, Junior

Treasury Department January 15th. 1796

Sir,

The question upon the Constitutionality of the Act imposing duties on Carriages,[1] will I expect be determined by the Supreme Court the next month.[2] I request you if possible to attend the trial as Counsel for the United States. Mr. Lee [3] the Attorney General is now here & will be able to inform you of the time when the trial will come on, and will concert with you the measures proper to be pursued.

I am with perfect respect Sir, Your Most Obedient Servant
Oliv. Wolcott Jr.

Alexander Hamilton Esquire

LS, Hamilton Papers, Library of Congress; ADf, Connecticut Historical Society, Hartford; copy, Connecticut Historical Society, Hartford.

1. For information on the Carriage Tax case (*Hylton* v *United States*), see 3 Dallas, *U.S. Reports,* 171; also in forthcoming Goebel, *Law Practice,* III. See also Tench Coxe to H, January 14, 19, 1795; H to Coxe, January 26, 28, 1795; William Bradford to H, July 2, August 4, 1795; Edmund Randolph to H, July 21, 1795; Wolcott to H, July 28, 1795; H to Wolcott, August 5, 1795.

2. *Hylton* v *United States* was argued before the Supreme Court of the United States at its February, 1796, term. The decision, handed down on March 8, 1796, declared the carriage tax constitutional (3 Dallas, *U.S. Reports,* 171–83).

3. For Charles Lee's appointment as Attorney General, see H to Wolcott, October 3, 1795, note 3.

To Maturin Livingston [1]

[New York, January 18, 1796]

Sir

I have been informed that not long since at Philadelphia, in presence of a number of persons, you made mention of the altercation which happened between us on the Eighteenth of July last,[2] and by direct comments or insinuations endeavoured to convey the idea that I had acted with want of spirit on that occasion. I owe it to myself to inquire of you what foundation, *if any*, there may be for this information. In a matter of this delicacy, you will be no doubt sensible of the propriety of explicitness; that it may be clearly understood whether there was any intention on your part directly or indirectly to throw such an imputation upon me.

I am Sir Your humble serv

Maturin Livingston Esqr   Jany 18. 1796

ADf, Hamilton Papers, Library of Congress.

1. Livingston, a New York lawyer, was the brother of Peter R. Livingston and son of Robert James Livingston, who was descended from a nephew of the original lord of Livingston Manor. His wife, Margaret Lewis, was the daughter of Morgan Lewis and a niece of Chancellor Robert R. Livingston and his brother Edward Livingston.

2. The incident to which H is referring is described in the following letter from Edward Livingston to his mother, Margaret Beekman Livingston, on July 20, 1795: ". . . Nothing can equal the Vexation of the tory party on discovering that their favorite leader [H] had lost his influence except the indecency with which the leader testified his Mortification—in the afternoon of Saturday a number of gentlemen of [both] parties accidentally stopped at my Door. We entered into Conversation on the politics of the Day, at first cooly and afterwards with some Warmth between Peter [Peter R. Livingston] & Jo. [Josiah Ogden] Hoffman. It at last grew personal & Mr. [Rufus] King, myself and others interposed begging that if there were any personal disputes they might be settled elsewhere. Hamilton then stepped forward declaring that if the parties were to contend in a personal Way, he was ready that he would fight the Whole party one by one. I was just beginning to speak to him on the Subject [of] this imprudent declaration when he turned from me threw up his arm & Declared that he was ready to fight the Whole *'Destestable faction'* one by one. — Maturin [Livingston] at this moment arrived, he stepped up to him told him very cooly that he was one of the party that he accepted the challenge & would meet him in half an hour where he pleased. Hamilton said he had an affair on his Hands already with one of the party (meaning a quarrel with Commodore Nicholson) & when that was settled he would call on him. Neither Nicholson nor Maturin have as yet heard from him. I mention this Circumstance particularly that you may Judge how much he must be Mortified at his loss of Influence before he would descend [to] language that would have become a Street Bully" (ALS, New-York Historical Society, New York City). For H's quarrel with James Nicholson, see the first letter from H to Nicholson, July 20, 1795, note 1.

To George Washington

[New York, January 19, 1796]

Sir

The Bearer of this letter is Doctor Bolman[1] whom you have heared of as having made an attempt for the relief of the Marquis la Fayette which very nearly succeeded. The circumstances of this affair, as stated by Doctor Bolman & Mr. Huger, son of B Huger[2] of St Carolina deceased, who assisted, do real credit to the prudence management and enterprise of the Doctor and shew that he is a man of sense and energy.[3]

He appears to have been induced to think that he attempted a service which would strongly recommend him to the *favour* of this Country; in which idea I have reason to believe that Mr Pinckney[4] among others encouraged him—and as a consequence of it he hopes for some civil employment under our Government. His expectations of what he may begin with are not high—it being principally his object to obtain some present provision in a way which may lead him, if he discovers talents to something better. He appears to be a man of education—speaks several languages converses sensibly is of polite manners & I dare say has the materials of future advancement.

I have not left him unapprised of the difficulties in his way, but he concludes to go to Philadelphia to ascertain what is or is not possible, relying at least on a kind reception from you.

He brought me letters from Mr & Mrs Church [5] which speak handsomely of him. I believe they had a chief agency in promoting his undertaking

At his request I give him this letter to you.

With respectful & Affecte Attachment   I have the honor to be Sir   Your very Obed ser   A Hamilton
Jany 19. 1796

P.S. The Doctor is a German

The President of The UStates

ALS, George Washington Papers, Library of Congress; copy, Hamilton Papers, Library of Congress.
1. Justus Erich Bollmann, a physician and adventurer, was a native of Hanover.
2. Francis Kinloch Huger was an English-educated medical student whose father, Major Benjamin Huger, had been killed at Charleston, South Carolina, in 1779.
3. In 1792 the Austrians arrested Lafayette and handed him over to the Prussians. In 1794 the Prussians returned Lafayette to the Austrians, who imprisoned him in the fortress of Olmütz in Moravia. See "Cabinet Meeting. Opinion on Writing to the King of Prussia Concerning the Marquis de Lafayette," January 14, 1794. For the unsuccessful efforts to arrange Lafayette's escape, see H to William Bradford, June 13, 1795; Bradford to H, July 2, 1795.
4. Thomas Pinckney, United States Minister Plenipotentiary to Great Britain.
5. John B. and Angelica Church were in England. In 1795 Angelica Church wrote to her sister Elizabeth Hamilton: "You will receive the letter by Dr. Bollman, a young gentleman of good sense and polite manners, his exertions for the Marquis de La Fayette have been so zealous and active that every good American must honor him for his generous conduct; his friend, Mr. Huger, is also greatly entitled to praise for what he has done. I hope that my Brother will afford them his best assistance in an introduction to General Washington and our distinguished men" (Hamilton, *Intimate Life*, 247–48).

From Maturin Livingston

[New York, January 20, 1796]

Sir

I this moment received your note of the 18th instant, and do not hesitate to give it an immediate answer. It is so long since the conversation alluded to in it took place, (and in which many of the company joined) that I can not now charge my memory with all that then passed. I well remember however generally, that the procedure of the town meeting at New York on the subject of the treaty, and what succeeded it relative to yourself Commodore Nicholson and me,[1] occupied a considerable part of that conversation. The *Manner* in which the altercation between yourself and me was introduced, I have been informed has been related to you by Mr B Livingston.[2] The relation must remove every impression of *my* having introduced the subject, nor have I any recollection of commenting upon it in the way you have been informed.

I am Sir   Your Humble Servt.   Maturin Livingston
Jany 20th 1796

Alexander Hamilton Esqr

ALS, Hamilton Papers, Library of Congress.
 1. For information on the meeting in New York City on the Jay Treaty and H's abortive duel with Commodore James Nicholson, see H to Nicholson, first letter of July 20, 1795, note 1.
 2. Brockholst Livingston, a New York City attorney, was the son of Governor William Livingston of New Jersey and a second cousin of Edward Livingston and Chancellor Robert R. Livingston. See H to Maturin Livingston, January 18, 1796, note 1.

To Maturin Livingston

[New York, January 21, 1796]

Sir

It is not my wish to cavil nor can I as a reasonable man have any desire to pursue the question between us further than a due regard to my own delicacy may demand. But having weighed maturely the contents of your letter of yesterday I am obliged to think that it is not sufficiently explicit. The course of your own ideas and conduct hitherto must afford you a consciousness whether on the occasion alluded to there could have been an intention on your part to throw at me the imputation menti⟨oned⟩ in my first letter,[1] and if there was any situation which may prevent a recollec⟨tion⟩ of what passed, it is still in your power at this time to satisfy what is due to delicacy by a disavowal of the exceptionable sentiment.

I am Sir   Your humble ser,

M Livingston Esq

ADf, Hamilton Papers, Library of Congress.
1. H to Livingston, January 18, 1795.

To Théophile Cazenove [1]

New York, January 22, 1796. "Upon Sounding the members of the Legislature, I find that great difficulties will attend a bill so formed as to confirm absolutely & without limitation, existing titles, notwithstanding the alienisation of those who may have acquired Lands[2]—But that a proposition to confirm them, upon the condition of a transfer, within a term of 15 a 20 years, to Citizens, or of the acquirers becoming Citizens within that term, is listened to with more favour.[3] If you think this will answer the purpose of your friends I will thank you to let me Know it as soon as may be. . . ."

LC, Gemeentearchief Amsterdam, Holland Land Company. These documents were transferred in 1964 from the Nederlandsch Economisch-Historisch Archief, Amsterdam.
1. Cazenove, a native of Holland, conducted a brokerage and commercial business in Amsterdam from 1763 to 1788. In 1789 he was appointed by four Dutch banking houses—Peter Stadnitski and Son, Nicholaas and Jacob Van Staphorst, P. and C. Van Eeghen, and Isaac Ten Cate and Hendrick Vollenhoven—to handle their speculations in American securities. Cazenove arrived in the United States in 1790. In 1792 he persuaded his employers to invest in western lands in the United States. For that purpose the Dutch bankers were joined by Wilhem and Jan Willink and Rutger Jan Schimmelpenninck. Although the banking firms did not formally organize as the Holland Land Company until February 13, 1796, Cazenove from 1792 to 1794 purchased five million acres of land in western New York and northern and western Pennsylvania for his Dutch principals.

H wrote this letter in his capacity as an attorney for the six Dutch banking firms. For the full text of this letter and for other relevant documents, see forthcoming Goebel, *Law Practice*, III.

2. This is a reference to Cazenove's efforts to secure legislation that would permit his Dutch employers to own land as aliens in New York State. For the rights of aliens to own land in New York State, see Robert Morris to H, June 7, 1795, note 37.

In 1794 the New York Senate passed, but the Assembly rejected, "An act to enable the persons therein named, being aliens, to take and hold for their own use certain lands within this state, for the purchase whereof they have already contracted and paid" (*Journal of the Senate of the State of New-York, At their Seventeenth Session, begun and held at the City of Albany, the seventh day of January, 1794* [Albany, 1794], 13; *Journal of the Assembly of the State of New-York, At their Seventeenth Session, begun and held at the City of Albany, the seventh day of January, 1794* [Albany, 1794], 87). The following year "Wilhem Willink and others, citizens of Amsterdam, in the Seven United Provinces," petitioned the legislature for a law to permit them "to take and hold to their own use, lands within this State, for the purchase of which, they have already contracted and paid" (*Journal of the Assembly of the State of New-York. At Their Eighteenth Session, Begun at the Town of Poughkeepsie, in the County of Dutchess, on Tuesday, The Sixth of January, 1795: And Held by Adjournment, at the City of New-York, Tuesday, January 20, 1795* [New York, 1795], 9). Although the petition was received favorably (*Journal of the Assembly of the State of New-York. At Their Eighteenth Session*, 61–62), "An Act to enable certain persons therein named to purchase and hold real estates within this State," which became law on April 8, 1795, while listing the names of several aliens, did not include the names of Willink and his associates (*New York Laws*, 18th Sess., Ch. LXVII). By 1796 H, as well as a few other prominent New Yorkers, was assisting Cazenove in in his campaign to have the legislature grant his clients permission to hold land in New York. On April 11, 1796, "An act for the relief of Wilhem Willinck, Nicolaas Van Staphorst, Christian Van Eeghen, Hendrick Vollenhoven, Rutger Jan Schimmelpenninck and Pieter Stadnitski being aliens" became law (*New York Laws*, 19th Sess., Ch. LVIII). This act reads: "Be it enacted *by the people of the state of New-York represented in Senate and Assembly*, That it shall be lawful for the persons by whom the lands for the purchase of which Wilhem Willinck, Nicolaas Van Staphorst, Christian Van Eeghen, Hendrick Vollenhoven, Rutger Jan Schimmelpenninck and Pieter Stadnitski being aliens, have already contracted and paid are now held to hold the same in fee simple as trustees for the said six persons above named, their heirs and devisees, and the heirs and devisees without limitation as to the number of descents or devises in succession, although the said six persons above named and such heirs and devisees may be aliens, and the law of this state whereby aliens are disabled from taking and hold lands to their own use notwithstanding. And to the end, that the lands herein intended may be known and ascertained.

"*Be it further enacted*, That the persons so holding as trustees shall execute declarations in writing to be acknowledged or proved, and thereupon to be recorded in the office of the Secretary of this state within one year after the passing of this act, specifying the lands held by them as trustees of the said six persons above named, and the lands to be specified in such declarations shall be deemed to be the lands for the purchase of which the said six persons above named have already contracted and paid, and which the persons executing such declarations are hereby enabled to hold in trust as aforesaid, and such trustees shall also at the time of executing such declarations make oath that no other lands are described in the said declarations respectively than such as were conveyed to them the said trustees, and were to the best of their knowledge and belief contracted and paid for by the said persons for whom they are so trustees before the passing of this act, and if such declarations shall not be recorded within the time for that purpose above limited that then this act shall be thenceforth void.

"*And be it further enacted,* That whenever any person holding the said lands in trust as aforesaid shall be minded to be discharged from the trust, or whenever the persons for whom the said lands shall be so held in trust shall be minded to change the trustees or any of them then in such case and as often as the same shall from time to time happen it shall be lawful for the trustees to be discharged or so to be changed to convey over in fee simple the lands so held by them in trust to new trustees to be also citizens of the United States and to be nominated for the purpose by the persons for whom the lands shall at the time be so held in trust. But in as much as the intent of this act is only to allow to the said six persons above named their heirs and devisees in succession as above mentioned if they shall not in the mean time themselves become citizens of the United States a reasonable time to sell the said lands to citizens of the United States, and to provide a mean whereby a title may be made to the vendees, free from the plea or pretence, of alienism in the vendors. Therefore,

"*Be it further enacted, and it is hereby expressly declared and provided,* That such of the said lands or rents issuing out of the same as shall after the expiration of seven years from the passing of this act be held in trust for the said six persons or their legal representatives aliens, shall be forfeited to and vested in the people of this state as lands held by aliens or to the use of aliens in like manner as if this act had never passed, any thing herein contained notwithstanding."

The following entry appears in H's Cash Book, 1795–1804, for August 1, 1796: "Theophilus Cazenove for consultations with Judge [Egbert] Benson & Mr. [Samuel] Jones concerning a certain Act of the Legislature   20" (AD, Hamilton Papers, Library of Congress).

3. An act with the provisions outlined by H became law on March 17, 1797. See "An Act providing a mean for procuring a sum to the Western Inland Lock Navigation company, to enable them more effectually and speedily to prosecute the improvements in the said navigation" (*New York Laws,* 20th Sess., Ch. XXXVI).

Finally, on April 2, 1798, the New York legislature passed "An Act to enable Aliens to purchase, and hold real Estates within this State, under certain restrictions therein mentioned" (*New York Laws,* 21st Sess., Ch. LXXII).

To Robert Morris

[*New York, January 22, 1796.* On February 10, 1796, Morris wrote to Hamilton: "I was preparing to answer your favour of the 22d ulto." *Letter not found.*]

To Charles Cotesworth Pinckney [1]

New York January 22. 1796

Dear Sir

Give me leave to recommend to your civilities Mr. Winstanly [2] the bearer of this an English Gentleman who came to this City some years. After former generosity and carelessness of temper disposes of a little fortune, he has assumed the business of Landscape Painting and in pursuance of his plan visits your County, which also he is desirous through curiosity of seeing before he goes to Europe. He appears to have a warm passion for his present pursuit, in which he may be said to be self taught—and what is more to his purpose, *talent*. With good opportunities I dare say he will arrive at eminence. In introducing him to you I give him a proof of my regard. With esteem & attachment

I am Sir   Your obed serv   A Hamilton

Jan 22. 1796

Charles C. Pinckney Esq

ALS, Pinckney Family Papers, Library of Congress.

1. Pinckney, a veteran of the American Revolution, was a member of the lower house of the South Carolina legislature in 1778 and 1782 and a member of the state senate in 1779. He was a delegate to the Constitutional Convention in 1787, and in 1788 he was a member of the South Carolina Ratifying Convention. He declined George Washington's offers of the post of Secretary of War in 1794 and of Secretary of State in 1795. In July, 1796, he accepted the appointment to be United States Minister Plenipotentiary to France to succeed James Monroe.

2. William Winstanley, an English landscape painter, came to the United States in the early seventeen-nineties. In 1793 and 1794 George Washington bought four of his pictures. Winstanley then proposed, among other projects, to paint pictures of the new Federal City. See Washington to the Commissioners of the District of Columbia, September 5, 1793 (*GW*, XXXIII, 83); H to ———, April 10, 1793; H to Robert Morris, May 6, 1793. In 1795 Winstanley put on permanent exhibition in New York a panorama of London, the first of its kind to be seen in the United States.

Certificate on John Hanson by Anthony L. Bleecker, Peter S. Curentius, Alexander Hamilton, John Lamb, and Hercules Mulligan [1]

[New York, January 24, 1796]

We the Subscribers do certify that we were acquainted with Capt John Hanson deceased in his life time, and at an early period of the Revolution of the United States, and have satisfactory grounds to believe that he was firmly attached to the cause of the Revolution and to the liberties of this Country. We also certify, that we particularly recollect as eye Witnesses his conduct on a certain Evening in the year MDCLXXVI, when cannon were removed from the battery in the City under the fire of a British Man of War, on which occasion the said Capt Hanson was distinguished by his activity in forwarding the Removal.[2] New York January 24. 1796.

> A Hamilton
> John Lamb
> Peter S. Curtenius
> Hercules Mulligan
> Anthony L. Bleecker

DS, in the handwriting of H and signed by H, John Lamb, Peter S. Curtenius, Hercules Mulligan, and Anthony L. Bleecker, from the original in the New York State Library, Albany.

1. Bleecker was an auctioneer and lawyer in New York City; Curtenius was state auditor; Lamb was collector of customs at New York; and Mulligan was a New York City merchant tailor.

This certificate was in support of a petition of Mary Hanson (Hansen), widow of John W. Hanson, that was received by the New York Assembly on February 1, 1796. The petition was "relative to a ballance due her said Husband, of £. 3,000 sterling on a pension granted by his Britannic Majesty, out of the quit rents arising with the colony of New-York." The petition was read and referred to a select committee. On February 19, 1796, the committee reported that "upon enquiring into the facts stated in the petition certain legal questions arise which materially affect the merits of the case, and as the committee feel themselves incompetent to decide the same, they would recommend that the present committee be discharged from any further consideration of the said petition, and that the same be referred to the Attorney General" (*Journal of the Assembly of the State of New-York. At Their Nineteenth Session*, 49, 85). In a report dated February 11 and submitted on February 20, 1797, Attorney General Josiah Ogden Hoffman, arguing that Mrs. Hanson's claim was a valid one, wrote: ". . . The King of Great-Britain could not revoke his grant, a specific fund being chargeable therewith: His revenue from quit-rents became forfeited to the people of this state: As they derive the benefit of such forfeiture, ought they not to satisfy all legal incumbrances thereon?" But the committee to which the petition was referred reported on March 15, 1797, "that the most material facts stated in the said petition, are not fully proven and substantiated to the satisfaction of the committee . . ." and that "considering the importance of the case to the petitioner, that she have leave to withdraw her said petition" (*Journal of the Assembly of the State of New-York; At their Twentieth Session,* 116, 159).

2. This is a reference to the events of the night of August 23–24, 1776, when a group of New Yorkers removed several cannon from the Battery despite shots of grape and ball from the British man-of-war *Asia*. Mulligan and H were well qualified to attest to Hanson's part in this episode, for both helped in the removal of the cannon. See Mulligan, "Narrative of Hercules Mulligan of the City of New York" (AD, Hamilton Papers, Library of Congress). This document is printed in *The William and Mary Quarterly,* 3rd ser., IV (April, 1947), 209–11.

From Jonathan Burrall [1]

[New York, January 25, 1796]

Dr Sir,

Our practice is to demand payment of Notes which fall due on the 4th. July, the day before, as in case of Sundays and Christmas days.[2] This practice has prevailed in this Office and at the New York Bank [3] from their first establishment.[4]

Yours respectfully

Jon: Burrall
Jany 25th 1796.

Alexr. Hamilton Esqr.

ALS, Hamilton Papers, Library of Congress.

1. Burrall was the cashier of the New York Office of Discount and Deposit of the Bank of the United States.
2. Section II of the "Ordinance and By-Laws for the Regulation of the Bank of the United States," printed on November 14, 1791, reads: "That the bank shall be open for the transaction of business every day in the year (Sundays, Christmas Day, and the Fourth of July excepted) during such hours as the board of directors shall deem advisable" (John Thom Holdsworth and Davis R. Dewey, *The First and Second Banks of the United States* [Washington, 1910], 133).
3. The rules of the Bank of New York, published on June 7, 1784, include the following provision: "The bank will be open every day in the year, except Sundays, Christmas-Day, New Year's-Day, Good Friday, the Fourth of July, and general holidays appointed by legal authority" (Henry W. Domett, *A History of the Bank of New York* [New York, 1884], 19).

4. H needed this information for the case of [Francis] *Lewis* v [Aaron] *Burr*, in which H appeared for the plaintiff. Burr had endorsed Roger Enos's promissory note for thirty-five hundred dollars to Francis Lewis. The note fell due on July 4, a holiday, and Lewis thus demanded payment on July 3. As Enos failed to make any payment on July 3, Lewis brought action to hold Burr liable as the endorser of the note. The verdict, filed in the New York Supreme Court on September 5, 1796, held that July 4 was a holiday and that the note fell due on July 3. Burr was therefore liable for the note. For additional information on this case, see Goebel, *Law Practice*, II, 17, note 64. See also Hamilton, *Intimate Life*, 160–62, and H's Law Register, 1795–1804 (D, partially in H's handwriting, New York Law Institute, New York City).

On March 14, 1797, the following entry appears in H's Cash Book, 1795–1804: "Cash Dr. to Account of Costs and Fees [for] this sum received of Lewis v Burr Trial fee 20" (AD, Hamilton Papers, Library of Congress).

From Théophile Cazenove[1]

Philadelphia, January 25, 1796. Acknowledges receipt of Hamilton's letter of January 22, 1796. Discusses legislation necessary for the ownership of land in New York State by aliens.

LC, Gemeentearchief Amsterdam, Holland Land Company. These documents were transferred in 1964 from the Nederlandsch Economisch-Historisch Archief, Amsterdam.

1. This letter, which is in French, was addressed to H in his capacity as an attorney for the six Dutch banking firms which formally organized as the Holland Land Company on February 13, 1796. For the full text of this letter and other relevant documents, see forthcoming Goebel, *Law Practice*, III.

From Charles Wilkes[1]

[New York] Monday Noon [January 25, 1796]

Sir

It has been the constant practice of the Bank, to demand payment on the 3d of July, for all notes which become payable on the 4th—that day being, by the regulations of the Bank, a holiday.[2]

I am with great respect   Your obet Servt   Chas Wilkes

Alexr Hamilton Esqe.

ALS, Hamilton Papers, Library of Congress.
1. Wilkes was cashier of the Bank of New York.
2. H needed this information for the case of *Lewis* v *Burr*. See Jonathan Burrall to H, January 25, 1796.

To Rufus King

[New York, January 29, 1796] [1]

My Dear Sir

If the News Papers till truth it would appear that Massachusettes has anticipated New York. But it is intended by our friends in the Legislature to give some pointed discountenance to the propositions.[2] It was expected that it would have been done to day, but by the divergings of some men who seek popularity with both sides, they have gotten into an unnecessary debate upon the propositions in detail, which will lose time; but in the result a handsome majority will do right.

Laurance is hurt, & as far as I see not without some reason from particular circumstances, at being left out of the Direction of the Bank.[3] It will be balm to his feelings to be put into the direction of the Office here [4] & I believe it will be an improvement of the Direction to do it. I wish you would endeavour to bring it about. Speak to Bayard [5] of our City and to Wharton [6] of Philadelphia. This is a suggestion of my own for Laurance rather rides a high horse upon the occasion.

Yrs. truly   A Hamilton

Ruffus King Esqr.

ALS, New-York Historical Society, New York City.
   1. Although H did not date this letter, it is postmarked "Jan 29" and endorsed by King "Jan 1796."
   King was United States Senator from New York.
   2. This is a reference to the action taken by the Massachusetts legislature on a resolution adopted by the Virginia legislature on December 12, 1795. The Virginia resolution reads: "*Resolved,* That the Senators representing this state in the Senate of the United States, be, and they are hereby instructed, and the Representatives requested to unite their utmost exertions, to obtain in their respective Houses, the following amendments to the Constitution, viz.

"1. 'That no treaty containing any stipulation upon the subject of the powers vested in Congress by the eighth section of the first article, shall become the supreme law of the land, until it shall have been approved in those particulars, by a majority in the House of Representatives; and, that the President, before he shall ratify any such treaty, shall submit the same to the House of Representatives.'

"2. 'That a tribunal, other than the Senate, be instituted for the trial of impeachments.'

"3. 'That the Senate of the United States shall be composed of two Senators from each state, chosen by the Legislature thereof for three years, and each Senator have one vote: Immediately after they shall be assembled in consequence of the first election, they shall be divided as equally as may be into three classes. The seats of the Senators of the first class shall be vacated at the expiration of the first year; the second class at the expiration of the second year; and of the third class at the expiration of the third year, so that one third may be chosen at the expiration of every year.'

"4. 'That no person holding the office of a Judge under the United States, shall be capable of holding at the same time any other office or appointment whatever.'" (*Journal of the House of Delegates of the Commonwealth of Virginia, Begun and Held at the Capitol, in the City of Richmond, on Tuesday, the Tenth Day of November, One Thousand Seven hundred and Ninety-five* [Richmond, 1795], 91.)

The Virginia resolution was then sent to other states for consideration. In Massachusetts on January 19, 1796, "The Secretary having communicated to the Hon. Senate, certain Resolutions of the Legislature of *Virginia*, proposing amendments to the Federal Constitution, &c. . . . The same was read, and a meeting to commit them, being negatived, they were sent down to the House.

"Being read in the House, it was moved, that the same be committed—which motion passed in the [negative], for it 24—against it 56.

"It was then moved, that they lie on the table, which passed in the affirmative, for it 42, against it 41." (*The* [Boston] *Columbian Centinel*, January 20, 1796.)

On January 21, 1796, Christopher Gore wrote to Rufus King: ". . . The disposal of the Virginia resolves, as related in the Centinel, is correct in every thing but the final vote of the House. After the question for commitment was lost, Doctr. [Charles] Jarvis moved that they might lay on the table till the answer to the Govr's speech was reported; with great difficulty this obtained a majority of one only" (King, *The Life and Correspondence of Rufus King*, II, 55).

On January 9, 1796, Governor John Jay laid before the New York legislature a letter "from his Excellency the Governor of Virginia, together with the resolutions mentioned in it." On March 22, 1796, the legislature adopted a resolution "That it does not appear . . . expedient to concur in behalf of this state in the propositions contained in the resolutions of the state of Virginia . . ." (*Journal of the Senate of the State of New-York. At Their Nineteenth Session*, 8, 30, 79–80).

3. John Laurance was a member of the House of Representatives from New York from 1789 to 1793 and United States judge for the District of New York from 1794 to 1796. The "bank" to which H is referring is the Bank of the United States. Laurance was a member of the bank's first board of directors.

4. The New York branch of the Bank of the United States. Laurance was a director of this branch in 1796.

5. William Bayard, a New York City merchant, was a director of the Bank of the United States.

6. Isaac Wharton, a Philadelphia merchant, was a director of the Bank of the United States.

To Thomas FitzSimons [1]

[*New York, February 4, 1796.* Hamilton endorsed a letter from FitzSimons dated December 17, 1795: "Ansr. Feby. 4 179[6] agreeing & naming Mr. Lewis [2]—Referees to decide as Judges in Chancellory Law & Fact." *Letter not found.*]

1. FitzSimons, a native of Ireland, was a Philadelphia merchant. He was a Federalist member of the House of Representatives from 1789 to 1795.
2. This is presumably a reference to William Lewis, a Philadelphia attorney and Federalist, who had been judge of the Federal District Court for the Eastern District of Pennsylvania from July 20, 1791, to April 11, 1792.

From Robert Morris

Alexr Hamilton Esqr Philada. Feby 10. 1796
New York

Dr Sir

I was preparing to answer your favor of the 22d ulto [1] when I was informed that you are to be here on the 17th of this month [2] which I am very glad of as it will give me the Oppy of adjusting the business personally & I hope to your Satisfaction.

I am most truly Yrs RM

LC, Robert Morris Papers, Library of Congress.
1. Letter not found.
2. The purpose of H's trip to Philadelphia was to argue the constitutionality of the carriage tax before the Supreme Court of the United States. See Oliver Wolcott, Jr., to H, January 15, 1796. On February 22, 1796, H "was admitted and sworn a Counsellor of . . . [the Supreme] Court" (RG 267, MS Minutes of the Supreme Court of the United States, National Archives). H argued the Government's case in the Supreme Court on February 24, 1796. His account with the United States "For his Compensation in attending the Argument on behalf of the said States, respecting the constitutionality of the Tax on Carriages" for five hundred dollars was submitted to the Treasury Department on March 7, 1796, and was paid on March 9, 1796 (RG 217, Miscellaneous Treasury Accounts, 1790–1894, Account No. 7712, National Archives). In H's Cash Book, 1795–1804, between the dates February 10 and March 3, 1796, is the following entry: "this sum expended on my journey 60." A second entry in H's Cash Book, 1795–1804, on March 10, 1796, reads: "Cash—Dr, to Account of Costs and fees for this sum received of the U. States for my attendance at Philadelphia a fortnight to argue the question of the constitutionality of the Carriage Tax 500" (AD, Hamilton Papers, Library of Congress).

From George Washington

Phila. 13th. Feby. 1796

My dear Sir,

In the moment I was closing & dispatching my letters to the Post Office, I learnt from the Attorney General of the U.S.[1] that you would be here on the 17th.[2] My mind being continually uneasy on Acct. of Young Fayette,[3] I cannot but wish (if this letter should reach you in time, and no reasons stronger than what have occurred against it) that you would request him, and his Tuter,[4] to come on to this place on a visit; without avowing, or making a mystery of the object—Leaving the rest to some after decision. In haste. Yours always & most
Affectionately

Go: Washington

Colo Hamilton

ALS, George Washington Papers, Library of Congress.
1. Charles Lee.
2. See Oliver Wolcott, Jr., to H, January 15, 1796; Robert Morris to H, February 10, 1796, note 2.
3. George Washington Motier Lafayette.
4. Felix Frestel. For information on Lafayette and Frestel, see H to Washington, October 16, 26, November 19, 26, December 24, 27–30, 1795; Washington to H, October 29, November 10, 18, 23, 28, December 22, 1795.

Draft on the Bank of the United States

[Philadelphia, February 18, 1796]

Cashier of The Bank of The United States   Dollars 46
Pay to Mr. Bicknel[1] or bearer Forty six Dollars

Philadelphia Feb. 18. 1796
Alexander Hamilton

ADS, Library Company of Philadelphia.
1. Robert Bicknell, a resident of Philadelphia, was proprietor of that city's New York and Baltimore stages.
For H's trip to Philadelphia, see Robert Morris to H, February 10, 1796, note 2.

From Angelica Church

[London, February 19, 1796]

My dear Brother

Your letters of January the 13th are received [1] but no plan of the lot, and no description of the house.[2] I am sensible how much I trouble I give you, but you will have the goodness to excuse it, when you know that it proceeded from a persuasion that I was asking from one who promised me his love and attention if I returned to America; If friendship is only a name, for what do I exchange ease and taste, by going to the New World, where politics excludes all society, and agreeable intercourse, where all that is not given to Fame seems to be regretted and forgotten. My Love to Betsey I do not write by this Ship but will by Monday.

I believe Mr. Marshall [3] has made no progress in settling the affairs of your HONORABLE friend.[4]

Adieu my dear and naughty Brother, it will be impossible for me to Charter a Vessel for how can I bring out furniture when I do not know the number of rooms my house contains. What an agreeable amiable fellow, has Jay's LITTLE treaty turned into a defender of what he never would himself have deigned to submit to. Voila mon sentiment, changes le si vous veules.

Adieu

Febr. 19. 1796.

AL, Hamilton Papers, Library of Congress.
 1. Letters not found.
 2. H was engaged in buying a house for John B. and Angelica Church. See Philip Schuyler to H, October 12, 1795.
 3. James Marshall, the brother of John Marshall, was married to Robert Morris's daughter Hetty.
 4. Robert Morris. See Morris to H, June 7, 1795, note 10. See also Morris to H, July 20, November 16, December 18, 1795, January 15, 1796.

Opinion on the Claim of Oliver Pollock [1]

[Philadelphia, February 27, 1796]

At the request of Mr. Pollock I certify that I have a distinct recollection that in the course of conversations with him, respecting his pecuniary claims on the United States, he expressed the idea of his having further claims on the United States beyond those admitted and liquidated; and that I have also some recollection, but indistinct and imperfect, that when a warrant came to be issued for the balance due to him, he objected to the wording of it, as amounting to a declaration that the sum to be paid was *to be in full of all demands;* and that in consequence of his representation, either words were added to the first warrant, or a new one was made out, altered in conformity to the within copy, that is to say, so as to import in the warrant *a full satisfaction for claims liquidated and credited only.*[2]

Alexander Hamilton,
February 27, 1796.

Augustus B. Woodward, *A Representation of the Case of Oliver Pollock* (Washington, D.C.: Printed by Samuel Harrison Smith, 1803), 54.

1. For background to this letter, see Pollock to H, February 15, 1792.
In June, 1777, the secret committee of Congress appointed Pollock commercial agent of the United States at New Orleans, a position which he held until 1781. During this period he also served as commercial agent for Virginia. In May, 1783, he became an agent of the United States at Havana, Cuba, where he remained for eighteen months. In both posts he advanced large sums of money. In 1791, "An Act making Appropriations for the Support of Government for the year one thousand seven hundred and ninety-two" provided for "payment of the principal and interest on a liquidated claim of Oliver Pollock . . . for supplies of clothing, arms, and military stores, during the late war, one hundred and eight thousand, six hundred and five dollars, and two cents" (1 *Stat.* 227 [December 23, 1791]). Pollock, however, was not satisfied with this settlement and continued to press his claim. Pollock's petition was one of ninety-nine which H returned to the House of Representatives shortly before he resigned as Secretary of the Treasury. See H to Frederick A. C. Muhlenberg, January 5, 1795. For the final settlement of Pollock's claim, see "An Act for the relief of Oliver Pollock (6 *Stat.* 65 [March 3, 1807]). For Pollock's life, see James Alton James, *Oliver Pollock: The Life and Times of an Unknown Patriot* (New York, 1937). For the history of Pollock's claim along with many of the appropriate documents, see Woodward, *A Representation of the Case of Oliver Pollock.*

2. H's "recollection" of this warrant was correct. See "Warrant number 1684," which is printed in full in Woodward, *A Representation of the Case of Oliver Pollock,* 53. This warrant is dated April 13, 1792, and is signed by H.

From Charles Cotesworth Pinckney

[*Charleston, South Carolina, March 3, 1796.* On June 5, 1796, Pinckney wrote to Hamilton: "I wrote to you the 3d: of last March." *Letter not found.*]

From John Jay

New York 4th. March 1796.

Sir

In pursuance of a concurrent Resolution of the two Houses of the Legislature of the third and fourth instant[1] I desire You as a Counsellor at Law to defend in behalf of this State a certain Suit brought against Lewis Cornwall by or in behalf of Alexander Colden for the Recovery of a Farm sold to the said Lewis by the Commissioners of Forfeitures for the Southern District.[2]

You will herewith receive a Copy of the said Resolution, and of the Petition of Lewis Cornwall which gave Occasion to it.

I have the Honor to be   Sir   Your Most Ob. & H'ble Servt.

John Jay.

Alexander Hamilton Esqr.

LS, Hamilton Papers, Library of Congress; LC, from the original in the New York State Library, Albany.

1. On March 3, 1796, the New York Senate resolved: "That his Excellency the Governor be and he is hereby requested to cause proper counsel to be employed in behalf of this State, to defend the suit brought against Lewis Cornwall, by or in behalf of Alexander Colden for the recovery of a farm sold to the said Lewis Cornwall by the commissioners of forfeitures for the Southern District" (*Journal of the Senate of the State of New-York. At Their Nineteenth Session,* 59). On March 4, 1796, the New York Assembly concurred with the Senate's resolution (*Journal of the Assembly of the State of New-York. At Their Nineteenth Session,* 111).

2. The appointment of commissioners of forfeitures for the various districts of New York State was required by the act of attainder of October 22, 1779, which declared forfeit the estates of New York Loyalists (*New York Laws,* 3rd Sess., Ch. XXV). The business of the commissioners, who were finally organized by an act of May 12, 1784 (*New York Laws,* 7th Sess., Ch. LXIV), was to sell "at public Vendue to the highest Bidder" the lands of those named

in or subsequently convicted under the act of attainder. One of the earliest entries in their ledger ("New York, Commissioners of Forfeiture, Southern District, Abstract of sales, New York City and Vicinity," 3 [New-York Historical Society, New York City]) records the location on May 13, 1784, of Lewis Cornwell, a member of a prominent Flushing family, on "The Lands and Tenements situate in Queens County on Nassau Island" formerly belonging to David Colden, and Cornwall's subsequent purchase of them for £1,800. Colden, a son of the former lieutenant governor of New York, Cadwallader Colden, had lived at Spring Hill Farm, Flushing, and was one of the fifty-nine Loyalists named in the act of 1779. He died in England on July 10, 1784. His widow, after unsuccessfully petitioning the legislature for the use of her husband's estate, died the following year at the house of her brother-in-law, Cadwallader Colden, of Coldenham, Orange County. The identity of the plaintiff in this suit is not clear, since two members of the immediate family were named Alexander Colden. It seems likely, however, that the plaintiff was David Colden's nephew, the fourth son of Cadwallader Colden of Coldenham, who farmed in Orange County. The other Alexander Colden was a sea captain and a grandson of David Colden's oldest brother, Alexander. Other sources apparently give the name of the buyer of this land as William Cornwell. See H. B. Yoshpe, *The Disposition of Loyalist Estates in the Southern District of the State of New York* (New York, 1939), 46, 137.

From Gouverneur Morris [1]

London 4 March 1796

My dear Hamilton

I have just now written to the President to communicate some Intelligence lately receiv'd from Paris.[2] This I have done in Abstract but my Correspondent has written to me as follows: "The Government here are highly displeas'd with ours. You may easily guess the Reason. It is come to a very serious State. A Fleet is to be sent to our

ALS (incomplete), Hamilton Papers, Library of Congress; LC, Gouverneur Morris Papers, Library of Congress; copy, in the handwriting of H, George Washington Papers, Library of Congress.

1. On October 24, 1794, Morris, who had been replaced by James Monroe as United States Minister Plenipotentiary to France in August, 1794, left Paris. He remained in Europe until 1798, traveling on the Continent and in England.

2. Morris is referring to the following section of his letter to Washington dated March 4, 1796: ". . . I hasten to communicate my latest Advices from Paris. These are, that a Fleet is to conduct to you the new french Minister, who will be directed to exact in the Space of fifteen Days a categorical Answer to certain questions. What these are I can only conjecture, but suppose that you will, in Effect, be called on to take Part decidedly with France. Mr. Monroe will no Doubt endeavor to convince the Rulers of that Country that such Conduct will force us into the War against them, but it is far from impossible that the usual Violence of their Councils will prevail" (ALS, George Washington Papers, Library of Congress).

Shore with a new minister. A definitive Answer must be given in fifteen Days. The Government are to declare to us within a few Days that our Treaty with them is annulled. This will put Mr. Munroe in a cruel Dilemma. He is already much displeas'd and a War will probably be the Consequence. The British will be glad of this. Perhaps we may have here a Revolution from the Industry ⟨of th⟩e ³ Jacobins. The Finances are worse than ever they cannot stand ⟨much longer."⟩ This letter is dated in Paris the 15th. ⟨of la⟩st Month.⁴ You may be sure by my communicating this to you that I have Confidence in the Source from whence it is derived. Now my dear Friend I have barely stated to the President the Intention as to the new Minister. His late Declaration as to the existing french Government ⁵ has prevented me from saying a Word to him on a

3. The material in broken brackets has been taken from the copy in the George Washington Papers.
4. On May 17, 1796, the [New York] *Minerva, & Mercantile Evening Advertiser* printed an "Extract of a letter from an American citizen, dated Paris, Feb. 14th, 1796." Despite the difference in dates, this is presumably the letter to which Morris is referring. The extract reads: "Could you imagine, my dear Sir, that any American citizens could be so abandoned as to invite France to attempt, by coertion, to prevent the free exercise of the judgment of our country concerning its own interests, and to awe it into a surrender of its opinion to the mandate of a foreign country? Yet so the fact undoubtedly is. Influential men on your side of the water, have invited the French government to speak to ours a decided language against the execution of the treaty with Great Britain and even to go so far, as to claim our guarantee of the French West Indies; placing before us the alternative of war with France or Great Britain. The idea has been listened to by the government, and it has been in contemplation to send a new Minister with a fleet to carry the plan into effect; tho' I am inclined to hope that it has been recently laid aside. The extreme embarrassments of the affairs of their country, especially with regard to its finances, and more serious reflections on the hazard of driving us into an election to take side with Great Britain, as well from the exposed state of our commerce, as from the resentment which a dictatorial conduct would naturally inspire, have at least produced a halt, and, I trust, that the hesitation which has begun, will end in a resolution not to risk so unjust and so mad a proceeding. Would to heaven that the war was at an end! for we shall not be safe from the machinations of this wicked portion of the globe till that event takes place—justice and morality have fled from Europe—but alas! are they flying from America also? I dare not trust to this mode of conveyance the persons supposed to be the authors of this nefarious plot. But a few months may enable me to make the disclosure with more certainty, where I can do it with perfect safety."
5. Morris was presumably referring to a public letter which Washington wrote to Pierre Auguste Adet, the French Minister to the United States, on January 1, 1796. Washington's letter was an acknowledgment of the presentation by the French Directory of the colors of France to the United States. In the course of this letter Washington wrote: "I rejoice that the interesting revolutionary movements of so many years have issued in the formation of a

Subject where he has I think committed himself. To you I will declare my Conviction that this Government cannot stand whether the Monarchy be restor'd or not. The People in general are averse to it. The Adherents to the royal Cause grow daily more numerous. If I knew decidedly the Steps to be taken in Aid of them I could tell you almost with Certainty whether they would be successful for the State of that Country now presents sufficient Data on which to reason soundly. I need not say to you that if the french Rulers persist in the Measures which are above mentioned, America will probably be obligd to take Part in the War. On a former Occasion when they talk⟨ed somewhat⟩ highly I told them that they could certainly force us into the Contest but as certainly it would be against them, let the Predelections in their Favor be ever so great, because it would be Madness in us to risque our Commerce against the navy of the world. That to join them would do them no Good and must do us much Evil. *That* Time they beleived me. What Representations Mr. Munroe may make I cannot pretend to divine and much less the Effect of them. Supposing however that you should be driven to make this Election *you* will naturally weigh not only the naval Force but also the financial Resources of the opposed Powers. The noisy Folks with you will undoubtedly be loud on our Obligations to France and on the long List of our Grievances from England. As to the former I think we should always seek to perform Acts of Kindness towards those who at the Bidding of their Prince s⟨tept forw⟩ard to fight our Battles. Nor would I ever permit a frigid Reasoning on political motives to damp those Effusions of Sentiment which are as laudable in a nation as they are decorous to a private Citizen. But would it be kind to support that Power which now tyrannizes over France and reduces her Inhabitants to unheard of Misery? Would it be grateful to mix with, much less to league with those whose Hands are yet red with the Blood of him who was our real Protector? Would it be decent? As to the Conduct of Britain towards us, altho I see as clearly as others the Grounds which we have to complain and can readily account for the Resentments which have been excited, yet I give due Weight to the Causes by which that Conduct was instigated: and if in some Cases I find it unjustifi-

---

constitution designed to give permanency to the great object for which you have contended. I rejoice that liberty . . . now finds an asylum in the bosom of a regularly organized government . . ." (*GW*, XXXIV, 413).

able, I cannot consider it as in all Cases inexcusable. Provided therefore that our Honor be saved, I am so far thinking that the Injuries we have endured should become the source of inextinguishable Hatred and perpetual War that I would rather seek in future Amity and good Offices the fair Motive for consigning them to utter Oblivion. I have not my dear Hamilton any such View of our present political Machinery as to judge what may be the Effect of lofty Menace. I apprehend that some feeble Counsels will be given: Whether they will be receivd and pursued you best know and will doubtless act accordingly. What I have to ask is that you would put yourself in the Way of being consulted. I mean locally, for should you be at a Distance the Time may be too short for Communication.

It is possible after all that the Demand may turn on a single Point viz: that we shall no longer pretend to claim an Exemption from Seizure for those Goods of an Enemy [6] [which may be found in our Ships. If so the Case is plain and easy. We slide back to the Law of Nations which it is our Interest to preserve unimpeached. Probably we shall be called on for our Guarantee of St Domingo [7] and here many questions will arise in the Course of which we shall see perhaps some wise and virtuous Slave Masters contending for the propriety of general emancipation with all its consequent Train of Crimes. It appears certain to me that the french Directory would not risque high Language to us if they had not receiv'd previous Assurances that the People would force our Government to sacrifice the national Interest. Those Assurances were I presume given and the present Plan propos'd while victory seem'd yet bound to the french Standards; and while you receiv'd official Assurances of the prosperous State of their internal Affairs. The Scene is now not only chang'd but almost revers'd, and I presume that the Language if not the Conduct of certain Persons will experience a similar Change. Adieu I am forc'd to conclude thus abruptly. You know I am always and truly yours—]

Alexander Hamilton Esqr.

6. The MS is incomplete. The bracketed material has been taken from the letter book copy in the Library of Congress.
7. This is a reference to Article 11 of the Treaty of Alliance between the United States and France of February 6, 1778, in which the United States guaranteed French possessions in America (Miller, *Treaties*, II, 39).

To Robert Morris

[*New York, March 5, 1796.* On March 6, 1796, Morris wrote to Hamilton: "I am glad to see by your line of yesterday." *Letter not found.*]

From Robert Morris [1]

Alexander Hamilton Esqre N York   Phila 6 March 1796

Dear Sir

I am glad to see by your line of yesterday [2] that you had got safe home.[3] I am at present in treaty for the Sale of some Lands of Pennsa & perhaps some of the Tracts I proposed to you may be included in the sale. If they are, others shall be Substituted & you may rely that I will not lose a day unnecessarily in preparing & transmitting the Mortgages, but instead of putting the whole into one Mortgage I think it will be best to put one parcel of contiguous Tracts into one Mortgage & another in another & so on—then if any one of those Parcels should be sold, I can pay or exchange the Security without affecting the others.

You omitted to Return the Copy of Mr Greenleafs Deed for the Washington Lotts.[4] The Original is gone to be recorded & I have no other Copy, therefore I request you to send it to me. I am very busy but you shall soon hear again from

Yrs   RM

LC, Robert Morris Papers, Library of Congress.

1. This letter concerns Morris's debt to John B. Church. For the nature of this debt and Morris's efforts to pay it, see the introductory note to Morris to H, June 7, 1795. See also Morris to H, July 20, November 16, December 18, 1795; January 15, 1796.

2. Letter not found.

3. H had been in Philadelphia to appear before the Supreme Court of the United States to argue the constitutionality of the carriage tax. See Morris to H, February 10, 1796.

4. For James Greenleaf, see H to Morris, March 18, 1795, note 21; Morris to H, June 7, 1795, note 7.

Beginning in 1793, Morris, James Greenleaf, and John Nicholson purchased

7,234¾ lots in the City of Washington, each lot consisting of 5,265 square feet. They then sold 769¼ lots, leaving a total of 6,465½ lots. On July 10, 1795, Morris and Nicholson bought Greenleaf's share of these lots as well as 376 acres of land which Greenleaf owned in Washington. When this transaction was completed, Morris and Nicholson jointly owned 7,756 lots in the City of Washington (Morris, *In the Account of Property,* 7–8).

To George Washington

[New York, March 7, 1796]

Introductory Note

This letter contains the first references in Hamilton's extant correspondence to what proved to be a protracted dispute over the Jay Treaty in the House of Representatives. The Senate approved the Jay Treaty on June 24, 1795, and the United States ratified it on August 14, 1795. Following British ratification on October 28, 1795, the ratifications were exchanged at London on that date. Washington proclaimed the treaty on February 29, 1796,[1] and on March 1, 1796, he sent the following message to the Senate and House of Representatives: "The Treaty of Amity, Commerce, and Navigation, concluded between the United States of America and His Britannic Majesty, having been duly ratified, and the ratifications having been exchanged at London on the 28th day of October, 1795, I have directed the same to be promulgated; and herewith transmit a copy thereof for the information of Congress."[2]

Although Washington had proclaimed the treaty, all of its provisions could not be put into effect until Congress voted appropriations for the three commissions provided for in Articles 5, 6, and 7.[3] Despite this fact, the debate in the House began on a somewhat different note on March 2, 1796, when Edward Livingston, a New York City Republican, stated "that it was generally understood that some important Constitutional questions would be discussed when the Treaty lately concluded between this country and Great Britain should come into consideration; it was very desirable, therefore, that every document which might tend to throw light on the subject should be before the House. . . ." He then made the following motion: "*Resolved,* That the President of the United States be requested to lay before this House a copy of the instructions given to the Minister of the United States who negotiated the Treaty

Four copies, Hamilton Papers, Library of Congress.
1. Miller, *Treaties,* II, 245.
2. *Annals of Congress,* V, 48.
3. For the text of Articles 5, 6, and 7 of the Jay Treaty, see "Remarks on the Treaty . . . between the United States and Great Britain," July 9–11, 1795, notes 12, 13, 39. For the text of Article 8, which dealt with the payment of the commissioners and "all other Expences attending the said commissions," see "Remarks on the Treaty . . . between the United States and Great Britain," July 9–11, 1795, note 42.

with Great Britain, communicated by his Message of the first instant, together with the correspondence and other documents relative to the said Treaty." [4]

At this time not all the opponents of the Jay Treaty in the House necessarily agreed with Livingston's resolution. On March 6, 1796, James Madison wrote to Thomas Jefferson: ". . . A motion has been laid on the table by Mr. Livingston, calling on the President for the instructions to Jay &c. The policy of hazarding it is so questionable that he will probably let it sleep or withdraw it. Notice of direct propositions on the Treaty will probably be given tomorrow. The purport & form of them create much diversity of ideas among the opponents of the Treaty. The state of the business as it now presents itself, with the uncertainty of the particular way of thinking in several quarters of the House, make it truly difficult to decide on the course most acceptable to the body of anti-treaty members." [5] On the following day, in deference to "gentlemen to whose opinions he paid the highest respect," Livingston amended his motion by adding the following phrase: "Excepting such of said papers as any existing negotiation may render improper to be disclosed." [6] Madison, who wished to "throw the resolution into such form as not to bear even the appearance of encroaching on the Constitutional rights of the Executive," suggested a more moderate amendment which read: "Except so much of said papers as, in his [the President's] judgment, it may not be consistent with the interest of the United States, at this time, to disclose." [7] Madison's proposal was, however, defeated, and the House turned to the consideration of the resolution which had been made and amended by Livingston.[8] Following more than two weeks of debate, the House, on March 24, 1796, adopted Livingston's resolution by a vote of 62 to 37.[9]

On the day after Livingston's resolution had been introduced, Washington began to gather information concerning its possible import and significance. On March 3, 1796, he wrote to Oliver Wolcott, Jr.: "I perceive by Bache's Paper [10] of this Morning that Mr. Livingston has laid a Resolution on the Table, requesting the President to lay before the House a copy of the Instructions to Mr. Jay. . . . A request somewhat similar to this *was* made, or *about* to be made, I do not now recollect which—nor the conduct that was observed upon the occasion, as it was 2, 3 or more years ago; [11] but as Colo. Hamilton was privy to it,

4. *Annals of Congress,* V, 400–01.
5. ALS, James Madison Papers, Library of Congress.
6. *Annals of Congress,* V, 426.
7. *Annals of Congress,* V, 438.
8. *Annals of Congress,* V, 438.
9. *Annals of Congress,* V, 759–60.
10. Benjamin Franklin Bache was publisher of the [Philadelphia] *Aurora. General Advertiser.*
11. See "Cabinet Meeting. Opinion on Communicating to the Senate the Dispatches of Gouverneur Morris," January 28, 1794. For an earlier request made by a House committee to investigate Major General Arthur St. Clair's expedition against the Indians, see Washington to H, April 6, 1792; Joseph Nourse to H, May 1, 1792, note 1.

I would thank you, if he has not left the City,[12] to see & converse with him thereon—learn what the case & result was—and what he thinks ought to be the conduct of the President if Mr. L—— motion reaches him."[13] The letter to Washington printed below may have been in response to the request the President made through Wolcott, or Hamilton may have offered his suggestions without having been asked for them.

On March 22, in a letter which has not been found, Washington wrote to Hamilton and apparently suggested that he planned to comply with the request in Livingston's resolution.[14] On March 24, in reply to the President's letter, Hamilton wrote: "In the course of this day I shall endeavour to concenter my ideas & prepare something—the premises of which may be in any event proper, admitti⟨ng⟩ of the conclusion being modified & adopted to your eventual determination." Hamilton, however, did not send his draft of Washington's message until March 29,[15] and by then it was too late, for Washington had already agreed to a draft which had been drawn up by Secretary of State Timothy Pickering with minor revisions by Attorney General Charles Lee.[16] The message prepared by Pickering, which refused the House request on constitutional grounds and for reasons of expediency, was sent to the House on March 30.[17] On the following day Washington wrote to Hamilton to explain why he had not used Hamilton's draft. The fact that in this particular instance the President did not rely on his former Secretary of the Treasury fooled even the experts, for on April 4, 1796, Madison wrote to Thomas Jefferson: "There is little doubt in my mind that the message came from N.Y.,"[18] and two weeks later he wrote: "I have no doubt that the advice & even the message were contrived in New York."[19]

On April 7 the House responded to the President's message by approving, by a vote of 57 to 36, two resolutions which had been introduced on the preceding day by Thomas Blount of North Carolina[20] and which asserted the House's "Constitutional right and duty . . . to deliberate on the expediency or inexpediency of carrying such treaty

---

12. H, who had been in Philadelphia to argue the constitutionality of the carriage tax before the Supreme Court of the United States, had left that city for New York on February 24. When Washington wrote to Wolcott on March 3, he may have believed that H was still in the city. On the other hand, H may have returned to Philadelphia for a short visit at the end of February or the beginning of March.

13. ALS, Connecticut Historical Society, Hartford.

14. See H to Washington, March 24, 1796.

15. For this document, see the enclosure in H to Washington, March 29, 1795.

16. ADf (undated, but filed under March 30, 1796), George Washington Papers, Library of Congress.

17. LC, George Washington Papers, Library of Congress. This message is printed in *Annals of Congress*, V, 760–62, and *GW*, XXXV, 2–5.

18. AL, James Madison Papers, Library of Congress.

19. Madison to James Monroe, April 18, 1796 (AL, James Madison Papers, Library of Congress).

20. *Annals of Congress*, V, 782–83.

into effect. . . ." [21] Then, after a week during which it considered other matters, the House on April 14 finally (that is, a month and one-half after Washington had submitted the treaty to Congress) considered the substantive question of appropriations for the implementation of Articles 5, 6, and 7 of the Jay Treaty.[22] Following two weeks of debate, on April 29, 1796, the Committee of the Whole House divided 49 to 49 on a "resolution, which . . . was in substance as follows: *Resolved*, That it is expedient to make the necessary appropriations for carrying the Treaty with Great Britain into effect." Because of the tie, "it remained for the Chairman, Mr. [Frederick A. C.] Muhlenberg [of Pennsylvania] to decide. He said he did not feel satisfied with the resolution as it now stood; he should, however, vote for it, that it might go to the House and there be modified. The resolution was consequently agreed to and reported to the House."[23] On April 30, after defeating by a vote of 50 to 49 a preamble to the motion which was proposed by Henry Dearborn of Massachusetts and which stated among other things that the treaty was "highly objectionable,"[24] the House passed the resolution of the Committee of the Whole by a vote of 51 to 48.[25] On the same day the House "*Ordered* that a bill or bills be brought in pursuant to the said resolution, and that Mr. [James] Hillhouse [of Connecticut], Mr. [Theodore] Sedgwick [of Massachusetts], and Mr. [Albert] Gallatin [of Pennsylvania] do prepare and bring in the same."[26] On May 2 Hillhouse "reported a bill," and on May 3 the House passed the measure.[27] The House bill was adopted by the Senate on May 4,[28] and it became law on May 6. Entitled "An Act making an Appropriation towards defraying the Expenses which may arise in carrying into effect the Treaty of

---

21. The Blount resolutions read: "*Resolved*, That, it being declared by the second section of the second article of the Constitution, 'that the President shall have power, by and with the advice of the Senate, to make Treaties, provided two-thirds of the Senate present concur,' the House of Representatives do not claim any agency in making Treaties; but, that when a Treaty stipulates regulations on any of the subjects submitted by the Constitution to the power of Congress, it must depend, for its execution, as to such stipulations, on a law or laws to be passed by Congress. And it is the Constitutional right and duty of the House of Representatives, in all such cases, to deliberate on the expediency or inexpediency of carrying such Treaty into effect, and to determine and act thereon, as, in their judgment, may be most conducive to the public good.

"*Resolved*, That it is not necessary to the propriety of any application from this House to the Executive, for information desired by them, and which may relate to any Constitutional functions of the House, that the purpose for which such information may be wanted, or to which the same may be applied, should be stated in the application." (*Annals of Congress*, V, 771–72.)

22. *Annals of Congress*, V, 970.
23. *Annals of Congress*, V, 1280.
24. *Annals of Congress*, V, 1282, 1289.
25. *Annals of Congress*, V, 1291.
26. *Annals of Congress*, V, 1291.
27. *Annals of Congress*, V, 1293, 1295.
28. *Annals of Congress*, V, 79–80.

Amity, Commerce and Navigation, made between the United States and the King of Great Britain," it "appropriated a sum not exceeding eighty thousand eight hundred and eight dollars" to cover "the expenses which may arise in carrying into effect the treaty." [29]

[New York, March 7, 1796]

Sir,

I found Young La Fayette here and delivered him your Letter which much relieved him.[30] I fancy you will see him on the first day of April.

Mr. Livingston's motion in the House of Representatives, concerning the production of papers has attracted much attention. The opinion of those who think here is, that if the motion succeeds, it ought not to be complied with. Besides that in a matter of such a nature the production of the papers cannot fail to start [a] new and unpleasant Game—it will be fatal to the Negotiating Power of the Government if it is to be a matter of course for a call of either House of Congress to bring forth all the communication however confidential.

It seems to me that something like the following answer by the President will be advisable.

"A right in the House of Representatives, to demand and have as a matter of course, and without specification of any object all communications respecting a negotiation with a foreign power cannot be admitted without danger of much inconvenience. A discretion in the Executive Department how far and where to comply in such cases is essential to the due conduct of foreign negotiations and is essential to preserve the limits between the Legislative and Executive

---

29. 1 *Stat.* 459.

30. George Washington Motier Lafayette. Washington confirmed his original invitation to Lafayette in the following letter, written from Philadelphia on February 28, 1796: "My dear young friend, My desire to see you, is such, that I request that you and Mr. Festal, will make me a visit about the first of April at this City; by that time the weather will be settled, the roads good, and the travelling pleasant.

"Colo. Hamilton will be the channel thro' which this letter will be conveyed to you; and my wish is that you and Mr. Festal could come by the way of New York to this City, and there make necessary arrangements with that Gentleman with respect to your proceeding hither. . . ." (ADfS, George Washington Papers, Library of Congress.) Felix Frestel (not Festal) was George Washington Motier Lafayette's tutor. For information on Lafayette and Frestel, see H to Washington, October 16, 26, November 19, 26, December 24, 27–30, 1795; Washington to H, October 29, November 10, 18, 23, 28, December 22, 1795, February 13, 1796.

Departments. The present call is altogether indefinite and without any declared purpose. The Executive has no cases on which to judge of the propriety of a compliance with it and cannot therefore without forming a very dangerous precedent comply.

It does not occur that the view of the papers asked for can be relative to any purpose of the competency of the House of Representatives but that of an impeachment. In every case of a foreign Treaty the grounds for an impeachment must primarily be deduced from the nature of the Instrument itself and from nothing extrinsic. If at any time a Treaty should present such grounds and it shall have been so pronounced by the House of Representatives and a further inquiry shall be necessary to ascertain the culpable person, there being then a declared and ascertained object the President would attend with due respect to any application for necessary information."

This is but a hasty and crude outline of what has struck me as an eligible course. For while a too easy compliance will be mischievous, a too peremptory and unqualified refusal might be liable to just criticism.

Most Respectfully & Affectionately I have the honor to be Sir your Obed sert A Hamilton

The President of the U. States.

To Oliver Wolcott, Junior

[New York, March 7–10, 1796]

Dr. Sir

Inclosed are two letters which I will thank you to hand on.

I have just seen *Livingston's* Motion [1] concerning Instructions &c. My first impression is that the propriety of a compliance with the call, if made, is extremely doubtful. But much careful thought on the subject is requisite.

Yrs truly A Hamilton

PS. I hand you also a letter from Mrs. Church [2] to Mr. Beametz [3]— which I will thank you to send to Mr. Talleyrand.[4]

Ol Wolcott Esqr

ALS, Connecticut Historical Society, Hartford.
1. See the introductory note to H to George Washington, March 7, 1796.
2. Angelica Church.
3. Bon-Albert Briois, Chevalier de Beaumetz, had been elected to the National Assembly as a deputy for the nobility of Artois on April 30, 1789, and had become president of the Constituent Assembly on May 30, 1790. Although originally a monarchist, on the outbreak of the French Revolution he joined the constitutional party. Accused of treason in 1792, he fled first to Germany and then to England, where he met Talleyrand. He and Talleyrand sailed for the United States in March, 1794. See H to George Washington, May 5, 1794; Angelica Church to H, September 19, 1794. In Philadelphia he became involved in the affairs of the Holland Land Company, and in May, 1796, he set sail for Calcutta, where he tried unsuccessfully to find purchasers for the company's lands.
4. In September, 1792, Charles Maurice de Talleyrand-Périgord fled from Paris to England. Expelled from England in the spring of 1794, he sailed for the United States, where he became friendly with H. He remained in the United States until June, 1796.

To Robert Morris

[*New York, March 8, 1796.* On March 12, 1796, Morris wrote to Hamilton and referred to "your letters of the 10th & 8th Inst." *Letter of March 8 not found.*]

From William Greene [1]

New York, March 9, 1796. States his determination to abide by whatever opinion Hamilton "should form" in "the case of Messr. John Calogan & Sons." [2] Discusses his dispute with the firm of Shaw and Randall [3] over a cargo of wine and the writ issued against him for £10,000 damages.

ALS, Hamilton Papers, Library of Congress.
1. Greene, a native of England, was a New York City merchant with an extensive overseas trade. See William Bradford and H to Edmund Randolph, November 4, 1794.
2. On April 23, 1796, the New York Supreme Court ordered the sheriff to produce Greene within four days to answer as defendant in a case brought by Thomas and Bernard Cologon (MS Minutes of the New York Supreme Court, January 19–November 5, 1796 [Hall of Records, New York City]). No record has been found that Greene appeared as ordered, but the following entry for May 11, 1796, appears in H's Cash Book, 1795–1804: "William Greene for attending Trial & assisting in compromise" (AD, Hamilton Papers, Library of Congress).

3. This is apparently a reference to the New York City firm of Samuel Shaw, who had died in May, 1794, and Thomas Randall. See Randall to H, August 14, 1791; October 15, 1792; July 15, 1793. See also Goebel, *Law Practice*, II, 234.

To George Clinton [1]

[New York, March 10, 1796.[2] Letter not found.]

1. Clinton, a veteran of the American Revolution, was a member of the Continental Congress from 1775 to 1776. He served as governor of New York from 1777 to 1795.
2. MS list of letters entitled "General Hamilton to Governor George Clinton," Columbia University Libraries.

To John Jay

New York March 10. 1796

Sir

I had the honor duely to receive Your Excellency's letter of the 4th instant. I did not immediately answer it from an indistinct and confused recollection that a state of things existed in reference to the opposite party which did not permit my being concerned for the State. It now appears that I was not mistaken, and that I cannot with propriety execute Your Excellency's desire.

With perfect respect I have the honor to be Sir Yr. very obed servant

ADf, Hamilton Papers, Library of Congress.

To Robert Morris

[New York, March 10, 1796. On March 12, 1796, Morris wrote to Hamilton and referred to "your letters of the 10th and 8th Inst." Letter of March 10 not found.]

To William Loughton Smith [1]

[New York, March 10, 1796]

Dear Sir

I observe Madison brings the power of the House of Representatives in the case of the Treaty to this Question   Is the Agency of the House of Representatives on this subject *deliberative* or *Executive?* [2] On the sophism that this Legislature and each Branch of it is *essentially deliberative* & consequently must have discretion will he, I presume, maintain the freedom of the House to concur or not.[3]

But this sophism is easily refuted. The Legislature & each branch of it is *deliberative* but with *various* restrictions not with *unlimited discretion*. All the injunctions & restrictions in the constitution for instance abrige its *deliberative* faculty & leave it *quoad hoc* merely *executive*. Thus the Constitution enjoins that there shall be a fixed allowance for the Judges which shall not be diminished. The Legislature cannot therefore deliberate whether they will make a permanent provision & when the allowance is fixed they cannot deliberate whether they will appropriate & pay the money. So far their deliberative faculty is abriged. The *mode* of raising & appropriating the money only remains matter of deliberation.

So likewise the Constitution says that the President & Senate shall make Treaties & that these Treaties shall be supreme laws. It is a contradiction to call a thing a law which is not binding. It follows that by constitutional injunction the House of Representatives *quoad* the stipulations of Treaties, as in the case cited respecting the Judges are not deliberative, but merely executive *except* as to the *means of executing*.

Any other Doctrine would vest the Legislature & each House with *unlimited discretion* & destroy the very idea of a Constitution limiting its discretion. The Constitution would at once vanish!

Besides the *legal* power to refuse the execution of a law is a *power to repeal* it. Thus the House of Representatives must as to Treaties concenter in itself the whole legislative power & undertake without the senate to repeal a law. For the law is *complete* by the action of the President & Senate.

Again a Treaty which is a contract between nation & nation abriges even the legislative discretion of the whole legislature by ⟨the⟩ moral obligation of keeping its faith; a fortiori that of one branch. In theory there is no method by which the obligations of a Treaty can be annulled but by mutual consent of the contracting parties—by ill faith in one of them or by a revolution of Government which is of a nature so to change the condition of parties as to render the Treaty inapplicable.[4]

Yrs. A H

March 10. 1796
Wm. Smith Esq

ALS, William Loughton Smith Papers, Library of Congress.
1. Smith was a Federalist member of the House of Representatives from South Carolina, a close friend of H, and one of the leading advocates in the House of the policies which H had introduced as Secretary of the Treasury.
For background to this letter, see the introductory note to H to George Washington, March 7, 1796.
2. This is a reference to a speech by James Madison on March 7, 1796, in the House of Representatives on a motion by Edward Livingston requesting that the President submit to the House papers relating to the negotiations of the Jay Treaty (see the introductory note to H to Washington, March 7, 1796). In the course of this speech Madison said: "The proposition now before the House . . . might be considered as closely connected with this important question. It was to be decided whether the general power of making Treaties supersedes the powers of the House of Representatives, particularly specified in the Constitution, so as to take to the Executive all deliberative will, and leave the House only an executive and ministerial instrumental agency? He was not satisfied whether it was expedient at this time to go into a consideration of this very important question" (*Annals of Congress*, V, 437–38).
3. H was essentially correct in his prediction concerning the position that Madison would take. In a speech in the House on March 10, Madison considered that "construction [of the Constitution], which left with the President and Senate the power of making Treaties, but required at the same time the Legislative sanction and co-operation, in those cases where the Constitution had given express and specific powers to the Legislature." He then said: "It was to be presumed that in all such cases the Legislature would exercise its authority with discretion, allowing due weight to the reasons which led to the Treaty, and to the circumstances of the existence of the Treaty. Still, however, this House, in its Legislative capacity, must exercise its reason; it must deliberate; for deliberation is implied in legislaton. If it must carry all Treaties into effect, it would no longer exercise a Legislative power; it would be the mere instrument of the will of another department, and would have no will of its own. Where the Constitution contains a specific and peremptory injunction on Congress to do a particular act, Congress must, of course, do the act, because the Constitution, which is paramount over all the departments, has expressly taken away the Legislative discretion of Congress. The case is essentially different where the act of one department of Government interferes with a power expressly vested in another, and no where expressly taken

away: here the latter power must be exercised according to its nature; and if it be a Legislative power, it must be exercised with that deliberation and discretion which is essential to the nature of Legislative power" (*Annals of Congress*, V, 493).

4. The contents of this letter should be compared with those of H to Washington, March 7, 29, 1796; H to Rufus King, March 16, 1796.

On March 10, 1796, Smith replied to Madison's speech of the same day. Smith raised most of the points mentioned by H in the above letter, but he also advanced several other arguments in opposition to Livingston's motion (*Annals of Congress*, V, 495-99).

From Robert Morris [1]

Alexander Hamilton Esqre   Phila 12 March 1796

dear Sir

I am concerned to perceive by your letters of the 10th & 8th Inst [2] a degree of solicitude which I did not expect or intend to excite. You will recollect that it was a point conceded by you that even after the Mortgage I might sell & change the Security for one equally Satisfactory, and as I was in Treaty for a Sale, I thought a delay untill that Treaty finished one way or the other was not of Consequence Sufficient to create uneasiness. I also intended to have the Mortgages drawn & sent to you, but as you prefer having a list of the Lands & their Valuation I will send you the same by Mondays Mail & in the mean time I am as ever

Yours   RM

LC, Robert Morris Papers, Library of Congress.

1. This letter concerns Morris's efforts to pay a debt which he owed to John B. Church. For this debt and Morris's attempts to pay it, see the introductory note to Morris to H, June 7, 1795. See also Morris to H, July 20, November 16, December 18, 1795; January 15, March 6, 1796.

2. Neither letter has been found.

From Robert Morris [1]

Alexander Hamilton Esqre   Phila 14 March 1796

Dear Sir

Agreeably to my promise I enclose herewith a List of the Lands which I propose to mortgage to you as Security for the debt due to

Mr Church and I think the value more than Sufficient. For some of these Lands the Patents are issued, for some they are not issued, but the Patents are only considered as Evidence of Title, because when Warrants of Survey are granted the money is paid & a return of the Survey upon the Warrants vests the absolute Fee Simple Title in the Warantee who conveys by Deed Poll to whom he pleases. These Deeds Poll are commonly assigned from one person to another & he that holds them is always entitled to the Land and has the right to take out the patents when he pleases and it is only done *when he pleases,* so that many of the Oldest Estates in Pennsylvania are held to this day without having taken out the Patents. In all decisions in the Courts of Law such Titles have been recognized and confirmed. I have mentioned this matter that you may know every thing respecting the business and at the same time that every Objection may be Removed. I have given Orders for taking out the Patents which is a work of some time owing to the quantity of Business in the Land Office and the slow mode of doing it. In your last letter [2] you supposed that Lands in the preferable Situations might be sold to the Injury or impairing of the Security offered. This was never intended by me, because if any of the Tracks proposed to be mortgaged should be sold either before or after the mortgage takes effect my intention is to substitute other property to your entire Satisfaction otherwise I could not think of making such sales. I believe the Lands standing in my name in the state of new york near Chemung [3] or near the Pennsa Line as marked on DeWitts New Map [4] are now worth about 2 of York Curry P Acre, and I expect soon to be in a Situation to sell the whole, that is about 38000 Acres. If you incline to buy Lands for Mr Church perhaps we may agree for those or some others, so as to discharge this debt with advantage to Mr Church, & in the mean time I am ready to execute the Mortgage as soon as you please.

I am Dr Sir Yrs &c. RM

LC, Robert Morris Papers, Library of Congress.
1. This letter concerns Morris's debt to John B. Church. For this debt and for Morris's efforts to pay it, see the introductory note to Morris to H, June 7, 1795. See also Morris to H, July 20, November 16, December 18, 1795; January 15, March 6, 12, 1796.
2. Letter not found.
3. The town of Chemung was founded in 1788 in what was then part of Tioga County and is now Chemung County, New York.

4. In 1792, Simeon DeWitt, surveyor general of New York, published *A Map of the State of New York* (Albany, 1792). In the following year he published a similar map in New York City. Morris is referring to the second of these two maps.

To Rufus King [1]

New York March 16. 1796

My Dr. Sir

I thank you for letter of the   .[2] My opinion on the resolution [3] when it first appeared was that the President should answer in substance as follows. (viz)

"That it could not be admitted as a right of course in the House of Representatives to call for & have papers in the Executive department essentially those relating to foreign negociations which frequently embrace confidential matters. That under all the circumstances & upon so indefinite a call without any declared specific object he did not think it proper nor consistent with what he owed to a due separation of the respective Powers to comply with the call. That if in the course of the proceedings of the House a question of their competency should arise for which any of the papers in question might be necessary an application made on that ground would be considered with proper respect &c." [4]

But after what has taken place in the discussion, if it can with propriety be got in as to form, I think a stand ought to be made by the President against the usurpation. The following propositions comprise an obvious ground

I The constitution empowers the President with the Senate to make Treaties.

II A treaty is a perfected contract between two nations obligatory on both.

II That cannot be a perfected contract or Treaty to the validity of which the concurrence of any other power in the state is constitutionally necessary. Again—

III The Constitution says a Treaty is a *law*.

IV A law is an obligatory rule of action prescribed by the competent authority. But

V That cannot be such a rule of Action or a *law* to the validity of which the assent of any other power is requisite. Again

VI The object of the *Legislative* Power is to prescribe a rule of Action for our own Nation which includes foreigners coming among us.

VII The object of the Treaty Power is by agreement to settle a rule of Action between two Nations binding on both.

VIII. These objects are essentially different and in a constitutional sense cannot interfere.

IX The Treaty Power binding the *Will* of the nation must within its constitutional limits be paramount to the Legislative power which is that Will; or at least the last *law* being a Treaty must repeal an antecedent contradictory law. And

X If the Legislative power is competent to repeal this law by a subsequent law—this must be the whole legislative power, by a solemn act in the forms of the Constitution, not one branch of the legislative power by disobeying the law.

XI The foregoing construction reconciles the two powers and assigns them distinguishable sp[h]eres of Action. While

XIII The other construction, that claiming that a right of assent is sanction for the House of Representatives, destroys the Treaty making Power & negatives two Propositions in the Constitution *to wit* I that The President with the Senate are competent to make Treaties. II That a Treaty is a Law.

On these grounds with the Presidents name a bulwark not to be shaken is erected. The propositions amount in my judgment to irresistable demonstration.

Yrs.   A Hamilton
                                       March 16. 1796

ALS, New-York Historical Society, New York City; copy, William Cabell Rives Papers, Library of Congress.

1. For background to this letter, see the introductory note to H to George Washington, March 7, 1796. See also H to William Loughton Smith, March 10, 1796.

2. Space left blank in MS. King's letter to H has not been found.

3. H is referring to Edward Livingston's resolution introduced in the House of Representatives on March 2, 1796, requesting that the President submit to the House the papers relating to the negotiation of the Jay Treaty. See the introductory note to H to Washington, March 7, 1796.

4. The contents of this paragraph should be compared with H to Washington, March 7, 1796.

Receipt from Morgan Lewis [1]

[New York, March 18, 1796]

Received New York March 18th 1796 of Alexander Hamilton [Four thousand two hundred & fifty] [2] Dollars in full for the consideration money of a lot and part of a lot of Ground adjoining thereto situate on the Broadway and Marketfield Street in the City of New York [3] as particularly described in a certain indenture bearing date the first day of May MDCCXCIII made between Carlisle Pollock William Rogers and Samuel Corp of the one part and myself of the other part [4] and according to a deed of Partition for ascertaining the said Part of a lot bearing date the twenty second of November MDCCXCIII made between Isaac Bronson and myself [5]—and I promise forthwith to make and deliver to the said Alexander Hamilton a good and sufficient deed in the Law for conveying and assuring to him his heirs and assigns the lot and part of a lot aforesaid with a Covenant of General Warranty for the same according to the metes and bounds in the said deed specified.   Morn: Lewis.

DS, Hamilton Papers, Library of Congress.
  1. Lewis, who had been deputy quartermaster general in the Northern Department during the American Revolution, was the brother-in-law of Chancellor Robert R. Livingston. He was a member of the New York Assembly from 1789 to 1790, attorney general of New York from 1791 to 1792, justice of the New York Supreme Court from 1792 to 1801, and chief justice of the New York Supreme Court from 1801 to 1804.
  2. The words within brackets are in H's handwriting.
  3. The lot and half-lot described in this transaction were part of four lots on the east side of Broadway to the north of Marketfield Street, which H secured for John B. and Angelica Church before their arrival from England in 1797. Lewis sold the middle lot of three lots facing Broadway, approximately 27 by 103 feet in size, and an L-shaped portion of another lot at the rear, the southerly part of which adjoined Marketfield Street. H presumably did not draw up a deed with Lewis for this property, for on August 28, 1797, Morgan and Gertrude Lewis conveyed the lots directly to John B. Church for seventeen hundred pounds, the equivalent of which H had already paid (copy, Conveyances in the Office of the Register, City of New York, Liber 60, 173–76, Hall of Records, New York City). H, however, bought the adjacent lots in trust for the Churches. The history of these lots is told in a conveyance dated May 24, 1798, from H and his wife and Isaac and Ann Bronson to John B. Church. On March 1, 1796, H had bought from Isaac Bronson, a New York City merchant, for two thousand pounds the lot to the south of Lewis's main lot on Broadway and Marketfield Street, together with the re-

mainder of the lot at the rear which Lewis had previously divided with Bronson. In the indenture H and Bronson guaranteed possession of this lot and a half to the Churches, and, in addition, H conveyed to them the lot to the north of Lewis's main lot, which he had bought on May 20, 1796, from John Lasher, inspector of the port of New York, for fifteen hundred pounds (copy, Conveyances in the Office of the Register, City of New York, Liber 60, 176–79, Hall of Records, New York City). An entry in H's Cash Book, 1795–1804, for May 27, 1796, states that H paid Lasher $2,500 and gave him a note for $1,250 for "a lot purchased of him for the said JBC." An entry for September 12, 1796, states that H paid Lasher $1,274.79 for the "principal & Interest of my Note to John Lasher dated May 27, 1796" (AD, Hamilton Papers, Library of Congress).

4. Copy, Conveyances in the Office of the Register, City of New York, Liber 50, 1–3, Hall of Records, New York City.

5. Copy, Conveyances in the Office of the Register, City of New York, Liber 50, 3–4, Hall of Records, New York City.

To Barent Bleecker [1]

New York March 20. 1796

Sir

I presume you have been informed that pursuant to the power given to me by yourself and the other parties concerned, I purchased at Auction the lands in Cosbys Manor claimed by the Trustees of the Ringwood Iron Company. These lands being in the whole 6761 acres cost £2422.13.10 payable ¼ part down one other ¼ on the first Tuesday of next month (April) one other ¼ on the First Tuesday of October next and the remaining ¼ on the first Tuesday of April 1797. The first installment I have paid—and I have therefore to request that you will without delay forward to me your ¼ of that installment and also of the second which will become payable on the 5th of next Month. To preserve the right we have acquired punctuality is essential.

With esteem I am Sir Your obedt servant Alex Hamilton

The sum you are to forward is £302.18.5½

Barent Bleecker Esquire
Albany

ALS, from a typescript furnished by The Detroit Public Library; ADfS, MS Division, New York Public Library.

1. For an explanation of the contents of this letter, see the introductory note to Philip Schuyler to H, August 31, 1795. See also H to Phineas Bond, September 1, 1795; H to Robert Morris, September 1, 1795.

Bleecker was an Albany merchant and land speculator.

From Timothy Pickering

Department of State March 22. 1796.

Dear Sir

The President is anxious to ascertain whether the gentlemen he has thought of for Commissioners under the 6th & 7th articles of the British treaty [1] will accept of those employments. He has concluded to appoint Egbert Benson Esqr.[2] one of the Commissioners for executing the 6th article, relative to the debts owing to British subjects —if he will accept of the employment. He is held in such high estimation for his abilities & integrity, as to render it extremely desirable that the appointment might meet his acceptance. The compensation will not be less than £1000. sterling a year; & it may rise to £1500: we do not yet know what agreement will be made on this head, under the 8th article of the treaty.[3] The continuance of the employment you and he can judge of better than I. Whether he can hold his present office of Judge on the New-York Bench and the office of commissioner, at the same time, you and he can also determine. But should his acceptance of the latter employment necessarily vacate his seat on that bench, it would naturally conduct him to one more important—in the supreme court of the U.States.

I forbear to intimate any other considerations to induce Mr. Benson's acceptance of the proposed office: you will more accurately estimate every motive of expedience and public utility which can properly influence his decision.

I hope Judge Benson is in New-York that his immediate determination may be given; if not, you will be so obliging as to write to him for the purpose. In the mean time the President will be obliged by your acknowledging the receipt of this letter, and embracing the earliest moment to communicate Judge Benson's decision.[4]

I am with sincere respect & esteem   yours   Timothy Pickering

Colo. Hamilton.

ALS, Hamilton Papers, Library of Congress; copy, Massachusetts Historical Society, Boston.

1. For the text of Article 6 of the Jay Treaty, which dealt with the pre-Revolutionary debts owed by Americans to British merchants, and of Article 7, which dealt with the capture and condemnation of United States vessels by the British during the war between Great Britain and revolutionary France, see "Remarks on the Treaty . . . between the United States and Great Britain," July 9-11, 1795, notes 13 and 39.

2. Benson, a New York City attorney, was attorney general of New York from 1777 to 1789, a member of the Assembly from 1777 to 1781 and in 1788, a member of the Continental Congress from 1784 to 1788, an associate judge of the New York Supreme Court from 1794 to 1801, a member of the New York Ratifying Convention in 1788, and a member of the House of Representatives from 1789 to 1793.

3. For the text of Article 8 of the Jay Treaty, see "Remarks on the Treaty . . . between the United States and Great Britain," July 9-11, 1795, note 42.

4. Benson declined the appointment. On March 31, 1796, the President nominated Thomas FitzSimons of Pennsylvania and James Innes of Virginia as the United States representatives on the debt commission, and the Senate confirmed the appointments on the following day (*Executive Journal*, I, 204, 205). See also George Washington to Innes, April 4, 1796 (LC, George Washington Papers, Library of Congress); Timothy Pickering to Innes, April 6, 1796 (LC, RG 59, Domestic Letters of the Department of State, Vol. 9, October 12, 1795–February 28, 1797, National Archives); and Innes to Washington, April 8, 1796 (ALS, George Washington Papers, Library of Congress).

Subsequently, Benson agreed to serve on the St. Croix boundary commission authorized by Article 5 of the Jay Treaty. See Pickering to Benson, September 10, 1796 (LC, RG 59, Domestic Letters of the Department of State, Vol. 9, October 12, 1795–February 28, 1797, National Archives); Pickering to Washington, September 20, 1796 (ALS, RG 59, Miscellaneous Letters, 1790-1799, National Archives).

From George Washington

[*Philadelphia, March 22, 1796.* On March 24, 1796, Hamilton wrote to Washington: "I had the honor to receive yesterday your letter of the 22." *Letter not found.*]

To George Washington[1]

New York March 24 1796

Sir

I had the honor to receive yesterday your letter of the 22.[2] The course you suggest has some obvious advantages & merits careful consideration. I am not however without fears that there are things in the *instructions* to Mr. Jay³ which good policy, considering the matter *externally* as well as *internally*, would render it inexpedient to communicate. This I shall ascertain to day. A middle course is under consideration—that of not communicating the papers to the house but of declaring that the Secretary of State is directed to permit them to be *read* by the *members individually*. But this is liable to a great part of the objections which militate against a full public disclosure. I throw it out however here that you may be thinking of it, if it has not before occurred. In the course of this day I shall endeavour to concenter my ideas & prepare something— the premisses of which may be in any event proper, admitti⟨ng⟩ of the conclusion being modified & adapted to your eventual determination.⁴

Respectfully & Affecty Sir Yr Obed ser   A Hamilton

The President

ALS, Hamilton Papers, Library of Congress; copy, Hamilton Papers, Library of Congress.
   1. For background to this letter, see the introductory note to H to Washington, March 7, 1796. See also H to William Loughton Smith, March 10, 1796; H to Rufus King, March 16, 1796.
   2. Letter not found.
   3. For Secretary of State Edmund Randolph's instructions to John Jay as envoy extraordinary to negotiate a treaty with Great Britain, see H to Washington, April 23, 1794, note 13. See also H to Jay, May 6, 1794.
   4. See H to Washington, March 29, 1796.

*To George Washington*¹

[New York] March 26 1796²

Sir

I perceived by the News Paper that the resolution has been carried. I have not been idle as far a⟨s⟩ my situation would permit but ⟨it⟩³ will not be in my power as I had hoped to send you what I am preparing by this day's Post. The next will carry it. It does not however appear necessary that the Executive should be in a hurry.

The final result in my mind, for reasons I shal⟨l⟩ submit in my next is that the Papers ought all to be refused. I am persuade⟨d⟩ the

Communication of the ins⟨tructions⟩ in particular would do ha⟨rm⟩ to The President & to the Govern⟨ment⟩.

Respecty & Affecty

AL[S], George Washington Papers, Library of Congress; copy, Hamilton Papers, Library of Congress.
 1. For background to this letter, see the introductory note to H to Washington, March 7, 1796. See also H to William Loughton Smith, March 10, 1796; H to Rufus King, March 16, 1796; H to Washington, March 24, 1796.
 2. In *JCHW*, VI, 96, this letter is dated "March 26th, 1799."
 3. The material within broken brackets has been taken from the copy in the Hamilton Papers, Library of Congress.

To George Washington[1]

N Y March 28. 1796

Sir

I am mortified at not being able to send you by this post a certain draft.[2] But the opinion that reasons ought to be given & pretty fully has extended it to considerable length & a desire to make it accurate as to *idea* & expression keeps it still upon the anvil. But it is so far prepared that I can assure it by tomorrow's Post. Delay is always unpleasant. But the case is delicate & important enough to justify it.

I mentioned as my opinion that the instruction to Mr. Jay if published would do harm.[3] The truth unfortunately is that it is in general a crude mass—which will do no credit to the administration. This was my impression of it at the time—but the delicacy of attempting too much reformation in the work of another head of Department, the hurry of the moment, & a great Confidence in the person to be sent prevented my attempting that reformation.

There are several particular points in it which would have a very ill effect to be published.[4]

I   There is a part which seems to admit the idea that an adjustment might be made respecting the spoliations which should leave that matter finally to the *ordinary course of* the British Courts. This is obscurely & ambiguously expressed but the least colour for such a construction would give occasion for infinite clamour.

II   The negotiator is expressly instructed to accede to the *intire abolition* of *alienism* as to inheritances of land. You have seen what clamour has been made about the moderate modification of this idea in the Treaty [5] & can thence judge what a load would fall on this part of the instruction.

III He is instructed to enter into an article against the employment of Privateers in War. This is manifestly against the policy of a Country which has no *navy* in a Treaty with a Country which has a large navy. For it is chiefly by privateers that we could annoy the trade of Great Britain. Some would consider this as a philosophic whim; others as an intentional sacrifice of the interests of this Country to G B.

IV There are several parts which hold up the disreputable & disorganising idea of not being able to *restrain our own Citizens*.

V There are parts which though proper to our own Agent, the publication of which would be a violation of decorum towards G Britain—after an amicable termination of the affair & offensive because contrary to the rules of friendly & respectful procedure.

VI The instructions have too little point (in the spirit of the framer who was in the habit of saying much & saying little) & would be censured as altogether deficient in firmness & spirit.

On the whole I have no doubt that the publication of these instructions would do harm to the Executive & to the character & interest of the Government.

If the President concludes to send papers—they ought only to be the Commissions & Mr. Jay's *correspondence;* saying that these are all, that it appears to him for the public interest to send.

But he may be then prepared for as much clamour as if he sent none. It would be said that what was done shewed that the *principle* had not been the obstacle & that the instructions were witheld because they would not bear the light. Or at most only that part of the instruction should go which begins at these words. "4 This enumeration presents generally the objects which it is desireable to comprise in a Commercial Treaty &c." to the end of the instructions.

But after the fullest reflection I have been able to give the subject (though I perceive serious dangers & inconveniencies in the course) I entertain a final opinion that it will be best, after the usurpation attempted by the house of Representatives, to send none & to resist in totality.⁶

Affecty & respecy   Yr Obed ser   A Hamilton

The President

ALS, George Washington Papers, Library of Congress.
1. For background to this letter, see the introductory note to H to Washington, March 7, 1796. See also H to William Loughton Smith, March 10, 1796; H to Rufus King, March 16, 1796; H to Washington, March 24, 26, 1796.
2. This is a reference to the draft which H had promised in his letter to Washington on March 24. This draft was for the reply to the request of the House of Representatives for the papers relating to the negotiation of the Jay Treaty. See the introductory note to H to Washington, March 7, 1796.
3. See H to Washington, March 24, 1796.
4. For Edmund Randolph's instructions to John Jay as envoy extraordinary to negotiate a treaty with Great Britain, see H to Washington, April 23, 1794, note 13. See also H to John Jay, May 6, 1794.
5. See H's discussion of Article 9 of the Jay Treaty in "The Defence No. XVII," September 22, 1795.
6. In the margin opposite the last three paragraphs of this letter H wrote: "The draft will be so framed as to admit of this conclusion."

To George Washington

[New York] March 29 [1796]

Sir

I wish the inclosed could have been sent in a more perfect State.¹ But it was impossible. I hope however it can be made out & may be useful.

It required more time to say all that was proper in a more condensed form.

ALS, George Washington Papers, Library of Congress.
1. For background to this letter, see the introductory note to H to Washington, March 7, 1796. See also H to William Loughton Smith, March 10, 1796; H to Rufus King, March 16, 1796; H to Washington, March 24, 26, 28, 1796.
In this letter H enclosed his draft of the President's reply to the resolution introduced into the House of Representatives by Edward Livingston on March 2, 1796, and passed by the House on March 24. This resolution requested the President to submit to the House the papers relating to the negotiation of the Jay Treaty. Washington, in submitting his reply, however, used a draft prepared by Timothy Pickering and revised by Charles Lee rather than the draft sent by H. For Washington's reasons for not using H's draft, see Washington to H, March 31, 1796.

In considering the course to be pursued by the President it may be well he should be reminded that the same description of men who call for the papers have heretofore maintained that they were not bound by any communication in confidence but were free afterwards to do as they pleased with papers sent them.

Respect & Aff A Hamilton

[ENCLOSURE]²

Gentlemen

I have received your resolution   ³ and have considered it with the attention always due to a request of the House of Representatives. I feel a consciousness (not contradicted I trust by any part of my conduct) of a sincere disposition to respect the rights privileges and authorities of Congress collectively and in its separate branches—to pay just deference to their opinions and wishes—to avoid intrusion on their province—to communicate freely information pertinent to the subjects of their deliberation. But this disposition, keeping steadily in view the public good, must likewise be limited and directed by the duty, incumbent upon us all, of preserving inviolate the constitutional boundary between the several de-

2. ADf, George Washington Papers, Library of Congress; ADf, Hamilton Papers, Library of Congress; copy, in the handwriting of H and in an unknown handwriting, Hamilton Papers, Library of Congress.

The draft in the Hamilton Papers, Library of Congress, which is shorter than the other two versions, was prepared by H as a working paper for the document which he eventually sent to Washington. The draft in the George Washington Papers, Library of Congress, is the version which H sent to the President and which is printed above. Because H did not retain a copy of this document (see H to Rufus King, April 2, 1796), he wrote to Washington on April 2, 1796: "If there is time, I should like to have the paper lately sent to correct prune guard & strengthen." H, however, did not have time to revise this draft, and he returned it to Washington on April 8. See H to Washington, April 8, 1796.

Before returning the draft to Washington on April 8, H and an assistant made a copy of it. This is the copy which is now in the Hamilton Papers, Library of Congress. It is possible that this copy was sent to Rufus King, to whom H had promised it. See H to King, April 12, 1796. If so, the following note in H's handwriting that appears on a separate page at the end of the copy was directed to King: "If any use is made of this it must be in a way intirely consistent with the state of the thing—so that it may never appear that it has been communicated. The assistant copier knows nothing of the object ⟨&⟩ is altogether discreet."

3. Space left blank in MS. The resolution was passed on March 24, 1796. See note 1.

partments of the Government: a duty enjoined by the very nature of a constitution which defines and distributes the powers delegated among different dipositories, enforced by the solemn sanction of an oath, and only to be fulfilled by a regard no less scrupulous for the rights of the Executive than for those of every other Department.

When I communicated to the House of Representatives the Treaty lately made with Great Britain,[4] I did not transmit the papers respecting its negotiation, for reasons which appeared to me decisive.

It is contrary to the general practice of Governments to promulge the intermediate transactions of a foreign negotiation without weighty and special reasons. The motives for great delicacy and reserve on this point are powerful. There may be situations of a Country, in which particular occurrences of a negotiation, though conducted with the best views to its interest and even to a satisfactory issue, if immediately disclosed, might tend to embarrassment and mischief in the interior affairs of that Country. Confidential discussions and overtures are inseparable from the nature of certain negotiations and frequently occur in others—essays are occasionally made by one party to discover the views of another in reference to collateral objects—motives are sometimes assigned for what is yielded by one party to another: which, if made public, might kindle the resentment or jealousy of other powers, or might raise in them pretensions not expedient to be gratified. Hence it is a rule of mutual convenience and security among nations that neither shall without adequate cause and proper reserves promulge the details of a Negotiation between them: otherwise one party might be injured by the disclosures of the other, and sometimes without being aware of the injury likely to be done.

Consequently, The general neglect of this rule in the practice of a Government would naturally tend to destroy that confidence in its prudence and delicacy—that freedom of communication with it; which are so important in the intercourses between Nation and Nation, towards the accommodation of mutual differences, and the adjustment of mutual interests.

Neither would it be likely to promote the advantage of a Nation, that the Agents of a foreign Government, with which it was at any

4. The treaty was communicated on March 1, 1796 (*Annals of Congress*, V, 48).

time in Treaty, should act under the apprehension that every expression, every step of theirs would presently be exposed, by the promulgation of the other party, to the criticism of their political adversaries at home. The disposition to a liberal and perhaps for that very reason a wise policy in them might be checked by the reflection that it might afterwards appear from the disclosures on the other side, that they had not made as good bargains as they might have made. And while they might be stimulated by this to extraordinary effort and perseverance; maxims of greater secrecy and reserve in their Cabinet would leave their competitors in the negotiation without the same motive to exertion. These having nothing to fear from the indiscretion of the opposite Government would only have to manage with caution their communications to their own. The consequences of such a state of things would naturally be an increase of obstacles to the favourable close of a negotiation, and the probability of worse bargains for the Nation, in the habit of giving indiscreet publicity to its proceedings.

The Agents of such a Nation, themselves, would have strong inducements to extreme reserve in their communications with their own government; lest parts of their conduct might subject them in other quarters to unfriendly and uncandid constructions—which might so narrow the information they gave as scarcely to afford sufficient light either with regard to the fitness of their own course of proceeding or the true state and prospects of the negotiation with which they were charged.

And thus in different ways the channels of information to a Government might be materially obstructed by the impolitic practice of too free disclosure in regard to its foreign negotiations.

Moreover—It is not uncommon for the instructions to negotiating Agents, especially where differences are to be settled, to contain observations on the views and motives of the other party, which after an amicable termination of the business, it would be contrary to decorum, unfriendly and offensive, to make public. Such instructions also frequently manifest views, which, if disclosed, might renew sources of jealousy and ill will which a Treaty had extinguished—might exhibit eventual plans of proceeding which had better remain unknown for future emergencies, & might even furnish occasion for suspicion, and pretext for discontent, to other powers. And, in general, where more had been obtained by a Treaty than the *ultimata* prescribed to the negotiation, it would be inexpedient to publish those *ultimata:* Since, among other ill effects, the publication of them might prejudice the interest of the Country in future negotiations with the same or with different powers.

These reasons explain the grounds of a prevailing rule of Conduct among prudent Governments, (viz) not to promulge without weighty cause nor without due reserves the particulars of a foreign negotiation. It so happens indeed that many of them have no immediate application to the case of the present Treaty. And it would be unadviseable to discriminate here between such as may and such as may not so apply. But it would be very extraordinary, situated as the UStates were in relation to Great Britain, at the commencement of the negotiation if some of them did not operate against a full disclosure of the papers, in which it is recorded.

Connected with these general reasons against the transmission of the papers with the Treaty, it was proper to consider if there were any special reasons which recommended in the particular case a departure from the rule, and especially whether there was any purpose to which the house of Representatives is constitutionally competent, which might be elucidated by those papers.

This involved a consideration of the nature of the constitutional agency of that house, in regard to Treaties.

The Constitution of the U States empowers the President with the advice and consent of the Senate two thirds concurring to "MAKE Treaties." It no where professes to authorise the House of Representatives, or any other branch of the Government, to partake with the President and Senate in the making of Treaties. The whole Power of making Treaties is therefore by the terms of the Constitution vested in the President and Senate.

To *make* a Treaty, as applied to Nations, is to *conclude* a contract between them *obligatory on their faith*. But that cannot be an (obligatory) contract, to the validity and obligation of which the assent of another power in the state is constitutionally necessary.

Again: The Constitution declares that a Treaty made under the authority of the U States shall be a supreme law of the land—let it be said "a law." A law is an obligatory rule of action prescribed by the competent authority: But that cannot be an obligatory rule of action, or a *law*, to the validity and obligation of which the assent of another power in the state is constitutionally necessary.

Hence, a discretionary right in the House of Representatives, to assent or not to a Treaty, or what is equivalent to execute it or not, would negative these two important propositions of our constitution I That the President and Senate shall have power to make Treaties II That a Treaty made by them shall be a law—and in the room of them would establish this proposition "That the power of making Treaties resides in the President, Senate and House of Representatives." For whatever coloring may be given a right of discretionary assent to a contract is in substance a right to participate in the making of it.

Is there any thing in the constitution which by *necessary* implication changes the force of the express terms that regulate the deposit of the Power to make Treaties?

If there is, it must be found in those clauses which regulate the deposit of the Legislative Power. Here two questions arise—

I Can the Power of Treaty reach and embrace objects upon which the legislative power is authorised to act, as the regulation of Commerce, the defining of piracy &c or are these objects virtually excepted out of the operation of that power?

II If it can reach and embrace those objects, is there any principle which as to them gives to Congress or more properly the House of Representatives, a discretionary right of assent or dissent?

The affirmative of the first question is supported by these considerations.

I The words which establish the Power of Treaty are manifestly broad enough to comprehend all Treaties.

II It is a reasonable presumption, that they were meant to extend to all treaties usual among nations, and so to be commensurate with the variety of exigencies and objects of intercourse which occur between nation and nation; in other words that they were meant to enable the Organ of the Power to manage with efficacy the external affairs of the Country in all cases in which they must depend upon compact with another nation.

III The Treaties usual among nations are principally those of Peace, Alliance and Commerce. It is the office of Treaties of peace to establish the cessation of hostilities and the conditions of it, including frequently indemnifications, sometimes pecuniary ones. It is the office of Treaties of alliance to establish cases in which nations shall succour each other in war stipulating a union of forces, the furnishing of troops, ships of war, pecuniary and other aids. It is the office of Treaties of Commerce to establish rules and conditions according to which nations shall trade with each other, regulating as far as they go the external commerce of the nations in Treaty— whence it is evident that Treaties naturally bear in different ways upon many of the most important objects, upon which the legislative power is authorised to act, as the appropriation of money, the raising of armies, the equipment of fleets, the declaring of war, the regulation of Trade. But

IV This is no objection to the Power of Treaty having a capacity to embrace those objects [5] 1 Because that latitude is essential to the great ends for which the Power is instituted 2 Because un-

---

5. In the draft in the Hamilton Papers, Library of Congress, this and the following three paragraphs read as follows: "IV. This is no objection to allowing the power a latitude equal to the embracing of such objects—Because that latitude is essential to the great national ends for which the power is instituted—Because the sphere of action of the legislative Power is intrinsically and inherently united to the jurisdiction of the Nation of which it is—and its arm too short to reach a single case in which a common obligatory rule of action for two nations is to be established—Because the establishment of such a rule of action, which from the independence of nations can only be by compact must be of the office of that power in the state which is charged to make treaties or compacts—Because this power acts by pledging the faith of the nation and binding its will by the obligation of a promise; while the legislative power acts by prescribing laws and enforcing them by sanctions—Because there is no incongruity or contradiction in supposing the Treaty Power in the establishment of a joint or common rule of action with another nation to act upon the same subject which the legislative power may act upon in the establishment of a separate rule of action for our own Nation—Because the stipulations of a Treaty can only be exceptions *quoad hoc* to the discretion of the legislative power and it will always still have a wide field of action beyond and out of the exceptions of Treaty—Because there is no difficulty in considering the stipulations of a Treaty as restraints upon the legislative discretion inasmuch as those stipulations operate by pledging the faith of a nation and laying it under a moral obligation—and the will of a nation as of an individual may be bound by the moral obligation of a contract—Because the organ of the Treaty Power is an organ of national will as well as the organ of the legislative power and there is no incongruity in supposing that its discretionary will through one organ may be bound by the pledge of its faith through the other organ: consequently the supposition that the Treaty Power acting in one sphere and the legislative Power acting in a different sphere may embrace in their action the same objects involves no collision in the theory of the constitution—but on the contrary reconciles the different parts of it and leaves a consistent and salutary latitude to each."

less the Power of Treaty can embrace objects upon which the legislative power may also act, it is essentially nugatory—often inadequate to mere treaties of Peace—always inadequate to Treaties of Alliance or Commerce   3 Because it is the office of the legislative power to establish separate rules of action for the nation of which it is—[6]its arm being too short to reach a single case in which a common obligatory rule of action for two nations is to be established   IV Because inasmuch as a common rule of action, for independent nations can only be established by compact, it necessarily is of the office of the Power of Treaty to effect its establishment   V Because the power of legislation being unable to effect what the power of Treaty must effect, it is unreasonable to suppose that the former was intended to exclude the action of the latter   VI Because on the other hand there is no incongruity in the supposition that the Power of Treaty, in establishing a joint rule of action with another nation, may act upon the same subject which the Legislative Power may act upon, in establishing a separate rule of action for one nation   VII Because it is a common case for the different powers of Government to act upon the same subject within different spheres and in different modes. Thus the legislative power lays and provides for the collection of a particular tax—the Executive Power collects the tax and brings it into the Treasury.[7] So the power of Treaty may stipulate pecuniary indemnification for an injury and the Legislative power may execute the stipulation by providing & designating the fund out of which the indemnification shall be made. As in the first case the Executive Power is auxiliary to the Legislative, so in the last legislative Power is auxiliary to the Power of Treaty. VIII Because this doctrine leads to no collision of powers, inasmuch as the stipulations of a Treaty may reasonably be considered as restraints upon the legislative discretion. Those stipulations operate by pledging the faith of a nation and restricting its will by the force of moral obligation, and it is a fundamental principle of social right that the will of a nation as well as that of an indi-

6. A this point in the copy in the Hamilton Papers, Library of Congress, "(the organ)" was added.
7. At this point in the copy in the Hamilton Papers, Library of Congress, the following sentence was written and crossed out: "So the legislative power may prescribe a regulation of Trade by law, and the Treaty Power may establish one by agreement."

vidual may be bound by the moral obligation of a contract. IX Because the organ of the Power of Treaty is as truly the Organ of the Will of a Nation as that of its legislative Power; and there is no incongruity in the supposition, that the will of a Nation, acting through one organ, may be bound by the pledge of its faith through another Organ. From these different views of the subject it results, that the position that the Power of Legislation, acting in one sphere, and the power of Treaty, acting in another sphere, may embrace in their action the same objects, involves no interference of constitutional Powers; and of course that the latter may reach and comprehend objects which the former is authorised to act upon; which it is necessary to suppose it does do since the contrary supposition would essentially destroy the Power of Treaty: whereas the stipulations of Treaties being only particular exceptions to the discretion of the Legislative Power, this power will always still have a wide field of action beyond and out of the exceptions.

The latitude of the Power of Treaty granted by analogous terms in the articles of our late confederation as practiced upon for years in treaties with several foreign Powers and acquiesced in by the Governments and citizens of these states, is an unequivocal comment upon the meaning of the provision in our present constitution and a conclusive evidence of the sense in which it was understood by those who planned and those who adopted the Constitution—supporting fully the foregoing construction of the Power. That latitude cannot be indebted to the circumstance of all the power granted by the confederation being in one body—for that body had legislative power in but very few cases & none in some very important cases embraced by its treaties. The examples of past practice under our present Government without the least question of its propriety afford a further corroboration of the intended & accepted sense of the Constitutional instrument.

The negative of the second question above stated is supported by these considerations.

I A discretionary right of assent in the House of Representatives (as before shewn) would contradict the two important propositions of the Constitution—That the President with the Senate shall have power to make Treaties—That the Treaties so made shall be laws.

II It supposes the House of Representatives at liberty to contravene the faith of the Nation engaged in a Treaty made by the declared constitutional Agents of the Nation for that purpose—and thus implies the contradiction that a Nation may rightfully pledge its faith through one organ, and without any change of circumstances to dissolve the obligation may revoke the pledge through another organ.

III The obvious import of the terms which grant the Power of Treaty can only be controuled, if at all, by some manifest necessary implication in favour of the discretionary right which has been mentioned. But it has been seen that no such implication can be derived from the mere grant of certain powers to the House of Representatives *in common* with the other branch of the legislative body. As there is a rational construction which renders the due exercise of these powers in the cases to which they are competent compatible with the operation of the power of Treaty in all the necessary latitude, excluding the discretionary cooperation of the house of Representatives, that construction is to be preferred. It is far more natural to consider the exercise of those powers as liable to the exceptions which the power of Treaty granted to the President and Senate may make; than to infer from them a right in the House to share in this power in opposition to the terms of the grant and without a single expression in the constitution to designate the right. It is improbable that the constitution intended to vest in the house of Representatives so extensive a controul over treaties, without a single phrase that would look directly to the object. It is the more improbable, because the Senate being in the first instance a party to treaties, the right of discretionary cooperation in the House of Representatives, in virtue of its legislative character, would in fact terminate in itself, though but a part of the legislative body—which suggests this question,—Can the House of Representatives have any right in virtue of its *general* legislative character which is not effectually participated [in] by the Senate?

IV The claim of such a right on the ground that the Legislative power is essentially deliberative, that wherever its agency is in question it has a right to act or not—and that consequently where provision by law is requisite to execute a Treaty there is liberty to refuse it—cannot be acceded to without admitting in the legislative body and in each part of it an absolute discretion incontroulable by any constitutional injunctions limits or restrictions; thereby overturning the fabric of a fixed & definite constitution and erecting upon its ruins a legislative Omnipotence.

It would, for example, give to Congress a discretion to allow or not a fixed compensation to the Judges, though the constitution expressly enjoins "that they shall at stated times receive for their services a compensation, which shall not be diminished during their continuance in office"; and would sacrifice this solemn & peremptory command of the Constitution to the opinion of Congress respecting a more essential application of the public money. Can this be true? Can any thing but absolute inability excuse a compliance with this injunction, and does not the constitution presuppose a moral impossib[il]ity of such inability? [8] If there be a legal discretion in any

---

8. The remainder of the draft in the Hamilton Papers, Library of Congress, reads: "Can any thing but absolute inability excuse the compliance with this injunction & which the assent or sanction of any other power in the state is constitutionally requisite.

"A right in the House of Representatives to participate in giving validity to a treaty is a right to cooperate in the making of treaties. The power to make treaties would then not be in the President & Senate as the Constitution declares but in the President & the two houses of Congress.

"A legal discretion to refuse the execution of a law is virtually to repeal it & a power to repeal a law cannot under our constitution be claimed by either branch of Congress. The House of Representatives therefore cannot constitutionally refuse to execute a Treaty made by the President with the advice and consent of the Senate which is consistent with the Constitution.

"To say that the Legislative body & consequently each member of it is essentially deliberative and wherever its cooperation is requested is free to refuse it—is to say that there is an unlimited discretion in Congress, that there are and can be no constitutional restrictions on its discretions and consequently that there is no Constitution or fundamental law—for the very idea of a Constitution or fundamental law presupposes restraints on the Legislative discretion and that as far as those restraints extend it is not free to act, it is not deliberative but executive and ministerial. The opposite doctrine erects a legislative omnipotence upon the ruins of a limited constitution.

"The truth must then be that, each branch of the legislature is only free to act as it pleases where the constitution and the laws impose no restraint. Its legal discretion is limited by all the injunctions and prohibitions in the constitution and by all the provisions of antecedent laws until they are abrogated by the competent authority.

"The obligation of a law continues until it is repealed or annulled by the proper authority. Till then it is binding on all; for it is a vital principle of a free Government that the will of no individual or delegated body in the state shall be above the law or uncontrouled by it—except in so far as the legislature by an authentic act within the limits & in the forms of the constitution may repeal a law.

"It follows that though a Treaty made by the P with the advice & consent of the Senate containing matter not permitted by the Constitution to be con-

case to contravene this injunction, what limit is there to the legal discretion of the legislative body? What injunction, what restriction

tained in it may for that reason be unconstitutional and void—yet if it contains nothing but what the constitution permits it to contain, it is then valid and conclusive & can require no other consent or sanction to its perfection & complete obligation. As a Treaty it must bind the faith of the Nation, as a law it must bind the will of all, till it ceases to be a Treaty & a law by regular abrogation or repeal.

"Questions may arise as to the cases in which & the authority by which in our constitution a Treaty consonant with the Constitution once perfected may lose or be divested of its obligatory force—but nothing is discernable in the constitution to authorize one branch of the Legislature or the house of representatives in particular to pronounce the existence of such cases—still less to refuse compliance with such a Treaty from the beginning and without the pretence of any events having happened to change the intrinsic & original obligation.

"While the claim for the House of a Representatives of a right of assent or sanction to Treaties negates the two important propositions of the Constitution that the President with the Senate shall have power to make Treaties & that the Treaties so made shall be supreme laws of the land the contrary doctrine gives the Constitution its true effect leaves all the powers of Government free to act in their proper spheres.

"Tis the province of the legislative power to prescribe rules of action for the Nation of which it is to regulate the affairs of that Nation separately. Its arm is too short to reach the establishment of a common rule for its own Nation & a foreign Nation.

"Tis the province of the Treaty power to establish this common rule, which operating by way of contract binds the faith of a Nation, and binding its faith binds its will by the strongest bond of moral obligation.

"Trade P & the Treaty power are both powers to make laws. Whether one be supposed paramount to the other or both coordinate—the law made by one must at least oblige till abrogated by the other.

"Since then it is the province of the legislative power to establish rules of action for our own nation and the province of the Treaty-power to establish joint rules of action of our own and another nation, it follows that their spheres of action being different, in a constitutional sense there can be no collision.

"To avoid a collision in fact, it is only necessary to follow a very clear principle of morality to wit that the will of a nation is bound legally & morally though not physically bound by its contracts—that the legislative power which is the internal organ of the national will is bound by the Treaty power which is the external organ of its will—that a separate rule which the national will is free to abrogate ought to yield to a joint rule which is enforced by the obligation of good faith—and that both these organs of the national Will are subordinate to the constitution which creates them and is the common Commission.

"This general doctrine of morality is enforced by that provision of our constitution which ordains that treaties shall be ipso facto laws; a provision, I believe peculiar to our constitution. It is a different thing whether Treaties binding the faith of the Nation shall morally oblige the Legislative power to execute them & whether they shall have immediately & without any further sanction the force of laws. The latter is the case in our government by force of a fundamental law and is a very material ingredient in the force of our Treaties.

of the constitution may they not supersede? If the Constitution cannot direct the exercise of their authority in particular cases how can it limit it in any? What becomes of the appeal to our Courts on the constitutionality of a legislative act? What becomes of the power they solemnly assert to test such an act by the constitutional Commission and to pronounce it operative or null according to its conformity with a repugnance to that Commission? What in fine becomes of the Constitution itself?

This inquiry suggests a truth fundamental to the principles of our Government and all important to the security of the People of the U States—namely that the legislative body is not deliberative in all cases, that it is only deliberative and discretionary where the constitution and the laws lay it under no command nor prohibition —that where they command, it can only execute—where they prohibit it cannot act. If the thing be commanded and the means of execution are undefined it may then deliberate on the choice of the means—but it is obliged to devise some means. It is true that the Constitution provides no method of compelling the legislative body to act, but it is not the less under a Constitutional legal and moral obligation to act, where action is prescribed, & in conformity with the rule of action prescribed.

In asserting the authority of laws as well as of the constitution to direct and restrain the position is to be understood with this difference. The constitution obliges always—the laws 'till they are annulled or repealed by the proper authority. But till then they oblige the legislative body as well as individuals; and all their antecedent effects are valid and binding. And the abrogation or repeal of a law must be by an act of the regular organ of the national will for that purpose in the forms of the constitution; not by a mere refusal to

---

"A treaty being a law must of necessity abrogate all antecedent contrary laws and must legally as well as morally obey all parts of the Government.

"If we suppose the legislative Power coordinate with the Treaty power it will only follow that the Legislative Body by a legislative act may repeal or annull a Treaty; it will not follow that a part of that body by doing nothing may repeal or annull it—for the legislative power reposes in the whole body, not in any part of it.

"The proposition before stated seems to be universally true that a law must operate & oblige all till repealed or annulled by another law.

"It is another question what a Treaty may constitutionally embrace—or whether it may act upon matters which the Legislative power may also act upon."

give effect to its injunctions and requisitions; especially by a part of the legislative body. A legal discretion to refuse the execution of a preexisting law is virtually a power to repeal it—and to attribute this discretion to a part of the legislative body is to attribute to it the whole instead of a part of the legislative power in the given case. When towards the execution of an antecedent law further legislative provision is necessary, the past effects of the law are obligatory; and a positive repeal or suspension by the whole legislature is requisite to arrest its future operation. The idea is essential in a government like ours that there is no body of men or individual above the law; not even the legislative body till by an act of legislation they have annulled the law.

The argument from the principle of an essentially deliberative faculty in the legislative body is the less admissible, because it would result from it that the Nation could never be conclusively bound by a Treaty. Why should the inherent discretion of a future legislature be more bound by the assent of a preceding one than this was by a pledge of the public faith through the President & Senate.[9]

Hence it follows that the house of representatives have no moral power to refuse the execution of a treaty, which is not contrary to the constitution, because it pledges the public faith, and have no legal power to refuse its execution because it is a law—until at least it ceases to be a law by a regular act of revocation of the competent authority.

The ingredient peculiar to our Constitution, in that provision, which declares that Treaties are laws, is of no inconsiderable weight in the question. It is one thing whether a Treaty pledging the faith of the Nation shall by force of moral duty oblige the legislative will to carry it into effect; another whether it shall be of itself a law. The last is the case in our constitution which by a fundamental decree gives the character of a law to every Treaty, made under the authority which it designates. Treaties therefore in our government of themselves and without any additional sanction have full legal perfection as laws.

Questions may be made as to the cases in which and the authority

9. At this point the following sentence is added in the copy in the Hamilton Papers, Library of Congress: "Even the Senate itself after having assented to a Treaty by two thirds in one capacity might in another by a bare majority refuse to execute; a contradiction not to be vindicated by any just theory."

by which under our constitution a Treaty consonant with it may be pronounced to have lost or may be divested of its obligatory force; a point not necessary now to be discussed. But admitting that authority to reside in the legislative body—still its exercise must be by an act of Congress declaring the fact and the consequence, or declaring war against the power with whom the Treaty is. There is perceived to be nothing in our constitution, no rule of Constitutional law, to authorise one branch alone, or the House of Representatives in particular, to pronounce the existence of such cases, or from the beginning to refuse compliance with such a Treaty without any new events to change the original obligations. A right in the whole Legislative body consisting of the two houses of Congress by a collective act to pronounce the cases of non operation & nullity of a Treaty asserts every thing that can reasonably be claimed in favour of the legislative Power, presents a consistent rule & obviates all pretence of collision.[10]

How discordant might be the results of a doctrine that the House of Representatives may at discretion execute or not a constitutional Treaty! What confusion, if our Courts of Justice should recognise & enforce as laws treaties, the obligation of which was denied by the House of Representatives!—and that on a principle of inherent discretion which no decision of the Courts could guide. We might see our commercial & fiscal systems disorganised by the breaches made

10. At this point in the draft in the Hamilton Papers, Library of Congress, H wrote and crossed out the following two paragraphs: "Arguments opposed to this reasoning drawn from the practice of any other Government must be apt to mislead. If such government have not a precise written constitution delineating the powers of its several departments—if it has been subjected to frequent struggles between the prerogatives of one department & the authorities and privileges of another—if innovations on its primitive principles from time to time have been the result of those struggles—there is not sufficient analogy between that Government and ours to admit of a just inference from one to the other. It is natural to expect in such a Government a mixture and confusion of powers which are inapplicable to a Government founded on a written constitution; one main object of which is to define and distribute its power.

"But there is a peculiar ingredient in our constitution, serving as an additional source of discrimination in that provision, which makes Treaties *ipso facto* laws. It is one thing whether a Treaty pled[g]ing the faith of the Nation shall by the force of moral duty oblige the legislative will to carry it into effect—another whether it shall be of itself a law. The last is expressly the case of our constitution, which by the fundamental decree of the Nation, gives the full force of law to every treaty made under the authority designated in its constitution."

in antecedent laws by posterior treaties, through the want of some collateral provisions requisite to give due effect to the principle of the new rule.

Can that doctrine be true which may present a Treaty operating as a law upon all the citizens of a country and yet legally disregarded by a portion of the legislative body?

The sound conclusion appears to be—that when a Treaty contains nothing but what the constitution permits, it is conclusive upon ALL and ALL are bound to give it effect. When it contains more than the constitution permits it is void either in the whole or as to so much as it improperly contains.

While I can discover no sufficient foundation in the constitution for the claim of a discretionary right in the House of Representatives to participate in giving validity to Treaties; I am confirmed in the contrary inference by the knowlege I have that the expediency of this participation was considered by the Convention which planned the Constitution and was by them overruled.

The greatness of the power of Treaty under this construction is no objection to its truth. It is doubtless a great power, and necessarily so, else it could not answer those purposes of national security and interest in the external relations of a Country for which it is designed. Nor does the manner in which it is granted in our constitution furnish any argument against the magnitude which is ascribed to it—but the contrary. A treaty cannot be made without the actual cooperation and mutual consent of the Executive and two thirds of the Senate. This necessity of positive cooperation of the Executive charges him with a high responsibility, which cannot but be one great security for the proper exercise of the Power. The proportion of the Senate requisite to their valid consent to a treaty approaches so near to unanimity, that it would always be very extraordinary, if it should be given to one really pernicious or hurtful to the State. These great guards are manifest indications of a great power being meant to be deposited. So that the manner of its deposit is an argument for its magnitude rather than an argument against it, and an argument against the intention to admit with a view to security the discretionary cooperation of the House of Representatives rather than in favour of such a right in them.

Two thirds of the two houses of Congress may exercise their

whole legislative power, not only without but against the consent of the Executive. It is not evident on general principles, that in this arrangement, there is a materially greater security against a bad law than in the other against a bad Treaty. The frequent absolute necessity of secrecy not only in the conduct of a foreign negotiation, but at certain conjunctures as to the very articles of a Treaty is a natural reason why a part and that the least numerous part of the legislative body was united with the Executive in the making of Treaties in exclusion of the other and the most numerous. But if the deposit of the Power of Treaty was less safe & less well guarded, than it is conceived to be, this would not be a good argument against its being in fact exclusively deposited, as the terms of the Constitution which establish it import it to be. It would only be an argument for an amendment to the Constitution modifying the deposit of the power differently & superadding new guards.

If the House of Representatives called upon to act in aid of a Treaty made by the President & Senate believe it to be unwarranted by the cons[ti]tution which they are sworn to support—it will not be denied that they may pause in the execution; until a decision, on the point of constitutionality, in the Supreme Court of the United States shall have settled the question.

But this is the only discretion in that House, as to the obligation to carry a Treaty made by the President & Senate into effect, in the existence of which I can acquiesce, as being [11] within the intent of the constitution.

Hence there was no question in my opinion of the competency of the House of Representatives, which I could presuppose likely to arise, to which any of the papers now requested could be deemed applicable; nor does it yet appear that any such question has arisen, upon which the request has been predicated.

Were even the course of reasoning which I have pursued less well founded than it appears to me to be—the request of papers, as a preliminary proceeding of the House, would still seem to be premature.

A question on the Constitutionality of a Treaty can manifestly only be decided by comparing the instrument itself with the Constitution.

11. In MS, "been."

A question whether a Treaty be consistent with or adverse to the interests of the U States must likewise be decided by comparing the stipulations which it actually contains with the situation of the U States in their internal and external relations.

Nothing extrinsic to the Treaty, or in the manner of the negotiating, can make it constitutional or unconstitutional, good or bad, salutary or pernicious. The internal evidence it affords is the only proper standard of its merits.

Whatever therefore be the nature of the duty or discretion of the house, as to the execution of the Treaty, it will find its rule of action in the Treaty. Even with reference to an animadversion on the conduct of the Agents who made the Treaty—the presumption of a criminal mismanagement of the interests of the U States ought first it is conceived to be deduced from the intrinsic nature of the Treaty & ought to be pronounced to exist previous to a further inquiry to ascertain the guilt or the guilty.

Whenever the House of Representatives, proceeding upon any Treaty, shall have taken the ground that such a presumption exists in order to such an inquiry, their request to the Executive to cause to be laid before them papers which may contain information on the subject will rest on a foundation that cannot fail to secure to it due efficacy.

But under all the circumstances of the present Request (circumstances which I forbear to particularise) and in its present indefinite form, I adopt with reluctance and regret but with intire conviction the opinion that a just regard to the Constitution and to the duty of my office forbid on my part a compliance with that request.[12]

(G W)

If the President should conclude to send the papers reserving parts not proper to be sent instead of the last paragraph the conclusion may be this

"But though under all the circumstances of the present request (circumstances which have produced great hesitation) I should deem myself warranted in witholding the papers—I am nevertheless induced by a desire to cultivate harmony and to obviate unfavourable inferences in a case which has excited so much sensi-

12. The copy in the Hamilton Papers, Library of Congress, ends at this point.

bility, to transmit to the House all such parts of the papers requested as can be material in any event for their information and as can be communicated without impropriety. These comprehend the commissions given to our Envoy, so much of the instructions to him as shew the extent & limits of his discretion & all the material parts of his correspondence."

(G W)

From Robert Morris

Alexander Hamilton Esqre   Philada 30 March 1796

Dear Sir

I delivered your letter to Wm Lewis Esqre [1] together with yours to me [2] and a draft of the Mortgage.[3] He promised attention but as the Supreme Court is Sitting I believe he is much hurried. It will be over in a few days & then I suppose we shall get the business finished. In the mean time I drop this line that you may know that no delay occurs on my part. On the Contrary I wish to put you perfectly at ease & always am

Dr Sir Yrs Sincerely   RM

LC, Robert Morris Papers, Library of Congress.
1. Letter not found.
2. Letter not found.
3. See Morris to H, March 14, 1796. This mortgage was to secure the payment of a debt which Morris owed to John B. Church. See the introductory note to Morris to H, June 7, 1795. See also Morris to H, July 20, November 16, December 18, 1795; January 15, March 6, 12, 14, 1796.

From George Washington [1]

Philadelphia 31st Mar: 1796

My dear Sir,   (Private)

I do not know how to thank you sufficiently, for the trouble you have taken to dilate on the request of the House of Representatives for the Papers relative to the British Treaty; [2] or how to apologize for the trouble (much greater than I had any idea of giving) which you have taken to shew the impropriety of that request.

From the first moment, and from the fullest conviction in my own mind, I had resolved to *resist the principle* wch. was evidently intended to be established by the call of the House of Representatives; and only deliberated on the manner, in which this could be done, with the least bad consequences.

To effect this, three modes presented themselves to me—1. a denial of the Papers in toto, assigning concise, but cogent reasons for the denial; 2 to grant them in whole; or 3. in part; accompanied with a pointed protest against the rights of the House to controul Treaties, or to call for Papers without specifying their object; and against the compliance being drawn into precedent.

I had as little hesitation in deciding that the first was to most tenable ground, but from the peculiar circumstances of *this case* It merited consideration, if the *principle* could be saved, whether facility in the provisions might not result from a compliance. An attentive examination however of the Papers and the subject, soon convinced me that to furnish *all* the Papers would be highly improper; and that a *partial* delivery of them would leave the door open for as much calumny as the entire refusal—perhaps more so—as it might, and I have no doubt would be said, that all such as were essential to the purposes of the House, were withheld.

Under these impressions, I proceeded, with the heads of Departments and the Attorney General, to collect materials; & to prepare an answer, subject however to revision, & alteration, according to circumstances.[3] This answer was ready on Monday [4]—and proposed to be sent in on Tuesday but it was delayed until I should receive what was expected; not doing it definitively on that day, the delivery of my answer was further postponed till the next; notwithstanding the anxious solicitude which was visible in all quarters, to learn the result of Executive decision.

Finding that the draft I had prepared, embraced most, if not all the principles which were detailed in the Paper I received yesterday; though not the reason⟨in⟩gs—That it would take considerable ⟨t⟩ime to copy the latter—and above all, hav⟨ing⟩ understood that if the Papers were refused a fresh demand, with strictures might be expected; I sent in the answer wch. was ready; reserving the other as a source for reasoning if my information proves true.

I could not be satisfied without giving you this concise acct. of the business. To express again my sincere thanks for the pains you have been at to investigate the subject, ⟨and to assure you, over & over, of the warmth of my friendship and of the affectionate regard with which

I am   Your Affectionate   G Washington⟩ [5]

AL[S], Hamilton Papers, Library of Congress; ADfS, George Washington Papers, Library of Congress.

   1. For background to this letter, see the introductory note to H to Washington, March 7, 1796. See also H to William Loughton Smith, March 10, 1796; H to Rufus King, March 16, 1796; H to Washington, March 24, 26, 28, 29, 1796.
   2. See H to Washington, March 29, 1796.
   3. On March 25, 1796, the day after the House had adopted Edward Livingston's resolution requesting that the President submit the papers relating to the negotiation of the Jay Treaty, a committee composed of Livingston and Albert Gallatin delivered the resolution to the President, who informed them that he would take it "into consideration" (*Annals of Congress*, V, 760). On the same day, the President wrote to the members of the cabinet: "The Resolution moved in the House of Representatives, for the Papers relative to the Negotiation of the Treaty with G. B having passed in the affirmative I request your opinion,
   "Whether that Branch of Congress hath—or hath not a right, by the Constitution, to call for those Papers?
   "Whether, if it does not possess the right, it wd. be expedient under the cricumstances of this particular case to furnish them?
   "And, in either case, in what terms would it be most proper to comply with or to refuse the request of the house?
   "These opinions in writing, and your attendance, will be expected at ten oclock tomorrow." (ADfS, RG 59, Miscellaneous Letters, 1790–1799, National Archives.)
   Of the cabinet members only Charles Lee thought that the President should comply with the request of the House (LC, dated March 26, 1796, George Washington Papers, Library of Congress).
   4. The draft was prepared by Timothy Pickering, and it was delivered to Washington on March 29, 1796. See the introductory note to H to Washington, March 7, 1796.
   5. Material within broken brackets has been taken from the draft in the George Washington Papers, Library of Congress.

From Rufus King

[*Philadelphia, April 1, 1796.* On April 2, 1796, Hamilton wrote to King: "Thank you for yours of yesteday." Letter not found.]

To Rufus King

[New York] April 2. 1796

Thank you for yours of yesteday.[1] I have no copy of the paper sent.[2] The greatest part went in the original draft though considerably reformed according to joint ideas & somewhat strengthened by new thoughts. A letter I have received [3] tells me that it came to hand after the ground which was acted upon had been formally considered & taken in Council & that it is reserved for future use in the event of an expected criticism of the message.

I have asked for it *conditionaly* to prune correct &c.[4] If I get it you shall have a copy. But you must take care that there is no crossing of path. Yrs. truly   A. Hamilton

ALS, New-York Historical Society, New York City.
  1. Letter not found.
  2. This is a reference to the draft of a message to the House of Representatives which H enclosed in his letter to George Washington on March 29, 1796.
  3. Washington to H, March 31, 1796.
  4. See H to Washington, April 2, 1796.

To George Washington

New York April 2d. 1796

Sir

The express is this morning gone off with your letter to Young LaFayette.[1] I foresaw when in Philadelphia certain machinations on this subject.[2]

I rejoice in the decision you have come to, in regard to the papers.[3] Whatever may happen, it is right in itself—will elevate the character of the President—and inspire confidence abroad. The contrary would have encouraged a spirit of usurpation the bounds of which could not be foreseen.

If there is time, I should like to have back the paper lately sent to correct prune guard & strengthen.[4] I have no copy. But of the expediency of this the circumstances on the Spot will decide. There is great fitness in the message to the House. I see only one point the least vulnerable, the too direct notice of the debate in the house—which may be attacked as contrary to parliamentary usage.[5] I hear the criticism here among the L——s.[6] But this cannot be very material.

Most respectfully & Affectny   I have the honor to be Sir   Yr very obed ser   A Hamilton

The President of the UStates

ALS, George Washington Papers, Library of Congress; copy, Hamilton Papers, Library of Congress.

1. When this letter was written, George Washington Motier Lafayette, who had arrived in the United States in October, 1795, was living with his tutor, Felix Frestel, at Ramapo, New Jersey. On repeated occasions H and Washington had exchanged letters on the possibility of political repercussions if Washington were to entertain young Lafayette at Philadelphia. See H to Washington, October 16, 26, November 19, 26, December 24, 27-30, 1795, March 7, 1796; Washington to H, October 29, November 10, 18, 23, 28, December 22, 1795, February 13, 1796. On February 28, 1796, Washington wrote to Lafayette inviting him and his tutor to Philadelphia. See H to Washington, March 7, 1796, note 31. But the situation was then altered by a resolution which Edward Livingston of New York introduced in the House of Representatives on March 4, 1796. The resolution reads: "That a committee be appointed to inquire whether the son of Major General Lafayette be within the United States, and also whether any, and what, provision may be necessary for his support" (*Annals of Congress*, V, 423). On March 10, before any action had been taken on this resolution, Livingston sent a copy of it to Lafayette and urged him to come to Philadelphia so ". . . that the legislature of America may no longer be in doubt wether the son of la Fayette is under their protection and within the reach of their gratitude" (copy, in the handwriting of Lafayette, George Washington Papers, Library of Congress). Lafayette replied to Livingston on March 28, 1796, with a polite letter (copy, in the handwriting of Lafayette, George Washington Papers, Library of Congress). On the same day he wrote to Washington, enclosing copies of Livingston's letter and the resolution and expressing his wish to do whatever Washington advised (ALS, George Washington Papers, Library of Congress). On March 31, 1796, Washington replied and repeated his earlier invitation to Lafayette and his tutor to "proceed immediately to this City, and to my house; where a room is prepared for you & him" (ALS, letterpress copy, George Washington Papers, Library of Congress).

2. For H's trip to Philadelphia, see Oliver Wolcott, Jr., to H, January 15, 1796. See also Robert Morris to H, February 10, 1796, note 2.

3. See the introductory note to H to Washington, March 7, 1796; Washington to H, March 31, 1796.

4. This "paper" was enclosed in H to Washington, March 29, 1796.

5. In his message to the House on March 30, 1796, in response to the demand for papers relating to the negotiation of the Jay Treaty, Washington wrote: "The course which the debate has taken, on the resolution of the House, leads to some observations on the mode of making treaties under the

Constitution of the United States" (LC, George Washington Papers, Library of Congress).

6. This is a reference to the members of the Livingston family who were opponents of Washington's administration. Edward Livingston had opened the House debate on the implementation of the Jay Treaty on March 2, 1796. See the introductory note to H to Washington, March 7, 1796.

Admission to Practice Law in the United States Circuit Court for the New York District in the Eastern Circuit

[New York, April 6, 1796]

Ordered,

That Alexander Hamilton, Josiah Ogden Hoffman, Brockholst Livingston and Peter Stephen Du Ponceau be and they are hereby respectively admitted to practice as Counsellors of this Court. Whereupon they were respectively qualified as Counsellors and respectively subscribed the oath on the roll of Counsellors.[1]

D, RG 21, Minutes, Trial Notes, and Rolls of Attorneys of the United States Circuit Court for the Southern District of New York, 1790–1841, National Archives.

1. On April 6, 1796, H signed the roll of counsellors (RG 21, Minutes, Trial Notes, and Rolls of Attorneys of the United States Circuit Court for the Southern District of New York, 1790–1841, National Archives).

To George Washington

[New York, April 8, 1796]

Sir

I have done something but not what I intended. The sitting of two Courts [1] & my professional engagements there prevent the execution of my plan. I no longer withold the paper lest circumstances should render it of any use.[2]

Most Affecy & resp   A H

April 8. 1796
President

ALS, Hamilton Papers, Library of Congress.
1. The New York Court of Chancery met in New York City on the last Tuesday in March; the New York Supreme Court held its April term in New York City.
2. The "paper" was H's draft of Washington's answer to a request by the House of Representatives for papers relating to the negotiation of the Jay Treaty. This draft was enclosed in H to Washington, March 29, 1796. H had asked Washington to return the draft so that he could revise it (H to Washington, April 2, 1796).

To George Washington

New York April 9. 1796

Sir

It gives me great pleasure to have the opportunity of announcing to you one whom I know to be so interesting to You as the bearer of this Mr. Motier La Fayette.[1] I allow myself to share by anticipation the satisfaction which the Meeting will afford to all the parties—the more, as I am persuaded, that time will confirm the favourable representation I have made of the person & justify the interest you take in him.

I have pleasure also in presenting to You Mr. Frestal who accompanies him & who more and more convinces me that he is intirely worthy of the charge reposed in him and every way intitled to esteem.

With the most respectful & Affectionate Attachment   I have the honor to be   Sir   Your very Obed servt   A Hamilton

The President of The UStates

ALS, George Washington Papers, Library of Congress; copy, Hamilton Papers, Library of Congress.
1. For background to this letter, see H to Washington, April 2, 1796.

From Justus Erich Bollmann

[*Philadelphia, April 10, 1796.* On April 13, 1796, Bollmann wrote to Hamilton: "A few days ago I had the pleasure to inclose You a copy of a letter which I had written to the President of the United States." [1] *Letter not found.*]

1. Bollmann to Washington, April 10, 1796 (ALS, George Washington Papers, Library of Congress).

From Fisher Ames [1]

[*Philadelphia, April 13–14, 1796.* On April 15, 1796, Hamilton wrote to Rufus King and referred to "A letter by yesterday's Post from our Friend Ames. *Letter not found.*]

1. Ames was a Federalist member of the House of Representatives from Massachusetts.

From Justus Erich Bollman [1]

Philadelphia April 13. 1796

Sir,

A few days ago I had the pleasure to inclose You a copy of a letter which I had written to the President of the United States.[2] In consequence of that I was called on Friday last to the State office, where Mr. Pickering told me that the President had some inclination to make a new effort to relieve the Marquis, and desired me at the same time to communicate to him by writing my Ideas on this subject. This occasioned a letter to the Secretary of State,[3] of which I take the liberty to send You again a Copy, repeating once more that I always shall be very glad if You will enable me to regulate my Conduct with respect to myself as well as to the marquis, after your advice!

It was impossible not to have myself in view when I wrote the 8th paragraph of the inclosed letter,[4] but I am so much convinced of what it asserts being essential and strictly true, that I would have written it exactly the same were I myself entirely out of the question!

It would be precious if this message were connectible with some other commercial and political object; it would be advantageous

APRIL 1796

even, because the principal object, being in somewhat a secret one, would be more covered! I have received great kindness and attention from Prince Henry,[5] when I was in Germany, and I am personally acquainted with the two sons of Count Bernstorf;[6] of which the eldest is envoy extraordinary at the Court of Berlin!

I have the honor to be with the highest esteem Sir Your most obt. & hbe. st. J. Erich Bollmann
170 Market street

ALS, Hamilton Papers, Library of Congress.

1. For background to this letter, see H to George Washington, January 19, 1796.
2. Bollmann to Washington, April 10, 1796 (ALS, George Washington Papers, Library of Congress). Bollmann's letter to H, presumably dated April 10, 1796, enclosing a copy of his letter to Washington, has not been found.
3. Bollmann to Timothy Pickering, April 10, 1796 (copy, in Bollmann's handwriting, Hamilton Papers, Library of Congress). In this letter Bollmann gave his "Ideas respecting the means that might be used in order to rescue Gen. Lf. from imprisonment."
4. The eighth paragraph of Bollmann's letter to Pickering reads: "It appears to me that the success of these new endeavours to rescue the General from imprisonment will in a great measure depend on the choice of a person sufficiently calculated for this purpose. The better he is acquainted with Gen. Lafayette, his character, his merits, the attachment which this Country at large and the President personally bears to him; the more fully he is informed of the causes of his Captivity, and the disposition of those on whom his fate depends; the better he will be able to furnish in Copenhague and Berlin the Data for the application to be made at Vienna. And besides I think it may be advisable to choose in preference a person well acquainted with the German language and some connexions in the Country where he is to be send to, because, the necessity of taking various kinds of information, and of maintaining a secret intelligence in Vienna and Olmütz with the friends of the marquis; the great advantage that may arise from the opportunity of making through these friends some communications to the Marquis himself; and the occasion there may be for employing other persons in order to assist the marquis and to receive him after he has been furnished with an opportunity to absent himself—all these circumstances together make such knowledge of the German language and such connexions in the Country where the marquis is imprisoned, of no trifling importance to a desirable Completion of this business!" (copy, in Bollmann's handwriting, Hamilton Papers, Library of Congress).
5. Prince Henry of Prussia, brother of Frederick the Great.
6. The two sons of Count Andreas Peter von Bernstorff, Danish Minister for Foreign Affairs and President of the German Chancery, were Count Christian Günther von Bernstorff and Count Joachim Frederik von Bernstorff. The former had been Danish ambassador in Berlin from 1791 to 1794. When this letter was written, he was ambassador in Stockholm. The latter was Secretary for Foreign Affairs in Copenhagen from 1793 to 1798.

To John Marshall [1]

[*New York April 14, 1796.* On April 25, 1796, Marshall wrote to Hamilton: "Yours of the 14th only reached me by the mail of this evening." *Letter not found.*]

> 1. Marshall was practicing law in Richmond, Virginia, at this time. In February, 1796, he had made his first and only appearance before the Supreme Court of the United States as an advocate for the defendant in the case of *Ware v Hylton*, in which he argued against the collection of a British debt (3 Dallas, *U.S. Reports*, 209–14).

To Rufus King [1]

New York April 15. 1796

My Dear

A letter by yesterday's Post from our Friend Ames [2] informed me that the Majority (57 concurring) had resolved in a private Meeting to refuse appropriations for the Treaty.[3] A most important crisis en-

ALS, New-York Historical Society, New York City.
> 1. This letter concerns the debate in the House of Representatives concerning the implementation of the Jay Treaty. For a discussion of this protracted controversy, see the introductory note to H to George Washington, March 7, 1796.
> 2. Fisher Ames's letter to H has not been found.
> 3. On the evening of April 2, 1796, Republicans in the House held a caucus (John Beckley to James Monroe [?], April 2, 1796 [ALS, MS Division, New York Public Library]) to consider the President's refusal to make available to the House the papers relating to the negotiation of the Jay Treaty. See the introductory note to H to Washington, March 7, 1796. Little is known about this caucus, but long after the event Albert Gallatin wrote the following about two Repubican caucuses in the seventeen-nineties: ". . . The first was after the House had asserted its abstract right to decide on the propriety of making appropriations necessary to carry a treaty into effect, whether such appropriations should be made with respect to the treaty with England of 1794. The other was in the year 1798, respecting the course proper to be pursued after the hostile and scandalous conduct of the French Directory. On both occasions we were divided; and on both the members of the minority of each meeting were left to vote as they pleased, without being on that account proscribed or considered as having abandoned the principles of the party" (Henry Adams, ed., *The Writings of Albert Gallatin* [New York, 1879], III, 553). On April 7, the House adopted by a vote of 57 to 36 two

sues. Great evils may result unless good men play their card well & with promptitude and decision. For we must seize and carry along with us the public opinion—& loss of time may be loss of everything.

To me our true plan appears to be the following (I presuppose that a certain communication has been made).[4]

I The President ought immediately after the House has taken the ground of refusal to send them a solemn Protest. This protest ought to contain reasons in detail against the claim of the House in point of Constitutional right and ought to suggest summarily but with solemnity and energy the danger to the interests & Peace of the Country from the measures of the House—the certainty of a deep wound to our character with foreign Nations & essential destruction of their confidence in the Government concluding with an intimation that in such a state of things he must experience extreme embarrassment in proceeding in any pending or future negotiations which the affairs of the UStates may require inasmuch as he cannot look for due confidence from others nor give them the requisitite expectation that stipulations will be fulfilled on our part.

A copy of this protest to be sent to the Senate for their information. The Senate by resolutions to express strongly their approbation of his principles, to assure him of their firm support & to advise him to proceed in the execution of the Treaty on his part in the confidence that he will derive from the virtue & good sense of the people, constitutionaly exerted, eventual & effectual support—& may still be the instrument of preserving the Constitution the Peace & the Honor of the Nation.

Then the Merchants to meet in the Cities & second by their resolutions the measures of the President & Senate further addressing their fellow Citizens to cooperate with them. Petitions afterwards to be handed throughout the U States.

The Senate to hold fast & consent to no adjournment till the

---

resolutions which had been introduced by Thomas Blount of North Carolina on the previous day (*Annals of Congress*, V, 781). For the text of the Blount resolutions, see H to Washington, March 7, 1796, note 21.

4. This is apparently a reference to a letter from Phineas Bond, British chargé d'affaires in the United States, to Timothy Pickering, March 26, 1796. Bond requested that an article be added to the Jay Treaty invalidating certain parts of the treaty concluded at Greenville in the Northwest Territory between the United States and the Northwest Indians on August 7, 1795 (*ASP, Foreign Relations*, I, 551–52). See H to Oliver Wolcott, Jr., April 20, 1796.

expiration of the term of service of the present House unless provision [is] made.

The President to cause a confidential communication to be made to the British stating candidly what has happened; his regrets, his adherence nevertheless to the Treaty, his resolution to persist in the Execution as far as depends on the Executive & his hope that the faith of the Country will be eventually preserved.

I prefer that measures should begin with a Protest of the President —as it will be in itself proper & there will be more chance of success if the Contest appears to be with him & the Senate auxiliaries than in the reverse.

But in all this business celerity decision & an imposing attitude are indispensable. The Glory of the President, the safety of the Constitution, the greatest interests depend upon it. Nothing will be wanting here. I do not write to the President on the subject.

An idea has come from *Cooper*[5] of an intention in our friends in the House of Representatives to resist the execution of the other Treaties, the Spanish & Algerine, unless coupled with the British.[6] But this will be altogether wrong & impolitic. The misconduct of the other party cannot justify in us an imitation of their principles. Tis best I think that the first course should be given to the other Treaties. Or at most if a *feint* of opposition is deemed adviseable it

5. William Cooper, the founder of Cooperstown, was one of the largest landholders in New York State. H served as his attorney in many of Cooper's land transactions (see forthcoming Goebel, *Law Practice*, III). In 1791 Cooper became a judge of Otsego County. From 1795 to 1797 and from 1799 to 1801 he was a Federalist member of the House of Representatives.

6. If Cooper wrote to H about this proposal, his letter has not been found.
The Treaty of Friendship, Limits, and Navigation between Spain and the United States was signed at San Lorenzo el Real, near Madrid, on October 27, 1795 (Miller, *Treaties*, II, 318). The Treaty of Peace and Amity with Algiers was signed at Algiers on September 5, 1795, and consented to by the Senate on March 2, 1796 (Miller, *Treaties*, II, 275). On April 13, 1796, Theodore Sedgwick, a Federalist member of the House of Representatives from Massachusetts, proposed the following resolution: ". . . That provision ought to be made by law for carrying into effect, with good faith, the Treaties lately concluded between the Dey and Regency of Algiers, the King of Great Britain, the King of Spain, and certain Indian tribes Northwest of the Ohio" (*Annals of Congress*, V, 940). This attempt to maneuver the House into passing appropriations for the Jay Treaty was, however, unsuccessful. On April 14, Sedgwick's resolution was defeated, and on the same day separate agreements were made to carry into effect all the treaties except for that with Great Britain (*Annals of Congress*, V, 969, 974-75).

ought to be left to the Senate by postponement &c. But even this is very delicate & very questionable.

Let us be *Right,* because to do right is intrinsically proper & I verily believe it is the best means of securing final success & let our adversaries have the whole glory of sacrificing the interests of the Nation.

Yrs Affecly   A Hamilton

P.S. If the Treaty is not executed the President will be called upon by regard to his character & the public good to *keep his post* till another House of Representatives has pronounced.

Rufus King Esq

From Robert Cowper [1]

Suffolk Virginia Apl. 16 1796

Sir

About three weeks past I Recd two letters, one from the post Master of Philadelphia Coining one bearing the Signature of A.

ALS, Hamilton Papers, Library of Congress.
1. Cowper apparently lived in the Upper Parish of Nansemond County, Virginia, from before 1790 until his death on March 23, 1812. The report of his death refers to him as "Captain" (*Virginia Magazine of History and Biography* [October, 1899], VII, 213; [July, 1955], LXIII, 335).

Accompanying this letter are five enclosures, all of which are copies in Cowper's handwriting and all of which are located in the Hamilton Papers, Library of Congress. These enclosures are William E. Van Allen to Stephen Graham, February 6, 1796; H to Cowper, March 3, 1796; Robert Patton to Cowper, March 14, 1796; Deposition of Caleb Haskins, April 9, 1796; Cowper to Patton, April 17, 1796.

This letter concerns two letters (Van Allen to Graham, February 6, 1796, and H to Cowper, March 3, 1796) which were forged to discredit H. The letter to Graham contains a report that H had told the writer that he was planning to run for the Presidency in 1796. The letter to Cowper purports to be "a Discussion and Vindication" of H's "political Sentiments and official Conduct" and concludes: "In my next I will be more particular. . . . The president resigns next June—my Countrymen are Solicitous that I Should become a Candidate for office—this I should at least have been persuaded to do but wished first to Know the Sentiments of the Southern states—will you give me some information on the Subject you may rely on it I shall not be ungrateful."

In April, 1796, the two recipients of the forged letters instituted a suit in

Hamilton True Copy of which I now Send you with the Deposistion of Caleb Haskins who Recd the letters at Suffolk and dld. them to Robert Patton post master Philadelphia. Also Send you Copys two others which Came at the Same time and was Conveyed to Philadelphia and back to Suffolk in the Same manner as those above) directed to Doctor Stephen Graham his letters as you See is Sign'd Wm. E. Van Allen from which you will Sufficiently Comprehend the Infamous procedure.[2] Attempts to injure Charecters in this manner must Excite the Execrations of men of all parties and Descriptions and whatever difference of Sentiments may Exist upon great political Subjects there Can be but one Sentiment upon a business of this nature, that is that it becomes a duty Incumbent in my opinion

---

the Suffolk District Court against Dr. Richard H. Bradford of Suffolk as the alleged author of the forgeries. The records of this court were destroyed by fire in 1866, but the deposition of Haskins throws some light on how the forged letters were mailed and discovered. This deposition reads in part: ". . . This deponant . . . Saith that on the Second day of March last . . . Doctor Richard H. Bradford accompanyed by a man unknown to this Deponant Came to this deponant in the Street of Suffolk and gave him a Packett of Letters directed to the post office Philadelphia which packet the Said Bradford requested this deponant to Take Charge of, and there to deliver them Safely Stating that they were letters of Great Importance. this deponant further Saith that he received the Said packet of Said Bradford and promised him that he would do as was requested, and . . . on his arrival at Philadelphia he took the Same Packet which was Sealed and on the 14th. day of the Same month delivered, the said packet in post office at Philadelphia to Robert Patton the post master.

"This deponant Saith that Patton the post master after opening the Said Packet ask'd this deponant where he got them from this Deponant answered from Suffolk. Said Patton then asked this deponant who it was that Gave them to him and this deponant told him that Doctor Bradford gave them to him and desired him to be particularly Carefull of them which he had been. this deponant being ask'd by Robert Cowper if he was personally acquainted with Doctor Bradford answered in the affirmative . . .

". . . this deponant Saith that the man who accompanied Bradford was a tall genteel man dressed in a mixed Coloured Coat and that the Said man Took the Packet out of his Pocket and Gave it to the Said Bradford who deliverd it to this deponant with the Charge aforesaid. . . ." (AD, Hamilton Papers, Library of Congress.)

On the same day on which Haskins delivered the forged letters to the Philadelphia post office, Patton wrote to Cowper, described what had happened, and stated that he was "apprehensive there is some trick intended." On April 17, 1796, Cowper wrote to Patton thanking him for his letter of March 14, and describing the contents of the forged letters.

2. The forger made a mistake in signing the letter "William" E. Van Allen. He intended the letter to appear to come from John Evert Van Allen (Alen), a member of the House of Representatives from Rensselaer County, New York.

on all Concern'd, to unite their Exertions in bringing to Justice men So Maliciously Inclined. This man Bradford, as you will See by the Deposistion of Haskins was accompanied by a tall Genteel man Dressed in a mix'd Coloured Coat who took the letters from his pocket and dld them to Sd. Bradford who deld them to Haskins with the Charge. Now sir permit me to observe as to the proof against Bradford the papers here Inclos'd will I hope bear Sufficient Testimony and with reference to his Companion I shall here observe, that the Description Haskins gives of the man, and from a Similitude of handwriting of the letter Signd A. Hamilton with that of a Certain Gentleman who is the Intimate friend and acquaintance of Bradford—with other Strong Circumstances such as asking one or two of his acquaintances on post days the Questions, have you been to the post office—are there no large Packets from the north— upon being Answer'd no he Express'd his Surprise and upon the arrival of those letters this Gentlemen finding the Transaction was like to take a Serious Turn was frequently Seen in Close Conversation with Sd. Bradford. I must here observe that Some Eighteen months ago there was Several letters of a Similar nature Recd. by many Gentlemen in Norfolk and this place. Doctor Graham and myself at that time was favour'd with two Each. Doctor Grahams was in the Same Stile of his last—mine was on a different Subject, but upon Shewing those last letters to the Gentlemen Generally, who Recd the first it was Concluded that their was a Great Likeness in the hand writing. Upon this the parties met together and Sent for Doctor Bradford and upon asking him Questions Respecting those letters he declared and Said he was willing to make oath that he Knew nothing of the first letters—Laying Great Stress on the words first letters—and did not positively deny the last nor would he own or acknowlede them—during this Examination a Gentleman answering the description of that, Haskins Gave of the one in Company with Bradford when the letters was deliver'd without being Call'd upon or Even told by any of the parties Concernd that he was Suspected Solicited an Interview with one of the Gentlemen who had Recd. Two of the first letters they accordingly met when this Gentleman observed I Know the nature of your meeting today and I know I am Suspected of writing those letters when he observd much as Bradford had done as to the first I declare I Know nothing about them and will make oath to it not denying or owning the last, the Gentleman Eluded to is of Consequence in this County (Nansemond) and Shall be made Known to you or your attorney if you think proper to prosecute in this Case and for this I pledge my honour. The Signatures of the letter in your name; there are Gentlemen who is well acquainted with the Hand writing of this nameless Gentleman) of Respectibility, that I believe would Swear to it if required at least they have tolled me they would. Now Sir you will I make no doubt agree with me and Say that Conduct like this merits punishment—you therefore perceive I have Instituted a prosecution against Bradford for the purpose above mentioned— Wheather you or myself are most injured or attempted to be injured I Know not. Shall Therefore make you a Tender of my Services on this oration and will with a Singular Satisfaction afford all the aid within the Compass of my power to any person who you may Charge with a prosecution on your behalf. The whole design of these letters I have not as yet been Enabled to develope but have a Conviction that a Sufficient degree of malignity is Discovered to Call for punishment for it Such practices are permitted to pass with impunity, the power of Society is ever exposed to the assaults of every person thus disposed. I was Desired by Doctor Graham who is Called to No Carolina on Business to forward you Copys of his letters as your name is therein involved and that you are at Liberty to use them but he requests that Mr. Van Allen and Mr. Baily [3]

---

3. Theodorus Bailey, a Republican member of the House of Representatives from Dutchess County, New York. The part of the forged letter which Van Allen was supposed to have written to Graham referring to Bailey and H reads: ". . . I must in the first Place inform you that your Cousin Theodorus Bailey is reelected a member of Congress, his Election is the more pleasing as I am Satisfied he will help his old Friends all he Can and may procure us Some lucrative post under the Government. But to Come at once to the main Subject of my letter. I must relate to you a Conversation I yesterday had with our best friend A Hamilton I waited on him Early yesterday morning on motives entirely of friendship, to enquire of his and family's welfare &c. I had marked on my entrance his Brow clouded and rivetted into Some uncommonly important reflections as Soon as we were alone he unbosomed himself thus 'I have Certain information that the president will resign in the progression of the next Summer and that Jefferson will be thrust into his place— this as you must be well aware Does not Coincide with my System and must by Some mean or other be averted, that Cool Casuistic Frenchified fellow will in a little time undo what I have been so many years labouring to accomplish I have Come to the resolution of offering myself a Candidate for that place. I hold it (says he) as a principle that when the object we have in view is

may also have the Use or Recourse to them—that if they think proper to take any Steps in this Infamous Transaction they may be assisted thereby. The Originals I Shall take Care of which will be at all times Subject to you and your attorneys Inspection your determination on this business I will thank you to Communicate as Soon as may be Convenient as I have determined to have them publish'd Should you not be disposed to take any Steps therein otherwise I Shall be Governd by you; Haskins is a Seafaring man and Hath a family liveing in Broadway New york and at present sails with a Capt. Decker [4] who will deliver you this. Decker lives on Staten Island and is Imployd. in the Shingle Trade between this and New york. The Circumstances attending this Transaction hath made me lenthy which I hope will plead an Excuse. This man Bradford is of Sufficient Consideration to merit punishment, as is also the other with whome you are more Imediately Concernd. If the fact Can be Established of this time and Circumstances will determine the practice is an Infamous one and ought to be noticed.

With Every Sentiment of Respect I am Sir Yr. mo. Ob Hume Serv
Robert Cowper

---

a good one, we may take any measure whatever to obtain it to this end you may well imagine that the dollars I have heapd together whilst handling the governments Cash will not be without their use. You understand me: write to your Friends disclose my intentions and hint to them that they shall not loose by their attachment to me I understand your Cousin Stephen Graham has Settled very advantageously in Virginia his Connexions are probably Extensive and influential write him, assure him, his purse Shall not be lighter for his Good wishes.' . . ."

4. Isaac Decker, a resident of Port Richmond, Staten Island, was a Loyalist during the American Revolution. After the war, he moved to Shelburne, Nova Scotia. He subsequently returned to Staten Island and remained there until shortly before his death.

From Germain Pierre Decrosses [1]

New York, April 16, 1796. "J'ai eu l'honneur de me presenter chez vous ce matin, mais je nai pas eu celui de vous y rencontrer. je quitte sous huit-jours cette terre hospitaliére pour aller dans un pays ou se trouvent réunis tous les fléaux qui peuvent affliger l'humanité. des raisons d'une grande importance me font desirer d'être recû citoyen americain. je suis resident ici dans cette ville de New-york depuis six ans,² et cent temoins peuvent le certifier et le cautioner. la ⟨cour supr⟩ême federale est-elle assemblée. dans ce cas rien de plus aisé,³ mais si elle ne l'est pas, n'y at-il pas un moyen dy suppleer, et de pouvoir me faire jouir des droits priviléges et immunités que ma bien certainement acquis un aussi long sejour. . . . j'ai eu l'honneur de vous être presenté par le colonel walker,⁴ et sur les bontés et l'interêt particulier dont veut bien M'honorer Mr. jay votre ami et si digne de l'etre. . . ." ⁵

ALS, Hamilton Papers, Library of Congress.

1. Decrosses had been a landowner in Santo Domingo before the outbreak of the slave revolt in 1791. In a letter of April 23, 1795, Robert R. Livingston wrote to James Monroe in Paris: "Mr. De Crosses has requested me again to trouble you with a recommendation of him to you under an apprehention that his former Letters may have miscarried & I comply with pleasure with his request as I am satisfied were you fully acquainted with his circumstances & character you would find much satisfaction in promoting his interest. This Gent. resided here with his wife & family a long time before the disturbances broke out in the Island of St. Domingo where he resided & possessed a very considerable property. His character & conduct here have been irreproachable. His property has been Wholy in the hands of the slaves & he now hopes, by the restoration of order, under the protection of the french republic, to be enabled to recover a part of it; & in this view he begs me to solicit your aid in puting his papers into the proper channel to gain the attention of the French Government from whose justice & moderation he flatters himself he has much to hope" (ALS, James Monroe Papers, Library of Congress).

2. Decrosses's name appears in a New York directory for the first time in 1792 (William Duncan, ed., *The New York Directory, and Register, for the Year 1792* [New York: Printed for the Editor, by T. and J. Swords, No. 27, William-Street, 1792], 35).

3. On April 20, 1796, Decrosses became a United States citizen in the United States Circuit Court for the New York District (D, RG 21, Records of the United States District Court for the Southern District of New York, Circuit Court Minutes, 1790–1808, 74, National Archives).

For the conditions under which aliens might become naturalized citizens of the United States, see "An Act to establish an uniform rule of Naturalization; and to repeal the act heretofore passed on that subject" (1 *Stat*. 404 [January 29, 1795]).

4. A native of London, Benjamin Walker had emigrated to America before the American Revolution and settled in New York City. During the war he had served as aide-de-camp to Baron von Steuben. In 1788 Walker was appointed commissioner to settle the accounts of the hospital, marine, and clothing departments. He was closely associated with Steuben and William Duer in business and like H served as a director of the Society for Establishing Useful Manufactures. In December, 1790, he visited Paris to investigate the affairs of the Scioto Company (H to Walker, September 10, 13, 1790; Walker to H, December 28, 1790). From March 21, 1791, to February 20, 1798, he was naval officer for the port of New York. In May, 1795, Walker became a representative of the Pulteney Associates, a London company that speculated in lands in the Genesee country of western New York.

5. In 1792 Decrosses borrowed money from John Jay (Decrosses to Jay,

November 11, 1792 [ALS, Columbia University Libraries]; Jay to Decrosses, November, 1792 [ADf, Columbia University Libraries]). Jay subsequently offered further help, which Decrosses accepted in order to pay the passage of two relatives from Santo Domingo to New York (Decrosses to Jay, January 25, 1794 [ALS, Columbia University Libraries]).

From Rufus King [1]

[Philadelphia] Monday Morning 17[-18]. Ap. [1796] [2]

In general I agree in the Course you recommend.[3] Separate Bills will be reported to the House this morning, providing for the Sp. Ind. & Alg. Treaties—they will pass the H. and be sent to the Senate by the middle of the week.[4] I percive no impropriety in adding to the first of these Bills recived by the Senate, and in succession to each of them if requisite, a Provision for the Br. Treaty. Such amendment, if recd. in the House before they take a Question, it is beleived would have influence.

The Merchants & traders Petition is signed with unexampled unanimity.[5] Baltimore have prepared a similar petition wh. will be very generally signed. Genl. Smith, who is now there, writes that the Treaty has gained many Friends, that they are next to unanimous in favor of its execution, that Annapolis is likewise unanimous, & that he thinks that Nine tenths of the State are for carrying it into Effect.[6] He adds that a memorial has been drawn up and signed by most of the respectable People in Baltimore, approving the Presidents Conduct in refusing the Papers; that he thinks a counter memorial could be obtained, but that he has discouraged it, seeing the necessity of unanimity at the present Crisis. He returns tomorrow or next Day & will be zealous for the execution of the Treaty.

Van Cortland [7] will leave this place on Wednesday. Would it not be well to prepare a Reception for him which may return him in favor of the Treaty. His Friends may be induced to act upon his Mind, which balances, so as to decide it.

Adieu

R King

ALS, Hamilton Papers, Library of Congress.

1. This letter concerns the efforts of supporters of the Jay Treaty both in and out of the Government to secure adoption by the House of Representatives of legislation for the implementation of that treaty. For an account of

the struggle in the House over this legislation, see the introductory note to H to George Washington, March 7, 1796.

2. As Monday fell on April 18, King was mistaken in dating this letter April 17. In *JCHW*, V, 630, this letter is incorrectly dated "1795."

3. See H to King, April 15, 1796.

4. See H to King, April 15, 1796, note 6. The bills for carrying into effect the treaties with Spain and the northwest Indians were introduced in the House on April 18 and passed on April 20 (*Annals of Congress*, V, 1025, 1094-95). The bill to appropriate funds for implementing the Algerian treaty was introduced on April 20 and passed on April 22 (*Annals of Congress*, V, 1095, 1140).

5. The petition of Philadelphia merchants, which was drawn up at a meeting on April 15, 1796, "at the Coffee-House, . . . at twelve o'clock, John Nixon, Esq. in the chair," reads: "That they have waited, with anxious expectation, to see the necessary measures adopted by your honorable House, for carrying into operation the Treaty concluded between the United States and Great-Britain, and are now seriously alarmed least the measures should be further delayed or entirely omitted.

"Under that impression, they deem it incumbent on them to represent, That property of the Merchants of the United States, amounting, upon a moderate computation, to more than five millions of dollars, has been taken from them by the subjects of G. Britain, the restitution of which, they verily believe, depends, in a great measure, upon the completion of the Treaty on our part.

"Independent of this immense sum, they have embarked the principal part of their remaining fortunes in vessels and adventures, the safety of which will, as they apprehend, be materially affected by a refusal or neglect on the part of the United States to comply with stipulations so solemnly entered into. Besides their particular interests as Merchants and Traders, they feel an interest, in common with their fellow-citizens of other descriptions, in the preservation of Peace, on which the prosperity of this country depends; and they should deem themselves wanting in that spirit and independence which ought ever to characterize freemen, if they forbear, on so interesting an occasion as the present, to express their wishes and expectations. They, therefore, with all due respect for the Representatives of the people of the United States, beg leave to recommend, that no partial considerations of policy may influence their decision on this important question; but that the Faith, the Honor, and the Interest of the Nation, may be preserved by making the necessary provisions for carrying the Treaty into fair and honorable effect." ([Philadelphia] *Gazette of the United States*, April 16, 1796.) The petition was received by the House of Representatives on April 20 and read on April 21, 1796 (*Journal of the House*, II, 518). Ten committee members were also appointed at the meeting in Philadelphia to correspond with merchants in other towns and cities of the United States and with the western counties of Pennsylvania. The committee members were: Thomas FitzSimons, Joseph Ball, Walter Stewart, George Latimer, Samuel Sterett, Israel Whelen, Robert Waln, Joseph Anthony, Samuel Breck, and Francis Gurney (*Gazette of the United States*, April 18, 1796).

6. Samuel Smith, a Baltimore merchant who had been appointed a brigadier general of militia in 1794, was a Democratic member of the House of Representatives. He initially opposed the appropriations for the Jay Treaty, but on April 22, 1796, he announced that he would support the treaty because "it would tend to restore harmony and unanimity to our public measures" (*Annals of Congress*, V, 1157). See also Rufus King to H, April 20, 1796.

7. Philip Van Cortlandt was a Republican member of the House of Representatives from New York, who first opposed and then supported the imple-

mentation of the Jay Treaty by the House. On March 24, 1796, he voted in favor of Edward Livingston's resolution that the papers concerning the negotiation of the treaty should be laid before the House (*Annals of Congress,* V, 759). He continued to vote with the Livingston faction on the question of whether or not Washington's refusal should be referred to a Committee of the Whole (*Annals of Congress,* V, 762), and he supported Thomas Blount's resolutions of April 6 (H to Washington, March 7, 1796, note 21; *Annals of Congress,* V, 771), concerning implementation of the treaty (*Annals of Congress,* V, 1291). It was suggested at the time that his defection came less from any new-found conviction concerning the treaty's merits than from the wish to placate his Westchester constituents. See John Beckley to DeWitt Clinton, April 11, 1796 (ALS, Columbia University Libraries).

To Rufus King [1]

New York April 18. 1796

Dear Sir

I thank you for your letter received to day.[2] Our Merchants here are not less alarmed than those of Philadelphia & will do all they can.[3] All the insurance people meet to day. The Merchants & Traders will meet tomorrow or the next day. A Petition will be prepared & circulated among the other citizens.

I regret that a certain communication was not made.[4] Indeed I think the Executive will be hereafter blamed for keeping back the fact in so critical a posture of things.

Yrs. truly A Hamilton

Rufus King Esq

ALS, New-York Historical Society, New York City.
1. For background to this letter, see the introductory note to H to George Washington, March 7, 1796. See also H to King, April 15, 1796; King to H, April 17–18, 1796.
2. Although it might be assumed that H was acknowledging King to H, April 17–18, 1796, this is not the case, for H acknowledged the receipt of that letter in H to King, April 30, 1796. The letter which H is acknowledging in the letter printed above has not been found.
3. See H to King, April 15, 1796.
4. See H to King, April 15, 1796.

From Woodbury Langdon [1]

Portsmouth [New Hampshire] April 18, 1796. "I conceive it will be necessary for you to have the original note which I hold against Michael Wentworth deceased, in order to settle matters with Mr. Edward Goold.[2] I intended to have left it with you on my return from Philadelphia, but forgot it when I was with you last. . . ."

ALS, Hamilton Papers, Library of Congress.
1. Langdon was a Portsmouth, New Hampshire, merchant, a former member of the Continental Congress, and an unsuccessful Republican candidate for Congress in 1796.
2. This refers to the New York Supreme Court case between John Langdon, Woodbury Langdon's brother, and Edward Goold, as administrator of the estate of Michael Wentworth, deceased. Goold was a New York City merchant and land speculator. Wentworth, a native of England, had come to America in 1767, lived in Portsmouth, where he married the widow of Governor Benning Wentworth, and died in New York on September 25, 1795. The case, in which H acted as attorney for the plaintiff, was heard on May 7, 1796, in New York (MS Minutes of the New York Supreme Court, January 19–November 5, 1796 [Hall of Records, New York City]). On October 5, 1797, H made the following entry in his Cash Book, 1795–1804: "received of Woodbury Langdon in cause v. Gould 81.16" (AD, Hamilton Papers, Library of Congress). See also H's Law Register, 1795–1804, 98 (D, partially in H's handwriting, New York Law Institute, New York City).

From Oliver Wolcott, Junior

[*Philadelphia, April 18, 1796.* On April 20, 1796, Hamilton wrote to Wolcott: "I have received your letter of the 18th. instant." *Letter not found.*]

From Rufus King

Wednesday
[Philadelphia] 20. Ap. [1796]

The Petitions of the Merchants and others will be printed today, and it is said they have been signed by almost every Merchant & Trader in the City [1]—Pettit,[2] Barclay,[3] & some few others are exceptions. A counter Petition has been very industriously carried through the City and its Suburbs; [4] and though very few merchants, Traders, or principal mechanicks have signed it, it will shew a long catalouge of Names. The Persons engaged in this service have been very successful in the northern & southern Liberties, and taking their stands upon the Wharves, they have collected the names of Sailors and others, as well forigners as Citizens. Baltimore has become very zealous, and I fear from their displeasure at the Conduct of Colo. Smith,[5] they have hazarded his vote and influence whatever it may [be],[6] in the Question of Provision for the Treaty. They have drawn up a Paper, which is signed by almost the whole Body of Merchants in which they request *and instruct* him to promote by the proper provisions the Executions of the Treaty [7]—his inclination was in favor of a Provision, but I am apprehensive his Pride will be so wounded by *this instruction,* that he may vote agt. his Jugement, to prove his independence.[8] We shall probably receive from the House today a Bill making an appropriation for defraying the Expences of carrying into Effect the Sp. Treaty.[9]

We shall amend it by adding a provision for the Br. Treaty. If the House disagree, we shall adhere, and they will lose the Bill by refusing our Amendment. We shall then add to the Algerine Bill [10] an amendment providing for the British and Span. Treaties. The House will also decide the Fate of this Bill. We shall then add to the Bill providing for the In. Treaty an amendment providing, for, the British, the Spanh. and the Algerine Treaties. The House will also decide the Fate of this Bill. We shall then Offer them a Bill providing for all the Treaties. This likewise they may reject—but my Belief is that the Opposition will give way before we have gone through this course.

Yrs. &c   Rufus King

ALS, Hamilton Papers, Library of Congress.
1. See King to H, April 17–18, 1796, note 5.
2. Charles Pettit was a Philadelphia merchant.
3. John Barclay was a Philadelphia merchant and a former alderman and mayor of that city.
4. The petition to which King is referring was adopted on April 16 "at a respectable meeting of citizens" of which Stephen Girard was chairman. The address denounced the Jay Treaty as "unequal in its stipulations, derogatory to our national character, injurious to our general interests, and as offering insult instead of redress" and complimented the treaty's congressional opponents for "asserting their constitutional prerogatives" and executing their trust,

"as the guardians of our dearest rights" ([Philadelphia] *Aurora. General Advertiser,* April 20, 1796).

5. Samuel Smith. See King to H, April 17–18, 1796, note 6.

6. In MS, "me."

7. The instructions which his Baltimore constituents sent to Smith are described in the following letters, which were printed in the [Philadelphia] *Gazette of the United States* on April 22, 1796: "Extract of a letter from a gentleman in Baltimore to his friend in this city, dated 19th April.

" '. . . We have, in some measure, anticipated your proceedings, by instructions to our delegate Gen. Smith, pointedly calling upon him to vote for the appropriations, and carrying into effect the treaty; considering an opposite conduct as a breach of the national faith, and pregnant with the most fatal consequences. The instructions to Gen. Smith . . . will have an influence; indeed it is my opinion, from what has fallen from him, that it was and has been his intention so to do.'

"Extract of a letter from Baltimore, dated April 18, to a House in this city.

" '. . . an address, or rather instructions have been given by a large majority of the mercantile characters of our town to Gen. Smith to vote for the appropriations. . . . We have about 600 signers, and might have obtained as many more. . . .' "

8. King need not have worried, for Smith voted for the implementation of the Jay Treaty. See King to H, April 17–18, 1796, note 6.

9. See H to King, April 15, 1796, note 10. On April 20, 1796, the House passed and sent to the Senate ". . . bills for making appropriations for defraying the expenses which may arise in carrying into effect the Treaties lately concluded between the United States and the King of Spain, and with certain Indian tribes Northwest of the river Ohio . . ." (*Annals of Congress,* V, 1094–95). The Indian treaty had been concluded on August 7, 1795, at Greenville in the Northwest Territory.

10. See King to H, April 17–18, 1796, note 4.

To Rufus King

[New York, April 20, 1796]

Dr. Sir

Yesterdays Post brought me a letter from you [1] which gave me pleasure. The papers will apprize you of the proceedings of the Merchants & Traders here on yesterday.[2] There is among them also "unexampled unanimity" [3] & as far as I can judge the current is in our favour throughout the City. Persons to day are going through the different wards.

Yrs. sincerely

A Hamilton

April 20. 1796

P.S. Our friends in the House will do well to *gain time.*

Rufus King Esq

ALS, New-York Historical Society, New York City.
1. King to H, April 17–18, 1796.
2. See H to King, April 15, 18, 1796.
On April 19, "at a meeting of the Merchant and Traders of the City of New York, convened by Public Notification, at the Tontine Coffee-House," the following resolution was adopted: ". . . that it is expedient to present a respectful address to . . . [the House of Representatives], expressive of the sentiment that it deeply concerns the commerce, agriculture, peace and honor of the United States—that provision be made for the execution of the . . . treaty [with Great Britain] with punctuality and good faith.

"That it is also expedient to appoint a Committee for corresponding with the other trading towns in the United States, and also with the other Counties of this state on the abovementioned subject.

"That Gulian Verplanck, James Watson, Edmond Seaman, William Nelson, Moses Rogers, John B. Coles, Isaac Clason, John Thurston, Thomas Pearsal, and Cornelius Ray, be the said committee, and that they be instructed to appoint a suitable number of proper characters to proceed through the different Wards of this city to obtain the signatures to the said address of all those of our fellow-citizens who shall agree in opinion with this meeting.

"And thereupon the following address having been produced, read and considered, the same was agreed to by the meeting.
"By order of the meeting
Gulian Verplanck, Chairman.
"To the *Honourable* HOUSE *of* REPRESENTATIVES *of the* UNITED STATES, *now convened*.

"We the undersigned, Merchants, Traders, and other Citizens of the City of New York, being of the number of your constituents and deeply interested in the issue of every public measure that can affect the essential interests of our country, find ourselves impelled by that consideration, to address you on the subject of certain resolutions now depending in your house respecting the Treaty made with Great Britain, which fills our minds with very serious apprehensions, which have already given occasion to very serious embarrasments, and which in our opinion threaten very extensive and complicated evils—the whole magnitude of which it is not easy to foresee or to calculate.

"Whatever difference of sentiment may at any time have existed among us respecting particular public measures, yet on this occasion and at this time, we all unite in one opinion—and that opinion is, that the abovementioned treaty ought to be provided for, and executed on the part of the United States with punctuality and good faith.

"We forbear to enter into the question what are the boundaries of the constitutional authority of the several branches of our government on the subject of this address; but however these may stand, we are convinced after full and mature deliberation, that no existing considerations are of sufficient weight, to render it adviseable to refuse making provision for the execution of the said treaty, and that it deeply concerns the Agriculture, Commerce, Peace, Character and Honour of our Nation, that such provision shall be promptly made.

"The compleat execution of the treaties with Great Britain, Spain and Algiers, by extinguishing all matters of controversy and war, which have heretofore existed between us and any foreign powers, appears to us a point of the greatest consequence to this young and rising country—affording a prospect of durable peace; and of an uninterrupted progress to that maturity and strength, which will enable us to defy the enmity of foreign powers, without those immense sacrifices which war in our present situation, must inevitably produce. And tho' we shall be at all times disposed to encounter with the spirit and fortitude of FREEMEN, the calamities of a war, necessary as well as just, we could not but look forward with extreme regret and dissatisfaction to one, of which either justice or the necessity was doubtful.

"Thus impressed, we respectfully offer our sense of the momentous subject to the solemn and dispassionate consideration of the House of Representatives; firmly trusting that no impartial views or impressions will interfere with the true interest of our country; that its peace will be carefully cherished; and that its faith and honor will be preserved inviolable and unblemished." ([Philadelphia] *Gazette of the United States*, April 21, 1796.)

3. This is a quotation from King to H, April 17–18, 1796.

To Oliver Wolcott, Junior

New York April 20. 1796

Dr. Sir

I have received your letter of the 18th. instant.[1] The money paid me for you shall be placed to your Credit in the Office of Discount & Deposit as you desire.

The British Ministry are as great fools, or as great rascals, as our Jacobins—else our Commerce would not continue to be distressed as it is by their Cruisers, nor would the Executive be embarrassed as it now is by the new proposition.[2]

ALS, Connecticut Historical Society, Hartford; copy, Hamilton Papers, Library of Congress.

1. Letter not found.

2. The "new proposition" of the British government was made by Phineas Bond to Timothy Pickering. On March 26, 1796, Bond wrote to Pickering: "The undersigned, His Britannic Majesty's chargé des affaires, has the honor of representing to the Secretary of State of the United States, that the King his master has been informed that a treaty was concluded on the 3d of August last [actually August 7, 1795], between the United States and certain tribes of Indians, living on the northwestern frontier of those States, which treaty appears to His Majesty to contain certain stipulations repugnant to the due execution of the provisions of the treaty between His Majesty and the United States of America, signed at London, on the 19th of November, 1794, and particularly that, by the eighth article of the said treaty between the United States and the Indians above-mentioned, it is agreed that no person shall be admitted to reside among, or to trade with, those tribes of Indians, unless they be furnished with a licence for that purpose from the Government of the United States; and that any person, so trading without such licence, shall be delivered up by the Indians to a superintendent appointed by the Government of the United States, to be dealt with according to the laws of the United States: whereas the third article of the treaty of amity, commerce, and navigation, concluded between His Majesty and the United States, expressly provides, 'that it shall, at all times, be free to His Majesty's subjects and to the citizens of the United States, and also to the Indians dwelling on either side of the boundary line, freely to pass and repass, by land or inland navigation,

Not knowing the precise form of that proposition, I cannot have an opinion what is right on the part of the Executive. But if I under-

---

into the respective territories and countries of the two parties on the continent of America, (the country within the limits of the Hudson's Bay Company only excepted) and to navigate all the lakes, rivers, and waters, thereof, and freely to carry on trade and commerce with each other.'

"The undersigned is directed to state that the King his master is fully persuaded that the said Indian treaty was concluded in consequence of instructions given by the Government of the United States at a time when that Government had not yet been apprised of the terms and stipulations of the treaty entered into by the respective plenipotentiaries, at London, on the 19th of November, 1794. Even if any doubt could arise on this subject in His Majesty's mind, His Majesty, in claiming the full execution of the said last mentioned treaty, would rely, with the utmost confidence, on the justice and good faith of the Government of the United States, and on the universally admitted rule of the law of nations, that no stipulations of existing treaties can be superseded by any engagements subsequently concluded by one of the parties with another State or nation; but when the particular circumstances connected with this important subject, and the influence which they may have on the lives and properties of so many, both of His Majesty's subjects, and of the citizens of the United States, are fairly and impartially considered, His Majesty can entertain no doubt that the Government of the United States will be equally anxious with himself that all possible misconstruction or doubt on this point, on the part either of His Majesty's subjects, or of the citizens of the United States, and still more on the part of the Indians, should be completely and authentically removed: and that this may be done with as little delay as possible, in order that less time may be left for the effect of any misrepresentations, which evil designing persons may have labored to impress on the minds of those, whose situation renders them peculiarly liable to such impressions. His Majesty trusts, therefore, that the Government of the United States will readily agree in the propriety of an explanation, which, under the circumstances above stated, appears to be of such indispensable necessity; and the undersigned is directed to propose, on His Majesty's part, that an article should, for that purpose, be added to the treaty of amity, commerce, and navigation, between His Majesty and the United States, so as to form a part thereof, conformably to the provisions contained in the 29th article of that instrument, by which it shall be declared that no treaty, subsequently concluded by either party with any other State or nation, whether European or Indian, can be understood, in any manner, to derogate from the rights of free intercourse and commerce secured by the aforesaid treaty of amity, commerce, and navigation, to the subjects of His Majesty and to the citizens of the United States, and to the Indians on both sides of the boundary line; but that all the said persons shall remain at full liberty freely to pass and repass into the countries on either side of the said boundary line, and to carry on their trade and commerce with each other, freely, and without restriction, according to the stipulations of the third article of the said treaty, which stipulations are, by the said treaty, declared to be permanent.

"If this measure, which appears to His Majesty conformable to the principles of justice and good faith, and indispensably required by the circumstances of the case, should meet the approbation of the Government of the United States, the undersigned is instructed and authorized to arrange the terms of such article, with any person who may be appointed by the Govern-

stand it, it ought to be sufficient for the Executive to declare that the article in the Treaty with the Indians can never operate nor will be permitted to operate in contravention of the Treaty with G Britain.³ It relates to a right reserved for our benefit which we can and will wave & being in a Treaty of subsequent date, it naturally gives way to another of prior date with which it is consistent. The Executive ought to be careful about admitting the propriety of a new condition though it ought to be ready to give all due satisfaction. It should not even shun a new explanatory article if reasonable in itself —but should agree to it upon the strength of its own reasonableness not as a new condition foreign to the Treaty. This affair requires great caution. But as I said I do not know enough to give advice worth much.

Yet the Government must take care not to appear pusyllanimous. I hope a *very serious* remonstrance has long since gone against the wanton impressment of our seamen. It will be an error to be too tame with this overbearing Cabinet.

Our City is in motion against the plan of the Majority in the House of Representatives with regard to the Treaty. The current

---

ment of the United States for the purpose, and to conclude and sign the same, subject to the ratification of the King his master: his Majesty being always desirous to take the earliest and most effectual means of removing any cause of uneasiness between the two Governments, and to maintain with the United States the most uninterrupted harmony and good understanding." (*ASP, Foreign Relations*, I, 551–52.)

3. Article 8 of the Treaty of Greenville reads: "Trade shall be opened with the said Indian tribes; and they do hereby respectively engage, to afford protection to such persons, with their property, as shall be duly licensed to reside among them, for the purpose of trade, and to their agents and servants; but no person shall be permitted to reside at any of their towns or hunting camps, as a trader, who is not furnished with a licence for that purpose, under the hand and seal of the superintendent of the department northwest of the Ohio, or such other person as the President of the United States shall authorize to grant such licences, to the end, that the said Indians may not be imposed on in their trade. And, if any licensed trader shall abuse his privilege by unfair dealing, upon complaint and proof thereof, his licence shall be taken from him, and he shall be further punished according to the laws of the United States. And if any person shall intrude himself as a trader, without such licence, the said Indians shall take and bring him before the superintendent, or his deputy, to be dealt with according to law. And, to prevent impositions by forged licences, the said Indians shall, at least once a year, give information to the superintendent, or his deputies, of the names of the traders residing among them" (*ASP, Indian Affairs*, I, 562–63).

For Article 3 of the Jay Treaty, see "Remarks on the Treaty . . . between the United States and Great Britain," July 9–11, 1795, note 8.

appears to be strong with us. The papers will tell you the measures in contemplation.[4]

But I was sorry to learn that a *proper qualified* communication was not made to the House of Representatives of the late communication from the British Agent. The Executive may hereafter be blamed for withholding so important a fact. Yet not knowing the whole affair I cannot judge well on this point more than on the other.

Yrs   A Hamilton

Oliver Wolcott Esq

4. See H to Rufus King, April 15, 18, 20, 1796.

To the Citizens Who Shall be Convened This Day in the Fields in the City of New York [1]

[New York, April 22, 1796]

Fellow Citizens

You have been called together by a description, which necessarily makes your meeting a partial one and excludes a great proportion of your Fellow Citizens, that is as those "who are determined to support the Constitution of the United States, and *approve of the proceedings of the House of Representatives with regard to the British Treaty.*" [2]

As to the first part of the description, those "who are determined

Copy, Hamilton Papers, Library of Congress.
1. This broadside was part of H's efforts to secure the adoption by the House of Representatives of legislation for the implementation of the Jay Treaty. For an account of the struggle in the House over this legislation, see the introductory note to H to George Washington, March 7, 1796.
2. H is quoting from the following handbill, dated April 21, 1796: "The citizens of New-York, who are determined to support the constitution of the United States, and approve of the proceedings of the House of Representatives, with regard to the British treaty, are requested to attend a meeting to be held in the fields, on Friday the 22d day of April, instant, at 12 o'clock. The present crisis is truly important. A punctual attendance is earnestly requested.

"☞ In opposition to the above, Good citizens, the real friends of our constitution and government, will not attend the meeting. The true sense of the citizens can be known only by the signatures to the petition now circulating." ([New York] *American Minerva; An Evening Advertiser*, April 21, 1796.)

to support the Constitution of the United States"—there is full evidence that those principally active in inviting you to meet have less title to this Character than those whom they meant to exclude, by the latter part of the description, and who have upon all occasions been the real and true friends of our Constitution.

Indeed it so happens that the two parts of the description are inconsistent with each other—for if there be any political truth demonstrable in itself, it is this—that if the House of Representatives refuse to provide for the Treaty, lately concluded with Great Britain, they will commit a manifest breach of those parts of our Constitution, which expressly grant the power of making Treaties to the President and Senate, and declare that the Treaties, they make, shall be laws of the Land. Unless you can believe that a thing may be a *bargain and not a bargain* at the same time—that a thing may be a *law and not a law* at the same time—you cannot but agree with me in the above conclusion. It is true this usurpation has been and will be covered by artful and plausible arguments—But when was a usurpation at a loss for such arguments? When did those who meant to overthrow a Constitution fail to find specious pretences to colour their designs?

The truth most assuredly is, Fellow Citizens, that the CONSTITUTION and PEACE are in one scale—the overthrow of the CONSTITUTION and WAR in the other. Which do you prefer? This is the true question. If you prefer the former—reject the advice which will be given to you to day. If the latter pursue it.

The Men, who ever since the present War in Europe broke out, have been trying to make our Country a party in it—tell you, to inflame your passions, that the Treaty with Great Britain was made under British Influence and to promote a British Interest. Can you seriously believe this, fellow Citizens? Can you be so cruel, so ungrateful as to think that George Washington, that veteran Hero and Patriot, who at the head of your Armies, with a halter about his neck, carried you successfully through a seven years war against Great Britain—that John Jay, who throughout our Revolution, was among the most conspicuous and useful of our Citizens in refusing British Tyranny—that the two thirds of the Senate who ratified the Treaty, almost all of whom during the same trying period were either in the Army, in Congress or in the State Legislatures supporting the common cause—that many other of your Fellow Citizens known to you to have been active in and out of the army in the same glorious cause—Can you, I ask, believe that all these Men have a sudden become the tools of Great Britain and Traitors to their Country? If you can, Fellow Citizens, then will Patriotism lose one of its strongest incentives and most precious rewards, the Esteem of those for whom it is exerted—Then will virtue and vice be confounded in the same undistinguishing opprobrium.

No, Fellow Citizens, these who made, and those who support the British Treaty did it and do it, merely as a *measure of peace,* to keep our Country out of one of the most dreadful Wars, that has hitherto scourged the Earth—and to gain time that we may securely reach a State of Manhood. They are willing to have peace and Trade with Great Britain as with the rest of the World—but they utterly disapprove and would firmly resist the idea of *political connection* or *alliance* with Great Britain. The true difference between them and their Opponents is this—They wish as far as our engagements already formed will permit to keep free from *political* connection with all EUROPE. Their Opponents wish to draw us into close alliance *offensive and defensive* with France, and thus involve us in all the Politics, Intrigues, Quarrels and Wars of Europe.

When as in our late Revolution, the Question was *Slavery* or *War* 'twas our duty to forget every other consideration and to put every thing to the hazard of the die—but when the question is to plunge into war, to avenge partial injuries which do not threaten either our Independence or our Liberty, Wisdom advises as to a very different course. Great sacrifices ought to be made for a great object, but to make them or hazard them for an inferior object would be folly in the extreme. It would be to surrender our reason and our interest to our pride and resentment, and in order to do our Enemy a small injury, to do ourselves a much greater.

Fellow Citizens! consider well your present situation If it be a good one, do not rashly risque a change—Do not second the ambition of a VIRGINIAN FACTION, constantly endeavoring to govern the United States—a Faction of which some of your Representatives are the Dupes—and are sacrificing very essential Interests of the State of New York, the recovery of your western Posts, the Furr trade, and the Trade of the two Canadas; all which from the course of the

Lakes and Rivers must necessarily fall into the Lap of the City of New York. May heaven by your guide and Preserver! [3]

NEW YORKER

3. The meeting in the Fields on April 22, 1796, adopted the following resolutions: "*Resolved*, That the treaty between the United States and Great Britain, is highly impolitic, disgraceful, and prejudicial to the true interests of the country. That in a variety of instances, it invades the delegated power of the House of Representatives, and infringes upon the rights and privileges of the people.

"II. *Resolved*, That we are and ever were anxious to preserve to our country the blessings of peace; that we deprecate unnecessary and unprovoked wars, and are conscious of their attendant calamities, but that when we protest against the idle clamours that artful and designing men have raised to induce a belief that war is the *inevitable* consequence of the non-execution of the treaty with Great Britain—we openly declare, that the constitution and liberties of our country are sacrifices we cannot submit to, even for the preservation of peace.

"III. *Resolved*, That the constitution of the United States is next to public liberty, the best inheritance of the citizens thereof, and that it is a duty incumbent upon every good citizen at all times to defend the same with his life and fortune.

"IV. *Resolved*, That the constitutional privileges of the House of Representatives is a trust consecrated to public liberty, and sacred to the welfare of the people, and that our representatives can never consent to submit to an invasion of these privileges in consistence with the duties they owe to their constituents.

"V. *Resolved*, That it is the constitutional right of Congress to make all necessary appropriations of money, and that they themselves are the proper judges of the justice, propriety and expediency of making those appropriations. And further, that all attempts to excite the apprehensions of the people to intimidate, and to influence the decision of their representatives, is unwarrantable and odious, and merits the marked detestation of a free and enlightened nation.

"VI. *Resolved*, That we highly applaud the resolution of Mr. Maclay submitted to the House of Representatives upon the subject of the British treaty; that we approve of the resolution of Mr. Livingston for indemnifying our merchants for the losses they have sustained in consequence of the British depredations and spoliations, and that we are willing to defray our full and equitable proportion of those losses.

"VII. *Resolved*, That we will ever support the House of Representatives in the exercise of their constitutional rights and authorities at the hazard of our lives and fortunes." (*The* [New York] *Argus, or Greenleaf's New Daily Advertiser*, April 23, 1796.)

For Edward Livingston's resolution, see the introductory note to H to Washington, March 7, 1796. For the resolution made on April 14, 1796, by Samuel Maclay of Pennsylvania, see *Annals of Congress*, V, 970–71.

From Walter Livingston [1]

Livingston Manor [*New York*] *April 22, 1796.* Asks Hamilton to serve as his attorney in a suit against "the Executors of my late brother Robt. C. L.² for the recovery of my ⅓ of three Bonds given to him by Mr. Robt. Morris for £3333 23/68 pensy. Curry. each— as a doceur for not biding for the Lands held by Massachusets in this State. . . .³ to Consult with Mr. Saml. Jones, respecting the Action commenced for me against Jno. R. Livingston for ½ of the Ship Somerset and her Cargo," and to "consult with Mr. Jones respecting the Suit commenced against Ben. Seixes on his Note in favor of P Colt for 10977 Dols. Defd. Debt."

LC, New-York Historical Society, New York City.
  1. For background to this letter, see Livingston to H, January 29, 1795.
  2. Robert Cambridge Livingston, a merchant, was the fourth son of Robert Livingston, Jr., the third lord of Livingston Manor. He died in 1794.
  3. For Morris's purchases of land in New York State from Massachusetts, see H to Morris, March 18, 1795, note 29.

To Fisher Ames

[*New York, April 23, 1796*. On April 23, 1796, Hamilton wrote to Rufus King: "I have written to *Ames* this day." *Letter not found.*]

To Rufus King

[New York, April 23, 1796]

Dr. Sir

I have received your two letters [1] & shall this day attend to the one which requires it.[2] I see however no objection to it as it stands & I do not now perceive how the further object you aim at could be accomplished in the *manner* you seem to desire.

I have written to *Ames* this day concerning the course of things in our City.[3] He will communicate to you as, I have not time to repeat. We are decidedly well. But it is intended today to continue the Petition in circulation & tomorrow it will be sent.[4] I thought it adviseable to publish an extract from your letter without naming you.[5]

Yrs. truly   A Hamilton

April 23 1796

R King Esqr

ALS, New-York Historical Society, New York City.

1. King to H, April 17–18, 20, 1796.
2. This is a reference to King to H, April 17–18, 1796.
3. H's letter to Fisher Ames has not been found.
4. See H to King, April 20, 1796, note 2. On April 25, 1796, the House of Representatives received "the petitions of sundry traders and other inhabitants of the city of New York, praying for a complete execution of the treaties with Great Britain, Spain, and Algiers" (*Journal of the House*, II, 521).
5. The extract from King's letter of April 17–18, 1796, which is entitled "Extract of a letter from a well informed character, in Philadelphia, dated 17th April, 1796," was published in the [New York] *American Minerva: An Evening Advertiser* on April 19, 1796. It reads: "The merchants & traders Petition is signed with unexampled unanimity—Baltimore have prepared a similar petition, which will be very generally signed—General Smith, who is now there, writes that the Treaty has gained many friends—that they are next to unanimous in favor of its execution—that Annapolis is likewise unanimous, and that he thinks that nine tenths of the State are for carrying it into effect. He adds that a memorial has been drawn up, and signed by most of the respectable People in Baltimore, approving the President's conduct in refusing the papers."

To Rufus King [1]

[New York] April 24 [1796] [2]

Dr. Sir

I return you a certain draft,[3] with a little substitute for the close of it proposed by Mr. J——[4] with an eye to your suggestion.

Our Petition went yesterday by express.[5] It had more than 3200 signers which is within about 300 of the highest poll we ever had in this City *on both sides,* at the most controverted election. Nothing can more clearly demonstrate our unanimity & I feel no doubt of equal or greater unanimity throughout the state.

The Meeting men have not dared to publish the names of this Committee, because it imprudently contained a considerable proportion of persons hostile to its object—several of them actually on our Petition.[6] You see by this their embarrassment & their weakness.

Yrs. A H

ALS, Hamilton Papers, Library of Congress.

1. This letter concerns the efforts of supporters of the Jay Treaty both in and out of the Government to secure the adoption by the House of Representatives of legislation for the implementation of the Jay Treaty. For an account of the struggle in the House over this legislation, see the introductory note to H to George Washington, March 7, 1796.

2. In *JCHW*, V, 632, and in *HCLW*, X, 98, this letter is incorrectly dated "1795."
3. This draft has not been found.
4. John Jay.
5. See H to King, April 20, 1796, note 2, and April 23, 1796, note 6.
6. For the meeting of April 22, 1796, see "To the Citizens Who Shall be Convened This Day in the Fields in the City of New York," April 22, 1796

From John Marshall [1]

Richmond April 25th. 96

Dear Sir

Yours of the 14th only reachd me by the mail of this evening.[2] I had been informed of the temper of the house of representatives & we had promptly taken such measures as appeard to us fitted to the occasion. We coud not venture an expression of the public mind under the violent prejudices with which it had been impressd, so long as a hope remaind that the house of representatives might ultimately consult the interest or honor of the nation. But now when all hope of this has vanishd, it was deemed adviseable to make the experiment however hazardous it might be. A meeting was calld which was more numerous than I have ever seen at this place & after a very ardent & zealous discussion which consumd the day, a decided majority declard in favor of a resolution that the welfare & honor of the nation requird us to give full effect to the treaty negotiated with Britain.[3]

This resolution with a petition [4] drawn by an original opponent of the treaty will be forwarded by the next post to Congress. The subject will probably be taken up in every county in the state or at any rate in very many of them. It is probable that a majority of the counties will avow sentiments opposd to ours—but the division of the state will appear to be much more considerable than has been stated. In some of the districts there will certainly be a majority who will concur with us & that perhaps may have some effect. As Man is a gregarious animal we shall certainly derive much aid from declarations in support of the constitution & of appropriations if such can be obtaind, from our sister States. The ground we take here is very much that of Mr. Hillhouse.[5] We admit the discretionary constitutional power of the representatives on the subject of appropriations but contend that the treaty is as completely a valid & obligatory contract when negotiated by the President & ratified by him with the assent & advice of the Senate as if sanctiond by the house of representatives also under a constitution requiring such sanction. I think it woud be very difficult perhaps impossible to engage Mr. H.[6] on the right side of this question. If you have any communications which might promote a concurrence of action we shall be proud to receive them.

With much respect & esteem I am dear Sir your Obedt.

J Marshall

ALS, Hamilton Papers, Library of Congress.

1. This letter concerns the efforts of supporters of the Jay Treaty both in and out of the Government to secure the adoption by the House of Representatives of legislation for the implementation of that treaty. For an account of the struggle in the House over this legislation, see the introductory note to H to George Washington, March 7, 1796.

On April 30, 1796, the [Philadelphia] *Gazette of the United States*, under the heading "Extract of a letter from a Gentleman in Richmond (Virginia) of April 25," printed most of the first paragraph and the first sentence of the second paragraph of Marshall's letter to H.

2. Letter not found.

3. The resolution and proceedings of the meeting of April 25, 1796, in Richmond are printed in *The* [Richmond] *Virginia Gazette, and General Advertiser*, April 27, 1796. The resolution reads: "Resolved, as the opinion of this meeting, That the peace, happiness and welfare, not less than the national honor of these United States depend, in a great degree, upon giving, with good faith, full effect to the Treaty lately negotiated with Great-Britain."

4. The petition is printed in *The* [Richmond] *Virginia Gazette, and General Advertiser*, April 27, 1796. There is no record in the *Journal of the House* that the House received this petition.

5. James Hillhouse was a member of the House of Representatives from Connecticut. For the speech by Hillhouse to which Marshall is referring, see *Annals of Congress*, V, 660–76.

6. Presumably Patrick Henry.

From Philip Schuyler [1]

Albany Monday April 25th 1796

Dear Sir

Unadvised of the measures pursuing at New York, relative to the treaty with Britain, It was not deemed prudent to convene the citizens here on the Subject, until we received information from your city.² On Saturday morning the mail arrived, and the Herald announced what had been done ³—about forty Citizens were immediately convened, and unanimously agreed to petition in the words of the new York petition, with no other variation than what was requisite to Accomodate It to the people in this quarter. Five hundred copies where immediately printed, proper persons appointed to invite the Signature of the Citizens individually, before sunset this was compleated, all having subscribed Except about ⁴ who declined, many decided Antifœdarelist concurred and signed.

A circular letter was prepared, directed to the Supervizers, Assessors & town Clerks, of the Several towns in this and the counties to the Eastward, northward & westward of this.⁵ Several of these, with copies of the petition are already dispatched, and the residue will be sent to day. We believe the Subscribers will be numerous.

The petition from this city will be sent to Philadelphia by this days mail.⁶

We are anxious to hear the result of the Application to the citizens of New York, and If favorable, wish It to ⟨be⟩ communicated in a formal manner, by the New York committee.⁷

The inclosed, is a copy of the letter, which accompanied the copy of the petition to the several towns.

Pray drop me a line, advising me of the latest intelligence from Philadelphia, on this important subject.

Adieu my Love to all with You   Yours most affectionately

Ph: Schuyler

Alexander Hamilton Esqr

ALS, Lloyd W. Smith Collection, Morristown National Historical Park, Morristown, New Jersey.

1. This letter concerns the efforts of supporters of the Jay Treaty both in and out of the Government to secure the adoption by the House of Representatives of legislation for the implementation of that treaty. For an account of the struggle in the House over this legislation, see the introductory note to H to George Washington, March 7, 1796.

2. For the petition of New York City's merchants urging that the House act to implement the Jay Treaty, see H to Rufus King, April 20, 1796, note 2.

3. See *The* [New York] *Herald; A Gazette for the Country*, April 20, 1796, which contains the texts of the New York merchants' petition and their accompanying resolution, which also appeared in the [Philadelphia] *Gazette of the United States*, April 21, 1796. See H to King, April 20, 1796, note 2.

4. Space left blank in MS.

5. A facsimile of this broadside is printed in Hamilton, *Intimate Life*, facing page 292.

6. On April 29, 1796, the House received "the memorials of sundry inhabitants of the City of Albany, and Town of Lansingburg, in the State of New York, whose names are thereunto subscribed, stating that certain resolutions now depending before the House of Representatives respecting the late treaty with Great Britain, have already given occasion to great embarrasments, and threaten very serious and complicated evils, the whole magnitude of which it is not easy to foresee or calculate, and that, in their opinion, it deeply concerns the agriculture, commerce, peace, character, and honor of America, that provision be made to carry the said treaty into effect" (*Journal of the House*, II, 527).

7. For public support given the New York City petition, see H to King, April 24, 1796.

From Richard Platt [1]

New York, April 26, 1796. Asks Hamilton to join with his attorneys, Robert Troup and Brockholst Livingston, in a case before the New York Supreme Court on the following day.[2] States that "The Amount of the Debt is too triffling to ask any interposition of you as Counsel, on the Defendant side, but the Consequences of it's *possible* result may involve a Question of the first magnitude to all persons in future subject to prosecution for Debt, when & where the hearts of Creditors . . . are instigated by the Devil."

ALS, Hamilton Papers, Library of Congress.

1. Platt was a New York City broker and speculator and a former business associate of William Duer.

2. There is no record that H appeared before the New York Supreme Court in Platt's case. According to the minute book of the court, the attorneys for the plaintiff were Richard Harison, Samuel Jones, and Thomas Smith, and those for the defendant were "Troup, B. Livingston and [Nicholas] Evertson" (MS Minutes of the New York Supreme Court, January 19–November 5, 1796 [Hall of Records, New York City]). This case, which was heard on April 27, 1796, was brought by John R. Myers and Helen Myers for assumpsit in the sum of four thousand dollars. After postponing the verdict for several days, the court met again on May 5 and discharged Platt from arrest (MS Minutes of the New York Supreme Court, January 19–November 5, 1796 [Hall of Records, New York City]). When Platt became bankrupt, however, he was declared indebted on November 26, 1800, to the estate of "Helena Myer" for $5,695.10, including interest (D, RG 21, District Court, Southern District of New York, Bankruptcy Act of 1800, Case Files, Richard Platt, National Archives).

Platt had a long history of debt. See William Lewis to H, June, 1794, note 1. Platt attempted as early as 1796 to get support for a declaration of insolvency, but was unsuccessful. See Platt to Walter Livingston, July 7, 1796 (ALS, New-York Historical Society, New York City).

From William Lewis

[*Philadelphia, April 27, 1796.* On April 27, 1796, Robert Morris wrote to Hamilton: "Mr. Lewis . . . says he has written you two letters, the last of them this morning." *Letter of April 27 not found.*]

From Robert Morris

[Philadelphia, April 27, 1796]

Introductory Note

This letter is the first in Morris's correspondence with Hamilton that refers to a debt which Benjamin Walker [1] was trying to collect from Morris. Hamilton became involved in this matter because both men consulted him about it on more than one occasion and because the debt in question became inextricably intertwined in Morris's efforts to pay a debt which he owed to John B. Church, who was the English husband of Elizabeth Hamilton's sister Angelica, and for whom Hamilton acted as agent or representative in the United States.[2]

The debt on which Walker was attempting to secure payment had been contracted by William S. Smith, John Adams's son-in-law, on behalf of the Pulteney Associates. In 1790–1791 both Smith and William Temple Franklin [3] were in England to promote the sale of American securities and lands. Their major customer proved to be William Johnstone Pulteney, a leading British capitalist and a member of the House of Commons, who in 1791 agreed to buy from Robert Morris 1.2 million acres in the Genesee country of western New York.[4] Associated in this purchase with Pulteney was William Hornby, who had been governor of Bombay. The man who served as intermediary and made the preliminary arrangements for Pulteney's purchase was Patrick Colquhoun, a merchant of Glasgow, who had once lived in Virginia. The organization which these men formed was variously known as the Pulteney Association, Pulteney Associates, London Associates and London Association. For his part in arranging the sale of Morris's property, Colquhoun was given an interest of one-twelfth in the purchase, while

LC, Robert Morris Papers, Library of Congress.
1. For Walker, see Germain Pierre Decrosses to H. April 16, 1796, note 4.
2. For Morris's debt to Church, see the introductory note to Morris to H, June 7, 1795. See also Morris to H, July 20, November 16, December 18, 1795; January 15, March 6, 12, 14, 30, 1796.
3. For Franklin, see Morris to H, June 7, 1795, note 48.
4. For this tract, see H to Morris, March 18, 1795, note 29.

Pulteney's and Hornby's interests were respectively nine-twelfths and two-twelfths.[5]

On his return to the United States in 1791, Smith in his capacity as agent for the Pulteney Associates loaned Morris $100,000 which belonged to Pulteney and Hornby. According to the terms of this loan Morris was to repay Smith with funded debt in two installments due on July 1, 1792, and January 1, 1793, together with interest payments. To secure the payment of this debt Morris conveyed to Smith the Morris Reserve [6] comprising some five hundred thousand acres of Genesee lands.[7] This transaction was accomplished by a deed and defeasance, which taken together constituted a mortgage. The deed was recorded in the office of the Secretary of State of New York, but the defeasance was not recorded. The defeasance stated in effect that if Morris paid his debt to Smith, the land pledged for the payment of the debt would be returned to Morris.[8]

Morris met the first of the two payments owed to Smith, but he failed to pay the remaining $50,000 when this obligation fell due.[9] This was the situation in May, 1795, when Smith assigned the mortgage to Walker, who had succeeded Smith as the representative of the Pulteney Associates.[10] On assuming his new responsibilities Walker was alarmed to learn that Morris had sold two tracts in the Reserve which had been mortgaged to Smith.[11] Accordingly, in October, 1795, Walker sued

5. For the standard account of the transactions described in this paragraph, see Helen I. Cowan, *Charles Williamson, Genesee Promoter: Friend of Anglo-American Rapprochement* (Rochester, 1941), 1–21.

6. For the Morris Reserve, see H to Morris, March 18, 1795, note 29.

7. Agreement, Robert Morris and William S. Smith, August 13, 1791 (copy, Hamilton Papers, Library of Congress); Bill, *Walker* v *Morris*, filed October 24, 1795, New York Chancery Decrees before 1800, W-174 (MS, Court of Appeals, Albany). For this agreement, see also Morris, *In the Account of Property*, 2.

8. Defeasance, William S. Smith to Robert Morris, August 13, 1791 (D, Hamilton Papers, Library of Congress). A defeasance is a collateral deed made at the same time as a conveyance and containing certain conditions. If these conditions are met, the conveyance is then nullified.
See Bill, *Walker* v *Morris*, filed October 24, 1795, New York Chancery Decrees before 1800, W-174 (MS, Court of Appeals, Albany). See also Morris, *In the Account of Property*, 4.

9. Bill, *Walker* v *Morris*, filed October 24, 1795, New York Chancery Decrees before 1800, W-174 (MS, Court of Appeals, Albany): Morris, *In the Account of Property*, 4.

10. Bill, *Walker* v *Morris*, filed October 24, 1795, New York Chancery Decrees before 1800, W-174 (MS, Court of Appeals, Albany); Morris, *In the Account of Property*, 4.

11. Morris had sold one of these tracts, comprising approximately one hundred thousand acres, to James Watson, James Greenleaf, and Andrew Craigie. See the introductory note to H to Morris, March 18, 1795. He had sold another tract of more than eighty thousand acres to Herman LeRoy and William Bayard. The second was the so-called Triangular Tract. See Morris to H, June 7, 1795, note 30.

in Chancery for an injunction to prevent additional sales of the Reserve by Morris and to foreclose Morris's equity of redemption.[12]

By 1796, the injunction sought by Walker had been issued,[13] and it was in the spring of that year that Hamilton became directly involved in the dispute between Walker and Morris. In the letter printed below Morris is proposing to secure the payment of his debt to John B. Church by mortgaging to Hamilton one hundred thousand acres of the Morris Reserve,[14] all of which had already been mortgaged to Smith (and was now mortgaged to Walker) and was tied up by Walker's suit in Chancery. To have the suit dismissed and thus clear the way for mortgaging the one hundred thousand acres to Hamilton, Morris needed $50,000 in cash to pay Walker. To secure this sum, as he mentions in the letter below, he asked Samuel Ogden [15] to act as his agent and to sell some of Morris's lands in the Morris Reserve.[16] On May 10, 1796, Morris was able to report to Hamilton that Ogden had sold fifty thousand acres to Othniel Taylor and Asa Danforth for $57,500 and that he had proposed to Walker that he "would convey the said 50,000 acres to him and assign to him the above mentioned Contract which binds the parties to pay $57,000 and interest." [17] Walker was apparently receptive to Morris's proposal, for Chancellor Robert Livingston, in response to a petition by Walker's attorney, gave Morris permission to mortgage the one hundred thousand acres to Hamilton to secure the debt to Church.[18] Accordingly, on May 16, Morris and Hamilton agreed on a mortgage to Hamilton of the one hundred thousand acres and a bond for the payment of $81,679.44 to Church.[19]

Morris soon had good reason to believe that whatever solutions he had devised merely served to create new problems. After he and Hamilton had agreed on the bond and mortgage for the debt to Church, Walker announced that he would not accept an assignment of the contract with

12. Bill, *Walker* v *Morris*, filed October 24, 1795, New York Chancery Decrees before 1800, W-174 (MS, Court of Appeals, Albany). "Equity of redemption" is defined as follows: "The right of the mortgagor of an estate to redeem the same after it has been forfeited at law, by a breach of the condition of the mortgage, upon paying the amount of debt, interest and costs" (Henry Campbell Black, *Black's Law Dictionary* [4th ed., St. Paul, 1951], 636).

13. Morris to Samuel Ogden, May 3, 1796 (LC, Robert Morris Papers, Library of Congress).

14. For Morris's debt to Church, see the introductory note to Morris to H, June 7, 1795.

15. For Ogden, see H to Morris, March 18, 1795, note 23.

16. Morris to Ogden, May 3, 11, 1796 (LC, Robert Morris Papers, Library of Congress).

17. Morris to H, May 10, 1796.

18. MS Minutes, New York Court of Chancery, 1793–1797, *sub* May 14, 1796 (Hall of Records, New York City); Order, *Walker* v *Morris*, June 6, 1797, New York Chancery Decrees before 1800, W-19 (MS, Court of Appeals, Albany).

19. See the introductory note to Morris to H, June 7, 1795.

Taylor and Danforth.[20] Because Walker's refusal among other things jeopardized Morris's agreement with Hamilton, Morris reneged on Ogden's sale to Taylor and Danforth and conveyed the fifty thousand acres to Garrett Cottringer, Morris's bookkeeper and business associate.[21] This, in turn, produced a delay in perfecting the mortgage of the one hundred thousand acres to Hamilton, for this property had a common border with the fifty thousand acres which had been conveyed to Cottringer. It was only after Cottringer's name had been inserted in the mortgage to Hamilton that the mortgage was perfected on May 31, 1796.[22]

Having reached an agreement concerning his debt to Church, Morris was then in a position to turn his attention to the $50,000 which he still owed to Pulteney and Hornby as a result of the loan made by Smith in 1791. Bypassing Walker, he worked out an arrangement with Charles Williamson, Pulteney's agent in the Genesee country, for Cottringer to convey the fifty thousand acres in Cottringer's name to Williamson.[23] For his part Williamson agreed that this conveyance would cancel Morris's debt of $50,000 to Pulteney and Hornby; that the four hundred and fifty thousand acres of the Morris Reserve, which remained after the conveyance of fifty thousand acres to Williamson, would be reconveyed to Morris; and that Walker's suit in Chancery would be dismissed. In announcing this agreement to Hamilton in a letter on January 7, 1797, Morris wrote: "I must request your immediate care and attention as a professional Man to see this done in all due Form & without loss of time for which I will chearfully pay the Compensation you say is right."

In March, 1797, Hamilton sent to Morris Williamson's deed of fifty thousand acres,[24] but Morris's troubles with Walker were still not over, for the suit in Chancery remained.[25] Morris was not completely relieved of this particular part of his financial misery until June 6, 1797, when the Chancellor directed that Walker's suit be dismissed.[26]

Alexander Hamilton Esqr Philada. April 27th 1796
New York

Dr. Sir

Your letter without date arrived within this half hour [27] & in consequence I run down to Mr Lewis [28] from whom I am just returned he says he has written you two letters, the last of them this morn-

20. Morris to H, May 31, 1796.
21. Morris to H, May 31, 1796.
22. See the introductory note to Morris to H, June 7, 1795.
23. Morris to H, January 7, 1797.
24. Morris to H, January 7, 1797.
25. Order, *Walker* v *Morris,* June 6, 1797, New York Chancery Decrees before 1800, W-19 (MS, Court of Appeals, Albany).
26. Order, *Walker* v *Morris,* June 6, 1797, New York Chancery Decrees before 1800, W-19 (MS, Court of Appeals, Albany).
27. Letter not found.
28. William Lewis. See Morris to H, March 30, 1796, note 1.

ing [29] & it was sent to the Post Office before I got there. If Mr Lewis does me justice he will tell you that I called on him more than once with a strong desire to finish the business.[30] I am mortified not a little to see your extreme anxiety & at the same time acknowledge that it is my duty to relieve you from it. I make it a point of honor to do so, and would now offer you as good a security in this City as that you gave up,[31] but I perceive the existing judgements would lead you to object. I will therefore send you a Mortgage upon one hundred thousand acres of the Genesee Land [32] adjoining that which I am now selling at 1 of your Curry ⅌ Acre in order to discharge the Mortgage to Colo. Walker. Mr Saml. Ogden will go over to New York in order to finish that business perhaps you can assist him in it. If that Mortgage is cleared away there is no other & the land I would not sell for less than two Dollr ⅌ Acre were it not to pay that cursed Mortgage. I must however stipulate with you that if at any time I should wish to change the security, you will allow me to do it upon giving one equally satisfactory. I wish also to know whether I should give the Bonds for 100,000 Drs deferred debt,[33] or if to be commuted to Money at what rate shall it be done or how will you settle the Acct. I will have the Mortgage drawn up immediately after hearing from you unless you choose to send me the draft of one & point out the formalities. Must Mrs Morris be a party, as there is no income arising from uncultivated Lands I suppose it is not necessary. You may rely you shall not have cause in any event to change your opinion of my honor or integrity if that opinion has been what I believe it always has been.

I am Dr. Sir   Y. O. h. S.   RM

29. Neither letter has been found, but see Lewis to H, May 4, 1796.
30. This is a reference to Morris's debt to Church and his efforts either to pay it or to offer a mortgage as security for it. See the introductory note to Morris to H, June 7, 1795. See also Morris to H, July 20, November 16, December 18, 1795; January 15, March 6, 12, 14, 30, 1796.
31. Morris had originally secured his debt to Church by mortgaging property in Philadelphia. This arrangement was subsequently altered. See the introductory note to Morris to H, June 7, 1795.
32. See Morris to H, June 7, 1795, note 17.
33. For Morris's agreement to pay Church in deferred debt, see Morris to H, June 2, 1795, and the introductory note to Morris to H, June 7, 1795.

From Stephen Rochefontaine [1]

West Point, April 28, 1796. Asks for Hamilton's "advice in a very disagreeable case" concerning the aftermath of an abortive duel between Rochefontaine and Lieutenant William Wilson.[2] Describes the case, his continuing difficulties with Wilson and other officers at West Point, and submits "a few Queries which I would wish you to favor with your opinion upon and as soon as convenient, in order that I may avoid if possible the Inconveniency of a writ, which may be served against me upon the application of my adversaries."

ALS, United States Military Academy Library.
1. Lieutenant Colonel Étienne Nicolas Marie Bechet, Sieur Rochefontaine, later known as Stephen Rochefontaine, was a French engineer who served in the Continental Army during the American Revolution. In 1792 Louis XVI appointed him Adjutant General of the Army of Santo Domingo. Following the death of Louis XVI in January, 1793, Rochefontaine returned to the United States, and on March 29, 1794, Secretary of War Henry Knox appointed him an engineer for the fortification of ports and harbors. On February 26, 1795, he was appointed to command the first regularly organized Corps of Artillerists and Engineers of the United States at West Point. See Edward Hagaman Hall, "Lieutenant Colonel Stephen Rochefontaine," *Twenty-Sixth Annual Report of the American Scenic and Historic Preservation Society, 1921* (Albany, 1922), 247–69.
2. William Wilson of Maryland was appointed a lieutenant in the Corps of Artillerists and Engineers on January 7, 1795, to rank from July 17, 1794 (*Executive Journal*, I, 167, 169).
A court of enquiry on the dispute was held at West Point in May and June, 1796. During the proceedings Rochefontaine suspected the men composing the court of being prejudiced against him and sought the advice of Timothy Pickering. In the end, however, no charges were brought against him. An account of the enquiry may be found in Rochefontaine to Pickering, May 28, 31, June 5, 7, 11, 19, July 1, 1796 (ALS, Massachusetts Historical Society, Boston).

From Oliver Wolcott, Junior

Phila. Apl. 29. 1796

Dr. Sir   Private
I have recd. your favour of the 20th. The affair with Bond [1] stands thus, & is truly attended with some perplexing circumstances.

ALS, Hamilton Papers, Library of Congress; copy, Connecticut Historical Society, Hartford.
1. Phineas Bond.

The communication states,² that provisional orders have been given for the surrender of the Posts whenever the House of Representatives shall have indicated an intention to give effect to the Treaty & when an article shall have been negociated explanatory of the sense of the two nations that the 8th article of our Treaty with the Indians³ shall not abrogate from the rights stipulated in favour of British subjects by the 3d. article of the Treaty with Great Britain.⁴ The style of the Memorial is respectful & the doubtful article in the Indian Treaty is attributed to want of information on our part of the Stipulation in the B. Treaty.

2. On March 26, 1796, Bond sent Timothy Pickering a memorial concerning a possible conflict between Article 8 of the Treaty of Greenville with the Indians northwest of the Ohio River and Article 3 of the Jay Treaty. See H to Wolcott, April 20, 1796, note 2. On April 9, 1796, Bond again wrote to Pickering: "Having, within these few Days, received Dispatches from the Rt. Hon: Lord Dorchester, His Majesty's Governor General of Canada, intimating his Lordship's Readiness to surrender, at the Period prescribed by the Treaty of Amity Commerce and Navigation, lately concluded between His Majesty and the United States, the Posts on the American Side of the Boundary Line, assigned to the United States by the Treaty of Peace; and finding that his Lordship has, already, given such preparatory Directions, as appeared to his Lordship, best calculated for the Completion of this Purpose, it seems expedient that I should, thus formally & explicitly, communicate to this Government . . . that any ulterior Measures, which His Majesty's Governor General is to pursue, must be considered as provisional.

"The Period, limited for the Surrender of the Posts, being so near at Hand, a precise Declaration of the Contingencies, upon which such ulterior Measures are to depend, may be satisfactory & eventually serve to prevent Inconvenience. . . .

"It . . . becomes indispensably necessary, that it should be ascertained, that this Treaty is, not only, held to be valid, and of binding Force, on the United States, but that every expedient legal Provision will be made, to carry the Stipulations of the Treaty into Effect, on the Part of this Government.

"The other Matter to be adjusted . . . is the Explanation, relative to the Indian Treaty, which was the Subject of my Memorial of the 26th Ult: about which, I was happy to find, from the Consideration you had given to my Application, you did not apprehend any Difficulty could arise. . . .

"As soon as these Contingencies shall have been brought to such an Issue, as shall be consistent with His Majesty's reasonable Expectations, & correspondent with His Majesty's sincere Wish to maintain Peace & Friendship with the United States, His Majesty's Governor General is authorized, and will be immediately ready, to form an Arrangement with the Person, the President of the United States may be pleased to appoint, to concert such Measures to effectuate the Provisions of the Treaty, as may be compatible with mutual Convenience & Accomodation." (LS, RG 59, Notes from the British Legation in the United States to the Department of State, 1791–1906, Vol. 2, January 10, 1796–November 19, 1803, National Archives.)

3. For Article 8 of the Treaty of Greenville, see H to Wolcott, April 20, 1796, note 3.

4. For Article 3 of the Jay Treaty, see "Remarks on the Treaty . . . between the United States and Great Britain," July 9–11, 1795, note 8.

I have thought that a declaration by the Executive, that we admit the doctrine of the Law of nations, ought to be sufficient, & that insisting upon an explanatory article was pressing a point rather unreasonably against us. As however Mr. Bond says that he is instructed to insist on an article, & as the terms can be adjusted so as compleatly to save the national honour, perhaps we are bound to consent.[5] I feel however that the Executive ought not to have been embarrassed at present.

There being two points to be settled, before we obtain the Posts, one concerning the Legislation & the other the Senate, it has appeared to me that a partial communication would be improper, & that a general one would be inexpedient. A message to the House would moreover unnecessarily stimulate the passions of the opposition. A resolution for giving effect to the Treaty is under consideration.[6] The presumption ought to be that they will do their duty. On this ground, the Senate have forborne to connect a provision for the B. Treaty with the bills which have been sent up respecting the other Treaties.[7] The principle which has governed the Senate, if correct, requires the Executive to forbear his interference.

Some difficulty may be apprehended in obtaining a ratification of the explanatory article in the present state of the Senate, but it will be surmounted.

5. An explanatory article was signed by Pickering and Bond on May 4, 1796. On May 5 President Washington submitted the article to the Senate (*ASP, Foreign Relations*, I, 551), which approved it on May 9 by a vote of 19 to 5 (*Executive Journal*, I, 207). For the text of the explanatory article, see Miller, *Treaties*, II, 346–47.

6. On April 29, 1796 (or the same day on which Wolcott wrote the above letter to H), the Committee of the Whole in the House of Representatives adopted by a vote of 50 to 49 a resolution "That it is expedient to make the necessary resolutions for carrying the Treaty with Great Britain into effect" (*Annals of Congress*, V, 1280). The following day the House passed the resolution by a vote of 51 to 48 (*Annals of Congress*, V, 1291). See the introductory note to H to Washington, March 7, 1796.

7. See H to Rufus King, April 15, 1796, note 6, and H to King, April 20, 1796, notes 10 and 11. On May 4, 1796, "The bill sent from the House of Representatives for concurrence, entitled 'An act making an appropriation towards defraying the expenses which may arise in carrying into effect the Treaty of Amity, Commerce and Navigation, made between the United States and the King of Great Britain,' was read the second time, and referred to the committee appointed the 20th of April, on the several bills making appropriations for carrying into effect the Treaties between the United States and the King of Spain, between the United States and the Dey and Regency of Algiers, and between the United States and certain Indian tribes, to consider and report thereon to the Senate" (*Annals of Congress*, V, 79).

I think the government will succeed in the present contest, but it remains doubtful whether order can be long preserved. Unless a radical change of opinion can be effected in the Southern States, the existing establishments will not last eighteen months. The influence of Messrs. Gallatin, Madison & Jefferson must be diminished, or the public affairs will be brought to a stand. No proper attention is paid to the current business of the Government by the House; every thing is in the hands of the Committees, nothing is understood & few matters of importance in a train for being compleated. Before the Treaty question commenced, the Treaty furnished a pretence for delay—the length of the session & the languor of the members will furnish another pretext, after that question shall have been determined.

Mr. Patten,[8] the Post Master, communicated to me yester day a singular circumstance.[9] Some time since, letters were delivered into his Office, for Robert Cowper & a Doctor Graham of Suffolk in Virginia. By some means Mr. Patten discovered that these Letters had been brought from Virginia, & this he says induced him to suspect some mischief & to write to Virginia. I have seen the answer which he (Patten) recd. from Robt. Cowper in which he says that the Letter to him was signed with your Name—that to Doct. Graham was signed with the name of Mr. Van Allen of Congress. It seems that the Letters were forgeries, & contain something which if true might injure yours & Mr. V Allens characters. This is doubtless some Jacobin Trick. I shall try to detect it & give you information. At present I have no particulars.

I am truely yrs. Oliv. Wolcott Jr.

Alex Hamilton Esq

8. Robert Patton was the postmaster at Philadelphia.
9. The remainder of this paragraph concerns two forged letters. See Robert Cowper to H, April 16, 1796.

From Rufus King [1]

[Philadelphia] Sunday 1 May [1796]

In committee of the whole on friday it was resolved by the casting vote of Muhlenburgh the chairman, to make provision by

Law for carrying the Treaty with England into Effect. Yesterday the Resolution of the Committee of the whole was passed in the House by 51. against 48.² A proposition to prefix to the Resolution a Preamble declaring the Treaty to be *injurious to the Interest* of the US. and assigning the short duration of its temporary articles as a reason why it should be permitted to go into Effect, was negatived by 50. against 49.³ and the Resolution was immediately, and without Division, referred to a Committee with instructions to prepare and report a Bill or Bills in conformity with the Resolution. The failure of the Party in their intention to denounce the Treaty, I am fearful will not discourage them in a second attempt. A majority of five or Six (If I am not mistaken) would join in a vote of condemnation, but in the shape in which the proposition was offered, some of the most inveterate Opponents of the treaty, voted in the negative because they said, if they voted for the Preamble, it would be then proper for them to vote for the Resolution which they were determined not to do. Though from the State in which the Business now is, I hope the attempt will not be made, yet if an independent Resolution shd. be offered, declaring the Treaty to be injurious &c &c I am apprehensive it would be adopted. This however would not defeat the Procession for the Execution of the Treaty—51 votes in the affirmative; the speakers vote with that of Mr. Freeman of Massachusetts,⁴ both of whom are in favor of the Provisions, make 53, affirmative voices, a Majority of the whole Number of Reps.

Yr's &c   RK

ALS, Hamilton Papers, Library of Congress.
 1. For background to this letter, see the introductory note to H to George Washington, March 7, 1796.
 2. On April 29, 1796, the Committee of the Whole in the House of Representatives passed a resolution "that it is expedient to make the necessary appropriations for carrying the Treaty with Great Britain into effect." The original vote was 49 to 49, with the tie being broken by Frederick A. C. Muhlenberg voting in his capacity as chairman of the committee (*Annals of Congress*, V, 1280). On April 30 the House approved the resolution by a vote of 51 to 48 (*Annals of Congress*, V, 1291). King's tabulation of the vote on April 30 is attached to his letter to H. It reads:
          "on passing Resolution

	Ayes	Noes	Absent
N. H.	3	0	1 on leave
Mass	10	3	1 Do
R I	2	0	0

Con	7	0	0
Ver	1	1	0
NY	7	3	0
NJ	5	0	0
Penn	7	5	1 skulked
Del	0	0	1 sick
Mar	6	1	1 resigned
Virg	1	18	0
NC.	1	9	0
SC.	2	4	0
Geo.	0	2	0
Kent	0	2	0
	52	48	5"

The affirmative vote of 52 rather than 51 is accounted for by King's inclusion under New Jersey of the vote of the Speaker of the House, Jonathan Dayton.

3. This resolution was proposed by Henry Dearborn of Massachusetts on April 30, 1796, and reads: "*Resolved,* That, although in the opinion of this House the Treaty is highly objectionable, and may prove injurious to the United States, yet, considering all the circumstances relating thereto, and particularly, that the last eighteen articles are to continue in force only during the present war, and two years thereafter, and confiding also in the efficacy of measures that may be taken for bringing about a discontinuance of the violations committed on our neutral rights, in regard to our vessels and seamen, therefore, &c." During debate on this resolution, Samuel Smith of Maryland moved "to strike out the word 'highly,' so as to read *objectionable,* instead of 'highly objectionable.' " The vote on Smith's resolution resulted in a tie of 48 to 48. The tie was broken by the affirmative vote of the Speaker of the House, Jonathan Dayton. Following a brief debate, the vote was taken on the amended motion and it was "decided in the negative, as follows: Yeas 49, Nays 50" (*Annals of Congress,* V, 1282, 1287, 1289).

4. Nathaniel Freeman was absent when the resolution for implementing the Jay Treaty was passed by 51 to 48 (*Annals of Congress,* V, 1291–92).

From Rufus King

[Philadelphia] Monday 2. May [1796]

The inclosed letter will give you all the information that we have on the Subject to wh. it relates. It seems problematical whether PH. can be induced to agree in the arrangement [1]—some circumstances of which I have lately heard incline me to believe that he will not. Our session will close by the first of June provided no farther impediment is thrown in the way of the Provision for giving Efficacy to the treaty with England—and it is much to be wished that a definitive arrangement should be made before we separate.[2]

Mr. Pinckney has asked leave to return home, and waits only for Permission.[3] To his former stock of Popularity, he will now add the

Good will of those who have been peculiarly gratified with the Sp. Treaty;[4] should we concur in him will he not receive as great, perhaps greater southern and western Support than any other man?

You must know that I am not a little tired with the separation from my Family, and drudging in the Senate. The work now before us being finished, I think I am intitled to a dismission. It would be agreeable to me to spend a few years abroad, and if I do not misconceive the interests of the Country, I think I could render some service to the Public at the present Period in England—will you converse with Mr Jay on this subject?

I can through no other channel communicate with the Executive —nor do I desire that either of you should suggest the measure, unless you both agree in its propriety and utility.

Farewel   Yrs very sincerely   Rufus King

[ENCLOSURE]

John Marshall to Rufus King [5]

Richmond April 19th 96

Dear Sir

I pray you to excuse my seeming inattention to the subject alluded to in yours by the last mail.

Having never been in habits of correspondence with Mr. H. I coud not by letter ask from him a decision on the proposition I was requested to make him without giving him at the same time a full statement of the whole conversation & of the persons with whom that conversation was held. In doing this I felt some difficulty. I am not positively certain what course that Gentleman might take. The proposition might not only have been rejected but mentioned publickly to others in such manner as to have become an unpleasant circumstance. Genl. Lee [6] corresponds familiarly with Mr. H. & is in the habit of proposing offices to him. I deemd it most adviseable to speak to that gentleman & to request him to sound Mr. H. as from himself or in such manner as might in any event be perfectly safe. He promisd to do so but said confidently that no answer woud be receivd to the the letter, nor was any answer receivd.

Mr. H. will be in Richmond on the 22d. of May. I can then sound him myself & if I find him (& suspect I shall) totally unwilling to engage in the contest, I can stop where prudence may direct. I trust it will not then be too late to bring forward to public view Mr. H. or any other gentleman who may be thought of in his stead.

Shoud any thing occur to render it improper to have any communication with Mr. H. on this subject, or shoud you wish the communication to take any particular shape you will be so obliging as to drop me a line concerning it.[7]

With great & sincere respect & esteem   I am dear Sir your Obedt.

J Marshall

ALS, Hamilton Papers, Library of Congress.
1. This is a reference to a proposal that Patrick Henry should be the Federalist candidate for President in 1796.
2. See King to H, May 1, 1796. On May 3, 1796, "the bill making appropriations towards defraying the expenses of carrying into effect the Treaty lately concluded between the United States and Great Britain was read a third time, the blanks filled up, and passed" by the House of Representatives. It was approved by the Senate on May 4 (*Annals of Congress*, V, 80, 1295) and became law on May 6, 1796 (1 *Stat.* 549). See the introductory note to H to George Washington, March 7, 1796.
3. Thomas Pinckney was United States Minister Plenipotentiary to Great Britain from 1792 to 1796. In addition, he served as envoy extraordinary to Spain in 1794 and 1795 to negotiate a treaty with that country. On October 10, 1795, Pinckney had written to Washington asking that his letters of recall "be expedited, so as to reach England by the middle of the month of June next" (ALS, George Washington Papers, Library of Congress).
4. The Treaty of Friendship, Limits, and Navigation was signed at San Lorenzo el Real by Spain and the United States on October 27, 1795 (Miller, *Treaties*, II, 318-38).
5. ALS, Hamilton Papers, Library of Congress.
Irwin S. Rhodes, ed., *The Papers of John Marshall, a Descriptive Calendar* (Norman, Oklahoma, 1969), I, 260, states incorrectly that this letter is from Marshall to H. Rhodes also wrongly attributes the same mistake to Albert J. Beveridge, *The Life of John Marshall* (Boston and New York, 1919), II, 156-57.
6. Henry Lee, leading Virginia Federalist, former governor of Virginia, and close friend of H.
7. On May 24, 1796, Marshall wrote to King: "Mr. Henry has at length been sounded on the subject you committed to my charge. Genl. Lee and myself have each conversed with him on it, tho' without informing him particularly of the persons who authorized the communication. He is unwilling to embark on the business. His unwillingness, I think, proceeds from an apprehension of the difficulties to be encountered by those who shall fill high Executive offices." King endorsed this letter: "Ansd. 1 June.—regretting &c and observing that it wd. be requisite to fix on another person without delay" (King, *The Life and Correspondence of Rufus King*, II, 48).

From William Tatham [1]

Confidential At the Court of Spain
Aranjuez 2d. May 1796.

Sir,

Being fully satisfied that the sentiments of our two *very young* Representitives in this Country holding the appointments of Charge de Affairs [2] and Consul,[3] of the United States are so different from those you have openly avowed that you will not be amongst the number of their correspondents, a knowledge of your public Character without a personal acquaintance induces me to communicate to you what concerns our Country at perhaps the most critical period it has experienced since our establishment.

The French Ambassadour *Perignon* [4] attended by The General Officer & his Suite late Comr. in Chief of the Army of Rousillon arrived here a few days ago & had his introduction at court which is said to have been less favourable above stairs than below; I do not feel myself at liberty to state particulars.

God only knows in what this european war will end. "Divide and Conquer" seems to me to be the ill judged maxim, and our fate will really be a hard one if we are compelled to take a part in it for want of firm unanimity and attention to our internal interests!

ALS, Hamilton Papers, Library of Congress.

1. Tatham, a native of England, was among many other things a lawyer and geographer. After his arrival in Virginia in 1769, he served as a clerk in a mercantile firm, and in 1776 he moved to Tennessee, where he was involved in the Watauga Association. In 1783, following an interlude in which he sought to become a merchant in Philadelphia, he returned to Virginia, where he became clerk of the council of state. He was subsequently admitted to the bar in North Carolina, and in 1787 he was a member of the General Assembly of North Carolina. In 1790 he became state geographer of Virginia, and in 1792 he again moved to the Tennessee country, where he divided his time between a law practice and mapping a large part of that region. By 1796 he was in Spain on a mysterious visit in which he was apparently attempting to promote his own interests and those of the United States in the West. In any event, he was expelled from Spain in July, 1796. He then went to England, where he wrote extensively on agriculture and engineering. He returned to the United States in 1805.

2. Charles Rutledge.
3. Joseph M. Yznardi was United States consul at Cadiz.
4. Dominique-Catherine, Marquis de Perignon.

I fear such a change in the War with England as to render our Country a principal Theatre of future operations: perhaps we may be compelled to seek safety in a closer connection with the Canadian Territories of our British Enemies unless the Nations who are now at Peace should all combine for a continuance of it under something like an Armed Neutrality; for if Spain should join the other side in this European contest thro' necessity *I have reason to* think that the destruction of Brittish naval power, a Revolution in England, the recapture of Canada (regardless of the King of France's stipulation) [5] and the surrender of Gibraltar tho' not agreed upon with the Cabinet of Madrid will at least be contemplated by that of Paris.

Here it is that I am at a loss to find the subsequent security which it behooves Spain and us to look to! for altho' the *Republic* of France *avows* the coequal Right of Countries to govern their own Affairs as the very essence of their Revolution, I cannot comprehend how the *purity* of that *principle* is any longer a basis when she goes abroad in search of foreign Colonization, or adopts measures of a dictatorial Complexion towards others who are acknowledged to be equaly free; or do I see how the Crown of Spain can be safe in relying on those successes of a People which go to destroy the Barrier which themselves have set up in their own *social* Contract, and to level the Power of Monarchy thro't the Universe in an Anarchy & Confusion beyond every calculation of certainty.

I inclose You in haste a Copy of my Letter to Mr. Rutledge by which You will see how I stand with him & conjecture his way of thinking. I would not have this understood as intended to injure him in his future consequence in life, for I have realy a high opinion of him as to his integrity and Heart; but regardless of private Freindship it is my duty to say as I beleive that unless one of our most temperate and experienced Statesmen is placed *here* we have no political Security! [6] for these are not Times to trust the Chariot of the Sun in the hands of Phaeton.

5. This is a reference to Article 4 of the Treaty of Paris of 1763 in which France ceded Canada to Great Britain "without restriction, and without any liberty to depart from said cession and guaranty, under any pretence" (*Parliamentary History*, XV, 1294).

6. On September 17, 1796, Tatham wrote to Rufus King: ". . . You will pardon me for troubling you . . . with a written explanation as it respects my conduct towards Mr. Rutledge. . . .

"The real Story is thus—Mr. Rutledge lives with the Family of the Prusian

I think also well of Young Yznardy *personally*, & he certainly in his Office supports our dignity under the indulgence of an amiable and gratefull Father with true Andalusian pride: It is however lucky for him to live in his native *luxurious* Climate in the Reign of Charles the 4th.; & still move so that *Long Island* is nearer to *New York* than to *Cadiz*.[7]

Between them I suppose I shall have to appear at the Bar of the supreme Court in a new Capacity on my return, & in this Case I must request that You will consider yourself retained for me.

As I have not nor never had a secret to hide from the old General (God knows if he is still President) beyond a temporary expediency, I leave you at perfect liberty to transmit this to Him; & if You enquire of my Freinds Colol. E. Carrington[8] or The Hone. J. Steele of the Virga. Council[9] I have no doubt that You will approve my political principles without tacking my faith to the Slave of any Foreign Power. My life is at Stake commit me not to any other living Soul?

I am in *haste* Yours *hastily*   Wm Tatham

Hone.
Alexr. Hamilton
N. York ☞ *News! be guarded & United if possible*   W.T.

Charge de Affairs, whose Lady "*Mrs. Tribotet*" is perhaps inferior to no Woman in Europe in point of political intrigue, & unbounded Ambition. . . .

"I . . . spent some evenings there at whist in company with the diplomatic Characters who frequented the Party, I confess in a very agreeable manner to me if I could have believed our political happiness safe in a Circle who under pretence of a friendly disposition seem'd evidently watching our rising importance with jealous fears; and I doubt not with an anxious wish to embrace every opportunity of checking our prosperity according to the abominably mistaken System of European policy.

"I . . . endeavour'd to get Mr. Rutledge frequently to my own Quarters . . . as I did not like the appearances which surrounded him. . . ." (ALS, RG 59, Miscellaneous Letters, 1790–1799, National Archives.)

7. This is a reference to the business activities of Yznardi, who was actively engaged in trade with the United States.

8. Edward Carrington was supervisor of the revenue for the District of Virginia.

9. John Steele, a veteran of the American Revolution, served for many years as a member of the Virginia Executive Council. In 1798 he was appointed a commissioner to negotiate a treaty with the Cherokees. He was secretary of the Mississippi Territory from 1798 to 1803 and acting governor from April to November, 1801.

P.S. Just as I am about to close this I am told that "a Courier arrived last night from the United States to Mr. Rutledge." I suppose he will not fail to let some of his Foreign Companions know more than he will confide to me as I have not seen him since my Letter to him. I shall in every event do all I can to keep our yet happy Country united & quiet.[10] *W.T.*

10. On July 30, 1796, Timothy Pickering wrote to Yznardi concerning Tatham: ". . . I should conjecture that whatever geographical information of the united States he is possessed of, he meant to communicate to the Spanish Government, for such reward as he can persuade that Government to give him. . . . He is an adventurer, a projector, who failing in his schemes in this Country, where he was well known, might hope for some success where he was a stranger" (LC, RG 59, Diplomatic and Consular Instructions of the Department of State, 1791–1801, Vol. 3, June 5, 1795–January 31, 1797, National Archives).

From Robert Morris

Alex Hamilton Esqre Phila May 3. 1796

Dear Sir

By a letter this moment received from Colo S. Ogden dated yesterday I learn that he was but then going to N York to accomplish the business I mentioned to you, the sale of 50,000 Acres of Genesee Lands in order to enable me to discharge Colo smiths mortgage.[1] This done, I can give you the Security mentioned in my last[2] and probably your influence with Mr Walker & Mr. seton[3] may help in point of accommodation from them to the purchasers. The Terms of Sale were fixed when I wrote to you[4] at 10/ p Acre part on time &ca.

I am Dr Sir Yrs Sincerely RM

LC, Robert Morris Papers, Library of Congress.

1. For an explanation of the contents of the preceding sentence, see the introductory note to Morris to H, April 27, 1796.
2. Morris to H, April 27, 1796. The "security" mentioned by Morris was for a debt owed to John B. Church. See the introductory note to Morris to H, June 7, 1795. See also Morris to H, July 20, November 16, December 18, 1795; January 15, March 6, 12, 14, 30, 1796.
3. William Seton, former cashier of the Bank of New York, was a partner of David Maitland in a New York City mercantile firm.
4. Morris to H, April 27, 1796.

To Rufus King

[New York, May 4, 1796]

My Dear Sir

Since my last[1] I have received two or three letters from you.[2] The late turn of the Treaty[3] question makes us all very happy. I hope no future embarrassment will arise.

I am intirely of opinion that P.H declining Mr. P—— ought to be our man. It is even an idea of which I am fond in various lights. Indeed on latter reflection, I rather wish to be rid of P.H, that we may be at full liberty to take up Pinckney.[4]

In the event of Pinck[n]ey's return to this Country, I am of opinion all circumstances considered, it is expedient you should replace him. I hope no great question will in a short period agitate our Councils & I am sure you will do much good on the scene in question. I have called on Jay, but happened not to find him disengaged. I shall quickly see him & shall with great pleasure do every thing requisite on my part.

We believe confidently our election in this City has succeeded; the other party however also claims success. Our Senator Ticket seems admitted on both sides to have prevailed & all accounts assure us of great success throughout the state. The *vile affair* of whipping Burke & McCredy made our election in the view of the common people a question between the Rich & the Poor.[5] You will easily conceive how much this must have embarrassed & jeoparded.

Yrs. Affectionately   A Hamilton

May 4 1796
Rufus King Esq

ALS, Hamilton Papers, Library of Congress.
 1. H to King, April 24, 1796.
 2. King to H, May 1, 2, 1796.
 3. This refers to the vote in the House of Representatives to approve legislation implementing the Jay Treaty. See the introductory note to H to George Washington, March 7, 1796; King to H, May 1, 1796.
 4. The references in this letter are to Patrick Henry and Thomas Pinckney.

Some leading Federalists were considering both men as possible candidates for the Presidency in 1796.

5. For information on Thomas Burk and Timothy Crady, see "Certificate on Robert Lenox," January 11, 1796, note 1.

From William Lewis [1]

Philadelphia, May 4, 1796. "When I wrote you a few lines some days since [2] I intended writing you more fully before this time, & this I should have done had I not soon after been informed by Mr. Morris that finding you to be very desirous to have security within the State of New York he had written to you offering you a security of lands within that state which he had no doubt but you would most willingly accept. On learning this I have waited in expectation of your answer being received either by Mr. Morris or myself, but not having since heard from you I have concluded to write to you without further delay. In Pennsylvania we have no Court of Chancery for a mortgagee to apply to in order to foreclose the equity of redemption in case of non-payment by the mortgagor but the remedy is by a scire facias issued under an act of Assembly which enacts that when any *lands or tenements* are mortgaged for securing the payment of monies if default shall be made by non-payment & it shall be lawful for the mortgagee after the expiration of one year thereafter to sue out a writ of scire facias to summon the mortgagor to shew cause why the mortgaged premises should not be levied on & sold to pay the monies due. This scire facias describes the mortgaged premisses by meets & bounds, courses & distances; the judgment is that execution be had of the premises so described; the writ of execution follows the description contained in the mortgage & the sale & Sheriff's deed must be equally particular. But as only part of Mr. Morris's warrant rights have been actually surveyed & located & as the applications & warrants describe no particular spots nor contain any other description than that of being on or near certain waters &c it is impossible for a mortgage to describe them & as an Execution must pursue the words of the mortgage no sale could be made in this way even tho' surveys should be made & returned & the Patents should issue after making the mortgage & before issuing the execution. Hence it is evident that unless you take a security in New York you must either wait till all the surveys are returned & allowed or another mode which I believe unexceptionable must be adopted, as has lately been done under my direction in another case. It is that a mortgage be taken of the warrant rights with a power for you, your heirs &c to sell in case of non payment by the mortgagor. In that case the mortgage after reciting the bond will proceed to grant & convey all the warrant rights. . . . Unless you take security on lands in your state I think the mode proposed by me much better than any other on the same property which I have thought of. You desire me to examine the title of Mr. Morris to these lands but this is impossible at present until the Patents issue since the claims of our Speculators very frequently clash & untill patents issue either party may enter his caveat agt. the other & untill a hearing takes place before the board of propy. it is impossible to procure the necessary materials to form judgt. on. As to the State of Judgts agt. Mr. M. I hardly know what to say except that they are certainly very numerous & I fear to a large amt. tho I rather suppose that but few if any of them are of a nature to affect your proposed security. If you conclude on taking a security here be so good as to inform me of it that I may (now that our Courts are over) set about the necessary enquiries & arrangements without loss of time, but if you can obtain satisfactory security elsewhere I think you had better take it. . . ."

ALS, Hamilton Papers, Library of Congress.
1. This letter concerns Robert Morris's debt to John B. Church and the validity of the title to lands which Morris owned and wished to mortgage to secure that debt. For Morris's debt to Church, see the introductory note to Morris to H, June 7, 1795. See also Morris to H, July 20, November 16, December 18, 1795; January 15, March 6, 12, 14, 30, April 27, May 3, 1796.
2. Letter not found, but see Morris to H, March 30, 1796.

To Rufus King

[New York, May 5, 1796]

Dr Sir.

After reading seal & hand on the inclosed.[1] If such things are to be you cannot leave the Senate.[2] *Jay* is against it at all events till the

European storm is over. We must all think well of this business.
Adieu   Yours Affey   A Hamilton

May 5 1796.
R. King Esqr

Copy, Hamilton Papers, Library of Congress.
1. The endorsement on this letter reads: "The enclosed letter was for the Pt. RK." The enclosure was a letter from H to Washington, May 5, 1796, which in turn enclosed a letter from Gouverneur Morris to H, March 4, 1796.
2. See King to H, May 2, 1796.

To George Washington

[New York, May 5, 1796]

Sir

The letter of which the inclosed is a copy contains such extraordinary matter that I could not hesitate to send it to you.[1] The writer is Mr. G—— M——. I trust the information it conveys cannot be true; yet in these wild times every thing is possible. Your official information may serve as a comment.

Very respectfully & affectly   I have the honor to be   Sir Yr Obed ser   A Hamilton

May 5. 179[6] [2]
The President

ALS, George Washington Papers, Library of Congress; copy, Hamilton Papers, Library of Congress.
1. The enclosure was Gouverneur Morris to H, March 4, 1796.
2. H incorrectly dated this letter "1795." In *JCHW*, V, 633, this letter is also misdated 1795.

From Edward Stevens [1]

[Philadelphia, May 7, 1796]

My dear Friend

Almost ever since your Departure I have been confined to my Chamber by a severe and obstinate Catarrh. Tho' much better, at present, my Health is still so much deranged, that I dread encountering the Warmth of the Summer Months in this City. I have therefore, determined to take a Voyage to Sea, and as I shall visit St. Croix, before my Return, Mrs. Stevens has concluded to accompany me with our little ones. Our Absence will be but short. If no unexpected Event takes place we shall certainly return by the Month of September. I could not, however, leave America without assuring you of our best Wishes for the Health and Prosperity of yourself and Family. May every Blessing attend you. Mrs. S. unites with me in affectionate Remembrance of Mrs. Hamilton. I remain with unfeigned Attachment.

My dear Sir   Your sincere Freind   Edward Stevens.

Philadelphia May 7th. 1796.

We embark this Day.

ALS, Hamilton Papers, Library of Congress.
   1. Stevens had been a childhood friend of H in St. Croix. See H to Stevens, November 11, 1769. He had later studied at King's College in New York and at Edinburgh, and he practiced medicine for ten years in St. Croix. See Stevens to H, October 5, 1791. In 1793 he moved to Philadelphia, and in September of that year was H's and Elizabeth Hamilton's doctor when both had yellow fever. See George Washington to H, September 6, 1793.

From George Washington

Philadelphia 8th. May 1796.

My dear Sir,   (Private & confidential)
   Your note of the 5th. instant accompanying the information given to you by G.—— M.—— on the 4th. of March, came safe on friday. The letter he refers to, as having been written to me, is not yet received;[1] but others from Mr. Monroe of similar complexion, and almost of as imperious a tone from that government, have got to hand.
   That justice & policy should dictate the measures with which we are threatned, is not to be conceived; and one would think that even

ALS (photostat), Princeton University Library; copy, Hamilton Papers, Library of Congress; copy (incomplete), Hamilton Papers, Library of Congress.
   1. See Gouverneur Morris to H, March 4, 1796, note 2.

MAY 1796

folly & madness on their part, would hardly go such lengths, without supposing a stimulus of a more serious nature than the Town meetings, & the partial resolutions which appeared in the course of last Summer & Autumn on ours. Yet, as it seems to be the Æra of strange vicissitudes, & unaccountable transactions; attended with a sort of irresistable fatality in many of them, I shall not be surprized at any event that may happen, however extraordinary it may be; and therefore, it may not be amiss to ruminate upon the information which has been received in its fullest latitude; and be prepared to answer the demands on the extensive scale wch has been mentioned.

What then do you think ought to be said in case G.—— M——s information should prove true, *in all its parts?* And what, if the proceedings, & Instructions of the French Directory should not exceed my conjecture, which is, that encouraged by the proceedings of last Summer on the Treaty (as already mentioned) and aided perhaps by communications of influencial men in *this* country, thro' a medium which ought to have been the last to engage in it,[2] that that government *may*, and I believe *will* send out an Envoy extraordinary, with Instructions to make strong remonstrances against the unfriendliness (as they will term it), and the tendency of our Treaty with Great Britain; accompanied probably, and expectedly, with discretionary powers to go farther, according to circumstances, and the existing state of matters when he shall have arrived here. Perhaps these Instructions may extend to a releasement from that part of our Treaty with *them*, which claims exemption from the seizure of Enemies goods in *our* Vessels.[3] Perhaps, to demand the fulfilment of our guarantee of their West India Islds.[4] as the most likely means of affording them relief, under the circumstances they labor at present. Perhaps too, to endeavor to render null & void our Treaty with G. Britain. Possibly *all of them*, or the dissolution of the Alliance. But I cannot bring my mind to believe that they seriously mean, or that they could accompany this Envoy with a Fleet, to *demand* the

---

2. James Monroe, United States Minister Plenipotentiary to France.
3. Washington is referring to Article 23 (originally 25) of the Treaty of Amity and Commerce concluded between the United States and France on February 6, 1778 (Miller, *Treaties*, II, 20–21).
4. This guarantee was included in Article 11 of the Treaty of Alliance between the United States and France, which was signed at Paris on February 6, 1778 (Miller, *Treaties*, II, 39).

annihilation of the Treaty with G. Britain in fifteen days; or that War, in case of refusal, must follow as a consequence.⁵

Were it not for the unhappy differences among ourselves, *my* answer wd. be short & decisive, to this effect. We are an Independent Nation, and act for ourselves. Having fulfilled, and being willing to fulfil, (as far as we are able) our engagements with other nations, and having decided on, and strictly observed a Neutral conduct towards the Belligerent Powers, from an unwillingness to involve ourselves in War—We will not be dictated to by the Politics of any Nation under Heaven, farther than Treaties require of us.

Whether the *present*, or any circumstances should do more than *soften* this language, may merit consideration. But if we are to be told by a foreign power (if our engagements with it are not infracted) what we *shall do*, and what we shall *not do*, we have Independence yet to seek, & have contended hitherto for very little.

If you have communicated the purport of G—— M——s letter to Mr. Jay, I wish you would lay this also before him, *in confidence*, and that you & he would be so good as to favor me with your sentiments, & opinions on both; and on the measures which you think would be most advisable to be taken, in case we should have to encounter the difficulties with which we are threatned: which, assuredly, will have been brought on us by the misconduct of some of our own intemperate people; who seem to have preferred throwing themselves into the arms of France (even under the present circumstances of that Country) to that manly, & Neutral conduct which is so essential, & would so well become us, as an Independent Nation.

Before, I close this letter, I will mention another subject, which, tho' in a smaller degree, is nevertheless embarrassing. This also is communicated in confidence. It respects the wishes of young Fayette, relative to his father.⁶ As is very natural, & what might have been expected, he is extremely solicitous that something should be attempted to obtain the liberation of him; and has brought forward

5. See Gouverneur Morris to H, March 4, 1796.
6. George Washington Motier Lafayette was the son of the Marquis de Lafayette, who was in prison in Europe. Young Lafayette had come to the United States in August, 1795. For information on Lafayette, see H to Washington, October 16, 26, November 19, 26, December 24, 27–30, 1795, March 7, April 2, 9, 1796; Washington to H, October 29, November 10, 18, 23, 28, December 22, 1795, February 13, 1796.

several plans (suggested by Doctr Ballman;[7] who, it is to be feared will be found a troublesome guest among us) to effect it.

These will be better understood by the Enclosures now sent, than by any details I could give, when I add to them—the supposition of Fayette & Frestal,[8] that the Doctor is without funds, and will be more embarrassing *to them* the longer he remains here. No mention, however, that has come to my knowledge of his going away.

The result of my reflection on this subject, and which I have communicated to the two young Men, is, that altho' I am convinced in my own mind that Mr. La Fayette will be held in confinement by the combined Powers until Peace is established; yet to satisfy them, & their friends of my disposition to facilitate their wishes, as far as it can be done with any propriety on my part, I would *as a private person*, express in a letter to the Emperor,[9] my wish, and what I believe to be the wishes of this Country towards that Gentleman; viz, that the liberation of him, conditioned on his repairing hither, would be a grateful measure. That this letter I would put under cover to Mr. Pinckney,[10] to be forwarded or not, according to the view he might have of its success; after conversing indirectly with the Diplomatic characters of the combined Powers in London. But that I could not, while in Public Office, have any Agency in, or even knowledge of, any projects that should require concealment, or that I should be unwilling to appear openly & avowedly in. That as Doctr. Ballman had committed an act (however meritorious & pleasing it might be to the friends of Mr. de la Fayette) which was viewed in a very obnoxious light by the Power in whose possession the prisoner was [11]—Had narrowly excaped condign punishment for it himself—and was released upon the express condition that he should never again appear in those Dominions, that I could neither shew him countenance—nor could I furnish him with money to extricate himself from difficulties (if he was in any). Seeing but little

7. See Justus Erich Bollmann to H, April 13, 1796.
8. Felix Frestel, George Washington Motier Lafayette's tutor.
9. Francis II, the Austrian Emperor. Washington wrote this letter on May 15, 1796 (*GW*, XXV, 45–46).
10. Thomas Pinckney, United States Minister Plenipotentiary to Great Britain. Washington's letter to Pinckney is dated May 22, 1796 (*GW*, XXV, 61–63).
11. For information on Bollmann's attempt to free Lafayette from prison, see H to Washington, January 19, 1796.

difference between giving before, or after, to a man who stands in the light he does between that Power & the Executive of the U States; but that, if he was disposed to quit the latter, I had no doubt, & he might be so assured, that the friends of Mr. de la Fayette would raise a sufficient sum to enable him to do this, and to defray his expences since he has been in this Country. What they will say to him, or he do in this matter, I know not.

If you & Mr. Jay see no impropriety in such a letter as I have mentioned, to be used at the discretion of Mr. Pinckney—I would thank either of you for drafting it. Mr. Jay in particular having been in the habit, & better acquainted with the stile and manner of addressing these sort of characters than I am, would be able to give it a better shape. To return the papers now sent, with the draught required, as soon as convenient, would be acceptable to

Dear Sir   Your Affecte Servt.   Go: Washington

Colo. A. Hamilton

To Robert Morris

[*New York, May 9, 1796.* On May 10, 1796, Morris wrote to Hamilton: "Your letter dated April 9th. but which was written yesterday, I presume, came to hand this Morning." [*Letter not found.*]

From Robert Morris [1]

Philada. May 10th. 1796

Dear Sir

Your letter dated April 9th. but which was written yesterday, I presume,[2] came to hand this Morning and I have since the receipt of it and of one from Colo Ogden seen Colo Walker who tells me that he left power with you to adjust with the latter the business of the Mortgage formerly granted by me to Colo W. Smith on behalf of Mr Pulteney &c., therefore I presume it has been settled in some way or other. Colo Ogden has sent me a Copy of the Articles of agreement made by him on my behalf with Othniel Taylor & Asa Danforth for the Sale of 50000 Acres of Land, and in order to have the affair compleatly finished, I proposed to Colo Walker that I would Convey the said 50,000 Acres to him and assign to him the above mentioned Contract which binds the parties to pay $57,500 and interest at the times therein mentioned. My debt to Mr. Pulteney for which the Mortgage was given is about fifty thousand Dollrs of Six ₱ Ct Stock now Worth about 17/4 in the pound, but that I would Commute it into Money at 20/ or par, and Colo Walker to pay the bale of the Account, & enter Satisfaction on the Mortgage discharging me of the demand. It appears to me that this is necessary in order to give Value to the Mortgage I am to make to you and I have thus explained myself lest Colo Walker might misunderstand or not Recollect clearly my proposition. I think it is fair, honorable and generous such as will be approved by the principal, and therefore I expect that you will advise his Concurrence. I will have the Mortgage to you immediately drawn[3] and the form you prescribe Shall be duly observed. I expect however to hear from you & Col Walker in answer to this letter, as I consider my hands to be tied up by the Chancery Suit, untill the Mortgage is discharged.

I am Dr Sir

AL[S], Hamilton Papers, Library of Congress; LC, Robert Morris Papers, Library of Congress.
1. For an explanation of the contents of this letter, see the introductory note to Morris to H, April 27, 1796. See also Morris to H, May 3, 1796.
2. Letter not found.
3. This is a reference to a mortgage on one hundred thousand acres of Genesee lands. The mortgage on this land was to secure Morris's debt to John B. Church. See the introductory note to Morris to H, June 7, 1795. See also Morris to H, July 20, November 16, December 18, 1795; January 15, March 6, 12, 14, 30, April 27, May 3, 1796.

To Timothy Pickering

[New York, May 10, 1796]

Dr Sir

Inclosed is a letter[1] which I will thank you to hand to its destination.

While I have my pen in my hand, give me leave to mention a particular subject to you. Mr. Pinckney, it is said, desires to return to the U States.² In this case a successor will be wanted. If we had power to make a man for the purpose, we could not imagine a fitter than Mr. *King*.³ He is tired of the Senate & I fear will resign at all events. I presume he would accept the mission to England. Can there be a doubt that it will be wise to offer it to him?

Yrs with much esteem & regard   A Hamilton

May 10. 1796
T Pickering Esq

ALS, Massachusetts Historical Society, Boston.
   1. The enclosure was H to George Washington, May 10, 1795.
   2. See Rufus King to H, May 2, 1796.
   3. See King to H, May 2, 1796; H to King, May 4, 1796.

From Stephen Rochefontaine [1]

West Point by Peekskill, May 10, 1796. "I have had the honor to transmit to you in the course of last week, a Letter detailing the affair which passed between Mr Wilson, a Lieut. in the Corps, and myself; the Injuries offered on both sides had been settled agreeably to the rules of honor adopted by gentlemen, and in consequence of a Particular agreement made by the two seconds; two days after I received a Challenge from Mr. Wilson by his second. . . . My answer was that I looked on that affair as settled. Some of the officers who are far from being my friends, and who are too Prudent to expose themselves to a gentlemanly explanation, took hold of that circumstance to revenge themslves without danger, they assembled the officers who . . . Sign'd a Sort of libel in which they declare that they will publish to the world, that after insulting Mr. Wilson, I refused to give him satisfaction; I refused the paper which was not authenticated by any signature, & I did not receive it back, but they Sent me a copy of some charges laid against me before the secretary of War. Mr. McHenry [2] has Sent me the copy of that accusation, and has not Informed me yet what plan he expected to proceed upon. I desired him by this post to grant me a Court of

Inquiry instead of a Court Martial. . . . I wish you would oblige me with your advice. . . ."

ALS, United States Military Academy Library.
1. For background to this letter, see Rochefontaine to H, April 28, 1796.
2. Secretary of War James McHenry.

To George Washington

[New York, May 10, 1796]

Introductory Note

The opening paragraph of this letter contains the first reference in Hamilton's extant correspondence to the preparation of Washington's Farewell Address. Washington first conceived of the idea of a valedictory address in 1792, when he thought that he would retire at the end of his first term in March, 1793. In May, 1792, he asked James Madison to draft a farewell address,[1] and Madison complied with the President's request on June 20, 1792.[2] When Washington continued in office for another term, Madison's draft was put aside.

As the letter printed below indicates, Washington spoke with Hamilton about drafting a farewell address in February, 1796, when Hamilton was in Philadelphia to argue the constitutionality of the carriage tax before the Supreme Court of the United States.[3] On May 15, 1796, the President sent Hamilton his first draft[4] of a farewell address, which consisted of the speech written by Madison in 1792 and a section written by Washington to explain the "considerable changes" that had "taken place both at home & abroad" since 1792.[5] Washington asked Hamilton

ALS, MS Division, New York Public Library.
1. "Substance of a Conversation with the President," May 5, 9, 25, 1792 (AD, James Madison Papers, Library of Congress).
2. ADf, MS Division, New York Public Library; printed in Paltsits, *Farewell Address*, 160–63, 227–29.
3. H was in Philadelphia from February 17 to February 24, 1796, to argue the constitutionality of the carriage tax before the Supreme Court. For information on the Carriage Tax case (*Hylton* v *United States*), see 3 Dallas, *U.S. Reports*, 171; also in forthcoming Goebel, *Law Practice*, III. See also Tench Coxe to H, January 14, 19, 1795; H to Coxe, January 26, 28, 1795; William Bradford to H, July 2, August 4, 1795; Edmund Randolph to H, July 21, 1795; Oliver Wolcott, Jr., to H, July 28, 1795, January 15, 1796; H to Wolcott, August 5, 1795; Robert Morris to H, February 10, 1796.
No evidence has been found to support Paltsits's assertion that H was in Philadelphia "shortly before May 10, 1796" (Paltsits, *Farewell Address*, 31).
4. ADfS, from the original in the New York State Library, Albany; printed in Paltsits, *Farewell Address*, 164–73.
5. ADfS, from the original in the New York State Library, Albany; see also Paltsits, *Farewell Address*, 168.

either to prepare an entirely new address or to revise the President's first draft. Hamilton decided to do both.

Between May 16 and July 5 Hamilton prepared an outline based on the Madison-Washington draft, which he endorsed "Abstract of points to form an address." By July 5 Hamilton had finished his own draft.[6] and on that date he wrote to the President: "I have completed the first draft of a certain paper & shall shortly transcribe correct & forward it. I will then also prepare & send forward without delay the original paper corrected upon the general plan of it so that you may have both before you for a choice in full time & for alteration if necessary." In 1811 John Jay, recalling that he and Hamilton had read and discussed Hamilton's draft, stated that some amendments had been made, but that none were of any consequence.[7] On July 30 Hamilton sent to the President his "Original Draft" of a farewell address. The first eight paragraphs closely follow the Madison-Washington draft, the middle section is Hamilton's own work, and the last six paragraphs are modeled on the concluding paragraphs of the Madison-Washington draft.

Hamilton then turned his attention to revising the Madison-Washington draft, and on August 10 he sent to the President a draft "on the plan of incorporating." Washington, however, did not use this second draft. Instead, on August 25 he returned Hamilton's "Original Draft," stating that he preferred it "greatly to the other draughts." Twelve paragraphs in Hamilton's two drafts are almost identical, and these have been indicated in the notes to Hamilton's "Draft on the Plan of Incorporating," which is printed as an enclosure to Hamilton to Washington, August 10, 1796.

On September 15 Washington submitted the address to the cabinet,[8] and Timothy Pickering wrote to the President on the same day: "The paper you put into my hands to-day was attentively perused by us all. I am now going over it by myself, but it will not be possible to get thro' in time to return it before bed-time. Before breakfast in the morning I will wait upon you with it." [9]

On the same day, Washington arranged with David C. Claypoole to have the Farewell Address printed in *Claypoole's* [Philadelphia] *American Daily Advertiser* on September 19, 1796. On February 22, 1826, Claypoole gave the following account of the publication of the address: "A few days before the appearance of this memorable document in print, I received a message from the President, by his private secretary [Tobias Lear] signifying his desire to see me. I waited on him at the appointed time, and found him sitting alone in the drawing-room. He received me kindly; and, after I had paid my respects to him, desired me to take a

---

6. H's "Draft of Washington's Farewell Address" is printed as an enclosure to H to Washington, July 30, 1796.

7. John Jay to Richard Peters, March 29, 1811 (copy, Historical Society of Pennslvania, Philadelphia); printed in Paltsits, *Farewell Address*, 264–71.

8. Timothy Pickering to James A. Hamilton, January 16, 1829 (Hamilton, *Reminiscences*, 33).

9. ALS, George Washington Papers, Library of Congress; printed in Paltsits, *Farewell Address*, 259.

seat near him—then addressing himself to me, said, that he had for some time past contemplated retiring from public life, and had at length concluded to do so at the end of the present term: that he had some thoughts and reflections on the occasion, which he deemed proper to communicate to the people of the United States, in the form of an Address, and which he wished to appear in the Daily Advertiser, of which I was editor. He paused, and I took the opportunity of thanking him for having preferred that paper as the channel of his communication with the people, especially as I viewed this selection as indicating his approbation of the principles and manner in which the work was conducted. He silently assented, and asked when the publication could be made. I answered, that the time should be made perfectly convenient to himself, and the following Monday was fixed on: he then told me that his secretary would call on me with the copy of the Address on the next (Friday) morning, and I withdrew.

"After the *proof sheet* had been compared with the copy, and corrected by myself, I carried another *proof*, and then a *revise*, to be examined by the President, who made but few alterations from the original, except in the punctuation, in which he was very minute.

"The publication of the Address, dated 'United States, September 17th, 1796,' being completed on the 19th, I waited on the President with the original; and, in presenting it to him, expressed my regret at parting with it, and how much I should be gratified by being permitted to retain it: upon which, in an obliging manner, he handed it back to me, saying that if I wished for it, I might keep it; and I then took my leave of him." [10]

Jared Sparks, in his edition of the *Writings of George Washington*, states that he copied the following endorsement in Washington's handwriting from a copy of Claypoole's newspaper: "designed as an instruction to the copyist, who recorded the Address in the letter-book: the letter contained in the gazette, addressed 'To the People of the United States,' is to be recorded, and in the order of its date. Let it have a blank page before and after it, so as to stand distinct. Let it be written with a letter larger and fuller than the common recording hand. And where words are printed with capital letters, it is to be done so in recording. And those other words, that are printed in italics, must be scored underneath and straight by a ruler." [11] Although the newspaper with Washington's endorsement has not been found, the copyist did follow his directions.[12] Washington's final manuscript is dated September 19, 1796.[13]

The Farewell Address was also printed on September 19 in John Fenno's *Gazette of the United States, & Philadelphia Daily Advertiser*.

10. Historical Society of Pennsylvania, *Memoirs*, I (republished Philadelphia, 1864), 265-67; also printed in Paltsits, *Farewell Address*, 290-91. The *Memoirs* were originally published in Philadelphia in 1826.
11. Quoted in *GW*, XXXV, 215.
12. LC, George Washington Papers, Library of Congress.
13. ADS, MS Division, New York Public Library; LC, George Washington Papers, Library of Congress; printed in Paltsits, *Farewell Address*, 139-59.

Benjamin Franklin Bache printed the address in two installments in the [Philadelphia] *Aurora. General Advertiser,* September 20, 21, 1796.[14]

After the deaths of Washington and Hamilton, controversy arose over the authorship of the Farewell Address. In 1810 Nathaniel Pendleton, one of the executors of Hamilton's estate, placed all of Hamilton's papers relating to the Farewell Address in the hands of Rufus King "to prevent their falling into the hands of the General's family," because of "the understood views of Mrs. Hamilton to endeavor to shew that General Hamilton, not General Washington, was the author and writer of the farewell address, ascribed to the latter. . . ."[15] In 1825 James A. Hamilton and John Church Hamilton tried to obtain these papers from King. In this endeavor they secured the assistance of Nicholas Fish,[16] also an executor of Hamilton's estate, and Timothy Pickering.[17]

The Hamilton family commenced a suit in the Chancery Court in 1825 to recover Alexander Hamilton's papers. On October 17, 1826, however, James A. Hamilton received from John Duer, on behalf of King, a bundle of papers endorsed "Papers received by Rufus King from Judge Pendleton in 1810, to be returned."[18] On the same day, Hamilton informed King that the Chancery suit "is ordered to be discontinued."[19]

On August 7, 1840, Elizabeth Hamilton reiterated her belief in her husband's authorship of the Farewell Address in the following statement: "Desirous that my children should be fully acquainted with the services rendered by their Father to our Country, and the assistance given by him to General Washington during his administration, for the one great object, the Independence and Stability of the Government of the United States, there is one thing in addition to the numerous proofs which I leave them and which I feel myself in duty bound to State; Which is: that a short time previous to General Washington's retiring from the Presidency in the year 1796 General Hamilton suggested to him the idea of delivering a farewell address to the people on his withdrawal from public life, with which idea General Washington was well pleased, and in his answer to General Hamilton's suggestion, gave him the heads of the subjects on which he would wish to remark, with a request that Mr Hamilton would prepare an address for him; Mr. Hamilton did so, and the address was written, principally at such times as his office was seldom frequented by his clients and visitors, and during the absence of his students to avoid interruption; at which times he was in the habit of calling me to sit with him, that he might read to me as he wrote, in order, as he said, to discover how it sounded upon

14. For additional information on the publication of Washington's Farewell Address in American and European newspapers, see Paltsits, *Farewell Address,* 55–74, 327–60.

15. Rufus King to Charles King, November 26, 1825 (King, *The Life and Correspondence of Rufus King,* VI, 618–19).

16. Hamilton, *Reminiscences,* 25–26.

17. Pickering to James A. Hamilton, September 5, 1825 (ALS, Massachusetts Historical Society, Boston).

18. Hamilton, *Reminiscences,* 26–27. Duer, the son of William Duer, was a former law clerk of H.

19. Hamilton, *Reminiscences,* 27.

the ear, and making the remark, 'My dear Eliza you must be to me, what Moliere's old nurse was to him.'

"The whole or nearly all the 'Address,' was read to me by him as he wrote it and a greater part if not all was written by him in my presence. The original was forwarded to Genl. Washington, who approved of it with the exception of one paragraph, of, I think, about four or five lines, which if I mistake not was on the subject of public schools, which was stricken out. It was afterwards returned to Mr. Hamilton who made the desired Alteration, and was afterwards delivered by General Washington, and published in that form, and has ever since been Known as 'General Washingtons farewell address.' Shortly after the publication of the address, my husband, and myself were walking in Broadway, when an old soldier, accosted him, with a request of him to purchase General Washington's Farewell address, which he did, and turning to me said, 'That Man does not Know he has asked me to purchase my own work.'

"The whole circumstances are at this moment, so perfectly in my remembrance, that I can call to mind his bringing General Washington's letter to me, which, returned the 'address,' and remarking on the only alteration which he (Genl Washington) had requested to be made." [20]

As early as 1827 James A. Hamilton and Jared Sparks had discussed the possibility of publishing all of the letters relative to the Farewell Address.[21] Sparks eventually gave John C. Hamilton copies of Alexander Hamilton's letters. But before John C. Hamilton printed them in 1860 in *The History of the Republic*,[22] Sparks allowed Horace Binney to print them in *An Inquiry into the Formation of Washington's Farewell Address* (Philadelphia, 1859). In 1850 James Lenox purchased Washington's final version of the Farewell Address at an auction held by the administrators of David Claypoole's estate,[23] and two months after purchasing the manuscript he published it.[24]

New York May 10. 1796

Sir

When last in Philadelphia [25] you mentioned to me your wish that I should *re dress* a certain paper which you had prepared.[26] As it is important that a thing of this kind should be done with great care and much at leisure touched & retouched, I submit a wish that as

20. DS, Hamilton Papers, Library of Congress. See also "Journal of John Silva Meehan," June 23, 1846 (AD, MS Division, Library of Congress).
21. Hamilton, *Reminiscences*, 28–31.
22. Hamilton, *History*, VI, 497–532.
23. See James Lenox to Jared Sparks, March 4, 1850 (ALS, MS Division, New York Public Library); printed in Paltsits, *Farewell Address*, 298–99.
24. *Washington's Farewell Address to the People of the United States of America* (New York, 1850).
25. See note 3.
26. H is referring to Washington's first draft of a farewell address. See the introductory note to this letter.

soon as you have given it the *body* you mean it to have that it may be sent to me.

A few days since I transmitted you the copy of a letter I had received from Mr G—— M——.[27]

It is rumoured, that Mr. Pinckney entertains a wish to return to this Country.[28] Give me leave to make known to you, that in such an event, I have ground to believe it would not be disagreeable to Mr. *King* to be the successor.[29] I verily believe, that a more fit man for the purpose cannot be found and I imagine Mr. King will in every event leave the Senate. Should you think well of his appointment, I presume he would be disposed by a *previous resignation* to make the way easy to his nomination by you. Considering the strong commercial relations of the two countries it is truly very important that each should have with the other a man able and willing to give fair play to reciprocal interests. From what I have seen of Mr. Liston the present Minister of G B [30] & from what Mr. Pinckney and others say of him to me—I believe he will be found a well disposed intelligent and agreeable man.

Very respectfully & affecty I have the honor to be Sir Your obed Servant A Hamilton

The President of the U States

27. Gouverneur Morris. See H to Washington, May 5, 1796.
28. Thomas Pinckney, United States Minister Plenipotentiary to Great Britain. See Rufus King to H, May 2, 1796.
29. See King to H, May 2, 1796; H to King, May 4, 1796; and H to Pickering, May 10, 1796.
30. Robert Liston, who succeeded George Hammond as British Minister to the United States, arrived in the United States on May 9, 1796, and presented his credentials to the President on May 16.

From George Washington

Philadelphia 15th May 1796

My dear Sir,

On this day week, I wrote you a letter on the subject of the information received from G—— M——, and put it with some other

Papers respecting the case of Mr. De la Fayette, under cover to Mr Jay: to whom also I had occasion to write.¹ But in my hurry (making up the dispatches for the Post Office next morning) I forgot to give it a Superscription; of course it had to return from N: York for one, & to encounter all the delay occasioned thereby, before it could reach your hands.

Since then, I have been favored with your letter of the 10th. instt.; & enclose (in its rough State) the paper mentioned therein,² with some alteration in the first page (since you saw it) relative to the reference at foot.³ Having no copy by me (except of the quoted part)—nor the notes from wch it was drawn, I beg leave to recommend the draught now sent, to your particular attention.

Even if you should think it best to throw the *whole* into a different form, let me request, notwithstanding, that my draught may be returned to me (along with yours) with such amendments & corrections, as to render it as perfect as the formation is susceptible of; curtailed, if too verbose; and relieved of all tautology, not necessary to enforce the ideas in the original or quoted part. My wish is, that the whole may appear in a plain stile; and be handed to the public in an honest; unaffected; simple garb.

It will be perceived from hence, that I am attached to the quotation.⁴ My reasons for it are, that as it is not only a fact that such an

---

ALS, Hamilton Papers, Library of Congress; two copies, Hamilton Papers, Library of Congress.

1. See Washington to H, May 8, 1796. Washington's letter to John Jay is also dated May 8, 1796 (ALS, George Washington Papers, Library of Congress; LC, George Washington Papers, Library of Congress).

2. This is a reference to Washington's first draft of a farewell address (ADfS, from the original in the New York State Library, Albany; printed in Paltsits, *Farewell Address*, 164–73). See the introductory note to H to Washington, May 10, 1796.

3. The "reference at foot" to which Washington is referring reads: "*Mr. Madison," with the asterisk referring to a crossed-out phrase in Washington's manuscript which reads: "(particularly in one who was privy to the draught)" (ADfS, from the original in the New York State Library, Albany; printed in Paltsits, *Farewell Address*, 164).

For James Madison's draft of a farewell address for Washington, which Madison wrote in 1792, see Paltsits, *Farewell Address*, 160–63.

4. The quotation in Washington's first draft of his Farewell Address is from a draft which Madison had prepared in the summer of 1792 when Washington believed that he would not seek a second term. See the introductory note to H to Washington, May 10, 1796, and Paltsits, *Farewell Address*, 160–63, 165–68.

Address *was written,* and on the point of being published, but *known also to one or two* of those characters [5] who are now stronger, & foremost in the opposition to the Government; and consequently to the person Administering of it contrary to their views; the promulgation thereof, as an evidence that it was much against my inclination that I continued in Office, will cause it more readily to be believed, that I could have *no* view in extending the Powers of the Executive beyond the limits prescribed by the Constitution; and will serve to lessen, in the public estimation the pretensions of that Party to the patriotic zeal & watchfulness, on which they endeavor to build their own consequence at the expence of others, who have differed from them in sentiment. And besides, it may contribute to blunt, if it does not turn aside, some of the shafts which it may be presumed will be aimed at my annunciation of this event; among which—conviction of fallen popularity, and despair of being re-elected, will be levelled at me with dexterity & keeness.

Having struck out the reference to a *particular character* [6] in the first page of the Address, I have less (if any) objection to expunging those words which are contained within parenthesis's in pages 5,[7] 7 & 8 [8] in the quoted part,[9] and those in the 18th page of what follows.[10]

5. Madison and Thomas Jefferson.
6. Madison. See note 3.
7. This is a reference to the following sentence: "May I be allowed further to add as a consideration far more important, that an early example of rotation in an office of so high and delicate a nature, may equally accord with the republican spirit of our Constitution, and the ideas of liberty and safety entertained by the people" (ADfS, from the original in the New York State Library, Albany; printed in Paltsits, *Farewell Address,* 166).
8. Washington is referring to the words in parentheses in the following paragraph on pages 7 and 8 of his first draft: "To confirm these motives to an affectionate and permanent Union, and to secure the great objects of it, we have established a common Government, which being free in its principles, being founded in our own choice, being intended as the guardian of our common rights—and the patron of our common interests—and wisely containing within itself a provision for its own amendment, as experience may point out its errors, seems to promise every thing that can be expected from such an institution; (and if supported by wise Councils—by virtuous conduct—and by mutual and friendly allowances, must approach as near to perfection as any human work can aspire, and nearer than any which the annals of mankind have recorded)" (ADfS, from the original in the New York State Library, Albany; printed in Paltsits, *Farewell Address,* 167).
9. This is a reference to Madison's draft, which was embodied in Washington's first draft. See notes 3 and 4.
10. Washington is referring to the last two sentences in the following paragraph of his first draft: "To conclude, and I feel proud in having it in my

Nor to the discarding the egotism (however just they may be) if you think them liable to fair criticism, and that they had better be omitted; notwithstanding some of them relate facts which are but little known to the Community.

My object has been, and must continue to be, to avoid personalities; allusions to particular measures, which may appear pointed; and to expressions which could not fail to draw upon me attacks which I should wish to avoid, and might not find agreeable to repel.

As there will be another Session of Congress before the Political existence of the *present* House of Representatives, or my own, will constitutionally expire, it was not my design to say a word to the Legislature on this subject; but to withhold the promulgation of my intention until the period, when it shall become indispensably necessary for the information of the Electors, previous to the Election (which, this year, will be delayed until the 7th. of December). This makes it a little difficult, and uncertain what to say, so long beforehand, on the part marked with a pencil in the last paragraph of the 2d page.[11]

---

power to do so with truth, that it was not from ambitious views; it was not from ignorance of the hazard to which I knew I was exposing my reputation; it was not from an expectation of pecuniary compensation that I have yielded to the calls of my country; and that, if my country has derived no benefit from my services, my fortune, in a pecuniary point of view, has received no augmentation from my country. But in delivering this last sentiment, let me be unequivocally understood as not intending to express any discontent on my part, or to imply any reproach on my country on that account. The first wd be untrue—the other ungrateful. And no occasion more fit than the present may ever occur perhaps to declare, as I now do declare, that nothing but the principle upon which I set out—and from which I have, in no instance departed—not to receive more from the public than my expences has restrained the bounty of several Legislatures at the close of the War with Great Britain from adding considerably to my pecuniary resources" (ADfS, from the original in the New York State Library, Albany; printed in Paltsits, *Farewell Address*, 172–73). In the margin next to the last two sentences, Washington wrote: "This may, or not, be omitted."

11. The pencil marks to which Washington is referring are no longer visible on the draft of his address. The last paragraph on the second page reads: "In this hope, as fondly entertained as it was conceived, I entered upon the execution of the duties of my second administration. But if the causes wch produced this postponement had any weight in them at that period it will readily be acknowledged that there has been no diminution in them since, until very lately, and it will serve to account for the delay wch has taken place in communicating the sentiments which were then committed to writing and are now found in the following words" (ADfS, from the original in the New York State Library, Albany; printed in Paltsits, *Farewell Address*, 154). The part that Washington marked with a pencil presumably referred to "postponement" and "delay" in making a decision about retiring from office.

All these ideas, and observations are confined, as you will readily perceive, to *my draft* of the validictory Address. If you form one anew, it will, of course, assume such a shape as you may be disposed to give it, predicated upon the Sentiments contained in the enclosed Paper.

With respect to the Gentleman you have mentioned as Successor to Mr. P——[12] there can be no doubt of his abilities, nor in *my mind* is there any of his fitness. But you know as well as I, what has been said of his political sentiments, with respect to another form of Government; and from thence, can be at no loss to guess at the Interpretation which would be given to the nomination of him. However, the subject shall have due consideration; but a previous resignation would, in my opinion, carry with it too much the appearance of Concert; and would have a bad, rather than a good effect.

Always, & sincerely   I am Yours   Go: Washington

Colo. A. Hamilton

12. This is a reference to H's suggestion that Rufus King succeeded Thomas Pinckney as United States Minister Plenipotentiary to Great Britain. See H to Washington, May 10, 1796.

Abstract of Points to Form an Address [1]

[New York, May 16–July 5, 1796] [2]

I   The period of a new Election approaching it is his duty to announce his intention to decline—

II   He had hoped that long ere this it would have been in his power and particularly had nearly come to a final resolution in the year 1792 to do it but the peculiar situation of affairs & advice of confidential friends dissuaded

<u>political cowardice</u>

ADf, Hamilton Papers, Library of Congress.

1. For an explanation of the contents of this document, see the introductory note to H to Washington, May 10, 1796.
2. H did not date this document, but it was written after May 15, 1796, when Washington had sent his first draft of a farewell address to H, and before July 5, 1796, when H completed his own draft of a farewell address for the President. See H to Washington, July 5, 1796.

III In acquiescing in a further election he still hoped a year or two longer would have enabled him to withdraw by a continuance of causes has delayed till now—when the position of our Country abroad and at home justify him in pursuing his inclination

IV In doing it has not been unmindful of his relation as a dutiful citizen to his Country nor is now influenced by the smallest diminution of zeal for its interest or gratitude for its past kindness but by a belief that the Step is compatible with both.

V The impressions under which he first accepted were explained on the proper occasion—[3]

VI In the execution of it has contributed the best exertions of a very fallible judgement—~an[ti]cipated his insufficiency~ experienced his disqualifications for the difficult trust & every day a stronger sentiment from that cause to yield the place—advance into the decline of life, every day more sensible of weight of years of the necessity of repose ~let~ the duty to seek retirement &c   Add

VII It will be among the purest enjoyments which can sweeten the remnant of his days to partake in a private station in the midst of his fellow Citizens the laws of a free Govert the ultimate object of his cares & wishes—

Qr. as to Rotation.

IX[4] In contemplating the moment of retreat cannot forbear to express his deep acknowlegements & debt of gratitude for the many honors conferred on him—the steady confidence which even amidst discouraging scenes & efforts to ~positin~ its ~poison~ ~source~ has adhered to supported him & enabled him to be useful—marking, if well placed the virtue and wisdom of his countrymen—All the return he can now make must be in the vows he will carry with him to his retirement I for a continuance of the divine beneficence to his Countryn. II for the perpetuity of their union & brotherly affection, for a good administration insured by a happy union of watchfulness & confidence III that happiness of people under auspices of liberty may be complete

3. See Washington's "First Inaugural Address," April 30, 1789 (*GW*, XXX, 291–96).
4. This document contains no paragraph VIII.

IV That by a prudent use of the blessing they may recommend to the affection the praise & the adoption of every nation yet a stranger to it—

X Perhaps here ~~it wo~~ he ought to end—But an unconquerable solicitude for the happiness of his Country will not permit him to leave the scene without availing himself of whatever confidence may remain in him to strengthen some sentiments which he believes to be essential to their happiness and to recommend some rules of conduct the importance of which his own experience has more than ever impressed upon him—

XI To consider the Union as the Rock of their salvation presenting summarily these ideas—

I ~~security against force or danger~~	I The strength & greater security from external danger
II ~~from interior tranquility~~	II Internal peace & avoiding the necessity of establishments dangerous to liberty—
Safety Peace & Liberty & commerce	III Avoidi[n]g the effects of foreign intrigue
	IV Bre[a]k the force of faction by rendering combination more difficult

   I Fitness of the parts for each other by their very discriminations
      I The North by its capacity for maritime streng[t]h & manufacture
      II The Agricultural South ~~nourishing the~~ furnishing materials & requiring those protection[s]
The Atlantic bound to the Western Country by the strong interest of peace &
The Western by the necessity of Atlantic maritime protection—
   cannot be secure of their great outlet otherwise—
   cannot trust a foreign connection
   Solid interests invite to Union—Speculation of difficul[t]y of Government ought not to be indulged nor momentary jealousies —lead to impatience
   Faction & individual ambition are the only advisers of Disunion

Let Confidence be cherished—Let the recent Experience of the West [5] be a lesson against impatience & distrust—

~~And above all Let the friends of Union wherever they reside avoid as far as possible attaching party spirit to Geographical discriminations—~~

XII Cherish the actual Government. ~~Change not~~ It is the government of our own choice, free in its ~~principles~~ the guardian of our common rights, the patron of our common interests & containing within itself a provision for its own amendment.

But let that provision be cautiously used not abused, changing only in any material points as experience shall direct—neither indulging speculations of too much or too little force in the system—& remembering always the extent of our Country—

   Time & Habit of great consequence to every Government of whatever structure.

   Discourage the spirit of Faction the bane of free Government—
    & particularly avoid founding it on geographical discriminations.
   Discountenance slander of <u>public Men</u>
    I Let the Departments of Governt. avoid interfering & mutual encroachment

XIII Morals religion—Industry Commerce œconomy—
Cherish public Credit—source of strength & security
adherence to systematic views—

XIV Cherish Good Faith ~~& ~~ Justice ₍Peace₎ with other Nations—
  1 Because Religion & morality dictate it
  2 Because Policy dictates it
If there could exist a nation invariably honest & fait[h]ful the benefits would be immense
But avoid national antipathies or national attachments
   display the <u>Evils</u>—~~source~~ fertile source of Wars
               <u>instrument of ambitious Rulers</u>

XV Republics peculiarly exposed to foreign intrigue those sentiments lay them open to it

5. This is a reference to the Treaty of Friendship, Limits, and Navigation between the United States and Spain, which was signed at San Lorenzo el Real on October 27, 1795 (Miller, *Treaties*, II, 318–38).

MAY 1796

XVI   The greater rule of our foreign politics ought to be to have as little political connections as possible with foreign Nations

establishing tempor[ar]y & convenient rules that commerce may be placed on a stable footing Merchants know their rights & Commerce how to support them— not seeking favors
}
Cultivating Commerce with all by gentle & natural means diffusing & diversyfing it but forcing nothing & Cherishing the sentiment of independence taking pride in the appelation of Ameri[c]a

XVII   Our seperation from Europe renders ~~alliance~~ standing alliances inexpedient—subjecting our peace & interest to the primaries to the primary & complicated relations of European interests—

Keeping constantly in view to place ourselves upon a respectable defensive & if forced into Controversy trusting to Connections of the Occasion

XVIII   Our Attidude imposing & rendering this policy safe

But this must be with the exception of ~~effee~~ existing engagements to be preferred but not extended—

XIX   It is not expected that these admonitions can controul the course of the human passions but if they only moderate them in some instances & now & then excite the reflections of virtue men heated by party spirit my endeavor is rewarded

XX   How far in the administration of my present Office my conduct has conformed to these principles the public records must Witness. My conscience assures me that I believed myself to be guided by them—

Touch sentiments with regard to conduct of belligerent Powers a wish that France may establish good Government— Time every thing

XXI   Particularly in relation to the Present War. The Proclamation of the 22 of April 1793 [6] is the key to my plan—Approved your Voice & that of your Representatives in Congress the spirit of that measure has continually guided me uninfluenced by & regardless of the Complaints & attempts of any the powers at War or their partizans to change them—

I thought our Country had a right under all the circumstances to

---

6. This is a reference to Washington's neutrality proclamation. For the text, see John Jay to H, April 11, 1793, note 1.

take this ground & I was resolved as far as depended on me to maintain it firmly—

XXII However in reviewing the course of my administration I may be unconscious of intentional errors I am too sensible of my own deficiencies not to believe that I may have fallen into many—I deprecate the evils to which they may tend & pray Heaven to avert or mitigate & abrige them—I carry with me nevertheless the hope that my motives will continue to be viewed with indulgence that after 45 years of my life devoted to public service with a good zeal & upright ~~use~~ views the ~~my~~ faults of deficient abilities will be consigned to obligion & myself must soon be to the mansions of rest—

XXIII Neither interest nor ambition has been my compelling motive—I never abused the power confided to me—I have not bettered my fortune retiring with it no otherwise improved than influence on prope[rt]y of the by the common blessings of my Country—I retire with undefiled hands & an uncorrupted heart and with ardent vows for the welfare of that Country which has been the native soil of myself & my ancestors for for four generations.

From John Browne Cutting [1]

Philadelphia, May 16, 1796. "You were good enough to offer me last Decr. what I little thought I should have occasion to accept in May—letters to any of your friends in Congress. Business of greater moment than my claim has incessantly occupied the Secretary of State ever since the documents that support it have been in his possession. . . . I therefore presume to request of you a single line to Mr. King [2] or any other Gentleman in Senate simply stating that you did thus examine my papers; and that you do think I zealously expended my own money in a public service and that this money at least should be repaid upon the proofs I have thus toild to accumulate. . . ."

ALS, Hamilton Papers, Library of Congress.
 1. During the American Revolution, Cutting was Apothecary General of Hospitals in the Eastern Department from 1777 to 1779 and in the Middle

Department from 1779 to 1780. In 1790, acting as a private citizen, he helped to free American seamen from impressment in British ports.

For background to this letter, see H to Timothy Pickering, December 26, 1795; H to George Washington, December 27–30, 1795.

2. Rufus King.

From Tench Coxe [1]

[*Philadelphia, May 17, 1796.* On May 31, 1796, Coxe wrote to Hamilton and referred to "my Letter of the 17th. inst." *Letter not found.*]

1. Coxe, who had been first a Loyalist and then a Patriot during the American Revolution, was a member of the Continental Congress in 1787 and 1788, Assistant Secertary of the Treasury from 1790 until the abolition of that office in 1792, and commissioner of the revenue from 1792 until his dismissal by President John Adams in December, 1797.

To Richard Harison [1]

[*New York*] *May 17* [*1796*]. "I have seen Mr. Blanchard. He will do what we talked of, except as to the loan of the further sum, which he intirely declines. I will thank you to send for *Bouvier* [2] and ascertain his final determination; in order that it may be known whether hostilities must ensue or not. . . ."

ALS, New-York Historical Society, New York City.
1. Richard Harison was United States attorney for the District of New York and recorder of the City of New York.
2. Presumably Julian (or Julien) Bouvier, a New York City physician who speculated in land.

From Robert Morris [1]

Alex Hamilton Esqre. N York   Phila May 17. 1796

Dear sir

When you received the Bond & Mortgage Deed transmitted here-

LC, Robert Morris Papers, Library of Congress.
1. This letter concerns Morris's debt to John B. Church. For this debt and

with which are dated the 16 Instant[2] you will perceive that there has been all the sincerity in my Professions which you could expect. I have from you experienced that degree of Confidence which consisted with my Character and I have been gratified thereby but the extreme solicitude that has lately appeared on your part leads me to suppose that Mr Churchs letters or the Common Reports have impaired that Confidence. You probably dread the Effects of the Judgements you have heard of but you need not, I have provided for them and so I shall continue to do whenever it becomes indispensible. I would never Suffer a Judgement to come against me, if I was alone in the business, but as I am now situated I cannot prevent it untill such time as solid relief shall arise from the abundant Property which I possess. I will seek the means of clearing away the Mortgage to Colo Smith[3] and I am sure the Principals in that Business would never have treated me as the Attorneys have done. Were I to act agreeably to my feelings a very different letter would be written by me to Mr Church than that which you will find inclosed herein & that such a letter is not written you may truly ascribe to yourself because I respect and esteem you. Be so kind to transmit with this letter your Advice of our new Arrangement & desire him to transfer the North American Land Company Shares agreeably to my request.[4] You did not leave with me the Deed of Conveyance of the 20290 Acres of Land but I still have the Patents & will either send them to you or deliver them to any Person you please.[5] I am Sincerely

Yrs RM

Morris's efforts to pay it, see the introductory note to Morris to H, June 7, 1795. See also Morris to H, July 20, November 16, December 18, 1795, March 6, 12, 14, 30, April 27, May 3, 10, 1796; William Lewis to H, May 4, 1796.

2. On May 16, 1796, Morris and his wife, Mary, signed an indenture by which Morris deeded to H one hundred thousand acres in Ontario County, New York, as security for his debt to Church (D3, Montague Collection, MS Division, New York Public Library). This mortgage had to be revised (Morris to H, May 31, 1796). In its final form it was dated May 31, 1796. See the introductory note to Morris to H, June 7, 1795, and the introductory note to Morris to H, April 27, 1796.

3. For this mortgage and its relationship to the debt which Morris owed to Church, see the introductory note to Morris to H, April 27, 1796. See also Morris to H, May 3, 10, 1796.

4. See Morris to H, June 7, 1795, note 7.

5. See the introductory note to Morris to H, June 7, 1795.

[ENCLOSURE]

Robert Morris to John B. Church[6]

via New York
Copy ⅌
Wm Penn

John B. Church Esqre (London)   Phila May 17. 1796

Sir

Colo Hamilton transmitted to me your letter of the 20 Febry last, wherein you complain that I had done wrong & treated you unfriendly "in having prevailed upon him to cancel the Mortgage I had given him on an Estate in Philadelphia, when the Agreemt was expressly made with my Son that the Mortgage should remain as Security to you untill the deferred stock was delivered in discharge of the Contract made with him." Be pleased to attend to the following state of Facts and your *astonishment* will probably cease & your Opinion become more favorable. The Origin of my Debt to you was a purchase of 100 Shares of Bank stock at £100 Stg ⅌ Share which gave you a profit of £16.13.4 Currency upon each Share. I then sold to Colo Hamilton 20290 Acres of Land at 7/6 Curry ⅌ acre which at the Par of Exchange amounted to £4565..5.. Stg and was to go according to his Agreement with me in part payment of the said Bank stock & for the Balance I gave a Bill on my Son in your favor being for £5434..15 Stg.[7] The 20290 Acres of Land sold to Colo Hamilton for your Account will now sell for thrice what I got for it and before he or I knew of the Agreement which took place between you and my Son, the Mortgage on the Philadelphia Estate was cancelled. I proposed & urged this being done because the sale of Lands paid nearly half the Debt due to you & because I had then good reason to expect that my Son to pay the Bill drawn upon him; & Colo Hamilton having the same Idea, was disposed to accomodate me, especially as I promised him to give a new Security for

---

6. LC, Robert Morris Papers, Library of Congress. This letter concerns Morris's debt to Church and his efforts to pay it. For an explanation of the contents of this letter, see the references cited in note 1.

7. "Exch. ⅌ 5434..15.0 Sterling.   Philadelphia May 31st. 1793.
At Eight months sight pay this first of Exchange (second, third and fourth not paid) to John Barker Church Esqre—or order Five thousand four hundred thirty four pounds fifteen shillings Sterling value received—which place to Account as ⅌ advice.
To Mr. Robert Morris Junr.   Robert Morris
London" (DS, Robert Morris Papers, Library of Congress).

the Amot of the bill in case my Son could not pay it or if from any cause whatever the said Bill should not be paid. My Son finding after the failure of J. Warder & Co [8] it would be inconvenient for him to pay that Bill and that the receipt of money from you for the Cost of the 20290 Acres of Land which I had sold to Colo Hamilton for you would be convenient to my Affairs in his hands, agreed with you to receive the Money for that Purchase & to commute the Original Debt contracted for 100 shares of Bank stock of the value of $40,000 Mexican to $100,000 of Deferred debt payable in February 1795 for which you demand $75000 Mexican with Interest of Six ₱ Cent ₱ Annum. Now sir, you will be good enough to attend to the Circumstance that the Mortgage was cancelled before Colo Hamilton or myself knew of the Agreement made by my Son Robert with you, consequently there was no violation of Faith or Friendship on my part nor any Neglect of Duty on the part of Colo Hamilton, who had obtained for you a real property of more Value than your stock, and my bill for £5434..15 Stg for which I was liable and had promised him a new security if necessary. My Promises I hold Sacred and I am always willing to fulfill them. I have therefore given to Colo Hamilton my Bond for $81679. $44/100$ payable in five Years from the 1st January last with six p Cent interest annually and an ample Security by Mortgage of Lands for the Payment of this Debt. I hope therefor that you will find cause to be Satisfied both with Colo Hamilton and myself, and in order to shew that your Money has not been unproductive I beg leave to submit to your Consideration the enclosed statemt, which I think ought to Satisfy any reasonable person.

You have threatened me with a Public sale of my North American Land Company Shares, which were entrusted to you by me in the expectation that they would on the terms of that Trust, have produced the discharge of my Debt, and it seems to me that the Act of transferring these Shares to your name ought to have convinced you that I never wished or designed you to be insecure. I disclaim any fears or Apprehensions from threats, and I will not use any, but as Colo Hamilton will advise you of our new arrangement and of the Security I have given, I must again request that you will transfer the 750 Shares in the North American Land Company to James Marshall

8. John Warder and Company was a London brokerage house.

Esqre or execute a power for him to transfer the same, being the shares which I had transferred to your name. Should Mrs. Church still remain in England, I pray you to present Mrs. Morris's and my thanks for her kind Attention to our Daughter [9] and that you will also accept the Same yourself. Should she be on her Passage to this Country as it is said she is, we will thank her in person, and a grateful Remembrance of her and your kindness will ever be retained in our minds.

My feelings it is true have been wounded at some part of your letter which I conceive to be unnecessarily harsh, but Still I am desirous as you say to wind up this business amicably, and I hope it will be so terminated as that we shall remain good Friends.

I am Sir   Yours &c.   RM

9. This is a reference to Morris's daughter Hetty, who was the wife of James Marshall. She and her husband had been in England and the Continent, where he had attempted—with little success—to sell both shares in the North American Land Company and lands belonging to Morris in the United States. See the introductory note to Morris to H, June 7, 1795, note 10.

To Charles Williamson [1]

[New York, May 17–30, 1796] [2]

Dr. Sir

Some arrangements which I have lately made with Robert Morris Esquire for the benefit of my Brother in Law Mr. Church [3] render it interest⟨ing⟩ to me to know from you the precise extent of the Western line of the tract of land you purchased of that Gentleman— I mean a line which was run from the Pensylvania line to Lake Ontario—by whom it was run, how far the accuracy of it may be depended upon—and likewise what is the course of Lake Ontario Westward of that line? [4] Is it ascertained whether it trends to the North or not and in what degree?

Have you ever had occasion to get explored a tract of land formerly mortgaged by Mr. Morris to Col. Smith for security of money due to Smith as Agent for Messrs. *Pultney & Hornby*— [5] extending with a breadth of six miles from Ontario to the Pensylvania line? If so what is the Nature of the land included in that tract North of the Pensylvania line to the distance of about 25 Miles?

I will ask for the favor of you to keep the Inquiry to yourself. The more particularly you answer it, to the extent of your information, the more you will oblige me.

With great esteem & regard   I am sir   Your Obed ser

Williamson Esq

ADf, Hamilton Papers, Library of Congress.

1. Williamson, who had served as a British officer during the American Revolution, in 1791 became the American agent of three English land speculators, the leader of whom was Sir William Pulteney, who had purchased a large amount of land in the Genesee country in western New York. For information about Williamson's activities, see Robert Troup to H, March 31, May 11, 1795.

2. The contents of this undated letter indicate that it was written after May 16, 1796, when Robert Morris had executed a mortgage to H, and before May 31, 1796, when that mortgage was perfected.

3. This is a reference to a mortgage on one hundred thousand acres of Robert Morris's property in the Genessee country. The mortgage was made out to H to secure a debt which Morris owed to John B. Church. For this debt and the mortgage, see the introductory note to Morris to H, June 7, 1795; Morris to H, April 27, May 17, 18, 31, 1796.

H wrote this letter to Williamson because he wished to determine the validity of the boundaries of the lands which Morris had mortgaged to him. One way to do this was to ascertain the boundaries of adjoining tracts. Through his connections with Pulteney and his associates, Williamson had a direct knowledge of the two tracts which H mentions in the course of this letter.

4. For this tract, see H to Morris, March 18, 1795, note 29.

5. For this tract and Morris's mortgage to William S. Smith, see the introductory note to Morris to H, April 27, 1796.

To Richard Harison [1]

[*New York*] *May 18, 1796.* "Do me the favour, if possible, to bring Bouvier to a decision this day. Much *alarm* & *suspicion* exist with the other party who is unwilling longer to leave unessayed measures of Coertion, if an arrangement cannot be made on the proposed basis."

ALS, New-York Historical Society, New York City.

1. For background to this letter, see H to Harison, May 17, 1796.

From Robert Morris [1]

Alex Hamilton Esqre. New York   Philada May 18, 1796

Dear Sir

I wrote a letter last night to you & one to Mr Church,[2] but as these must go by some private hand who will carry Safe my Bond & Mortgage [3] I send this by Post to let you know that those papers are duly executed & the Mortgage acknowledged by Mrs Morris & myself before Judge Wilson.[4] They shall be sent by the first safe Conveyance I can meet with by

Dr Sir   Yrs   RM

LC, Robert Morris Papers, Library of Congress.
1. This letter concerns Morris's efforts to secure his debt to John B. Church. For this debt and Morris's efforts to meet his obligations to Church, see the introductory note to Morris to H, June 7, 1795. See also Morris to H, July 20, November 16, December 18, 1795, January 15, March 6, 12, 14, 30, April 27, May 3, 10, 17, 1796; William Lewis to H, May 4, 1795; H to Charles Williamson, May 17–30, 1796.
2. Morris's letter to Church is printed as an enclosure to Morris to H, May 17, 1796.
3. This is a reference to the mortgage on one hundred thousand acres of Morris's lands in the Genesee country. This mortgage was to secure Morris's debt to Church. See the introductory note to Morris to H, June 7, 1795. See also Morris to H, July 20, November 16, December 18, 1795; January 15, March 6, 12, 14, 30, April 27, May 3, 10, 1796.
4. James Wilson, a resident of Philadelphia, was one of Morris's oldest and closest friends. Wilson had served successively as a member of the Continental Congress, Constitutional Convention, and Pennsylvania Ratifying Convention. From 1789 until his death in 1798 he was an associate justice of the Supreme Court of the United States. For "the Mortgage acknowledged . . . before Judge Wilson," see Morris to H, May 17, 1796, note 2.

To George Washington

New York May 20. 1796

Sir

A belief that the occasion to which they may be applicable is not likely to occur, whatever may have been once intended, or *pre-*

ALS, George Washington Papers, Library of Congress; copy, Hamilton Papers, Library of Congress.

tended in *terrorem*, has delayed the following observations in compliance with your desire [1]—and which are now the result of conferences with the Gentleman you named.[2]

The *precise form* of any *proposition* or *demand* which may be made to or of this Government must so materially influence the course proper to be pursued with regard to such proposition or demand, that it is very difficult by anticipation to judge what would be fit and right. The suggestions which can be submitted must therefore be very general and liable to much modification according to circumstances.

I It would seem in almost any case adviseable to put forward a calm exhibition of the views by which our Government have been influenced in relation to the present War of Europe—making prominent the great interest we have in peace in our present infant state—the limitedness of our capacity for external effort—the much greater injury we should have suffered than good we could have done to France by taking an active part with her—the probability that she would derive more advantage from our neutrality than from our direct aid—the promptitude with which, while all the world was combined against her, we recognised the new order of things [3] and the continuance of our Treaties [4] & before any other power had done so—the danger to which we exposed ourselves in so doing [5]—the fidelity with which we have adhered to our Treaties notwithstanding formal violations of certain parts of them on the other

1. See Washington to H, May 8, 1796.
2. John Jay.
3. On March 12, 1793, Thomas Jefferson instructed Gouverneur Morris, United States Minister Plenipotentiary to France, to recognize the National Assembly as France's legal government (ALS, letterpress copy, Thomas Jefferson Papers, Library of Congress).
4. In his opinion on the French treaties, April 28, 1793, Jefferson argued that the treaties of 1778 were binding and therefore could not be suspended (ADS, George Washington Papers, Library of Congress). H, who presented his opinion to Washington on May 2, 1793, favored suspension of the treaties, as they were not in his view applicable to existing circumstances. In this case Jefferson's opinion prevailed. For a description of the provisions of the 1778 Franco-American treaties, see H to John Jay, first letter of April 9, 1793, note 2. See also Washington to H, Jefferson, Henry Knox, and Edmund Randolph, April 18, 1793; "Cabinet Meeting. Opinion on a Proclamation of Neutrality and on Receiving the French Minister," April 19, 1793; H and Knox to Washington, May 2, 1793.
5. In the margin opposite the words enclosed by dashes, H wrote: "I believe this is the fact."

side [6]—our readiness to the utmost extent of our faculties to discharge our debt, without *hesitation in the earliest period of the revolution*,[7] and latterly having facilitated an anticipated enjoyment of the ballance [8]—the zeal and confidence of our Merchants by which they are now creditors for very large sums to France [9]—the patience with which we have seen infractions of our rights—the peculiar nature of the War as it regarded the origin of our relations to France (Quaere?)—the declaration of the War by France against the maritime powers [10]—her incapacity for maritime effort and to supply our deficiency in that particular so as to render a war not absolutely ruinous to us—the early expectations given to us by her Agents that we were not expected to become parties [11]—the exposed state of our commerce at this time with an immense property of our merchants afloat relying on the neutral plan which they have understood our Government to be pursuing [12] even with the concurrence of France

6. This is a reference to the French decrees of May 9 and July 27, 1793, which authorized the arrest of neutral vessels carrying provisions to enemy ports, and the decree of November 15, 1794, which ordered the seizure and confiscation of enemy goods found on board neutral vessels. For the texts of the decrees of May 9 and July 27, 1793, see Duvergier, *Lois*, V, 344–45; VI, 71. The decrees of May 9, 1793, and November 15, 1794, are printed in *ASP, Foreign Relations*, I, 749, 752.

7. H is referring to plans to defray the cost of supplies for the relief of Santo Domingo by using payments on the debt due to France which the United States had incurred during the American Revolution. See Jean Baptiste de Ternant to H, September 21, 1791, February 21, March 8, 10, 1792; H to Ternant, September 21, 1791, February 21, March 8, 11, 12, 1792; William Short to H, December 28, 1791, January 26, March 24, April 22, 25, May 14, June 28, August 6, 1792; H to Short, April 10, 1792; Gouverneur Morris to H, September 25, 1792, note 4; H to Washington, November 19, 1792; George Latimer to H, January 2, 1793.

8. This is a reference to the conversion of the French debt, which H proposed in his "Report on a Plan for the Further Support of Public Credit," January 16, 1795. See also H to Oliver Wolcott, Jr., April 10, June 13, 22, 1795; Wolcott to H, June 18, 1795.

9. In the margin opposite the words enclosed by dashes, H wrote: "Quaere?"

10. On February 1, 1793, France declared war against Great Britain, Holland, and Spain (Duvergier, *Lois*, V, 169–70).

11. In the period following his arrival in the United States in 1793, Edmond Charles Genet carefully refrained from even suggesting that the United States become a cobelligerent. See Jefferson to James Madison, May 19, 1793 (ALS, letterpress copy, Thomas Jefferson Papers, Library of Congress). Instead Genet proposed the liquidation of the United States debt to France and a "true family compact" on a "liberal & fraternal basis" (Genet to Jefferson, May 23, 1793 [letterpress copy, in Jefferson's handwriting, Thomas Jefferson Papers, Library of Congress]).

12. This is a reference to Washington's neutrality proclamation. For the text, see John Jay to H, April 11, 1793, note 1.

at least without its opposition—the extreme mischiefs to us of a sudden departure from this plan & the little advantage to France from our aid—the *merely peace* views which influenced our Treaty with Great Britain—the nature of that treaty involving no ingredient of political connection reserving the obligation of our prior Treaties the commercial articles terminating in two years after the present war; [13] nothing in it to change the nature of our relations to France. All this will of course require great caution & delicacy so as not to compromise the dignity of this Country or give umbrage elsewhere —and I think observations ought to hold out the idea that under all the circumstances of the case the Government of this Country thought itself a full liberty consistently with its Treaties with France to pursue a neutral plan and they ought to hold up strongly our desire to maintain friendship with France, our regret that any circumstances of dissatisfaction should occur—our hope that justice & reason will prevail & preserve the good understanding &c. The conclusion of this preliminary exposition will be according to the nature of the proposi[ti]on.

If it should claim a renunciation of the British Treaty—The answer will naturally be that this sacrifice of the positive & recent engagements of the country is pregnant with consequences too humiliating and injurious to us to allow us to believe that the expectation can be persisted in by France since it is to require a thing impossible & to establish as the price of the continuance of Friendship with us the sacrifice of our honor by an act of perfidy which would destroy the value of our friendship to any Nation. That, besides, the Executive, if it were capable of complying with a demand so fatal to us, is not competent to it—it being of the province of Congress by a declaration of War or otherwise in the proper cases to annul the operation of Treaties.

If it should claim the abandonment of the articles of the present Treaty respecting free ships free goods [14] &c the answer may be

That our Treaties with France are an intire work parts of a whole —that nevertheless the Executive is disposed to enter into a new

13. This is a reference to Article 28 of the Jay Treaty. For the text of that article, see "Remarks on the Treaty . . . between the United States and Great Britain," July 9–11, 1795, note 72.

14. See Article 23 (originally 25) of the Treaty of Amity and Commerce between France and the United States, February 6, 1778 (Miller, *Treaties*, II, 264).

negotiation by a new Treaty to modify them so as may consist with a due regard to mutual interest and the circumstances of parties and may even tend to strengthen the relations of friendship & good understanding between the Two Countries.

If the Guarantee of the West Indies [15] should be claimed—The answer may be—

"That the decision of this question belongs to Congress who if it be desired will be convened to deliberate upon it." I presume & hope they will have adjourned. For to ⟨gain⟩ [16] time is every thing.

The foregoing marks the general course of our reflections. They are sketched hastily because they can be only general ideas and much will depend on numerous circumstances.

I observe what you say on the subject of a certain diplomatic mission.[17] Permit me to offer with frankness the reflections which have struck my mind.

The importance to our security and commerce of good understanding with G Britain renders it very important that a man *able* and *not disagreeable* to that Government should be there. The Gentleman in question [18] equally with any who could go & better than any willing to go answers this description. The idea hinted in your letter will apply to every man fit for the mission by his conspicousness talents and dispositions. 'Tis the stalking horse of a certain party & is made use of against every man who is not in their views & of sufficient consequence to attract their obloquy. If listened to, it will deprive the Government of the services of the most able and faithful agents. Is this expedient? What will be gained by it? Is it not evident that this party will pursue its hostility at all events as far as public opinion will permit? Does policy require any thing more than that

15. This is a reference to Article 12 of the Jay Treaty. For the text of that article, see H to Rufus King, June 11, 1795, note 2.

16. This word has been taken from the copy.

17. This is a reference to the retirement of Thomas Pinckney as United States Minister Plenipotentiary to Great Britain and his replacement by Rufus King. See Washington to H, May 15, 1796.

18. Rufus King. Washington had decided to appoint King before he had received this letter from H. For H's earlier recommendations of King as Minister to Great Britain, see H to Timothy Pickering, May 19, 1796, and H to Washington, May 10, 1796. On May 19, 1796, the President nominated King "to be Minister Plenipotentiary of the United States at the Court of Great Britain, in the room of Thomas Pinckney, who desires to be recalled," and on the following day the Senate approved the nomination (*Executive Journal*, I, 209).

they shall have no real cause to complain? Will it do, in deference to their calumniating insinuations to forbear employing the most competent men or to entrust the great business of the Country to unskilful unfaithful or doubtful hands? I really feel a conviction that it will be very dangerous to let party insinuations of this kind prove a serious obstacle to the employment of the best qualified characters. Mr. King is a remarkably well informed man—a very judicious one —a man of address—a man of fortune and œconomy whose situation affords just ground of confidence—a man of unimpeached probity where he is best known—a firm friend to the Government— a supporter of the measures of the President—a man who cannot but feel that he has strong pretensions to confidence and trust.

I might enlarge on these topics but I have not leisure neither can it be necessary. I have thrown out so much in the fulness of my heart & too much in a hurry to fashion either the idea or the expression as it ought to be. The President however will I doubt not receive what I have said as it is meant—as dictated by equal regard to the public interest & to the honorable course of his administration.

I have the honor to be Very respectfully & affecty   Dr sir   Yr Obed ser   A Hamilton

The President

From Elisha Boudinot [1]

New Ark [New Jersey] 23 May. 1796

My dear sir

I am very happy that your endeavors to extricate Mr. Duer [2] will occasion your so far investigating his affairs, as to enable you to do justice to a very injured character. When the misfortunes of life, or the frowns of fortune have thrown a man in the shade the generality of the world have too little feeling to investigate before they Judge, and too great a propensity to censure unheard, he is therefore at

ALS, Hamilton Papers, Library of Congress.
  1. Boudinot, a Newark, New Jersey, lawyer, was the uncle of John Pintard, the subject of this letter.
  2. William Duer.

once condemned and kept in oblivion as long as malice & envy can have their effects. I know your conduct is swayed by entirely different motives; and that if convinced of the rectitude of a mans conduct, misfortunes will not prevent, but, urge, your helping hand to restore him to life again. It is this belief of your character that induces me to trouble you with what I know of my friend's [3] conduct in his connection with Mr. Duer. I *know* his *virtue*, his *integrity*, his *purity of intention*, and therefore if the whole world should forsake him, I would support him to the utmost of my ability, trusting for *his* and *my* vindication, to that awfull day when the secrets of all hearts will be revealed.

When Mr. Pintard first engaged in the line of a Broker, he was young, sanguine and full of spirits, his abilities soon introduced him to very handsome business. It was then Mr. Duer made a proposition to him, to go to Europe for him, offering him certain conditions. He consulted his Uncle,[4] who was cautious, and had not the best opinion of Mr. D.—he advised him against it—he sent for me. I told him, to make out an account of the profits of his business for two Months then past, to go to Mr. D. shew it to him, and inform him, "that he had a young growing family, was inexperienced, and threw himself entirely on his generosity—if he knew the business he wanted to send him upon, would be more advantageous to him than that in which he was in, he would go" and I was confident Mr. D. as a man of science, character and liberality would never deceive him. He did so, and Mr. D—— said at once, that his business was so good, he would not advise him to leave it and accept of his offers—but that he would advise him to continue in the line he was in, and he would increase his business by giving him his own—complaining that he had employed several agents who had made their own fortunes, and then turned their backs on him, and treated him with ingratitude. This frankness entirely won the heart of Mr. P—— and he soon after engaged in his business; but as I understood the matter, not to become bound for him in any instance. The saturday after

---

3. Pintard was a New York City merchant and stockbroker. In the seventeen-eighties Pintard prospered in the East India trade, but, as Boudinot states, he decided to abandon his own enterprises to enter into partnership with Duer. After Duer failed in March, 1792, Pintard fled to Newark. Duer's creditors followed him to New Jersey, and he went to debtors' prison for thirteen months.

4. Lewis Pintard, by whom John Pintard had been adopted.

our return from organizing the manufacturing Society at Trenton,[5] I received an express from Mr. P. that he wanted to see me; I went in, and found his Uncle with him in great distress—saying that during the weeks absence of Mr. D.[6] he had been called upon unexpectedly, to pay off several of his notes due at the bank, which Mr. D. had not given him any notice were due and that he might not be charged with *ingratitude,* in the absence of Mr. D—— he had been induced to indorse notes, to redeem those at the bank—and they wanted me to go to Mr. D. and endeavor to find out how his circumstances were &c. My answer was that from the little acquaintance I had with Mr D—— I believed him to be a man of honor, delicacy and pride—that he would feel himself hurt, at the Idea of Johnny's doubting his ability and his pride would be wounded at his communicating it to me—that I would therefore advise him to go with the same openness and candour as at first and know from himself his true situation, and whether he was safe in what he had done for him. This advise he said he would follow—and it being saturday afternoon, I left town. The result will appear in the extract of a few lines from two or three letters I received from him at that time which I kept, and which he does not know are in existence—and which will be more forcible than pages of comments from me—first giving an extract from a letter brought me by Mr. D. on his way to Trenton—as an inlet to what followed.

26 Novr. 1791. "You will find from Duer who is my friend & who has my best services; that his prospects are unbounded—and were I to work night & day he alone wd. furnish me ample employment & that profitable. I have unbounded confidence in him, which I believe is reciprocal and I am determined to conduct myself in such a way by strict attention to my accounts that I will be a Cæsars wife to him. I flatter myself he never was better served, I am sure never more honestly. I fear nothing whilst he has life, for as to resource he is a most wonderfull man, he is really an Atlas"!

---

5. This is a reference to a meeting on November 28, 1791, of the stockholders of the Society for Establishing Useful Manufactures. It was at this meeting that the society's first board of directors was elected. See "Minutes of the S.U.M.," 2.

6. Duer was one of the subscribers to the Society for Establishing Useful Manufactures and its first governor.

4 Decr. 1791 (the day after I left him to follow the advice I mentioned before)

"I have spent the whole of this afternoon with Col. Duer, who dined with me. You will be kind eno. not to drop a lisp of my communications to you to any one else in the world. With respect to contingencies, I must risk the event, but he assures me that he is solid & immensely rich. My greatest risk is his not investigating his accounts with me and leaving every thing to my discretion. However I shall walk strait and trust to an upright conduct of his affairs for his approbation."

6 Decr. 1791. "Col. Duer spent yesterday evening with me, when we had a long conversation and full investigation of his business committed to me. From every circumstance, his assurance, and more his honor, I feel perfectly secure in committing myself to any extent on his account. I consider him next to yourself my best friend, and where I fix my confidence is unbounded. I find a reciprocal sentiment on his part, indeed what proof so clear, as laying himself entirely at my mercy; I trust the issue will prove his opinion of my Zeal & friendship not misplaced. I shall from this moment go forward into every engagement on his account with as much alacrity as ever I undertook anything in my life."

I will not trouble you farther with extracts; these are sufficient to convince a candid mind; that he engaged in the business with a warm, inexperienced tho' sincere mind, and not that of a swindler or sharper. The consequence of this Zeal & confidence is too well-known—the sufferings, the torture of mind, as well as distress of body he has undergone for these four years past—if known, would be sufficient to soften the hearts of his most obdurate creditors even those of a LeRoy & Bayard,[7] altho' *they* ma⟨y⟩ suppose *their hearts & feelings* so incruscated with Gold, as to be impervious to the darts of distress & misfortune.

I have informed Mr. P. of your wish to have a short journal of his endeavors to satisfy Mr. D. and his creditors which he will make out and forward you immediately. He has constantly offered to surrender every farthing he has in the world to his creditors that his worst enemies might be the assignees—and that if ever it should appear a farthing was kept back, that the whole should be void. I

7. Herman LeRoy and William Bayard were New York City merchants.

am confident that if they had given him a letter of licence for ten years, from his exertions, he would have been enabled to have paid them all off—but nothing short of his death appears will be satisfactory to them and they would have been gratified in that long ago, if his lott had been cast anywhere, but where it is.

I should not have troubled you on any other subject with so long a letter but where humanity is engaged, I know, you will not only read it, but *interest* yourself in its behalf. If *your* endeavors fail—I give up all hopes of any thing being done, until a general bankrupt law takes place—and when that will be Heaven only knows.[8] I do not choose to trust my Clerks to copy this and am too much hurried to do it myself—you will therefore excuse the manner in which it comes.

I am dear sir   with esteem   Your most Obt. Servt

Elisha Boudinot

P. S. I set off tomorrow morning and shall be gone the remainder of the week, as soon as I return, will send ⟨- - -⟩ letter, if it is not forwarded before he will set about it, immediately.

8. The first bankruptcy act was passed by Congress on April 4, 1800 ("An Act to establish an uniform System of Bankruptcy throughout the United States" [2 *Stat.* 19–36]).

To Robert Morris

[*New York, May 26, 1796.* On May 31, 1796, Morris wrote to Hamilton and referred to "your letter of the 26 Inst." *Letter not found.*]

From James Watson[1]

New York, May 27, 1796. "Wishing to have the Benefit of your much esteemed Council as a Lawyer in important Cases, if unfortunately I should hereafter be involved in any, I have inclosed you my Note for one Thousand Dollars, payable in five years, with Interest at 5 ℔ Cent ℔ annum, which I beg you to accept. . . ."[2]

LS, Hamilton Papers, Library of Congress.

1. Watson, a native of Woodbury, Connecticut, had acted as agent and subcontractor for the firm of John Carter (John B. Church) and Jeremiah Wadsworth during the American Revolution. In 1786 he moved to New York City, where he practiced law, engaged in business, and served as director of the Bank of the United States and of the Society for Establishing Useful Manufactures. In 1791, 1794, and 1795 he represented New York City in the state Assembly.

2. H endorsed this letter: "Returned as being more than is proper. A H."

To Oliver Wolcott, Junior

New York May 27. 1796

Dr. Sir

The Patterson manufactory being defunct,[1] the persons heretofore employed are thrown out of business and among them Mr. Marshall who erected & directed the Cotton Mill.[2] As this man has proved that he understands himself & is a discreet well-moralled man I am loth that he should be under the necessity of leaving the Country. He is a man of some education. Besides a considerable knowlege of mechanics & some of surveying he writes a good hand and good English. I have thought that perhaps temporarily some employment as a copying Clerk in some one of the Offices might be found for him. Can this be? Let me hear from you in answer as soon as may be. He is a decent man in his demeanour.

Yrs. truly   A Hamilton

May 27. 1796

Oliver Wolcott Jur. Esq

Mr. Dickson, an American Citizen, by birth, who has been concerned in establishing & means to conduct in person the Cotton Manufactory at New Haven[3] is desirous of contracting to supply the army with Cotton shirts of his own fabric. As I cannot help still hoping this manufacture may succeed in a scene so favourable to it as New Haven—as it will have a fair chance under Mr. Dickson who is attentive industrious & has now had a good deal of experience, I think there would be a public policy in facilitating to him the supply he desires for a good proportion of the shirts which the army will require at a price which will allow a reasonable profit. This business may be detached from the general contract & be the subject of a particular agreement. Mr. Dickson assures greater strength & duration than India Cotton or than linnen. This idea may assist an experiment. General Knox [4] made one of *Cotton* shirts & I understood him thought well of it.

ALS, Connecticut Historical Society, Hartford.

1. By 1796 it was clear to all concerned that the Society for Establishing Useful Manufactures, in which H had played a prominent part and to which he had been elected a director on November 24, 1795 ("Minutes of the S.U.M.," 115), was not going to make a profit in the foreseeable future. At a meeting on January 25, 1796, the directors of the society resolved that in view of the fact that the society could not continue "any further without evident loss. . . , the Superintendant be directed to put a Stop to every species of manufacture as soon as the work in hand is so far compleated as to prepare them for Sale, & that the Superintendant be authorized to raise Money on the Goods of the Society by Sale at vendue or otherways as he shall Judge most prudent—and that he be authorized to discharge immediately every person not necessary to carry this resolution into execution" ("Minutes of the S.U.M.," 119). At a subsequent meeting the stockholders voted "that the Superintendant be authorized to advertise the works for renting" ("Minutes of the S.U.M.," 120).

2. Thomas Marshall, an Englishman, had been in charge of the society's cotton mill since 1791. See Marshall to H, July 19, 1791, note 1. At a meeting on April 19, 1796, the directors "Resolved that the Superintendant be authorised to discharge Mr. Thos Marshall from the Service of the Society" ("Minutes of the S.U.M.," 120).

3. In the early seventeen-nineties David Dickson, who was a native of England (and not of the United States, as H states), established a cotton mill in northeastern Manhattan on the East River. His partners were Andrew Stockholm, John R. Livingston, and John Leary, Jr. This enterprise was not a success, and in the winter of 1793–94, Dickson, Livingston, and William McIntosh opened a cotton mill in New Haven, Connecticut. See William R. Bagnall, *The Textile Industries of the United States* (Cambridge, Massachusetts, 1893), I, 184, 188–90.

4. Henry Knox, former Secretary of War.

From Marquis de Fleury [1]

à paris le 28. May 1796.

Dear hamilton,

I hope you have not quitte forgotten an old friend of yours; almost escaped to the misfortunes of our bloody revolution. I have preserved till now my head, but lost the greatest part of my fortune, and my most assured and important propriety is now, what is due to me by the united states.

Till the year 1789 I have touched at paris, by the hands of their banker *grand*² the interests of what was due to me by the united states.³

In the year 1793 governor morris minister of the united states informed the french officers, that those who would not be paid in france, should declare it in writing to the banker grand.⁴ I made that declaration, and mr. grand transmitted it to mr. morris, & wrott at the extract signed *j. nourse* which is in my hands, that I should be paid in america.

Since that time I have run so many dangers of all kinds, that I have not dared take any informations: and I depend now on your friendship, to learn, what I want very much to know about that affair: I hope you will not refuse your usefull services to your distressed friend.

1st. I persist to desire that was is due to me by the united states *remain in america*, and be placed with safety, either in the bank, the Loan office, or otherwise.

2e. I beg you would inquire, if what is due to me, is at the united states threasury, or in the bank, or in the Loan office, and if it is safe, and will be safe for the future.

3e. If since 1789 that I have received none, it produces interets, and what interets?

4e. If it would be possible to apoint either you or some of your honest friends to receive for me those interets in america *in hard money:* and transmit them to me in france by bills of exchange *in hard money*. I mean only the interets, for as to the Capital, I will Let it in america: as I may be obliged some day or other to return there, & should be happy to find something there, to buy a Corner of Land, and Cultivate it to Live quiet if not happy.

as soon as I shall have received those kindly informations of you I shall sent to you, or to the person which you will propose my power, to receive the interets, place the total summ in the bank or Loan office, & send me annualy the interets in france, in *hard money*.

I shall expect your answer with eagerness, as this affair is very important for me. You will be sensible of it.

I have a great deal forgotten my american (I will not tell english) but I hope yet to be understood.

My adress is as follows, being only accidentaly at paris. "au

Citoyen fleury marèchal de Camp retirè par la fertè sur marne à jouar, dèpartement de seine et marne."

Adieu, be happy as much as I desire and you deserve it.[5] fleury

ALS, Hamilton Papers, Library of Congress.

1. François Louis Teisseydre, Marquis de Fleury, who had served in the French army, was a veteran of the American Revolution. He was made a brigade major on the staff of Casimir Pulaski in 1777 after the Battle of Brandywine, and later that year he became a lieutenant colonel of engineers. He fought with Rochambeau at Yorktown in 1781. At the end of the war Fleury went to South America, and in 1784 he returned to France. See Fleury to H, October 15–19, 1777, August 4, 1784.
2. Ferdinand Le Grand, a banker in Paris.
3. On June 17, 1783, Secretary at War Benjamin Lincoln presented the following report, dated June 13, to Congress. "On the representation of Lieutenant Colonel Fleury, referred to the Secretary at War, I beg leave to observe that he was deranged by a resolve of Congress of the 31st December 1781, at which time all officers, who were not of the line of any particular State, nor annexed to any corps were deranged, excepting such as were reported by the Secretary at War as necessary to be retained.

"Although Lieutenant Colonel Fleury was not included in this return, yet, in consideration of his eminent services, which have merited and met the most honorary marks of the approbation of Congress, and on recurring to the furlough granted him by their resolves, which is unlimited, I am induced to recommend to the consideration of Congress the propriety of settling his account of arrears, and allowing him the emoluments of his commission in like manner as if the resolves of December 31, 1781, had not passed." (*JCC*, XXIV, 399–400.) For the resolutions of December 31, 1781, see *JCC*, XXI, 1186–87. For Fleury's unlimited furlough, see *JCC*, XX, 471.

The committee to which the recommendation was referred reported on October 3: "That as Lieut. Col. Fleury retired under the resolution of the 31st December 1781, of course he is entitled to pay till that time and to the half pay or commutation and other emoluments allowed to officers continuing in the service to the end of the war, or deranged by Congress subsequent to the half pay establishment" (*JCC*, XXV, 664).

On April 16, 1784, Congress resolved that the resolutions of January 22 and February 3, 1784, which dealt with pay to foreign officers, be extended to Fleury (*JCC*, XXVI, 239). The resolution of January 22 provided: "That the superintendant of finance [Robert Morris] take order for paying to the foreign officers of the late corps of engineers, and to the foreign officers lately belonging to the legionary corps, commanded by Brigadier-General [Charles Tuffin] Armand, also to Major Seconde [James Segonde], Captain [Louis Joseph de] Beaulieu, late of General Pulaski's corps, and to Captain [Louis de] Ponthiere, late aid to the Baron [Frederick William Augustus] Steuben, such sums on account of their pay as may be necessary to relieve them from their present embarrassment . . ." (*JCC*, XXVI, 43). The resolution of February 3 provided for the annual payment to the foreign officers listed above of "the interest of such sums as may remain due to them respectively, after the payments which shall have been made to them in consequence of the resolution of the 22d of January last" (*JCC*, XXVI, 65–66). The certificates which were issued in accordance with these resolves substituted for the depreciated certificates of 1782, which had been issued to foreign officers for the balance due to them after part of their demands had been paid in cash. See William Short to H,

August 3, 1790, note 5. For the certificates issued to Fleury, see the report of Joseph Nourse, register of the United States Treasury, July 28, 1790, which is part of Schedule B of H's "Report on Additional Sums Necessary for the Support of the Government," August 5, 1790.

In an effort to discharge this debt, Section 5 of "An Act supplementary to the act making provision for the Debt of the United States" provided: ". . . whereas the United States are indebted to certain foreign officers, on account of pay and services during the late war, the interest whereof, pursuant to the certificates granted to the said officers by virtue of a resolution of the United States in Congress assembled, is payable at the house of   Grand, banker at Paris, and it is expedient to discharge the same. *Be it therefore enacted*, That the President of the United States be, and he hereby is authorized to cause to be discharged the principal and interest of the said debt, out of any of the monies, which have been or shall be obtained on loan, in virtue of the act aforesaid, and which shall not be necessary ultimately to fulfil the purposes for which the said monies are, in and by the said act, authorized to be borrowed" (1 *Stat.* 282 [May 8, 1792]).

4. For H's instructions to Gouverneur Morris, see H to Morris, September 13, 1792.

5. H referred this letter to Secretary of the Treasury Oliver Wolcott, Jr. See Wolcott to H, September 1, 1796. On the cover of the letter printed above H wrote: "answered by General Pinckny."

Fleury wrote a similar letter to Timothy Pickering on May 25, 1795 (ALS, Massachusetts Historical Society, Boston). For copies in Fleury's handwriting of the documents sent in support of his claim, see the enclosures to Fleury to Pickering, June 1, 1796 (ALS, Massachusetts Historical Society, Boston). See also Fleury to Pickering, February 21, 1797 (ALS, Massachusetts Historical Society, Boston), and its enclosures.

From George Washington

[*Philadelphia, May 29, 1796.* On June 1, 1796, Hamilton wrote to Washington and acknowledged "Your letter of the 29th." *Letter not found.*]

To Oliver Wolcott, Junior

[New York, May 30, 1796]

Dr. Sir

I perceive Congress are invading the Sinking Fund system.[1] If this goes through & is sanctionned by the President the fabric of public Credit is prostrate & the Country & the President are disgraced. Treasury Bills & every expedient however costly to meet exigencies must be preferable in the event to such an overthrow of system.

Yrs truly					A Hamilton

May 30. 1796

ALS, Connecticut Historical Society, Hartford; copy, Hamilton Papers Library of Congress.
  1. "An Act making provision for the payment of certain Debts of the United States" provided "That it shall be lawful for the commissioners of the sinking fund, with the approbation of the President of the United States, to borrow, or cause to be borrowed, on the credit of the United States, any sum not exceeding five millions of dollars, to be applied to the payment of the capital, or principal of any parts of the debt of the United States now due, or to become due, during the course of the present year, to the bank of the United States, or to the bank of New York, or for any instalment of foreign debt; And that, for the whole, or such part of the said sum, as shall be borrowed, certificates shall be issued, purporting that the United States are indebted for the sums to be therein expressed, bearing an interest of six per centum per annum, payable quarter yearly; which sums, at the said rate of interest, are to remain fixed and irredeemable, until the close of the year one thousand eight hundred and nineteen, and to be redeemed thereafter, at the pleasure of the United States: And the Bank of the United States is hereby authorized to lend the whole, or any part, of the said five millions of dollars, and to sell the stock received for such loan. . . .
  "And it shall be lawful for the commissioners of the sinking fund, if they shall find the same to be most advantageous, to sell such and so many of the shares of the stock of the bank of the United States, belonging to the United States, as they may think proper; and that they apply the proceeds thereof to the payment of the said debts, instead of selling certificates of stock, in the manner prescribed in this act. . . ." (1 *Stat.* 488–89 [May 31, 1796].)
  For the debates on this bill in the Senate on May 17, 1796, and in the House on May 23, 24, and 28, 1796, see *Annals of Congress,* V, 95–96, 1430–50, 1466–72.

From Tench Coxe [1]

Philad. May 31. 1796

Sir

Mr. Whelen & I do not understand that he had made a proposition to you to let Mr. Church take back what remains in their Hands of Mr. Church's original interest in the lands sold him & Company. You will find on a revision of my Letter of the 17th. inst.[2] that it does not convey that Idea and you will perceive on reflection that it could not. The matter stood thus. When you were here at the supreme

Court[3] Mr. Whelen informed you I had made a proposition to take to a certain amount, being an undivided sixth or a sixth by lot of the whole lands, as well of those they bought of Patterson, as of those bought of me & Mr. Church & he offered that if I would take a third (instead of a sixth) they would agree to it & ⟨tend⟩ the matter. Mr. Church would then have to receive his balance on the Accot. I told you that I feared that it might not suit me to buy so largely as my Engagements stood, but I would think of it. On reflexion I called upon Mr. Whelen & told him I would buy of them that undivided third part, which was of their whole 88 tracts as above. I could not expect Mr. Church to be concerned in this purchase, without he should give his assent because, besides the lands he & I owned together, and five lots more of the same parcel, which I owned long before Wheelen & Miller's application, there would be many others, which had never belonged to him or me, but were all those sold by Mr. Patterson. I hear Nothing from them in reply to my offer, but I mean to call as soon as Congress rises, and if I can, will finish the Business. No endeavour of mine has ever been wanting. I then offered you the whole balance that would be due if Wheelen & Co had paid, to be taken out of another parcel of lands Mr Church & I had taken up together in 1793 at 2¼ acres for one. Calling Whelen & Co's as cash $1\tfrac{1}{10}$—the lands I would give would be about ⅝, tho the two parcels cost ℔ acre just the same.

I am, sir,   yr obedient Servant   T.C.

Alexander Hamilton Esqr.
Atty of J. B. Church Esq

ADfS, Tench Coxe Papers, Historical Society of Pennsylvania, Philadelphia.
  1. For an explanation of the contents of this letter, see the introductory note to Coxe to H, February 13, 1795. See also Coxe to H, February 17–18, 22, May 10, August 4, 1795; H to Joseph Anthony, March 11, 1795; Anthony to H, May 16, 1795.
  2. Letter not found.
  3. H argued for the Government before the Supreme Court of the United States on February 24, 1796, in the Carriage Tax case (*Hylton* v *United States*). For information on the Carriage Tax case, see 3 Dallas, *U.S. Reports*, 171, and the forthcoming Goebel, *Law Practice*, III. See also Coxe to H, January 14, 19, 1795; H to Coxe, January 26, 28, 1795; William Bradford to H, July 2, August 4, 1795; Edmund Randolph to H, July 21, 1795; Oliver Wolcott, Jr., to H, July 28, 1795, January 15, 1796; H to Wolcott, August 5, 1795; Robert Morris to H, February 10, 1796.

From Robert Morris [1]

Alexander Hamilton Esqre Philada May 31. 1796
New York

Dear Sir

I am sorry that the Omission & inaccuracy of description in the Mortgage Deed [2] as expressed in your letter of the 26 Inst.[3] should have occasioned you any farther Trouble in Mr Churchs Business.[4] The Omission of the name was owing to that Tract not having been conveyed to the parties for whom it was intended by Colo Ogden, who made an Agreement short of my terms the Object being to discharge thereby Colo Smiths Mortgage but as Colo Walker will not discharge the Mortgage I will not agree to the Bargain of Mr. Ogden as it was not consanant to my Orders either as to price or terms of Payment. I have therefore conveyed the Tract to Mr Garrett Cottringer whose name is now inserted in the new Mortgage executed by me, and as I want no other depositary than yourself I will send both Mortgages by the Young Gentn. you have sent hither.[5] It may be well however to have a line from you declaratory that the two are for the same purpose & that the Payment of the Bond will discharge both. Accept my thanks for the friendly terms of your last letter and be assured of my constant regard.

Yrs. RM

P.S. Suppose you were to make up a Company to purchase the 50,000 acres conveyed to Mr Cottringer, give me two Dollars ⅌ acre, discharge Colo Smith's mortgage which is for 50,000 Dolls Six ⅌ Cent stock and pay me the bal.? You will get four Dolls an acre in about 12 Mos. and Colo Walker will give longer credit than that I suppose, or I will sell at 2 Dolls ⅌ acre as much as will discharge that Mortgage altho my Son Tom [6] writes that Lands are risen so much that he advises me not to sell.

LC, Robert Morris Papers, Library of Congress.
1. This letter concerns two separate mortgages which Morris hoped would secure the payment of two separate debts. One of these mortgages was for

one hundred thousand acres in the Morris Reserve to H to secure payment of Morris's debt to John B. Church. The other was a mortgage of the entire Morris Reserve to William S. Smith—and then to Benjamin Walker—to secure the payment of Morris's debt to William Pulteney and William Hornby.

For the history of the mortgage to H and the debt to Church, see the introductory note to Morris to H, June 7, 1795. See also Morris to H, July 20, November 16, December 18, 1795, January 15, March 6, 12, 14, 30, April 27, May 3, 10, 17, 18, 1796; William Lewis to H, May 4, 1796; H to Charles Williamson, May 17–30, 1796.

For the mortgage to Smith and Walker and the debt to Pulteney and Hornby, as well as the relationship between this mortgage and debt to the mortgage to H and the debt to Church, see the introductory note to Morris to H, April 27, 1796. See also Morris to H, May 3, 10, 1796; H to Charles Williamson, May 17–30, 1796.

2. This is a reference to the mortgage of one hundred thousand acres to H. See note 1.

3. Letter not found.

4. For an explanation of the remainder of this letter, see the introductory note to Morris to H, April 27, 1796.

5. The following entry appears in H's Cash book, 1795–1804, for June 2, 1796: "Account of Expences—Dr. to Cash   John B. Church for expence of Clk sent to Philadelphia for Mortgage R. Morris [$]27" (AD, Hamilton Papers, Library of Congress).

6. Thomas Morris served as his father's agent in the Genesee country.

Design for a Seal for the United States

[May, 1796] [1]

A Globe with Europe and part of Africa on one side—America on the other—the Atlantic Ocean between. The portion occupied by America to be larger than that occupied by Europe. A COLOSSUS to be placed on this Globe, with one foot on Europe, the other extending partly over the Atlantic towards America, having on his head a *quintuple* crown in his right hand an *Iron*-Sceptre projected but broken in the middle—in his left hand a *Pileus* *[2] reversed, the staff intwined by a snake with its head downward having the staff in its mouth and folding in its tail (as if in the act of strangling) a label with these words "Rights of Man."

Upon a base, supported by fifteen columns, erected on the Continent of America, to be placed the *Genius* of America, represented by *Pallas*—a female figure with a firm composed countenance, in an attitude of defiance, cloathed in armour with a golden breast plate, a spear in her right hand and an *Ægis* or shield in her left, decorated with the scales of Justice instead of the Medusa's head—her helmet incircled with wreaths of Olive—her spear striking upon the Sceptre of the Colussus and breaking it obliquely over her head a radiated Crown or *Glory*.[3]

EXPLANATION

The Globe is an antient symbol of universal Dominion. This, with the Colossus alluding to the Directory, will denote the project of acquiring it—the position of one leg of the colussus will signify the *attempt* to extend it to America. The Columns will represent the American States. Pallas, as the Genius of America will denote, that though loving Peace (of which the Olive wreath is the emblem) yet guided by *Wisdom,* or an enlightened sense of her own rights and interests, she is determined to exert and does successfully exert her *valour,* in breaking the sceptre of the Tyrant. The *Glory* is the usual type of Providential interposition.

It would improve it if it did not render it too complicated to represent the Ocean in Tempest & Neptune striking with his Trident the projected leg of the Colussus.

But perhaps instead of all this it may suffice to have the figure of Pallas on horse back the harp placed on the Columns these on a small mount—her spear breaking a Sceptre projected by a *Herculean Arm.*

AD, American Antiquarian Society, Worcester, Massachusetts; ADf, Hamilton Papers, Library of Congress.

1. In *JCHW*, VII, 685, this document is dated "1799." Its contents, however, indicate that it was probably written at some time in 1796. Because H refers to fifteen states and Tennessee was admitted to the Union as the sixteenth state on June 1, 1796, it could not have been written after that date. In addition, H mentions the Directory, which was established on November 3, 1795, and "the *attempt* to extend it to America." This is apparently a reference to the receipt in early May, 1796, by the Administration of Gouverneur Morris's report that France planned to invade the United States. See George Washington to H, May 8, 1796. When these bits of information are combined, it is difficult to escape the conclusion that H wrote this document in May, 1796.
2. In the margin H wrote: "*Cap of Liberty."
3. In the margin opposite this paragraph H wrote: "Usual Insignia of Minerva on Pallas."

To James Watson

[New York, May, 1796]

Dr Sir

The handsome general retainer you have offered me & the handsome manner in which the Offer is made claim my acknowlegement.[1] But it will not consist with any rule of Action to avail myself of it. I have in other instances engaged for Individuals on these terms, to take as a retainer 100 £ and afterwards to charge services performed at the established rates. Though it was my intention to avoid this in future, yet if you desire it, I will add you to the list. But it must except the priorities already incurred which are of William Constable Alexander Macombe LeRoy Bayard & McEvers Williamson of Genesee.[2]

Yrs with esteem & regard   A Hamilton

P.S To prove to you however that I am not unmindful of my own interest I send you the following account

To opinion concerning arbitration Bond	Ds	5
To services in negotiating & settling your business with William Constable [3]		100
	Cr	105
March 3 By Cash		50
Ballance due AH		55

The first 50 dollars I consider as a Retainer & for my opinion given at the time.[4]

James Watson Esqr.

ALS, from a typescript supplied by an anonymous donor.

1. See Watson to H, May 27, 1796.
2. For the retainers paid to H by the individuals mentioned in this sentence, see H to Robert Troup, July 25, 1795, notes 24, 25, and 26.
3. See Watson to H, April 20, 1795, note 1.
4. An entry in H's Cash Book, 1795–1804, for June 10, 1796, reads: "Cash Dr. to James Watson

for this sum received of him for Retainer	250—
for this sum received of him for ballance of Account	55
	305"

(AD, Hamilton Papers, Library of Congress).

To Oliver Wolcott, Junior

[*New York, May–August, 1796.*] "I have been applied to for an opinion concerning the Georgia Claim. . . .[1] I will thank you for the Report of the Attorney General [2] on that subject, to Congress. . . ." [3]

Copy, Connecticut Historical Society, Hartford.

1. This is a reference to the claims of the Georgia Yazoo land companies which were organized in 1795. For information on these land grants and their revocation, see H to James Greenleaf, October 9, 1795, note 3. For information on the Yazoo land companies which were organized in 1789, see H's "Defence of the Funding System," July, 1795, note 24.

Robert G. Harper, a Federalist Congressman from South Carolina and a subscriber to the Georgia Mississippi Company, was preparing a pamphlet on the Georgia sales and had requested H's opinion (see H's endorsement on Harper's undated list of questions [AD, Hamilton Papers, Library of Congress]; for this document, see also forthcoming Goebel, *Law Practice* III). No evidence has been found that H responded to Harper's questions. In the appendix to his pamphlet, first published in 1797, however, Harper printed H's opinion on the Georgia grants, dated March 25, 1796, which H had prepared for William Constable (see Harper, *The Case of the Georgia Sales on the Mississippi Considered with a reference to Law Authorities And Public Acts; with an Appendix containing certain Extracts, Records And Official Papers* [Philadelphia: Printed by Richard Folwell, 1799], 88–89). Constable was involved in the Georgia grants as a subscriber to a new company, the Yazoo Company, and as a guarantor of Nathaniel Prime's sale of Georgia lands to Samuel Sewall, Samuel Dexter, and George Lane, all of Massachusetts (see H's opinion, March 25, 1796 [ADf, Hamilton Papers, Library of Congress]; for this document, see also forthcoming Goebel, *Law Practice*, III). Constable and Prime were New York City merchants. An entry in H's Cash Book, 1795–1804, under the date of March 17, 1796, reads: "for this sum recd—of Wm Constable on account of Retainer 150" (AD, Hamilton Papers, Library of Congress). For a discussion of the Georgia land sales along with relevant documents, see forthcoming Goebel, *Law Practice*, III.

2. Attorney General Charles Lee's report, dated April 26–28, 1796, with appended documents, was communicated to the Senate on April 29, 1796 (*ASP, Public Lands*, I, 34–67). On May 20, 1796, the Senate committee to which Lee's report was referred presented its report, and the Senate ordered that Lee's report be printed (*Annals of Congress*, V, 100–01). John Fenno printed the report, which was first advertised in his newspaper, the *Gazette of the United States, & Philadelphia Daily Advertiser*, on May 28, 1796.

3. The following note is written at the bottom of this letter in an unknown handwriting: "original Sent to Metropolitan Fair, March 1864." New York City's Metropolitan Fair was held in April, 1864, to raise money for the United

States Sanitary Commission. Laura Wolcott Gibbs, the daughter of Oliver Wolcott, Jr., was in charge of the Curiosity Shop at the fair (*The New-York Times*, April 4, 1864).

To James McHenry

New York June 1. 1796

My Dear Mc.

I am told the Executive Directory have complained of Mr. *Parish* our Consul at Hamburgh.[1] Perhaps the complaint may be ill founded but perhaps also he was indiscreet in giving colour for it. Admit too that he is a good man. Yet we must not quarrel with France for *pins* and *needles*. The public temper would not bear any umbrage taken where a trifling concession might have averted it. Tis a case for temporising, reserving our firmness for *great and necessary* occasions. Let Mr. Paris[h] be superseded, with a kind letter to him. I do not write to *Pickering* or the *President* because I am not regularly possessed of the information. But I hope you will attend to the matter, even if at the expense of being a little officious.

Yrs. truly   A Hamilton

James Mc.Henry Esq

ALS, The Huntington Library, San Marino, California; copy, Hamilton Papers, Library of Congress.

1. John Parish, an English merchant, was appointed United States vice consul at Hamburg on June 8, 1790, and consul at the same city on February 20, 1793 (*Executive Journal*, I, 49, 50, 130, 131). On July 6, 1795, James Monroe wrote to Timothy Pickering that Parish was reportedly "unfriendly to America; . . . absolutely unfriendly to France and the French Revolution . . . [and] an agent of England . . ." (*ASP, Foreign Relations*, I, 718). On December 22, 1795, Monroe wrote to Pickering that the French government had asserted that Parish was "granting passports for France to British subjects, equipping the emigrants, and acting in all cases as the English agent" and that "he not only equipped the emigrants, but did it in American bottoms, with a view of protecting them under our flag" (*ASP, Foreign Relations*, I, 728).

On May 31, 1796, Pierre Auguste Adet, the French Minister to the United States, transmitted to Pickering a request of the Directory that Parish be removed as consul at Hamburg. Adet's letter reads: "The executive directory has just sent me the order to demand formally of the government of the United States, the recall of Mr. Parish, the American consul at Hamburgh. I hasten to fulfill its intentions, and to state the motives on which the demand of my government is grounded. I think this cannot be done in a better manner, than by transmitting to you an extract of the dispatch which I have received on that subject.

"'The executive directory is informed, that Mr. Parish is not only the avowed agent of England for the fitting out of the French emigrants; but that in his quality of American consul he gives passports for France to Englishmen, under the title of Anglo-Americans. A conduct so reprehensible must needs excite the indignation of both governments. It is the extreme of perfidy; since, under the seal of an alliance we cherish, it accredits among us the spies of England.

"'The French Republic at war with an enemy, more to be dreaded because of his intrigues, than redoubtable by his arms, has in vain taken every precaution which a legitimate defence commands. The agents of the cabinet of St. James introduce themselves on our territory, sow there the seeds of disturbance and sedition; and the consul of a friendly power does not blush to abuse his character in order to favor Englishmen in France, by rendering himself guilty of the crime of forgery.'

"I shall not allow myself the liberty of adding a single reflection to that extract; It would be to insult the government of the United States, if I were to say more on that subject, in order to induce it to avenge that infringement upon the faith of treaties, that violation of the guarantee of nations." (Monroe, *A View of the Conduct of the Executive*, 367-38.)

On June 2, 1796, Pickering replied to Adet: "I have now Sir, the honor to inform you, that in consequence of a letter from Mr. Monroe, received the last autumn, suggesting some complaints against Mr. Parish, an inquiry was directed to be made, in order to ascertain how far they were founded, and whether any really exceptionable conduct of his required a change in the consulate at Hamburg. The information expected from the proposed inquiry has not been received. But some facts have otherwise become known, which altho' they do not impeach the integrity of Mr. Parish, or derogate from his mercantile reputation, yet in an *officer* of the United States, they deserve to be noticed.

"Mr. Parish is not, nor ever was a citizen of the United States. He is a foreign merchant, of great eminence, established at Hamburg. He had been particularly friendly to the United States, especially at the commencement of their Revolution. . . . The United States could not expect that a man of such extended correspondence in trade would confine his agency to the affairs of the United States alone. . . .

"*As a merchant*, then, Mr. Parish would naturally consider himself at liberty to transact, for any body, any business of the kind usually intrusted to the management of a merchant. And hence we may account for his agency for Great Britain, as mentioned in your letter. But the other information given to the Directory, that Mr. Parish, as an American Consul, gives passports to *Englishmen*, under the title of Anglo-Americans, *for the purpose of introducing into the French Territory, emissaries of the British Court*, imports a crime of so deep a die, as may well justify an opinion that the persons who gave the information were in an error. . . . Desirous, however, of maintaining a course of action as impartial as his principles, the President has for some time contemplated a change in the Consulate at Hamburg, and proposes to supply the place of a foreigner by an American citizen. This change will be made as soon as a fit character shall present to succeed Mr. Parish." (Copy, Massachusetts Historical Society, Boston.)

On June 2, 1796, Pickering wrote to Parish informing him of his dismissal and stating: ". . . The President will endeavor to fill the place with an American citizen" (LC, RG 59, Domestic Letters of the Department of State, Vol. 9, October 12, 1795-February 28, 1797, National Archives). On July 18, 1796, Pickering wrote to George Washington recommending his nephew, Samuel

Williams, of Salem, Massachusetts, as Parish's replacement (ALS, RG 59, Miscellaneous Letters, 1790–1799, National Archives). On December 21, 1796, Washington nominated Williams to the post at Hamburg, and the Senate confirmed the nomination the following day (*Executive Journal*, I, 217).

To George Washington

New York June 1. 1796

Sir

Your letter of the 29th [1] was delivered me by Mr. King [2] yesterday afternoon. I thought I had acknowleged the Receipt of the paper inquired for [3] in a letter written speedily after it—or in one which transmitted you a draft of a *certain letter* by Mr. Jay.[4] I hope this came to hand.

I am almost afraid to appear officious in what I am going to say; but the matter presses so deeply on my mind that fearing you may not recollect the situation of the thing and that it may happen not to be brought fully under your eye, I cannot refrain from making the suggestion to you. It regards a Bill which I am told has lately passed the two houses of Congress authorising a sale of *Bank Stock* for paying off a sum due to the Bank.[5] You will perceive by the 8th. and 9th Sections of the Act intitled "An Act making further provision for the support of public Credit and for the Redemption of the public Debt" passed the 3d. of March 1795 [6] that the dividends of the Bank Stock are appropriated to the Sinking Fund with all the force and solemnity of which language is capable and that to divert them in the manner proposed (and this too without any substitute in the act which so diverts) will be a formal express and unequivocal violation of the public faith—will subvert the system of the Sinking Fund and with it all the security which is meant to be given to the people for the Redemption of the Public Debt, and, violating the sanctity of an appropriation for the public Debt, will overturn at once the foundation of Public Credit. These are obvious and undeniable consequences, and though I am aware that great embarrassments may ensue to the Treasury, if the Bill by the objection of The President is lost and no substitute for it takes place towards the reimbursement of the Bank—Yet I am sure no consequences can ensue of equal moment from the rejection as from the principle of the Bill going into execution. All the Presidents administration has effected for establishing the Credit of the Country will be prostrate at a single blow. He will readily make all the necessary comments upon this position. It grieves my heart to see so much shocking levity in our Representative Body.

Most respectfully & Affecty I remain   Sir Yr very obed Ser

A Hamilton

The President of the U States

ALS, George Washington Papers, Library of Congress; copy, Hamilton Papers, Library of Congress.
  1. Letter not found.
  2. Rufus King.
  3. The "paper inquired for" was Washington's first draft of a farewell address (ADfS, from the original in the New York State Library, Albany; printed in Paltsits, *Farewell Address*, 164–73). See H to Washington, May 10, 1796; Washington to H, May 15, 1796.
  4. The draft by John Jay has not been found, but see H to Washington, May 20, 1796.
  5. See H to Oliver Wolcott, Jr., May 30, 1796, note 1.
  6. 1 *Stat.* 433–38.

From Charles Cotesworth Pinckney [1]

Charleston [South Carolina] June 5th: 1796

Dear Sr:

I beg leave to recommend to your attention the Bearer of this Letter Mr: Benjamin Huger,[2] a Gentleman of family & fortune in this State; he is the Son of Major Huger [3] who unfortunately fell at the lines of Charleston in 1779, & the Eldest Brother of the Mr: Huger [4] who was imprisoned by the Austrians for attempting the rescue of the brave Marquis la Fayette. He intends to travel with his Lady this Summer through the Middle & Eastern States and if he visits New York, I will be obliged to you for your attentions to them. I wrote to you the 3d: of last March [5] on Mr: Church's [6] affairs & enclosed to you a Bill for two thousand seven hundred & seventy dollars drawn by Jno: Price & Co of this City on Comfort Sands Esqr: of New York [7] in favour of Mr. George Lockey [8] & indorsed by him to you.[9] Be so good as to inform me whether it has been honoured. Mrs: Pinckney joins me in best respects to Mrs: Hamilton, & I remain with great regard & esteem

 Yrs truly   Charles Cotesworth Pinckney

Honble
Coll: Hamilton.

ALS, Hamilton Papers, Library of Congress.
 1. Pickney was practicing law in Charleston at this time.
 2. Huger, a wealthy rice planter, was elected to Congress in 1798 and served in the House of Representatives from March, 1799, to March, 1805.
 3. Major Benjamin Huger.
 4. Francis Kinloch Huger. See H to George Washington, January 19, 1796.
 5. Letter not found.
 6. John B. Church.
 7. Among other business activities, Sands engaged extensively in foreign trade. He was president of the New York City Chamber of Commerce from 1794 to 1798.
 8. Lockey was a British merchant.
 9. On March 28, 1796, H made the following entry in his Cash Book, 1795–1804: "To J B Church for this sum being the amount of a Bill on Comfort Sands accepted by him payable in 60 days & discounted at the Bank on account of Kinloch's bond 2770" (AD, Hamilton Papers, Library of Congress). "Kinloch's bond" had been delivered to Church by the executors of Francis Kinloch of South Carolina for a debt contracted during the American Revolution (Cleland Kinloch to H, September 20, 1785, and Church to H, April 5, 1786). Francis Kinloch was the father of Cleland, Francis, and Mary Kinloch and the grandfather of Francis Kinloch Huger.
 In "John B. Church's Account with Alexander Hamilton," June 15, 1797, is the following entry: "1796 October 11 By this sum received on account of Kinlock's Bond 340.4.6."

From Lawrence Kercado [1]

Philadelphia, June 6, 1796. States that he is the Vicomte de Kercado, a cadet member of the princely family of Rohon in Brittany, that he had lived in Santo Domingo, that he had come to Charleston, South Carolina, in 1791, and that he and his family are now living at Elizabeth, New Jersey. States that he has given orders for his property in Santo Domingo to be sold and that he wishes to go there to settle his affairs. Asks Hamilton to urge President Washington to grant him a Government commission which would assure him a safe passage to and from Santo Domingo and suggests that he be named agent for obtaining the release of American sailors imprisoned by the British.

ALS, Hamilton Papers, Library of Congress.
  1. This letter is written in French.

From Abraham Van Vechten [1]

[*Albany*] *June 6, 1796.* "The Cause of Guernsey [2] will not be tried until October Term. . . . It is to him a Cause of the greatest importance. His all is at Stake, and he is both able & willing to pay liberally for the Services of his Council."

ALS, Hamilton Papers, Library of Congress.
  1. Van Vechten was an Albany lawyer and Federalist politician. In 1796 Governor John Jay appointed him attorney for the Fifth District of New York.
  2. This is a reference to *James Jackson ex dem. William H. Ludlow and Mary, his wife* v *Nathan Guernsey,* a case in the New York Supreme Court concerning the title to lands in Saratoga County, New York. The hearing on the case was postponed from the August to the October, 1796, term. On October 20, 1796, the jury found for the defendant (MS Minutes of the New York Supreme Court, January 10–November 5, 1796 [Hall of Records, New York City]). The following entry appears in H's Cash Book, 1795–1804, for October 15, 1796: "this sum received of Nathan Garnsey for trying his cause 200—" (AD, Hamilton Papers, Library of Congress). See also H's Cash Book, 1795–1804, under the date of October 20, 1798. The plaintiff appealed the decision, and on October 27, 1802, the jury again decided in favor of Guernsey (MS Minutes of the New York Supreme Court, October 19–30, 1802 [Court of Appeals, Albany]).

From Jonathan Williams [1]

Philadelphia, June 8, 1796. "I thank you for your friendly offer [2] and, in conformity, request you to let me know what proposals Mr Macomb [3] is willing to make. My Demand is $17530 Dollars, being the difference arising on the unperformed Contract made with me by Mr. Duer on the Companys acct. agreeably to the terms of the partnership. I bought the $50000 six ⅌ Cents and paid for them in specie $63250. Dollars. The stock was tendered and the tender duely acknowledged on the Day the Contract became due. At that time the stock would not sell for its nominal amount, so that I am a real sufferer in the sum of $13250. . . ." 4

ALS, Hamilton Papers, Library of Congress.
1. Williams, a native of Boston and a great-nephew of Benjamin Franklin, had been prize agent and commercial agent for Congress at Nantes during the American Revolution. After the war he returned to the United States, settled in Philadelphia, and became an investor in various stock and land operations. In 1796 he was appointed associate judge of the Court of Common Pleas in Philadelphia.
2. H had been in Philadelphia from June 2 to June 8, 1796. An entry in his Cash Book, 1795–1804, for June 2, 1796, reads: ". . . June 9 for my expenses to Philadelphia 34" (AD, Hamilton Papers, Library of Congress).
3. Alexander Macomb, a native of Ireland, had engaged in trade with the Indians in the American West during the American Revolution and was a partner with his brother William and William Edgar in the Detroit firm of Macomb, Edgar, and Macomb, which supplied the British Indian department. After the Revolution he settled in New York where he became a wealthy businessman and speculator. In December, 1791, he formed a partnership for speculation in public securities with William Duer; both partners went to jail in 1792.
In the April, 1797, term of the United States Circuit Court for the District of New York Williams prosecuted Macomb and Duer. Williams's declaration stated that on January 16, 1792, he and Duer had signed agreements that Williams would deliver to Duer by April 15, 1792, fifty thousand dollars of United States stock at six percent, in exchange for a cash payment of "twenty seven shillings in the pound" by the same date. Duer and Macomb, however, refused to buy the stock, and Williams claimed damages of twenty thousand dollars (RG 21, Records of the United States Circuit Court for New York, National Archives [filed May 8, 1798]).
For the details of Williams's stock transactions with Duer and Macomb, see Clement Biddle's Account Books, 1790–1799, in the Columbia University Libraries.
4. An entry in H's Cash Book, 1795–1804, for February 9, 1797, reads: "Alexander McComb for opinion & retainer in the case of Jo Williams 15" (AD, Hamilton Papers, Library of Congress).

To Robert Morris

[*New York, June 9, 1796.* On the June 17, 1796, Morris wrote to Hamilton and referred to "your favor of the 9th." *Letter not found.*]

To Oliver Wolcott, Junior

New York June 9. 1796

Dr. Sir

I called at your house the morning of my departure [1] but you was not then up. While I was in the City we had a little conversation concerning an affair of an arrangement with *Swan* for effecting a remittance to Holland.[2] I intended to have resumed it for two reasons, one because it has been represented to the disadvantage of the Conduct of the Treasury, another because *Swan* who lodged at the same house with me begged me to converse with you on the subject and give my opinion both to you & him of what I thought of the matter. The latter I should of course have managed with due regard to all prudential considerations.

But I wished chiefly to apprise you that it is industriously circulated that Monroe [3] & Skipwith,[4] *as Agents for the Treasury* received Swan's money at Paris to remit to Holland, that they mismanaged the fund, produced besides delay, loss—and that the Treasury now endeavours to turn the loss on Swan.[5] If you have not been apprized of this it is requisite you should be.

Yrs. truly

A Hamilton

ALS, Connecticut Historical Society, Hartford.

1. H had been in Philadelphia between June 2 and June 8, 1796. See Jonathan Williams to H, June 8, 1796, note 2.
2. James Swan. See Wolcott to H, June 18, 1795, notes 6 and 7.
3. James Monroe, United States Minister Plenipotentiary to France. See Wolcott to H, July 10, 1795, note 9.
4. Fulwar Skipwith, United States consul general in France.
5. On December 14, 1795, in an attempt to pay off the current interest owing on the Dutch debt, Monroe applied to the French Minister of Finance, Guillaume Charles Faipoult de Maisoncelle, for permission to export one hundred and twenty thousand dollars in specie to Holland. A week later Faipoult refused Monroe's request (Faipoult to Monroe, December 21, 1795 [ALS, MS Division, New York Public Library]). Monroe then tried to find some other way to send the money. In a letter to Monroe, dated December 24, 1795, the Dutch bankers Willink, Van Staphorst, and Hubbard rejected a proposal by Monroe that the firm should draw on him for the equivalent of the amount owed, "no persons having at present to remit monies to France, at least for any sums of consequence. . . ." They then suggested that Monroe deposit Swan's money with the French treasury in exchange for bills on the government of

the Netherlands (LS, MS Division, New York Public Library). Monroe rejected this proposal and instead approached French bankers. One of them, Jean Frédéric Perregaux, refused to co-operate (Perregaux to Monroe, February 7, 1796 [ALS, MS Division, New York Public Library]), but three days later a letter from Jacob Van Staphorst approved "the proposal of Mess. Corsange and Co. . . , provided the Bills are not upon too long terms, which would occasion so much longer advances from the Bankers in Amsterdam and of consequence a loss of Interest for the United States" (ALS, MS Division, New York Public Library). It is not clear whether Monroe eventually transferred the money to Holland by means of Corsange, but he did complete the transaction before he received his letter of recall in November (Monroe to James Madison, January 8, 1797 [Hamilton, *James Monroe*, III, 63]), for Swan presented his account at the Treasury in January, 1797. See Wolcott to H, June 18, 1795, note 7.

Monroe tried to dispel the rumors mentioned in the letter printed above in the following letter to George Clinton, dated July 25, 1796: "I have just heard that some benevolent minded people in Philadelphia have circulated a report that I am engaged in speculations in this country in land &c. with Mr. Skipwith: and that I omitted to forward or neglected the remittance hence of a sum of money committed to me by draft of Swan upon the H. of Dallardt & Swan here to be remitted to Holland to our bankers. I enclose you the affadavit of Mr. Skipwith to disprove the first calumny, & the correspondence with this govt, our bankers in Holland &c to disprove the 2d" (Hamilton, *James Monroe*, III, 36). On December 25, 1797, Monroe wrote to Thomas Jefferson: "I had no other money entrusted to me for foreign officers: nor for any other purpose except a remittance of 120.000 dollars by a draft of Swan upon his house in favor of the Secretary of the Treasury to be remitted to our bankers in Holland. Upon this latter point an attempt was made to injure me in my absence, but abandoned when it was found that I could not be assailed. Still some injury was perhaps done me in the beginning in whispers. It therefore merits attention whether I ought not to take the subject up openly & pursue Mr. Wolcott, either to an explicit disavowal of calumnies, or to a conviction of being guilty of them, as I have the most ample proof of the rectitude & propriety of my own conduct in that respect. This is for your opinion" (Hamilton, *James Monroe*, III, 89).

From Oliver Wolcott, Junior

Phila. June 14th. 1796

Dear Sir

I am oblidged to you for the intimation in your Letter of the 9th. instant. I have known for some time that Mr. Swan has misrepresented my conduct—he knows that I have more than fullfilled my Contract, that it was an express agreement, that the risque & expence of transmitting the money from Paris to Amsterdam should be borne by him—that Mr. Monroe was a *mutual* Agent, not the Agent of the Treasury—that we neither of us intended that Mr. Skipwith should meddle with the business—& that the opinion of the Attorney General is against throwing the loss upon the United States.

It is true that there has been great mismanagement & delay & some loss, but it is not my fault, nor am I responsible for it. I am now paying as fast as the Treasury will admit, though nothing can yet be demanded according to Contract.

The plan of the French & our Patriots begins to develope, the history of the Captives of the Mount Vernon,[1] & the apology or rather hypothesis offered in Mr Baches paper[2] of this morning are important facts when taken in connection with what we before knew. If more seizures shall be made, or if Mr. Adet shall not give a satisfactory explanation, I do not see but that Mr. M *must* be recalled & a special confidential Minister sent. A short time will enable us to judge. I shall be glad to know your opinion of what is to be done—if a Minister is sent, who should it be?

Mr. Dawson[3] a confidential Clerk will be in New York a few days hence, to endeavour to ascertain whether or not Mr. Duer retains certain papers respecting the seven ranges of townships.[4] I will thank you to give him such advice as may be proper.

I am ever yrs   Oliver Wolcott

A. Hamilton Esq

ALS, Connecticut Historical Society, Hartford; LC, Connecticut Historical Society, Hartford.

1. On June 13, 1796, Timothy Pickering wrote to Pierre Auguste Adet, French Minister to the United States: "The merchants of Philadelphia are extremely alarmed by the conduct of a small Privateer called the Flying Fish, bearing, it is understood, a Commission from the French republic. It is said that she has been lying in this port for some time, preparing for sea: and it seems that after inquiring and observing that valuable vessels were to sail for foreign ports, she sailed herself to the Capes of the Delaware, and not far from thence lay in wait for the vessels she had marked for her prey. Accordingly, on the 9th instant, she seized on the Ship Mount Vernon, belonging to Mr. [Thomas] Murgatroyd, a merchant of Philadelphia, within two hours after the pilot had left her, and within about six leagues of Cape Henlopen, took possession of all her papers, and forced the master, mate, and all her crew, save two men to leave her, and, under these circumstances, she was sent they know not whither!" (LC, RG 59, Domestic Letters of the Department of State, Vol. 9, October 12, 1795–February 28, 1797, National Archives). For the protest of Captain George Dominick of the *Mount Vernon,* see Debrett, *A Collection of State Papers,* V, 240–42.

2. Wolcott is referring to the following letter from "A Citizen," which was published in Benjamin Franklin Bache's [Philadelphia] *Aurora. General Advertiser* on June 14, 1796: "The late capture of the ship MOUNT VERNON by the

French Privateer FLYING FISH, has excited just alarms and apprehensions, and given much room for speculation.

"It does not appear as yet upon what grounds this capture was made, nor whether it was authorized by the constituted authorities of the French Republic. The dispositions of France towards us are sufficiently known to convince us that it is neither their wish nor their interest to engage in hostilities with this country, but from the dissatisfaction and evident disgust which they have manifested at our late treaty with Great Britain and other acts of our government, we ought to be on our guard against such measures (short of actual hostility) as their resentment might induce them to pursue. By merely enforcing their *existing laws* respecting the navigation of neutral vessels, they have it in their power greatly to distress the navigation, and commerce of the United States, and it seems not improbable that they may have been induced to adopt such a measure. It appears therefore highly important that those laws should be made known to our fellow citizens in order to enable them to take such precautions as will secure them from their effects, in case France should be determined to put them in force. For this reason, I take the liberty to enclose to you for publication with a few explanatory notes and observations, a translation of the Regulation of the . . . [26] July 1778, concerning the navigation of neutral vessels, which having never been repealed I understand is still considered as a part of the laws of France and has only been suspended in practice during the present war out of respect to neutral nations and particularly to the United States, the ally of France. I shall be happy if this publication can prove useful to the merchants of the United States, and I will rejoice if it should be the means of saving a single ship from capture or detention."

The "Regulation Concerning the navigation of Neutral Vessels in *time of war*" is printed in the *Aurora. General Advertiser* immediately following the letter by "A Citizen."

3. Joshua Dawson.

4. This is a reference to "An Act providing for the Sale of the Lands of the United States, in the territory northwest of the river Ohio, and above the mouth of Kentucky river" (1 *Stat.* 464–69 [May 18, 1796]). On August 12, 1796, Wolcott wrote to Winthrop Sargent, acting governor and secretary of the Northwest Territory, respecting "the sale of the seven ranges of Townships in the North Western Territory . . . fixed for . . . the 24th day of . . . October" (Carter, *Territorial Papers*, II, 566).

From John Lowell, Junior [1]

[*Boston, June 15, 1796.* An entry in H's Law Register, 1795–1804, under the date of June 20, 1796, reads: "See Letter Lowel June 15." [2] *Letter not found.*]

1. Lowell was a Boston attorney and the son of John Lowell, United States judge for the District of Massachusetts.

For background to this letter, see Lowell to H, December 19, 1795.

2. AD, partially in H's handwriting, New York Law Institute, New York City.

To Oliver Wolcott, Junior

[New York, June 15, 1796]

Dr. Sir

The post of today brought me a letter from you.[1] From some recent information which I have obtained here, I have scarcely a doubt that the plan of the French is— 1 to take all enemy property in our Ships contrary to the Treaty [2] between the two Countries 2 to seize and carry in all our vessels laden with provisions for any English Port. Among this all that they choose to think enemy property will be seized & for the residue they will promise to pay.

This state of things is extremely serious. The Government must play a skilful card or all is lost. No doubt an explanation has been asked of Mr. Adet.[3] There is room enough for asking it & the result *if explanatory* ought in some convenient way to be made known.

Moreover the Government must immediately set in earnest about averting the storm. To this end a person must be sent in place of Monroe.[4] General Pinckney,[5] John Marshall, Mr. Dessaussure of St Carolina,[6] Young Washington the Lawyer,[7] McHenry, Secy at War, Judge Peters,[8] occurs as eligible in different degrees—either of them far preferable to Monroe. It may be understood that the appoint. is permanent or temporary at Choice of the person sent. Under this idea perhaps Pinckney may be prevailed upon—perhaps Marshall it being well urged as a matter of great importance to the Country.

I mentioned to Col. Pickering an idea which has since dwelt powerfully on my mind. Mr. King [9] ought not to be empowered to do any thing to prolong the Treaty beyond the two years after the war.[10] This will afford the Government a strong argument. I earnestly hope this idea will prevail in the Instructions.

Yours truly
                                                                A Hamilton
                                                                June 15. 1796

PS After turning the thing over and Over in my mind I know of nothing better that you have in your power than to send Mc.Henry. He is not yet obnoxious to the French and has been understood formerly to have had some kindness towards their Revolution. His present Office would give a sort of importance to the mission. If he should incline to an absolute relinquishment his mission might be temporary & Col Pickering could carry on his Office in his absence. He is at hand & might depart immediately & I believe he would explain very well & do no foolish thing. Though unusual, perhaps it might be expedient for the President to write himself a letter to the Executive directory explaining the policy by which he has been governed and assuring of the friendship. But this would merit great consideration. Our measures however should be prompt.

Sometimes I think of sending Pinckney who is in England [11] but various uncertainties & possible delays deter me from this plan.

Remember always as a primary motive of Action that the favourable Opinion of our own Country is to be se⟨cured.⟩

A frigate or two to serve as Convoys would not be amiss. If the English had been wise they would neither have harrassed our Trade themselves nor suffered their Trade with us to be harrassed. They would see this a happy moment for conciliating us by a clever little squadron in our Ports & on our Coast. A *hint* might not perhaps do harm.

O Wolcott Esq

ALS, Connecticut Historical Society, Hartford; copy, Hamilton Papers, Library of Congress.

1. Wolcott to H, June 14, 1796.
2. H is referring to the Franco-American Treaty of Amity and Commerce, February 6, 1778 (Miller, *Treaties*, II, 3–29).
3. On June 13, 1796, Timothy Pickering had addressed a letter of protest to Pierre Auguste Adet. See Wolcott to H, June 14, 1796, note 1.
4. James Monroe.
5. Charles Cotesworth Pinckney of South Carolina.
6. Henry William De Saussure, a Charleston lawyer and a member of the South Carolina legislature, had formerly been director of the United States Mint.
7. Bushrod Washington.
8. Richard Peters, United States judge for the District of Pennsylvania.
9. On May 20, 1796, Rufus King was appointed to succeed Thomas Pinckney as United States Minister Plenipotentiary to Great Britain (*Executive Journal*, I, 209).
10. This is a reference to Article 28 of the Jay Treaty. For the text of that article, see "Remarks on the Treaty . . . between the United States and Great Britain," July 9–11, 1795, note 72.
11. Thomas Pinckney.

To George Washington

[New York, June 16, 1796] [1]

Sir

I have received information this morning of a nature which I think you ought to receive without delay. A Mr. *Le Guen,* a Frenchman, a client of mine and in whom I have inspired confidence, and who is apparently a discreet and decent man, called on me this morning to consult me on the expediency of his becoming naturalized, in order that certain events between France and the U States might not prejudice him in a suit which I am directed to bring for him for a value of 160,000 Dollars.[2] I asked him what the events to which he alluded were. He made me the following reply under the strictest injunctions of confidence. "I have seen a letter from *St Thonax*[3] to Mr. *Labagarde*[4] of this City informing him that a plan was adopted to seize all American vessels carrying to any English Port provisions of any kind to conduct them into some French Port, if found to be British property to condemn them, if American, to take them on the *accountability* of the Government—adding that he must not thence infer that it was the intention to make war upon the U States—but it was with a view to retaliate the conduct of Great Britain, to keep supplies from her, and to obtain them for themselves, and was also bottomed on some political motives not necessary to be explained. That it was also in contemplation when Admiral Richery arrived, if the Ships could be spared to send five sail of the line to this Country."[5] Fearing he said that this might produce a rupture between the two Countries he had called to consult me on the subject &c.[6]

I asked his permission to make the communication to you He gave me leave to do it, but with the absolute condition that the knowlege of names was on no account to go beyond *you* and *myself*. I must therefore request Sir that this condition be exactly observed. He has promised me further information.

I believe the information, as well because the source of it under all the circumstances engages my confidence, as because the thing appears in itself probable. France wants supplies and she has not the means of paying & our Merchants have done creditting.

It becomes very material that the real situation should as soon as possible be ascertained & that the Merchants should know on what they have to depend. They expect that the Government will ask an explanation of Mr Adet [7] & that in some proper way the result will be made known.

It seems to become more and more urgent that the U States should have some faithful organ near the French Government to explain their real views and ascertain those of the French. It is all important that the people should be satisfied that the Government has made every exertion to avert Rupture as early as possible.[8]

Most respectfully & Affect I have the honor to be Sir Yr. Obed serv   A Hamilton

The President of the U States

ALS, George Washington Papers, Library of Congress; copy, in the handwriting of Washington, George Washington Papers, Library of Congress; copy, Hamilton Papers, Library of Congress.

1. Washington endorsed this letter: "without date *But* recd. the 23. June 1796." At the bottom of the copy which Washington made of this letter, he wrote: "This letter has no date; but came by the Post of Wednesday, to Alexandria, under cover from The Secretary of the Treasury." For evidence that H wrote this letter on June 16, 1796, see Oliver Wolcott, Jr., to H, June 17, 1796.

In Hamilton, *History*, VI, 466, this letter is dated June 26, 1796. In *JCHW*, VI, 133, and *HCLW*, X, 177, it is dated June, 1796.

2. Louis Le Guen was a merchant in New York City. The suit to which H is referring was one of a series of cases in which H served as Le Guen's attorney. For these cases, see Goebel, *Law Practice*, II, 48–164.

3. In the margin opposite "St. Thonax," H wrote "Santhonax." The reference is to Léger-Félicité Sonthonnax, one of the French commissioners appointed in the spring of 1792 to govern Santo Domingo.

4. This is apparently a reference to Peter Delabigarre, a native of France and a New York City merchant, who owned land at Red Hook, New York, and was a protégé of Chancellor Robert R. Livingston. Delabigarre also knew Jean Antoine Joseph Fauchet, former French Minister to the United States, for on June 30, 1794, he wrote to Livingston: "Notre envoy est enfin parti et fauchet m'a promis devenir passer quelques jours à Redhook . . ." (ALS, New-York Historical Society, New York City). Delabigarre, who took up various schemes, including a papermaking venture with Livingston and the foundation of a colony at Tivoli, New York, went bankrupt in 1800 and eventually moved to New Orleans.

5. Although a squadron commanded by Admiral Joseph de Richery conducted a successful campaign against the British fisheries in the North Atlantic in the summer of 1796, the rumor that he would send part of his squadron to the United States was unfounded.

6. A somewhat fuller version and a covering letter by "A Citizen" were printed in the [Philadelphia] *Gazette of the United States,* June 20, 1796. They read as follows: "Mr. [John] FENNO, I send you the substance of a letter from a man in public office under the French Republic at the Cape, to another Frenchman in this country, which was read by a confidential friend of his, and the particulars from memory communicated to me. It is very material that our merchants should be generally apprized of the plan, and as I have no doubt of the authenticity of the intelligence, I think it my duty to publish it thro the channel of the press. The manner in which it comes to me, does not permit me to disclose the source—but you who know your author will not I am sure, scruple to vouch for the goodness of the authority.

"A CITIZEN

" 'It is determined to seize and bring in all American vessels laden with provisions which shall be met with bound to any English port. These will undergo a severe examination, & when the property appears to be British, it will be confiscated; where it is clearly and without suspicion American it will be detained, but paid for, according as the means in our power furnish. For this conduct we have several motives—to keep the supplies from our enemies, to obtain them for ourselves. The embarassed state of the finances of the republic has much narrowed the means of paying for what is wanted from abroad, and after what has happened, we cannot expect much future succour from our credit with the American merchants. Besides we have some political reasons. It is well the merchants who have so zealously supported the treaty with Great Britain should see that there are two sides to the question, and that by temporizing with our enemy, they will not enjoy that full exemption from the inconveniences of war which they have promised themselves. It is also essential that we should support our friends in America, by fulfilling their predictions of evil from the treaty. Perhaps you may shortly see a French fleet on your coast.

" 'But do not imagine that there will be war with America. This will not happen. The republic has no disposition to a final rupture with that country, and we have no fears that it will come to an open breach with us. Notwithstanding the coalition between PITT and WASHINGTON, we are well assured by our confidential friends that the attachment of the American people to the French nation will oblige the government to be passive, that if its folly should prompt it to a rupture with us, there will be more to put on the tri-coloured cockade, than to join the standard of the hypocritical Washington.' "

This letter was reprinted in the [Philadelphia] *Aurora: General Advertiser,* June 21, 1796.

7. Pierre Auguste Adet.

8. Washington sent this letter to Timothy Pickering on June 24, 1796 (LC, George Washington Papers, Library of Congress). See also Washington to H, June 26, 1796.

To Oliver Wolcott, Junior

[New York] June 16. 1796

Dr. Sir

It appears to me material under our present prospects to complete the three frigates without delay.[1] They may be useful with reference to the Algerines—they may be useful to convoy our vessels out of the reach of pickeroon privateers hovering on our Coast. I know you want money [2] but could not the Merchants by secret movements be put in motion to make you a loan. I think something of this kind may be done here & I should presume at Philadelphia &c. The sole ostensible object may be the Algerines but the second object may circulate in whispers. If you conclude on any thing I will second you.

Perhaps no bad form of the thing may be to place in the hands of your Agents for building Treasury Bills from 100 to 1000 Dollars payable in a year with interest & to let it be known among the Merchants that they are lodged exclusively to facilitate the equipment of the Ships. But a more direct operation may be attempted & I should hope with success for the sum you may want for the frigates.

Yrs   A Hamilton

ALS, Connecticut Historical Society, Hartford; copy, Hamilton Papers, Library of Congress.

1. On March 27, 1794, Congress had passed "An Act to provide a Naval Armament" (1 *Stat.* 350–51) providing for the construction of six frigates. Progress was so slow that a year later only the hulls of three frigates had been completed, and construction on the hulls of two others had just begun. With the conclusion of a peace treaty with Algiers in 1795, work on the frigates stopped altogther. On April 20, 1796, however, "An Act supplementary to an act entitled 'An act to provide a Naval Armament'" authorized completion of three of the frigates, the *United States*, the *Constitution*, and the *Constellation* (1 *Stat.* 453–54). The frigates were not launched until the summer and fall of 1797.

2. In a communication to the Ways and Means Committee of the House of Representatives on May 6, 1796, on the need for additional revenue, Wolcott had stated: "It being known to the committee, that no loans can, at present, be negotiated in Europe, and that the high profits which reward commercial enterprise, though beneficial to the community, are obstacles to the success of domestic loans, beyond a limited amount, I cannot, consistently with my duty, omit expressing it as my opinion, that some effectual measures, for improving and extending the revenue, ought to be adopted during the present session of Congress" (*ASP, Finance,* I, 413). See also Wolcott to H, June 17, 1796.

From Walter Livingston

[*Livingston Manor, New York*] *June 17, 1796.* "In examining my fathers [1] papers yesterday I found a receipt of yours in the following words Viz. Received New York June 8. 1786 of Robert C. Livingston Esquire Twenty five Dollars as a retainer for the Manor of Livingston. Alex Hamilton.² I have taken the liberty to mention this because my brother, Henry ³ who is gone down with an intention to endeavour to procure your assistance in some of his ejectment Causes against his & Johns Tenants in the Manor which will be tried in July term at Albany—applied to me for information respecting the retainer. . . ."

LC, New-York Historical Society, New York City.
  1. Robert Livingston, Jr., third lord of Livingston Manor, died in November, 1790.
  2. Receipt not found. On February 25, 1795, after discussing a dispute with a group of tenants, John Livingston wrote to his brother Walter: ". . . I shall to day call on Mr Hamilton and give him a General Retainer for us in this & all other business. If he will take it—the complement must be paid him" (ALS, New-York Historical Society, New York City). No evidence has been found that H received this retainer.
  3. Henry (Hendrick) Livingston, sixth son of Robert Livingston, Jr.
  On June 22, 1796, Henry Livingston wrote to Walter Livingston from New York: ". . . [John] Wigram had found the charge against Hamilton for £ 10 . . . in the invoice Book. Since I have been in Town Mr. [John B.] Coles has Examined the Books of R[obert] C[ambridge] L[ivingston] where it is Charged, but Could not find the receipts amongst the papers" (ALS, New-York Historical Society, New York City). Wigram was the overseer of Livingston Manor; R. C. Livingston was the brother of Walter and Henry Livingston; Henry Coles was a New York City merchant.

From Robert Morris ¹

Alexander Hamilton Esqre   Phila June 17 1796
Dear Sir
  I was disappointed in not seeing you as expected before your departure.² In reply to your favor of the 9th.³ I must first tell you, that if certain Negotiations which I am working at succeed I will pay you sooner than you expect, but if they fall through as many others have done I will at all Events take up my Note by paying Principal and Interest within nine months from this date & as much sooner as I can, besides if at any particular time before the Period abovementioned you need a part, let me know it, and I will Struggle hard (if needful) to get it.
  I am Dr Sir Yrs   RM

LC, Robert Morris Papers, Library of Congress.
1. This letter concerns the repayment of a loan which H had made to Morris in 1794. For this loan and its repayment, see the introductory note to H to Morris, March 18, 1795. See also Morris to H, March 31, June 2, 23, 30, July 18, 20, 1795.
2. H had been in Philadelphia from June 2 to June 8, 1796. See Jonathan Williams to H, June 8, 1796, note 2.
3. Letter not found.

Receipt to Pierre Van Cortlandt, Junior [1]

[New York, June 17, 1796]

Received of Pierre Van Cortlandt Jun Esqr Two hundred Dollars on account of his fathers bond.[2]

June 17. 1796

A Hamilton

ADS, Mrs. Robert Crimmins, Darien, Connecticut.
1. Van Cortlandt, son of the first lieutenant governor of New York, had studied law in H's law office. See H's Cash Book, March 1, 1782–1791, note 3. He was a member of the New York Assembly from Westchester County in 1792, 1794, and 1795.
2. An entry in H's Cash Book, 1795–1804, for June 17, 1796, reads: "To Stock Account on account of this sum received on account of Pierre van Cortlands Bond 200" (AD, Hamilton Papers, Library of Congress). See also H to Robert Troup, July 25, 1795, note 14.

From Oliver Wolcott, Junior

Philadelphia June 17th. 1796

My Dear Sir,

I have your Letters of the 15th. & 16th. instant—that for the President will go on by the next mail.[1]

The affair of the Capture assumes a more equivocal character as respects the French Government than at first.[2] In a confidential way from some of our Merchants I have reason to believe, that proposals were made to Mr. Murgatroy who built the Ship, by a Mr. Dunkinson an English Gentleman not yet naturalised, to become the purchaser, that Dunkinson on finding that he could not obtain a Register in his own name, made a conditional purchase of the Vessell *deliverable in England;* after which the Vessell was registered in

Murgatroyds name. That the Loading though in the names of Willings & Francis is in fact British property & that these circumstances, were known or strongly suspected by the owner of the French Privateer.³ If these things are true, & the sole motives of the Capture, the thing though perhaps wrong, is not alarming. I do not find that any other capture has been made.

Mr. Adet I understand has written to Colo. Pickering that the Privateer was Commissioned by the French Government of Sn. Domingo, *but that he is ignorant what the orders of the Privateer are, or what orders the French directory in the West Indies are authorised to give in respect to Neutral Vessels.*⁴ This answer is neither satisfactory nor the contrary—it is nothing—except that it leaves ground to suspect that the West India Directory possess some discretionary authority, which may be used to distress us, if circumstances should render it expedient. What now gives me more concern than the capture, is the compliance of Baches paper, which is I think calculated to prepare the public mind, to expect a new course of conduct by the French, contrary to our Treaty, & distressing to our Commerce.⁵

I have for some time been inclined to think that Mr. Munroe ought to be recalled,⁶ but as others have doubted, & as the thing was not demonstrable I have not urged it, every event shews however new reasons for believing, that we must stop the channells by which foreign poison is introduced into our Country or suffer the government to be overturned—at all hazards the attempt must be made.

I have the power of the President to borrow,⁷ & have been making attempts in the manner you have intimated but without prospect of success.⁸ Bills can only be used in a case of the utmost emergency, as the discount would be ruinous. I will however carry on the public business this summer some way or other—though I know that we shall ultimately fail, unless some miraculous change in public measures, shall speedily take place.

I will write you if any thing occurs.

yrs. truly

Oliv. Wolcott Jr

Alexander Hamilton Esq

ALS, Hamilton Papers, Library of Congress; copy, Connecticut Historical Society, Hartford.

1. H to George Washington, June 16, 1796. Washington had left Philadelphia for Mount Vernon on June 13, 1796.
2. See Wolcott to H, June 14, 1796.
3. William M. Duncanson, who had arrived in the United States from England in August, 1794, invested heavily in real estate in the Federal City. From April 16, 1796, to June 13, 1797, Duncanson and James Ray, who had come to the United States in April, 1795, from England, were partners in a mercantile firm in Philadelphia.

In 1796 Duncanson and Ray purchased an American ship, the *Delaware*, from the Philadelphia mercantile firm of Thomas Willing and Tench Francis. Willing and Francis were the agents of Thomas Murgatroyd, a Philadelphia merchant and the owner of the *Delaware*. Duncanson renamed the ship *Mount Vernon*. In May, 1796, the firms of Duncanson and Ray and Willing and Francis loaded the ship with rum, and on or about June 1, 1796, the ship set sail for London. When only a short distance out from Philadelphia, the *Mount Vernon* was captured by the French privateer the *Flying Fish*. For additional information on the *Mount Vernon*, see Allen C. Clark, *Greenleaf and Law in the Federal City* (Washington, D. C., 1901), 278–82.

4. The letter from Pierre Auguste Adet to Timothy Pickering is dated June 14, 1796, and reads: "I have received the letter you did me the honor to write me, relative to the seizure of the ship Mount Vernon by the French privateer the Flying Fish. I am vexed, sir, not to have it in my power to give you the information you request of me. I cannot say whether the privateer, which is certainly a vessel commissioned by the republic, and came from St. Domingo to this port, has or has not acted conformably to orders which have been transmitted to her; I do not know the instructions given by the Directory to its commissioners in the colonies, nor do I know what conduct it has prescribed to them to cause to be observed, by the armed vessels under orders, in regard to neutrals trading with the enemies of the republic. It is impossible for me, at this moment, to furnish you with precise explanations; I shall, therefore, write to the colonies to obtain them, and I will immediately transmit to you what shall come to my knowledge, as well as to this point, as concerning the event which is the object of your letter" (*ASP, Foreign Relations*, I, 652).

5. See Wolcott to H, June 14, 1796. Wolcott's complaints about the "compliance of Bache's paper" were doubtless strengthened by a defense of the capture of the *Mount Vernon* which appeared in Benjamin Franklin Bache's newspaper, the [Philadelphia] *Aurora. General Advertiser*, on June 16, 1796. The article reads in part: "In the Philadelphia Gazette of last evening the protest of Capt. DOMINICK of the ship MOUNT VERNON 'is laid before the Merchants and Citizens of the United States for their full information in a point which both the *honor of the country* and the property of its *subjects* is so materially interested.'

"It is not a little remarkable, that as long as our property upon the high seas was seized *libelled* & CONDEMNED by the British only—the honor of the country was never spoken of by certain friends to peace and order; indeed more—when the word *honor* then happened to be mentioned by the advocates for a respectable and substantial neutrality, it was called a chimera, an empty bubble, and *interest, interest* was echoed from all quarters—but now that a *single* ship is only *captured* by the French, the *honor of the country* is in jeopardy, tho' it be not known yet upon what principles the capture is made, or whether the vessel or cargo will be condemned. Certainly we have not much lenity or generosity to expect from the French in our trade; for they have suffered materially by our deceptive neutrality, but if the claims of the owners of the MOUNT VERNON are founded in justice their property will no doubt be safe. . . ."

6. See H to Wolcott, June 15, 1796.

7. On June 10, 1796, Washington wrote to Wolcott: "I do hereby authorize and empower you, by yourself or any other person or persons to borrow on behalf of the United States, of the Bank of the Ud. States or any other body or bodies politic, person or persons, any sum not exceeding in the whole Three hundred and twenty four thousand, five hundred and thirty nine Dollars and six Cents; and to make or cause to be made for that purpose such contract or contracts as shall be necessary and for the interest of the said States" (*GW*, XXXV, 87). This authorization was pursuant to "An Act making further provision for the expenses attending the intercourse of the United States with foreign nations; and to continue in force the act, intituled 'An act providing the means of intercourse between the United States and foreign nations'" (1 *Stat.* 487–88 [May 30, 1796]).

8. See H to Wolcott, June 16, 1796.

To Angelica Church [1]

[New York, June 19–20, 1796]

Dear Angelica

If you knew the power you have to make happy You would lose no opportunity of writing to Betsey & me; for we literally feast on your letters.

But our impatience increases as the prospect becomes more promising; and you must permit us ever to chide Mr. Church for his tardiness. Expectations must be converted into realities. Life is too short to warrant procrasti[nati]on of the most favourite and precious objects.

Tis not easy that you and I should differ in any thing. On a certain subject we agree. And though I am in a minority here—It is gaining strength. Your Countrymen are zealous but they are not mad. All will go well here. Our own Jacobins have made a violent effort against me, but a complete victory has been gained to their utter confusion.

Yrs. as much as you desire   AH

ALS, Judge Peter B. Olney, Deep River, Connecticut.

1. The references in this letter are so vague that it could have been written either in the summer of 1795 or in May or June, 1796. H first learned of the Churches' plan to come to the United States in 1795 (Philip Schuyler to H, October 12, 1795), and they did not arrive in New York until May, 1797. See Robert Morris to H, May 23, 1797. H's statement concerning the "victory" over "Our own Jacobins" could be a reference to either the approval of the Jay Treaty in the Senate on June 24, 1795, or the passage in May, 1796, of leg-

islation implementing that treaty. In any event, the letter has been dated June 19–20, 1796, on the assumption that it was the letter H sent to England with Rufus King on June 20, 1796. See H to Angelica Church, June 25, 1796. It should perhaps also be mentioned that H's concluding remarks in the letter printed above appear to be a reply to Angelica Church's comments in the last paragraph of her letter of February 19, 1796, to H.

To Robert Morris

[*New York, June 20, 1796.* In a letter dated June 27–30, 1796, Morris wrote to Hamilton: "Your favor of the 20th I have received." *Letter not found.*]

[Opinion of William Rawle][1]

[Philadelphia, June 21, 1796]

ADf, Historical Society of Pennsylvania, Philadelphia.
 1. This is a draft of Rawle's opinion on Sections 4 and 7 of "An Act for the relief and protection of American Seamen" (1 *Stat.* 477–78 [May 28, 1796]). This document is endorsed, in an unidentified handwriting: "June 21. 1796 Draft of Opinion William Rawle for Alex. Hamilton Sec. of Treas." Rawle's opinion, however, was sent to Oliver Wolcott, Jr., not to H. See Wolcott to George Washington, June 28, 1796 (ADf, Connecticut Historical Society, Hartford; LC, George Washington Papers, Library of Congress).

From James Ricketts[1]

Elizabethtown [*New Jersey*] *June 24, 1796.* "Enclosed are the extracts of Mr. Jackson's letters, which you desired me to send you."[2]

ALS, Hamilton Papers, Library of Congress.
 1. Ricketts, a New Jersey businessman, had been a director of the Society for Establishing Useful Manufactures.
 2. John Jackson's two letters were written from London on March 4, 1794, and March 2, 1796, and refer to litigation over the will of Peter Van Brugh Livingston, Ricketts's father-in-law, who had died on October 16, 1792. Sarah Livingston's seventh child had married Ricketts in 1777. The extract dated March 4, 1794, reads: "The Question which you ask me concerning the good old Gentn. Mr. Livingstons claim—I answer, to the best of my recollection, that as he could not have recovered it in any other mode, from Jacob, it was secured

through your means, as a present to dear Mrs. R—in that settlement, and, her Father became exonerated from his engagements on your general accounts— he was to be fully indemnified—but, if he hath not noticed this in his Will, I fear the Executors will endeavour to establish the claim against you, unless they will rely upon our evidence as to the facts at the time, you should represent them to Philad—as they really occurred, with my concurrent testimony. . . ."

The extract dated March 2, 1796, reads: ". . . when I was settling the Old Gentn. claim against your Brothers and yourself . . . he mentioned to me repeatedly it was merely a matter of form to ascertain what was due, as the amt. should be for Mrs. R—and, the Children—I never considered it, but, as so disposed of by him, for, most assuredly he Confirmed it in my presence, in my situation, I cannot get out to make any affidavit before the Lord Mayor of the fact . . . and, as that, is the only authority, I apprehend, which will answer your purpose, I cannot, I am sorry to say, comply with it, but I shall be ever ready to give that testimony of the Fact, as it really occurred, and, as Mr. ph: Livington I presume, knows my writing you may show him this declaration. . . ." (copies, in Ricketts's handwriting, Hamilton Papers, Library of Congress.)

As attorney for Ricketts, H prepared a draft of a declaration to be filed during the July, 1796, term of the New York Supreme Court (ADf, Hamilton Papers, Library of Congress). The declaration, however, was not filed until May 22, 1798, and on April 1, 1799, in the New York Circuit Court the jury found ". . . a Verdict for the Plaintiffs Two thousand and ninety dollars and eighty six Cents debt and six Cents damages and six Cents costs" (H's Law Register, 1795–1804 [D, partially in H's handwriting, New York Law Institute, New York City]; MS Minutes of the New York Circuit Court, 1796–1799 [Hall of Records, New York City]). The cause was tried before Justice James Kent at the March, 1800, Circuit and ". . . a verdict was taken for the plaintiff, subject to the opinion of the court, as to the admissibility and effect of the evidence" (William Johnson, *Reports of Cases Adjudged in the Supreme Court of Judicature of the State of New-York; from January Term 1799, to January Term 1803, both inclusive; together With Cases Determined in the Court for the Correction of Errors, during that period* [New York: Banks, Gould & Co., 1848], II, 97–98). Under the heading of "July Circuit 1800," H made the following entry in his Cash Book, 1795–1804: "James Rickets for Trial & Argument of Cause v. Philip Livingston decision in his favor 100" (AD, Hamilton Papers, Library of Congress). For the report in favor of the plaintiffs in October, 1800, see 2 Johnson, *Cases*, 98–102.

To Angelica Church

[New York, June 25, 1796]

I cannot omit the opportunity My Dear Angelica of dropping you a line by your old acquaintance Colonel Noble [1] to inform you that we are all well, strongly agitated between Fear and Hope, but anxiously wishing for your Return. If you are not persuaded that this is one of the dearest objects to Eliza & myself you do us much injustice. The only rivalship we have is in our attachment to you and we each contend for preeminence in this particular. To whom will you give the apple?

I wrote you last by Mr. King who sailed a few days since for London as our Minister Plenipotentiary.[2] You must not think the less well of him for not being a *Jacobin*—for he is a very clever fellow and will do credit to your Country. He will not give me the trouble of defending any Treaty of his making—for to be sure of everybody's approbation he is instructed to do nothing but after a previous consultation with you. What do you say to this Madam? Will it have no charm for your ———? But I had forgotten. You have none.

His better self [3] accompanies him. She has not the proverb in her favour "*The nearer the bone* &c." But I dare say she is sweet enough.

How do you manage to charm all that see you? While naughty tales are told to you of us, we hear nothing but of your kindness, amiableness, agreeableness &c. Why will you be so lavish of these qualities upon those who forget them in six weeks & withold them from us who retain all the impressions you make, indelibly? But so the world goes. And we must submit to Destiny.

When we last heared from Albany all your family were well. Your father was gone to Fort Schuyler.

We have sent you by different opportunities sketches of your house & lot.[4] I repeat them under cover to Mr. Church.

Adieu Yr. ever Affect friend   A Hamilton

Eliza will write by this opportunity or at least I trust add a postscript. Yet She continues lazy at the pen.

June 25th.

ALS, Massachusetts Historical Society, Boston.

1. Arthur Noble, an Irishman, had come to the United States in 1783. After petitioning the New York legislature for a grant of two townships for settling Irish emigrants ("New York Assembly. Remarks on an Act for the Relief of Arthur Noble," February 9, 1787), he settled in 1790 on a 40,960-acre tract of land in Herkimer County, New York. See H to Robert Troup, July 25, 1795, note 11.

2. On May 20, 1796, Rufus King was appointed United States Minister Plenipotentiary to Great Britain. He sailed from New York on June 20, 1796. See H to Angelica Church, June 19–20, 1796.

3. Mary Alsop King.

4. See "Receipt from Morgan Lewis," March 18, 1796, note 2.

From Peter Goelet [1]

Alex Hambleton   N York June 25 1796

Sir

I have found Your Deeds for the Lands You Mentioned but no Receipt or other Papers with it.

Inclosed have a Copy of that part of the Conditions of the Sales You Request.

I am with Respt S Y Vy   P Goelet

[ENCLOSURE]

The Conditions of the Sales of the Lands belonging to the Am Iron Compy on the 10. 11 & 18 Decemr. 1795 was Vizt

¼ To be paid to Peter Goelet on or before 11 OClock to Morrow Morning
¼ On the first tuesday in April next with Lawfull Intrest.
¼ On the first tuesday in October next with Lawfull Intrest.
And the Residue on or before the first tuesday in April 1797 with Lawfull Intrest.

Copy, Miscellaneous Chancery Papers, American Iron Company, Clerk of the Court of Appeals, Albany, on deposit at Queens College, New York City.
1. For an explanation of the contents of this letter, see the introductory note to Philip Schuyler to H, August 31, 1795. See also H to Phineas Bond, September 1, 1795; H to Robert Morris, September 1, 1795; H to Barent Bleecker, March 20, 1796.

From George Washington

Mount Vernon 26th June 1796.

My dear Sir,

Your letter without date,[1] came to my hands by Wednesdays Post; and by the first Post afterwards I communicated the purport of it

ALS, Hamilton Papers, Library of Congress; copy, Hamilton Papers, Library of Congress.
1. H to Washington, June 16, 1796.

(withholding the names) to the Secretary of State;[2] with directions to bestow the closest attention to the subject, and if the application which had been made to the Minister of France, consequent of the Capture of the Ship Mount Vernon,[3] had not produced such an answer as to supercede the necessity, then to endeavor to obtain such explanation of the views of the French government relatively to our Commerce with Great Britain, as the nature of the case appeared to require.

That the fact is, as has been represented to you, I have very little, if any doubt. Many, very many circumstances are continually happening in confirmation of it: among which, it is evident Bache's Paper,[4] which *receives* and *gives* the hope, is endeavouring to prepare the Public mind for this event, by representing it as the *predicted*, and *natural* consequence of the Ratification of the Treaty with Great Britn.[5]

Let me ask therefore.

Do you suppose that the Executive, in the recess of the Senate,[6] has power in such a case as the one before us—especially if the measure should not be *avowed* by authority—to send a special character to Paris, as Envoy Extraordinary, to give, & receive explanations? And if there be a doubt, whether it is not probable—nay more than probable, that the French Directory would, in the present state of things, avail themselves of the unconstitutionallity of the measure, to decline receiving him? The policy of delay, to avoid explanations, would induce them to adopt any pretext to accomplish it. Their reliance upon a party in this country for support, would stimulate them to this conduct; and we may be assured they will not be deficient in the most minute details of every occurrence, and every opinion, worthy of communication. If then an Envoy cannot be sent to Paris without the Agency of the Senate, will the information you have received, admitting it should be realized, be sufficient ground for convening that body?

2. Washington to Timothy Pickering, June 24, 1796 (LC, George Washington Papers, Library of Congress).
3. See Oliver Wolcott, Jr., to H, June 14, 1796.
4. Benjamin Franklin Bache, editor of the [Philadelphia] *Aurora. General Advertiser*.
5. Such arguments appeared in the *Aurora* throughout the first weeks of June, 1796. See, for example, Wolcott to H, June 14, 1796, note 2, and June 17, 1796, note 6.
6. The first session of the Fourth Congress had adjourned on June 1, 1796.

These are serious things; they may be productive of serious consequences; and therefore require very serious & cool deliberation. Admitting, however, that the Powers of the President during the recess, were adequate to such an appointment, where is the character who would go, that unites the proper qualifications for such a Mission; and would not be obnoxious to one party or the other? And what should be done with Mr. M———[7] in that case?

As the affairs of this country in their administration, receive great embarrassment from the conduct of characters among ourselves; and as every act of the Executive is mis-represented, and tortured with a view to make it appear odious, the aid of the friends to government is peculiarly necessary under such circumstances; and at such a crises as the present: It is unnecessary therefore to add, that I should be glad upon the present, and all other important occasions, to receive yours: and as I have great confidence in the abilities, and purity of Mr. Jays views, as well as in his experience, I should wish that his sentiments on the purport of this letter; and other interesting matters as they occur, may accompany yours; for having no other wish than to promote the true and permanent interests of this country, I am anxious, always, to compare the opinions of those in whom I confide with one another; and these again (without being bound by them) with my own, that I may extract all the good I can.

Having from a variety of reasons (among which a disinclination to be longer buffitted in the public prints by a set of infamous scribblers) taken my ultimate determination "to seek the Post of honor in a private Station" I regret exceedingly that I did not publish my valedictory address the day after the Adjournment of Congress.[8] This would have preceeded the canvassing for Electors (wch. is commencing with warmth, in this State). It would have been announcing *publioly*, what seems to be very well understood, and is industriously propagated, *privately*. It would have removed doubts from the minds of *all*, and left the field clear for *all:* It would, by having preceeded any unfavorable change in our foreign relations (if any should happen) render my retreat less difficult and embarrassing. And it might have prevented the remarks which, more than

---

7. James Monroe. See H to Wolcott, June 15, 1796.
8. See the introductory note to H to Washington, May 10, 1796.

probable will follow a late annunciation—namely—that I delayed it long enough to see, that the current was turned against me, before I declared my intention to decline. This is one of the reasons which makes me a little tenacious of the draught I furnished you with,[9] to be modified & corrected.

Having passed, however, what *I now* conceive would have been the *precise* moment to have addressed my Constituents, let me ask your opinion (under a full conviction that nothing will shake my determination to withdraw) of the *next* best time, considering the present, and what may, probably, be the existing state of things at different periods previous to the Election; or rather, the middle of Octr, beyond which the promulgation of my intentions cannot be delayed. Let me hear from you as soon as it is convenient; and be assured always of the sincere esteem, and affecte. regard of

Go: Washington

Alexr. Hamilton Esqr.

9. See Washington to H, May 15, 1796.

To Oliver Wolcott, Junior

[New York, June 26, 1796]

Dr. Sir

I learn from a Gentleman of character that a prize brought into Boston by a French Privateer is about to be sold.[1] This being in direct breach of our Treaty with G Britain [2] how does it happen? Though no particular law passed, the Treaty being the law of the land, Our custom houses can & ought to prevent the entry & sale of prizes, upon Executive instruction. If any thing is wanting to this end for god sake, My Dr. Sir, let it be done & let us not be disgraced.[3]

Yrs. A Hamilton

June 26, 1796

ALS, Connecticut Historical Society, Hartford; copy, Hamilton Papers, Library of Congress.

1. On July 14, 1796, Pierre Auguste Adet wrote to Timothy Pickering: "The consul at Boston has just informed me that [Benjamin Lincoln] the collector

of customs there has prevented the unlading and sale of the prizes carried into that port by two French privateers. The consul has ineffectually complained to him. The collector founds his refusal upon a letter which he says he received from you" (*ASP, Foreign Relations*, I, 653). On July 19, Pickering replied that the behavior of the collector at Boston was justified on the ground that ". . . as soon as provision was made on both sides to carry into effect the treaty between the United States and Great Britain, it behoved the Government of the former to countermand the *permission* formerly given to French privateers to sell their prizes in our ports. Such sales, you have seen, the United States had always a *right* to prohibit; and by the above mentioned stipulation this right became a *duty*" (*ASP, Foreign Relations*, I, 654).

2. Article 24 of the Jay Treaty stipulated: "It shall not be lawful for any Foreign Privateers (not being subjects or Citizens of either of the said Parties) who have Commissions from any other Prince or State in Enmity with either Nation, to arm their Ships in the Ports of either of the said Parties, nor to sell what they have taken, nor in any other manner to exchange the same . . ." (Miller, *Treaties*, II, 262).

3. In the Connecticut Historical Society, Hartford, is a fragment of a letter in H's handwriting which has been attached to the letter printed above. This fragment reads: "Considering what is going on & may go on in the West Indies it appears to me *essential* that the President should be empowered to lay embargoes in the interval between the present & the next session of Congress.
"Yrs. truly   A. Hamilton."
In *JCHW*, VI, 135, and in George Gibbs, *Memoirs of the Administrations of Washington and John Adams: Edited from the Papers of Oliver Wolcott, Secretary of the Treasury* (New York, 1846), I, 363, this fragment is incorrectly printed as a postscript to the letter printed above.

From Peter Goelet [1]

Mr. Alexr Hambleton   New York June 27 1796

Sir

According to Your Request I have examind the Accounts and find that You paid the first Instalment on the 17 of December 1795
£605.13.4 is 1514.18

The Second payment on the 6 April 1796
£605.13.4 Int £14.2.4 is   619.15.9   1549.47
                                                                               £1225.9.2 Ds 3063.65

With Sentiments of Respect I am
   Sir Your Most Humble Servant   Peter Goelet

Copy, Miscellaneous Chancery Papers, American Iron Company, Clerk of the Court of Appeals, Albany, on deposit at Queens College, New York City.

1. For an explanation of the contents of this letter, see the introductory note to Philip Schuyler to H, August 31, 1795. See also H to Phineas Bond, September 1, 1795; H to Robert Morris, September 1, 1795; H to Barent Bleecker, March 20, 1796; Goelet to H, June 25, 1796.

From Robert Morris [1]

Alexander Hamilton Esqre   Phila. June 27 [–30] 1796

dear Sir

Your favor of the 20th [2] I have received & will most chearfully comply with your requisition by remitting $1500 which if I can shall go in this letter and if in the Course of my negotiations I can meet with notes or drafts upon New York suitable for the remaining Payment they shall be sent you, but if I do not obtain Such you may rely that I will fulfill my Promise in regard to that Payment or it shall be as you propose half in six & half in 12 mos.

Yrs.   RM

June 30   I could not bear to send this without the $1500. You will find herein a draft of Joseph Higbee [3] upon   [4] at 30 days for that sum you can get it discounted & charge me with the Cost letting me know the amount. You will see by this that I did not neglect you altho' you did not receive it immediately.   RM

LC, Robert Morris Papers, Library of Congress.

1. This letter concerns Morris's efforts to pay the balance of a debt which he owed to H. For this debt and Morris's attempts to pay it, see the introductory note to H to Morris, March 18, 1795. See also Morris to H, March 31, June 2, 23, 30, July 18, 20, 1795; June 17, 1796.
2. Letter not found.
3. For the details of this transaction, see the introductory note to H to Morris, March 18, 1795.
4. Space left blank in MS. The draft was on the firm of Hartshorne and Lindley of New York. See H to Morris, March 18, 1795, note 14.

From Oliver Wolcott, Junior

Phila. [June] 28 96 [1]

Dear Sir

No instructions have gone to the Collectors respecting the Entry of Prizes taken by French Privateers; [2] it was expected that a general regulation would have been established by Law; since the rising of

Congress³ every thing has recd. attention in the order which appeared to be most interesting—the point you mention⁴ was not forgotten, but it was supposed that as the Judiciary would interfere on application & as relief in this way would be most efficacious no inconvenience was to be expected. The absence of the President⁵ though perfectly proper, will always occasion some delay, in adjusting executive arrangements.

Though the capture of the Mt. Vernon⁶ is not a decided evidence that the French mean to contravene their Treaty with the U.S., yet other circumstances render it possible—a confidential character in France is therefore necessary. I do not think any of the persons mentioned by you⁷ would undertake the mission, some I know will not; Wm. Smith⁸ would go, his talents, integrity, knowledge of the affairs of the U.S. & acquaintance with the French language, (a thing important) iminently fit him for the Station—perhaps he would be unpopular in France; if so, this would be an objection. The French however are not a weak people, they know Mr. Smith to be a man of ability & respected character, & his declarations would have weight on these accounts. Will you inform me in confidence whether this appointment would in your opinion be a suitable measure under all circumstances. If not can Mr. Adams be transferred with propriety & without offence to the Portuguese government?⁹

I much fear that the new Stock will not sell, on the terms proposed, nor on any terms without an enormous discount, probably not in sufficient sums at more than 17/.¹⁰ Treasury drafts cannot be negotiated for the sums wanted, without a still greater loss, unless they are made payable at a short date say three or four months. This will endanger the public Credit, & affect the banks, especially that of the U.S. The consequence is, the Frigates must stop ¹¹—or the new stock must be sold on any terms. Sales of Bank Stock are strenuously urged, this idea has however been strenuously opposed by me.¹² There is but one other measure which I can think of & that is, to pledge sufficient sums of the new Stock, to be sold after the expiration of six or nine months if not then redeemed. To accomplish this the aid of some of the Banks, (say that of N. York) is necessary. The Bank at Pensylvania will do nothing being as they say prohibited from lending more than 50,000 Dolls. to the U.S. in any ⟨–⟩.¹³ I owe the B. of N.Y. 200.000 Dolls. which they require payment of in

Oct.¹⁴—this prevents *me* from applying to them. If the opinion of the Direction upon this or any other plan for raising money can be obtained by you, I shall be happy to receive it.

Yrs as ever   O Wolcott Jr

Colo. Hamilton

ALS, Connecticut Historical Society, Hartford; LC, Connecticut Historical Society, Hartford.
   1. Wolcott mistakenly dated this letter May 28, 1796.
   2. See H to Wolcott, June 26, 1796.
   3. The first session of the Fourth Congress had adjourned on June 1, 1796.
   4. See H to Wolcott, June 26, 1796.
   5. George Washington had left Philadelphia for Mount Vernon on June 13, 1796.
   6. See Wolcott to H, June 14, 17, 1796.
   7. See H to Wolcott, June 15, 1796.
   8. William Loughton Smith was a Federalist member of the House of Representatives from South Carolina.
   9. On May 28, 1796, Washington nominated "John Quincy Adams, at present Minister resident of the United States at the Hague, to be their Minister Plenipotentiary at Lisbon." The Senate confirmed the nomination on May 30, 1796 (*Executive Journal*, I, 212, 213).
   10. The "new Stock" had been authorized by "An Act making provision for the payment of certain Debts of the United States" (1 *Stat.* 488–89 [May 31, 1796]). See H to Wolcott, May 30, 1796.
   11. See H to Wolcott, June 16, 1796.
   12. See H to Wolcott, May 30, 1796; H to Washington, June 1, 1796.
   13. Section XI of "An Act to incorporate the subscribers to the Bank of Pennsylvania" states: "No loan shall be made by the said corporation, for the use or account of the government of the United States, to an amount exceeding fifty thousand dollars . . ." (*Pennsylvania Laws*, December, 1792, Sess., Ch. CXLVII [March 30, 1793]).
   14. This sum was borrowed from the Bank of New York in 1794 pursuant to "An Act making further provision for the expenses attending the intercourse of the United States with foreign nations; and further to continue in force the act intituled 'An Act providing the means of intercourse between the United States and foreign nations'" (1 *Stat.* 345 [March 20, 1794]). See H to Gulian Verplanck, September 28, 1794; H to Wolcott, September 29, 1794; Wolcott to H, October 11, 1794. In January, 1795, the Bank of New York extended the loan for eight months until October 8, 1795. See H to the Directors of the Bank of New York, January 25, 1795. The loan was subsequently renewed for another year (DS, RG 217, Miscellaneous Treasury Accounts, 1790–1894, Account No. 8297, National Archives).

From James McHenry

Philad. 4 July 1796

My dear Hamilton.

Wilkinson continues to heap charges upon Wayne; is condensing them into a consistent form, and I perceive will urge them in such a manner as may oblige the Executive, to determine whether a commander of the army can be tried by a court martial, or the affair examined by a court of inquiry, or if neither can be done by what authority the case is cognizable.[1]

Will you take the question into your consideration and help me with your opinion. I wish to be prepared, and will be extremely obliged to you if you will bestow a few thoughts upon it, and favour me with the result as soon as you can without interfering with professional engagements.

ADf, James McHenry Papers, Library of Congress.

1. Brigadier General James Wilkinson was second in command of the United States Army in the West under Major General Anthony Wayne. In the early summer of 1794 Wilkinson began a campaign to have Wayne's conduct reviewed before a court-martial or court of inquiry (Henry Knox to Wayne, December 5, 1794 [Richard C. Knopf, *Anthony Wayne: A Name in Arms; Soldier, Diplomat, Defender of Expansion Westward of a Nation; the Wayne-Knox-Pickering-McHenry Correspondence* (Pittsburgh, 1960), 396]). On October 6, 1794, George Washington wrote to Secretary of State Edmund Randolph: "It is but too evident, that there is a faction in the Army of the United States; at the head of which I believe it is a certain Genl W—— has placed himself, and is attempting the ruin of Genl. Wayne . . ." (*GW*, XXXIII, 521). Within two years enough material had accumulated for an inquiry to be held, and on July 1, 1796, the President, deciding that some action should be taken, wrote to McHenry: "It is my desire that the charges exhibited against General Wayne by Brigadier Wilkenson, with the letters of crimination on both sides, should be laid before the heads of Departments: and yours and their opinions reported to me on the measures necessary to be pursued to do justice to the Public; the accused; and the accuser; As also when, and by whom, the enquiry is to be made; with the preliminary steps necessary thereto" (*GW*, XXXV, 108). In addition to H's opinion, McHenry also sought the advice of Attorney General Charles Lee, Supreme Court Justice Samuel Chase, and William Vans Murray, member of the House of Representatives from Maryland (Steiner, *James McHenry*, 183). No report on Wilkinson's charges was ever made, for Wayne died on December 15, 1796, before the investigation had been completed.

To George Washington

New York July 5. 1796

Sir

I was in due time favoured with your letter of the 26 June & consulted the Gentleman you name on the subjects of it.

We are both of opinion there is *no* power in the President to appoint an Envoy Extraordinary, without the concurrence of the senate, & that the information in question is *not* a sufficient ground for extraordinarily convening the senate. If however the President from his *information collectively* be convinced that a dangerous state of things exists between us & France and that an envoy extraordinary to avert the danger is a necessary measure, I believe this would in the sense of the constitution warrant the calling of the Senate for the purpose. But this measure may be questionable in point of expediency, as giving a stronger appearance of danger than facts warrant. If further depredations on our commerce take place, if new avowals of the principle of the last capture should appear,[1] it may alter the case. But without something more the measure would scarcely seem adviseable.

Mr. Jay & Myself though somewhat out of your question talked of the expediency of removing Monroe,[2] and though we perceive there are weighty reasons against it, we think those for it preponderate—if a proper man can be found. But here we feel both immense embarrassment, for he ought to be at the same time a friend to the Government & understood to be *not unfriendly* to the French Revolution. General Pinckney is the only man we can think of who fully satisfies the idea, & unfortunately every past experiment forbids the hope that he would accept—though but for a short time.[3] But if a character of tolerable fitness can be thought of, it would seem expedient to send him. At any rate it is to be feared, if under the symptoms of discontent which have appeared on the part of the French Government, no *actual* & *full* explanation takes place, it will bring serious censure upon the Executive. It will be said that it did not display as much zeal to avoid misunderstanding with France as with G Britain—that discontents were left to rankle—that if the Agent of the Government in France was negligent or unfaithful some other mode ought to have been found &c.

As to your resignation, Sir, it is not to be regretted that the declaration of your intention should be suspended as long as possible & suffer me to add that you should *really hold the thing undecided to the last moment*.[4] I do not think it is in the power of party to throw any slur upon the lateness of your declar[a]tion. And you have an obvious justification in the state of things. If a storm gathers, how can you retreat? This is a most serious question.

The proper period now for your declaration seems to be *Two months* before the time for the Meeting of the Electors. This will be sufficient. The parties will in the mean time electioneer conditionally, that is to say, *if you decline*—for a serious opposition to you will I think hardly be *risked*.

I have completed the first draft of a certain paper & shall shortly transcribe correct & forward it.[5] I will then also prepare & send forward without delay the original paper corrected upon the general plan of it so that you may have both before you for a choice in full time & for alteration if necessary.[6]

With true respect & Affect Attachment I have the hon to remain Sir   Yr very Obed ser   A Hamilton

The Presi of the U States

ALS, MS Division, New York Public Library.

1. H is referring to the capture of the *Mount Vernon*. See Oliver Wolcott, Jr., to H, June 14, 17, 1796.
2. James Monroe. See H to Wolcott, June 15, 1796; Wolcott to H, June 17, 1796; Washington to H, June 26, 1796.
3. Charles Cotesworth Pinckney of South Carolina had declined an offer to be Secretary of War in 1794 (Washington to Pinckney, January 22, 1794 [LC, George Washington Papers, Library of Congress]; Pinckney to Washington, February 24, 1794 [ALS, George Washington Papers, Library of Congress]). Pinckney had also declined an offer to be Secretary of State after Edmund Randolph's resignation in 1795 (Washington to Pinckney, August 24, 1795 [ADfS, George Washington Papers, Library of Congress]; Pinckney to Washington, September 16, 1795 [ALS, George Washington Papers, Library of Congress]).
4. See Washington to H, May 15, June 26, 1796.
5. See the introductory note to H to Washington, May 10, 1796; "Draft of Washington's Farewell Address," printed as an enclosure to H to Washington, July 30, 1796.
6. See the introductory note to H to Washington, May 10, 1796; "Draft on

the Plan of Incorporating," printed as an enclosure to H to Washington, August 10, 1796.

From Oliver Wolcott, Junior

[*Philadelphia, July 6, 1796.* On July 8, 1796, Hamilton wrote to Wolcott: "I have just received your letter of the 6th." *Letter not found.*]

To Elias Boudinot [1]

[New York] July 7. 1796

My dear Sir

You will oblige me by letting me have an Extract from that part of your Mortgage law in New Jersey which regulates the mode of *cancelling* Mortgages [2]—also an extract from the Registering Book of the usual manner in which entries for cancelling were made about the years 1771, 1772 and 1773—and by informing me whether these Entries have been adjudged *conclusive*—though the order or certificate of the Mortgage is not to be found, the Mortgage money not paid, and the fact should appear that the Entry was a fraudulent act of the Registering Officer?

Excuse the trouble I give you and use me freely in a like case.

How are your Election prospects? Do not let the discontent with *Dayton* hazard the main point.[3] 'Tis better by a coalition with him to secure that, though you make some sacrifice of opinion, than to produce a dangerous schism.

Our affairs are critical, and *we* must be dispassionate and wise.

Yours truly   A. Hamilton

JCH Transcripts.

1. Because the original of this letter has not been found, it is impossible to determine whether it was sent to Elias or Elisha Boudinot. John Church Hamilton states that it was sent to Elisha Boudinot (*JCHW*, V, 138). Henry Cabot Lodge (*HCLW*, X, 182) and George Adams Boyd (*Elias Boudinot, Patriot and Statesman, 1740–1821* [Princeton, 1952], 229) state that it was written to Elias Boudinot.

Elias Boudinot, who had practiced law in New Jersey, was a member of the House of Representatives from 1789 to 1795 and director of the United States

Mint from 1795 to 1805. His brother Elisha was an attorney in Newark, New Jersey.

2. H is referring to Section 1 of "An Act for the more easy redemption and foreclosure of Mortgages" (*New Jersey Laws*, 19th Sess., Ch. DXVI [December 3, 1794]).

3. Jonathan Dayton was a member of the House of Representatives from New Jersey from 1791 to 1799 and Speaker of the House from 1795 to 1799. The "discontent" with Dayton arose from the fact that although he supported the House measure for implementing the Jay Treaty (see the introductory note to H to George Washington, March 7, 1796), he did so with a marked lack of enthusiasm. On April 29, 1796, in the course of a long speech to the House, he stated: "That the defects of this instrument of compact with Britain greatly exceeded its merits, was a truth which was strongly impressed upon his mind . . ." (*Annals of Congress*, V, 1274).

From David Hunter [1]

Martinburgh, Virginia, July 7, 1796. "A cause is now depending before the Supreme Court of the United States on an appeal from the Circuit Court of the United States for the district of Virginia, wherein I am Appellant & Denny Fairfax Appellee. . . .[2] I am informed that you practise in the supreme Court. I shoud therefore thank you to inform me whether you will undertake the Cause for me for a fee of Four Hundred dollars certain & made up to a Thousand if you succeed, or, if you think you can establish my right to the Land, I will give it to you as a Fee. It is worth about Two Thousand dollars. Mr. Marshall [3] of this State & the Attorney General of the United States Mr. Lee [4] will argue the cause on behalf of Fairfax. . . ." [5]

ALS, Hamilton Papers, Library of Congress.

1. Hunter was a Virginia planter.
2. For the case of *Hunter* v *Fairfax's Devisee*, see 3 Dallas, *U.S. Reports*, 305, and Henry Wheaton, *Reports of Cases Argued and Adjudged in the Supreme Court of the United States, February Term 1816* (New York, 1907), I, 304–81. See also Goebel, *Law Practice*, I, 525, note 198.
3. John Marshall.
4. Charles Lee.
5. On the cover of this letter H wrote: "Answer in the negative. It not being my general plan to practice in Supreme Court of U.S." H's letter to Hunter has not been found.

Conveyance from Isaac and Hannah Riley [1]

New York, July 7, 1796. "Isaac Riley and Hannah his wife for . . . the Sum of Two thousand Dollars . . .[2] have granted . . . unto the Said Alexander Hamilton . . . eight certain Lots of Land . . . in the Seventh Ward. . . ."

Copy, Conveyances in the Office of the Register, City of New York, Liber 71, 345, Hall of Records, New York City.
1. Isaac Riley was a New York City merchant.
2. On July 7, 1796, H made the following entries in his Cash Book, 1795–1804:
"Lots City of New York Dr. to Isaac Riley for purchase mony of 8 lots ℔ deed of this date   2000
"To Cash paid clerks of Supreme & Mayors Court for search for Mortgages & Judgmt   16.25
"Isaac Riley Dr to Cash for this sum paid him on account of above lots   1400
"Note there is a mortgage from Riley to you for Ballance." In the margin opposite these entries H wrote: "Mayors not paid 62.10 Qr." (AD, Hamilton Papers, Library of Congress).
John Barker Church was H's partner in this purchase. Church assumed one-half of all the expenses. See "Account with John Barker Church," June 15, 1797.

To Oliver Wolcott, Junior [1]

[New York, July 7, 1796]

Dr Sir

I have had some conversation with some influential Members of the Bank of New York who are disposed to do all that shall be found possible. But I wish to know without exaggeration the *least* sum that will be a *material* relief to you & when & how the payments will be desired.

Yrs.   A Hamilton

July 7. 1796

Oliver Wolcott Esq

ALS, Connecticut Historical Society, Hartford.
1. For an explanation of the contents of this letter, see H to Wolcott, May 30, 1796; H to George Washington, June 1, 1796; Wolcott to H, June 28, 1796.

To Oliver Wolcott, Junior

[New York, July 8, 1796]

Dr. Sir

I have just received your letter of the 6th.[1] The idea of selling Bank Stock is the worst of all & can only be urged on a plan of private speculation.[2] *Acquiescence* may tempt the Bank to oppress hereafter for speculation purposes. I have talked to some Directors of the Bank of New York conformably to your first suggestion, respecting the deposit of *Stock*[3] & it will not be expedient to change ground. The term of Credit I mentioned too was six months. You may safely deposit with the Bank of New York the directors of which would not sell at a sacrifice to the public *without necessity*. But confidence in the Government is impaired, and in addition, the Directors are apprehensive of falling too much under the power of the Bank of the U States. They will therefore want the deposit to give certainty to the operation.

I wait to have from you some idea of what sum will be a relief & when & how it will be wanted. As far as you can pospone transferrs from the B of NY to the B of the U States it will be comfortable to them. I have said nothing as yet of interest.

Yrs   A Hamilton
                   July 8th

O Wolcott Jnr Esq

ALS, Mr. Hall Park McCullough, North Bennington, Vermont.
1. Letter not found.
2. See H to Wolcott, May 30, July 7, 1796; H to George Washington, June 1, 1796; Wolcott to H, June 28, 1796.
3. See Wolcott to H, June 28, 1796.

To Charles Cotesworth Pinckney

[*New York*] *July 11, 1796.* "I received the letter [1] which you did me the favour to write me by Mr. Huger, whose acquaintance I was glad to make. The Bill for 2770 Dollars on Mr. Comfort Sands [2] was received & duly answered."

ALS, Pinckney Family Papers, Library of Congress.
1. Pinckney to H, June 5, 1796.
2. See Pinckney to H, June 5, 1796, note 9.

From Gerard Bancker [1]

New York, July 12, 1796. "I am content to dispense with Mrs. Rickets giving the Security you mention in your Note.[2] As Executors, Mr Livingston [3] & Myself have paid her Considerable Sums without thinking that kind of Security Necessary."

ALS, Hamilton Papers, Library of Congress.
1. Bancker was treasurer of the State of New York.
2. See James Ricketts to H, June 24, 1796.
3. Philip Livingston.

From Philip Schuyler

Albany, July 14, 1796. "The messenger with whom I sent Mr Morris's Mortgage [1] returned whilst I was at Fort Schuyler with a letter from the Clerk advising me that so many mortgages had been presented that he could not register the one in question so as to return It by the Messenger, but that as soon as he had done it, he would send It by a safe hand. . . ."

ALS, National Library of Scotland, Edinburgh.
1. The mortgage presumably was the one on western New York lands which Robert Morris sent to H on May 31, 1796. See Morris to H, May 17, 1796, note 2.

To James McHenry [1]

[New York, July 15, 1796]

My Dear Sir

I have considered the articles of War & rather think the case is not provided for by them. I incline to the opinion that The President *ex officio* as Commander in Chief has power to order a General Court Martial. But the exercise of this power would be liable to too much question & Criticism to be expedient.

What then is to be done? The President has a right to dis⟨miss⟩ Military Officers as holding their Comm⟨issions⟩ during pleasure—but the delicacy of the military character requires that ⟨– –⟩ should be exercised with Great Cauti⟨on⟩ & not till after very full investigation.

What then? When the Charges come forward let them be communicated to the Commanding General & he called upon to reply particularly to them. If there are facts to be proved & by persons with the army let three or five judicious Officers with the aid of the Judge Advocate & a Magistrate if to be had to administer oaths, be charged to collect testimony for the information of the Department of War to be laid before the President. Let the accuser & the accused be notified to attend the examination of the Witnesses to cross examine &c & let their testimony reduced to Writing by the Referrees or Commissioners with the Judge Advocate & certified by them with the observations of the Accuser & accused be transmitted to the War office & laid before the President who can afterwards act according to circumstances.

This is the best I can think of.

But you must by all means avoid the imputation of evading the inquiry & protecting a favourite.

Adieu   Yrs tr   A Hamilton
                                                          July 15 1796

Have you devised any mean of ensuring an ex[p]lanation to the French Government?[2] If it be not done & any thing amiss happens, I dont know what will befall you all.

Js Mc.Henry Esq

ALS, The Huntington Library, San Marino, California.
  1. This letter was written in reply to McHenry to H, July 4, 1796.
  2. See H to Oliver Wolcott, Jr., June 15, 1796; H to George Washington, June 16, July 5, 1796; Washington to H, June 26, 1796.

To William Tilghman [1]

[*New York*] *July 15* [*1796*] "I sent you about a fortnight since in a packet . . . a Deed to be executed by Mr and Mrs. R Morris & to be afterward recorded, requesting your attention to it. Not having heared from you concerning it, I fear it may have miscarried. Do me the favor to advise me by a line how this is, & if received what has been done."

ALS, James Monroe Law Office Museum, Fredericksburg, Virginia.
  1. Tilghman, a native of Maryland, had moved from Philadelphia on the eve of the American Revolution to his family's property in Chestertown, Maryland. He remained in Maryland, where he served in the Maryland Ratifying Convention and in the Maryland Assembly and Senate until 1794, when he opened a law office in Philadelphia.

To Oliver Wolcott, Junior [1]

[New York, July 15, 1796]

Dr. Sir

The application for a loan from the Bank of New York [2] though powerfully supported by some of the leading directors labours; owing to the jealousy & narrowness of certain ones who see in it a plan to increase the active capital of the Branch Bank & put them in its power. Unluckily the *President* [3] suddenly went off to R Island with his wife & some sick Children. I pursue the affair & I hope still to accomplish it.

There will be no difficulty in obtaining a postponement of the existing loan.[4] But this I tell them will not be sufficient.

Yrs.

AH
July 15

Oliver Wolcott Jun. Esq

ALS, Connecticut Historical Society, Hartford.
  1. For an explanation of the contents of this letter, see H to Wolcott, May 30, July 7, 8, 1796; H to George Washington, June 1, 1796; Wolcott to H, June 28, 1796.

2. See H to Wolcott, July 8, 1796.
3. Gulian Verplanck.
4. See Wolcott to H, June 28, 1796, note 14.

From Timothy Pickering

Philadelphia July 16. 1796.

Dear Sir,

Mr. Howell,[1] the Commissioner for settling the St. Croix boundary, has been here this week, & started the following questions.

1. "How far will it be proper for Mr. Howell to use his discretion in refusing to draw lots for the third Commissioner, in case the British Commissioner [2] shall persist in proposing a gentleman on his part who may be, in Mr. Howell's opinion, not an indifferent person?" [3]

2. "In case inhabitants of Massachusetts are thought objectionable on the part of the British, will not all inhabitants of New Brunswick & Nova Scotia be also, if not equally, objectionable?"

3. "Whether the authority of the commissioners can be legally executed, unless the three commissioners sign the declaration required of them by the treaty?" In other words, Whether if any two of the Commissioners agree, they can finally decide the question? [4]

I had previously received from Mr. Sullivan (the agent for the U States) [5] a letter stating the interview between Mr. Howell & Mr.

ALS, Hamilton Papers, Library of Congress; copy, Massachusetts Historical Society, Boston; copy, Columbia University Libraries.

1. On May 21, 1796, the Senate confirmed the President's nomination of "David Howell, of the State of Rhode Island, to be the Commissioner on the part of the United States, for the purpose of ascertaining the River St. Croix, agreeably to the fifth article of the treaty of amity, commerce, and navigation, between the United States and Great Britain" (*Executive Journal*, I, 210–11). Howell had been a delegate to the Continental Congress and a judge of the Supreme Court of Rhode Island. At the time of his appointment as United States commissioner, he was practicing law in Providence.

For the text of Article 5 of the Jay Treaty, see "Remarks on the Treaty . . . between the United States and Great Britain," July 9–11, 1795, note 12.

2. The British commissioner was Thomas Barclay of Nova Scotia, who had been a Loyalist during the American Revolution.

3. In the margin opposite this paragraph, John Jay wrote: "not at all."
4. In the margin opposite this paragraph, Jay wrote: "Yes."
5. On May 21, 1796, the Senate approved the nomination of "James Sullivan, of Massachusetts, to be the Agent on behalf of the United States, to manage the business of the fifth article of the treaty of amity, commerce, and navigation between the United States and Great Britain" (*Executive Journal*, I, 211). In

Barclay at Boston; in which it appeared that Mr. Barclay considered the appointment of a Commissioner from Massachusetts would be improper, because there was not one from New Brunswick. Yet (Judge Sullivan remarks) Nova Scotia, where Mr. Barclay resides, may be considered as a party, seeing he said that he could not take any steps towards the appointment of a third commissioner, until he consulted Sir John Wentworth, the Governor of that province, on the subject, as well as the governor of New Brunswick.[6] Judge Sullivan further remarks, "that the lands in New-Brunswick he considers as owned by proprietors in Nova Scotia, as those in Vermont are by proprietors in New-Hampshire; and that therefore Commissioners in New-Brunswick would be as eligible as in Nova-Scotia."

But the most unpleasant part of Judge Sullivan's information is, "That though the third commissioner is to be nominated and chosen or drawn by the two original commissioners, Mr. Barclay does not consider himself as acting judicially in the business, or as equally responsible to both nations on the point; but considers the appointment as a matter of negociation between the parties, *and that any advantages which may be gained will be honourable.*" Mr. Howell also informed me that Mr. Barclay did avow this extraordinary opinion: and if it were a just one, as founded on the treaty, it had been better to decide the question by the cast of a die: but 'tis so repugnant to the oath which each commissioner is to take, it is impossible that it should be the true construction of the article. I suppose it was chiefly the avowal of this principle, on the part of Mr. Barclay, that led Mr. Howell to propose his first quere: for while he should propose for the decision of the choice of the third commissioner by lot, a gentleman belonging to another state than Massachusetts, in order to obtain a *disinterested judge*, it would be with extreme repugnance that he would admit the name of an inhabitant of New Brunswick or Nova Scotia, on account of the direct interest of the former, & the probable interest of the latter, as above suggested by Judge Sullivan; especially as Nova Scotia already furnishes one of the Commissioners. If then it will consist with good faith to refuse to draw lots, on so partial a nomination by Mr. Barclay, it is desir-

---

1788 Sullivan had been appointed judge of probate for Suffolk County, and from 1790 to 1807 he served as attorney general of Massachusetts.
6. Thomas Carleton.

able that it might be done. In a report made to Congress by Mr. Jay, in April 1785, on this subject,[7] he proposed that his Britannic Majesty should name his half of the Commissioners, "being inhabitants of any of his dominions except those which are situated in & to the west and south of the gulph of St. Lawrence, and that the U. States should name the other half from any of their countries, except Massachusetts." The whole number of Commissioners then contemplated by Mr. Jay was 6. 8. 10. or 12.

The 3d question asked by Mr. Howell is in itself, as well as for the reasons contained in the preceding observations, highly important. The words in the article are "The said commissioners shall by a declaration under their hands & seals decide what river is the river St. Croix intended by the treaty:" Not the said Commissioners or *any two of them agreeing*. What is the legal construction of this article on this point? No such question arises on the 6th and 7th articles,[8] any three of the five commissioners being competent to a decision, the fifth commissioner being present. On one hand if *unanimity* be necessary, it will enable either party to counteract any flagrant partiality; on the other, it may defeat a great object of the article—putting a final end to a dispute that might have disagreeable consequences. Permit me to request your attention to this subject, and that you would converse with Mr. Jay upon it. In the course of two or three days I expect Mr. Howell will call on you both at New York.

I am very respectfully & affectionately yours   T. Pickering.

Alexander Hamilton Esqr.

7. On April 21, 1785, Jay, as "Secretary of the United States for the Department of foreign Affairs, to whom was referred the Papers . . . respecting the Eastern boundary Line of the United States," had reported "That in his Opinion effectual Measures should immediately be taken to settle all Disputes with the Crown of Great Britain relative to that Line.

"He thinks that Copies of the said Papers should be transmitted to the Minister Plenipotentiary of the United States at that Court, with Instructions to present a proper Representation of the Case, and to propose that Commissioners be appointed to hear and finally decide those Disputes. . . .

"That the Number of Commissioners should be six, or eight, or ten, or twelve at the Election of his britannic Majesty: the exact Number not being important." (*JCC*, XXVIII, 287–88.)

8. For the text of Articles 6 and 7 of the Jay Treaty, see "Remarks on the Treaty . . . between the United States and Great Britain," July 9–11, 1795, notes 13 and 39.

From William Tilghman

[*Philadelphia, July 16, 1796.* On July 18, 1796, Hamilton wrote to Tilghman: "I am favoured with your letter of the 16 instant." *Letter not found.*]

To William Tilghman [1]

[New York, July 18, 1796]

Dr. Sir

I am favoured with your letter of the 16 instant [2] and regret the occasion of my not having heard from you. I thank you for the attention paid to the business. If in the course of a fortnight a perfectly good opportunity should not occur you would oblige me by sending on the deed by a Trusty Express, the expence of which I will with pleasure defray, as I am desirous to have the affair completed.[3] Yrs. with esteem & regard   A Hamilton

July 18th.

ALS, Cornell University Library, Ithaca, New York.

1. For background to this letter, see H to Tilghman, July 15, 1796.
2. Letter not found.
3. Tilghman endorsed this letter: "A. Hamilton 18. July 96 Send Church's Deed to Luzerne by Express. ansd. 23. July." Tilghman's letter to H has not been found. This is a reference to John B. Church's speculations in Pennsylvania lands with Tench Coxe. For an explanation of these purchases, see the introductory note to Coxe to H, February 13, 1795.

Alexander Hamilton and Richard Harison to Richard Bayley [1]

New York 19th. July 1796.

Sir

We have looked into the Act to prevent the bringing in & spreading of Infectious Diseases in this State.[2] By one of its provisions every

Vessel arriving from parts beyond Sea, having on Board forty passengers, is subject to Quarantine of Cause, & may be removed to the place assigned for the same. We think that where the numbers of passengers is so great, the Health Officer may take a reasonable Time to satisfy himself as to the Danger of Infection from such Vessel—And of Course any prudent arrangements may be made in the Interim by Consent of parties. The Captain or owners of the Vessel would be subject to the Charges of Quarantine—other Expences must be provided for in some other Manner.[3]

We are respectfully, Sir,   Your Obedt Servts.   Alex Hamilton
Rich: Harison

Dr Richard Bayley
Health Officer &ca.

Copy, Municipal Archives and Records Center, New York City.

1. Harison was United States attorney for the District of New York. Bayley, a physician, was health officer of the City of New York.

2. The act was passed on April 1, 1796 (*New York Laws*, 19th Sess., Ch. XXXVIII).

3. On July 18, 1796, the ship *Nancy* arrived at New York from Newry, Ireland, with four hundred and fifty immigrants on board. A yellow fever epidemic, which was generally thought to have originated on foreign ships, had begun in the neighborhood of the docks in June. A paragraph in *The* [New York] *Minerva, & Mercantile Evening Advertiser*, July 19, 1796, on the *Nancy*'s arrival, expressed the hope that "those, *whose business it is,* will not forget the melancholy fate which attended the emigrants who landed in this city about this time last year." This was followed by a statement that ". . . measures are taking by the Health officer and other public characters to prevent the immediate landing of the Irish Emigrants in this city as their introduction at present might be attended with injurious consequences to themselves and the inhabitants."

On the same day Bayley wrote to Mayor Richard Varick asking if the City of New York would support the immigrants while they remained in quarantine (ALS, Municipal Archives and Records Center, New York City). Bayley's letter to Varick and the letter printed above were read to the Common Council on July 19, "Whereupon the Board determined to grant the Sum of 800 Dollars. . . .

"The following Case was then stated for the Opinions of Messrs Hamilton, Harison & Troup. . . ." (*Minutes of the Common Council of the City of New York* [New York, 1917], II, 263.)

"A Vessel lately arrived in the Port of New York with Four hundred and fifty Emigrants from Newry in Ireland on Board—it is supposed that it will be dangerous to permit them to land in the City, and that it is proper the Vessel should perform Quarrentine, but many of these Emigrants are unable to support themselves, and without some Assistance will probably suffer for Want of Necessaries. Your opinion is therefore requested—

"(1) Whether the Corporation of the City of New York are by Law bound to provide for and support persons in such Circumstances

"(2) If the Corporation is not who is bound to support them, and
"(3) What will be prudent for the Corporation to do in the present Case all Circumstances considered" (copy, Municipal Archives and Records Center, New York City).

The opinion of H, Harison, and Robert Troup, dated July 21, 1796, was read on July 25 (*Minutes of the Common Council*, II, 264). The opinion reads: "In answer to the questions annexed we are of opinion that whilst the Emigrants are performing quarantine, on board their Vessel the Corporation are not bound to support them—But they must be provided for by the owners or master of the Vessel, or themselves, according to the nature of the contract under which they embarked for America; Yet if the Corporation should cause any of them to be landed under any restraints or in any place except such as they themselves shall assign before their Quarantine is performed We think the Corporation would then be bound to support the persons landed. Considering, however, the present situation of the City—the distress to which those may be reduced on board of the vessel who are without the means of comfortable subsistence—the injury which may thereby be done to the health of the others —and the consequent danger of having the quarantine, at least in some degree, eluded—We do not hesitate to say it will be prudent in the Corporation to contribute to the support of the Emigrants whilst they shall continue on quarantine" (DS, Municipal Archives and Records Center, New York City). See also forthcoming Goebel, *Law Practice*, III.

To Timothy Pickering

[New York, July 21, 1796]

Dear Sir

I communicated your letter¹ to Mr. Jay & now give you our joint sense.

Considering the nature of the transaction and what must necessarily have been presumed to be the intent, & that the authority is on a public subject & between two nations, we think that a decision by two out of three commissioners must be sufficient.

We know nothing but an immediate personal interest in property which may be affected by the decision, that can be a conclusive objection to the person nominated—but this interest must be known not suspected. The rest must be matter of *negotiation*. In point of *propriety* neither Government ought to name a person, liable from local situation to the suspicion of particular interest or byass. But one cannot formally object to the nomination of the other on this general ground.

Declarations like those ascribed to Mr. Barkely,² if well authenticated & unequivocal, importing clearly that he thought himself at liberty to gain advantages & not bound to act impartially would justify the Government in stopping & representing the matter to the British Government. But we ought to act with great caution not to give occasion to impute to us a spirit of procrastination or subterfuge. Tis so much more important that the dispute should be settled than how it is settled (at least according to my idea of the object) that we should by no means seek for difficulties but rather facilitate than impede.

Yrs. respectfully & truly   A Hamilton
July 21. 1796

T Pickering Esq

ALS, Massachusetts Historical Society, Boston.
1. Pickering to H, July 16, 1796.
2. Thomas Barclay, British representative on the St. Croix boundary commission. See Pickering to H, July 16, 1796.

From William Tilghman

[*Philadelphia, July 23, 1796.* Tilghman endorsed a letter from Hamilton, dated July 18, 1796: "ansd. 23 July." *Letter not found.*]

From Oliver Wolcott, Junior

[*Philadelphia, July 26, 1796.* On July 30, 1796, Hamilton wrote to Wolcott and acknowledged "the Receipt of your letter of the 26th." *Letter not found.*]

From James Greenleaf [1]

Alexander Hamilton Esqr.   New York July 27th. 1796
Dear Sir,

The indispensible necessity of an immediate tho' short respite from business united with Motives of Interest and an unbounded Attachment to reputation induce me to make a proposition to you of a pretty extraordinary Nature but which after due Reflection I flatter myself will be deemed not unworthy your Attention. My engagements of every possible Nature do not exceed Twelve Hundred Thousand Dollars and my real and personal Estate may with ease be liquidated and made to produce Five Millions of Dollars—say rather a Million Dollars annually for Five consecutive Years—but in consequence of some important and unexpected delinquencies on the part of persons whose Engagements have become due to me and must be paid from Securities given, my own engagements become due more rapidly than my means (without having recourse to improper operations) can be made to answer. If you will now be induced to aid me with your name responsibility and talents in the liquidation of my Concerns and payment of my engagements, in such wise, that no undue sacrifice of property shall result and my name be borne thro' with the Credit and propriety it deserves The one third part of the net residue of my whole Estate both real and personal, after payment of my Engagements, shall become yours; provided you will consent that the Mass shall remain undivided for Ten years & constitute the Capital of a Banking House to be established either in this City, or at Philadelphia in our joint Names and under your sole guidance and the profits divided between us in equal portions.

I have reason to believe that with the aid of your name and our joint responsibility accompanied with the names of three other persons as trustees for deposited property, it will, by a reputable Mode of financing, I shall communicate, be practicable for me to obtain the use of a Million of Dollars at Legal Interest for the average term of five years, and with this Sum I should calculate on being able to pay off all my engagements with due Credit and Advantage, as considerable Amounts are due at distant periods and may be purchased in at a considerable discount.

If these Outlines so far meet your approbation as to induce you to wish my entering into a particular detail, it shall be done at such time as will best suit your liesure and convenience.

I am with great Esteem, Dear Sir, Your very Affectionate And Obedient Servant James Greenleaf.

LS, Hamilton Papers, Library of Congress.
1. Greenleaf, a native of Massachusetts, a member with James Watson of the former New York City mercantile firm of Watson and Greenleaf, and a former United States consul at Amsterdam, engaged in extensive land and securities speculations. In 1793, Greenleaf, Robert Morris, and John Nicholson made

vast land purchases in the Federal City. Greenleaf proved to be dishonest. He failed to honor notes endorsed by Morris; he did not meet the payments on his Washington lots; and he misused money entrusted to him by Morris. Morris and Nicholson eventually bought out Greanleaf's interests in the Federal City and the North American Land Company. See H to Morris, March 18, 1795, note 21; Morris to H, June 7, 1795, note 7.

To Oliver Wolcott, Junior

[New York, July 28, 1796]

Dr. Sir

I have not lost sight of the negotiation with the Bank [1] though it labours & I have thought it best to let it lie bye till the President [2] returns. *Mc.Cormick* [3] is violent against it & plays on little jealousies, & what is still more efficacious private *interests;* representing the consequent inability of the Bank to accommodate the Merchants, many of whom from the unfortunate issue of some late speculations are likely to want *much aid.*

Yrs. truly   A Hamilton
July 28. 1796

Ol Wolcott Esq

ALS, Connecticut Historical Society, Hartford.
1. The Bank of New York. See Wolcott to H, June 28, 1796; H to Wolcott, July 7, 8, 15, 1796.
2. Gulian Verplanck.
3. Daniel McCormick, a New York City merchant, was a director of the Bank of New York.

From James Greenleaf

Alexander Hamilton Esqr.   [New York] 30 July. 96

Dear Sir

I must leave the City for Philada on Monday, to return in about a week—if before my departure you can with convenience give an answer on the proposition made to you,[1] it will oblige me. If the general principle marked by me should meet your approbation, I shall have no objection to making very important alterations to square with your wishes relative to the pursuit of other objects. believe me with great Esteem   Dr Sir   Yr very obedt Servant

James Greenleaf.

ALS, Hamilton Papers, Library of Congress.
1. See Greenleaf to H, July 27, 1796; H to Greenleaf, July 30, 1796.

To James Greenleaf [1]

New York July 30 1796

Dr. Sir

I have carefully reflected upon the subject of your letter of the 27th. instant.

Though the data which it presents authorise an expectation of large pecuniary advantage and though I discover nothing in the affair which an Individual differently circumstanced might not with propriety enter into—yet in my peculiar situation, viewed in all its public as well as personal relations, I think myself bound to decline the overture.

With great regard I am Dr. Sir   Yr. Obed serv   A H

James Greenleaf Esqr

ADfS, Hamilton Papers, Library of Congress.
1. H wrote this draft at the bottom of Greenleaf's letter to him of July 27, 1796.

To George Washington [1]

New York July 30. 1796

Sir

I have the pleasure to send you herewith a certain draft [2] which I have endeavoured to make as perfect as my time and engagements

ALS, MS Division, New York Public Library.
1. For an explanation of the contents of this letter and its enclosure, see the introductory note to H to Washington, May 10, 1796. See also Washington to H, May 15, 1796; "Abstract of Points to Form an Address," May 16–July 5, 1796; H to Washington, June 1, 1796.
2. See the enclosure to this letter.

would permit. It has been my object to render this act *importantly* and *lastingly* useful, and avoiding all just cause of present exception, to embrace such reflections and sentiments as will wear well, progress in approbation with time, & redound to future reputation. How far I have succeeded you will judge.

I have begun the second part of the task—the digesting the supplementary remarks to the first address ³ which in a fortnight I hope also to send you—yet I confess the more I have considered the matter the less eligible this plan has appeared to me. There seems to me to be a certain awkwardness in the thing—and it seems to imply that there is a doubt whether the assurance without the evidence would be believed. Besides that I think that there are some ideas which will not wear well in the former address, & I do not see how any part can be omitted, if it is to be given as the thing formerly prepared. Nevertheless when you have both before you you can better judge.

If you should incline to take the draft now sent—and after perusing and noting any thing that you wish changed & will send it to me I will with pleasure shape it as you desire. This may also put it in my power to improve the expression & perhaps in some instances condense.

I rejoice that certain clouds have not lately thickened & that there is a prospect of a brighter horison.⁴

With affectionate & respectful attachment I have the honor to be Sir   Yr. Very Obed Serv   A Hamilton

The President of the UStates

[ENCLOSURE]

Draft of Washington's Farewell Address ⁵

The period for a new election ˄being not very distant and the ˄of a Citizen to administer the Executive Gov of the U States

---

3. H is referring to his "Draft on the Plan of Incorporating" in which he revised Washington's first draft of his Farewell Address. See the introductory note to H to Washington, May 10, 1796.

4. This is presumably a reference to relations between the United States and France.

5. ADf, Hamilton Papers, Library of Congress; ADf, facsimile (tracing), Hamilton Papers, Library of Congress.

time actually when the thoughts ~~of my fellow Citizens~~ must be employed in designating ~~the Citizen who is to administer the Executive Government of the United States~~ ^the person who is to be cloathed with that important trust for another term, ~~it may conduce to~~ ^it appears to me proper, and ^especially as it may conduce to a more distinct expression of the public voice, that I should now apprize you of the resolution I have formed to ~~desire~~ decline being considered ^among ~~of~~ the number of those ^out of whom a choice is to be made.

I beg you nevertheless to be assured ^at the same time that the resolution, which I announce, has not been taken without a strict regard to all the considerations attached to the relation which|as|^connected with a dutiful Citizen|I ^connected with [6] ^bears to|my|^his Country; and that in withdrawing the tender of my service, which silence in my situation might imply, I am influenced by no diminution of zeal for its future interest nor by any deficiency of grateful respect for its past kindness, but by a full conviction that ~~my retreat~~ ^such a step is compatible with both.

The ^acceptance of and continuance hitherto in the office to which your ~~unanimous~~ suffrages have twice called me has been a uniform sacrifice of private inclination to ^the opinion of public duty coinciding with ~~your~~ what appeared to be your wishes ~~and to the opinion of public duty~~ ^combined with a deference for. I |had| ~~constantly~~ ^constantly hoped that it would have been much earlier in my power ~~consistently~~ consistently with motives which I was not at liberty to disregard to return to that retirement from which those ^they motives had reluctantly drawn me.

~~The conflict betwe between those motives and inclination previous to the last election~~

The strength of my desire to withdraw previous to the last election had even led to the preparation of an address to declare it to

---

6. In the margin opposite these insertions H wrote: "inseparable from" and "incident to."

you—but deliberate reflection on the very critical and perplexed posture of our affairs with foreign nations and the unanimous advice of|men of every way|intitled to my confidence obliged me to abandon the idea.
(with "mature" inserted above "deliberate"; "persons" above "men"; "impelled" above "intitled")

I rejoice that ~~that~~ the state of your national Concerns external as well as internal no longer ~~appa~~ renders the pursuit of my inclination incompatible with the sentiment of duty or propriety, and that ~~the~~ partiality ~~which~~ any portion of ∧ ~~my fellow citizens~~ may still ~~cherish~~ for my services, ~~will not~~ they, ~~will~~ under the existing circumstances of ~~the~~ Country, ∧ not disapprove the resolution I have formed.
(with "whatever" above "the"; "You" above "my fellow citizens"; "retain" above "cherish"; "our" above "of the"; "will" and "my" and "to retire" inserted)

The impressions under which I first accepted the arduous trust|of chief Magistrate [7] of the U States|were explained on the proper occasion.[8] In the discharge of this trust I can only say that I have ∧ contributed ~~towa~~ towards the organisation and administration of the Government the best exertions of which a very fallible judgment was capable. ~~I am not uncon~~ Not unconscious|at|the outset of the inferiority of my qualifications|for the station|, experience in my own eyes and perhaps still more in those of others has not diminished ~~the~~ in me the diffidence of myself—and every day the increasing weight of years admonishes me more and more that the shade of retirement is as necessary ∧ as it will be welcome|to me.|~~If any circumst~~ Satisfied that if any circumstances have given|a|peculiar value to my services they were temporary, I have the ~~satisfaction~~ to believe that ~~patriotism~~ while inclination and prudence urge me to recede from the political scene patriotism does not forbid∧—|May I
(with "with pure intentions" inserted; "in" above "at"; "to me" inserted; "consolation" above "satisfaction"; "it[9]" above "forbid")

---

7. In MS, "Masistrate."
8. See Washington's "First Inaugural Address," April 30, 1789 (*GW*, XXX, 291–96).
9. A brace encloses the material from this point to the end of the paragraph. In the margin Washington wrote: "omitted in address." Washington crossed out the same material in his final draft of the Farewell Address (ADS, MS Division, New York Public Library; printed in Paltsits, *Farewell Address*, 140).

also have that of perceiving in my retreat that ~~my invol~~ the involuntary errors which I have probably committed have been the causes of no serious or lasting mischief to my Country and thus be spared ˄the anguish of regrets which would disturb the repose of my retreat and embitter the remmant of my life! I may then expect to realize ˄without alloy the purest enjoyment of partaking, in the midst of my fellow citizens ˄of the benign influence of good laws under a free Government; the ultimate object of all my wishes and|to which I look as|the happy reward ˄I hope of our mutual cares labours and dangers.

In looking forward to the moment which is to terminate the carreer of my public life, my sensations do not permit me to ~~suppress~~ suspend the deep acknowlegements required by that debt of gratitude which I owe to my beloved country for the many honors it has conferred upon me ˄still more for the distinguished and ˄steadfast ~~persevering~~ confidence it has reposed in me and for the opportunities I have thence enjoyed it has thus afforded me of manifesting my inviolable attachment by services ~~at least~~ faithful and persevering—however the inadequateness of my faculties may have rendered these efforts unequal to my ˄my fellow Citizens have ill seconded my zeal.¹⁰ If benefits have resulted to you ˄ from these services, let it always be remembered to your praise and as an instructive example in our annals that the constancy of your support¹¹ amidst appearances ~~sometimes~~ ~~frequently~~ sometimes dubious ~~discouraging~~ vicissitudes of fortune˄and ~~not infrequently~~ ~~want of success~~ often discouraging in situations in which not infrequently want of success has seconded the ~~suggesti~~ criticisms of malevolence was the essential prop ~~and guarantee~~ of ~~of~~ the efforts and˄the guarantee of the measures by which they were atchieved. ~~I will not be restrained by personal considerations of personal del-~~

10. In the margin opposite this sentence H wrote: "disproportioned."
11. At this point H placed an asterisk and wrote in the margin: "under circumstances in which the passions agitated in every direction were liable to the greatest fluctuations."

~~icacy from paying you the tribute of declaring~~ Profoundly penetrated with this idea, I shall carry it with me to my retirement and to my grave as a lively incitement to unceasing vows (the only returns I can henceforth make) that Heaven may continue to You the choicest tokens of the beneficence merited by national piety and morality —that your union and brotherly affection may be perpetual—that the free constitution, which is the work of your own hands may be sacredly maintained—that its administration in every department may be stamped with wisdom and virtue—that in fine the happiness of the People of these States under the auspices of liberty may be made complete by so careful a preservation & so prudent a use of this blessing as will acquire them the glorious satisfaction of recommending it to the affection the praise—and the adoption of every nation which is yet a stranger to it.

Here perhaps I ought to stop. But a solicitude for your welfare, which cannot ~~expire~~ end but with my life, ~~urges me to offer~~ and the fear that ∧there may exist projects unfriendly to it ~~are in train~~ against which it ~~is very important~~ may be necessary you should be ~~carefully~~ guarded, urge me ~~to~~ in taking leave of you to offer to your ∧solemn consideration and frequent review some sentiments the result of mature reflection confirmed by ∧observation & experience which appear to me ~~all import~~ essential to the permanency of your felicity as a people. These will be offered with the more freedom as you can only see in them the ~~advice~~ disinterested advice of a parting friend who can have no personal motive to tincture or byass his counsel.

Interwoven as is the love of Liberty ~~in~~ with every fibre of your hearts no recommendation ~~can be~~ is necessary to fortify your attachment to it. ~~After~~ Next to this ~~and as very materially connected with it~~ that unity ∧of Government ∧ ~~of that Republic~~ which constitutes you one people claims your ~~most cordial affection and~~ anxious care ~~and vigilant~~ vigilant & guardianship— as ~~one of the~~ a main pillars of ~~so~~ your real independence of your peace safety ~~liberty~~ freedom and happiness ~~and as the one against which the efforts of your internal and external enemies will be most constantly & actively but insidiously levelled.~~ ~~though covertly and~~ most

This being the point in your political fortress against which the batteries of internal and external enemies will be most constantly and actively however covertly and insidiously levelled, it is of the utmost importance that you should appreciate in its full force the immense value of your political Union to your national and individual happiness—that you should cherish towards it an affectionate and immoveable attachment and that you should watch for its preservation with jealous ~~and eagle eyed~~ solicitude.

For this you have every motive of sympathy and interest. Children for the most part of a common country, that country ~~ought~~ claims and ought to concentrate your affections. The name of American must always ~~exalt your character~~ & gratify and exalt the just pride of patriotism more than any denomination which can be derived from local discrimination. ~~Religion morality~~ You have with slight shades of difference the same religion manners habits & political ~~laws~~ institutions & principles. You have in a common cause fought and triumphed to gether. The independence and liberty you enjoy are the work of ~~your united~~ joint councils efforts—dangers sufferings & successes. By your Union you atchieved them, by your union you will most effectually maintain them. ~~This~~ The ~~name of American is more flattering more exalting and ought to be more dear to you than any which you derive from the discriminations of State boundaries.~~

~~But considerations addressed to your sensibility, however persuasive to virtuous minds~~

The considerations which address themselves to your sensibility are greatly strengthened by those which apply to your interest. even outweighed Here every portion of our Country will find the most urgent and commanding motives for ~~cherishing~~ guarding and preserving the Union of the Whole.¹²

The North in ~~an~~ intercourse with the South under the equal laws of one Government will ^free & unfettered^ find vast additional resources ^in the production of the latter many of them peculiar^ of maritime and commercial enterprise ^and precious materials of their manufacturing industry.^ The South in the same intercourse will share in the benefits of the Agency of the North will find its agriculture promoted and its commerce extended by ^turning into its own channels~~those~~^ ~~the employment of those~~ means of Navigation which the North more abundantly affords and while it contributes to extend ^the national^ navigation ~~which~~ will participate in the protection of a maritime strength to which itself is unequally adapted. The East in a like intercourse with the West finds and in the progressive improvement of internal navigation will more & more find, a valuable vent for the commodities which it brings from abroad or manufactures at home. The West derives through this Channel an essential supply of its wants—and what is ^far^ more important to it, it must owe the secure and permanent enjoyment of the ~~essent~~ indispensable outlets for its own productions to the weight influence & ~~and future marine~~ ^maritime resources & ~~indissol~~^ of the Atlantic States directed by an indissoluble community of interest. The tenure by which it could hold this advantage either from its own separate ~~power~~ strength or by an apostate and unnatural connection with any foreign Nation must be intrinsically & necessarily precarious at every moment liable to be disturbed by the ^fluctuating^ combinations of those primary ^European^ interests which ~~every portion of Europe must~~ constantly ~~be governed by regulate the conduct of every portion of Europe~~— ^And where every part finds a particular interest in the Union^ All the parts of our Country will find in their Union greater independence from the superior abundance & variety of production incident to ~~different~~

12. At this point in the MS there is a double dagger which H presumably made between September 1 and September 5, 1796, to indicate the insertion he planned of an additional passage on education. See Washington to H, September 1, 1796; H to Washington, September 5, 1796.

~~soils~~ the diversity of soil & climate, all the parts of it must find in the aggregate assemblage & reaction of their mutual population production [13] ^greater^ strength, proportional security from external danger, ~~less frequency of foreign wars~~ less ^frequent^ interruption of their peace with foreign nations and what is far more valuable an exemption ~~those~~ from those broils & wars between the parts if disunited which their ^own^ rivalships ~~of inflamed~~ fomented by foreign intrigue, or the opposite alliances ~~with which mu~~ with foreign nations engendered by their mutual jealousies would inevitably produce—a ~~corespondent~~ ^consequent^ exemption from the necessity of those military establishments upon a large scale which bear in every country so menacing an aspect toward Liberty.

These considerations speak a conclusive language to every ~~considerate an~~ virtuous and considerate mind. ~~The diversities~~ They place the continuance of our Union among the first objects of patriotic desire. Is there a doubt whether a common government can long embrace so extensive a sphere? Let Time & Experience decide the question. Speculation in such a case ought not to be listened to—And tis rational to hope that the auxiliary ^agency of the^ governments of the subdivisions, ~~if~~ with a proper organisation of the whole will secure a favourable issue to the Experiment. Tis allowable to believe that the spirit of party the intrigues of foreign nations, the corruption & the ambition of Individuals are likely to prove more formidable adversaries to the unity of our Empire than any inherent difficulties in the scheme. Tis against these that the guards of ^mounds^ national opinion national sympathy national prudence & virtue are to be erected. With such obvious motives to Union there will be always cause from the fact itself to distrust the <u>patriotism</u> of those who ^in any quarter^ may

---

13. At the bottom of this page H wrote: "in the aggregation & reaction of their mutual resources & advantages." Although in Paltsits, *Farewell Address*, 185, this phrase is inserted in the fourth sentence of the following paragraph to read "Let Time & Experience in the aggregation & reaction of their mutual resources & advantages decide the question," it seems more likely that H meant these words to be used at this point as a possible alternative.

JULY 1796

endeavour to weaken its bands. And by all the love I bear you My fellow Citizens I ~~exhort~~ ^{conjure} you as ~~far~~ ^{often} as it appears to frown upon the attempt.

Besides the more serious causes which have been hinted, as endangering our Union there is ~~one~~ another ^{at} less dangerous but against which it is necessary to be on our guard. I mean the petulance ^{collisions & disgusts} of party differences of Opinion. It is not uncommon to hear the irritations which these excite vent themselves in declarations that the different parts of the Union are ill assorted and cannot remain together—in menaces from the inhabitants of one part to those of another that it will be dissolved by this or that measure. Intimations of the kind ar[e] as indiscreet as they are intemperate. Though frequently made with levity and without being in earnest they have a tendency to produce the consequence which they indicate. They teach the minds of men to consider the Union as precarious as an object to which they are not to attach their hopes and ~~desires~~ fortunes and thus weaken the sentiment in its favour. By rousing the resentment and ~~piquing the~~ alarming the pride of those to whom they are addressed they set ingenuity to work to depreciate the value of the object and _∧^{to} discover motives of Indifference to it. This is not wise. Prudence demands that ~~all our words~~ we should habituate ourselves in all our words and actions to reverence the Union as a sacred and inviolable palladium of our happiness ~~as a thing which in even~~ and should discountenance ~~the supposed~~ whatever can lead to a suspicion that it can in any event be abandonned.[14]

^{Tis matter of serious concern}
~~There is cau much cause to regret that the organisation of parties has for some~~ that parties in this Country for some time past have been too much characteristed by ~~local and~~ geographical discriminations—Northern and Southern States Atlantic and Western Country.[15] These discriminations which are the mere artifice of the spirit ^{of party}

---

14. In the margin opposite this paragraph Washington wrote: "Omitted in address." In his final draft of the Farewell Address, Washington crossed out this paragraph and wrote beside it: "not important enough" (ADS, MS Division, New York Public Library; printed in Paltsits, *Farewell Address*, 145).

15. In the margin opposite the remainder of this paragraph Washington

274   JULY 1796

always
of party (~~over~~ dexterous to avail itself of every source of sympathy of every handle by which the passions can be taken hold of and which has been careful to turn to account the circumstance of
sympathy of neighborhood
territorial vicinity) have furnished ~~in the difference of p~~ an ~~evidence in the difference of party opinions~~ an argument against the Union as evidence of a real difference of local interests and views and serve to hazard it by organising large districts of country under the direction
the leaders of
of ˄different factions whose passions & prejudices rather than [16] the true interests of the Country, will be too apt to regulate the use of their influence. If it be possible to correct this poison in the affairs of our Country
˄it is worthy the best endeavours of moderate & virtuous men to effect it.

One of the expedients which the partisans of Faction employ to‐
within local spheres
wards ~~fostering~~ strengthening their influence by local discriminations is to misrepresent the opinions and views of rival districts—The People at large cannot be too much on their guard against the jealousies which grow out of these misrepresentations. ~~The~~ They tend to render aliens to each other those who ought to be tied together by fraternal affection. The Western Country have lately had
in the negotiation by the Executive &
a useful lesson on this subject. They have seen˄in the unanimous ratification of the Treaty with Spain by the Senate [17] ~~the conclusive~~
in all parts of the Country
~~proof~~ & in the universal satisfaction at that event˄a decisive proof
propagated
how ~~in~~ unfounded have been the suspicions [that] have been instilled
among
in them of a policy ~~hostile~~ in the Atlantic States & in the different
departments of the General Government
~~states~~ hostile to their interests in relation to the Mississipian. They

---

wrote: "not in address." Washington crossed out this material in his final draft of the Farewell Address (ADS, MS Division, New York Public Library; printed in Paltsits, *Farewell Address*, 145–46).

16. In MS, "that."

17. The Treaty of Friendship, Limits, and Navigation between the United States and Spain was signed on October 27, 1795 (Miller, *Treaties*, II, 318–38). It was ratified by the Senate on March 3, 1796 (*Executive Journal*, I, 203).

have seen, too two treaties formed which secure to them every thing that they could desire to confirm their prosperity. Will they not henceforth rely for the preservation of these advantages on that union by which they were procured? Will they not reject those counsellors who would render them alien to their brethren & connect them with Aliens?

To the duration and efficacy of your Union a Government extending over the whole is indispensable. ~~Without this~~ No alliances however strict between the parts could ~~have the necessary solidity or afford the necessarily~~ be an adequate substitute. These could not fail to be liable to the infractions and interruptions which all alliances in all times have suffered. Sensible of this important truth ~~and with a view to a more intimate Union~~ you have lately established a Constitution of General Government, better calculated than the former ~~one~~ for an intimate union and more adequate to the direction of your common concerns. This Government the offspring of your own choice uninfluenced and unawed, completely free in its principles, in the distribution of its powers uniting energy with safety and containing in itself a provision for its own amendment is well entitled to your confidence and support—~~Complian~~ Respect for its authority, compliance with its laws, acquiescence in its measures, are duties dictated by the fundamental maxims of true Liberty. The basis of our political systems is the right of the people to make and to alter their constitutions of Government.[18] But the ~~existing~~ constitution for the time, and until changed by an explicit and authentic act of the whole people, is sacredly binding upon all. The very idea of the right and power of the people to establish Government presupposes the duty of every individual to obey ~~it~~ the established Government.

All ~~irregular~~ obstructions ~~therefore~~ to the execution of the laws— all <u>combinations</u> and <u>associations</u> under whatever plausible character with the real design to ₍direct₎ counteract countroul ₍influence₎ or awe the regular deliberation or ₍action of the constituted authorities are contrary to ~~the true principles of a representative Government~~ this fundamental principle & of

18. In the margin next to this and the preceding sentence H wrote: "ordinary management of affairs to be left to Represent."

the most ~~dangerous~~ tendency.[19] They serve to organise Faction‸and to put in the stead of the delegated will of the whole nation the will of a party. ~~A~~ often a small‸minority of the community—and according to the alternate ~~victories~~ of ~~party~~ different ~~factions~~ to make the public administration ~~reflecting~~ the‸schemes and projects of faction rather than the wholesome plans of common councils and deliberations. However combinations or assoc[i]ations of this description may occasionally promote popular ends and purposes they are likely to produce in the course of time and things the most effectual engines by which artful ambitious and unprincipled ~~in~~ men will be enabled to subvert the power of the people and usurp the reins of Government.

(margin insertions: "fatal to give it an artificial force;" · "but artful & enterprising" · "triumphs" · "parties" · "ill concerted")

Towards the preservation of your government and the permanency of your present happy state, it is not only requisite that you steadily discountenance irregular oppositions to its authority but that you should be upon your guard against the spirit of innovation upon its principles however ~~plausible~~ the pretexts. One method of assault may be to effect alterations in the forms of the constitution tending to impair the energy of the system and so to undermine what cannot be directly overthrown. In all the changes to which you may be invited remember that time and habit are as necessary to fix the true character of governments as of any‸human institutions, that experience is the surest standard by which the real tendency of existing constitutions of government can be tried—that changes upon the credit of mere hypothesis and opinions exposes you to perpetual change from the ~~exsessive~~ and endless variety of hypothesis and opion—and remember‸that for the efficacious management of your common interests in a country so extensive as ours a Government of as much force and strength as is consistent with the perfect security of liberty is indispensable. Liberty itself will find in

(margin insertions: "specious" · "other" · "facility in" · "success" · "ni" · "also" ~~always~~)

---

19. In the margin next to this sentence H wrote: "direct."

such a Government, ~~its surest~~ with powers properly distributed and arranged, its surest guardian—and protector. In my opinion the real danger in our system is that the General Government organised as at present will prove too weak rather than too powerful.

I have ^already^ observed the danger to be apprehended from ~~characterising~~ ^founding^ our parties ~~by~~ on Geographical discriminations. Let me now enlarge the view of this point and caution you in the ^most^ solemn manner against the baneful effects of party spirit in general. This spirit unfortunately is inseperable from human nature and has its root in the strongest passions of the human ^heart^—It exists under different shapes in all governments ~~more or l~~ but ^in different degrees stifled controuled or repressed^ in those of the popular form it is always seen in its ~~most~~ ^utmost^ vigour & rankness and it is their worst enemy.[20] In republics of narrow ~~dimensions, the combination of a~~ ^extent^ it is ~~easy for those~~ ~~who at any time possess the power of the State~~ ^usual^ ^rule^ it is not difficulty for those who at any time possess the reins of administration, or even for partial combinations of men, who from birth riches and other sources of distinction have an ~~habitual influence~~ extraordinary influence by ~~having~~ ^possessing^ or acquiring the direction of the military ^force^ or by sudden efforts of partisans & followers to overturn the established order of things and effect a usurpation. But in republics of large extent the one or the other is scarcely possible. The powers and opportunities of resistance of a numerous and wide extended nation ~~compared with the ordinary~~ defy the successful efforts of the ordinary military force or of any ^assemblages^ collections which wealth and patronage may call to their aid especially if there be no city of overbearing for[c]e resources and influence. In such Republics it is perhaps safe to ~~say~~ ^assert^ that the conflict of popular faction offer the only avenues

20. H wrote in the margin the four sentences which follow from this point. Above this marginal material Washington wrote "omitted in address" and drew a hand pointing to H's insertion. Washington crossed out this material in his final draft of the Farewell Address (ADS, MS Division, New York Public Library; printed in Paltsits, *Farewell Address*, 149).

to ~~usurpation & tyrann~~ tyranny & usurpation. ~~Perhaps it may be safely asserted that in those which occupy a large extent of territory it is the only channel through which tyranny~~ & usurpation ~~can approach~~. The ~~dep desposition of one faction despotic~~ domination of one faction over another stimulated by that spirit of Revenge which is apt to be gradually ~~and invariably~~ engendered and which in different ages and countries have produced the greatest enormities is itself a frightful despotism. But this leads at length to a more formal and permanent despotism. The disorders and miseries which ~~resolution~~ result predispose the minds of men to seek repose & security in the absolute power of a single man. And ~~the~~ some leader of a prevailing faction more able or more fortunate than his competitors turns this disposition to the purpose of an ambitious and criminal self aggrandisement.

Without looking forward to such an extremity (which however ought not to be out of sight) the ordinary and continual ~~fact~~ mischief of the spirit of party ~~demand the endeavours of moderate~~ make it the interest and the duty of a wise people to discountenance and repress it.

It serves always to distract the Councils & enfeeble the administration of the Government. It agitates the community with ~~false alarms~~ ill founded jealousies and false alarms ~~and~~ embittering one part of the community against another, & producing occasionaly riot & insurrection. It opens inlets for foreign corruption and influence—which find an easy access through the channels of party passions—and cause the true policy & interest ~~interests~~ of our own country to be ~~sacrificed to~~ made subservient to the policy and interest of one and another foreign ~~Power~~ Nation; sometimes enslaving ~~the~~ our own Government to the will of a foreign Government.

There ~~It~~ is an opinion ~~which has some vogue and is intirely without true~~ that parties in free countries are salutary checks upon the administration of the Government & serve to ~~keep alive~~ invigorate the spirit of Liberty. This within certain limits is true and in governments of a particular kind patriotism may look with some favour on the spirit of party. But in those of the popular in those purely elective, it is a spirit not to be fostered & encouraged. From the natural tendency of such governments, it is certain there will always be enough of it for every salutary purpose and there being constant danger of excess the effort ought to be by force of public opinion to mitigate & correct it. Tis a fire which cannot be quenched but demands a uniform vigilance to prevent its bursting into a flame—lest it should not only warm but consume.

It is important likewise that the habits of thinking of the people should tend tend to produce caution in their public agents in the several departments of Government, to retain each within its proper shere sphere and not to encr[o]ach one upon the another—The spirit of approach encroachment in this particular and that every attempt of the kind are should meet with the discountenance of community, so and that in every case in which a precedent of encourage encroachment should have been given, a careful election of (revocation be effected by) a careful attention to the choice next choice of public Agents. The spirit of encroachment ab tends to absorb the powers of the several branches and departments, and thus to establish under whatever forms a despotism. A just knowlege of the human heart, of that love of power which predominates in it, is alone sufficient to establish this truth. Experiments ancient and modern— some in our own country and under our own eyes serve to confirm it. If in the public opinion the distribution of the constitutional powers be in any instance and wrong or inexpedient—let it be corrected by the authority of the people in a legitimate constitutional way—Let there be no change by usurpation, for though this may

be the instrument of good in one instance, it is the ordinary ∧and natural ~~ord~~
~~death~~
instrument of the destruction of free Government—and the influence of the ~~presede~~ precedent is always infinitely ~~worse~~ more pernicious than [21] any thing which it may atchieve can be beneficial.

To all those dispositions which promote ~~the~~ political happiness, prosperity
Religion and Morality are essential props. In vain does ~~he~~ ∧that man claim the praise of patriotism who labours to subvert or undermine these great pillars of human happiness these ~~sure foundations~~ firmest foundations of ~~all~~ the duties of men and citizens. The mere politician equally with the pious man ought to respect and cherish them. A volume could not trace all their connections with private and public happiness. Let it simply be asked where is the security for ~~reputation~~ property for reputation for life if the sense of moral and religious obligation deserts the oaths which are administered in ~~the~~ the instruments of Investigation Courts of Justice? Nor ought we to flatter ourselves that morality can be separated from religion. Concede as much as may be asked to the effect of refined education in minds of ∧a peculiar structure—can we believe—can we in prudence suppose that national morality can be maintained in exclusion of religious principles? Does it not require the aid of a generally received and divinely authoritative Religion?

Tis essentially true that virtue or morality is ∧a main & necessary spring ~~an indispensable prop~~ of popular or republican Governments. The rule indeed extends with more or less force to all free Governments. Who that is a prudent & sincere friend to them can look with indifference on the ravages which are making in the foundation of the Fabric? [22] Religion? The uncommon means which of late have been directed to this fatal end seem to make it in a particular of manner the duty of the Retiring Chief of ~~his~~ ∧a nation to warn his country against tasting of the poisonous draught.

Cultivate also industry and frugality. They are auxiliaries of good

21. In MS, "that."
22. Washington bracketed the remaining material in this paragraph and wrote in the margin: "omitted in address."

morals and ~~sour~~ great sources of private and national prosperity. Is there not room for regret that our propensity to expence exceeds the maturity of our Country for expense? Is there not more luxury among us, in various classes, than ~~the~~ suits the actual period of our national progress? Whatever may be ₍the apology for₎ ~~said of~~ luxury in a Country mature ~~in wealth and~~ in all the arts which are its ministers and the means of national opulence—can it promote the advantage of a young agricultural Country little advanced in manufactures and not much advanced in wealth? [23]

Cherish public Credit as a mean of strength and security. ~~But œconomise the resource by the using it as little as possible~~ As one method of preserving it, use it as little as possible. Avoid occasions of expence by cultivating peace—remembering always that the preparation ₍against danger₎ ~~for danger defence~~ by timely and provident disbursements is often a mean of avoiding greater disbursements to repel it. Avoid the accumulation of ~~expence~~ debt by avoiding occasions ₍of₎ ~~and~~ expence and by vigorous exertions in time of ₍peace₎ to discharge the debts which unavoidable wars may have occasionned—not transferring to posterity the burthen ₍which₎ we ought to bear ourselves. Recollect that towards the ~~dischar~~ payment of debts there must be Revenue, that to have revenue there must be taxes, ~~and that a chearful acquiescence which in those whic~~ that it is impossible to devise taxes which are not more or less inconvenient and unpleasant—that they are always a choice of difficulties—that ~~from~~ the intrinsic embarrassment which ~~always~~ never fails to attend a selection of objects ought to be a motive for a candid construction of the conduct of the Government in making it—and that a spirit of acquiescence in those measures for obtaining revenue which the public exigencies dictate is in an especial manner the duty and interest of the citizens of every State.

Cherish good faith and Justice towards, and peace and harmony

---

23. In the margin next to the end of this sentence H wrote: "in the infancy of the arts & certainly not in the manhood of Wealth."
In Washington's final draft of the Farewell Address he crossed out the entire paragraph and bracketed it as follows: "not sufficiently important" (ADS, MS Division, New York Public Library; printed in Paltsits, *Farewell Address*, 152).

with all nations. Religion and morality ~~demand~~ enjoins this conduct And It cannot be, but that true policy equally_∧_ demands ~~demands~~ ~~dictates~~ it. It will be worthy of a free enlightened and at ~~not~~ no distant period a great nation to give_∧to mankind_ the magnanimous and too novel example ~~to mankind~~ of a people ~~and go~~ invariably governed by those exalted views _an exalted justice & benevolence._. Who can ~~say~~ a doubt that in ~~the~~ long course of time and events the fruits of such a conduct would richly repay any temporary advantages which might be lost by a steady adherence to the plan? Can it be that Providence has not connected the_∧ permanent felicity_ ~~happiness~~ of a nation with its virtue? The experiment is ~~worthy~~ _recommended by_ of every sentiment ~~that~~ _which_ ennobles human nature. Alas! is it rendered impossible by its vices?

Toward the execution of such a plan [24] nothing is more essential than that antipathies against particular nations and passionate attachments ~~towards~~ _for_ others should be ~~discarded~~ avoided—and that instead of them we should_∧ cultivate_ just and amicable feelings towards all. That nation, which indulges towards another a habitual hatred or a habitual fondness is in some degree a slave. It is a slave to its animosity or to its ~~attach~~ affection—either of which is sufficient to lead it astray from its duty and interest. Antipathy against one nation which never fails to beget a similar sentiment in the other disposes each more readily to ~~violate the rights~~ offer injury and insult to the other—to lay hold of slight causes of umbrage and to be haughty and intractable when accidental or trifling differences arise. Hence frequent quarrels and bitter and obstinate contests _broils_. The nation urged by resentment and rage sometimes impels the Government to War

24. An asterisk appears at this point in the document, and H wrote in the margin as an alternative: "it is very material that while we entertain proper impressions of particular cases, of friendly or unfriendly conduct of different foreign nations towards us, we nevertheless avoid fixed and rooted antipathies against or passionate attachments for any—instead of these cultivating as a general rule just & amicable feelings towards all." Washington did not use H's alternative material in his final draft of the Farewell Address (ADS, MS Division, New York Public Library; printed in Paltsits, *Farewell Address*, 153).

contrary to its own calculations of policy ~~& interest~~. The Gover[n]ment ~~frequ~~ sometimes participates [25] in this propensity & does through passion what reason would forbid—at other times it makes the animosity of the nations ~~subservient~~ subservient to hostiles projects which originate in ambition & other sinister motives. The peace often and sometimes the liberty of Nations has been the victim of this cause.

~~In like manner~~ So likewise a passionate attachment of ~~one~~ one nation to another produces multiplied ills. Sympathy for the favourite nations, ~~promote~~ facilitating promoting the illusion of a supposed common interest in cases where it does not exist and a ~~participation in the enmities of the favourite leads to embark commun~~ and communicating to one the enmities of the one betrays into a participation in its quarrels & wars without adequate inducements or justifications. It leads to the concession of privileges to one nation and to the denial of them to others—which is apt doubly to injure the nation making the concession by an unnecessary ~~sacrifice~~ yielding of what ought to have been retained and by exciting jealousy ill will and retaliation in the party from whom an equal privilege is witheld. And it gives to ambitious ~~or~~ corrupted or deluded citizens, who devote themselves to the views of the favourite foreign ~~nation the~~ power, facility in betraying or sacrificing the interests of their own country even with ~~the advantage of~~ without odium & gilding with the appearance a virtuous popularity ~~to themselves~~ of ~~virtue &~~ impulse yieldings ~~justness of sentiment~~ the base ~~sacrifices~~ of ambition ~~of~~ or corruption.

As avenues to foreign influence in ~~innume~~ innumerable Ways such attachments are peculiarly alarming to the enlightened independent Patriot do they ~~friend of his Country~~. How many opportunities ~~does it~~ afford to intrigue with domestic factions ~~to seduce even~~ to practice with suc seduction—to mislead cess the arts of ~~success—to misdirect the~~ public opinion—to influence or awe the public Councils! Such an attachment of a small or weak towards a great & powerful Nation destines the former to revolve round the latter as its satellite.

25. In MS, "particaples."

Against the Mischiefs of Foreign Influence all ~~are~~ the Jealousy of a free people ought to be constantly ^continually ~~directed~~ exerted. All History & Experience ~~in different ages and nations~~ has proved that foreign influence is one of the most ~~formidable~~ ^baneful foes of republican Governt— but the jealousy ^at ^of it to be useful must be impartial else it becomes an instrument ~~instead of a defence~~ of ~~that~~ ^the very influence ^to be avoided instead of a de- ~~guard~~ ^it fence against.

~~An~~ Excessive partiality for one foreign nation & excessive dislike of another, leads to see danger only on one side and serves to viel ^& second the arts of influence on the other. ~~This is a mo~~ Real Patriots who resist the intrigues of the favorite become suspected & odious. Its tools & dupes usurp the applause & confidence of the people to betray their interests.

The great rule of conduct for us in regard to foreign Nations ought to be to have as little <u>political</u> connection with them as possible —so far as we have already formed engagements let them be fulfilled —with circumspection indeed but with perfect good faith. ~~But~~ Here let us stop.

Europe has a set of primary interests ~~foreign to us~~ which have none or a very remote relation to us. Hence she must be involved in frequent contests the causes of which will be essentially foreign to us. Hence therefore it must necessarily be unwise ~~in us~~ on our part to implicate ourselves by an artificial connectione in the ordinary vicissitudes of European politics—in the combination, & collisions of her friendships or enmities.

Our detached and distant situation invites us to a different course & enables us to pursue it. If we remain a united people under an efficient Government the period is not distant when we may defy material injury from external annoyance—when we may take such an attitude as will cause the neutrality we shall at any time resolve to observe to be ~~duly~~ violated with caution—~~when menacing more than ear~~ when it will be the interest of belligerent nations under the impossibility of making acquisitions upon us to be very careful how either forced us to throw our weight into the opposite scale—when we may choose peace or war as our interest guided by justice shall dictate.

Why should we forego the advantages of so ~~ha~~ felicitous a situation? Why ~~should we~~ quit our own ground to stand upon ~~European~~ Foreign ground? Why by interweaving our destiny with any part of Europe should we intangle our ~~prospect~~ prosperity and peace in the nets of European Ambition rivalship interest or Caprice?

Permanent alliance, intimate connection with any part of the foreign ~~ea~~ world is to be avoided. ~~I mean~~ so far (I mean) as we are now at liberty to do it: for let me never be understood ~~as infedily to~~ as patronising infidelity to preexisting engagements. These must be observed in their true and genuine sense. But tis not necessary nor will it be prudent to extend them. Tis our true policy as a general principle to avoid permanent or ~~a~~ close alliance—Taking care always to keep ourselves by suitable establishments in a respectably defensive posture we may safely trust to occasional alliances ~~in~~ for extraordinary emergencies. ~~But I mean to submit to you my fellow citizens a general principle of policy which I think ought to govern you as far as you are at present free. In extraordinary exigencies temporary alliances will suffice for the occasion.~~

Harmony liberal ~~friendly~~ intercourse and commerce with all nations are recommended by justice humanity & interest. But even our commercial policy should hold an equal hand—neither seeking nor granting ~~particular~~ exclusive favours or preferences—consulting the natural course of things—diffusing and diversifying by gentle means the streams of Commerce but forcing nothing—establishing ~~by treaty~~ with powers so disposed in order to give to a stable course, Trade to ~~trade~~ define the rights of our Merchants and enable the Government to support them— ~~temporary~~ conventional rules of intercourse the best that present circumstances and mutual opinion of interest will permit but temporary— and liable to be abandonned or varied as time experience & future circumstances may dictate—remembering that tis folly ~~to expect a dis-~~ alway

~~interested~~ in one nation to expect disinterested favour in another—that to accept any thing under that character ~~it~~ is to part with a portion of ~~our~~ its independence—and that ~~we~~ may ~~frequently~~ find ~~ourselves~~ it itself in the condition of having given ~~an~~ equivalents for nominal favours and of being reproached with ingratitude in the bargain. There can be no greater error in national policy than to desire expect or calculate upon real favours. Tis an illusion that experience must cure, that a just pride ought to discard.

In offering to you, My Countrymen! ~~fellow Citizens~~ these counsels of an old and affectionate friend—counsels suggested by labourious reflection and matured by a various experience—I dare not hope that they will make the strong and lasting impressions I wish—that they will controul the current of the passions or prevent our nation from running the course ~~of~~ which has hitherto marked the destiny of all nations. But if they ~~may~~ I may flatter myself that even produce some partial ~~benefits~~, occasional some good—~~if the shall~~ that they sometimes recur to moderate the violence of party spirit—to warn against the evils of foreign intrigue—to guard against the impositions of pretended patriotism—the having offered them must always afford me a precious consolation.

How far in the execution of my present Office I have been guided by the principles which have been ~~recommended~~ inculcated the public records & the external evidences of my conduct must witness. ~~to an~~ My conscious assures me that I have at least believed myself to be guided by them.

In reference to the present War of Europe my Proclamation of the 22d of April 1793 [26] is the key to my ~~sentiments~~ plan. Sanctioned by your approving voice and that of your representatives in Congress ~~has continually governed me~~ the spirit of that measure has continually governed me uninfluenced and unawed by the attempts of any of the warring powers their agents or partizans to deter or divert from it.

26. This is a reference to Washington's neutrality proclamation. For the text, see John Jay to H, April 11, 1793, note 1.

After deliberate consideration and the best lights I could obtain (and from men who did not agree in their views of the original progress & nature of that war) I was satisfied that our Country, ~~had~~ under all the circumstances of the case, had a right and was bound in propriety and interest to take a neutral position—And having taken it, I determined as <ins>far as</ins> should depend on me to maintain it steadily and firmly.[27]

Though in reviewing the ~~events~~ <ins>incidents</ins> of my administration I am unconscious of intentional error—I am yet too sensible of my own deficiencies not to think it probable that I have committed many errors. I deprecate the evils to which they may tend—and fervently implore the Almighty to avert or mitigate them. I shall carry with me nevertheless the hope that my motives will continue to be viewed by my Country with indulgence & that after forty five years of my life devoted with an upright zeal to the public service the faults of inadequate abilities will be consigned to oblivion as myself must soon be to the mansions of rest.

Neither Ambition nor interest has been the impelling cause of my actions. I never designedly misused any power confided to me. The fortune with which I came into office is not bettered otherwise than by that ~~value~~ improvement in the value of property which the natural progress and peculiar prosperity of our country have produced. I retire with ~~an~~ a pure heart <ins>without cause for a blush—</ins> ~~with no sentiment alien to your true interests~~ with no alien sentiment to the ardor of those vows for the

---

27. At this point in H's draft he left a large blank space. In his final draft of the Farewell Address, Washington inserted the following three paragraphs: "The considerations, which respect the right to hold this conduct, it is not necessary on this occasion to detail. I will only observe, that according to my understanding of the matter, that right, so far from being denied by any of the Belligerent Powers has been virtually admitted by all.

"The duty of holding a Neutral conduct may be inferred, without any thing more, from the obligation which justice and humanity impose on every Nation, in cases in which it is free to act, to maintain inviolate the relations of Peace and amity towards other Nations.

"The inducements of interest for observing that conduct will best be referred to your own reflections and experience. With me, a predominant motive has been to endeavour to gain time to our country to settle and mature its yet recent institutions, and to progress without interruption, to that degree of strength and consistency, which is necessary to give it, humanly speaking, the command of its own fortunes." (*GW*, XXXV, 237.)

happiness of his Country which is so natural to a Citizen who sees in it ²⁸ ~~with undefiled hand and with ardent~~ vows for ~~the happiness of~~ ~~which is~~ himself his ~~a Country,~~ ₍the native soil of ~~myself~~ and₍progenitors for four generations.²⁹

28. Washington crossed out this paragraph in his final draft of the Farewell Address and wrote in the margin opposite it: "This paragraph may have the appearance of self distrust and mere vanity" (ADS, MS Division, New York Public Library; printed in Paltsits, *Farewell Address*, 159). Washington ended his address with the following paragraph: "Relying on its kindness in this as in other things, and actuated by the fervent love towards it, which is so natural to a Man, who views in it the native soil of himself and his progenitors for several Generations; I anticipate with pleasing expectation that retreat, in which I promise myself to realize, without alloy, the sweet enjoyment of partaking, in the midst of my fellow Citizens, the benign influence of good Laws under a free Government, the ever favourite object of my heart, and the happy reward, as I trust, of our mutual cares, labours and dangers" (*GW*, XXXV, 238).
29. H endorsed this draft: "Original Draft Copy considerably amended."

To Oliver Wolcott, Junior ¹

[New York] July 30th 1796

Dr Sir

I had written you a short line previous to the Receipt of your letter of the 26th ² to which indeed I can add nothing material.

It will, as things stand, be imprudent to push the point of a further loan till the President arrives ³—for though a majority of the Directors are well disposed to the thing, they are afraid of *McCormick's* clamours ⁴ and want the sanction of the President to controul & counterballance him. All I am told that can now be relied upon is a postponement of the payment of the 200 000 Dollars heretofore lent ⁵—to which McCormick assents.

Yrs. truly   A Hamilton

Oliver Wolcott Esq

ALS, Connecticut Historical Society, Hartford.
1. For an explanation of the contents of this letter, see Wolcott to H, June 28, 1796; H to Wolcott, July 7, 8, 15, 28, 1796.
2. Letter not found.
3. Gulian Verplanck.
4. Daniel McCormick.
5. See Wolcott to H, June 28, 1796, note 14.

From Oliver Wolcott, Junior

[*Philadelphia, August 1, 1796.* On August 3, 1796, Hamilton wrote to Wolcott: "I have received your letter of the 1st." *Letter not found.*]

From Catharine Bedlow [1]

New York, August 2, 1796. "Inclosed is the Letter of Helena Soyer [2] which I Should have been Sent you before, but being daily in Expectation of Seeing you, it was defered to be given you till then. I could wish a Leasure Houre will permit you to call & See us as Mr Bedlow Continues Ill unable to transact any Business."

ALS, Hamilton Papers, Library of Congress.
1. Catharine Bedlow, the oldest daughter of Hendrick Rutgers, was the wife of William Bedlow (Bedloe), grandson of Isaac Bedlow of Bedloe's Island in New York Harbor. William Bedlow, a former sea captain and merchant, in 1784 became postmaster of New York City.
The following entry under the date of June 11, 1796, appears in H's Cash Book, 1795–1804: "for retainer of *Wm. Bedlow* adsm. *Medcaff Eden* 10." Another entry on July 8, 1796, records the receipt of the additional sum of ten dollars (AD, Hamilton Papers, Library of Congress). See also H's Law Register, 1795–1804 (D, partially in H's handwriting, New York Law Institute, New York City).
2. H's endorsement of this letter reads: "with Helena Sawyers letter."

To Oliver Wolcott, Junior

[New York, August 3, 1796]

Dr Sir

I have received your letter of the 1st.[1] I deplore the picture it gives and henceforth wish to *forget* there is a Bank or a Treasury in the U States, though I shall not forget my regard to individuals.

I do not see one argument in any possible shape of the thing for the sale of Bank Stock or against that of the other stock, which does not apply *vice versa* & I shall consider it as one of the most infatuated steps that ever was adopted.²

God bless You   A Hamilton
                                                             Aug 3. 1796

It will be known on Thursday whether any thing is to be expected here.³

Oliver Wolcott Jun Es

ALS, Connecticut Historical Society, Hartford.
   1. Letter not found.
   2. H is referring to the provisions of "An Act making provision for the payment of certain Debts of the United States" (1 *Stat.* 488–89 [May 31, 1796]). For the provisions of that act to which H took exception, see H to Wolcott, May 30, 1796, note 1; H to George Washington, June 1, 1796. See also Wolcott to H, June 28, 1796; H to Wolcott, July 8, 1796.
   3. For information on negotiations for a loan by the Bank of New York to the United States, see Wolcott to H, June 28, 1796; H to Wolcott, July 7, 8, 15, 28, 30, 1796.

To Oliver Wolcott, Junior

[New York, August 5, 1796]

Dr. Sir

The Bank of New York is willing to make the loan of 324 000 Dollars to you (I mean the exact sum of about this amount, if you desire it, which one of the laws you mentioned authorises to borrow)¹ on these terms to advance all but two hundred thousand Dollars when you please—to advance the two hundred thousand Dollars, by way of reloan, when that sum, payable in October, becomes due.² The term of credit to be in each case six months from the time of the advance. The interest six per Cent, with a deposit of Stock (6 ℔ Cent) at par so placed as to permit the sale of it at the *market price*, if there be a failure of reimbursement at the stipulated periods. The Treasury, upon honor, to draw immediately upon the Bank as the money is wanted for expenditure not to transfer it before hand. On this point sincerity and delicacy will be expected.

It was mentioned too as desirable, *though not made a condition*, that it should be understood that in case a real pressing emergency in the course of the Winter should exist the Bank on giving previous notice of the necessity to the Treasury might be at liberty to sell the stock at the then market price. The Directors to be *upon honor* not to use this permission but in case of *real necessity*. Their *honor*, I know, may be intirely relied upon & it may be well to gratify.

The deposit of Stock was suggested by myself upon your first letter.[3] It is an ingredient in the negotiation which the Bank values.

Yrs. truly   A Hamilton
Aug 5. 1796

The Bank wishes a speedy decision.[4]

Oliver Wolcott Junr. Esq

ALS, Connecticut Historical Society, Hartford.

1. H is suggesting that the United States borrow from the Bank of New York in accordance with the provisions of "An Act making further provision for the expenses attending the intercourse of the United States with foreign nations; and to continue in force the act, intituled 'An act providing the means of intercourse between the United States and foreign nations'" (1 *Stat.* 487–88 [May 30, 1796]). Section 5 of this act provided that the President "be authorized to borrow . . . a sum not exceeding three hundred and twenty-four thousand five hundred and thirty-nine dollars and six cents, at an interest not exceeding six per centum per annum, reimbursable at the pleasure of the United States, to be applied to the purposes of this act. . . ." In actuality the United States borrowed three hundred and twenty thousand dollars under the terms of "An Act making provision for the payment of certain Debts of the United States" (1 *Stat.* 488–89 [May 31, 1796]). For this act, see H to Wolcott, May 30, 1796, note 1. For the terms of the loan, dated August 16, 1796, negotiated with the Bank of New York under this act, see Rafael A. Bayley, *The National Loans of the United States, From July 4, 1776, to June 30, 1880* (Washington, 1882), 40; *ASP*, Finance, I, 584, 691.

For information on H's efforts to aid Wolcott in securing a loan from the Bank of New York, see Wolcott to H, June 28, 1796; H to Wolcott, July 7, 8, 15, 28, 30, August 3, 1796.

2. See Wolcott to H, June 28, 1796, note 14.
3. Wolcott to H, June 28, 1796.
4. Wolcott wrote at the top of this letter: "recd. & ansd. the 7th." Wolcott's answer has not been found.

From Rufus King

[*London, August 6, 1796.*[1] *Letter not found.*]

1. "List of Letters from . . . Mr. King" to H, Columbia University Libraries.

From Oliver Wolcott, Junior

[*Philadelphia, August 7, 1796.* At the top of a letter from Hamilton, dated August 5, 1796, Wolcott wrote: "recd. & ansd. the 7th." *Letter not found.*]

To Richard Hatfield [1]

New York, August 9, 1796. "I have in my hands two bonds one from Joseph *Lyon* of White Plains, in WestChester for £ 82.10 dated the 9th of Feby 1770—the other from Joseph Lyon and Daniel Lyon dated the 2nd. of may in the year 1768 both to General Schuyler. . . . As well from finding your name mentioned in the matter as from the belief that you are more likely than any other to know the situation of the Parties and the state [of] facts I am induced to trouble you with a request that you will be so good as to make the necessary inquiry and assist me with all the light you can collect to enable me to Judge of the probability of recovering the money. . . ."

Copy, Hamilton Papers, Library of Congress.
   1. Hatfield was county clerk of Westchester County, New York, from 1777 to 1802. He was also a member of the New York Assembly in 1794 and of the New York Senate in 1795.

From George Washington [1]

Mount Vernon 10th Augt. 1796.

My dear Sir,

The principal design of this letter, is to inform you, that your favor of the 30th. Ulto, with its enclosure,[2] got safe to my hands by the last Post, and that the latter shall have the most attentive consideration I am able to give it.

A cursory reading it has had, and the Sentiments therein contained are extremely just, & such as ought to be inculcated. The doubt that occurs at first view, is the length of it for a News Paper publication; and how far the occasion would countenance its appearing in any other form, without dilating *more* on the present state of matters, is questionable. All the columns of a large Gazette would scarcely, I conceive, contain the present draught. But having made no accurate calculation of this matter, I may be much mistaken.

If any matters should occur to you as fit subjects of communication at the opening of the next Session of Congress [3] I would thank you for noting and furnishing me with them. It is my wish, and my custom to provide all the materials for the Speech in time that it may be formed at leizure.

With sincere esteem and affectionate regard   I am always Yours

Go: Washington

Alexr: Hamilton Esqr.

ALS, Hamilton Papers, Library of Congress.
1. For an explanation of the contents of this letter, see the introductory note to H to Washington, May 10, 1796.
2. Washington is referring to H's "Draft of Washington's Farewell Address," which is printed as an enclosure to H to Washington, July 30, 1796.
3. Congress was scheduled to convene on December 5, 1796.

To George Washington [1]

[New York, August 10, 1796]

Sir

About a fortnight since, I sent you a certain draft.[2] I now send you another on the plan of incorporating.[3] Whichever you may prefer, if there be any part you wish to transfer from one to another any part to be changed—or if there be any material idea in your

ALS, MS Division, New York Public Library.
1. For an explanation of the contents of this letter, see the introductory note to H to Washington, May 10, 1796. See also Washington to H, May 15, 1796; "Abstract of Points to Form an Address," May 16–July 5, 1796; H to Washington, June 1, July 30, 1796.
2. This is a reference to H's "Draft of Washington's Farewell Address," which is printed as an enclosure to H to Washington, July 30, 1796. See also the introductory note to H to Washington, May 10, 1796.
3. See the enclosure to this letter. See also the introductory note to H to Washington, May 10, 1796.

own draft which has happened to be omitted and which you wish introduced—in short if there be any thing further in the matter in which I can be of any, I will with great pleasure obey your commands.

Very respectfully & Affecty I have the honor to be Sir Yr Obed ser
A Hamilton
Aug 10. 1796

[ENCLOSURE]

Draft on the Plan of Incorporating [4]

The strength of my desire to resume a private station had led, previous to the last election, to the preparation of an address to declare it to you, which it was my intention to have published in the year 1792 early enough to have made the knowlege of it general in due time for that Election. But mature reflection on the very critical and perplexed posture of our affairs with foreign nations and the unanimous advice of persons intitled to my confidence impelled me to abandon the idea, and to resolve, in the event of being again ~~honored~~ designated by your suffrages, to devote to you my services for a year or two longer; hoping that ~~when~~ within this period all obstacles to a justifiable and becoming retreat would be removed.

~~I rejoice that the state of your national~~ Though the fit moment has been ₍retarded₎ postponed by ₍particular₎ circumstances beyond my ~~hope~~ expectation—I rejoice that the state of your national concerns, external as well as internal, no longer renders the pursuit of ~~my~~ inclination incompatible with the sentiment of duty or propriety, and that whatever partiality any portion of you may yet retain for my services, even they in the present situation of ~~y~~our Country will not disapprove my resolution to retire.

Under this ₍pleasing₎ impression, I now communicate that resolution; employing for the purpose the language of the address already mentioned, as having been prepared for an earlier occasion, and which is in these words—

4. ADf, MS Division, New York Public Library; printed on Paltsits, *Farewell Address*, 200–08.

"The period &c (take in the whole address) [5]

Had not particular occurrences intervened to exhibit our political situation in some respects under new ^attitudes ~~aspects~~ I should have thought it unnecessary to add any thing to what precedes—But there have been circumstances and events of a nature to awaken anxiety for the future in every considerate and patriotic mind, which on an occasion like the present urge me to lay before you some further reflections and sentiments dictated by an ardent concern for your welfare.

Let me then conjure you, ^fellow Citizens, still more earnestly than I have done to hold fast to that <u>Union</u> which ~~now~~ constitutes you one ~~one~~ people. It is now justly dear to you. It cannot be too much so. You ought to prize it as a main pillar in the edifice of your real independence peace liberty and happiness. And being the point in your political ^fortress against which the batteries of internal and external enemies will be most actively, though often ^covertly & insidiously aimed, it is the more essential that you should properly estimate the immense value of your Union to your national and individual welfare—that you should cherish towards it an affectionate and immoveable attachment—that you should watch for its preservation with jealous solicitude—that you should habituate yourselves to ~~entertain~~ think and speak of it as the palladium of your prosperity & should frown upon whatever may lead to a suspicion that it can in any event be abandonned.

To the efficacy & duration of your Union a Government extending over the whole is indispensable. No alliance however intimate between the parts can be an adequate substitute. These must experience the infractions and interruptions, which all alliances in all times have experienced. Sensible of this important truth you have lately organised a Constitution of General Governt. better fitted than your former for a solid Union and for the efficacious management of your common concerns. ~~This Government, the offspring of your own choice, uninfluenced and unawed, completely free in~~

5. This is a reference to the draft of a farewell address which James Madison had prepared for Washington in June, 1792, and which Washington had used in his own first draft of a farewell address. See the introductory note to II to Washington, May 10, 1796; Washington to H, May 15, 1796.

~~its principles, in the distribution of its powers uniting energy with safety, and cir~~ I have before touched on the motives which entitle it to your Confidence. Let me add that Respect for its authority, compliance with its laws, acquiescence in its measures are duties enjoined by the fundamental maxims of true Liberty The basis of our political systems is the right of the People to make and to alter their constitutions of Government. But the Constitution which at any time exists, until changed by an explicit and authentic act of the whole people is sacredly binding upon all. The very idea of the right & the power of the people to establish Government presupposes the obligation of every individual to obey the established Government.[6]

All obstructions to the execution of the laws. All combinations and associations under whatever plausible character, with the real design to direct ^influence counteract ^or controul the regular deliberation or action of the constituted authorities are contrary to this fundamental principle and of the most fatal tendency. They serve to organise faction, to give ^to it an artificial and extraordinary force, to put in the stead of the delegated will of the Nation the will of a party, often a small but artful & enterprising minority of the ~~peop~~ community; and according to the alternate triumphs of different parties to make the Public Administration the Mirror of the ill concerted and incongruous projects of faction rather than ^an organ of ~~the well~~ ~~digested and~~ wholesome plans ^digested by ~~of~~ common councils & modified by mutual interests. However combinations and associations of this description may occasionally answer popular ends, they are likely in the course of time and things to prove potent engines by which cunning ambitious and unprincipled men will be enabled to erect their own greatness on the ruins of public Liberty; destroying afterwards the very engines by which they have been lifted to unjust dominion.[7]

6. This paragraph, with minor changes in wording, is the same as paragraph 18 of H's "Draft of Washington's Farewell Address," which is printed as an enclosure to H to Washington, July 30, 1796.
7. This paragraph, with minor changes in wording, is the same as paragraph 19 of H's "Draft of Washington's Farewell Address," which is printed as an enclosure to H to Washington, July 30, 1796.

Towards the preservation of Your Government, and with it your present happy condition, it is requisite not only that you steadily discountenance irregular oppositions to its authority, but also that you ~~should~~ be upon your guard against a spirit of Innovation upon its principles however specious the pretexts. One method of assault may be to effect alterations in the forms of the constitution tending to impair the energy of the System and so to undermine what cannot be directly overthrown. In all the changes to which you may be invited, remember that Time and Habit are at least as necessary to fix the true character of a Government as of any other human institution—that Experience is the surest standard by which to determine the real tendency of an existing constitution, that facility in changes upon the mere credit of hypothesis and opinion, exposes to ^perpetual ~~endless~~ change from the endless variety of hypothesis and opinion: And remember especially that for the efficacious management of your common concerns, in a country so extensive as ours, a Government of as much Vigour as is compatible with the perfect security of Liberty is indispensable. Liberty itself in such a Government, with powers properly distributed and adjusted, will find its best guardian and protector.[8]

Let me, ~~then, conjure you fellow Citizens~~ ^extort you in the next place, ~~in the most earnest manner~~ ^to be upon your guard against the baneful effects of party Spirit. This Spirit unfortunately is inseparable from human Nature having its root in the strongest passions of the mind. It ^exists ~~is seen~~ under different shapes in all Governments more or less stifled controuled or repressed, but in those of the popular form it is always seen in its greatest rankness, and ~~it~~ is truly their worst enemy. However easy it may be in Republics of narrow extent for those who ^at any time administer the ~~power~~ Government and command the ordinary public force, or for partial combinations of men, who from birth riches or other sources of distinction possess extraordinary influence and numerous retainers to overturn the established order in favour of their own aggrandisement—in Republics of large

---

8. This paragraph, with minor changes in wording, is the same as paragraph 20 of H's "Draft of Washington's Farewell Address," which is printed as an enclosure to H to Washington, July 30, 1796.

extent, the one or the other is rarely possible. The powers & opportunities of resistance of a great and widely extended nation defy the successful efforts of the ordinary military force or of any collections which wealth and patronage may call to their aid. In such Republics, it is perhaps safe to assert that the Conflicts of popular Factions open the only avenues to usurpation and Tyranny.

The domination of one faction over another sharpened by that spirit of Revenge which it always engenders, and which in different ages and countries has produced the most horrid enormities is itself a frightful despotism. But this leads at length to a more formal and permanent despotism. The disorders and miseries which result prepare the minds of men to seek security and repose in the absolute power of an Individual. And some leader of a prevailing faction more able or more fortunate than his competitors converts this disposition to the purposes of an aspiring and unprincipled ambition.[9]

But without looking forward to such an extremity (which however ought not to be intirely put out of sight) the common and continual mischiefs of the Spirit of Party make it the interest and the duty of a wise people to discountenance and repress it.[10]

It serves always to distract the public councils and enfeeble the public administration—agitates the community with ill founded jealousies and false alarms—embitters one part against another, and produces occasionally riot and insurrection. It opens inlets for foreign corruption and influence, which find a facilitated access through the channels of party passions; causing the true policy and interest of our own country to be subservient to the policy and interest of a foreign country and enslaving the will of our own Government to the Will of a foreign Government.[11]

---

9. This paragraph, with minor changes in wording, is the same as the last part of paragraph 21 of H's "Draft of Washington's Farewell Address," which is printed as an enclosure to H to Washington, July 30, 1796.

10. This paragraph, with minor changes in wording, is the same as paragraph 22 of H's "Draft of Washington's Farewell Address," which is printed as an enclosure to H to Washington, July 30, 1796.

11. This paragraph, with minor changes in wording, is the same as paragraph 23 of H's "Draft of Washington's Farewell Address," which is printed as an enclosure to H to Washington, July 30, 1796.

There is an opinion that parties in free countries are salutary checks upon the administration of the Government and serve to keep alive the spirit of Liberty. This within certain bounds is probably true, and in governments of a monarchical cast, patriotism may look with indulgence on the spirit of Party. But in governments of the popular character, in those purely elective, it is a spirit not to be fostered. From the natural tendency of such Governments, it is certain, that there will always exist enough of it for every salutary purpose; and there being constant danger of excess, the effort ought to be by force of public opinion to mitigate and assuage it: A Fire not to be quenched, it demands a uniform vigilance to prevent its bursting into a flame, lest it should not only warm but consume.[12]

It is in a particular manner to be regretted that our parties for some time past have been too much characterised by Geographical discriminations—<u>Northern</u> and <u>Southern</u>—<u>Atlantic</u> and <u>Western</u>. These discriminations, the mere artifice of the spirit of party (always dexterous to avail itself of every handle by which to wield the passions and too skilful not to turn to account the sympathy of neighbourhood, have furnished an argument against the Union, as ~~the~~ evidence of a real difference of local interests and views, and serve to hazard it by organising large districts of Country under the direction of the leaders of different parties, whose passions and prejudices rather than the real interests of the Country will be apt to regulate the use of their influence. If it be possible to correct this poison in the habit of our body politic, it is worthy the endeavours of the moderate and the good to effect it.[13]

One of the Expedients, meriting a special notice, which the partisans of faction employ towards fortifying their influence within local spheres is to misrepresent the principles and opinions of other Districts. The People at large cannot too carefully shield themselves against the jealousies, which grow out of these misrepresentations.

---

12. This paragraph, with minor changes in wording, is the same as paragraph 24 of H's "Draft of Washington's Farewell Address," which is printed as an enclosure to H to Washington, July 30, 1796.

13. This paragraph, with minor changes in wording, is the same as paragraph 16 of H's "Draft of Washington's Farewell Address," which is printed as an enclosure to H to Washington, July 30, 1796.

They tend to render alien to each other, those who ought to be bound together by fraternal affection. The Western Country have lately had a useful lesson on this subject. They have seen in the negotiation by the Executive and in the unanimous ratification by the Senate of the Treaty with Spain,[14] and in the universal satisfaction at that event throughout in U States how unfounded have been the suspicions propagated among them of a policy in the General Government and in the Atlantic States inimical to their interests in regard to the Mississippi. They have seen two Treaties concluded, that with Great Britain [15] and that with Spain which secure to them every thing they could desire, with respect to our foreign relations, towards confirming their prosperity. Will they not henceforth rely for the preservation of these advantages on that Union by which they were procured? Will they not reject those advisers, if any there are, who would ⟨sever⟩ ~~render~~ them ⟨from⟩ ~~alien to~~ their Brethern and connect them with Aliens? [16]

In controuling, fellow Citizens, as far as possible the spirit of party it is ~~essential~~ indispensable that you should cultivate ⟨towards⟩ ~~for~~ each other mutual good will, mutual forbearance, mutual candour—that you should ⟨not⟩ construe differences of opinion about the ~~best~~ means of advancing the public good ~~as~~ ⟨into⟩ infallible indications of enmity to the Government, enmity to Liberty, want of Integrity and patriotism. Inferences of this kind are often as false as they are uncharitable and exasper ⟨at⟩ ing. I have before hinted the necessity of blending with ~~a~~ due watchfulness over the conduct of your public Agents a just confidence in them. This is a point of great moment to your safety. Calumny will never spare even those who are most faithful and able, and if it find too ready credit with you, the consequence will be not only to disable from serving you usefully good men whom you may have entrusted with your affairs, but it will gradually banish

14. See H to Washington, July 30, 1796, note 17.
15. This is a reference to the Jay Treaty, signed at London, November 19, 1794 (Miller, *Treaties*, II, 245–64).
16. This paragraph, with minor changes in wording, is the same as paragraph 17 of H's "Draft of Washington's Farewell Address," which is printed as an enclosure to H to Washington, July 30, 1796.

from them persons of this character and leave you a prey to unskilful and undeserving pretenders to your favour.¹⁷ Among the various evils ~~other evils which~~ which ensue from the wanton indulgence of obloquy against your public Agents_∧not the least is the discrediting of them in the eyes of foreign Governments, ~~so as deprive them of~~ so as to ~~we~~ lessen their weight in promoting your ~~interests~~ _∧affairs abroad, and even to invite from foreign powers enterprizes against your Government, your peace safety and interests.

It is very important likewise that the habits of thinking of the people should tend to inspire caution in their Agents, in the several departments of the Government, to avoid encroachment upon each other. ~~and that as often as any precedent of the kind might occur that it should marked~~ The spirit of encroachment in this respect leads to the consolidation of the powers of all the departments into one; and thereby, under whatever forms, to the establishment of a despotism. A just knowlege of that love of power_∧and proneness to abuse it which predominate in the human heart_∧are alone ~~is~~ sufficient to convince us of this truth. The necessity of mutual checks in the organisation of political power by dividing and distributing it into different depositories has been evinced by experiments ancient and modern, some of them in our own country and under our own eyes. If necessary to institute them, it is equally necessary to maintain them in practice. If in the public opinion the destribution of_∧~~any of~~ the powers of the Government be in any particular wrong, let it be corrected by an ~~adm~~ amendment in the course indicated by the Constitution. Let there be no change by usurpation; for though this may be the instrument of good in one instance it [is] the usual and the fatal weapon by which free Government is destroyed. The evil of the precedent must always greatly exceed the partial benefit which the use of that instrument can at any time afford.¹⁸

~~Be faithful to all~~

17. Opposite this part of the paragraph H wrote: "This is not in the first may be interwoven."
18. This paragraph, with minor changes in wording, is the same as paragraph 25 of H's "Draft of Washington's Farewell Address," which is printed as an enclosure to H to Washington, July 30, 1796.

Let fidelity to your Engagements be the characteristic of our Nation. Cherish public credit as a mean of strength and security. As one method of preserving it, use it as little as possible. Avoid occasions of Expence by cultivating peace, ‸but remembering always that timely and provident disbursements to ~~provide against~~ prepare for danger frequently prevent much greater disbursements to repel it. Avoid the accumulation of Debt not only by avoiding occasions of Expence but by vigorous exertions in time of peace to discharge the debts which unavoidable wars may have occasionned; not ungenerously throwing upon posterity the burthens which we ourselves ought to bear. The execution of these maxims belongs to your Representatives; but ~~is necessary~~ a coincidence [19] of sentiments on your part will tend to render their task much easier.[20]

Cherish, with peculiar care, good faith and justice towards and harmony with all Nations. Religion and Morality enjoin this Conduct. Can it be that true policy does not equally demand it? It will, at least, be worthy of a free, enlightened, and at not distant period, a great Nation to give to mankind the magnanimous and too novel example of a people invariably governed by an exalted justice and benevolence. ~~Whenever~~ It is to be doubted that the fruits of such a conduct would richly repay any temporary advantages which might be lost by a steady adherence to the plan? Can it be that providence has not connected the permanent felicity of a Nation with its Virtue? The Experiment is recommended by every sentiment which ~~ennobles~~ ennobles human nature? Alas! It is rendered impossible by its Vices?[21]

Towards the execution of such a plan, it is material that while our impressions and sentiments make the proper distinctions between a friendly or unfriendly conduct of different foreign nations towards us—we nevertheless avoid‸rooted & permanent antipathies against or passionate attachments for any; as a general rule cultivating just and amica-

19. In MS, "cononcidence."
20. This paragraph, with minor changes in wording, is the same as paragraph 29 of H's "Draft of Washington's Farewell Address," which is printed as an enclosure to H to Washington, July 30, 1796.
21. This paragraph, with minor changes in wording, is the same as paragraph 30 of H's "Draft of Washington's Farewell Address," which is printed as an enclosure to H to Washington, July 30, 1796.

                                                               against
ble feeling towards all. The nation which indulges ~~towards~~ another
                            for another
a habitual hatred or ₐa habitual fondness is in some degree a slave. It is &c [22]

                                              to the end as in the former

22. Opposite this paragraph H wrote: "varied from the first sent & I think for the *better*. If the first be preferred tis easy to incorporate this."

From Joseph Strong [1]

Cooperstown [*New York*] *August 11, 1796.* "I having been lately imployed by several Defendants in Actions of Trespass recommended by Joshua Mercereau in Tioga County [2] for fishing in the Susquehannah River where he owned the Soil on both sides thereof and on argument thereof befor *Balthazar De Haert Esqr.* (your late partner in business while I were under your Tuition) [3] as an umpire, being disappointed in his decision for the plaintiff in Support of the Actions, in private conversation with him afterwards we offered to submit the same to your Opinion—in consequence whereof as well as to satisfy myself & employers I transmit you the foregoing Case [4] comprising the whole question. . . . Permit me Sir to request your Opinion on the Case. . . ."

ALS, Hamilton Papers, Library of Congress.
1. Strong was a clerk in H's law office from 1786 to 1789 ("Certificate of Clerkship," January 20, 1789 [ADS, Hall of Records, New York City]). When Strong wrote this letter, he was an attorney in Albany.
2. Mersereau, a native of France, had been deputy commissary of prisoners during the American Revolution. He served in the New York Assembly from Richmond County in 1777, 1778, 1779 to 1783, and 1784 to 1786. He subsequently moved to Otsego County and then to the town of Union in that part of Tioga County which later became part of Broome County.
3. Although Balthazar De Haert, who had been a New York lawyer since 1773, had been associated with H in several of his cases, it is not clear whether they even established a formal partnership. But at the very least De Haert had a "working arrangement" with H. See Goebel, *Law Practice*, I, 1.
4. The enclosure to this letter, which was written by Strong and is entitled "Case," reads: "The River Susquehannah is a River navigable with Boats, Canoes and other small Craf and is constantly so used by every person wishing to pass and repass therein; (and by the 11th Sessn. chap. 45 § 30. 2 Vol Laws of New York p 214) it is used and occupied as a common & public Highway for all the Citizens of this State &ca. and there are also in said River Shad and

other valuable Fish. The Soil adjoining the River is owned by private Individuals & in many paths on both sides thereof.

"Question—Can the Citizens of this State lawfully take the fish in the said River and also pass up and down the same—and for this purpose go upon the *Banks* thereof, notwithstanding the Right of property be in Individuals, who refuse their Consent thereto?" (AD, Hamilton Papers, Library of Congress.)

Strong is referring to "An Act directing the Settlement of Public Accounts, and for other Purposes therein mentioned," which reads in part: "*And whereas,* it is represented to the Legislature, that divers persons have . . . [been] guilty of raising wiers and other obstructions in the Susquehannah river within this State, whereby the navigation thereof has been rendered dangerous, and the free course of the fish up the same river impeded and diverted: *For remedy whereof,*

"XXX. *Be it further enacted by the authority aforesaid,* That if any person or persons shall raise, erect or build, or cause to be raised, erected or built any such wier or other obstruction whatsoever in the same river, in any part of this State, he or they shall respectively forfeit the sum of *five pounds* for each offence, to be recovered with costs of suit, before any court, having cognizance thereof, by any person or persons who will sue for the same." (*New York Laws,* 11th Sess., Ch. XCV [March 22, 1788].)

From Jonathan Williams

Mount Pleasant[1] [*near Philadelphia*], *August 18, 1796.* "I wrote you, on the day of my last Interview relative to my affair with Mr Macomb, June 8. 1796. . . . By your silence it is evident that, as counsel for Mr Macomb you did not think yourself justifiable to enter farther into the Matter. My only reason for troubling you now, is to request your remembrance of the measures I have taken to procure an amicable arrangement; and at the future day you will do me the justice to allow, that I am not bound by politeness, or any principle of regard to the parties, to vary in the smallest degree any kind of rigour that the Laws will Support."

ALS, Hamilton Papers, Library of Congress.
1. This was the name of Williams's estate, which was located on the east bank of the Schuylkill River and had belonged to Benedict Arnold.

From Pierre Auguste Adet[1]

[New York, August 25, 1796]

the Minister plenipotentiary of the french Republic presents his best compliments and his grateful thanks to M. hamilton for the Letters of introduction he was kind enough to give to him,[2] and is very Sory to be prevented by a previous Engagement to call upon him on Saturday next to dine according to his polite invitation.

the Minister before he leaves this city shall pay his Respects to Mr hamilton.

25 august 1796.

AL, Hamilton Papers, Library of Congress.

1. In mid-August, 1796, Adet left Philadelphia for a trip through the middle and New England states. On August 19, 1796, the Secretary of the French Legation wrote to the French Minister of Foreign Relations describing the purpose of Adet's trip: "Attaché au progrès des Sciences et des arts, et savant lui-même le Citoyen Adet n'a rien négligé depuis son arrivée aux Etats Unis pour recueillir tout ce qu'ils renferment de découvertes utiles: il y a consacré le très petit nombre d'instans dont le courant des affaires lui a permis de disposer; je n'anticiperai point sur les rapports qu'il aura à faire du bruit de ses efforts à l'Institut National; le voyage qu'il exécute en ce moment, Citoyen Ministre, et dont vous connaitrez les motifs et les résultats enrichera sans doute sa collection déjà très précieuse" (Turner, "Correspondence of French Ministers," 945).

In a letter dated September 24, 1796, Adet described the object of his trip to the French Foreign Minister: "Obligé de chercher des moyens de remplir la caisse consulaire épuisée par une foule de dépenses, je me suis rendu à Boston dans l'espérance d'y trouver des secours que je ne pouvais obtenir à Philadelphie. J'ai profité de cette circonstance pour avoir une juste idée de l'opinion du peuple dans le moment actuel et savoir ce que nous devons espérer ou craindre, si, comme on nous annonce, Washington retire son nom de la liste des candidâts pour la présidence . . ." (Turner, "Correspondence of French Ministers," 947).

2. See H to Stephen Van Rensselaer, August 25, 1796.

From Rufus King

London Aug. 25. 1796

Dear sir,

It would have been agreeable to this Government if we would have agreed to the appointment of Doct. Swabey as the fifth commissioner; he is really a very candid and honorable man, but for the same reason that we could not satisfy the Commissioners on the part of G.B. with the appointment of our Country man Colo Trumbull, an equally candid and honorable character, they have been unable to convince us that under all circumstances it would be adviseable that we should accept Doctr. Swabey.[1]

The utmost propriety of conduct has been shewn on both sides, and out of several Names proposed by each, the British Commissioners selected Colo. Trumbull and our Commissioners Doctr. Swabey, as the names to be put in the urn—the lot has decided in our favor, and Colo Trumbull who is on the spot is the fifth Commissioner. The Board being now complete will proceed to Business without unnecessary Delay.

Knowing the immense importance of this Commission to our Commerce, and navigation, I take the earliest Opportunity to give you this information. The surrender of the Posts which has taken place,[2] and the very explicit assurances that I have received from the highest authority in this nation, of a Resolution to carry into Effect the Treaty with the most scrupulous Fidelity, make me anxious that nothing should take place on our side that should furnish even a pretence, much less a Justification, for arresting the further and complete execution of the Treaty—the very extraordinary situation of Europe at this moment should inspire us with great caution; and those whose Property depend on the Treaties being permitted to go into full Effect, should feel, and be influenced by, this Reflection.

Farewell!   Very sincerely yr's   Rufus King

Col. Hamilton

ALS, Hamilton Papers, Library of Congress.

1. Article 7 of the Jay Treaty provided for a five-man commission to settle the claims of United States citizens against Great Britain and the claims of British citizens against the United States. The commission was to consist of two representatives from Great Britain and two from the United States. The four commissioners were then authorized to choose a fifth commissioner by a unanimous vote. If this proved impossible, each side was to nominate a candidate with the choice between these two being determined by lot (Miller, *Treaties*, II, 252–53).

The British members of the commission were John Nicoll and John Anstey; the United States members were Christopher Gore and William Pinkney. After the four commissioners had failed to agree on a candidate for the fifth commissioner, the British nominated Maurice Swabey and the Americans nominated John Trumbull.

2. Article 2 of the Jay Treaty reads in part: "His Majesty will withdraw all His Troops and Garrisons from all Posts and Places within the Boundary Lines assigned by the Treaty of Peace of the United States. This Evacuation will take place on or before the first Day of June One thousand seven hundred and ninety six . . ." (Miller, *Treaties*, II, 246). This deadline was not met because of the delay caused by the debate in the House of Representatives over the implementation of the Jay Treaty (see the introductory note to H to George Washington, March 7, 1796). On December 7, 1796, Washington reported to

Congress: "The period during the late session at which the appropriation was passed for carrying into effect the treaty of amity, commerce, and navigation, between the United States and his Britannic Majesty, necessarily procrastinated the reception of the posts stipulated to be delivered, beyond the date assigned for that event. As soon however, as the Governor General of Canada [Guy Carleton, Lord Dorchester] could be addressed with propriety on the subject, arrangements were cordially and promptly concluded for their evacuation, and the United States took possession of the principal of them, comprehending Oswego, Niagara, Detroit, Michilimakinac, and Fort Miami, where such repairs and additions have been ordered to be made, as appeared indispensable" (*ASP, Foreign Relations,* I, 30).

To Stephen Van Rensselaer [1]

[*New York, August 25, 1796.* "I embrace with pleasure the opportunity of making you acquainted with Mr. Adet Minister P: of the French Republic,[2] for whom it is unnecessary for me to ask your particular attentions as they are equally due to his public and personal character. I will only add that I shall take a particular interest in whatever you may do to render his visit to Albany [3] agreeable to him." [4] *Letter not found.*]

ALS, sold at American Art Association, March 12, 1920, Lot 383.

1. Van Rensselaer, who was the husband of Elizabeth Hamilton's sister Margaret (Margarita), was lieutenant governor of New York.
2. See Pierre Auguste Adet to H, August 25, 1796.
3. The following item appeared in the *Gazette of the United States, & Philadelphia Daily Advertiser* on September 9, 1796: "Albany. September 5. The French Minister, his Excellency Citizen ADET, arrived in this city, since our last —he has proceeded on his journey to Lake George. During his stay here, he was waited on by the Lieut. Governor, the Chief Justice and many other of our most respectable citizens."
4. Extract taken from dealer's catalogue.

From George Washington [1]

Private   Philadelphia 25th. Augt. 1796

My dear Sir,

I have given the Paper herewith enclosed,[2] several serious & attentive readings; and prefer it greatly to the other draughts, being more copious on material points; more dignified on the whole; and with less egotism. Of course less exposed to criticism, & better calculated to meet the eye of discerning readers (foreigners particularly, whose curiosity I have little doubt will lead them to inspect it attentively & to pronounce their opinions on the performance).

When the first draught was made, besides having an eye to the consideration above mentioned, I thought the occasion was fair (as I had latterly been the subject of considerable invective) to say what is there contained of myself—and as the Address was designed in a more especiall manner for the Yeomanry of this Country I conceived it was proper they should be informed of the object of that abuse; the silence with which it had been treated; and the consequences which would naturally flow from such unceasing & virule⟨nt⟩ [3] attempts to destroy all confidence in the Executive part of the Government; and that it was best to do it in language th⟨at⟩ was plain & intelligable to their understand⟨ing.⟩

The draught now sent, comprehends the most, if not all these matters; is better expressed; and I am persuade⟨d⟩ goes as far as it ought with respect to any personal mention of myself.

I should have seen no occasi⟨on⟩ myself, for its undergoing a revision. But as your letter of the 30th. Ulto. whi⟨ch⟩ accompanied it, intimates a wish to do this—and knowing that it can be more correctly done after a writing has been out of sight for sometime than while it is in hand, I send it in conformity there⟨to⟩—with a request, however, that you w⟨d.⟩ return it as soon as you have carefully re-examined it; for it is my intention to hand it to the Public before I leave this City,[4] to which I came for the purpose of meeting General Pinckney [5]—receiving ministers from Spain [6] & Holland [7]—and for the dispatch of other business which could not be so well executed by written communications between the heads of Departments & myself as by oral conferences. So soon as these are accomplished I shall return; at any rate I expect to do so by or before the tenth of next month for the purpose of bringing up my family for the Winter.

I shall expunge all that is marked in the paper as unimportant &ca. &ca. and as you perceive some marginal notes, written with a pencil, I pray you to give the sentiments so noticed mature consideration.[8] After which, and in every other part, if change or alteration takes place in the draught, let them be so clearly interlined—erazed—or referred to in the Margin as that no mistake may happen in copying it for the Press.

To what Editor in *this* City do you think it had best be sent for Publication? Will it be proper to accompany it with a note to him, expressing (as the principal design of it is to remove doubts at the next Election) that it is hoped, or expected, that the State Printers will give it a place in their Gazettes—or preferable to let it be carried by my private Secretary [9] to that Press which is destined to usher it to the World & suffer it to work its way afterwards? If you think the first most eligable, let me ask you to sketch such a note as you may judge applicable to the occasion. With affectionate regard

I am always   Yours   Go: Washington

Colo. A. Hamilton.

ALS, Hamilton Papers, Library of Congress; ALS, facsimile (tracing), Hamilton Papers, Library of Congress; copy, Hamilton Papers, Library of Congress.

1. For background to this letter, see the introductory note to H to Washington, May 10, 1796.

2. This is a reference to H's "Draft of Washington's Farewell Address," which is printed as an enclosure to H to Washington, July 30, 1796.

3. Material within broken brackets has been taken from the facsimile in the Hamilton Papers, Library of Congress.

4. On September 19, 1796, the day that Washington's Farewell Address was printed in *Claypoole's* [Philadelphia] *American Daily Advertiser*, the President left Philadelphia for Mount Vernon.

5. Having decided to recall James Monroe as United States Minister Plenipotentiary to France, Washington offered that post to Charles Cotesworth Pinckney on July 8, 1796 (ALS, George Washington Papers, Library of Congress; LC, George Washington Papers, Library of Congress), and Pinckney accepted it on July 27 (ALS, George Washington Papers, Library of Congress). As Congress was not in session at the time of Pinckney's appointment, his nomination was not sent to the Senate until December 21, 1796 (*Executive Journal*, I, 217). The Senate agreed to his appointment the following day (*Executive Journal*, I, 217). Monroe's letter of recall is dated August 22, 1796 (Timothy Pickering to Monroe [copy, Massachusetts Historical Society, Boston]).

6. The new Spanish Minister, Carlos Martinez, Marquis de Casa Yrujo, presented his credentials to the President on August 25, 1796 ([Philadelphia] *Aurora. General Advertiser*, August 26, 1796).

7. Washington received the new minister from the United Netherlands, Roger Gerard Van Polanen, on August 30, 1796 ([Philadelphia] *Aurora. General Advertiser*, August 31, 1796). Van Polanen was employed in the East India service and served as a member of the legislature for the province of Zeeland. After arriving in the United States in January, 1791, he bought an estate in Pennsylvania in 1792 and became a United States citizen in the New York Mayor's Court on May 8, 1793. The government of the Batavian Republic appointed him Minister Resident to the United States in September, 1795.

8. For these marginal notations, see H's "Draft of Washington's Farewell Address," which is printed as an enclosure to H to Washington, July 30, 1796.

9. Tobias Lear.

From David Howell [1]

Halifax [Nova Scotia] Aug. 31. 1796

Sir,

Col. Barclay [2] & myself after 7 or 8 days canvassing have agreed upon the Hon. Egbert Benson of N.Y. [3] as 3d Comissr.

As he is your friend as well as ours let me request your influence with him to accept this appointment. We never shall agree on any other person. The alternative is not very ⟨promising⟩ [4] nor likely to prove satisfactory to either Country.

I hope your State will suspend their claim on Mr. Benson only for a few weeks this fall. The Cause Col. Barclay & myself have agreed Shall be tried in the City of N. York.

It is not likely that the Surveys can be compleated till late in this fall. The Agents must then have time to prepare—and the Commissioners & Agents cannot meet in the Winter conveniently so that the trial will probably be in N. York next Spring. This we have agreed to for Mr. Bensons convenience—so he will see how entirely he has *our* Confidence & may hope to give Satisfaction to both Countries.

We have sent a Vessel to bring him to attend merely in answering the Court & opening the business—to sit only a few days & adjourn.

As you delight in doing public Service I assure myself of your attention to the object of this Letter. I need only add that when I parted with you I requested you to consult Mr. Benson & to write me whether he would accept or not & that from your Silence I had some reason to hope he would accept.

With great esteem & respt Sir your very He Sert   David Howell

Hon. A. Hamilton.

ALS, Public Archives of Canada, Ottawa, Ontario.
1. For background to this letter, see Timothy Pickering to H, March 22, July 16, 1796; H to Pickering, July 21, 1796.
2. Thomas Barclay of Nova Scotia was the British representative on the St. Croix River boundary commission provided for under Article 5 of the Jay Treaty. For the text of Article 5 of the Jay Treaty, see "Remarks on the Treaty . . . between the United States and Great Britain," July 9-11, 1795, note 12.

3. When this letter was written, Benson was a justice of the New York Supreme Court. Although Benson had refused to serve as an American commissioner on the debt commission authorized by Article 6 of the Jay Treaty, he did serve on the St. Croix boundary commission. See Pickering to H, March 22, 1796, note 4.
4. This word has been taken from Hamilton, *Intimate Life*, 269.

From George Washington

Private   Philadelphia 1st. Septr. 1796

My dear Sir,

About the middle of last Week I wrote to you;[1] and that it might escape the eye of the Inquisitive (for some of my letters have lately been pried into) I took the liberty of putting it under a cover to Mr. Jay.

Since then, revolving on the Paper that was enclosed therein;[2] on the various matters it contained; and on the just expression of the advice or recommendation which was given in it, I have regretted that another subject (which in my estimation is of interesting concern to the well-being of this country) was not touched upon also: I mean Education *generally* as one of the surest means of enlightening & givg. just ways of thinkg to our Citizens, but particularly the establishment of a University; where the Youth from *all parts* of the United States might receive the polish of Erudition in the Arts, Sciences & Belle Letters; and where those who were disposed to run a political course, might not only be instructed in the theory & principles, but (this Seminary being at the Seat of the General Government) where the Legislature wd. be in Session half the year, and the interests & politics of the Nation of course would be discussed, they would lay the surest foundation for the practical part also.

But that which would render it of the highest importance, in my opinion, is, that the Juvenal period of life, when friendships are formed, & habits established that will stick by one; the Youth, or

ALS, Hamilton Papers, Library of Congress; ALS, facsimile (tracing), Hamilton Papers, Library of Congress; two copies, Hamilton Papers, Library of Congress.
1. Washington to H, August 25, 1796.
2. Washington is referring to H's "Draft of Washington's Farewell Address," which is printed as an enclosure to H to Washington, July 30, 1796.

young men from different parts of the United States would be assembled together, & would by degrees discover that there was not that cause for those jealousies & prejudices which one part of the union had imbibed agains[t] another part: of course, sentiments of more liberality in the general policy of the country would result from it. What, but the mixing of people from different parts of the United States during the War rubbed off these impressions? A century in the ordinary intercourse, would not have accomplished what the Seven years association in Arms did: but that ceasing, prejudices are beginning to revive again, and never will be eradicated so effectually by any other means as the intimate intercourse of characters in early life, who, in all probability, will be at the head of the councils of this country in a more advanced stage of it.

To shew that this is no *new* idea of mine, I may appeal to my early communications to Congress;[3] and to prove how seriously I have reflected on it since, & how well disposed I have been, & still am, to contribute my aid towards carrying the measure into effect, I enclose you the extract of a letter from me to the Governor of Virginia on the Subject,[4] and a copy of the resolves of the Legislature of that State in consequence thereof.[5]

3. Washington had proposed the creation of a national university in his first annual message to Congress, January 8, 1790 (LC, George Washington Papers, Library of Congress).

4. On March 16, 1795, Washington wrote to Governor Robert Brooke of Virginia: "Ever since the General Assembly of Virginia were pleased to submit to my disposal fifty shares in the Potomack, and one hundred in the James River company, it has been my anxious desire to appropriate them to an object, most worthy of public regard.

"It is with indescribable regret that I have seen the youth of the United States migrating to foreign countries, in order to acquire the higher branches of erudition and to obtain a knowledge of the Sciences. Altho it would be injustice to many to pronounce the certainty of their imbibing maxims, not congenial with republicanism; it must nevertheless be admitted that a serious danger is encountered by sending abroad among other political systems those who have not well learned the value of their own.

"The time is therefore come when a plan of Universal education ought to be adopted in the United States. Not only do the exigencies of public and private life demand it; but if it should ever be apprehended that prejudice would be entertained in one part of the Union against another; an efficacious remedy will be, to assemble the youth of every part under such circumstances, as will, by the freedom of intercourse and collision of sentiment, give to their minds the direction of truth, philanthropy and mutual conciliation.

"It has been represented, that an University, corresponding with these ideas is contemplated to be built in the federal city; and that it will receive considerable endowments. This position is so eligable from its centrality—so

I have not the smallest doubt that this donation (when the Navigation is in complete operation, which it certainly will be in less than two years) will amount to twelve or £1500 Sterlg a year, and become a rapidly increasing fund. The Proprietors of the Federal City have talked of doing something handsome towards it likewise [6] and

convenient to Virginia, by whose legislature the shares were granted, and in which part the federal district stands—and combines so many other conveniences, that I have determined to vest the Potomack shares in that University.
"Presuming it to be more agreeable to the general assembly of Virginia, that the shares in the James River company should be reserved for a similar object in some part of that State, I intend to allot them for a Seminary to be erected at such place, as they shall deem most proper. . . .
"I must beg the favor of your Excellency to lay this letter before that honorable body, at their next Session; in order that I may appropriate the James River shares to the place which they may prefer. . . ." (ADfS, George Washington Papers, Library of Congress; LC, George Washington Papers, Library of Congress.)

5. Washington's letter to Brooke of March 16, 1795, was presented to the Virginia House of Delegates on November 10 and 11, 1795 (*Journal of the House of Delegates of the Commonwealth of Virginia, Begun and Held at the Capitol, in the City of Richmond, on Tuesday, the Tenth Day of November, One Thousand Seven Hundred and Ninety-Five* [Richmond, 1795], 3, 5).

On December 1, 1795, the House of Delegates agreed to the following resolutions:

"Whereas the migration of American youth to foreign countries, for the completion of their education, exposes them to the danger of imbibing political prejudices disadvantageous to their own republican forms of government, and ought therefore to be rendered unnecessary and avoided.

"1. *Resolved*, that the plan contemplated for erecting an University at the Federal City where the youth of the several states may be assembled, and their course of education finished, deserves the countenance and support of each state.

"And whereas, when the General Assembly presented sundry shares in the James river and Patowmac Companies to George Washington, as a small token of their gratitude for the great, eminent and unrivalled services he had rendered to this commonwealth, to the United States, and to the world at large, in support of the principles of liberty and equal government, it was their wish and desire that he should appropriate them as he might think best. And whereas the present General Assembly retain the same sense of his virtues, wisdom, and patriotism:

"2. *Resolved therefore*, that the appropriation by the said George Washington of the aforesaid shares in the Patowmac Company to the University intended to be erected in the Federal City, is made in a manner most worthy of the public regard and of the approbation of this commonwealth.

"3. *Resolved also*, that he be requested to appropriate the aforesaid shares in the James river Company to a Seminary at such place in the upper country as he may deem most convenient to a majority of the inhabitants thereof."
(*Journal of the House of Delegates of the Commonwealth of Virginia. . . ,* 63–64).

6. See the Memorial of the Commissioners of the District of Columbia,

if Congress would appropriate so⟨me of⟩ ⁷ the Western lands to the same uses, funds sufficient, and of the most permanent and increasing sort might be so established as to invite the ablest Professors in Europe, to conduct it.

Let me pray you, therefore, to introduce a Section in the Address expressive of these sentiments, & recommendatory of the measure—without any mention, however, of my proposed personal contribution to the plan.

Such a Section would come in very properly after the one which relates to our religious obligations, or in a preceding part, as one of the recommendatory measures to counteract the evils arising from Geographical discriminations.⁸

With Affecte regard   I am always Yours   Go: Washington

Colo. A. Hamilton

November 21, 1796 (*ASP, Miscellaneous*, I, 153–54); Washington to the Commissioners of the City of Washington, December 1, 1796 (ALS, letterpress copy, George Washington Papers, Library of Congress; LC, George Washington Papers, Library of Congress).

7. Material within broken brackets has been taken from the facsimile in the Hamilton Papers, Library of Congress.

8. See the introductory note to H to Washington, May 10, 1796; H to Washington, July 30, 1796, note 12.

From Oliver Wolcott, Junior ¹

Treasury Department
September 1st. 1796

Sir

Lieutenant Colonel Fleury has credit on the Books of the Treasury as a foreign Officer for Seven thousand, five hundred & Seventy Dollars & fifty eight Cents principal, for which there exists an appropriation; this sum will therefore be paid at any time on the production of a power of Attorney and the original Certificates.

If however a transmission of the original Certificates would be attended with too great risque they may be lodged with our Minister in Paris and a Certificate from him that this is done, with a proper power of Attorney will be Sufficient.

The Interest on this debt ceased on the last day of December 1792, the sum then due was, One thousand eight hundred & Sixteen Dollars & Ninety four Cents, for the payment of which provision was made at Paris—this sum may be yet received at Paris by application to our Minister Mr. Munroe or His Successor General Pinckney ² when he shall have arrived.

If payment of the Interest last mentioned, is however preferred in the United States, it will be so made, on the production of a Certificate from our Minister, mentioning that the claim for payment in Paris, has been renounced.

It will be best for Colo Fleury to obtain payment here as soon as possible, for although his Monies are perfectly safe, they are in their present state entirely unproductive. As soon as payment shall be obtained from the Treasury, the monies may if he chooses, be advantageously invested in the purchase of Stock.

I am with perfect respect   Sir   Your most Obedient Servant

Oliv. Wolcott Jr.

Alexander Hamilton Esqr.

LS, Hamilton Papers, Library of Congress; ADf, Connecticut Historical Society, Hartford.
1. For background to this letter, see the Marquis de Fleury to H, May 28, 1796.
2. See George Washington to H, August 25, 1796, note 5.

From Amanda Coe

New York, September 2, 179(6). Encloses ten dollars and asks for Hamilton's assistance in securing her release from prison.¹

ALS, Hamilton Papers, Library of Congress.
1. Amanda Coe had been found guilty of forgery in the New York Supreme Court in May, 1796. Soon afterwards the Court made the following ruling: "The people vs. Amanda Coe. On Conviction of Felony, Forgery & uttering &c. The Crime of which the prisoner was convicted appearing to have been committed before the Statute entitled an Act making alterations in the criminal Law of this State and for erecting State prisons was passed, and the said prisoner praying openly that sentence might be pronounced against him according to the provisions of the said Statute thereupon it is Ordered and adjudged that the said Convict be imprisoned for life in the State prison to be built in the City of New York, and that until the State prison aforesaid shall be built and ready for

the reception of prisoners the said Convict be confined in the Goal of the City and County of New York" (MS Minutes of the New York Supreme Court, January 19–November 5, 1796, under the date of May 7, 1796 [Hall of Records, New York City]).

Amanda Coe was sentenced according to the provisions of "An Act making alterations in the Criminal law of this State, and for erecting State Prisons," which reads in part: "And that every person who shall hereafter commit and be duly convicted or attainted of any other felony now punishable with death for the first offence, except the crime of stealing from a Church, shall instead of being punished with death be punished with imprisonment for life in one of the State Prisons herein after mentioned; and the justices who shall give judgment in any such case shall upon consideration of all the circumstances thereof adjudge the offender to imprisonment only, or to be kept in the said prison to hard labour or in solitude or both" (*New York Laws*, 19th Sess., Ch. XXX [March 26, 1796]). This act superseded "An Act for preventing and punishing Forgery and Counterfeiting," which stipulated that offenders be sentenced to death (*New York Laws*, 11th Sess., Ch. XX [February 7, 1788]).

H endorsed this letter: "Amanda Coe Sept. 2, 1796. Answered I could do nothing more in her affair & sent back her money." H's letter has not been found.

To George Washington

New York Sepr. 4. 1796

Sir

I have received your two late letters,[1] the last but one transmitting me a certain draft.[2] It will be corrected & altered with attention to your suggestions[3] & returned by Monday's or Tuesday's post. The idea of the university is one of those which I think will be most properly reserved for your speech at the opening of the session.[4] A general suggestion respecting education will very fitly come into the address.

With respectful & Affect attach: I have the honor to remain   Sir Yr. very obedt. Servt   A Hamilton

The President

ALS, MS Division, New York Public Library.
1. Washington to H, August 25, September 1, 1796.
2. H's "Draft of Washington's Farewell Address," which is printed as an enclosure to H to Washington, July 30, 1796.
3. See Washington to H, September 1, 1796.
4. In his eighth annual message to Congress, December 7, 1796, Washington proposed the creation of a national university and a military academy (LC, George Washington Papers, Library of Congress).

From Isaac Sherman [1]

New York, September 5, 1796. "I have defered troubling you with a detail relative to the property which Mrs Sherman (my wife) claims in this city. . . . I am fully satisfied, in my own mind, that Mrs Sherman (my wife) has a clear title to a lot in this city, situate in Liberty Street, between Nassau Street and Broadway, primarily derived from Richard Ashfield deceased, who was her grandfather. . . . This lot lay vacant many years. A blacksmith's shop was erected thereon by Mr. Clilend, about five or Six years ago; who now is in possession of it. Judge Richard Morris had, it seems, prior possession thereof, and was the person who permitted Mr. Cliland to erect the blacksmith's Shop aforementioned thereon, and gave him, the said Cliland possession of said lot; but afterwards tried to dispossess him, and could not; because Mr. Cliland having, by some means, discovered, that Judge Richd. Morris had no legal claim thereto. . . . I sincerely wish that such means may be used as your wisdom shall dictate, to reinstate the proper Heirs in their right. . . . Mrs. Sherman can shew, I believe, that the legal right to the lot . . . is solely vested [in] Her."

ALS, Hamilton Papers, Library of Congress.
1. For background to this letter, see Sherman to H, July 2, 1795.

To George Washington [1]

New York Sept. 5. 1796 [2]

Sir

I return the draft [3] corrected agreeably to your intimations. You will observe a short paragraph added respecting *Education*.[4] As to the establishment of a University, it is a point which in connection with military schools, & some other things, I meant, agreeably to your desire to suggest to you, as parts of your Speech at the opening of the session.[5] There will several things come there much better than in a general address to The People which likewise would swell the address too much. Had I had *health* enough, it was my intention to have written it over, in which case I could both have improved & abriged. But this is not the case. I seem now to have regularly a period of ill health every summer.

I think it will be adviseable *simply* to send the address by your Secretary [6] to *Dunlap*.[7] It will of course find its way into all the other papers. Some person on the spot ought to be charged with a careful examination of the impression by the proof sheet.

Very respectfully & Affect I have the honor to be   Sir   Yr. very obed serv   A Hamilton

The President

ALS, MS Division, New York Public Library.

1. For an explanation of the contents of this letter, see the introductory note to H to Washington, May 10, 1796. See also Washington to H, August 25, September 1, 1796; H to Washington, September 4, 1796.

2. In *HCLW*, X, 190, this letter is dated September 4, 1796. Henry Cabot Lodge attributes the source of this letter to Hamilton, *History*, VI, 530, where it is correctly dated.

3. H's "Draft of Washington's Farewell Address," which is printed as an enclosure to H to Washington, July 30, 1796.

4. This paragraph has not been found. See H to Washington, July 30, 1796, note 12.

In his final draft of the Farewell Address, Washington wrote the following paragraph on education: "Promote then as an object of primary importance, Institutions for the general diffusion of knowledge. In proportion as the structure of a government gives force to public opinion, it is essential that public opinion should be enlightened" (ADS, MS Division, New York Public Library; printed in Paltsits, *Farewell Address*, 152).

5. See H to Washington, September 4, 1796, note 4.

6. Tobias Lear.

7. John Dunlap, in partnership with David C. Claypoole, had been publisher of *Dunlap and Claypoole's American Daily Advertiser* in Philadelphia. H presumably did not know that Dunlap had retired on December 31, 1795, and that the *American Daily Advertiser* had become *Claypoole's American Daily Advertiser*, published by David C. and Septimus Claypoole.

From George Washington [1]

Philadelphia 6th. Septr. 1796.

My Dear Sir,

I received yesterday, your letter of the 4th. instant. If the promised paper [2] has not been sent before this reaches you, Mr. Kitt [3] the bearer of it, who goes to New York partly on mine, and partly on his own business, will bring it safely. I only await here, now, and shall in a few days do it impatiently, for the arrival of General Pinckney.[4]

If you think the idea of a University had better be reserved for the Speech at the opening of the Session,[5] I am content to defer the communication of it until that period. But even in *that* case, I would pray you (as soon as convenient) to make a draught for the occasion; predicated on the ideas with which you have been furnished—looking at the sametime into what was said on this head in my *second* Speech to the *first* Congress [6]—merely with a view to see what was said on the subject at that time, and this you will perceive was not so much to the point as I want to express now—though it may, if proper, be glanced at, to shew that the subject had caught my attention early.

But to be candid, I much question whether a recommendation of this measure to the Legislature will have a better effect *now* than *formerly*. It may shew indeed my sense of its importance, and that is a sufficient inducement with *me* to bring the matter before the public in some shape or another, at the closing Scenes of my political exit. My object for proposing to insirt it where I did [7] (if not improper) was to set the People to ruminating on the importance of the measures ⟨as the⟩ [8] most likely means of bringing it to pass.

With much truth   I am Your Affectionate   Go: Washington

Colo. A. Hamilton

ALS, Hamilton Papers, Library of Congress; ALS, facsimile (tracing), Hamilton Papers, Library of Congress; copy, Hamilton Papers, Library of Congress.

1. For background to this letter, see the introductory note to H to Washington, May 10, 1796.
2. Washington is referring to H's "Draft of Washington's Farewell Address," which is printed as an enclosure to H to Washington, July 30, 1796. H returned this draft to Washington on September 5, 1796.
3. Frederick Kitt (Kitts) was Washington's household steward.
4. Charles Cotesworth Pinckney. See Washington to H, August 25, 1796. Pinckney arrived in Philadelphia on September 15, 1796.
5. See Washington to H, September 1, 1796; H to Washington, September 4, 5, 1796.
6. Washington is referring to his first annual address to Congress, January 8, 1790 (*GW*, XXX, 491–94). His first speech to Congress was his first inaugural address on April 30, 1789 (*GW*, XXX, 291–96).
7. See Washington to H, September 1, 1796.

8. Material within broken brackets has been taken from the facsimile in the Hamilton Papers, Library of Congress.

From George Washington

[Philadelphia, September 6, 1796. Second letter of September 6 [1] not found.]

1. In the "List of Letters from G—— Washington to General Hamilton," Columbia University Libraries, two letters from Washington to H September 6, 1796, are listed.

From Isaac Sherman

New York, September 7, 1796. "I have not been able to get money to pay my rent for the quarter which became due on the first day of august last, amounting to thirteen pounds fifteen shillings, and the Landlord is extreamly pressing for the money, I have therefore no other alternative than to refer him to you for the money. . . ."[1]

ALS, Hamilton Papers, Library of Congress.
1. Under the date of September 7, 1796, the following entry appears in H's Cash Book, 1795–1804: "Account of Donations Dr. to Cash for this sum paid on account of rent for Isaac Sherman 37.50." A second entry on January 14, 1797, reads "Account of Donations for paid ballance of indem for Rent for I Sherman 12.50" (AD, Hamilton Papers, Library of Congress).
On other occasions H had loaned money to Sherman. See Sherman to H, October 16, 1790; January 23, 1792.

To George Washington [1]

New York Sepr. 8. 1796

Sir

I have received your letter of the 6th. by the bearer. The draft was sent forward by Post on Tuesday.[2]

I shall prepare a paragraph with respect to the University & some others for consideration respecting other points which have occured.

With true respect & attachment   I have the honor to be Sir   Yr. very obed serv   A Hamilton

The President

ALS, MS Division, New York Public Library.
1. For background to this letter, see the introductory note to H to Washington, May 10, 1796. See also Washington to H, September 1, 6, 1796; H to Washington, September 4, 5, 1796.
2. H returned the draft to Washington in H to Washington, September 5, 1796. It was sent by post on Tuesday September 6, 1796.

From Rufus King

London Sep. 10. 1796

Dear Sir

I received this morning a Letter from Mr. Monroe dated Paris August 28.[1] of which the following is an extract—"As soon as *the order of this Government*, as notified by the minister of foreign Affairs [2] to Barthelemi [3] the present Ambassador at Basle appeared in the Papers,[4] for it was never notified to the foreign ministers here, I applied for information whether orders were issued for the Seizure of neutral *vessels*, stating Equally as the motive of my application a report apparently well authenticated, that one of our vessels had been lately taken near our own coast,[5] and was informed that no such order was issued, and further that none such would be, in case the British did not seize our vessels. I am happy to give you this information, because I flatter my self the Knowledge of this fact may be useful in respect to our commerce with the Country in which you reside." I have in a former Letter [6] told you that the British Government deny that any order has been lately issued, or that any order exists, authorising the seizure of neutral Cargoes bound to the french ports as was alledged to be the case in the Letter from the french Minister of for. Affairs to Barthelemi. The foregoing Extract is all I know from Mr. Monroe respecting the Resolution of the french Government communicated by their Minister of for. Affairs to their Ambassador at Basle. You will have seen the Letter to Barthelemi, which is undoubtedly authentic, and you now have what mr. Munroe reports as the result of his Application on the Subject. I make no comments nor inferences—you have the Materials and can make your own interpretations.

Very sincerely Yrs   R. King

PS. I have seen Mrs. Church [7] and family this morning at Mr. Pinckney's they are all well. Mr. Pinckney [8] will sail for Carolina about the 22d. or 25th. of this month.

ALS, Hamilton Papers, Library of Congress.
   1. James Monroe's letter was written in reply to the following letter from King to Monroe, August 11, 1796: ". . . a few days since a paper was published in the English Gazettes, purporting to be a letter from the Directory to Mr. Barthelemi, in which the French government announces their intention to stop the cargoes of all neutral vessels bound to the English ports, and assigns as the cause and justification of this measure a recent order of the British government to stop the cargoes of all neutral vessels bound to French ports . . ." (King, *The Life and Correspondence of Rufus King*, II, 78). Monroe's letter of August 28 is printed in Monroe, *A View of the Conduct of the Executive*, 364.
   2. Charles Delacroix.
   3. François (later Marquis de) Barthélemy was French Ambassador to Switzerland until his election to the Directory in 1797.
   4. Delacroix's letter of August 7, 1796, to Barthélemy reads: "The French government is informed that the English, after having stopped, during the war, under the most frivolous pretexts, every neutral vessel, have just given the most positive orders to the commanders of their ships of war, to seize, indiscriminately, all the cargoes which they may suppose to be destined for the French.

"Whatever injury France may have sustained from this conduct, she has, nevertheless continued to give the only example of the most inviolable respect for the law of nations, which constitutes the pledge and security of their civilization. But, after having long tolerated the offence of this Machiavelian system of policy, she at length finds herself compelled, by the most urgent motives, to have recourse to reprisals against England.

"The Executive Directory, therefore, orders all the political agents of the French Republic to inform the different governments, that the squadrons and privateers of the Republic will act against the ships of every country, in the same manner in which those governments suffer the English to act against them.

"This measure ought not to surprise them, since it would be very easy to demonstrate that it is imperiously prescribed by necessity, and is only the effect of a lawful defence. If these powers had known how to make their commerce respected by the English, we should have had no occasion to have recourse to this afflicting extremity.

"They will recollect, that the French Republic, ever generous, proposed to all the belligerent powers to respect commerce; but that this proposition, honourable to the government which made it, and dictated by the most perfect philanthropy, was rejected with pride, by a government accustomed to treat with contempt the most sacred laws of humanity, &c." (Debrett, *A Collection of State Papers*, V, 76.)

5. On August 15, 1796, Monroe wrote to Timothy Pickering: "I lately received an account from England of the capture of one of our vessels upon our coast, on the point of entering one of our ports, taken by a french privateer, upon a presumption she had English property on board, as she was cleared out of that country. Although this report was not so well authenticated nor accompanied with the necessary details to enable me to act officially on it, yet . . . I communicated it immediately to the Minister of Marine asking him whether such orders were given. He appeared astonished at the report and declared that none such were issued . . ." (LC, RG 59, Despatches from United States Ministers to France, 1789–1869, Vol. 4, August 15, 1794–October 21, 1796, National Archives). This is a reference to the seizure of an American ship, the *Mount Vernon*, by the *Flying Fish*, a French privateer. See Oliver Wolcott, Jr., to H, June 14, 17, 1796.

6. Letter not found.

7. Angelica Church, H's sister-in-law.

8. Thomas Pinckney, whom King had succeeded as United States Minister Plenipotentiary to Great Britain.

From Rufus King

London Sep. 11. 1796

Immediately after the publication of the Letter from the french Government to their Minister Barthelemi at Basle, announcing their determination to seize the cargoes of neutral vessels destined to the English Ports, I wrote to Mr. Monroe [1] informing him that the Br. Gov. disavowed the having issued any recent order for the capture of neutral Cargoes bound to french Ports as alledged in the letter to Barthelemi—and by a Letter that I received today from Mr. Monroe under date of the 28. of August he says that on application for Information whether the fr. Gov. have issued an order for the capture of neutral Vessels he has been informed that no such order has been issued, and further that none will be, *in case the British did not seize our vessels.*

I am not quite able to explain this Transaction, I therefore give you fresh Facts as I know—you must seek for interpretations.

very sincerely and affectionately   Yr. ob. Ser.   Rufus King

Colo. Hamilton

ALS, Hamilton Papers, Library of Congress.

1. See King to H, September 10, 1796, note 1.

To Charles Cotesworth Pinckney

[New York, September 12, 1796]

Dr Sir

I have received your letter[1] transmitting me a draft on H & S Johnson & Co.[2] for 857 Dollars & 14 Cents on account of Kinloch's debt to Mr. Church.[3] Lest I should not see you here give me leave to request information in whose care the affairs of Mr. Church have been left by you—& whether any thing more has been done with Mrs Cattle's alias Bowman's note.[4] The above bill has been accepted.

I trouble you with two letters, one to an old military acquaintance *Fleury* [5]—another to a person who not knowing what to do with his money when he left this Country deposited it with me upon my bond in duplicates between 6 & 700 pounds.[6] It is very long since I have heared any thing of him. Perhaps he may not exist. You will oblige me by inquiry & if dead concerning his relations, as I am disposed to exonerate myself of my charge.

My best wishes for your happiness & success will follow you every where

Yrs. truly

A Hamilton

Sepr 12. 1796

P.S. You will excuse the use I make of your Name in these letters. Ducher was a member of the *National Convention* [7]

Charles C. Pinckney Esq

ALS, Pinckney Family Papers, Library of Congress.

1. Letter not found.
2. Horace and Seth Johnson were New York City merchants.
3. The following entry appears in H's Cash Book, 1795–1804, under the date of October 11, 1796: "To J. B. Church for this sum received of H & S Johnson in payt. of Draft received on account of Kinlochs Bond 850.57" (AD, Hamilton Papers, Library of Congress). For information on "Kinloch's debt to Church," see Pinckney to H, June 5, 1796.
4. Sabina Lynch, the daughter of Thomas Lynch of South Carolina, married William Cattell, who died in 1778. She then married John Bowman.
5. See the Marquis de Fleury to H, May 28, 1796. H endorsed Fleury's letter of May 28: "answered by General Pinckny." For a statement of Fleury's ac-

count with the United States, see Oliver Wolcott, Jr., to H, September 1, 1796.

6. This letter, which has not been found, was addressed to Gaspard Joseph Armand Ducher. Ducher was appointed vice consul *ad interim* at Portsmouth, New Hampshire, in 1786. In 1788 he was transferred to Wilmington, North Carolina, and in June, 1790, he returned to France. See H's Cash Book, March 1, 1782–1791.

7. H was mistaken. Ducher was not a member of the Convention. See H to Robert Troup, July 25, 1795, notes 9 and 10.

To Phineas Bond [1]

New York Sepr. 15. 1796.

Sir.

Two days since a letter was delivered to me with a declaration of the bearer that it came from Mr. Lyston.[2] On opening the cover, I found nothing except a letter from Capt Cochran (which though not addressed would appear to have been written to some public agent of Great Britain) and a declaration of *David Wilson* and *Thomas Marshall* respecting the ship *Eliza*.[3] The superscription of the packet resembling your hand writing, I concluded that it might have come from you & that by some mistake the letter you had written me had been omitted and that on discovery of the omission,

ALS, Hamilton Papers, Library of Congress.

1. This letter concerns the ship *Eliza*, originally a British transport vessel, which had been captured by a French privateer commanded by Joshua Barney. After it was condemned, Barney sold it to George G. Hussey, an American. The *Eliza* was then captured by the British frigate *Thetis*, commanded by Captain Alexander F. Cochrane. A few weeks later, it was recaptured by a group of men led by Hussey. At this point Cochrane retained H as counsel.

For an explanation and discussion of the contents of this letter, see Goebel, *Law Practice*, II, 905–08. See also Robert Liston to Lord Grenville, first letter of September 6, 1796 (PRO: F.O. [Great Britain] 5/14). For a reproduction of this letter as it was written by H, see Goebel, *Law Practice*, II, 908–10.

Bond had served in the United States as a representative of the British government since 1786. His first appointment was as British consul for the states of New York, New Jersey, Pennsylvania, Delaware, and Maryland. In addition, he was commissary for commercial affairs of all the states. The Continental Congress, however, recognized him only as British consul for Philadelphia. From February, 1793, until 1812 or 1813, Bond was British consul general for the middle and southern states, and from August, 1795, until May, 1796, he served as Britain's chargé d'affaires.

2. Robert Liston, British Minister to the United States.

3. Wilson and Marshall were British seamen who were members of the prize crew on the *Eliza* when it was recaptured by Hussey.

it would have been forwarded by another opportunity. Finding after two days waiting that this expectation has not been realized, I have determined to write to you on the subject.

Mr. Charles Wilkes [4] had previously applied to me concerning this affair and had submitted to my consideration various papers. The result was that I discouraged a judicial prosecution.

My reasons are these—

Taking it to be true as stated that Cap Hussey brought from *the shore within our territory* persons who *by force* aided him to rescue the captured Vessel, I am of opinion that *this circumstance* would give jurisdiction of the case to our Courts on the application of the Capturing party.

But when on such application any of our Courts should hold jurisdiction it would in my judgment go into the merits and examine the validity of the Capture.

Here these facts occur, that the Eliza, being a transport Vessel in the service of Great Britain, was captured by a French privateer fitted out of some port of France by *Barney* [5] an American Citizen in quality of *Armateur, Le Veillé* probably a Frenchman, Captain by Comission—and was afterwards condemned as prize by the sentence of a Court of Admiralty at Dunkirk—and as far as the direct proof goes purchased in virtue of that sentence by an American Citizen.

It is conjectured that two thirds of the Vessel may have belonged to a French house Messrs. *Debaques;* because it appears that Hussey paid two thirds of the purchase money in a Bill drawn by that House. But this is evidently a mere circumstance of suspicion & wholly inconclusive. Why may not the *Debaques* have been factors or Agents for *Hussey?* Why may not *Hussey* have purchased their draft towards the payment? One or the other of the two latter sup-

4. Wilkes was cashier of the Bank of New York.
5. After a distinguished career in the Navy during the American Revolution, Joshua Barney tried a variety of ventures, including agriculture, commerce, and exploration. In 1794 he was named one of six captains to command the six new frigates authorized by Congress, but he declined the commission because he was outranked by a man who previously had been his junior. He returned to the merchant service and took command of the ship that carried James Monroe to France in 1794. He then offered his services to the French navy, and while waiting for a commisson he outfitted three privateers which preyed on British commerce. It was one of these privateers that seized the *Eliza*. Barney served as a captain in the French navy from 1796 to 1802.

positions would no doubt prevail with the Court, if there was no collateral proof to the contrary.

It is also conjectured that the Eliza may even have continued the property of Barney. But all the documents now in the power of the Captor speak a contrary language. This suspicion then, however just it may be in fact, cannot be supported.

The question then is Would the Equipment of the Privateer by *Barney* be sufficient to invalidate the purchase by a neutral Citizen under the sentence of a Court of the Capturing Power?

No opinion of any theoretic Writer, nor as I believe, any usage of any Nation, nor the decisions of Courts of Admiralty will authorise, in any judgment, an affirmative answer to that Question.

If Mr. *Barney* comes within the 21st. Article of our Treaty with Great Britain,[6] it would make him liable, if *taken by Great Britain* to be punished *as a pirate*. But it will be observed that the stipulation would not oblige the U States to treat him as such. And the article being confined to personal punishment may be supposed not to contemplate the confiscation of property captured by such a person.

But it would be to go an unheard of length to pronounce null the prize made under such circumstances by a Vessel fitted out of the Ports of the Belligerent power & regularly commissioned & after a sentence of condemnation.

Therefore, and as the property in question is of little value, & as smart damages would be likely to attend a failure of the prosecution, I advised against it, as I now still do.

Yet, if Capt. Cochran or any person acting on his behalf shall *desire the experiment to be made*, however unpromising in my view, I shall esteem it a professional duty, and due to justice to a foreign power, to put the affair in a course of judicial investigation.

With esteem   I am Sir   Yr very Obed serv   A Hamilton

Phineas Bond Esqr

6. Article 21 of the Jay Treaty states that if any subject or citizen of Great Britain or the United States ". . . shall accept any Foreign Commission or Letters of Marque for Arming any Vessel to act as a Privateer against the other party, and be taken by the other party, it is hereby declared to be lawful for the said party to treat and punish the said Subject or Citizen, having such Commission or Letters of Marque as a Pirate" (Miller, *Treaties*, II, 261).

From Abraham Van Vechten

[*Albany*] *September 16, 1796.* "In the Causes of Mr Duane [1] agst. the Tenants of Voght [2] two Questions are likely to arise, on which I am directed to request your opinion as early as possible. The inclosed is a Copy of the only Writing which Mr Duane has from the Patentee to vest the Title in him.[3] Quer. Does a legal Title pass by it, so as that we can recover on Mr. Duanes sole demise? In one of the Causes the Ancestor of Defts was a Tenant for Years of Mr. Duane. He died a Year or two ago & left Defts. in his possession, who agreed to deliver it up to Mr Duane by a certain Day. On the Day appointed Mr. Duane sent a person to receive the possession, who met the Defts. at the Door on a Cart going off with their last Load of Furniture &c. The Defts. declared they delivered up the possession to the person sent by Mr Duane, and then rode away. When Mr Duane's Agent or new Tenant came up to the Door of the House he found Voght & another person in it, by whom he was deterred from entering it. Thus situated Mr Duane's Agent &c went off & informed his principal that he could not obtain the possession, as a few Days after Defts. reentered as Tenants under Voght. Quer. Are not Defts. Precluded by their original Tenancy from controverting our Title? Their Transactions with Voght savour strongly of Fraud & Collusion. . . ."

ALS, Hamilton Papers, Library of Congress.

1. Before the American Revolution, James Duane had been an attorney in New York City. During the war he was a member of the Continental Congress. He was mayor of New York City from 1784 to 1789, a member of the New York Senate from 1782 to 1785 and from 1788 to 1790, a member of the New York Ratifying Convention, and United States judge for the district of New York from 1789 to 1794. He owned a large estate named Duanesburg in the vicinity of Schenectady, New York.

2. This is a reference to a protracted dispute between Duane and John Voght. The Voght family owned the Thomas Brain Patent on the eastern border of Duanesburg. During the American Revolution the Voghts sided with the British, and Duane attempted to purchase their property. The Voghts not only retained their lands but also claimed some farms on the Duanesburg side of the line. It was not until April, 1803, six years after Duane's death, that his family were victors in this dispute in the case of *Maria Duane* v *John Voght* before the New York Supreme Court. See the endorsement on "Subpoena to William Cockburn," March 7, 1803 (DS, Detroit Public Library).

Under the date of October 15, 1796, the following entry appears in H's Cash Book, 1795–1804: "this sum received of James Duanes fee in his controversy with Voght 100" (AD, Hamilton Papers, Library of Congress).

3. "Lieutenant John Butler. Conveyance to James Duane for 2000 Acres of Land he is entitled to by Virtue of the royal Proclamation of 7th October 1783" (DS, Hamilton Papers, Library of Congress).

From Hall and Stimpson [1]

[*Boston, September 20, 1796.* On October 24, 1796, Hall and Stimpson wrote to Hamilton: "We wrote you the 20th. Septr." *Letter not found.*]

1. James Hall and Charles Stimpson were partners in a mercantile firm located at No. 67, Long Wharf, Boston.

To John Steele [1]

[*New York, September 20, 1796.* On September 23, 1796, Steele wrote to Hamilton: "I have the honor to acknowledge your letter of the 20th. inst." *Letter not found.*]

1. On July 1, 1796, when Congress was not in session, Timothy Pickering informed John Steele, a Federalist member of the House of Representatives from North Carolina from 1789 to 1793, of his appointment as comptroller of the Treasury (LC, RG 59, Domestic Letters of the Department of State, Vol. 9, October 12, 1795–February 28, 1797, National Archives). The Senate confirmed his appointment on December 22, 1796 (*Executive Journal*, I, 217).

To Timothy Pickering

New [York] Sepr. 21. 1796

Dr Sir

Some time since Mr. McCormick [1] spoke to me about the case of his Kinsman Mr. Pitcairn whom Mr. Monroe had prevented from exercising the functions of Consul.[2] I can, in justice, inform you that this Gentleman is well considered in our City and that his political principles have been understood to be very friendly to the

French Revolution; nor have we any doubt that his sentiments towards our own Government are altogether American. So that in truth there can be no shadow of political objection to him as to the Office for which he was intended.

With respect & esteem   Dr. Sir   Yr Obed Serv   A Hamilton

Col Pickering

ALS, Massachusetts Historical Society, Boston.
  1. Daniel McCormick was a New York City merchant and a director of the Bank of New York.
  2. On November 24, 1794, the Senate confirmed Joseph Pitcairn's appointment as vice consul of the United States at Paris (*Executive Journal*, I, 164). On March 6, 1795, James Monroe, United States Minister Plenipotentiary to France, wrote to Secretary of State Edmund Randolph: "I was advised by your favor of the 2nd. of December that Mr. J. Pitcairn of New York was appointed Consul for this city. . . . Permit me to ask: Is he an American citizen, and if so, whether by birth or naturalization; and, in the latter case, whether he became such since the Revolution? If of the last description, his arrival will subject me to great embarrassment. . . . I candidly think, if his situation is known, being a person deemed by the English law a subject of that crown, he will not be recognized, or if recognized, not without great reluctance. . . ." On May 17, 1795, Monroe wrote to Randolph that Pitcairn had arrived in Paris, but that he ". . . thought it best to withhold the official communication of his appointment from the government" (Hamilton, *James Monroe*, II, 226–27, 256).
  For the mission for which Pickering was considering Pitcairn at this time, see Pickering to H, September 24, 1796.

From Baron de Rou[1]

Frederick County, Virginia, September 23, 1796. States that he has failed at agriculture in both Virginia and Long Island. Proposes that Hamilton ask his friends to subscribe to a fund for de Rou's support.

ALS, Hamilton Papers, Library of Congress.
  1. This letter is written in French.

From John Steele

Philada. Septemr. 23d. 1796

My dear sir,

I have the honor to acknowledge your letter of the 20th. inst.[1] and to return you my unfeigned thanks for the polite and friendly manner in which you were pleased to speak of my appointment. Next to the pleasure which attends a faithfull discharge of duty, it will always afford me the highest gratification to be classed among those who are favored with your approbation.

John Sitgreaves the united States's Judge for the district of North Carolina[2] being in this city, I have concieved that it might be satisfactory to you to be furnished with his information upon the point stated in your letter. His notes are herewith enclosed for your perusal,[3] and as circumstances which entitle them to consideration, it

ALS, Hamilton Papers, Library of Congress.

1. Letter not found.

2. Sitgreaves served as United States judge for the District of North Carolina from 1789 until his death in 1802.

3. In an undated letter to Steele, Sitgreaves wrote: "North Carolina having never passed an Act of naturalization, the mode of complying with the requisites of the Constitution to obtain the rights of Citizenship has been very loose & irregular. The oath has heretofore been often taken before a *single Justice* in his Chambers, & his Certificate of it the sole evidence of the fact. I do not remember in the course of my practice that any Question has arisen & been divided in the Superior Courts touching the validity or regularity of such Certificates, altho it may have happened.

"The Legislature in directing the Oath of Allegiance to be taken by suspicious persons at the commencement of the war prescribed, that it should be *taken and subscribed in open Court*. By an Act in April 1784 relative to Quakers, they permitted an affirmation made before a Justice of the peace of the County where they resided as sufficient to entitle them to Citizenship—& by a subsequent Act of 1784 to take Effect in April 1785 they have directed persons desirous to become Citizens to *take and subscribe* the Oath of Allegiance, which was then altered in its form—but are silent with respect to the Court or person before whom it is to be taken or the manner certifying the fact.

"You know that our Justices never keep any Records but I am inclined to think that a Certificate from one known to be a Justice; of the party having *taken & subscribed* the Oath of Allegiance before him in his *proper County* would be admitted in the *Courts of the State* as an Evidence of the fact, *if it bore date with the fact*, but I should doubt much of the propriety of admitting the memory of the Justice to relate to a fact of Eight or nine Years' standing on a point of such moment it certainly is not the best evidence, the nature of the case would admit. . . ." (Copy, Hamilton Papers, Library of Congress.)

may not be improper to add that before his present appointment he was a lawyer of respectable standing in that state, and a member of the Legislature.

In addition to his letter you will also herewith receive the transcripts of three laws which I have caused to be prepared, and which are forwarded with an expectation that the expression of the legislature upon the subject will prove more satisfactory to your mind, than the information, or opinion of any individual.

During the revolution war many laws were passed to ascertain the description of persons entitled to citizenship, but these laws having a particular reference to the then circumstances of the country are decred to be obsolete, and having been dictated by the spirit of the times, it is right that they should be so considered.

An opinion prevailed in North Carolina until the appearance of the late insurrection in Pennsylvania, *that not having a population equal to the extent of our territory it would be expedient to open the door to european emigrants as wide as possible,* and to this mistaken policy it must be ascribed that the important subject of naturalization has been so little attended to by the legislature.

The evidences of citizenship I have often known to be the subject of interesting discussions at elections, and although the Judges of the elections do not like the courts of justice settle the law for the State their decisions nevertheless serve to shew the opinions entertained by the best informed men among the people. In consequence of their decisions, in the part of the country where I lived, emigrants of distinction who either from a sense of personal rights, or from the nature of their pecuniary transactions were desirous to be armed at all points, have been usually advised to take the oath of allegiance before some Justice of the peace (out of court) capable of granting a certificate in decent form. This certificative is immediately presented to the Clerk of the court of pleas, and quarter sessions at his office who upon the payment of a perquisite 2/8 will subjoin a testimonial under the county seal in this form.

North Carolina } ss
Anson County }

Be it remembered that A: B esquire who administered the foregoing oath of allegiance to C. D was at the time of doing so, and is at this time one of the acting Justices of the peace for the county aforesaid, and being legally authorised to hold the courts, to administer oaths, and to keep the peace within the said county full faith and credit are due to his official attestation.

In testimony whereof &ca. &ca.

Seal of the County

A certificate of this kind supported by the requisites of the constitution I have never known to be disputed either in the courts of law, or by the Judges of the elections, the only tribunals where the rights of a citizen are usually scrutinized; but in all cases where the certificate is to be used out of the state or even out of the county the seal and attestation of the Clerk have been considered indispensable for this obvious reason, *that the office of the clerk of the county, and the office of the private Sectry. of the Governor are the only two places in the state where the fact that a man is an acting justice of the peace can be legally authenticated.*

Sometimes I have known, men who intended to travel, or for greater caution apply to the Court by petition, or motion of counsel to have their certificates admitted to record; this is attended with expence but never refused, unless it shoud appear that the certificate was obtained collusively.

It will afford me peculiar pleasure to understand that you have recevd. this letter safe, and that its contents are in any respect useful to you.

I have the honor to be, My dear sir, With perfect respect, Your obliged friend and hume. Servt.   Jno. Steele

The honble.
Colonel Hamilton
New York.

To Angelica Church

[New York, September 24, 1796]

At length, Dear Angelica our apprehensions are realized and your coming is deferred.[1] But though life is too short to render it agreeable to lose even a winter in the passage from hope to enjoyment in any thing which materially interests us—yet if you do really come in the Spring and bring with you Mr. Church it will afford us consolation, because it will leave less ultimately at hazard and may give us earlier the pleasure of seeing him. But prithee do not let the Winter freeze the inclination, and produce more procrastination. For one cannot always live on hope. Tis thin diet at best.

Your friend, Mrs. Grattan, is strongly tempted to remain in Philadelphia.[2] But we are trying to form a counterplot. She will be an acquisition to us, if what we hear is true.

Adieu Give our Love to the younger part of your family, to Caty[3] in particular mine. I am told she justifies all my anticipations of her. I take credit to myself for having discerned her worth in embryo when no one else had yet found it out.

Adieu Yrs. Affect   A Hamilton

Sepr. 24. 1796

ALS, Judge Peter B. Olney, Deep River, Connecticut.

1. The Church family had originally planned to return to the United States in 1796 (Philip Schuyler to H, October 12, 1795; Angelica Church to H, February 19, 1796; H to Angelica Church, June 19–20, 1796). On July 9, 1796, however, Angelica Church wrote to Elizabeth Hamilton: "We shall not meet before the Spring . . ." (ALS, Hamilton Papers, Library of Congress). The Churches arrived in the United States in May, 1797. See Robert Morris to H, May 23, 1797.

2. A typical advertisement for Mrs. Grattan's concerts reads: *"Mrs. GRATTAN Respectfully informs the Ladies and Gentlemen of the City, that the 4th LADIES' CONCERT will be on TUESDAY, the 14th day of February at the Assembly-Room. . . .*

"Mrs. Grattan begs leave to inform the Ladies and Gentlemen, that the subscription-book is at her house No 39, North Sixth-street, for the reception of those names who wish to honor her with their commands.—A subscription for eight nights 16 dollars, including a Gentleman and Lady's ticket, each transferable—Half-subscriptions 8 dollars, including one ticket.—single ticket, 2 dollars.

"*/* The Concert to begin at half past six; and at half past eight, the music will attend for the Ball." (*Gazette of the United States, & Philadelphia Daily Advertiser,* February 14, 1797.)

3. Catharine, one of Angelica Church's four children.

From Timothy Pickering

Department of State Sept 24. 1796.

Dr Sir,

I have just received your letter of the 21st relative to Mr. Pitcairn. As soon as the President had determined to change our Minister at Paris, I considered it not less necessary to make a change in the Consulate; and Mr Pinckney [1] will go thither with the requisite powers on this subject. I have mentioned to him Mr Pitcairn as the gentleman whom he may safely and advantageously employ in the preliminary investigations of Mr. Skipwith's proceedings with respect to the immense property of American citizens which has been committed to his management.[2] This investigation, and measures, for securing the property, I thought should precede any change in the Consulate. The mode suggested will naturally introduce Mr Pitcairn to his proper place, with this view I had some days since made particular enquiry about his character, and received such information as enabled me to recommend him to the confidence of Gen'l Pinckney in the proposed investigation, and with an assurance, that his agency would be acceptable to our mercantile citizens.[3] I am glad to receive your additional testimony in his favor, which I shall give to Gen'l Pinckney.

With great respect & esteem, I am, &c   Timothy Pickering

P.S. I shall be obliged, by your communicating this to Mr McCormick, to whom I am indebted for an answer to his letter concerning Mr Pitcairn [4] but which this may now supercede. But as it respects Mr Skipwith I think nothing should be made public.

Copy, Massachusetts Historical Society, Boston; LC, RG 59, Domestic Letters of the Department of State, Vol. 9, October 12, 1795–February 28, 1797, National Archives.
  1. Charles Cotesworth Pinckney.
  2. Fulwar Skipwith had been appointed consul general of the United States in France in 1795. On June 25, 1795, George Washington, in a letter nominating Skipwith for this position, wrote to the Senate: "It has been represented by our Minister Plenipotentiary, near the French Republic, that such of our commercial relations with France as may require the support of the United

States, *in detail*, cannot be well executed without a Consul General. Of this I am satisfied, when I consider the extent of the mercantile claims now depending before the French government; the neecssity of bringing into the hands of one agent the various applications to the several Committees of Administration, residing at Paris; the attention which must be paid to the conduct of Consuls and Vice-Consuls; and the nature of the services which are the peculiar objects of a Minister's care, and leave no leisure for his intervention in business to which consular functions are competent. I therefore nominate Fulwar Skipwith, to be Consul General of the United States, in France" (*Executive Journal*, I, 189).

3. Daniel McCormick.

4. On September 24, 1796, Pickering wrote to Pinckney: "You will find by the papers now delivered to you, that Mr. Joseph Pitcairn of New York was about two years ago appointed vice Consul of the united States, to reside at Paris, and you will also at the same time see by what means he has been excluded from the office. I have on this occasion made particular inquiries of his character, and am satisfactorily assured that it is unblemished. In addition to the testimony before received, I am happy to give you that of Colo. Hamilton in his letter of the 21st. instant . . ." (LC, RG 59, Domestic Letters of the Department of State, Vol. 9, October 12, 1795–February 28, 1797, National Archives).

To Jeremiah Wadsworth [1]

New York Sep 29. 1796

Dear Sir

Permit me to introduce to your acquaintance and recommend to your Civilities the bearer of this, Mr. Hoffman,[2] our Atty General who goes to Connecticut on the question of the Connecticut Gore.[3] He will wish to engage the assistance of one of your Lawyers; will you assist him with your advice?

Yrs. Affectly   A Hamilton

J Wadsworth Esq

ALS, Blumhaven Library and Gallery, Philadelphia.

1. Wadsworth, a friend of H for many years, was a Federalist member of the House of Representatives from Connecticut from 1789 to 1795 and a member of the Connecticut Executive Council from 1795 to 1801.

2. Josiah Ogden Hoffman.

3. This is a reference to the dispute between Connecticut and New York over a narrow strip of land running the length of the Pennsylvania–New York border, along the Southern Tier of New York. For an account of this dispute and H's part in it, see Goebel, *Law Practice*, I, 657–84.

From Robert Liston [1]

Philadelphia 30th September 1796

Sir,

Mr Bond has communicated to me a letter written by you to him on the 15th of this month, on the Subject of the Ship Eliza, captured by Captain Cochrane, and afterwards retaken by the Master and carried into New York.

The letter signed by Captain Cochrane and enclosing a declaration of David Wilson and Thomas Marshall, which you received under a Blank Cover, was in fact intended for you, though not addressed, and was forwarded by me at his desire.

Mr. Cochrane had previously made an application to me on that business, and transmitted to me copies of a letter of Captain Barney to Mr. George G. Hussey, dated at Ostend the 8th of April, and of a receipt of the said Barney for the value of the Ship Eliza, said to have been purchased in the *port of Flushing;* requesting that I would take such steps as I might think proper in a case which appeared to him to be of national importance.[2]

I accordingly presented a memorial to the American Secretary of State (on the 12th inst.) [3] claiming the restitution of the Eliza to the British Captors, on the ground that the original capture by an armament fitted out by an American citizen must have been illegal and that no regular trial, and consequently no legitimate sale, could take place in a port of Holland, into which it appeared that the vessel had been carried. I urged that these circumstances at least created a suspicion of the fair neutrality of the property, and of course justified the detention of the Ship, with a view to a discussion of the question in a Competent Court of Justice; that the violent recapture by the Captain became therefore a breach of the Law of Nations, which called for redress.

I had judged however from the two abovementioned documents alone. You, Sir, appear to have had other information; since you state as a fact that the Eliza was condemned by the Sentence of a Court of Admiralty in Dunkirk. If this is the case, the question is essentially altered; and though I cannot admit of the regularity or propriety of the conduct of Captain Hussey, yet I agree with you in thinking it inadvisable to endeavour to obtain redress in a Court of Law in New York: at all events, as a friend of Captain Cochrane's, I frankly give it is as my opinion that no step should be taken in the matter till you are expressly authorized by some person acting on his behalf.

I am, with perfect truth and regard, Sir, Your most obedient humble servant, Rob. Liston.

Alexander Hamilton Esqe

LS, Hamilton Papers, Library of Congress.
1. For background to this letter, see H to Phineas Bond, September 15, 1796.
2. Copies of the documents mentioned in this paragraph may be found in RG 59, Notes from the British Legation in the United States to the Department of State, 1791–1906, Vol. 2, January 10, 1796–November 19, 1803, National Archives.
3. AL, RG 59, Notes from the British Legation in the United States to the Department of State, 1791–1906, Vol. 2, January 10, 1796–November 19, 1803, National Archives.

Timothy Pickering referred Liston's memorial of September 12 to William Rawle, United States attorney for the District of Pennsylvania. On September 24, 1796, Pickering wrote to Rawle: "I request you to read the enclosed papers relative to the capture & recapture of the ship Eliza, George G. Hussey, master, and to favor me as early as you can with your opinion on the question submitted by the British Minister, Mr. Liston, 'Whether a strict regard to justice, and a faithful observance of the law of nations, does not require that she should be re-delivered to the British captors?' And if the government of the United States is under any obligation to interpose, whether it must not be by the judiciary not the executive department? . . ." (LC, Massachusetts Historical Society, Boston).

Rawle replied to Pickering on September 28, 1796, that ". . . the point of view in which the question strikes me forbids the application of the Executive to the Judicial authority and leaves it to the British captor in his own person and founded on his own right to represent his case to the District court of New York and to procure that redress which if he is entitled to it will be imparted as freely and as fully on his application as on that of the Executive authority of the union" (LS, RG 59, Miscellaneous Letters, 1790–1799, National Archives). On October 1, 1796, Rawle sent to Pickering the opinion of William Lewis "on the subject of the Elizabeth on my requesting him . . . to favor me with his sentiments on the question stated abstractedly.

"As he gives a more enlarged construction to a clause in the treaty than I can bring myself to do it is proper to lay it before you. But admitting it to be according to his construction I cannot discover the right of Executive interference." (ALS, RG 59, Miscellaneous Letters, 1790–1799, National Archives.) See also Lewis to Rawle, September 29, 1796 (ALS, RG 59, Miscellaneous Letters, 1790–1799, National Archives).

After receiving the two opinions, Pickering wrote to Liston on October 5, 1796: "That there exists no constitutional power in the Executive branch of the Government, to effectuate a delivery of the ship, without intervention of the judiciary; and that if resort be had to the judiciary, the British captors must themselves represent their case to the District court of New York, from which they may expect a just decision on their claim" (LC, Massachusetts Historical Society, Boston).

The War in Europe
[September–December, 1796]

Every step of the progress of the present war in Europe has been marked with horrors. If the perpetration of them was confined to those who are the acknowleged instruments of despotic Power, it would excite less surprize—but when they are acted by those who profess themselves to be the Champions of the rights of man, they naturally occasion both wonder and regret. Passing by the extreme severities which the French have exercised in Italy, what shall we think of the following declaration of *Jourdan* to the inhabitants of Germany [1]

Good God! is it then a *crime* for men to defend their own Government and Country? Is it a punishable offence in the Germans that they will not accept from the French what they offer as liberty, at the point of the bayonet? This is to confound all ideas of morality and humanity; it is to trample upon all the rights of man and nations. It is to restore the ages of Barbarism. According to the laws and practice of modern war, the peasantry of a Country, if they remain peaceably at home, are protected from other harm than a contribution to the necessities of the invading army. Those who join the armies of their Country and fight with them are considered and treated as *other soldiers*. But the present French Doctrine is, that they are to be treated as *Rebels* and *Criminals*. German *patriotism* is a heinous offence in the eyes of French PATRIOTS. How are we to solve this otherwise than by observing that the French are influenced by the same spirit of Domination which governed the antient Romans! These considered themselves as having a right to be the Masters of the World and to treat the rest of mankind as their vassals.

How clearly is it proved ⟨by⟩ all ⟨–⟩ that the praise of a ⟨–⟩ world is justly due to Christianity. War, by the influence of the humane principles of that Religion, had been stripped of half its terrors. The *French* renounce christianity & they relapse into Barbarism. War resumes the same hideous and savage form, which it wore in the ages of *Roman* and Gothic Violence.

AD, Hamilton Papers, Library of Congress.
    1. This is a reference to a proclamation made by General Jean Baptiste Jourdan to the inhabitants of the country beyond the Rhine, July 4, 1796. The proclamation reads: "The repeated victories of the armies of the French Republic, the cry of the nations exhausted by a war, which brings with it only ruin and desolation, the voice of humanity, which incessantly exclaims, that it is time to dry up the streams of blood which inundate your fields, have not yet moved the hearts of your sovereigns to solicit a peace which may restore tranquillity and happiness to Europe. Since, then, blood must continue to flow, the French armies must carry the war into the heart of Germany. But fear not, peaceable inhabitants of these unhappy countries, we are not your enemies, we mean not to destroy your laws or your religion, as some falsely endeavour to persuade you. The presence of the armies will undoubtedly cause you to suffer some inconveniences; but imagine not that we mean to avenge upon you the cruelties which the people of France suffered when that country was made the theatre of war. Your property shall not be plundered, nor your houses reduced to ashes. Take no part in the contest, remain peaceably in your houses, and you and your property shall be protected by the generals of the Republic. But should you take arms, you must expect the severest punishment, and to be made a terrible example.

    "A regulation, consisting of seven articles, is annexed, which orders the French troops to observe the strictest discipline. Every soldier who shall plunder any of the inhabitants shall be put to death. The inhabitants, however, must remain quiet in their houses, and deliver up their arms: if they are taken flying with their effects or cattle, they will be arrested, and their property confiscated for the use of the Republic. The inhabitants of the villages, who shall take arms against the French, shall be shot, and their houses burnt, as shall likewise all who bear arms without permission from the French generals." (Debrett, *A Collection of State Papers*, V, 45–46.)

Account with Archibald Drummond [1]

New York Octobr. 4th. 1796.

Col: Hamilton		To Archibd Drummond, Dr.	
1795			
Decr. 22d.	1 large slate	4/6	£
"	2 Pencils	2/6	
	1 Copy	2/0	11.6
	1 Ashes Grammr.[2]	2/6	
24	1 Espinasses [3]		1.18. .
	4 papers ink powdr.		6.

OCTOBER 1796

Jany.	4th	1 box pounce	1.
	12	1 Sett bills Exchange	3.
	13	1 Qr. Imperiel papr.	16.
	14	1 Powel & Devises [4]	1.16.
Feby.	1	1 pen knife	8.
	"	½ Hund Quills 6/ Wafers 1/6	7.6
	18th.	¼ Do. Do.	3.
	25	Slate pencil	1
March	2d.	2 Hundd. Quills	1.4
	5	1 Ream thick 4to. posts	2.2
	7	Wafers	3.
	11	6 Sheets bills Exchange	6.
	21st	1 box pounce	6
April	2	1 Kyd. on bills [5]	15.
	6	1 Stick wax	1.
	19th	1 Slate pencil	6
May	11th.	12 Skins parchments	2.16.
		1 Ream fools cap	2.4.
		1 Do 4to. Posts	1.18
		1 Do. fools cap No. 4	1.3
June	6th.	¼ Hundd. Quills	6.6
		1 Stick wax	1.
	20	6 Skins parchment 5/	1.10.
	25th	6 Sticks wax	6.
	29th	1 tin box wafers	7.
July	1st	1 blk book	3.6
	20th.	1 Greek Testament	9.
	28th.	1 Hundd. Quills	14.
		Sand	2.
		India rubr.	6
		Pounce	1.
Augt.	23d.	1 blank book	7.
	30th.	10 Skins parchment 5/.	2.10.
Septr.	3d.	6 papers Ink powdr.	5.
	8th.	½ Hundd. Quills	3.
	13th.	8 Volms. Spectator [6]	2.0.0
			£28.9.6 [7]

D, Hamilton Papers, Library of Congress.

1. Drummond was a bookseller and stationer whose store was located at 132 Water Street, New York City.

2. John Ash, *Grammatical Institutes: or an Easy Introduction to Dr. Lowth's English Grammar. Designed for the Use of Schools. With an Appendix, Containing, I. The Declension of Irregular and Defective Verbs. II. The Application of the Grammatical Institutes. III. Some Useful Observations on the Ellipsis. IV. Exercises of Bad English. V. Lessons on the English Language. To This Edition is Added, an Essay on Punctuation, and an Explication of Tropes and Figures, Used in Writing the English Language* (Philadelphia: Printed and sold by John M'Culloch, No. 1, North Third street, 1795). Ash's *Grammatical Institutes* was first printed in London in 1763.

3. Isaac Espinasse, *Cases, Argued and Ruled at Nisi Prius, in the Courts of Kings Bench, and Common Pleas, from Easter Term 33 George III—Hillary Term 34 George III with Some Additional Cases of an Earlier Period* (Baltimore: Reprinted by Clayton, Dobbin, & Co. for Keating's Book-store, 1795).

4. John Joseph Powell, *An Essay upon the Learning of Devises, from Their Inception by Writing, to Their Consummation by the Death of the Devisor* (London: P. Uriel, 1788).

5. Stewart Kyd, *A Treatise on the Law of Bills of Exchange and Promissory Notes* (3rd ed., London: J. Johnson, 1795).

6. Joseph Addison and Richard Steele, *The Spectator*. Volumes 1-8 included Nos. 1-635, March 1, 1711–December 20, 1714.

7. Under the date of October 11, 1796, H made the following entries in his Cash Book, 1795–1804:

"Account of Expences Dr. to Cash. . .
This sum paid Archibald Drummond for stationary   21.20."
"Account of Books purchased Dr. to Cash
for this sum paid Archibald Drummond for sundry books ₽ account   50"
(AD, Hamilton Papers, Library of Congress).

Receipt from Peter Goelet [1]

[New York, October 4, 1796]

Received New York Octo 4 1796 of Alexander Hambleton Esqr. Six Hundered and fourty One pounds being principle and Interest on the third Instalment of the Purches Money for Lands bught at Acction belonging to the American Iron Company as mentioned in the Receipt of the first payment.   PG

£ 641

Copy, Miscellaneous Chancery Papers, American Iron Company, Clerk of the Court of Appeals, Albany, on deposit at Queens College, New York City.

1. For an explanation of the contents of this document, see the introductory note to Philip Schuyler to H, August 31, 1795. See also H to Phineas Bond, September 1, 1795; H to Robert Morris, September 1, 1795; H to Barent Bleecker, March 20, 1796; Peter Goelet to H, June 25, 27, 1796.

From Benjamin Walker [1]

New York, October 4, 1796. "It is six months since I furnished Col Smith with a Copy of the inclosed accounts and pressed him for a settlement. . . . Col Smith himself cannot require this nor can he be surprized that I desire you to commence process against him without any further delay this and nothing else will bring this tedious business to an issue. . . ."

ALS, Hamilton Papers, Library of Congress.
 1. This letter refers to debts which William S. Smith owed to William Pulteney and William Hornby when Smith was acting as the representative of the Pulteney Associates. Pulteney and Hornby subsequently employed Benjamin Walker, not only to succeed Smith, but also to collect the money which Smith owed to them. Walker, in turn, hired H and Robert Troup, H's college friend and a lawyer, to represent Walker, Pulteney, and Hornby in their efforts to recover the money owed by Smith. For the Pulteney Associates and the relation to them of Smith and Walker, see Walker to H, September 15, 1793, note 1, and the introductory note to Morris to H, April 27, 1796.
 A biased, but detailed, account of Smith's relationship with Pulteney and Hornby is contained in a letter, dated November 30, 1823, from William Coleman, editor of the *New-York Evening Post,* to Timothy Pickering. In response to a request from Pickering, Coleman enclosed the following decidedly unfriendly view of Smith's activities from an unidentified correspondent who, Coleman stated, was "in the 68th. year of his age & therefore allowances must be made for time & failure of memory; but verily believes the facts may be relied upon as stated. . . . *Implicit reliance may be placed on his statement.*" The statement reads: ". . . Col. Smith, soon after the funding system was established by Congress & a national Bank was organized went to England, with statements said to have been furnished by Mr [William] Duer & others of a nature to shew that capitalists could advantageously employ their monies in the purchase of our funded debt & of Bank stock. Smith after his arrival in England, got introduced to Sir Wm. Pulteney, a great capitalist & to his friend Mr. Wm. Hornby, commonly called governor Hornby, from his having been in the East Indies & governor, I think of Bombay. Mr. Hornby was also a respectable capitalist. Smith put into the hands of these gentlemen his statements. It is very likely the statements recommended the investment of monies in wild lands, as well as in funded debt & bank stock.
 "Smith, through his address & by the influence of some one of the Adams family then in London, as I believe in some public character, induced Sir Wm. Pulteney & Gov. Hornby to put into his hands the *enormous sum* of £60,000 stg: that is, to say, Sir Wm. entrusted him with £30,000 & Govr. Hornby entrusted him with a like sum.
 "With this money in his pocket, Smith, always light-headed, got completely ballooned. He soon afterwards returned to New York with a large family coach big & heavy enough for 4 horses to draw without himself or any of his family in it. He set up a wondrous establishment of horses, dogs & servants in the style of many of the English noblemen. Soon afterward, he purchased a

large parcel of ground about 5 miles out of New York, & began to erect on it a large building, (with a cellar cut of solid rock that alone cost $5000 & the money to pay for it borrowed at 3 per cent a month) that was immediately nicknamed Smith Folly.

"Smith, forthwith, after his return from England, went into the most dashing speculation in the funds—in Bank stock, in wild lands, & in loans of money on hypothecations, according to report. Among his speculations in lands, he purchased of this state upwards of one hundred & three thousand acres of wild lands in that part of the state then called the Chenango country. These lands, he is understood to have purchased for aliens *at a quarter of a dollar per acre*. The purchase was made with his trust monies as above acquired. It ought here to be mentioned that Smith was, by his agreement with Sir Wm. Pulteney & Gov. Hornby to employ their monies on certain commissions which Smith was to receive for his services. The lands thus purchased by Smith he obtained patents for, in his own name, whereby the lands were vested in him in *fee simple*. The lands, before they were patented, were divided into townships, & a patent issued for each township.

"Since writing the above, I have recurred to deeds & papers & find that Smith purchased several tracts of wild lands; & a number of lots in New York. He went on in a course of extravagant speculation & extravagant living for a considerable time; always confused, careless & irregular in his business, or rather what he used ridiculously to term his *modus agendi*. He finally got involved head over heels in pecuniary embarrassments of every sort. His credit soon afterwards was destroyed. . . .

"Sir Wm. Pulteney & Gov. Hornby received no monies whatever from Smith nor any accounts whatever respecting the application & use of their funds. At length despairing of any accounts or remittances from him, they employed Charles Williamson then in the Genesee country to apply to him for a settlement of his accounts & for a surrender of their property in his hands. Mr. Williamson was the person then entrusted with what Mr. Pickering calls Sir Wm. Pulteney's 'vast landed estate in New York.' This 'vast landed estate' was situated in the western part of the state of New York generally called the Genesee country. Smith never had any concern with this 'vast landed estate.' The monies entrusted to him formed altogether a separate concern, & Mr Williamson the general had no control over Smith or connection with him. Gen. Williamson received instructions to apply to Smith at a time when there was a general scramble among his creditors to get what property they could find in payment of their debts, it being then known that he was deeply insolvent. Mr. Williamson having been bred an officer in the British army, was not much a man of business & he employed Col. Benja. Walker to make the application to Smith. . . .

"The effort of Col. Walker to get back the property in Smith's hands was exactly like the effort commonly made at dwelling houses much on fire to save the furniture. A great deal was lost & a little comparatively speaking was saved. As to any account from Smith relative to the execution of his trust none was rendered. No funded debt, nor any bank stock that I ever heard of was transferred to Col. Walker or any body else on account of the trust monies. All that Col. Walker got out of the 303,000 acres of wild lands was about 41,000, and the remainder, Smith had disposed of. . . ." (Copy, in the handwriting of William Coleman, Massachusetts Historical Society, Boston.)

From Benjamin Walker

New York, October 4, 1796. "I wrote you this morning directing you to proceed against Col Smith—you will observe the ballances are stated to be

	due to Mr Pulteney	$151022 57
	Mr Hornby	79792 92
		$230815 49

there will be deducted from this the property he conveyed to me say about 48000 Dollars which I agreed to take and about $90000 of Virginia Land which it was to be at the option of the Gentlemen to take or not as they should choose. . . . Either Colo Smith has property sufficient to pay or secure all his Debts or he has not—if he has he should do it—at least he should give security for as to time I will not press him. If he has not sufficient let him come forward candidly & disclose his situation. . . ."

ALS, Hamilton Papers, Library of Congress.

From James Wilson

[*Philadelphia, October 6, 1796.* On October 12, 1796, Hamilton wrote to Théophile Cazenove: "I have received two letters of the 6th & 10th of October from Judge James Wilson." *Letter of October 6 not found.*]

From James Wilson

[*Philadelphia, October 10, 1796.* On October 12, 1796, Hamilton wrote to Théophile Cazenove: "I have received two letters of the 6th & 10th of October from Judge James Wilson." *Letter of October 10 not found.*]

To Théophile Cazenove [1]

[*New York, October 12, 1796.*] "I have received two letters of the 6th & 10th of October from Judge James Wilson [2] respecting certain tracts of land . . . to which I reply That some of the conditions in the Contracts between Mr. Wilson & the Holland Company not being yet fulfilled they are not at present obliged nor prepared to make the elections which those contracts reserve to them. . . . [3] I cannot advise the Trustees for the Holland Company to execute, nor will they I am persuaded excuted the deed. . . ." [4]

AL, Gemeentearchief Amsterdam, Holland Land Company. These documents were transferred in 1964 from the Nederlandsch Economisch-Historisch Archief, Amsterdam.

1. H wrote this letter in his capacity as attorney for the Holland Land Company. Cazenove was the agent in the United States for the company. For background to this letter, see Cazenove to H, January 22, 1796, note 1. For other documents and letters concerning H's relationship with the Holland Land Company, see forthcoming Goebel, *Law Practice*, III.

2. Letters not found.

3. On December 25, 1792, James Wilson contracted to sell to the Holland Land Company either five hundred thousand acres at two and one-half shillings Pennsylvania currency per acre or seven hundred thousand acres at three shillings per acre in the Six Districts of Pennsylvania east of the Allegheny River. The Dutch chose the second option. Wilson agreed to pay the costs of warranting, surveying, and patenting the land. Wilson, however, was unable to fulfill the contract, and the Holland Land Company was forced to pay $8,000 in excess of the purchase price to secure title to the seven hundred thousand acres. In addition, on August 21, 1793, Wilson contracted with the same associates to secure patents for 499,660 acres of land west of the Allegheny River at three shillings four pence Pennsylvania currency per acre. At the time of the contract Wilson received $191,660 from the Holland Land Company. As Wilson was able to provide only 431,240 acres, he remained in debt to the company for $47,162. On February 12, 1794, Cazenove purchased from Wilson an additional two hundred thousand acres in the Six Districts at one-third of a dollar per acre. For information on Wilson's transactions with the Holland Land Company, see Evans, *Holland Land Company*, 31–33, 88–89.

4. Cazenove endorsed this Letter: "Substance de la lettre ecrite a M Wilson le 13 8bre."

To Nicholas Low [1]

[New York, October 12, 1796]

Mr. Hamilton will thank Mr. Low if not inconvenient for the loan of 100 Dollars for a few days.

October 12. 1796

AL, The Sol Feinstone Collection, Library of the American Philosophical Society, Philadelphia.

1. Low, a New York City merchant and land speculator, had been a director of the Bank of New York and of the Society for Establishing Useful Manufactures. In 1796 he was a director of the New York Office of Discount and Deposit of the Bank of the United States.

From William Heth

Berm Hundred [Virginia] 14th Octr 1796

Dear Sir

I have only three minutes allowd to ask whether you received a private letter [1] with part of a news paper enclosed some time last Winter addressed to the particular care of Capt Stratton. The piece alluded to was written by yr Hble servt—and the letter contained observations, intended only for yourself. Let me hear from you on this subject I pray.

You have herewith one of our papers, containing some pieces, which it is hoped by many in this part of the world, will be republished in the Northern papers.

It is the duty of every honest Man to exert himself at the present crisis. Every little may help.

Yrs truly   W Heth

ALS, Hamilton Papers, Library of Congress.
1. Heth to H, January 11, 1796.

To Benjamin Walker [1]

[*New York*] *October 15* [*1796*]. "Troupe & I have conferred. We think, considering the magnitude of the concerns, the diversifications of it into sub-branches—the ability of parties &c.—We may reasonably expect each of us as a Retainer for each of your principals £50. that is to

	To Hamilton
	NY Curry
For Pulteney	£50
For Horneby	50
Same to Troupe	£100 = 250 Ds.[2]

We shall consider this as a retainer in all matters with Smith or growing out of his Agency. . . ."

AL, Montague Collection, MS Division, New York Public Library.

1. For background to this letter, see Walker to H, first letter of October 4, 1796.

2. Under the date of October 15, 1796, H made the following entry in his Cash Book, 1795–1804: "Cash Dr. to Account of *Costs & Fees* for this sum received of Benjamin Walker as retainer for Pulteney & Hornby 250" (AD, Hamilton Papers, Library of Congress). See also H's Law Register, 1795–1804 (D, partially in H's handwriting, New York Law Institute, New York City).

From Oliver Wolcott, Junior

(Private)   Philada. October 17. 1796

Dear Sir,

Permit me to ask your opinion on the following points.[1]

1. Ought we or ought we not to permit Sales of Prizes to French *national* Ships of War, as formerly, in payment of duties?

Copy, Connecticut Historical Society, Hartford; LC, Connecticut Historical Society, Hartford.

1. Wolcott requested this information to assist him in the preparation of a Treasury Department circular to the collectors of the customs. The circular, dated November 26, 1796, reads: "For regulating the conduct of the Officers of the Customs respecting prizes to French privateers commissioned against the subjects of Great Britain, I am directed to communicate the following instructions:

2. In case of an affirmative answer to the first question; What is to be regarded as evidence of a national Ship? Will the Certificate of a French Commissioner in the West Indies, or of a Consul or the French Minister in the United States be sufficient provided nothing appears in the Commission of the Vessel *contradictory* to their Certificate.

"1st. The privilege of unloading the said prize vessels when they are so damaged as to be totally incapable of reparation, is to be permitted; but in such cases the unloading and storing of the cargoes must be done with the permission and under the inspection of the proper Officers of the United States.
"2d. The cargoes of prize vessels found to be totally incapable of reparation, may be permitted to be exported in American or other vessels; but such cargoes so exported, must be described in the *Manifests, Clearances, Bills of Lading*, & other documents of vessels as *French property*.
"3d. A prize vessel being damaged and reported to be in a situation capable of and requiring reparation, may be unloaded and her cargo stored as abovementioned, and so much of her cargo may be permitted to be sold as shall be *bona fide* requisite to defray the expenses of necessary reparations. Upon the quantities sold, duties are to be collected as in other cases. Of the quantities and amount in value to be sold for the purpose of making necessary reparations, the Collectors are to be the sole judges—except that in doubtful cases special references may be made to this Department.
"4th. The surveys in cases of alledged damage are to be invariably made by men of reputation, to be designated by the Collectors, who are to report the condition of the prize vessels, whether they be irreparable or not & if reparable, their opinion of the expenditures which such reparations will require.
"5th. All goods or merchandize unladen from prize vessels are to be deposited in Stores, secured with two locks, one key of which is to remain with the Collector, and the other with the agent of the prize. All expenses of unlading and storage, other than the compensation of inspectors and other officers of the Customs, are to be defrayed by the agents of the prizes.
"6th. The proceedings relative to the unlading, storage, and sale of any part of the cargoes of prize vessels, are to be governed as nearly as may be practicable by the rules established by the 38th Section of the collection law, for vessels arriving in distress.
"7th. During the continuance of prize vessels in the ports of the United States, they are to be subject to constant inspection at the expense of the United States, and in case goods or merchandize shall be unladen without permission, they are to be seized.
"8th. Reports are to be made to this Department of all prizes to French vessels arriving in the ports of the United States specifying their condition as requiring reparation or otherwise; of the articles composing their cargoes; of all goods unladen & stored conformably to the foregoing regulations—of all sales or any part of the said cargoes for the purpose of defraying the expense of necessary reparations, and of all shipments in neutral or other vessels, permitted in consequence of condemnations of prize vessels.

"It being the object of the foregoing regulations to protect the revenue from loss, to preserve the property of prizes from destruction, and to secure their departure from our ports, subject to the risk of recapture, the strict and impartial attention of the Collectors is specially requested." (Copy, RG 59, Miscellaneous Letters, 1790-1799, National Archives.)

3. May we keep an Inspector of the Revenue on board a prize during her continuance in our Ports?

4th. In case a prize requires reparation, may a *part* of her Cargo be sold, sufficient to defray expences, on payment of duties?

5th. In case a prize Vessell is condemned, as incapable of reparation, may the Prize goods be exported in one or other Neutral Vessells as French Property?

6th. Who is to Judge when it is necessary to unlade a Vessell for the purpose of making reparations, is the suggestion of a French Prize Master or Consul sufficient?

7th. Shall the Cargoes of Prizes be sold or any part of them for the reparation of any Vessell, or the payment of any expence, not incident to the identical Vessell in which the Cargoes arrived?

8th. Who is to Judge of the quantity sufficient for making reparations, in case any Sale is lawful?

9th. If after a Vessell is condemned as incapable of reparation She should be notwithstanding repaired, is she to be permitted to depart?

10th. Is it or is it not, the right of a Collector, to treat French Prizes, in the same manner as Vessells, which report themselves as bound to a Foreign Port or which arrive in distress: See Sect. 18th. & 38th. of the Collection Law.[2]

2. These sections of "An Act to provide more effectually for the Collection of the duties imposed by law on goods, wares and merchandise imported into the United States, and on the tonnage of ships or vessels" read: "Sec. 18. *And be it further enacted*, That it shall be lawful for the said ship or vessel to proceed with any goods, wares or merchandise brought in her which shall be reported by the said master or other person having the charge or command of the said ship or vessel, to be destined for any foreign port or place from the district within which such ship or vessel shall first arrive, to such foreign port or place, without paying or securing the payment of any duties upon such of the said goods, wares or merchandise, as shall be actually re-exported in the said ship or vessel accordingly; any thing herein contained to the contrary notwithstanding. *Provided always*, That the said master or person having the charge or command of the said ship or vessel shall first give bond with one or more sureties, in a sum equal to the amount of the duties upon the said goods, wares and merchandise, as the same shall be estimated by the collector to whom the said report shall be made, to the satisfaction of the said collector, with condition that the said goods, wares or merchandise, or any part thereof, shall not be landed within the United States, unless due entry thereof shall have been first made, and the duties thereupon paid or secured according to law, which bond shall be cancelled in like manner as bonds herein after directed to be given for obtaining drawbacks of duties. *Provided nevertheless*, That such bond shall not be required in respect to the goods on board of any ship or vessel which shall have put into the United States from necessity, to be made appear in manner herein after prescribed. . . .

The 18th. & 38th. Sections of the Collection Law appear to have provided for cases not very dissimilar from those of Prizes to Privateers, which in contemplation of Law must be considered as coming into our Ports merely for refreshments; the requiring of a Bond on their departure may not however be proper.

We shall on the subject of these Prizes be vexed with every kind of uncandid ingenuity—there is danger of loosing the Revenue, while at the same time Sales may not be prevented. You will see that not only public questions which affect our neutrality, but Revenue questions are concerned. There are too many who will not miss a good opportunity to purchase West India produce when it can be had below the market price. In every point of view the subject is embarrassing. Please to reply as soon as possible.

In haste I remain   Yrs with much respect   O. W.

Alexander Hamilton Esquire

"Sec. 38. *And be it further enacted,* That if any ship or vessel from any foreign port or place, compelled by distress of weather or other necessity, shall put into any port or place of the United States, not being destined for the same; and if the master or person having charge or command of such ship or vessel, together with the mate or person next in command, shall, within twenty-four hours after her arrival, make protest in the usual form upon oath before a notary public, or other person duly authorized, or before the collector of the district where the said ship or vessel shall so arrive, who is hereby empowered to administer the same, setting forth the cause and circumstances of such distress or necessity, and shall within forty-eight hours after such arrival, made report to the said collector, of the said ship or vessel and her cargo as in other cases. And if it shall be made appear to the said collector, by the certificate of the wardens of the port, or other officers usually charged with, and accustomed to ascertaining the condition of ships and vessels arriving in distress, if any such there be, or by the certificate of any two reputable merchants, to be named for that purpose by the said collector, if no such wardens or other officers there be, that there is a necessity for unlading the said ship or vessel, the said collector shall grant a permit for that purpose, and shall appoint an inspector or inspectors to oversee such unlading. And all goods so unladen shall be stored under the direction of the said collector; who, upon request of the master or other person having charge or command of such ship or vessel, or of the owner thereof, shall grant a license to dispose of such part of the said cargo as may be of a perishable nature (if any there be) or as may be necessary to defray the expenses attending such ship or vessel, and her cargo; *Provided,* That the duties thereupon be first paid. And the said goods, or the remainder thereof, may afterwards be reladen on board the said ship or vessel, and the said ship or vessel may proceed with the same to the place of her destination, free from any other charge than for the storing and safekeeping of the said goods." (1 *Stat.* 159–60, 167 [August 4, 1790].)

From Elizabeth Hamilton

[*New York, October 21, 1796.* On October 26, 1796, Hamilton wrote to Elizabeth Hamilton: "I received yours of Friday last." [1] *Letter not found.*]

1. H was in Albany to attend the October session of the New York Supreme Court, which met in that city between October 18 and November 5, 1796. See H to Elizabeth Hamilton, October 25, 26, 1796.
   In H's Cash Book, 1795–1804, under the date of October 11, 1796, H wrote:
"Account of Expences   Dr to Cash
This sum dld Mrs. Hamilton on going to Albany	100
This sum on my return November 1	20
my expences to and from Albany	40
	160"

(AD, Hamilton Papers, Library of Congress).

From Hall and Stimpson

Boston, October 24, 1796. "We wrote you the 20th. Septr.[1] respecting the cause that was left in your hands by Mr Stimpson against Mr Isaac Riley [2] as a partner of Seth Wetmore; [3] but not having heard from you respecting it and there being a report that you have since been engaged in behalf of Riley—the Gentlemen who are Creditors here and have supposed that you was taking the necessary steps of the Law in their behalf, are anxious to hear how the bussiness is situated. . . ." [4]

ALS, Hamilton Papers, Library of Congress.
1. Letter not found.
2. Isaac Riley was a New York City merchant.
3. Wetmore was a Boston merchant.
4. This is a reference to the case of *Hall and Stimpson* v *Riley and Wetmore.* See H's Law Register, 1795–1804 (D, partially in H's handwriting, New York Law Institute, New York City).
   H endorsed this letter: "Answered Nov 5. 1796." H's letter has not been found.

To Elizabeth Hamilton

Albany 25. [October] [1] 1796

The extreme hurry in which I have been My Dear Eliza since my arrival here has prevented my writing to you. This serves merely to inform you that my health is as good as when I left you & let me add that your father is much better than he was & the rest of your family in good health. I need not add that I am impatient to be restored to your bosom & to the presence of my beloved Children. Tis hard that I should ever be obliged to quit you & them. God bless you my beloved. Take care of yourself.

Yrs. with unbounded Affec   A Hamilton

Mr. Renselaer sets out for the City this day. I have asked him to stay at our house.[2]

Mrs. H

ALS, Hamilton Papers, Library of Congress.
   1. H mistakenly dated this letter "25. Aug 1796." On August 25, 1796, he had been in New York and Stephen Van Rensselaer had been in Albany. See Pierre Auguste Adet to H, August 25, 1796; H to Van Rensselaer, August 25, 1796. See also H to Elizabeth Hamilton, October 19, 26, 1796.
   2. H addressed this letter to his wife at 26 Broadway, a rented house to which the Hamiltons had moved in 1796.

To Elizabeth Hamilton

[Albany, October 26, 1796]

My Dear Eliza

I wrote you yesterday by Mr. Rensselaer.[1] Since that I received yours of Friday last [2] which gave me much pleasure. I was consoled to hear that you & our darling little ones were well—though I shall be anxious till I rejoin you lest there should be a relapse or some new attack.

Your father is really better and as I hope in no present danger. His breaking out looks less & less like mortification & his appetite strength & spirits are good. A fit of the gout will probably relieve him from the breaking out. Peggy³ has promised to have your beef prepared. Eggs are more scarce & nearly as dear as at New York. I shall see what can be done as to butter.

Yr. ever tender & devoted AH
October 26. 179⟨6⟩

I expect to leave this on Friday by Water.

Mrs E H

ALS, Coburn Library, Colorado College, College Springs.
  1. H to Elizabeth Hamilton, October 25, 1796.
  2. Letter not found.
  3. Margaret (Margarita) Van Rensselaer, H's sister-in-law.

To Oliver Wolcott, Junior

Albany October 27
1796

Dear Sir

Your letter of the 17th instant found me at Albany attending the Supreme Court. I have no copy of the Treaty with G B at hand, but I am well satisfied from memory that the true interpretation of that Treaty, enforcing in this respect the true Rule of neutrality, forbids our permitting the sale of a prize taken & brought in by a *French National* Ship, equally as if by a *Privateer*—and that the *prise vessel* herself with her Cargo ought to depart our Ports.¹ I hasten to give you my opinion thus far. I reserve to consider more at leisure what exceptions absolute necessity may justify. But this is clear, that as far as it may admit any, the exception must be *measured* & *restricted* by the *necessity* & as soon as possible you must return into the path of the Treaty.

Thus if the prize Vessel was absolutely insufficient to proceed to sea—her cargo ought to be sent out of the Country in another Vessel & care ought to be taken that it **does** not go out under false colours. Our Own Officers no doubt must *inspect* & *ascertain* any case of necessity which may be suggested.[2]

Pray my good friend Let there be no evasions.

Yrs. Affecty   A Hamilton

O W Esq

ALS, Connecticut Historical Society, Hartford; copy, Hamilton Papers, Library of Congress.

1. Article 24 of the Jay Treaty reads: "It shall not be lawful for any Foreign Privateers (not being Subjects or Citizens of either of the said Parties) who have Commissions from any other Prince or State in Enmity with either Nation, to arm their Ships in the Ports of either of the said Parties, nor to sell what they have taken, nor in any other manner to exchange the same, nor shall they be allowed to purchase more provisions than shall be necessary for their going to the nearest Port of that Prince or State from whom they obtained their Commissions" (Miller, *Treaties*, II, 262). See also "Remarks on the Treaty . . . between the United States and Great Britain," July 9–11, 1795, in which H indicated his approval of the clause forbidding the sale of prizes in the port of one party by privateers in the service of the enemies of the other. In the "Remarks" H made no distinction between French privateers and French national ships, suggesting that the prohibition covered all French ships.

2. See Article 25 of the Jay Treaty, which reads in part: ". . . No Shelter or Refuge shall be given in their Ports to such as have made a Prize upon the Subjects or Citizens of either of the said Parties; but if forced by stress of weather or the Dangers of the Sea, to enter therein, particular care shall be taken to hasten their departure, and to cause them to retire as soon as possible" (Miller, *Treaties*, II, 262).

From Pierre August Caron de Beaumarchais[1]

Mr hamilton avocat.   Paris le 8 Briumaire an 5 répondant
                                       au 29 8bre, 1796. (vieux Stile)

Monsieur   *Triplicata.*

Un des hommes de mon pays que jai le plus honorés, estimés et chéris, L'ancien évêque D'autun, *Taillerand Périgord,* est revenu de

ALS, Bibliothèque et Archives Municipales, Lille, France; ALS (marked "Duplicata"), The Andre DeCoppet Collection, Princeton University Library.

1. This letter concerns the efforts of Beaumarchais, the French dramatist, to obtain payment for his services as an agent for procuring supplies for the United States Government during the American Revolution. Beaumarchais was also concerned with recovering the so-called "lost million." For Beaumarchais's earlier efforts to settle his accounts with the United States, see the introductory note to Oliver Wolcott, Jr., to H, March 29, 1792; H to Thomas Jefferson, June 10, 1793.

In the interval between the American Revolution and the French Revolution, Beaumarchais was out of politics. On September 22, 1792, he left Paris

L'amérique en france.² Indépendament du plaisir de retrouver un ami Bienveillant échappé comme moi a la hache de nos Boureaux; j'etais fort empressé d'acquérir par lui les lumières qu'un homme de Sa force pouvait me transmettre a Paris, Sur L'esprit qui compose et gouverne aujourd'hui le peuple Américain; Ce Peuple avec lequel mon Entousiasme connu pour la cause qu'il Soutenait, m'a mis il y a plus de vingt ans en liaison Si utile a Ses plus puissans intérèts; mais dont les désirs de justice accumulés depuis vingt ans, ont causé en partie la ruine de ma Fortune!

Ce qui m'a le plus ranimé, dans la conférence amicale du très obligeant *Taillerand*, est, de Sa part, la certitude qu'il m'a donnée d'avoir vécu deux ans dans la liaison la plus intime avec *le colonel Alexandre hamilton*, ex ministre, et l'homme Selon lui, le plus Supérieur en tous genres dont votre Amérique S'honore. (je cite Sa propre expression) A quoi je me Suis écrié, plein de joie; ah! c'est bien le Seul homme aussi de l'équité duquel j'aye a me louer dans ce pays!

Mon ami m'a félicité d'avoir eu l'occasion de pouvoir rendre un juste hommage aux qualités de *M hamilton;* car il a lu chez un de nos amis, *Casenove* ³ a Philadelphie, le mémoire en forme de lettre que, dans ma détresse a hambourg, je vous ai adressé en mars 1795.⁴ Ce *Mr hamilton*, cet homme juste, m'a t'il dit, que vous invoquiés alors comme ministre, en craignant qu'il n'abandonnat Ses fonctions avant la fin de vos affaires, les a trop tot, pour vous, abandonnées.

---

with a commission from the French government to purchase a consignment of muskets at Terweren (Veere) in the Netherlands. He returned briefly to France in 1793, and had his commission renewed by the Committee of Public Safety. Later, however, he was proscribed as an émigré. Beaumarchais continued to negotiate for the guns until the British seized them in October, 1794. He then moved to Hamburg, and on July 5, 1796, with the permission of the Directory he returned to Paris.

This letter was enclosed in Charles Maurice de Talleyrand-Périgord to H, November 12, 1796.

2. Talleyrand became Bishop of Autun in 1788. After the overthrow of the French monarchy in 1792, he left France for England, where he learned that a decree of the Convention prohibited his return. Expelled from England early in 1794, he sailed for the United States, where he became friends with H (see H to George Washington, May 5, 1794). In June, 1796, he returned to Europe, and after spending a month in Hamburg, he arrived in Paris in September, 1796.

3. Théophile Cazenove.

4. Beaumarchais to H, March 9, 1795. This letter is in the possession of the Beaumarchais family in Paris and to date has not been made available.

Aujourdhui ce mesme *hamilton,* rentré modestement dans la classe des Citoyens non fonctionnaires publics, mais ayant conservé le respect général, est, dans le continent du nord, le plus grand des jurisconsultes, et le premier des avocâts Sous la clientelle de qui tout ce qui Souffre vont Se mettre. heureux les clients qu'il adopte! Et je vous regarderais comme un des plus heureux vous mesme, Si vous parvenés a l'engager de Se faire votre effenseur officiel. Je vais joindre, a t'il ajouté, toutes mes instances aux vôtres. Et en effet, Monsieur, cet ami généreux consent a vous écrire pour imprimer une plus grande force a ma prière, par la Sienne, c'est ce que Sa lettre vous prouve.

Je charge donc mon correspondant, *Mr Chevâlié* [5] de Newyork, de vous remettre cette lettre, dont l'intention Sans réserve est de vous Supplier, Monsieur, de m'accepter comme client, Soit pour

5. John A. Chevallié, a partner with Anthony Rainetaux in the New York mercantile firm of Chevallié and Rainetaux, had assumed the responsibility for collecting the debt which the state of Virginia had contracted with his father, Pierre François Chevallié, in his capacity as supercargo for Beaumarchais in delivering a consignment of military stores to Yorktown in 1778. See Chevallié *fils* to Thomas Jefferson, January 19, 1787 (Julian P. Boyd, ed., *The Papers of Thomas Jefferson* [Princeton, 1950–], XI, 55), and *The Commonwealth of Virginia v Beaumarchais* (Daniel Call, *Reports of Cases Argued and Adjudged in the Court of Appeals of Virginia* [Richmond: Thomas Nicolson, 1805], III, 122–80).

Chevallié also acted as Beaumarchais's agent in the negotiations concerning Beaumarchais's claim against the United States. On December 11, 1794, Wolcott, at that time comptroller of the Treasury, wrote to Chevallié: "In reply to your Letter of the 4th. instant, I think it proper to observe, that I am possessed of an official Copy of a Rect. signed by Mr. Beaumarchais dated the 10th. of June 1776 for One million of Livres.

"It must not be disputed that this money was charged to the United States by the French Government and acknowledged by our Minister in a Contract concluded at Versailles on the 25th. of February 1783.

"It remains for you to show on behalf of Mr. Beaumarchais, that he ought not to account with the United States, for monies recd. by him for their use, or that he has accounted or remains otherwise accountable for the sum in question." (ADf, Connecticut Historical Society, Hartford.) On February 17, 1796, Wolcott wrote to Timothy Pickering: "It is said to be a matter of record in your Dept. that the Minister of France stated in an Official conference or in a Letter some time in June 1779. that the supplies recd. from France during the late war which were *drawn from the Royal Magazines were not to be paid for by the United States to Mr. Beaumarchais.* This declaration being thought to be important to a right decision soon to be made at the Treasy upon Mr. Beaumarchais accounts, I have to request a certified extract of [what] relates to the subject to be filed as a Voucher in [this] Dept" (ADf, Connecticut Historical Society, Hartford). For information on the French government's loan of a million livres tournois to the United States through a firm operated by Beaumarchais, see the introductory note to Wolcott to H, March 29, 1792.

Soutenir tous mes droits, Sous quelque forme judiciaire qu'ils doivent être deffendus: Soit pour arranger mon affaire avec le congrés général par voie de conciliation, tant Sur la liquidation de mes créances avérées, que Sur la forme des paiemens dont je vous constitue L'arbitre; vous promettant et m'engageant, *comme j'ai déja eu L'honneur de vous l'écrire,* de n'en appeler a nul autre, Sur toutes les conditions auxquelles votre prudence m'aura Soumis, lorsque vous les aurés payées en pleine connaissance des fâits. C'est moins ma cause que je plaide, moi qui touche presqu'a la fin mon orageuse carrière, que celle de ma fille unique que jai *Léguée* par vous aux Américains, *a doter* avec la dette Si Sacrée qu'ils ont contractée Envers moi! [6]

Je vais donc joindre a cette lettre un pouvoir Spécial offert au très honorable homme, Mr Le Colonel *Alexandre hamilton,* aux fins d'établir, Soutenir, deffendre et règler tous mes droits dans la grande affaire des Services que j'ai rendus au Peuple Américain; avec liberté de passer mon pouvoir a telle personne qu'il voudra, S'il croit qu'il Soit utile aux intérèts de Son client, qu'un tiers en Soit plutot chargé, pour faire toutes les démarches; en Se réservant Seulement le titre de mon deffenseur et c'est le conseil que me donne non Bienveillant instituteur, *Taillerand*.

Je fais mon instante prière; jenjoins, j'ordonne au Zélé *Mr chevalié* mon correspondant de Newyorck, de vous passer, Monsieur, *toutes les instructions intimes* qu'il a recues de moi en divers tems; car la nature des lumières qu'il a du transmettre a mon juge quand vous l'étiés; et quand vous avés prononcé que j'étais au 1er janvier 1792, créancier du congrès depuis 17 années, *Au moins de 2 millions 2*

---

6. Amelie Eugénie Beaumarchais. On April 10, 1795, Beaumarchais addressed a petition to the American people "Dans Sa personne Collective, Et celle de Ses Representans, quels qu'ils Soient . . ." (ADS, RG 76, Records of the Boundary and Claims Commissions and Arbitrations, Records Relating to French Spoliation Claims, Miscellaneous Envelope 3, Folder 38, National Archives). A lengthy justification of his claim against the United States, the petition ended with the following plea for his daughter: "Souffrés donc qu'en mourant, *je vous lègue ma fille a doter avec ce que vous me devés.* Peut-être qu'après moi, par d'autres injustices que je ne peux plus relever, il ne lui reste rien au monde; Et peut-être la Providence a-t-elle voulu lui ménager, par vos retards d'acquittement, une ressource après ma morte, contre une infortune complette! Adoptés la comme une digne Enfant de l'Etat! Sa Mère aussi malheureuse et ma veuve; *Sa Mère vous la conduira* qu'elle Soit regardée chez vous comme la fille d'un citoyen!" Immediately after Beaumarchais returned to Paris from Hamburg, however, on July 11, 1796, Eugénie married André-Toussaint Delarue, an officer and a former aide-de-camp to the Marquis de Lafayette.

cent quatrevingt mille livres tournois,⁷ peut S'accroitre. Et, pardonnés Généreux homme! ce n'est pas par dèffiance de vos lumières que j'ai refusé d'adopter le résultat fautif de votre compte. Mais c'est parce que la perte en Serait énorme pour moi! Revoyés le.

Les instructions que *Chevalié* vous a transmises comme juge, ne Sont pas telles qu'il n'en puisse ajouter beaucoup d'autres, quant il parle a mon deffenseur. *Mr chevalié* puisera donc dans toutes mes correspondances tant anterieures que posterieures, tout ce qui pourra vous prouver de combien mes justes créances S'élèvent au dela de votre premier apperçu, quand vous éxaminiés L'affaire comme chef de la trésorerie. mais, avec un arbitre aussi équitable que vous, toutes les erreurs Se relèvent Sans aucune difficulte. Le titre de mon avocat, Si toutefois vous L'acceptes, comme *Mr De Tallerand* m'en flatte, éxige Seulement que vous envisagiés mes demandes Sous un point de vue different.

7. No report by H on Beaumarchais's claim has been found. In May, 1793, however, Richard Harrison, auditor of the Treasury, reported that Beaumarchais's claim was settled on May 24, 1793, and he recommended that the balance of payment should be suspended until steps were taken to determine who had received the million livres (*Reports of Committees*, 18th Cong., 1st Sess., No. 64 [February 16, 1824], 5). In a "Statement of the domestic debt of the United States, as due on the first of January 1794 including the sums passed to the credit of the Trustees of the Sinking Fund," which Wolcott prepared for the 1794 congressional investigation of the Treasury Department, Wolcott noted ". . . a claim of Caron de Beaumarchais for supplies furnished during the late war for Dollars 422,265..18 Cents which is now depending in the Comptroller's Office" (copy, RG 217, Oliver Wolcott's "Explanation of Accounts, 1792-1794," Comptroller of the Treasury, National Archives). See also H to Jefferson, June 10, 1793. For information on the investigation of the Treasury Department in 1794, see the introductory note to H to Frederick A. C. Muhlenberg, December 16, 1793.

After Beaumarchais's death in 1799, his heirs unsuccessfully petitioned Congress nineteen times for a settlement of his accounts. See *Digest Summary and Alphabetical List of Private Claims Which Have Been Presented to the House of Representatives From the First to the Thirty-First Congress, Exhibiting the Action of Congress on Each Claim With References to the Journals, Reports, Bills, &c., Elucidating its Progress, Compiled by Order of the House of Representatives* (Washington, D.C., 1853), I, 496-97; *ASP, Claims*, 314 19, 332, 341-42, 343-46, 433-35, 538 41, 559-81, 859-61; Wharton, *Revolutionary Diplomatic Correspondence*, I, 380-87.

The documents and letters concerning Beaumarchais's claim may be found in RG 76, Records of the Boundary and Claims Commission and Arbitrations, Records Relating to French Spoliation Claims, Miscellaneous Envelope 3, Folder 38, National Archives. Beaumarchais's claim was finally settled between 1835 and 1837. In compliance with the provisions of the Convention of 1831, the French government paid the United States five million dollars for spoliations of American commerce. Out of this fund the heirs of Beaumarchais

En effet le plus beau de mes titres, en épousant il y a vingt deux ans, les intérêts du Peuple Américain, ayant été d'avoir généreusement dédaigné les précautions minutieuses que le commerce prend toujours quand il envoie des objets prohibés, a un peuple opprimé qui Secoue L'esclavage, (Précautions qui m'auraient Semblé une très grave insulte a la Brave nation a qui je consacrais mes Soins;) il ne doit en Solliciter le remboursement rigoureux, qu'au titre du premier Ami que les Américains ayent rencontré en France, et qui ait Servi chaudement les intérêts de leur libération; car j'avais cru devoir laisser a ce peuple, *avant mesme qu'il eut usé de mes envois,* la plus immense latitude Sur la forme, le fonds et la nature des paiemens qu'il adopterait envers moi, en reconnaissant mes Services! nul ne Sait mieux que vous, Monsieur, quels Sont mes droits Sur l'amitié de ce grand Peuple, Et avec quels dangers pour moi j'ai tout bravé pour me les acquérir! ma Lettre a vous et ma dernière pétition en ont accumulé les preuves Sous vos yeux: Et cependant vingt ans Se Sont passés, Sans que ce peuple, excepté vous, m'en ait fait la moindre justice! vous L'obtiendrés, j'y compte et vous en rends graces d'avance. Le Peuple Américain, en vous voyant plaider ma cause, reconnaitre enfin qu'il est plus que tems de faire droit a de tels Services rendus, remis après vingt ans, pour la centième fois Sous L'oeuil de Ses représentans, Et par un homme tel que vous: il Sentira qu'il est de Son honneur de ne point laisser exhaler, publier

---

received eight hundred thousand francs and agreed to abandon any further claims. For the text of the Convention between the United States and France, July 4, 1831, see Moore, *International Adjudications*, V, 315-19. See also Charles J. Stillé, "Beaumarchais and the Lost Million," *Pennsylvania Magazine of History and Biography,* XI (1887), 1-36; Moore, *International Adjudications*, V, 333-34, 337. No record of this final payment on Beaumarchais's claim has been found in the accounts of the United States. On March 12, 1951, F. E. Manning of the General Accounting Office reported on the payments that the United States had made to Beaumarchais and his heirs. In that report Manning wrote: "Examination of the Treaty brings out the fact that claims of citizens of France against the U. S. for *'ancient supplies or accounts'* were provided for by allowing France under Article III of the Treaty to withhold 1,500,000 francs from the amount due the U. S. under Article II.

"Article V further provided that the claims of the citizens of both nations would be prosecuted in their respective countries before competent judicial and administrative authority.

"Hence, it would appear that if the Beaumarchais claim was allowed under the Treaty of 1831 it would have been paid by France from the moneys withheld under Article III, and no accounts of the U. S. would be involved." (LS, RG 217, Records of the United States General Accounting Office, National Archives.)

en Europe les justes plaintes d'un vieillard ruiné pour avoir consacré Sa vie, Sa plume et Sa fortune, au Soutien de la liberté du Peuple qu'il invoque, et qui borne Sa récompense a demander un payement qui Seul peut assurer du Pain, *oui du pain* a Sa fille unique.

je vous Salue, vous respecte, et vous aime.

> Caron Beaumarchais
> Citoyen français, rappelé
> honorablement dans Sa patrie,
> apres 3 ans de proscription.

Ne Sachant pas, Monsieur, Si vous accepterés, ou non, la défense de mes intérèts; Je laisse a votre profonde Sagesse a règler avec Mr Chevalié mon agent, chargé de ma procuration, Sous quelle forme il conviendra que ma Clientelle vous Soit remise Sans réserve; M'en rapportant parfaitement a vous.

To Oliver Wolcott, Junior

[New York, November 1, 1796]

Dr Sir

I wrote you a line from Albany¹ expressing an opinion from *Memory*, that our Treaty with G B prohibitted the sale of prizes made by French *National* Ships. Being just returned to Town I have looked into the article which relates to the point & I *fear* that opinion was wrong. In a day or two I will write you more particularly.

Adets late communication² demands a very *careful* & *well managed* answer.

Yrs. A H

November 1. 1796

ALS, Connecticut Historical Society, Hartford.
1. H to Wolcott, October 27, 1796. See also Wolcott to H, October 17, 1796.
2. On October 27, 1796, Pierre Auguste Adet sent Timothy Pickering "a resolution taken by the executive directory of the French republic on the 14th Messidor, 4th year (July 2, 1796) relative to the conduct which the ships of war of the republic are to hold towards neutral vessels." The resolution stated that "the flag of the republic will treat the flag of neutrals in the same manner as they shall suffer it to be treated by the English" (*ASP, Foreign Relations*, I, 576). In his letter accompanying the resolution, Adet denounced British policy toward neutral nations and argued that since the United States had not

taken steps "in favor of her violated neutrality" the resolves of the Directory were "dictated by imperious circumstances, and approved by justice." Adet assured Pickering "that the neutral Governments, or the allies of the republic, have nothing to fear as to the treatment of their flag by the French, since, if, keeping within the bounds of their neutrality, they cause the rights of that neutrality to be respected by the English, the republic will respect them." But, he warned, "if, through weakness, partiality, or other motives, they should suffer the English to sport with their neutrality, and turn it to their advantage, could they then complain, when France, to restore the balance of neutrality to its equilibrium shall act in the same manner as the English? No, certainly; for the neutrality of a nation consists in granting to belligerent Powers the same advantages; and that neutrality no longer exists, when, in the course of the war, that neutral nation grants to one of the belligerent Powers advantages not stipulated by treaties anterior to the war, or suffers that Power to seize upon them . . ." (*ASP, Foreign Relations,* I, 577).

From George Washington

Private   Philadelphia 2d. Novr. 1796.

My dear Sir,

On Monday Afternoon I arrived in this City, and among the first things which presented themselves to my view, was Mr. Adets letter to the Secretary of State,[1] published by his order,[2] in the moment it was presented.

The object in doing this is not difficult of solution; but whether the *publication* in the manner it appears, is by order of the Directory, or an act of his own, is yet to be learnt. If the first, he has executed a duty only; if the latter, he has exceeded it, and is himself responsible for the indignity offered to this Government by such publication, without allowing it time to reply—or to take its own mode of announcing the intentions of his country towards the Commerce of these United States.

In either case, should there be in your opinion, any difference in my reception & treatment of that Minister, in his visits at the public Rooms (I have not seen him yet, nor do not expect to do it before tuesday next), and what difference should be made if any?

ALS, Hamilton Papers, Library of Congress.
1. See H to Oliver Wolcott, Jr., November 1, 1796.
2. Pierre Auguste Adet's letter to Timothy Pickering, October 27, 1796, was published in the [Philadelphia] *Aurora. General Advertiser* on October 31, 1796, and in *Claypoole's* [Philadelphia] *American Daily Advertiser* on November 1, 1796.

He complains in his letter, that he had received no answers to the remonstrances in former communications (the dates of which are given).³ The fact is, that one at least of those remonstrances, were accompanied by as indecent charges, and as offensive expressions as the letters of Genet were ever marked with; and besides, the same things on former occasions, had been replied to, (as the Secretary of State informs me) over & over again.

That the letter which he has now given to the public will be answered and (to a candid mind) I hope satisfactorily, is certain; but ought it to be published *immediately*, or *not?* This question has two sides to it; both of which are important. If the answer does not accompany the letter, the antidote will not keep pace with the poison —and it may, & undoubtedly would be said, it is because the charges are just, and the consequences had been predicted. On the other hand —may not the dignity of the Government be committed by a Newspaper dispute with the Minister of a foreign Nation, and an apparent appeal to the People? And would it not be said also that we can bear *everything* from one of the Belligerent Powers, but *nothing* from another of them? I could enlarge on this subject, but add nothing, I am certain, that your own reflections thereon will not furnish. Whether the answer is published now, or not, would it be proper do you conceive, at the ensuing Session, which will close the political Scene with me, to bring the French affairs, since the controversy with Genet fully before Congress? In doing this it is to be noticed, that there is such a connexion between them and our transactions with Great Britain as to render either imperfect without the other; and so much of the latter as relates to the Treaty with that country has already been refused to that body: ⁴ not because there was any

3. In his letter of October 27, 1796, to Pickering, Adet complained that six weeks after the signing of the Jay Treaty the British still refused "to abandon the plan they had formed" and continued "to stop and carry into their ports all American vessels bound to French ports, or returning from them." Adet stated that this conduct was the subject of an unanswered note which he had addressed to the United States Secretary of State on September 29, 1795. He also denounced British impressment of American seamen, charging that "the Government of the United States" had failed to make known "to the undersigned the steps they had taken to obtain satisfaction for this violation of neutrality, so hurtful to the interests of France as the undersigned had set forth in his despatches to the Secretary of State" of March 29, April 8, and April 20, 1796, "which have remained without an answer" (*ASP, Foreign Relations*, I, 577).

4. Washington is referring to a motion of March 24, 1796, by Congressman

thing contained therein that all the world might not have seen, but because it was claimed as a matter of right, and the compliance therewith would have established a dangerous precedent.

Since I wrote to you from Mount Vernon,[5] on the eve of my departure from that place, and on my way hither,[6] I received a letter from Sir John Sinclair[7] an extract of which I enclose you—on the subject of an Agricultural establishment.[8] Though not such an enthusiast as he is, I am nevertheless deeply impressed with the benefits which would result from such an institution, and if you see no impropriety in the measure, I would leave it as a recommendatory one in the Speech at the opening of the Session;[9] which, probably, will be the last I shall ever address to that, or any other public body.

It must be obvious to every man who considers the Agriculture of this country, (even in the best improved parts of it) and compares the produce of our lands with those of other countries, no ways superior to them in *national fertility*, how miserably defective we are in the management of them; and that if we do not fall on a better

---

Edward Livingston of New York that the President be requested to submit to the House of Representatives the documents relating to the negotiation of the Jay Treaty. On March 30 Washington sent a message to Congress in which he refused to accede to the request. See the introductory note to H to Washington, March 7, 1796. See also H to Washington, March 26, 28, 29, 1796; H to William L. Smith, March 10, 1796; H to Rufus King, March 16, 1796.

5. Letter not found.
6. On September 19, 1796, Washington left Philadelphia for Mt. Vernon. He arrived back in the capital city on October 31.
7. Sinclair, a Scotsman and Member of Parliament for Caithness, was an authority on statistics and a scientific agriculturalist. An adherent of Pitt, he received his baronetcy in 1786. Ten years later he advised Pitt to open a loyalty loan, and he strongly advocated peace with France. He became the first president of the British board of agriculture in 1793.
8. The pertinent part of Sinclair's letter, dated September 10, 1796, reads: ". . . The People of this Country, as well as of America, learn with infinite regret, that you propose resigning your situation as President of the United States. I shall not enter into the Discussion of a Subject, of which I am so incompetent to judge; but if it is so, I hope that you will recommend one Agricultural Establishment, on a great Scale, before you quit the Reins of Government. By that I mean, *A Board of Agriculture* or some such Establishment at Philadelphia, with Societies of Agriculture in the capital of each State to correspond with it. Such an establishment would soon enable the farmers of America to acquire Agricultural Knowledge, and what is of importance, the ability of communicating what they learnt, to their Countrymen" (LS, George Washington Papers, Library of Congress).
9. The President had requested H's assistance in preparing his last annual message. See Washington to H, August 10, September 6, 1796; H to Washington, September 4, 1796.

mode of treating them, how ruinous it will prove to the landed interest. Ages will not produce a systematic change without public attention & encouragement; but a few years more of increased Sterility will drive the Inhabitants of the Atlantic States Westwardly for support; whereas if they were taught how to improve the old, instead of going in pursuit of new & productive Soils, they would make those acres which now scarcely yield them any thing, turn out beneficial to themselves—to the Mechanics, by supplying them with the staff of life on much cheaper terms—to the Merchants, by encreasing their Commerce & exportation—and to the Community generally, by the influx of Wealth resulting therefrom. In a word, it is in my estimation, a great national object, and if stated as fully as the occasion & circumstances will admit, I think it must appear so. But whatever may be the reception, or fate of the recommendation, I shall have discharged my duty, in submitting it to the consideration of the Legislature.

As I have a very high opinion of Mr. Jay's judgment, candour, honor and discretion (tho' I am not in the habit of writing so freely to him as to you) it would be very pleasing to me if you would shew him this letter (although it is a hurried one, my time having been much occupied since my arrival by the heads of the Departments, & with the Papers which have been laid before me) and let me have, for consideration, your joint opinions on the several matters herein Stated.

You will recollect that the conduct to be observed towards Mr. Adet must be decided on before tuesday next; that is, if he comes to the public room, whether he is to be received with the same cordiality as usual, or with coolness; and you will do me the justice to beli⟨eve⟩ that in this instance, and every other, I wi⟨sh⟩ it to be such as will promote the true policy ⟨and⟩ interest of the country, at the sametime th⟨at⟩ a proper respect for its dignity is preserved. My own feelings I put out of the question.

There is in the conduct of the Fr⟨ench⟩ government relative to this business is i⟨ncon⟩sistency, a duplicity, a delay, or a someth⟨ing⟩ else, which is unaccountable upon honor⟨able⟩ ground. It appears that the order under ⟨which⟩ Mr. Adet has acted is dated in July (early) [10] ⟨and⟩ yet Mr. Monroe has been led to believe (tho⟨ugh⟩

10. The order was dated July 2, 1796. See H to Oliver Wolcott, Jr., November 1, 1796.

much dissatisfaction he says has appeared) that no such order had, or would be issue⟨d un⟩less Great Britain set the example; and in a ⟨letter⟩ of August the 28th. he writes Mr. King [11] to that effe⟨ct⟩ as the latter officially informs the Secretary of State: [12] But I am fatigued with this and other matters which crowd upon me, and shall only add that I am

Very Affectionately Yo⟨urs⟩   Go: Washing⟨ton⟩

Colo. A. Hamilton

PS. I find I have not time before the hour for closing the Mail arrives, to take the promised extract from Sir John Sinclairs letter, I therefore send the original, with a request that it may soon be returned as I have given it no acknowledgment yet. The articles which he requests my acceptance of are not yet come to hand.[13] G W——

11. See Rufus King to H, September 10, 1796.
12. King to Pickering, September 10, 1796 (ALS, RG 59, Despatches from United States Ministers to Great Britain, 1792–1870, Vol. 5, August 10, 1796–December 28, 1797, National Archives).
13. In his letter of September 10, 1796, Sinclair wrote that he was sending to Washington ". . . a parcel, with some papers we have lately printed, and a Sandwich Box with the Egyptian wheat, and some Straw Rings of which I request your acceptance" (LS, George Washington Papers, Library of Congress).

From George Washington [1]

Private   Philadelphia 3d. Novr. 1796

My dear Sir,

After my letter of yesterday was despatched to you, the draught of the answer to Mr. Adet [2] was presented for my approbation, with the opinions of the Gentlemen about me, that it would be expedient to publish it, and without delay.

It appeared also, by information from the Secretary of State, that as far as public opinion had been expressed on the occasion, that this measure was looked to, & expected. These considerations, and a conviction if the publication was to take place o⟨ther⟩wise than through the medium of Congress, the sooner it happened the more likely it would be to obviate the bad impressions it was calculated to make on the public mind; induced an acquiescence on my part. I do not, nevertheless, think it free from those objection⟨s⟩ which I mentioned in my last; as it is not probable that the correspondence will end wi⟨th⟩ the Secretarys letter.

I give you the trouble of this note & ⟨a⟩ccount for the Publication which you will find in the Gazettes of this Morning;³ and to rescue my conduct from the imputation of inconsistency.

There are other parts of my letter not involved in this determination, which await the opinions I have asked, and on which I should be glad to hear from you (and in the manner which has been required in preceeding letters) as soon as it is convenien⟨t.⟩

I am Your affectionate friend   Go: Washington

Alexr. Hamilton Esqr

ALS, Hamilton Papers, Library of Congress.
1. For background to this letter, see H to Oliver Wolcott, Jr., November 1, 1796, note 2; Washington to H, November 2, 1796.
2. Timothy Pickering to Pierre Auguste Adet, November 1, 1796 (LC, RG 59, Domestic Letters of the Department of State, Vol. 9, October 12, 1795–February 28, 1797, National Archives). Pickering's letter is printed in *ASP, Foreign Relations*, I, 578.
3. See, for example, [Philadelphia] *Aurora. General Advertiser*, November 3, 1796, and *Claypoole's* [Philadelphia] *American Daily Advertiser*, November 3, 1796.

To Oliver Wolcott, Junior

[New York, November 3, 1796]

Dr. Sir

I have more carefully examined our Treaty with G Britain & I return to the opinion given you from Albany.¹ My hesitation yesterday² arose from the terms of the 24th article³ which were confined to *privateers*, a word that has an appropriate sense, meaning *ships of private persons commissioned to cruise*. But the following article⁴ contains the equivalent one to that with France,⁵ upon which we refused all bringing in and sale of prizes by her enemies. The words are "no refuge &c."; the *major* including the *minor*. And though France by our Treaty with her may *bring in* prizes; yet the Treaty gives her *no right to sell*.⁶ The clause in question in the English Treaty cannot take away the right she before had to *bring in* her prizes, but as she has not a positive right to sell, it will oblige her to *depart* with them—in other words, it will preclude her from whatever she has not a positive right to.[7] This also is Mr. Jay's opinion [8] & it is certainly agreeable to the whole spirit of the Treaty.

Yrs. A H

Nov 3. 1796

ALS, Connecticut Historical Society, Hartford; copy, Hamilton Papers, Library of Congress.

1. See H to Wolcott, October 27, 1796.
2. See H to Wolcott, November 1, 1796.
3. See H to Wolcott, October 27, 1796, note 1.
4. See H to Wolcott, October 27, 1796, note 2.
5. H is referring to Article 22 (originally 24) of the Treaty of Amity and Commerce between the United States and France, February 6, 1778, which reads: "It shall not be lawful for any foreign Privateers, not belonging to Subjects of the most Christian King nor Citizens of the said United States, who have Commissions from any other Prince or State in enmity with either Nation to fit their Ships in the Ports of either the one or the other of the aforesaid Parties, to sell what they have taken or in any other manner whatsoever to exchange their Ships, Merchandizes or any other lading; neither shall they be allowed even to purchase victuals except such as shall be necessary for their going to the next Port of that Prince or State from which they have Commissions" (Miller, *Treaties*, II, 19–20).
6. This is a reference to Article 17 (originally 19) of the Franco-American Treaty of Amity and Commerce, February 6, 1778, which reads: "It shall be lawful for the Ships of War of either Party & Privateers freely to carry whithersoever they please the Ships and Goods taken from their Enemies, without being obliged to pay any Duty to the Officers of the Admiralty or any other Judges; nor shall such Prizes be arrested or seized, when they come to and enter the Ports of either Party; nor shall the Searchers or other Officers of those Places search the same or make examination concerning the Lawfulness of such Prizes, but they may hoist Sail at any time and depart and carry their Prizes to the Places express'd in their Commissions, which the Commanders of such Ships of War shall be obliged to shew: On the contrary no Shelter or Refuge shall be given in their Ports to such as shall have made Prize of the Subjects, People or Property of either of the Parties; but if such shall come in, being forced by Stress of Weather or the Danger of the Sea, all proper means shall be vigorously used that they go out and retire from thence as soon as possible" (Miller, *Treaties*, II, 16–17).
7. But see "Remarks on the Treaty . . . between the United States and Great Britain," July 9–11, 1795, in which H pointed out that the right to sell French prizes in United States ports had previously been granted, not because the treaty of 1778 had expressly permitted it, but because there was no law against it.
8. In the margin opposite these words, H wrote: "Send the enclosed immediately."

From Robert G. Harper [1]

Raleigh No. Carolina Novr. 4th. 1796

In passing thro' this state, My dear sir, and South Carolina, I have taken some pains to ascertain the state of public opinion respecting the leading points of federal politicks, and have enjoyed considerable opportunities of doing so, particularly in the latter state. I believe it will not be disagreeable or wasteful to you to hear the result.

I do not believe the states east of the Hudson are more decidedly correct in all the great points than these two. The people are not so well acquainted with Characters & measures, but they have received a great accession of light during the last 18. Months; and a proportion as they better understand the system & its authors they are more attached to both. Certain names in the opposition still possess a certain degree, and not an inconsiderable one, of respect here, but their principles, are very unfashionable, and their late Conduct very unpopular. Instead of their maxims being received as the oracles of truth, their errours are merely pardoned, in consideration of what is supposed to be the purity of their intentions. This you know is the regular transition: It is going on, and were two or three more trying occasions to occur, occasions which would oblige men to come forward & expose their principles to public view, Jefferson & Madison would be as well understood on this side of the Potomac as they are on the other.

On the subject of the treaty & the treaty-making power, Ames himself is not more orthodox than the people of these two states.[2] Most of them are now perfectly well satisfied with the expediency of the measure. As to its constitutional sanction, there is very little, if any, more decision on that point in south Carolina than in New Eng-

ALS, Hamilton Papers, Library of Congress.

1. Harper, a Federalist member of the House of Representatives from South Carolina, was en route to Philadelphia to attend the second session of the Fourth Congress, which was scheduled to assemble on December 5, 1796.

2. Fisher Ames, a Federalist Congressman from Massachusetts, was a staunch supporter of the Jay Treaty. On April 28, 1796, in the course of the debate over a bill authorizing funds to carry the treaty into effect, Ames defended the treaty in what is generally regarded as the most brilliant speech of his career (*Annals of Congress*, V, 1239-63).

land. In North Carolina I believe the case is nearly the same. They very generally understand the dilemma in which the government was placed, of either making an accommodation, such as could be effected or continuing the quarrel at the hazzard of war. If there be any individual who ballances between the treaty and war, or even the hazzard of it, he does not choose to avow his sentiments. The people say that they are not capable of dividing this question, but they are perfectly content that the President and Senate should decide it for them. They are fully perswaded that the House of Representatives had nothing to do in the decision. Many of those who declared themselves the most warmly against the treaty before it was ratified by the President, are most severe in their censure on the opposition in the house of representatives, which they regard, as indeed it is generally regarded here, in the light of a most unconstitutional attack on the other departments of the government. It is commonly said that the house was as much bound to execute the treaty, as to vote money for fulfilling any other contract entered into by the government. On the question relative to the call for papers,[3] the public opinon here is decidedly in favour of the Minority; though I believe the Thirty-eighth vote, as our friend Jerry Smith [4] Called it, the Presidents message, had more effect in fixing this opinion that all that was said beside. It gave us a most decided majority.[5]

The old man never stood higher or firmer than he does throught these states. Tatom,[6] one of the north Carolina members, lost his election for speaking dis-respectfully of him. The principal objection urged against Franklin,[7] who has also been turned out, was that he voted in favour of the call for papers. That a man should oppose the treaty they could account for and bear; it was natural, they said,

---

3. On March 2, 1796, Congressman Edward Livingston from New York moved that the President be requested to submit copies of Jay's instructions and other relevant papers. This resolution was adopted by the House on March 24. On March 30, the President's message in which he refused to comply with the House resolution was delivered to the House. See the introductory note to H to George Washington, March 7, 1796.

4. Jeremiah Smith was a Federalist member of the House of Representatives from New Hampshire.

5. On April 30, 1796, the House of Representatives approved an appropriation for carrying the Jay Treaty into effect by a vote of 51 to 48 (*Annals of Congress*, V, 1291).

6. Absalom Tatum.

7. Jesse Franklin.

for men to differ in opinion on such subjects; but it was ⟨inconceivable⟩ to them that any man, without improper motives, a bad heart, or a most perverted judgment, should speak with disrespect of the old man, as they call him, or do any act which implied a want of confidence in his integrity. I am assured that many of their other members obtained their re-election merely for want of respectable opposition. The Election for Electors in this state is made by the people. While it was understood that General Washington would consent to be reelected, no man however popular, had the least Chance of becoming an Elector if he was understood to be opposed to the old man. Ever since he has declined, some very popular Candidates, it is thought, will be very much injured in the election, by their known dislike to him.

In this detail I speak of the great mass of the people, who are and have been, unconnected with the politicks of the Union. Most of the politicians, tho' not all, have espoused the opinions & prejudices of the opposition. Many of them are much respected, but their opinions in this particular are very little in fashion.

On french affairs, and our relations with that Country, the people of these states particularly south Carolina, are very correct. They applaud the conduct of our government in resisting all the foreign and domestic attempts to establish french influence in our councils. In fine, they perfectly understand the destinction made by Pacificus [8] between good wishes and alliance; between gratitude and subserviancy. "All for love or the world well lost" is not a maxim of their politicks.[9]

As to President, Jefferson is generally spoken of. Some say Adams will get two or three votes in this state, but I think it very doubtful. In south Carolina, I believe he is sure of two; perhaps three. His chance was very good for three till genl. Pinckney left the state.[10]

8. This is a reference to the "Pacificus" essays which H wrote in 1793 in defense of Washington's neutrality proclamation. The specific reference is to "Pacificus No. IV," July 10, 1793.
9. Writing on the subject of the gratitude which the United States owed to France, H remarked in "Pacificus No. IV," July 10, 1793, that ". . . it is at this shrine that we are continually invited to sacrifice the true interests of the Country; as if 'All for love and the world well lost' were a fundamental maxim in politics."
10. Charles Cotesworth Pinckney, James Monroe's successor as United States Minister Plenipotentiary to France, sailed from Philadelphia on September 25, 1796.

Jefferson will unite Georgia. I believe however you may rely upon Pinckney's [11] securing a vote from every elector in the three Southern states. South Carolina I am sure of. Georgia I think not doubtful, or very little so, and they tell me north Carolina is equally certain. Patrick Henry is spoken of in Virginia, but Pinckney will get a number of votes there also. Upon the whole, if the Pensylvania election for Electors should turn out well, I think Adams will beat Jefferson; but Pinkney you are sure of, if you support him North of the Delaware. I have declared that you will do so. Jeffersons friends would infinitely rather see Pinkney President than Adams, and many of them will support him with that view.

Farewell. I fear I have tired you; but you must submit to be pestered a little sometimes.

Yours most sincerely   Rob: G: Harper

Alexr. Hamilton Esqr.

11. Thomas Pinckney was the Federalist candidate for Vice President.

To George Washington

[New York, November 4, 1796]

Sir

I have lately been honored with two letters from you, one from Mount Vernon [1] the other from Philadelphia,[2] which came to hand yesterday. I immediately sent the last to Mr. Jay & conferred with him last night. We settled our opinion on one point—(viz) That whether Mr Adet acted with or without instruction from his Government in publishing his communication, he committed a disrespect towards our government which ought not to pass *unnoticed*, and would most properly be *noticed* to him as the Representative or Agent. That the manner of noticing it, in the first instance at least, ought to be *negative*, that is, by the *personal conduct* of the President towards the Minister. That the true rule on this point would be to receive the Minister at your levies with a *dignified reserve*, holding an *exact medium* between an *offensive coldness* and *cordiality*. The *point* is a nice one to be hit, but no one will know better how do it than the President.

Self respect, & the necessity of discouraging further insult, requires that *sensibility* should be manifested; on the other hand, the importance of not widening a breach, which may end in rupture, demands great *measure* and *caution* in the mode.

Mr. Jay & myself are both agreed also, that no immediate publication of the reply which may be given ought to be made—for this would be like joining in *an appeal* to the Public—would countenance & imitate the irregularity & would not be dignified—nor is it necessary for any present purpose of the Government.[3] Mr. Jay *inclined* to think that the reply ought to go through Mr. Pinckney[4] to the Directory with only a short note to Adet acknowleging the reception of his paper & informing him that this mode will be taken. I am not yet satisfied that this course will be the best. We are both to consider further and confer. You will shortly be informed of the result.

But whatever be the mode adopted it is certain that the reply will be one of the most delicate papers that has proceeded from our Government—in which it will require much care and nicety to steer between *sufficient* and too *much justification,* between *self respect* & the *provocation* of further insult or injury—and that will at the same time save a great political interest which this step of the French Government opens to us. Did I not know how guarded you will yourself be, I should be afraid of Mr. Pickerings *warmth.* We must if possible avoid rupture with France—who if not effectually checked will in the insolence of power become no less troublesome to us than to the rest of the world.

I dedicate *Sunday* to the execution of your commands in preparing certain heads.[5] You will speedily hear again from me

Most Affecty & respectly   I have the honor to be Sir   Yr. very Obed serv   A Hamilton

November 4. 1796

The President

ALS, George Washington Papers, Library of Congress.
1. Letter not found.
2. Washington to H, November 2, 1796. See also Washington to H, November 3, 1796.
3. H's and John Jay's opinion arrived too late. Timothy Pickering's reply to Pierre Auguste Adet's letter of October 27 was given to the newspapers on the morning of November 3, 1796. See Washington to H, November 3, 1796.
4. Charles Cotesworth Pinckney.

5. These were "heads" for topics for Washington's address at the opening session of Congress in December. See Washington to H, August 10, September 6, November 2, 1796; H to Washington, September 4, 1796.

To Hall and Stimpson

[*New York, November 5, 1796.* On the back of a letter from Hall and Stimpson, dated October 24, 1796, Hamilton wrote: "Answered Nov 5, 1796." *Letter not found.*]

To George Washington

[New York, November 5, 1796]

Sir

Yesterday after the departure of the Post I received your letter of the 3d.[1] I have since seen the answer to *Adet*. I perceive in it nothing intrinsically exceptionable—but something in the manner a little epigrammatical and *sharp*. I make this remark freely, because the Card now to be played is perhaps the most delicate that has occurred in your administration. And nations like Individuals sometimes get into squabbles from the manner more than the matter of what passes between them. It is all important to us—first, if possible, to avoid rupture with France—secondly, if that cannot be, to evince to the People that there has been an unequivocal disposition to avoid it. Our discussions therefore ought to be *calm smooth* inclined to the argumentative, when remonstrance and complaint are unavoidable, carrying upon the face of them a *reluctance* and *regret*—mingling a steady assertion of our rights and adherence to principle with the language of moderation, and as long as it can be done, of friendship.

I am the more particular in these observations because I know that Mr. Pickering, who is a very worthy man, has nevertheless something warm and angular in his temper & will require much a vigilant moderating eye.

I last evening saw Doctor Bayley[2] our health Officer, who tells me, that the French Consul here,[3] in a conversation with an assistant of the Doctors, who is a refugee from St Domingo, expressed a desire to make arrangements for the sick of a French fleet expected shortly to arrive in this port. I thought this circumstance worth communication.

With the most respectful Attachment   I have the honor to be Sir Yr. very Obed servant   A Hamilton
Nov. 5. 1796

The President of the U States

ALS, Hamilton Papers, Library of Congress.
1. See also H to Oliver Wolcott, Jr., November 1, 1796; Washington to H, November 2, 3, 1796; H to Washington, November 4, 1796.
2. See H and Richard Harison to Richard Bayley, July 19, 1796.
3. Jean Antoine Bernard Rozier.

From Oliver Wolcott, Junior [1]

Phila. Nov. 6th. 1796

Dear Sir

I fear that your opinion of Nov. 3d has been founded on a partial view of the case.

You will remember that it has all along been a recd. opinion that the French had a right by Treaty to enjoy an *indefinite asylum* in our Ports: but that they could not claim the privilidge of *selling Prizes in our Ports*. The privilidge of an indefinite asylum in was also granted to British *Ships of War & Letters of Marque, provided they had not made Prizes of French Vessells*.

I do not therefore see, that the 25th. article of the British Treaty can be construed to abridge a right which we have acknowledged to be accorded to France under our prior Treaty [2] especially as this article saves the rights of France expressly.

The right of *selling Prizes* stands on different ground. It might have been refused to France in *all cases:* it was however granted by the President in *all cases*. The British Treaty takes away this privilidge from *Privateers;* but it leaves the cases of Prizes to *N. Ships* as formerly. The United States may pass a *Law* to take away the privilidge of selling Prizes to National Ships; but they have passed no Law on the subject. The Presidents decisions now, must be consistent with his former decisions except where Treaties or Laws require a change. As before mentioned there is no *Law;* the British Treaty speaks only of *Privateers* and it has been ever held that a stipulation affecting *Privateers* could not be extended to affect *N. Ships.*

In short though I wish that your opinion may be found tenable, yet I do not at present see how it can be maintained. This you will see renders some of the other questions proposed by me both difficult & important. There was no inclosure in your Letter. Have we done right with Mr. Adet.³ I wish to know as we may hear further. Must we or must we [not] publish further in the Papers if so under what circumstances?

The Federal Ticket is lost here. There are still hopes that Mr. Adams will be elected, but nothing more. I hope Mr. P.⁴ will be supported as the next best thing which can be done. Pray write to our Eastern friends.

In haste yours. Oliv Wolcott Jr.

ALS, Hamilton Papers, Library of Congress; ADfS, Connecticut Historical Society, Hartford; LC, Connecticut Historical Society, Hartford.
   1. For background to this letter, see Wolcott to H, October 17, 1796; H to Wolcott, October 27, November 1, 3, 1796.
   2. See H to Wolcott, November 3, 1796.
   3. See H to Wolcott, November 1, 1796; George Washington to H, November 2, 3, 1796; H to Washington, November 4, 5, 1796.
   4. Thomas Pinckney, Federalist candidate for Vice President.

To  ¹

[New York, November 8, 1796] ²

Our excellent President, as you have seen, has declined a re-election.³ 'T is all-important to our country that his successor shall be a safe man. But it is far less important who of many men that may be named shall be the person, than that it shall not be Jefferson. We have every thing to fear if this man comes in, and from what I believe to be an accurate view of our political map I conclude that he has too good a chance of success, and that good calculation, prudence, and exertion were never more necessary to the Federal cause than at this very critical juncture. All personal and partial considerations must be discarded, and every thing must give way to the great object of excluding Jefferson. It appears to be a common opinion (and I think it a judicious one), that Mr. Adams and Mr. Pinckney (late minister to England) are to be supported on our side for President and Vice-President. New York will be unanimous for both. I hope New England will be so too. Yet I have some apprehensions on this point, lest the fear that he may outrun Mr. Adams should withhold votes from Pinckney. Should this happen, it will be, in my opinion, a most unfortunate policy. It will be to take one only instead of two chances against Mr. Jefferson, and, well weighed, there can be no doubt that the exclusion of Mr. Jefferson is far more important than any difference between Mr. Adams and Mr. Pinckney. At foot, is my calculation of chances between Adams and Jefferson. 'Tis too precarious. Pinckney has the chance of some votes southward and westward, which Adams has not. This will render our prospect in the main point, the exclusion of Jefferson, far better.[4]

Relying on the strength of your mind, I have not scrupled to let you see the state of mine. I never was more firm in an opinion than in the one I now express, yet in acting upon it there must be much caution and reserve.

HCLW, X, 195; Hamilton, *History*, VI, 538.
1. See Oliver Wolcott, Jr., to H, November 6, 1796; H to Jeremiah Wadsworth, November 8, 1796.
2. In *HCLW*, X, 195, and in Hamilton, *History*, VI, 538, this letter is dated "1796."
3. Washington's Farewell Address had been published on September 19, 1796. See the introductory note to H to Washington, May 10, 1796.
4. For information on the selection of members of the Electoral College and the electoral votes for President in 1796, see Appendices A-D in Stephen G. Kurtz, *The Presidency of John Adams: The Collapse of Federalism, 1795-1800* (New York, 1961), 409-14.

To Jeremiah Wadsworth

New York Nov 8. 1796

Dr Sir

A few days since I wrote you my opinion concerning the good policy of supporting faithfully *Pinckney* as well as *Adams*.[1]

The following extract of a letter from Mr. Wolcott of the 6th instant serves to confirm it—

"The Fœderal Ticket is lost in this State. There are still *hopes* that Mr. Adams will be elected but nothing more. I hope Mr. Pinckney will be supported as the next best thing which can be done. Pray write to our Eastern Friends."

Yrs. truly   A Hamilton

ALS, Mr. Pierce W. Gaines, Fairfield, Connecticut.

1. Letter not found, but see H to ———, November 8, 1796.

To Oliver Wolcott, Junior

[New York, November 9, 1796]

Dr. Sir

I received yesterday your letter of the 6th & immediately wrote some additional letters to the Eastward [1] enforcing what I had before written. Pensylvania does not surprise me.

I have reconsidered the opinion given to you on the 3d,[2] & see no reason to change it. The reasoning which leads me to the conclusion has not been sufficiently explained. I will therefore be more particular.

The articles in our Treaty with France which respect the subject are the 17th and 22.[3]

The 17th consists of two parts—1st It grants *asylum* in our ports for French Ships of War and privateers, *with their prizes,* and with liberty *to carry them freely thence to their own ports.* 2 It prohibits the giving refuge in our ports to *such as shall have made prize of the subjects or property of the French*. It grants no right to sell prizes in our ports—neither does the *letter* of the article prohibit *prizes* made of the French from coming into our ports—it only prohibits *the instrument* of making the prizes. But the construction justly adopted by the President was that the prohibition, in its true spirit, excluded the *bringing in of prizes* whether coming with or without the capturing Vessels.[4] Tis upon this part of the Treaty alone that prizes made by *national Vessels* of G Britain were excluded from our Ports. For

The 22d. article with France is wholly confined to *privateers*—

prohibitting those of other nations to *fit*, or to sell their *prizes*, in our ports. This article, if it had stood alone, would have left us as free to admit British *national* Ships, with *their prizes*, into our ports, as our 24th article with Great Britain leaves us free to admit French National Ships with their prizes.[5] For these articles are the exact equivalent of each other. So that, as before remarked, the prohibition to the *coming in* or *sale in* our ports *of prizes made upon the French by British National Ships* was derived *by construction* & *implication* from the 17 article of our Treaty with France.

It follows that this article was considered as competent to prevent the *coming in and sale* of Prizes.

If so, the same or equivalent terms in the British Treaty must be competent to the same thing.

Now the 25th article of our Treaty with Great Britain[6] has equivalent terms. We there read that "no shelter or refuge shall be given in their ports to *such as have made a* prize upon the subjects or citizens of either of the contracting parties, but if forced by stress of weather or the danger of the sea to enter therein, particular care shall be taken to hasten their departure and to cause them to retire as soon as possible." This prohibition includes here, as in the 17th article of our Treaty with France, a prohibition to sell prizes in our ports, not the prizes of privateers only but prizes generally.

But France, it is answered, had a prior right by the 17th article of our Treaty with her, to come and bring prizes into our ports.

True, she had this right, and must have it still, notwithstanding the 25 article of our Treaty with Great Britain, but she had no prior right by Treaty *to sell prizes* in our ports and consequently, as the 25 article of our Treaty with Great Britain excludes, as the *minor* of a *major*, the selling of prizes in our ports—the exclusion so far is in force, because it contravenes no *prior right* of France. As far as the Treaty with France gives a right inconsistent with the above 25 article, that right forms an exception, but the exception must be only coextensive with the right. The conclusion is that France retains the right of *Asylum*, but is excluded from the right of selling. This gives effect to the 25 article with Great Britain—as far as the Treaty-right of France does not require an exception.

And this construction ought to be favoured, because it best comports with the rule of neutrality.

It will also best agree with the Presidents former decisions. He permitted France to sell prizes, not because Treaty gave her a right —but because he did not see clearly any law of the Country or of Nations that forbid it. But consistency does not require that this permission shall continue if there be any thing in the Treaty with G Britain against it. Consistency however does require that the same latitude of construction should be given to the 25 article of our Treaty with G Britain as was before given to the 17th article of our Treaty with France. The same latitude will, as I apprehend, exclude the sale of Prizes by France in the case in question.

I regret extremely the publication of the Reply to *Adet*,⁷ otherwise than through the channel of Congress. The sooner the Executive gets out of the news Papers the better. What may now be in its power will depend on circumstances which *are to occur*.

Yrs.   A Hamilton
Nov. 9. 1796

Oliver Wolcott Jun Esq

ALS, Connecticut Historical Society, Hartford; copy, Hamilton Papers, Library of Congress.
    1. See H to ———, November 8, 1796; H to Jeremiah Wadsworth, November 8, 1796.
    2. H to Wolcott, November 3, 1796. See also Wolcott to H, October 17, 1796; H to Wolcott, October 27, November 1, 1796.
    3. For the text of these articles, see H to Wolcott, November 3, 1796, notes 5 and 6.
    4. The "construction . . . adopted by the President" was announced in "Treasury Department Circular to the Collectors of the Customs," August 4, 1793.
    5. See H to Wolcott, October 27, November 3, 1796.
    6. See H to Wolcott, November 3, 1796.
    7. See George Washington to H, November 2, 3, 1796.

To Robert Morris

[*New York, November 10, 1796.* On November 19, 1796, Morris wrote to Hamilton: "I . . . find your letter of the 10 Inst." *Letter not found.*]

To George Washington

[New York, November 10, 1796]

Sir

I have been employed in making and have actually completed a rough draft on the following heads "*National University, Military Academy, Board of Agriculture, Establishment of such manufactories* on *public account* as are relative to the equipment of army & navy, *to the extent of the public demand for supply,* & excluding all the branches already well established in the country.— The *gradual & successive* creation of a Navy, compensations to public Officers.— *Reinforcement* of provision for public Debt" [1] I send you this enumeration that you may see the objects which I shall prepare for. But I must beg your patience till the beginning of the next week for the transmission of the draft, as I am a good deal pressed for time.

The Legislature having appointed Mr. Laurance district Judge— a succession will of course be to be provided.[2] A conviction of his competency, a high opinion of his worth, and a long established personal friendship induce me to take the liberty of *precipitating* a recommendation to you of Mr. Troupe,[3] the present Clerk of the District and Circuit court (the *Attorney* of the District [4] being known to be disinclined to the Office). Mr. Troupe is a lawyer, professionally very respectable, so that his practice is inferior in productiveness to no other—but he has by the most unexceptionable means acquired a property sufficient to make it reasonable in him to withdraw from practice upon a salary such as that of the District Judge & latterly his health has somewhat suffered from a long course of *excessive application.* His moral character is without an imputation of any sort—indeed no man in the state is better esteemed than this Gentleman. So that, I believe, the appointment would be considered as altogether fit. I trust however that in expressing myself thus strongly it will not occasion to you a moment's embarrassment, if any candidate more agreeable to you shall occur.

Very respectfully & Affecty   I have the honor to be Sir   Yr. Obed servant   A Hamilton
                                                N York Nov 10th 1796

The President of the U States

ALS, George Washington Papers, Library of Congress.
1. H was preparing this material for Washington's eighth annual address to Congress. See Washington to H, August 10, September 6, November 2, 1796; H to Washington, September 4, November 4, 1796. See also H's "Draft of George Washington's Eighth Annual Address to Congress," November 10, 1796.
2. John Laurance had been appointed United States judge for the District of New York on May 6, 1794 (*Executive Journal*, I, 153). On November 9, 1796, he was elected United States Senator by the New York legislature (*Journal of the Assembly of the State of New-York; At their Twentieth Session*, 28–29). Laurance resigned as United States judge on November 30, 1796 (Laurance to Washington, November 30, 1796 [ALS, RG 59, Miscellaneous Letters, 1790–1799, National Archives]).
3. On December 10, 1796, Robert Troup was appointed United States judge for the District of New York (*Executive Journal*, I, 215).
4. Richard Harison had declined the nomination in May, 1794 (*Executive Journal*, I, 153).

Draft of George Washington's Eighth Annual Address to Congress [1]

[New York, November 10, 1796]

That among the objects of labour and industry, Agriculture considered with reference either to individual or national welfare is first in importance may safely be affirmed without derogating from the just and real value of any other branch.[2] It is indeed the best basis

ADf, Hamilton Papers, Library of Congress.
1. This draft of Washington's eighth annual message to Congress is the "rough draft" mentioned in H's letter to the President on November 10, 1796. As early as August 10, 1796, Washington had written to H: "If any matters should occur to you as fit subjects of communication at the opening of the next Session of Congress I would thank you for noting and furnishing me with them. . . ." During September and November, the two men exchanged ideas on what subjects should be included in the President's message. See Washington to H, September 6, November 2, 1796; H to Washington, September 4, November 4, 10, 1796. H's draft was incorporated into the President's message with minor variations. The message was delivered to Congress on December 7, 1796 (*Annals of Congress*, VI, 1591–97; LC, George Washington Papers, Library of Congress).
2. For Washington's suggestion that remarks on the encouragement of agri-

of the prosperity of every other. In proportion as nations progress in population and other circumstances of maturity this truth forces itself more & more upon the conviction of Rulers and makes the cultivation of the soil more and more an object of public patronage and care. Institutions for promoting it sooner or later grow up supported by the public purse—and the fruits of them when judiciously conceived and directed have fully justified the undertaking. Among these none have been found of greater utility than BOARDS composed of proper characters charged with collecting and communicating information and enabled to stimulate enterprise and experiment by premiums and honorary rewards. These have been found very cheap instruments of immense benefits. They serve to excite a general spirit of discovery & improvement to stimulate invention to excite new & useful experiments—and accumulating in one center the skill and improvement of every part of the nation they spread it thence over the whole nation at the same time promoting new discovery and diffusing generally the knowlege of all the discoveries which are made.

In the U States hitherto no such institution has been essayed though perhaps no country has stronger motives to it. Agriculture among us is certainly in a very imperfect state. In much of those parts where there have been early settlements the soil impoverished by an unskilful tillage yields but a scanty reward for the labour bestowed upon it, and leaves its possessors under strong temptation to abandon it and emigrate to distant regions more fertile because they are newer and have not yet been exhausted by an unskilful use. This is every way an evil. The undue dislocation of our population from this cause promotes neither the strength the opulence nor the happiness of our Country. It strongly admonishes our national Councils to apply as far as may be practical by natural & salutary means an adequate Remedy. Nothing appears to [be] so unexceptionable & likely to be more efficacious than the institution of a Board of Agriculture with the views I have mentioned & with a moderate fund towards executing them. After mature reflection I am persuaded it is difficult to render our country a more precious and general service than by such an institution.

---

culture be included in his annual message, see Washington to H, November 2, 1796.

I will however observe that if it be thought expedient the objects of the Board may be still more comprehensive. It may embrace the encouragement of the mechanic and manufacturing arts by means analogous to those for the improvement of Agriculture & with an eye to the introduction from abroad of useful machinery &c. Or there may be separate Boards one charged with one object the other with the other.

I have heretofore suggested the expediency of establishing a national university and a Military Academy.[3] The vast utility of both these measures presses so seriously and so constantly upon my mind that I cannot forbear with earnestness to repeat the recommendation.

The Assembly to which I address myself will not doubt that the extension of science and knowlege is an object primarily interesting to our national welfare. To effect this is most naturally the care of the particular local jurisdictions into which our country is subdivided as far as regards those branches of instruction which ought to be universally diffused and it gives pleasure to observe that new progress is continually making in the means employed for this end. But can it be doubted that the General Government would with peculiar propriety occupy itself in affording neutriment to those higher branches of science which though not within the reach of general acquisi[ti]on are in their consequences and relation, productive of general advantage? Or can it be doubted that this great object would be materially advanced by a University erected on that broad basis to which the national resources are most adequate & so liberally endowed as to command the ablest professors in the several branches of liberal knowlege? It is true and to the honor of our Country that it offers many colleges and Academies highly respectable and useful—but the funds upon which they are established are too narrow to permit any of them to be an adequate substitute for such an institution as is contemplated & to which they would be excellent auxiliaries. Amongst the motives to such an institution the assimilation of the principles opinions manners and habits of our countrymen by drawing from all quarters our youth to participate

3. For the correspondence between H and Washington on the establishment of a national university and a military academy, see H to Washington, September 4, 1796; Washington to H, September 6, 1796.

in a common Education well deserves the attention of Government. To render the people of this Country as homogeneous as possible must lend as much as any other circumstance to the permanency of the Union & prosperity.

The eligibleness of a Military Academy depends on that evident maxim of policy which requires every nation to be prepared for war while cultivating peace and warns it against suffering the military spirit & military knowlege wholly to decay. However particular instances superficially viewed may seem exceptions it will not be doubted by any who have attentively considered the subject that the military art is of a complicated and comprehensive nature, that it demands much previous study as well as practice and that the possession of it in its most improved state is always of vast importance to the security of a Nation. It ought therefore to be a principal care of every Government however pacific its general policy to preserve and cultivate indeed in proportion as the policy of a Country is pacific & it is little liable to [be] called to practice the rules of the Military Art does it become the duty of the Government to take care by proper institutions that it be not lost. A Military Academy instituted on proper principles would serve to secure to our country though within a narrow sp[h]ere a solid fund of military information which would always be ready for national emergencies & would facilitate the diffusion of Military knowlege as those emergenc[i]es might require.

A systematic plan for the creation of a moderate navy appears to me recommended by very weighty considerations. An active external Commerce demands a naval power to protect it—Besides the dangers from War in which a state is a party. It is a truth which our Experience has confirmed that the most equitable and sincere neutrality is not sufficient to exempt a state from the depredations of other nations at war with each other. It is essential to induce them to respect that neutrality that there shall be an organised force ready to vindicate the national flag. This may even prevent the necessity of going into war by discouraging from those insults and infractions of right which sometimes proceed to an extreme that leave no alternative. The U States abound in Materials. Their Commerce fast increasing must proportionably augment the number of their seamen and give us rapidly the means of a naval power respectable if not great. Our relative situation likewise for obvious reasons would render a moderate force very influential more so perhaps than a much greater in the hands of any other power. It is submitted as well deserving consideration whether it will not be prudent immediately and gradually to provide and lay up magazines of Ship Timber and to build & equip annually on[e] or more ships of force as the developpement of resources shall render convenient & practicable—so that a future War of Europe, if we escape the present storm may not find our Commerce in the defenceless situation in which the present found it.

There is a subject which has dwelt long & much upon my mind which I cannot omit this opportunity of suggesting. It is the compensations to our public Officers; especially those in the most important stations. Every man acquainted [with] the expence even of the most frugal plan of living in our great cities must be sensible of their inadequateness. The impolicy of such defective provision seems not to have been sufficiently weighed.

No plan of governing is well founded which does not regard man as a compound of selfish and virtuous passions. To expect him to be wholly guided by the latter would be as great an error as to suppose him wholly destitute of them. Hence the necessity of adequate rewards for those services of which the Public stand in need. Without them the affairs of a nation are likely to get sooner or later into incompetent or unfaithful hands. If their own private wealth is to supply in the candidates for public Office the deficiency of public liberality then the sphere of those who can be candidates especially in a country like ours is much narrowed and the chance of a choice of able as well as upright men much lessened. Besides that it would be repugnate to the first principles of our government to exclude men from the public trusts because their talents & virutes however conspicuous are unaccompanied by wealth. If the rewards of the Government are scanty those who have talents without wealth & are too virtuous to abuse their stations cannot accept public offices without a sacrifice of interest which in ordinary time may hardly be justified by their duty to themselves and their families. If they have talents without virtue they may indeed accept offices to make a dishonest & improper use of them. The tendency then is to transfer the management of public affairs to wealthy but incapable hands or to hands which if capable are as destitute of integrity as of wealth. For a time particular circumstances may prevent such a course of things and hitherto the inference has not been verified in our experience. But it is not the less probable [4] that time will prove it to be well founded. In some Government men have many allurements to office exclusive of pecuniary rewards—but from the nature of our government pecuniary reward is the only aliment to the interested passion, which public men who are not vicious can expect. If then it be essential to the prosperous course of every Government that it shall be able to command the services of its most able & most virtuous citizens of every class, it follows that the compensations which our Government allows ought to be revised & materially increased. The character & success of Republican Government appear absolutely to depend on this policy.

Congress have repeatedly directed their attention to the encouragement of manufactures, and have no doubt promoted them in several branches. The object is of two much importance not to assure a continuance of their efforts in every way which shall appear proper & conducive to the end. But in the present state of our Country we cannot expect that our progress in some essential branches will be as expeditious as the public welfare demands—particularly in reference to security & defence in time of War. This reflection is the less pleasing when it is remembered how large a proportion of our supply the course of our Trade derives from a single nation. It appears very desireable that at least with a view to security and defence some measures more efficacious than have heretofore been adopted should be taken. As a general rule manufactories carried on upon public account are to be avoided. But every general rule may admit of exceptions. Where the state of things in our Country leaves little expectation that certain branches of manufacture will for a great length of time be sufficiently cultivated—when these are of a nature to be essential to the furnishing and equipping of the troops and ships of war of which we stand in need—are not establishments on the public account, to the *extent of the public demand* for supply, recommended by very strong considerations of national policy? Ought our country to be dependent in such cases upon foreign

4. In MS, "probably."

supply precarious because liable to be interrupted?⁵ [If the necessary Supplies should be procured in this mode at great expense in time of Peace—will not the Security and independence arising from it very amply compensate? Institutions of this Kind commensurate only with our peace Establishments, will in time of War be easily extended in proportion to the public exigencies. And they may even perhaps be rendered contributary to the Supply of our citizens at large so as greatly to mitigate the privations arising from the interruption of trade. The idea at least is worthy of the most serious consideration. If adopted, the plan ought of course to exclude all those branches which may be considered as already established in our Country, and to which the efforts of individuals appear already as likely to be Speedily adequate.

A reinforcement of the existing provisions for discharging our public Debt was mentioned in my address at the opening of the last Session.⁶ Congress took Some preliminary steps,⁷ the maturing of which will no doubt engage their zealous attention during the present. I will only add, that it will afford me heartfelt Satisfaction to concur in such auxiliary measures as will ascertain to our country, the prospect of a Speedy extinguishment of the Debt. Prosperity may have Cause to regret, if, from any motive, intervals of tranquility are left unemployed, for accelerating this valuable end.]

5. The bracketed material that follows at this point is taken from a separate page in the Hamilton Papers, Library of Congress, written in an unknown handwriting.
6. December 8, 1795 (LC, George Washington Papers, Library of Congress).
7. See "An Act making provision for the payment of certain Debts of the United States" (1 *Stat.* 488 [May 31, 1796]). H disapproved of this measure. See H to Oliver Wolcott, Jr., May 30, 1796.

From George Washington

[*Philadelphia, November 11, 1796.* On November 21, 1796, Washington wrote to Hamilton: "Having written to you on Saturday the 11th. instant." *Letter not found.*]

To George Washington [1]

[New York, November 11, 1796]

Sir

My anxiety for such a course of things as will most promise a continuance of peace to the country, & in the contrary event a full justification of the President, has kept my mind dwelling on the late Reply to Mr. Adet & though it is a thing that cannot be undone, yet if my ideas are right the communication of them may not be wholly useless for the future. The more I have considered that paper the less I like it.

I think it is to be regretted that answers were not given to the preceding communications of Mr. Adet.[2] For silence commonly carries with it the appearance of *hauteur* and *contempt*. And even if the paper to be answered is offensive tis better & less hazardous to harmony to say so with calmness & moderation, than to say nothing. Silence is only then to be adopted when things have come to such a state with a Minister that it is the intention to break with him. And even in this case, if there is still a disposition to maintain harmony with his Government a Reply ought to go through our own Organ to it so as to distinguish between the Minister & the Government.

The reason given for not having answered the inquiry respecting the impressment of our seamen is too broad.[3] When two nations have relations to each other, & one is at war, the other at peace, if the one at peace suffers liberties to be taken wth it by the enemy of the one at war which turns to the detriment of the latter, it is a fair subject of inquiry & discussion. The questions may be asked—how does this happen, what measures are taking to prevent a repetition or continuance? There is always possibility of *connivance* & this possibility gives a right to inquire, and imposes an obligation to enter into friendly explanation. Tis not a matter of indifference to our friend, what conduct of its enemy we permit towards ourselves. Much indeed in all these cases depends on the manner of the Inquiry. But I am satisfied the principle is as I state it & the ground assumed by Mr. Pickering in the latitude of the expression untenable.

These opinions are not confined to me. Though most people like the air of what is called Spirit in Mr. Pickerings letter, but some of the best friends of the cause whisper cautiously remarks similar to the above.

It is a question, now, well worth considering whether if a handsome opportunity of rectifying should not occur with Mr. Adet, it may not be expedient specially to instruct Mr. Pinckney to make the explanations; putting our backwardness here to the score of the manner of the inquiry & qualifying the generality of our principle— without giving up our right of judging of the measure of our compliance in similar cases.

I know you will so well appreciate the motives to these observations that I run no risk of being thought officious, & I therefore freely transmit them being always

with true respect & attachment   Sir   Yr. very obed ser

A Hamilton
Nov. 11. 1796

The President

ALS, George Washington Papers, Library of Congress.
1. For background to this letter, see H to Oliver Wolcott, Jr., November 1, 1796; Washington to H, November 2, 3, 1796; H to Washington, November 4, 5, 1796.
2. See Washington to H, November 2, 1796, note 3.
3. H is referring to Timothy Pickering's reply on November 1, 1796, to Pierre Auguste Adet's complaints that the United States had failed to reply to his remonstrances. Pickering wrote to Adet: "You are also pleased to refer to your letters of March and April last, relative to impresses of American seamen by British Ships, and complain that the Government of the united States had not made known to you the steps they had taken to obtain satisfaction. This, Sir, was a match which concerned only that Government. As an independent nation, we were not bound to render an account to any other, of the measures we deemed proper for the protection of our own citizens, so long as there was not the slightest ground to suspect that the Government ever acquiesced in any aggression" (LC, RG 59, Domestic Letters of the Department of State, Vol. 9, October 12, 1795–February 28, 1797, National Archives).

From Tench Coxe [1]

[Philadelphia, November 12, 1796]

Sir,

Owing to the absence of Mr Whelen the matter with his concern was not settled till just before my late illness. I am now just getting out. The Pattersons take back their balance, about 10,000 Ds in their Lands and we take a moiety of the remainder. Out of these Mr Church will have to the amount of his remaining 17¾ tracts, taking none but what have been ours, and by a fair draughting Lot. I gave them their choice of this, a suit or a reference. As soon as they execute the papers I will advise you. I shall have 20 tracts, which were to have been sold and to square the account by near £1100. It is very inconvenient to me, but as the Lands are well worth the money & would be rising to a much greater Value, while the Matter was pending, it is much most profitable to proceed as has been done.

I shall be glad to see Mr Church & if my advice or *assistance* in regard to any of his Pennsylvania property, can be useful, I shall always be ready to afford it.

I am Sir, your mo. obt. st   Tench Coxe

Philada. Novr 12th. 1796

Copy, RG 21, Records of the United States Circuit Court for the Eastern District of Pennsylvania, Equity Records, Case Files, 1790–1911, National Archives.

1. For an explanation of the contents of this letter, see the introductory note to Coxe to H, February 13, 1795. See also Coxe to H, February 17–18, 22, May 10, August 4, 1795, May 31, 1796; H to Joseph Anthony, March 11, 1795; Anthony to H, May 16, 1795.

From Charles Maurice de Talleyrand-Périgord

paris 12 nov. 1796

alexander hamilton   New york

Duplicata

Cher colonel hamilton

Vous recevres en même tems que cette letter une réclamation de M. de beaumarchais [1] qui se confie avec un entier abandon a vous pour obtenir de l'amerique une justice qu'il invoque infructueusement depuis 20 ans. Vous aves apprécié dans le tems les services qu'il a rendus a votre pays. Il pense qu'un nouvel examen de son affaire conduiroit encore a des resultats plus favorables. Je n'ai pas craint de lui promettre votre interêt et vos conseils pour la suite de son affaire. Il sera heureux pour lui d'etre défendu par vous: ce sera le plus sur garant de l'équité de sa demande. Beaucoup de personnes s'y interessent ici: je partage sincerement cet interêt, et desire vivement pouvoir vous l'inspirer. Du reste en reclamant vos lumieres et vos conseils dans le cours de cette affaire, Mr. de beaumarchais n'a garde de vous demander les démarches qu'elle pourra entrainer: c'est de diriger qu'il vous prie: il doit s'en remettre pour toute la partie active a Mr. Sterret[2] qu'il sait que vous estimes et a qui son intention est d'offrir un interêt proportionné au succès de sa reclamation.

Quoique je suis depuis deux mois en france, le pays est encore bien nouveau pour moi; je passe mon tems a l'etudier voila au vrai ce que j'y fais, et pas autre chose. A mon arriveè les papiers publics francois et anglois se sont amusés a beaucoup prononcer mon nom, a me supposer des vues, même des occupations: de tout cela il n'y a pas un mot de vrai. Il faut savoir la langue d'un pays, avant d'oser y parler: et j'en suis encore bien loin.

On m'a beaucoup questionné sur l'amèrique au moment de mon arriveè. J'ai repondu, comme je le devois, et en des termes qui, je crois, vous auroient convenu. Je n'ai pas manqué surtout de dire que je ne croyois point a l'éloignement des americains pour les francois; mais que, quand même cet éloignement èxisteroit il n'y auroit rien de plus naturel d'apres la conduite folle et audacieuse des agents de la france qui s'etoient toujours montrés l'ennemi de votre gouvernement.

Adieu, cher colonel hamilton: en reclamant vos bons offices pour mr. de beaumarchais j'use avec toute confiance du droit que me donne l'amitiè que vous m'aves toujours montrée. Vous m'aves promis de disposer de moi dans toutes les occasions; je vous somme de votre promesse pour vous et pour vos amis.

Soyez assez bon pour presenter mes hommages respectueux a Madame hamilton, me rappeler au souvenir de votre famille, et faire mes meilleurs compliments a MM. Seton, nic. low, hamond.[3] Votre petit jean[4] a t'il toujours autant de génie? Vous vous souviendres toujours, j'esperc, que vous m'aves promis de m'envoyer dans quelques années votre fils aine[5] pour lui faire faire son voyage de france.

Je vous renouvelle, cher Colonel hamilton, l'assurance des sentiments d'amitiè et respect
avec lesquels j'ai l'honneur d'être   votre &c &c

ch. mau. talleyrand.

ALS, Hamilton Papers, Library of Congress; copy (marked "Triplicata"), Bibliothèque et Archives Municipales, Lille, France.

1. Pierre August Caron de Beaumarchais to H, October 29, 1796.
2. Samuel Sterett was a Baltimore merchant who was a member of the House of Representatives from 1791 to 1793 and a naval agent in 1794. Following the failure of his business in Baltimore, he established a partnership in Philadelphia with George Harrison. In addition, he was employed by the six Dutch banking firms which formed the Holland Land Company in 1796.
3. This is a reference to three New York merchants: William Seton, Nicholas Low, and Abijah Hammond.
4. John Church Hamilton, born on August 22, 1792.
5. Philip Hamilton, born on January 22, 1782.

From George Washington

Philadelphia 12th. Novr. 1796.

My dear Sir,

In due time, and in good order, I received your letters dated the 4th 5th & 10th. instt: and shall be mindful of their contents.

What construction do you put upon the information received through the assistant of D——r B——?[1] and what notice, if any, should it meet with *now*, or hereafter, if application should be made for leave, or the event take place without?

Having sometime since, called upon the different Secretaries for such matters (within their respective departments) as required to be communicated to Congress at the opening of the Session,[2] the enclosed papers are from two of them;[3] one has given a shape to the ideas. From the Treasury department I have received nothing yet; and presume nothing will come from the Secretary of it except such matters as are of the fiscal kind, founded upon facts and statements.

The Secretary of War has closed his notes, or draught, with a communication, a declaration, and an invocation, which I had no intention of introducing, if such sentiments could be avoided with that decent respect wch. is due to such members of both houses as have been uniform & steady in their support of those measures of government which I have thought the interest & welfare of this country required, and accordingly recommended.

The reasons which have operated a reluctance in my mind to touch this subject at the *opening* of the Session, are two—First, that it might not be supposed it was introduced for the purpose of a complimentary notice of the event, by those who might feel a disposition to offer it; and secondly, that it might not embarrass others, who had rather be silent; much less put it in the power of a third set, to oppose (if it should be attempted) sentiments of this sort, in the answer to the Speech.

These being my reasons, judge of their force. If they outweigh what may be considered as indifference—slight—or disrespectful in me, towards the body to whom the Address is made, let them prevail. If not, adopt in whole, or in part, or new model altogether to your liking, the sentiments, or expressions of Mr. McHenry.

Among the things noted in my Memorandums, & not to be found in the enclosures is an intimation to this effect—viz—that from the best information I have been able to obtain, and from the best view I have of the general system of European Politics, and of the state of matters in the Mediterranean in particular, our Commerce in that quarter will always be upon a precarious establishment unless a protecting force is given to it. If Congress in their investigation of the subject should coincide in this opinion, it will rest with their wisdom to decide whether that trade, in particular, is of sufficient importance to countervail the expence of its protection. How much beyond this to extend the view towards a navy, in the present uncertain State of our Fiscal concerns, merits consideration. My own sentiments lead strongly to the means of Commencement.

This last article in addition to the several matters contained in the enclosures, and what will naturally flow from the texts mentioned in your letter,[4] together with a general reference to the proper Officers for estimates—Papers—&ca.—alluded to in the Speech will comprehend every thing that has occured to me, as necessary to be mentioned at the *opening* of the Session; and I would thank you much for letting me have the whole as early in next week as your convenience will permit—at any rate on Saturday; with your opinion on the propriety of giving Congress a full statement relatively to the Situation of our affairs with France, as suggested in my letter of the   [5] instant.

With Affectionate regard   I am always Yours   Go: Washington

PS. I was in the very Act of closing this letter when yours of yesterday's date came to hand—due consideration shall be given to the Contents of it.

ALS, Hamilton Papers, Library of Congress.
1. Doctor Richard Bayley. See H and Richard Harison to Bayley, July 19, 1796; H to Washington, November 5, 1796.
2. Washington requested this material from Timothy Pickering on July 18, 1796 (LC, George Washington Papers, Library of Congress), from James McHenry on August 8 (ALS, George Washington Papers, Library of Congress; LC, George Washington Papers, Library of Congress), and from Oliver Wolcott, Jr., on August 10 (ALS, Connecticut Historical Society, Hartford; LC, George Washington Papers, Library of Congress). On October 19, 1796, Washington wrote to Pickering from Mount Vernon: "As the meeting of the Congress is fast approaching, and I shall want to collect all the materials for the speech at the opening of it by, or soon after my arrival, that there may be time to consider and to digest them. Let me request your attention to this matter" (ALS, Massachusetts Historical Society, Boston). Washington wrote a similar letter to McHenry on the same date (Steiner, *James McHenry*, 187–88). Washington had also requested H's assistance in the preparation of his annual message. See Washington to H, August 10, September 6, November 2, 1796; H to Washington, September 4, November 4, 10, 1796.
3. The papers submitted to the President by Pickering and McHenry have not been found.
4. See H to Washington, November 10, 1796.
5. Space left blank in MS. Washington is referring to his letter to H of November 2, 1796.

From John C. Glover [1]

New York, November 16, 1796. Asks what action should be taken in regard to damages "sustained" by the ship *Mary* "in case the Broker [2] will not pay the damages when due." [3]

L, in the handwriting of Richard Hughes, Hamilton Papers, Library of Congress.
1. Glover was a New York City merchant.
2. John Henry, an insurance broker.
3. Under the date of November 12, 1796, the following entry appears in H's Cash Book, 1795–1804: "Cash received for opinion concerning Insurance—Ship Mary 10" (AD, Hamilton Papers, Library of Congress).

From David Ross [1]

Bladensburgh [Maryland] Novr. 16. 1796

Dear Sir

Being engaged in electioneering prevented my writing as soon as I intended that a Mr. Reese (formerly of Baltimore & now connected with a Whole sale Store in Philadelphia) [2] is said to have circulated in George Town, that he had seen, or heard of, a letter of yours to your friends in one of the West India Islands, in which you boasted of the hand you had in promoting our General Government but that it was not yet to your liking & that you had hopes still of introducing a King & Nobility and that you had keept up a correspondence for three years with the British Minister Mr Pitt, but as to the nature of it that was left to every one to draw his own inference. I thought it proper you should know this & judge for yourself whether it was worth your notice. One of Co. Mercers[3] party came full of it from George Town to this place.

I have lately heard it hinted that you had acquiesced in Co. Mercers charge of your having through motives of friendship favor'd the Contractor for supplying the Western Army with Provisions,[4] by your declining the issue it had been put on, by your correspondence with him. I took the liberty of asserting that if nothing farther had passed than what I knew of, that I had no doubt but that you considered any thing Co. Mercer could say of you was not worth your notice after I had enclosed to you Capt. Campbells[5] & my answer lodged at the Printing office at Annapolis, to Co Mercers "Detail"[6] —mentioning at the same time what those answers were.[7] If anything farther has passed between you than what I know of I shall be glad to be informed and if there has not, whether I am right as to your motives for not doing what your correspondence intimated as I have no doubt but the subject will become more public & I wish to have it in my power to contradict & prevent the inference that may be otherwise drawn to your prejudice.

Co Mercer has done as to Mr Adams ⟨–⟩ as to yourself charging him in a late public sp⟨eech – –⟩ District with being an advocate for monarc⟨hy –⟩ partial quotations from his Works, and that he held the poorer classes of People in the greatest contempt—& gave in evidence of it, that Mr Adams at a sumptuous entertainment, told Co Mercer that that was too good for him & that such a Democrat (or Republican) ought to be satisfied with black broth and brown bread. I was present.

If any thing of this sort did pass Mr Adams was ridiculing Co Mercers pretensions to equality & Popularity as I have no doubt he enjoyed the entertainment as much, & showed as much as if not more aristocratical self-importance than, any one of the Company.

This party now assume the name of Republican & those that oppose them are monarchy men & Aristocrats: & these very men that were such opposers of the existing Government now profess the greatest attachment to it & alarm the People with apprehensions for their Government & liberties if they do not elect Mr Jefferson. And as the great body of the People have no knowledge of the characters & as Mr Jeffersons advocates are in general much the most active I should not be surprized if they should be imposed on to do what is so much against their own interest by risking the Peace & happiness of this Country in one who appears not to have been attached to the measures of Government which have keept us clear of European quarrels & secured to us the benefits of Neutrality.

In our *District* we have had the pleasure of defeating Co. Mercers & Mr Masons speeches [8] by electing one who is for persevering in our present measures of Government;[9] altho' they had a majority in this County owing to the great confidence some of our leading characters have *still* in Co Mercer & his Politicks.

In haste   Your friend & obedt Servt.   David Ross

ALS, Hamilton Papers, Library of Congress.

1. Ross had served during the American Revolution as a major in Grayson's Additional Continental Regiment. After the war he had practiced law and managed his family's extensive estates in Frederick County, Maryland. From 1786 to 1788 he was a delegate to the Continental Congress from Maryland.

2. Probably David Rees, listed as a merchant in the Philadelphia directory for 1796 (*Stephen's Philadelphia Directory, For 1796* . . . [Philadelphia, n.d.], 150).

3. John F. Mercer, a member of a prominent Virginia family, had served during the American Revolution as an aide-de-camp to Major General Charles Lee and as a lieutenant colonel in the Virginia militia. After the war he studied law at Fredericksburg, was elected to the Virginia House of Delegates, and represented Virginia in the Continental Congress. In the mid-seventeen-eighties he moved to Maryland and was a delegate from that state to the Constitutional Convention of 1787, where he was an outspoken Antifederalist. A member of the Maryland House of Delegates for the terms 1788–1789 and 1791–1792, he was elected in 1791 to the United States House of Representatives. He served until his resignation on April 13, 1794. Mercer and H were inveterate political enemies. For the protracted dispute between them in 1792, see the introductory note to H to Mercer, September 26, 1792.

4. William Duer. For information on this charge by Mercer, see the introductory note to H to Mercer, September 26, 1792.

5. William Campbell. For Campbells' role in H's dispute with Mercer in 1792, see David Ross to H, November 23, 1792.

6. This is a reference to a publication by Mercer in the fall of 1792. According to a letter which Ross wrote to H on November 23, 1792, Mercer stated that "'a full detail of these and other circumstances (relative to Capt.

Campbell) is lodged with the Printers.'" When Ross applied on November 15 "for a copy of this detail" he was "informed by the Gentlemen of the office that no such thing was ever lodged and that on observing this assertion in his Publication a note was sent from the office that no such detail was lodged and his reply was that it was not ready."

7. If Ross sent H a copy of the answer which he and Campbell "lodged at the Printing office at Annapolis," neither the answer nor the letter in which it was enclosed has been found.

8. Presumably Stevens Thomson Mason, United States Senator from Virginia from 1794 to 1803. Mason's speeches in opposition to the Jay Treaty and other Federalist measures were widely circulated.

9. This is a reference to William Craik, a Federalist from Maryland's third district, which included a part of Ross's home county, Frederick. Craik, who was elected to fill the vacancy caused by the resignation of Jeremiah Crabb, took his seat on December 5, 1796, at the beginning of the second session of the Fourth Congress (*Annals of Congress*, VI, 1589).

From Oliver Wolcott, Junior

(Private) Phila. Nov. 17. 1796

Dear sir

You must feel interested in knowing how our affairs stand with France, I give you a summary of them.

The Note to Colo. Pickering[1] contains a summary of all the complaints of France since the commencement of the present War. They are as follows. That the Courts of the United States have taken Cognizance of Prizes to French Vessells. That the Treaty has been misconstrued, by permitting the admission of British Ships which have at *some time* made Prizes of French Vessells. Mr. Adets construction is that a B. Ship which at *any time* or in *any place* has made a Prize ought to be denied Asylum. Complaints are made of the proclamation of Neutrality & of the *promptness* with which the President requested Congress to enact Laws for preserving our Neutrality. The questions proposed by the President before Genets arrival are recited at length, & commented on as evidences of unfriendliness to France.

Lists of almost all the particular cases respecting privateers &ca are made out & the decisions of the Executive censured.

It is said that the Government has manifested partiality against France, by the alacrity which marked its conduct, in enforcing the Laws against them, & by tardiness in prosecuting the British.

That the American Government *deceived* France in respect to Mr Jays mission.

That the Treaty with G. B. is a violation of the Treaty with France, is equivalent to a Treaty of Alliances, & ought not have been made during the War.

A fulfillment of the 11th. article of our Treaty with France [2] is required which stipulates that favours granted to other nations shall become common—this Mr. A. says will justify the French in taking British property on board of American Vessells, & in intending contraband as defined by the B. Treaty.

For these reasons, the commercial relations founded on Treaty are to be suspended untill the *Government returns to itself.* Nevertheless the French Nation regards *the People* as its friends.

The *people* in a declamatory rhapsody are directly addressed, in this ⟨style⟩ "O ye Americans"—an appeal is made to their passions; the injuries of the British during the last War are recounted, & the assistance of the French nation extolled; it is said that the suspension of the ministers functions is not to be regarded as an Act of *hostility* but of *just resentment* against the *Government*—when the Government *returns to itself,* the French will forget the injury.

France is said to be terrible to its enemies but magnanimous to its Friends, quick to resent injuries, but easily appeased.

The Executive & Mr. Jay are treated with personal indignity.[3]

On the whole this is by far the most bold attempt to govern this Country which has been made. It is necessary to come to issue. Measures to prevent any panick or depression of the public opinion are necessary. We have the right of the question, but whether we shall be overuled by force will partly depend on the spirit of the people, partly on the issue of the Campaign in Italy & Germany.[4]

I am ever yours   Oliv Wolcott Jr

Colo. Hamilton

ALS, Hamilton Papers, Library of Congress; copy, Connecticut Historical Society, Hartford.

1. This is a reference to Pierre Auguste Adet's reply to a letter from Timothy Pickering, dated November 1, 1796. See George Washington to H, November 3, 11, 1796. Adet's reply, with numerous supporting documents, is dated November 15, 1796, and is printed in ASP, *Foreign Relations,* I, 579–667.

2. Wolcott was mistaken, for he meant to refer to Article 2 of the Franco-American Treaty of Amity and Commerce of 1778. That article reads: "The most Christian King, and the United States engage mutually not to grant any particular Favour to other Nations in respect of Commerce and Navigation, which shall not immediately become common to the other Party, who shall enjoy the same Favour, freely, if the Concession was freely made, or on allowing the same Compensation, if the Concession was Conditional" (Miller, *Treaties*, II, 5).

3. Adet's protest contains several implied criticisms of Washington. Wolcott was probably referring to the following part of Adet's letter in which both Washington and Jay were criticized: "These wrongs of the American Government towards the republic . . . will soon be aggravated by new ones. It was a little matter only to allow the English to avail themselves of the advantages of our treaty; it was necessary to assure these to them by the aid of a contract which might serve at once as a reply to the claims of France, and as peremptory motives for refusals, the true cause of which it was requisite incessantly to disguise to her under specious pretexts.

"Such was the object of Mr. Jay's mission to London; such was the object of a negotiation, enveloped, from its origin, in the shadow of mystery, and covered with the veil of dissimulation. Could the executive directory have any other idea of it, on examining its issue; on seeing all the efforts made by the American Government to conceal the secret from every eye? . . ." (*ASP, Foreign Relations*, I, 581.)

4. See Rufus King to H, November 30, 1796, notes 1 and 2.

From Oliver Wolcott, Junior

[*Philadelphia, November 17, 1796.* On December 21 1796, Hamilton wrote to Wolcott: "I did not understand by your letter of the 17th. of November whether you meant or not to authorise the immediate commencement of the sale of the Stock." *Letter not found.*]

From Robert Morris

Alexander Hamilton Esqre   Phila 19 Novr 1796

Dear Sir

I am but just returned from the City of Washington [1] after a long absence, and find your letter of the 10 Inst [2] with others awaiting me, as yet I hardly know my Position, what I can or cannot do, but after looking round and counting Claims & Resources I will write to you again and you may rest assured that I will do all I can for your Convenience,[3] for I am your constant & faithful Friend & Servt   RM

LC, Robert Morris Papers, Library of Congress.

1. Morris had gone to Washington in connection with his large holdings in that city. For Morris's property in Washington, see Morris to H, March 6, 1796, note 4.

2. Letter not found.

3. This is a reference to the balance of a debt which Morris owed to H. For this debt and Morris's efforts to pay it, see the introductory note to H to Morris, March 18, 1795. See also Morris to H, March 31, June 2, 23, 30, July 18, 20, 1795; June 17, 27–30, 1796.

From Rufus Putnam [1]

Marietta [Territory Northwest of the River Ohio]
November 19th. 1796

Sir

The eight acre Lot No. 305 belong to one of the rights Drawn in your Name in the Ohio Companys Purchas [2] Lies adjoining to one owned by Commedore Abraham Whipple [3] (Late of Rhode Island) who is desierous of purchasing it from you, Commedore Whipple after being much reduced in his property (by the failure of public Credit: like most of us who Served there Country in the late War), has retired to this Country where he wishes to accommodate himself with a little farm Neer the Town of Marietta and could he add your eight acre lot above mentioned to the one he has adjoining, and on which he is building a House and makeing improvemint he concives he sould be compleatly accommodeted: at his Desire therefore I requst to know if you will Sell this Lot and if so at what price. And for your information on the Subject I take the Liberty to give you a Description of the lot on which you may rely viz It lies on the West Bank of Muskingum river about two mile from its mouth or junction with the Ohio, the Soil is of the first quality and has about thirty rods front on the Muskingum, there is no Stream or Spring ariseing in or runing throug it, nor any thing more to recommend it than what I have Stated.

As Lands of the Same quality are Sold neer this town it is worth ten Dollars an acre and if you are disposed to part with it at this or any other price you will oblige Commedore Whipple (and me as his frind) to give him the refusal.

I have the honor to be with very great esteem & respect   Sir your most obedient Sert   Rufus Putnam

P.S. an answer is requested.

Colo. Hamilton

ALS, Hamilton Papers, Library of Congress.
1. Putnam, a veteran of the American Revolution, was a founder of the Ohio Company and surveyor general of the United States from 1796 to 1803.
2. H owned five and one-half shares in the Ohio Company (Archer Butler Hulbert, *The Records of the Original Proceedings of the Ohio Company* [Marietta, Ohio, 1917], II, 238).
3. Whipple, a sea captain from Providence, was in charge of the fifty men who burned the British schooner *Gaspée* in 1772 after it had run aground near Pawtucket, Rhode Island. During the American Revolution he served with distinction as a captain in the Continental Navy. He moved to the Ohio country after the formation of the Ohio Company and remained there until his death in 1819. Whipple owned two shares of stock in the Ohio Company (Hulbert, *The Ohio Company*, II, 242).

From Theodore Sedgwick [1]

Stockbridge [Massachusetts] 19. Nov. 1796

My dear sir

The letters inclosed will explain themselves. I will only add one fact—the young man "who was going to transact some business up the north river" came directly here in the stage which communicates with New York and of course went not nigh the river at all & is now waiting *only* for my answer. I need not say that this information must be kept secret, for however proper it may be, and I esteem it highly so, Dayton would doubtless deem it a breach of confidence.

I am sincerely & affectionately your friend   Theodore Sedgwick

Mr. Hamilton.

ALS, Hamilton Papers, Library of Congress.
1. Sedgwick, one of the nation's leading Federalists, was a member of the House of Representatives from March 4, 1789, to June, 1796. He was elected to the United States Senate to fill the vacancy caused by the resignation of Caleb Strong and served from June 11, 1796, to March 3, 1799.

[ENCLOSURE]

Jonathan Dayton to Theodore Sedgwick [2]

[November 12, 1796]

I cannot forbear my dear friend to congratulate you on your appointment to a seat in the Senate, altho it is impossible for me not to lament your separation from the House of Representatives where you could have been more useful.

I know you too well to suppose that you can regard with indifference the preparations which are making for the approaching election of a President. Is not the success of Mr. Adams to be more than doubted, and *that* of Mr. Jefferson, without some decisively counteracting measures to be seriously apprehended? If all our efforts will not avail to effect the former, ought they not nevertheless to be directed to prevent the latter? To me it appears that they ought, but I wish to know the result of your own calculations, & your opinion as to the expedient it may be proper to adopt before I suggest the only adviseable one which has occurred to my mind. Mr. Adams will have I presume, the first votes of all the Electors of your State and of mine, but even with them & all that he can get from other Quarters his chance is a desperate one, since Pennsylvania will be unanimous in it's opposition to him. To whom should their other votes be given with the view of excluding *him* from the Presidency whom of all the Candidates you and I should be the last to prefer? Think of these things, and write to me immediately. I shall wait your answer & give you another letter, if time be afforded me, previously to the day of election.

In our friendship towards Mr. Adams, & in our decided opposition to Mr. Jefferson we are certainly agreed, and on this account I flatter myself that upon a communication and comparison of our views & opinions, we may harmonize in some plan which will gratify our wishes in part at least, if not entirely. You certainly well know that we have only to chuse between Jefferson, Burr & Pinckney, and

2. Copy, Hamilton Papers, Library of Congress.
Dayton was a New Jersey Federalist and a member of the House of Representatives from March 4, 1791, to March 3, 1799, and Speaker of the House from March 4, 1795, to March 3, 1799.

cannot *now* be ignorant that Mr. Burr will have the votes of the Southern States very generally, & will find some friends also in the middle as well as Eastern. It is pretty well ascertained that So. Carolina will entirely abandon Mr. Adams, owing to two causes, their anxiety to place Mr. Pinckney³ at least the second upon the list, & their sensibility (if I may so call it) as to the slave system & trade.

[ENCLOSURE]

*Jonathan Dayton to Theodore Sedgwick*⁴

[November 13, 1796]

Dr. Sir,

This will be delivered to you by a young man who was going to transact some business up the North river, & whom, since writing the other letter, I have engaged to call upon you with it, & to bring me your answer. Every moments reflection serves only to impress me more with the importance of our fixing upon some plan of cooperation to defeat the designs of Mr. J——'s friends. If Mr. A. cannot succeed, is it not desirable to have at the helm a man who is personally known to, as well as esteemed & respected by us both? I assure you that I think it possible for you & me with a little aid from a few others to effect this.

[ENCLOSURE]

*Theodore Sedgwick to Jonathan Dayton*⁵

[Stockbridge, Massachusetts, November 19, 1796]

Last evening, my dear sir, I had the pleasure to receive your favours of the 12th. & 13th. insts. accept for them and for your friendly congratulation on my appointment to a seat in the senate, my sincere acknowledgments. Believe me, that event, however grateful to my friends, is not pleasing to me. I preferred a seat in the

---

3. Thomas Pinckney of South Carolina was the Federalist candidate for Vice President.
4. Copy, Hamilton Papers, Library of Congress.
5. Copy, Hamilton Papers, Library of Congress.

house to any public station whatever, but I had firmly decided to retire from that, on the fourth of March next. How far my resolution may be altered, by any possible event, I can at present hardly conjecture.

I have been for some time past almost blind by an inflamation in my eyes, yet I cannot avoid attempting at least to answer to the interesting subject of your Letters.

Indeed I do not regard with indifference the preparations which are making for the approaching election of a President. Probably the peace and happiness of our country, possibly its freedom depend on the result. You expect reasonably, therefore and shall receive a free communication of my views and opinions on this important subject.

I believe for a thousand reasons, and particularly to impress a conviction on the authors of disorganisation & confusion, that success is not to be ensured by misrepresentation and falsehood, that Mr. Adams should be elected as President; and that to harmonize with the southern States, it is essential that the Vice President should be chosen from that part of the Community. By firmness, union, and adherence to the plan which seems to have been agreed on, we have every reason, I think, to expect success; for I perceive by the Philadelphia papers, which I received last evening of the 11th. that, not withstanding the immense weight of votes against us in that City, and in the County of Philad. there is, from the votes which are known, a ballance of more than 3,600 in our favour—a number which cannot, I think, be counterballanced by the votes which remain to be Computed. It seems to me, then, that you desponded too much, when you believed that Pensylvania would be unanimous in the opposition. Should I however be here mistaken, I feel a confidence, that Mr. Adams will receive, at least, twelve votes on the other side of the Delaware, which will, I have no doubt, secure his election; for he will have the first votes of all the electors not only of your State and of mine, but of all the other states east of that boundary. If there should be no election, in the first instance, Jefferson will undoubtedly be chosen by the present Jacobin House of Representatives. But to avoid that I feel confident that we should not deviate, from the course, which the federalism of the country is persuing. For I cannot bring myself to believe, for a moment, that the federal electors in So. Carolina; and that there will be seven of that description is past a doubt, can act so faithless and insidious a part, as to throw away their votes, preferably to giving them to Mr. Adams. Every consideration of duty and of interest, will concur in inducing them to act fairly and honorably on this occasion. If they now conduct as you suppose, they never hereafter can expect our confidence or support, and without them they must be overwhelmed by their adversaries in that part of the United states, nor without our aid can they expect to continue their favorite candidate in the administration. Be assured they can never act so absurd & stupid a part. It ought; and I presume will be sufficient for them, that the eastern Gentleman have left to them, wholly uninfluenced, the designation of their man. And if no confidence can be placed in their honor, it is impossible even to act extensively, in concert. On the other hand should we deceive their just expectations, and obtain a President and Vice-President from this part of the U.S. it would produce and continue, for the four succeeding Years, an incurable jealousy and hatred, between those, whose union and mutual confidence, are indispensable to the welfare, and probably the very existence of the Government. Rather, then, infinitely rather, if that be the alternative, had I been the injured, than the injuring party.

From every view, indeed, which I have been able to take of the subject, I have the most clear conviction, that every Elector on this side of the Delaware should give his suffrages for Adams & Pinckney. In that case we have every reason to conclude that they will be elected—we shall certainly know that we have performed our duty. To this it may be answered, that Mr. Pinckney may have the greatest number of votes, and of course be the President, contrary to the intention of a great majority of his electors. This may undoubtedly happen, but if so, it is, if I may so express it, a constitutional mischief, and we must console ourselves with the purity and federalism of our chief Magistrate. But on the other hand, the mischiefs of a breach of faith, I do not mean expressly, but impliedly given, for ⟨they certainly expe⟩ct and with reason that one of those offices will be filled by a southern man are innumerable and will, probably, be endless in their efforts. But I do not believe that event to be probable, for I think we have reason to expect that there will be several votes for Mr. Adams in Virginia, and none for Mr. Pinckney.

Respecting Mr. Burr, no man better than yourself knows the estimation in which I hold him. But in my concience I do not believe that every vote in Massachusetts would give him the least chance of an election to either of the offices; and the reason of my opinion I will detail to you. The party with which he has generally acted, altho' they covet the aid of his character & talents, have not the smallest confidence in his hearty union to their cause. Indeed it is my firm belief that their veiws and his are not only distinct but opposite. Their want of confidence in him was incontrovertibly demonstrated in the support which the party gave to the appointment of Monroe.[6]

You remember how anxious you was that Burr should be gratified by that office, and how complete the evidence was to both our minds, that he was defeated by the insidious machinations of that party. And wherefore was it that they prefered Monroe to him? Had they more confidence in monroe's talents? They are not so stupid. In his integrity? no. But they knew the one would & the other would not condesend to Act as their tool. They doubtless respect Burr's talents, but they dread his independence of *them*. They know, in short, he is not one of them, and of course they will never support but always effect to support him.

I am sorry I cannot dwell longer on this subject. If it be agreeable to you, you will please to deliver the inclosed. I feel extremely anxious that we should not appear to play false with our ⟨–.⟩ [7]

6. This is a reference to George Washington's canvass of candidates in May, 1794, to replace Gouverneur Morris as United States Minister Plenipotentiary to France. Among those considered were Chancellor Robert R. Livingston, Aaron Burr, and James Monroe. See H to Richard Harison, May 16, 1794, note 7; "List of Names From Whence to Take a Minister for France," May 19, 1794, note 1. Monroe accepted the appointment on May 26, 1794, after Secretary of State Edmund Randolph had assured him that the President would not consider the appointment of Burr (Monroe to Thomas Jefferson, May 27, 1794 [ALS, Thomas Jefferson Papers, Library of Congress]).

7. On the back of this letter H wrote: "Concerning Dayton's intrigue for Burr."

To George Washington

[New York, November 19, 1796]

Sir

I duly received your letter of the 12th. instant. My avocations have not permitted me sooner to comply with your desire. I have looked over the papers & suggested alterations & corrections;[1] and I have also numbered the paragraphs I. II. III &c in the order in which it appears to me eligble they should stand in the Speech.[2]

I thought upon full reflection you could not avoid an allusion to your retreat in order to express your sense of the support of Congress—but that the simplest manner of doing it was to be preferred. A paragraph is offered accordingly.[3]

I believe the commencement of a Navy ought to be contemplated. Our fiscal concerns if Congress please can easily be rendered efficient. If not tis their fault & ought not to prevent any suggestion which the interest of the Country may require. The Paragraph in your letter respecting our Mediterranean Commerce may well be incorporated in this part of the communication.[4]

You will observe a paragraph I have framed contemplates a full future communication of our situation with France.[5] At present it seems to me that this will best be effected in the following mode.

Let a full reply to Mr Adets[6] last communication be made containing a particular review of our conduct & motives from the commencement of the Revolution. Let this be sent to Mr. Pinckney[7] to be imparted to the Directory & let a copy of it with a short auxiliary statement of facts if necessary be sent to the House of Representatives. As Mr. Adet has suspended his functions[8] I presume no reply can be made to him; but not having seen his paper I cannot judge.

The crisis is immensely important to the glory of the President & to the honor & interest of the Country. It is all important that the Reply to Adets last communication to whomsoever made should be managed with the utmost possible prudence & skill—so that it may be a solid justification—an inoffensive remonstrance—the expression of a dignified seriousness reluctant to quarrel but resolved not to be humbled. The subject excites the greatest anxiety.

I have the honor to be very respectfully & Affectly Sir Your obed ser   A Hamilton

NYork November 19. 1796

The President of the U States

ALS, George Washington Papers, Library of Congress.
1. H is referring to suggestions for the President's annual message to Congress submitted to Washington by Secretary of State Timothy Pickering and Secretary of War James McHenry. These papers have not been found. See Washington to H, November 12, 1796.
2. This is a reference to the President's annual message to Congress on which Washington had asked for H's help as early as August, 1796. See Washington to H, August 10, September 6, November 2, 12, 1796; H to Washington, September 4, 6, November 4, 10, 1796; "Draft of George Washington's Eighth Annual Address to Congress," November 10, 1796.
3. This paragraph has not been found.
4. See H's "Draft of George Washington's Eighth Annual Address to Congress," November 10, 1796; Washington to H, November 12, 1796.
5. This paragraph has not been found.
6. This is a reference to Pierre Auguste Adet's letter of November 15, 1796, to Pickering. See Oliver Wolcott, Jr., to H, November 17, 1796.
7. Charles Cotesworth Pinckney, United States Minister Plenipotentiary to France.
8. In his letter to Pickering of November 15, 1796, Adet stated: "The undersigned minister plenipotentiary . . . declares that the executive directory regards the treaty of commerce concluded with Great Britain as a violation of the treaty made with France in 1778, and equivalent to a treaty of alliance with Great Britain; and that, justly offended at the conduct which the American Government has held in this case, they have given him orders to suspend, from this moment, his ministerial functions with the Federal Government" (*ASP, Foreign Relations*, I, 582).

From George Washington

Philadelphia 21st. Novr. 1796

My dear Sir

Having written to you on Saturday the 11th. instant[1] (accompanying it with enclosures) without hearing any thing from you in the course of last week, or by the Mail of this day, I begin to have uneasy sensations for the fate of my letter. To this cause, & to my solicitude to have the Papers returned, you must ascribe the trouble of receiving this letter.

If my last got safe to your hands, & indisposition, business, or any other cause should have prevented your looking into the Papers;[2] I wish, even under these circumstances, that they may be returned to me immediately; for I have no copies, and have but little time to digest, and to put the several matters therein contained into form, that the whole may be revised again and again, before it is presented. Among these Papers do not forget to place Sir John Sinclairs letter to me,[3] as I am desirous of giving it an acknowledgement.

You will perceive by the publication of Mr. Adets letter to Colo. Pickering[4] (in Claypools Gazette of this date)[5] that the French Government are disposed to play a high game. If other proofs were wanting, the *time*, and *indelicate mode & stile*, of the present attack on the Executive, exhibited in this laboured performance—which is as unjust as it is voluminous—would leave no doubt as to the primary object it has in view; but what consequences it may ultimately produce, is not so accessible to human foresight, as it may depend upon various contingencies & events. I have not seen the writer since my return to the City—nor is it presumable I shall do it under present circumstances, unless courted on my part.

The letter of Mr. Adet having been committed to the keeping of Mr. Bache, by him—Extracts having already been given to the public and other parts promised to be eked out[6] (as would, it is presumed, subserve the purposes in view) induced an opinion that it was best to give the *entire* letter to the Public from Authority, and without delay, that the well informed part of the Community might judge for themselves.

The necessity of bringing the matter fully before Congress[7] is now rendered indispensable and through that Medium it is presumed it will make its way to the Public with proper explanations. I am, as you know me to be, always and sincerely

Your affectionate   Go: Washington

P.S. Since writing the above, your letter of the 19th. with its enclosures have been sent to me. Accept my thanks for them. On account of the other matter contained in this letter I forward it—

being written. Your sentimts. in this interesting crisis will always be thankfully received.

ALS, Hamilton Papers, Library of Congress; ADfS, George Washington Papers, Library of Congress.
1. Letter not found.
2. Washington to H, November 12, 1796. See also H to Washington, November 19, 1796.
3. Washington to H, November 2, 1796.
4. Pierre Auguste Adet to Timothy Pickering, November 15, 1796 (*ASP, Foreign Relations*, I, 579–667). See also Oliver Wolcott, Jr., to H, November 17, 1796; H to Washington, November 19, 1796.
5. Washington was mistaken, for on November 19, 1796, Pickering wrote to George W. Craik, Washington's secretary: "I will thank you to send me a letter to be addressed to Mr. Adet, concerning some prizes sent into Charleston & Wilmington; if the President approves of the draught, Mr. Adets last long note will be in Brown's paper on Monday morning; & I wish to acknowledge its receipt before hand" (AL, RG 59, Miscellaneous Letters, 1790–1799, National Archives). "Brown's Paper" was *The Philadelphia Gazette and Universal Daily Advertizer*, which was published by Andrew Brown. Adet's letter to Pickering appeared in the issue of Monday, November 21, 1796.
6. A summary of Adet's letter was published in Benjamin Franklin Bache's [Philadelphia] *Aurora. General Advertiser* on November 18, 1796. It is preceded by the following paragraph: "To relieve in some degree the impatience of the Public as to Mr. ADET's last note to our Executive we promised an outline of its contents. We fulfil the task with as much accuracy as is compatible with the brevity we are obliged to observe and the intricacy of the subject."
7. A report which Washington communicated to Congress on January 19, 1797, included Adet's letter (*Annals of Congress*, VI, 914). The report is printed in *ASP, Foreign Relations*, I, 559–748.

To Oliver Wolcott, Junior

[New York] Nov 22. 1796

Dr. Sir

I thank you for your Note sending me *Adet's* letter.[1] The present is in my opinion as critical a situation as our Government has been

ALS, Connecticut Historical Society, Hartford; copy, Hamilton Papers, Library of Congress.
1. Letter not found. As Pierre Auguste Adet's letter to Timothy Pickering of November 15, 1796, was printed in *The Philadelphia Gazette and Universal Daily Advertiser* on November 21, Wolcott's "Note" to H presumably was dated November 21, 1796. See George Washington to H, November 21, 1796, note 5.

in—requiring all its prudence all its wisdom all its moderation, all its firmness.

Though the thing is now passed, I do not think it useless to say to you that I was not well pleased with the Secretary of State's answer to Adets note [2] communicating the order respecting neutral Vessels. There was something of hardness & epigrammatic sharpness in it—neither did I think the position true that France had no right to inquire respecting the affair of seamen.[3] I am of opinion that whenever a neutral power suffers liberties to be taken with it by a belligerent one which turns to the detriment of the other belligerent party, *as the acquiring strength by impressing our seamen,* there is a good ground of inquiry demanding candid explanation.

My opinion is that our communications should be *calm reasoning* and *serious,* shewing steady resolution more than feeling having force in the idea rather than in the expression.

I am very anxious that our Government should do right on the present occasion.

My ideas are these—

As *Adet* has declared his functions suspended,[4] the reply ought not to be to him but through Mr. Pinckney [5] to the Directory.

It ought to contain a review of our conduct from the beginning—noticing our first & full acknowlegement of the Republic & the danger we run by it—also the danger we incurred by other large interpretations of the Treaty in favour of France adverting to the sale of prizes.

It should meet all the suggestions of the Minister correct his misstatements of Facts & meet argumentatively his principles. Where arguments already used are repeated, it ought to be in new language or by quotations in the body of the Reply not by referrence to other communications annexed or otherwise which embarrass the reading & attention.

It should review calmly the conduct of France & her Agents pointing out fully & clearly the violations of our rights & the spirit which was manifested—but in terms the most cautious & inoffensive.

2. Pickering to Adet, November 1, 1796. See Washington to H, November 2, 3, 1796.
3. See Washington to H, November 2, 1796, note 3; H to Washington, November 11, 1796, note 3.
4. See H to Washington, November 19, 1796, note 8.
5. Charles Cotesworth Pinckney.

It should advert to the policy of moderation towards the enemies of France which our situation & that of France, especially as to maritime power imposed upon us. It should briefly recapitulate the means of obtaining redress from G Britain employed by our Goverment & the effects they have produced.

It should explain why the Goverment could not safely adopt more *expeditious* modes why the Executive could not controul the judiciary & should shew that in effect the opposite Party as well as France suffered the inconven[ien]cies of Delay.

It should make prominent the consequences upon the peace & friendship of Governments if all accidental infractions from situation, from the negligences &c of particular officers are to be imputed with severity to the Government itself & should apply the remark to the case of the injuries we have suffered in different ways from the Officers & Agents of France.

It should make prominent two ideas, the situation in which we were with Great Britain prior to the last Treaty—so as to shew that by the *laws* of Nations as *admitted* to us & declared to France & the world prior to that Treaty, all the things complained of as resulting from that Treaty previously existed & it should dwell on the exception in that Treaty of prior Treaties.

It should point out strongly the idea that the inconvenience at particular junctions of particular stipulations is no reason for one party superseding them; but should intimate that the President is willing to review the *relations* between the two Country and by a new Treaty if the same shall be approved by the Senate to readjust the terms of those *relations*.

The article in the Treaty with France respecting an admission of the same privileges which are granted to other powers [6] should be examined. This plainly means where there is any *concession* of a positive privilege which the U States were free to refuse, not where there is a mere recognition of the principles of the laws of Nations.

It should be made prominent, that the U States have always wished & still wish to cultivate the most amicable relations & are still disposed to evince this disposition by every method in their power. That in what they have said they mean only to shew that they have acted with sincerity & good faith & have rather received than given

6. See Wolcott to H, November 17, 1796.

cause to complain. That they have been disposed to make a candid construction of circumstances which might seem inconsistent with a friendly conduct in France & claim a similar candour in the estimate of their situation & conduct.

There should be an animadversion upon the unfitness of looking beyond the Government to the Citizens.

And there should be these ideas properly couched that the UStates cannot admit that a just cause of resentment has been given that they appeal from the misapprehension which dictated this sentiment to the justice and mag[na]nimity of France for a retraction for it and for meeting them freely in the complete restoration of friendly intercourse; that France will not deliberately expect that they could make a sacrifice of self respect since she must be sensible that a Free People ought in every event to cherish it as a sacred duty & to encounter with firmness every danger & calamity which an attempt to make them forget it or degrade them from their Independent character may involve.

This would be the general complexion of the reply which I would give. The manner should be extremely caution smooth, even friendly, but yet solemn & dignified.

Yrs. A H

The alliance in its future operation must be against our Interest. A door to escape from it is opened. Though we ought to maintain with good faith our engagements—if the conduct of the other party releases us, we should not refuse the release, so far as we may accept without compromitting our peace. This idea is very important.

O Wolcott Esq

To Stephen Higginson [1]

[*New York, November 28, 1796.* On December 9, 1796, Higginson wrote to Hamilton: "Your Letter of 28 of last month I received." *Letter not found.*]

1. Higginson, who had commanded a privateer during the American Revolution and had been a delegate to the Continental Congress from Massachusetts

in 1782 and 1783, was one of Boston's wealthiest merchants and a prominent Federalist.

From Rufus King

London 30 Nov. 1796

My Dear sir

The Arch Duke having expelled Jourdan & Moreau from Germany[1] the Parties are in respect to territory in this Quarter where they were when the campaign began. Buonaparte by the latest accounts from Italy is critically circumstanced, and it seems not improbable that he likewise will be compelled to retire from Lombardy.[2] The mission of Lord Malmesbury remains undecided, and though the negotiation is not promising, it does not appear as desperate as it did a fortnight past.[3] Paper has intirely *ceased* as a medium in France, what their ability is to prosecute another Campaign you, as well as I can, may conjecture. New Projects are to be brought forward in this country, and if for no other reason than that they are novelties, they will be hazardous in a society where the Force of habit is stronger than that of Reason. The minister's[4] Plan is not definitively settled, but enough is known to authorise a Belief that it cannot be approved by the monied men—the three per Cents are at about 56. pr Ct. the minister is unwilling to augment the Debt already enormous by borrowing on such Terms—he intends proposing a Loan, which is to be advanced by *patriotic* Capitalists, upon Terms more advantageous to the Government.[5] What Patriotism may do I can't say, but unless there exists a real conviction in the minds of wealthy men, that their Wealth is in Danger, I should suspect that this virtue pure & dignified as it is, will in this Country prove an unproductive Source when Millions are required. It is Time to make peace for all sides are weary with the war. We must sincerely desire it, since Peace alone will afford us the Tranquillity we wish, and ought, to enjoy.

I do not think it prudent to write my Opinions so far as I have formed them, concerning certain subjects interesting to our Rights, and respecting which you will naturally wish for information from this Quarter. The casualties to which Letters are liable require a caution that between Friends is unpleasant and sometimes inconvenient—you know my Opinions respecting this Country—we have often endeavoured to explain appearances that we disliked, and to preserve our Respect for a nation Who have done much to improve the Condition & happiness of Mankind. I still hope that I have not been deceived, and that experience will prove that the Opinions of those from whom we differed were, as we believed them, partial and erroneous.

We are anxious to hear the Result of the presidential Election—much, very much, will depend on that Event.

Farewell yrs very sincerely   Rufus King

Col Hamilton

ALS, Hamilton Papers, Library of Congress.
1. After their victories in eastern France and Flanders in May, 1796, the French armies commanded by generals Jean Baptiste Jourdan and Jean Victor Moreau advanced toward Germany and Austria. Jourdan was to engage the Austrians with the army of the Sambre and Meuse, while Moreau occupied southern Germany with the army of the Rhine and Moselle. By July, Jourdan had driven the Austrian army eastward across the Rhine, but in late August and early September Archduke Charles recouped with two victories at Amberg and Würzburg, forcing Jourdan's army back into France. Soon afterward Moreau, who had reached Bavaria, also turned and retreated across the Rhine.
2. In the late summer of 1796, Napoleon left a blockade around Mantua, and moved eastward toward the Julian Alps. He had originally planned to reach Lower Austria by way of Trieste, but orders from the Directory diverted him toward Moreau's army in Bavaria, and on September 8 he defeated Dagobert Siegmund, Count von Wurmser, at Bassano. He was not, however, to advance any farther to the east. By the end of October he had massed defensive forces in Lombardy, the Veneto, and the Friuli, but in early November a concerted Austrian attack forced the French armies westward to the Adige. On November 12, Josef Alvinczy, Baron von Barberek, the Austrian general, withstood an attack by the French and drove them back to Verona, where he hoped to merge his forces with the other column of the Austrian army under Baron Paul Davidovich. Napoleon, however, moving eastward from Verona to Vicenza, met Davidovich's forces, and at Arcola, from November 15 to 17, 1796, he fought a decisive battle, eventually turning back both the Austrian armies.
3. On October 17, 1796, James Harris, first Earl of Malmesbury, left England with instructions to make peace with France provided that the French agreed to restore the Netherlands to Austria. The Directory, however, refused this provision. The negotiations, which were conducted at Lille, broke down, and on November 13 Malmesbury wrote to Lord Grenville, the British Foreign Secretary, that it was likely that he would be ordered to leave France (*Dropmore Papers*, III, 268). On November 28 he wrote to Grenville from Paris asking for latitude in negotiating the treaty and suggesting that the negotiations might succeed "Should the emperor consent to an equivalent in lieu of the Austrian Netherlands" (*Dropmore Papers*, III, 279). Grenville, however,

stuck to his original condition, and on December 19 the Directory ordered Malmesbury home.

4. William Pitt, first lord of the Treasury.

5. On December 7, 1796, Pitt received the approval of the Ways and Means Committee for his project of a "loyalty" loan of eighteen million pounds to be raised by annuities at five and five-eighths percent interest toward the cost of defense against a possible invasion (*Parliamentary Register*, LX, 262, 275, 293). He had, however, already proposed unofficially that subjects in their private capacity, rather than contractors, should meet the loan. By December 1 a group of six London bankers had agreed to raise three hundred thousand pounds. See Thomas Coutts to the King, December 2, 1796 (A. Aspinall, ed., *The Later Correspondence of George III* [Cambridge, 1963], II, 521).

From Henry Sadler and Company [1]

New York, November, 1796. "We take the liberty of inclosing Copy of an obligation given for payt. of Commission on a certain contract made with the Agents of the French Republic [2]—copy of which contract you have also herewith. As the F Republick would not pay for the Leather immediately on delivery—nor in Specie, and not having yet paid for the Amount of Leather delivered agreeable to said Contract—We conceive it has not been compiled with on its part & that the obligation given for payment of Commission is thereby annulled. We therefore request your opinion. . . ."

ALS, Hamilton Papers, Library of Congress.

1. Henry Sadler and Company was a firm of merchants located at 81 Water Street, New York City.

2. On August 12, 1794, Henry Sadler and Company and Townsend and Franklin, also a New York mercantile firm, signed a contract with Louis Arcambal, vice consul of the French republic at New York, "to deliver to the french republic . . . four Hundred Thousand Wheight of tanned inspected sole Leather . . . at the rate of one Half of a dollar for every pound of fourteen french ounces . . . payable in specie of gold or Silver immediately after the delivery of each Cargo . . ." (DS, Hamilton Papers, Library of Congress). On the same day Henry Sadler and Company signed an "obligation" in which the firm promised to pay Peter Delabigarre, a New York City merchant, a five percent commission "on the whole amount of a Contract made this day between Us and L. Arcambal . . . in consideration of the preference given to Us and of his trouble in the settling of said contract—said Commission amounting to Ten thousand Dollars . . ." (copy, Hamilton Papers, Library of Congress).

An entry in H's Cash Book, 1795-1804, for July 3, 1795, reads: "for this sum received for advice of Townshend & Franklin & Sadler respecting contract with Mr. Fauchet M Plenipotentiary 50." An entry for July 20, 1796, reads: "for advice concerning contract with French Consul some time since given 15" (AD, Hamilton Papers, Library of Congress). H's opinion, dated December 2, 1795, states: ". . . I incline to the opinion that upon So much of *the contract money* as the contractors or their agents have *discharged the french government from* . . . they must pay the full commission on in specie *pro rata*. It does not appear to me that they are to pay Commission on the balance unreceived or unextinguished. . . . I think they are bound to pay the Commission *pro rata* without waiting for payment of the whole Contract money" (copy, Hamilton Papers, Library of Congress).

A final entry in H's Cash Book, 1795–1804, on November 12, 1796, reads: "Ditto [cash received for opinion] from Sadler & Co. contract with french Republic 20" (AD, Hamilton Papers, Library of Congress).

To Jeremiah Wadsworth

[New York, December 1, 1796]

Dr. Sir

I have lately received a line from you.[1] I had been apprised of the machination to cheat us into Mr Burr[2] but I have no apprehension of its success. My chief fear is that the attachment of our Eastern friends to Mr. Adams may prevent their voting for *Pinckney* likewise, & that some irregularity or accident may deprive us of *Adams* & let in Jefferson.

Judge *Tichener*[3] in passing through informed me that from something which had occurred to his recollection while here he feared that the votes of Vermont would be lost for want of being warranted by a subsisting legislative Act.[4] If so, Adams will not have sufficient votes to prevent the question going to the House of Representatives & then we can be at no loss for the result. The whole number I venture to *depend* on for Adams (including Vermont & *two* in Pensylvania) is 73. Take off Vermont and there will be 69 which is less by one than the whole number of Electors.

It may be said Georgia also is irregular.[5] This I do not consider as certain. But if so at first there was time enough to discover & rectify it. Not so as to Vermont. Besides who will take care to have the necessary *authentic* proof from Georgia? From *Vermont* it can be had & our patriots are not likely to neglect it.

Tis therefore a plain policy to support Mr. Pinkney equally with Mr. Adams.

Yrs. truly

A Hamilton
Dec. 1. 1796

J Wadsworth E

ALS, Mr. Pierce W. Gaines, Fairfield, Connecticut.
1. Letter not found, but see H to Wadsworth, November 8, 1796. See also H to ———, November 8, 1796.
2. See the enclosures to Theodore Sedgwick to H, November 19, 1796.
3. Isaac Tichenor, United States Senator from Vermont, was associate justice of the Vermont Supreme Court from 1790 to 1794 and its chief justice in 1795 and 1796. In October, 1796, he was elected to the United States Senate, where he served until October, 1797, when he resigned to become governor of Vermont.
4. In *The* [New York] *Minerva, & Mercantile Evening Advertiser,* November 26, 1796, the following item appeared: "We have good authority to believe the election of Electors in Vermont is invalid—being grounded only on a *Resolve* of the Legislature, not a law. This is supposed to have been known to the 'Patriots,' of that State at the time. It being now too late to correct the mistake, it has leaked out in whispers." This item was reprinted in the [Boston] *Columbian Centinel* on December 7, 1796. On December 28, 1796, the *Columbian Centinel* printed the following paragraph, dated December 14, from a correspondent in Vermont: "We have seen in the Centinel a doubt of the validity of our votes for President and Vice-President, but we can have no idea on what ground that doubt is founded. There is a law in this state which points out the mode of appointing Electors, and they were made agreeably to that law. . . ."
Vermont's electoral votes were cast and counted for John Adams.
5. Although in the election of 1796 four western counties in Georgia voted for the Federalist ticket, the state's four electoral votes were cast for Thomas Jefferson and Aaron Burr.

From Catharine Miller [1]

Mulberry Grove [Georgia] Decembr. 3d 1796

I regret that I have only time to tell my beloved friend Colo Hamilton what he already knows—that my best affections—my liveliest gratitude, and purest friendship are his and that I send him a Small Box of Oranges from My Own Garden. I hope they may arrive Safe—and if the frost should spare them, I will insure them to be exlent.

With My Compliments to Mrs Hamilton and love to the Dear Children I have the honor

to be Your obliged and very obedt. Sarvant   Cathe Miller

ALS, Hamilton Papers, Library of Congress.
1. Catharine Miller was the widow of Major General Nathanael Greene. See "Report on the Petition of Catharine Greene," December 26, 1791. See also Catharine Greene to H, May 10, 1794. In June, 1796, she married Phineas Miller, her children's tutor.

To Oliver Wolcott, Junior

[New York, December 6, 1796]

Dr Sir

The President of the Bank of New York [1] called upon me yesterday and manifested considerable anxiety about the State of the Bank. It seems the course of things lately, and their large accommodation to the Government, have produced a heavy ballance against them in favor of the Office of Discount at this place, which has lately called for 100000 Ds in specie & it is apprehended may speedily call for more.[2]

The *President* mentioned this situation generally with only this view to shew that the Bank would probably be under a *necessity* of selling the Stock pleged with them,[3] if the Government should not be punctual. It was at the same time declared that nothing but necessity would lead to any measure inconvenient to the Government yet it was thought adviseable to admonish of the probable necessity.

A *Director*, two or three days since, also mentioned to me that there was a sum of about 26000 Dollars of interest due to the Bank of which an account had been rendered but which was not paid—adding that in the present situation every little would help. Observations like these are of course confidential.

But the situation requires & will make it good policy that if in your power you should come to the *aid* of the Bank of New York. It would be wise if possible to anticipate a partial payment. It will also be useful to arrest for a time too free calls from the Office.

Friendly attentions & good offices on your part will inspire confidence & embolden the Bank to assist in future emergencies & it is very much the policy of the Treasury not to be exclusively dependent on one institution.

Yrs.

A Hamilton
Decr. 6. 1796

Let me hear from you shortly on this subject. What is doing with *Adet?*[4]

O. Wolcott Junr. Esquire

ALS, Connecticut Historical Society, Hartford.
1. Gulian Verplanck.
2. As H indicates in this paragraph, the Bank of New York was in difficulty. In the first place, as a result of an increase in its discounts, the bank was unable to meet its obligations to other banks, and the directors of the Bank of New York had turned to the New York branch of the Bank of the United States for assistance. In the second place, the Bank of New York had recently made a "large accomodation to the Government." See H to Wolcott, August 5, 1796.
3. See H to Wolcott, August 5, 1796.
4. Pierre Auguste Adet. See Wolcott to H, November 17, 1796; H to George Washington, November 19, 1796; Washington to H, November 21, 1796; H to Wolcott, November 22, 1796.

The Answer [1]

[New York, December 8, 1796] [2]

For The Minerva.

The French republic have, at various times, during the present war, complained of certain principles, and decisions of the American government, as being violations of its neutrality, or infractions of the treaty made with France in the year 1778. These complaints were principally made in the year 1793, and explanations, which, till now, were deemed satisfactory, were made by Mr. Jefferson's correspondence, in August of that year.[3] They are now not only

The [New York] *Minerva, & Mercantile Evening Advertiser,* December 8, 1796.
1. H wrote "The Answer" to refute the points raised by Pierre Auguste Adet in his letter to Timothy Pickering on November 15, 1796. In this letter Adet criticized United States policy toward French privateers. Adet's letter, with its supporting documents, is printed in *ASP, Foreign Relations,* I, 579–667.
2. This document is dated December 6, 1796, in *JCHW,* VII, 600, and in *HCLW,* VI, 215.
3. The correspondence between Edmond Charles Genet and Thomas Jefferson during the summer of 1793 is printed in *ASP, Foreign Relations,* I, 147–67. See also Jefferson to Gouverneur Morris, August 16, 1793 (*ASP, Foreign Relations,* I, 167–72).

renewed with great exaggeration, but the French government have directed that it should be done *in the tone of reproach, instead of the language of friendship.*⁴ The apparent intention of this menacing tone, at this particular time, is to influence timid minds to vote agreeable to their wishes in the election of president and vice-president, and probably with this view, the memorial was published in the news-papers. This is certainly a practice that must not be permitted. If one foreign minister is permitted to publish what he pleases to the people, in the name of his government, every other foreign minister must be indulged with the same right. What then will be our situation on the election of a president and vice president, when the government is insulted, the persons who administer it, traduced, and the electors menaced by public addresses from these intriguing agents? Poland, that was once a respectable, and powerful nation, but is now a nation no longer, is a melancholy example of the danger of foreign influence in the election of a chief magistrate. Eleven millions of people have lost their independence from that cause alone. What would have been the conduct of the French directory, if the American minister had published an elaborate, and inflammatory address to the people of France against the government, reprobating the conduct of those in power, and extolling that of the party opposed to them? They would have done as the Parliament of England did in 1727, when the Emperor's resident presented an insolent memorial to the king, and published it next day in the newspapers. "All parties concurred in expressing the highest indignation and resentment at the affront offered to the government by the memorial delivered by Monsieur Palm, and more particularly at this audacious manner of appealing from the government, to the people under the pretext of applying for reparation and redress of supposed injuries."⁵ In consequence of an address from

4. See note 1. See also Oliver Wolcott, Jr., to H, November 17, 1796; H to George Washington, November 19, 1796; Washington to H, November 21, 1796.

5. At the opening of Parliament on January 17 (O.S.), 1727, George I devoted his speech to an attack on the King of Spain, who was currently besieging Gibraltar and who had also supposedly acquiesced in the Austrian usurpation of British trading rights at Ostend by his treaty of 1726 with the empire. On March 2 (O.S.), 1727, the Emperor's resident in England, Karl Joseph von Palm, sent George I a memorial "couched in a very indecent and injurious stile, altogether unusual and very unbecoming the majesty of crowned heads" (*Parliamentary History*, VIII, 554). Acting on instructions from the imperial

both houses, Monsieur Palm was ordered to quit England immediately.⁶ And is it not necessary that we should adopt some remedy adequate to this evil, to avoid these serious consequences which may otherwise be apprehended from it?

The conduct of the American government to preserve its neutrality, has been repeatedly justified by arguments drawn from the law of nations; and in the application of its principles, they have gone as far, in every instance, and in one particular instance, farther in favor of France, than the strict rule of neutrality would justify.⁷ It would therefore answer no valuable purpose, to state the same principles, and deduce the same consequences, in order to justify ourselves on the same ground, that we have already done; but as the *reproaches* of the French republic are founded on an idea, that our construction, and application of the law of nations, is erroneous, partial, and inimical; it may be worth while to examine, whether we cannot justify ourselves by the example of the French nation itself. I presume a better rule of justification against any charge, cannot be required, than the conduct of those who have made it, in like cases.

I propose therefore, to compare the decisions of the American government, in the several points wherein they have been complained of in Mr. Adet's memorial, with the laws of France on the same points.

It is asserted that the American government has violated the 17th article of the treaty of 1778, by arresting French privateers, and their

---

chancellor, Ludwig Philipp, Graf von Zinzendorf, Palm defended the Spanish actions at Gibraltar and Ostend and demanded reparation for the injury done to Austria by the King's speech (*Parliamentary History*, VIII, 554–57). The following day, Palm pubilshed both his memorial and Zinzendorf's letter of authorization. On March 15 (O.S.), 1727, both houses of Parliament presented an address to the King expressing "the highest resentment at the affront and indignity" which he had suffered (*Parliamentary History*, VIII, 561–62). H is quoting from this address to the King.

6. The King ordered Palm from the country on March 4, 1727 (*The London Gazette*, March 4, 1727).

7. H is referring to the fact that the United States gave to France "a doubtful privilege, to which she was not entitled by treaty—that of *selling the prizes* made by her armed vessels in their ports; the treaty stipulating nothing more than a free *access* and *egress*" ("No Jacobin No. IV," August 10, 1793). For a discussion of the question of the sale of French prizes in the United States, see Charles M. Thomas, *American Neutrality in 1793: A Study in Cabinet Government* (New York, 1931), 219–20, note 3.

prizes; and that it has exercised *shocking persecutions* towards them.[8]

It will be found on an accurate inquiry, that all the prizes brought in under French commissions, that have been restored, have been found to be in one, or the other, of the following descriptions:

1. Those captured within a marine league of the shores of the United States.

2. Where the capturing vessel was owned, and principally manned, by American citizens.

3. Where the capturing vessel was armed in our ports.

As to the jurisdiction exercised by the U. States, over the sea contiguous to its shores, all nations claim and exercise such a jurisdiction, and all writers admit this claim to be well founded; and they have differed in opinion, only as to the distance to which it may extend. Let us see whether France has claimed a greater, or less extent of dominion over the sea, than the United States. Valen, the king's advocate at Rochelle, in his new commentary on the marine laws of France, published first in 1761, and again by approbation in 1776,* after mentioning the opinions of many different writers on public law on this subject, says "As far as the distance of two leagues the sea is the dominion of the sovereign of the neighboring coast; and that, whether there be soundings there or not." It "is proper to observe this method, in favor of states whose coasts are so high, that there are no soundings close to shore; but this does not prevent the extension of the dominion of the sea, *as well as in respect to jurisdiction as the fisheries* to a greater distance, by particular treaties, or the rule herein before mentioned, which extends dominion as far as there are soundings, or as far as the reach of a cannon shot; *which is the rule at present universally acknowledged.*" [9] The effect of this

---

* Book 5. Title 1.

8. For the text of Article 17 (originally 19) of the Franco-American Treaty of Amity and Commerce, February 6, 1778, see H to Wolcott, November 3, 1796, note 6.

Adet wrote: "In contempt of these stipulations, the French privateers have been arrested in the United States, as well as their prizes; the tribunals have taken cognizance of the validity or invalidity of these prizes. It were in vain to seek to justify these proceedings under the pretext of the right of vindicating the compromitted neutrality of the United States. The facts about to be stated will prove that this pretext has been the source of shocking persecutions against the French privateers, and that the conduct of the Federal Government has been but a series of violations of the 17th article of the treaty of 1778" (*ASP, Foreign Relations*, I, 579).

9. René-Josué Valin, *Nouveau Commentaire Sur L'Ordonnance de La Marine*,

dominion, the same author says, "According to the principles of Puffendorf, which are incontestible, is, that every sovereign has a right to protect foreign commerce in his dominions, as well as to secure them from insult, by preventing others from approaching nearer to a certain distance." [10] In extending our dominion over the sea to one league, we have not extended it so far, as the example of France, and the other powers of Europe would have justified. They therefore can have no right to complain of our conduct in this respect.

The second description of cases, which has induced the American government to restore prizes claimed by the French, is, where our citizens have made the capture under a French commission.

The third article of the ordinances of the marine of France, which the commission now given to French privateers require to be observed, (Valin, 2 Vol. 235) is as follows: "We prohibit all our subjects from taking commission from foreign kings, princes, or states, to arm vessels for war, and to cruize at sea under their colors, unless

---

Du Mois D'Août 1681. Où se trouve la Conférence des anciennes Ordonnances, des Us & Coutumes de la Mer, tant du Royaume que des Pays étrangers, & des nouveaux Réglemens concernans la Navigation & le Commerce maritime. Avec des Explications prises de l'esprit du Texte, de l'Usage, des Décisions des Tribunaux & des meilleurs Auteurs qui ont écrit sur la Jurisprudence nautique. Et des Notes historiques & critiques, tirées de la plupart des divers Recueils de Manuscrits conservés dans les dépôts publics (La Rochelle, 1776), II, 688. The first edition of this work, entitled *Commentaire* . . . , was published at La Rochelle in 1760.

Valin wrote: "Il faut avouer neanmoins que nul potentat n'a prétendu sérieusement excepté le salut de son pavillon, s'arroger le domaine de l'Océan, comme Océan; mais seulement à raison de commerce, qui pouvoit être entrepris à son prejudice sur ses possessions contigues à l'Océan" (Valin, *Nouveau Commentaire*, II, 688).

10. This is apparently a free translation of the following passage in Valin: "Car enfin l'Océan n'est à personne, & la conclusion qui se tire delà naturellement, c'est qu'il est permis è toutes les nations d'y naviger; en telle sorte que cette liberté ne sauroit être ôtée par une nation à une autre, sans injustice & sans un ambition démesurée même extravagante, comme le prouve, d'une maniere sans replique, Pufendorff, . . § 9" (Valin, *Nouveau Commentaire*, II, 687). Valin is referring to Samuel von Pufendorf, *Of the Law of Nature and Nations. Eight Books. Written in Latin by the Baron Pufendorf, Counsellor of State to his late Swedish Majesty, and to the late King of Prussia. Done into English by Basil Kennett, D. D. late President of Corpus Christi College in Oxford. To which are added All the large Notes of Mr. Barbeyrac, Translated from the best Edition; Together with Large Tables to the Whole. The Fourth Edition, carefully Corrected* . . . (London: Printed for J. Walthoe, R. Wilkin, J. and J. Bonwicke, S. Birt, T. Ward, and T. Osborne, 1729), Book IV, Ch. 5, Sec. 9.

by our permission, on pain of being treated as pirates." The commentator says these general and indefinite prohibitions have no exception. They extend to commissions taken from friends or allies, as well as neutrals, and those that are equivocal: and they were considered as necessary consequences of the laws of neutrality.

"If, says Valin, the commission of the foreign prince be to cruize against *his enemies* who are *our allies, or those with whom we intend to preserve neutrality*, it would afford just ground of complaint on their part, and might lead to a rupture." [11] The rule extends as well to subjects domiciliated as not domiciliated in the kingdom, and foreign countries; "for Frenchmen are not the less Frenchmen, for having gone to live in foreign countries." [12] If France may rightfully prohibit her citizins from accepting foreign commissions to make prize of the property of her friends, why should the United States be *reproached* for exercising a similar right? A necessary consequence of this wise and just prohibition is, that all prizes taken contrary to it should be restored with damages to the party injured.

The third description of prizes restored, is where they have been fitted, and armed in the ports of the United States.

I find no direct, positive provision by the marine laws of France, prohibiting this; but the whole tenor of those laws suppose that vessels of war, are armed in the ports of the sovereign who give the commission. French privateers must not only fit out in a French port, but are bound to bring all prizes made by them into some particular port, or ports expressed in their commissions. Valin. 2 Vol. 276. And it is certain that the king of France, previous to his alliance with the United States, delivered up some American prizes, to the English, because the capturing vessel had been armed in a French port.[13]

11. Valin, *Nouveau Commentaire*, II, 236.
12. Valin, *Nouveau Commentaire*, II, 236.
13. On August 23, 1777, for example, Silas Deane wrote to Robert Morris: ". . . Soon after Mr. [William] Hodge's arrival, we bought a lugger at Dover, and sent her to Dunkirk. Mr. Hodge went after her, and equipped her with great secrecy, designing a blow in the North Sea. He sent Captain [Joseph] Cunningham in her, and ordered him to intercept the packet between England and Holland, and then to cruise northward toward the Baltic. Cunningham fell in with the packet in a day or two after leaving Dunkirk, and took her. As she had a prodigious number of letters on board, he imagined it was proper he should return to Dunkirk instead of continuing his course. In his return he also took a brig of some value, and brought both prizes into port.

Mr. Adet's memorial charges that the English have been permitted to arm their vessels, and bring their prizes into our ports.[14]

As to this charge, the fact is simply denied. In the cases mentioned,[15] the vessels said to have taken in guns for their defence, were gone, before he made his representation: yet he complained, and the government did nothing. I ask what could they have done? Mr. Adet will answer, they might have declared war, against Great Britain: and it is certain, this was the only remedy that remained, in such a case: but neither our interest, nor our duty would have permitted us to have adopted it. Our interest did not permit us to give up our neutrality, and engage in a foreign war, the event of which would have produced many and certain evils, and could not by any possibility have produced any good; and it was contrary to every principle by which a just nation would desire to act, to have made war on a whole people, because one or two of them had clandestinely taken arms on board for their defence, in one of our ports, without the knowledge of their government, or of ours.

The memorial complains that we have infringed the 17th article of the treaty of 1778, by restraining the prohibition therein contained only to the ships of war, and privateers of their enemies, who should come into our ports, *with their prizes.*

The literal sense of the 17th article, is, that no armed ship *who shall have made prizes* from the French people, shall receive an asylum in our ports.[16] The 22d article [17] says that no privateer, fitted

---

This spread the alarm far and wide, and gave much real ground of complaint, as he had been entirely armed and equipped in Dunkirk, and had returned thither with his prizes. The ministry, therefore, to appease England, ordered the prizes to be returned, and Cunningham and his crew to be imprisoned, which gave the English a temporary triumph" (Wharton, *Revolutionary Diplomatic Correspondence,* II, 380).

14. Adet wrote: "Not satisfied with permitting the 17th article of the treaty to be violated by its agents and tribunals, the Federal Government also suffered the English to seize upon the advantages interdicted to them by that article. They armed in the ports of the United States, brought in and repaired their prizes, and, in a word, found in them a certain asylum" (*ASP, Foreign Relations,* I, 580).

15. Adet wrote: ". . . the English privateer Trusty, Captain Hall, was armed at Baltimore, to cruise against the French, and sailed, notwithstanding the complaints of the consul of the republic. At Charleston, one Bermudian vessel, several English vessels, and one Dutch vessel, from the 24th of May, to the 6th of June, 1793, took in cannon for their defence, and sailed without opposition" (*ASP, Foreign Relations,* I, 580).

16. See H to Wolcott, November 9, 1796.

17. For the text of Article 22 (originally 24) of the Treaty of Amity and

under a commission of the enemy of either, shall have asylum in the ports of the other. Neither of these articles say any thing of prizes. The literal application of them therefore would exclude the capturing vessels, but give admission to their prizes; which would never have been the intention of the parties. The law of nations, expressly adopted by France, relative to the right of asylum, may illustrate these articles of the treaty. Ord. Louis XIV. art. XIV. declares, "That no prizes made by Captains under a foreign commission, shall remain in our ports, longer than twenty-four hours, unless detained by bad weather, or unless the prize shall have been made from our enemies." But this article, says Valin, is only applicable to prizes carried into a neutral port, "and not at all to armed vessels, whether neutrals or allies, who have taken refuge there, *without prizes*, either to escape the pursuit of enemies, or for any other cause. They may, in this case remain as long as they please." [18] By the law of neutrality, simply, French prizes could only have remained twenty-four hours in our ports, but by the treaty they have obtained the priviledge of remaining as long as they please. This privilege has not only been allowed them in its fullest extent, but we had gone a step further, and as a favor permitted them to sell their prizes, which neither the treaty nor the law of nations required; and which was of more importance than all the rest put together. This favor, as favors generally are, is now claimed as a right, and the withholding is considered as an injury. Let us see what the ordinances of the French marine have said on this point. Ord. Louis XIV Tit prises. Art. XV. "If in the prizes brought into our ports by vessels armed under a foreign commission, there be any merchandizes belonging to our subjects, *or allies*, those belonging to our subjects shall be restored, *and the rest shall not be put into any store house, or be purchased by any person under any pretext whatsoever.*" "And all this, says Valin, is founded on the law of neutrality." By the treaty of Utrecht, Louis XIV, and his grandson, the king of Spain, agreed mutually, to permit the prizes made by one to be brought in *and sold* in the ports of the other. But this the same author says, was only

---

Commerce between the United States and France of February 6, 1778, see H to Wolcott, November 3, 1796, note 5.

18. Valin, *Nouveau Commentaire*, II, 272–73.

a particular arrangement, so much the less to be proposed for a general rule, as the two nations had given up the duties on prize goods sold in their dominions; which however did not last long, on account of the abuses to which it gave rise.[19] Abuses similar, I presume, to those to which the same permission gave rise in this country.

The next ground of complaint is the British treaty and its consequences. This treaty is said to deprive France of all the advantages stipulated in a preceding treaty; and this is done by an abandonment of the modern law of nations.

If we may credit the declaration of the king of France, there were no exclusive advantages stipulated for France, in that treaty. His ambassador delivered a paper to the British court, dated the 13th of March 1778, wherein after announcing the treaty between France and the United States, he says, "His majesty declares at the same time, that the contracting parties have paid great attention *not to stipulate any exclusive advantages in favor of the French nation: and that the United States have reserved the liberty of treating with every other nation whatever, upon the same footing of equality and reciprocity.*" [20]

The injury supposed to have resulted from an abandonment of the modern public law, assumes two propositions, neither of which is true: 1st. That neutral ships make neutral property: 2d. That materials for building ships, are not among the articles considered as contraband of war. By the marine laws of France, *Reg. Dec.* 1744,[21] Art. 5, it is directed that "If there are found on board of neutral vessels, of whatever nation they may be, merchandizes or effects, belonging to the enemies of his majesty, they shall be good prize, even tho they are not of the growth or manufacture of the enemy's country; but the vessels shall be released." Previous to this regulation, and contrary to the law of nations, as Valin acknowledges, if either the ship or the cargo, or any part of it, was enemy's property, the whole was confiscated, by the laws of France."[22] And at this day,

19. Valin, *Nouveau Commentaire*, II, 275-76.
20. *The Annual Register, Or a View of the History, Politics, and Literature, For the Year 1778* (3rd ed., London, 1796), 299.
21. "Reglement, Concernant les prises faites sur mer, & la navigation des vaisseaux neutres pendant la guerre," October 21, 1744 (Valin, *Nouveau Commentaire*, II, 250-52).
22. Valin, *Nouveau Commentaire*, II, 252-54.

neutral property on board of enemy's ships, are, by the same laws, liable to confiscation.[23]

As to contraband of war, timber is enumerated among the articles that are so, by Vattel [24] Lib. III, chap. VII, but Valin is much more particular, 2 Vol. 264. "In the treaty of commerce concluded with the king of Denmark, the 23d of August, 1742, pitch and tar were declared contraband; *as also rosin, sail-cloth, hemp, cordage, masts and timber, for the building of ships.* There would have been, therefore, no reason to complain of the conduct of the English, if they had not violated particular treaties; *for of right (de droit) these things are contraband at present, and have been so, since the beginning of this century, which was not the case formerly.*" By the modern law of nations, expressly adopted by France, enemies property on board neutral ships is good prize; and by the same law, the number of contraband articles has been increased so as to include the materials for ship building. All the situations were probably foreseen, in which the treaty might operate favorably or unfavorably for France, at the time it was made. It might have been stipulated that materials for ship-building should be deemed contraband, instead of declaring that they should not; or, that the United States should not enter into any treaty in which they should be made so. Neither of these being the case, there is no ground of complaint, except *that the consequence is inconvenient,* at present, to France, and the belligerent powers allied to her. If timber and naval stores are contraband by the law of nations, to declare them to be so by a treaty, cannot be considered as a privilege granted to one nation, or as injury to any other. The French nation will not persist in asserting, that because the exercise of rights which she has claimed as legitimate on similar occasions, becomes inconvenient when exercised by others, she may therefore refuse to acknowledge and

23. Article 7 of the *Ordonnance de la Marine* of August, 1681, reads: "Tous navires qui se trouveront chargés d'effets appartenans à nos ennemis, & les marchandises de nos sujets ou alliés qui se trouveront dans un navire ennemi, seront pareillement de bon prise" (Valin, *Nouveau Commentaire,* II, 252). The part of this article allowing for the confiscation of neutral goods found in enemy ships was not repealed, and the same principle was restated in Article 14 (originally 16) of the Treaty of Amity and Commerce of February 6, 1778, between France and the United States (Miller, *Treaties,* II, 14–15).
24. Emeric de Vattel, *Law of Nations: or Principles of the Law of Nature: Applied to the Conduct and Affairs of Nations and Sovereigns* (London, 1759–1760).

respect them. This would be the language of an haughty despot, in a conquered country, not of justice, honor and good faith from one friend to another.

It is said that the 18th article of the treaty with Great-Britain,[25] suspends all the commercial relations between the United States and France, by preventing the supplies looked for by France from this country.

This article has not introduced any new case, in which provisions may be contraband; It only alters the consequence resulting from a seizure of them, when they are so. Valin (2 vol. 264) says, "By our law, and the law of nations, provisions are not prohibited, *except to places besieged or blockaded.*" The article complained of, says explicitly, that when provisions and other articles *not generally contraband*, are become so, *according to the existing law of nations*, and shall, *for that reason*, be seized, they shall not be confiscated, but the owners shall be completely indemnified, and receive besides a reasonable mercantile profit. This principle operated as an encouragement for American vessels to seek the French markets, by insuring them against loss, if they happened in any instance to be interrupted in the voyage—France, I presume, might consider our vessels bound with provisions to a place besieged or blockaded, liable to seizure, after due notice of the fact; if, instead of this, they contend for the privilege of paying for them according to the terms of the treaty with Great-Britain, I suppose it will not be denied to them. But, if *under pretence that a vessel is bound to a besieged or blockaded port,* when she is not, either France or Great Britain should seize or detain her, it is an injury not authorized by the treaty, or the law of nations. This is what both nations have done, when their interest or necessities required it—sometimes with, and often without any apology—and what they will often continue to do, I fear, as long as they know we cannot punish them for it.

These injuries are said to have been received while every object around reminds us of the tyranny of Britain and the generous Assistance of France, during the American war.

The generosity of France and the ingratitude of the United States have been often suggested by some of our own Citizens, and we are

25. For the text of Article 18 of the Jay Treaty, see "Remarks on the Treaty . . . between the United States and Great Britain," July 9-10, 1795, note 63.

now *reproached* with it by France herself. Gratitude is due for favors received; and this virtue may exist among nations as well as among individuals: but the motive of the benefit must be solely the advantage of the party on whom it was conferred, else it ceases to be a favor. There is positive proof that France did not enter into the alliance with us in 1778 *for our advantage;* but for her own. The whole course of the negociation, as well as a positive knowledge of the fact, proves this. She resisted all our solicitations for effectual assistance for near three years; and rose in her demands during the campaign of 1777, when our affairs presented the most threatening aspect. Memorials were presented in August and September of that year, while General Burgoyne was advancing from Canada, in a stile of importunity, proportioned to the danger we were in from a junction of the two armies; and they were received with increased coldness from the same cause.[26] But when the knowledge of the capture of Burgoyne's army arrived in December; fearing we might be able to do the business without them, the French Court began to change its tone. In January the British minister gave notice in the House of Commons, that he meant to propose terms of accomodation with America.[27] The French ministry, on the arrival of this in-

26. No record has been found that the United States commissioners in Paris, Silas Deane, Benjamin Franklin, and Arthur Lee, presented a memorial to the French court in August, 1777. In late September, however, the commissioners presented a memorial to Count Vergennes, the French Foreign Minister, in which they asked for a loan of fourteen million livres and recognition of American independence. On October 1, 1777, Arthur Lee noted in his diary: ". . . Mr. [Ferdinand Le] Grand [the intermediary] reported that Count Vergennes had not yet laid the memoire before the king . . . ; that he seemed to think the sum of fourteen millions of livres a great demand; that he talked of an alliance as a thing yet to be considered of; that it would involve all Europe, and assist us much less than we imagined" (Richard Henry Lee, *Life of Arthur Lee, LL.D.* [Boston, 1829], I, 335). Two days later, Le Grand reported that Vergennes could give no answer before he had consulted Spain. The commissioners appear to have heard nothing more until early December, when news reached Paris of Burgoyne's surrender at Saratoga on October 17, 1777. On December 6, Conrad-Aléxandre Gérard, Vergennes's first secretary, called on the American commissioners with congratulations and an invitation to renew their proposal for a Franco-American alliance. At the same time he promised a contribution of three million livres from Spain. The commissioners sent off their memorial on December 8 and resumed discussions, which were eventually to lead to an alliance on December 12, 1777 (Lee, *Life of Arthur Lee*, 336, 357–62).

27. This is a reference to Lord North's speeches in the parliamentary debate of December 10, 1777, on a motion made by John Wilkes in favor of granting the American colonies their independence from Great Britain. North

telligence in France, immediately pressed the conclusion of the treaty which they had resisted for three years, and proposed terms much more favorable for us, than those our Commissioners had offered, and they had refused three months before. The treaty was signed on the 8th February.[28] I perceive no generosity in all this. They did then, as we have done now, and as every discerning nation will do, they regarded only their own interest and advantage, and not that of any other nation. In the interval between the declaration of independence and the alliance, with France, that Court sometimes ordered away our privateers, and sometimes restored their prizes: They refused to receive an ambassador, or acknowledge our independence: All of which was for fear of bringing France prematurely into the war. The fact is, that the French spoke of very different terms, as the condition of their assistance, before the Capture of Burgoyne, from those actually agreed on afterwards. There can be no doubt, that our success on that occasion, and the disposition it appeared to have produced in the British ministry, were the immediate causes of that alliance. It was certainly the interest of the French to unite with America in the war against Great Britain. They therefore acted right in doing this at last, tho with too much refinement in putting it off so long; but it is not the interest of the United States to be engaged in any war whatsoever—much less do they desire to imbrue their hands in the blood of one nation, to gratify the hatred, or serve the interest of another. We have acted right hitherto, in laying it down as a principle, not to suffer ourselves to be drawn into the wars of Europe, and if we must have a war, I hope it will be for refusing to depart from this principle.

Our government has acted with firmness, consistency, and modera-

---

opposed the motion on the ground that it was "unseasonable, and ill-timed" but conceded that he would be ready to make peace in different circumstances, which must "arise out of the state of the war; from domestic situation; from the disposition of both countries" (*Parllamentary Register*, VIII, 143-44). When Wilkes contended that Great Britain "should lose nothing" by withdrawing from the war, North replied that "he did not yet despair of gaining America; and hoped to be in force, or have such a force, in the course of the ensuing campaign, as would enable us both to offer terms with dignity, and enforce an acceptance, should America refuse to listen to reasonable terms of accomodation, with success" (*Parliamentary Register*, VIII, 145).

28. The treaties of Amity and Commerce and of Alliance, as well as a secret treaty concerning Spain, were signed on February 6, 1778 (Miller, *Treaties*, II, 1-41).

tion, in repelling the unjust pretensions of the belligerent powers, as far as reason and argument could have weight. If it has not attempted, in every instance, to preserve our rights by force, wherein the remedy would have been worse than the disease, they have not yielded them by concession, in any instance. Into whosoever hands the administration of the government may now come, they are called on by the suggestions of a wise policy, and the voice of their country to pursue the same general line of conduct, that has been hitherto pursued, without yielding to the violence of party on either side.

They will then be sure of the approbation and support of the most virtuous, which it is hoped are the most numerous part, of all parties. On the contrary, if, departing from these principles, they unnecessarily involve their country in the horrors of war, they will meet the merited execration of good men, and in the end, the punishment justly due to such conduct, from an injured people.   AMERICANUS.

From Robert Morris [1]

Alexander Hamilton Esqr   Philada Decemr 8. 1796

Dear Sir

I intended to have sent you Bank notes. Disappointments which are in this City day by day happening have prevented, but the above draft of Joseph Higbie in favor of Garrett Cottringer for $1000 will be honored and you can have it discounted, so that I hope this Remittance will answer the Purpose and you will Credit me for the same.

I am truly Yrs   RM

J Higbies draft 8 Decr at 30 ds on Robinson & Hartshorne $1000.

LC, Robert Morris Papers, Library of Congress.

1. This letter concerns the payment of the balance of a debt which Morris owed to H. For an explanation of the transaction and for the identification of the individuals mentioned in this letter, see the introductory note to H to Morris, March 18, 1795. See also Morris to H, March 31, June 2, 23, 30, July 18, 20, 1795; June 17, 27–30, November 19, 1796.

From Oliver Wolcott, Junior

[Philadelphia, December 8, 1796]

Dr. Sir

I have recd. your Letter of Decr. 6th. The Warrant for the sum *due* to the Bank of New York [1] was issued punctually,[2] by some neglect or accident in the Treasurers Office, it remained undischarged. I have taken measures for the payment.

By a Letter from Mr. Wilkes [3] I find that the Bank claim a payment of Interest by way of *discount* and the 200.000 Dollars continued on Loan on the security of a deposit of Stock.[4] This was not understood by me, nor does it appear a reasonable condition, I will however take measures to prevent any disadvantage to the Bank from the misconception of what was their construction.

The Loan of 120.000 Dolls.[5] has really operated as an advance by the *Branch Bank,* & has been no other relief, than as it enabled me to assist the Bank *here* in a critical moment. These Institutions have all been mismanaged, I look upon them with terror, they [are] at present the curse, & I fear they will prove the ruin of the Government. Immense operations depend on a triffling Capital fluctuating between the Coffers of the different Banks; At present business in this City is on the point of stagnation.

I will thank you to inform the President of New York Bank or any other confidential person, that they may rest assured of as full & cordial assistance in any pressure of their affairs, as shall be in my power. I think however that they must principally rely on Sales of Stock, & in my opinion any sacrifice ought to be preferred to a continuance of temporary expedients. In the present state of the Treasy. anticipated payments are not practicable.

It is matter of importance that the proxies for electing Directors should not be placed in improper hands; some attention to this will be useful, if you find it convenient without exciting suspicions of Treasy. interference.

The Treasy. of N. York might have a number of Votes, which would be useful.

436   DECEMBER 1796

Perhaps intimations from the Bank of N York had best to come through you, they will be confidential.

The President will lay the correspondence with France since Genets time, before Congress.[6] A Letter is preparing by Colo. Pickering to Mr. Pinckney in answer to Adet.[7]

Tom Payne has published a book against the President [8] containing the most infamous calumnies: it is a systematical measure of France to destroy the publick confidence in the Friends of Govt. or *"Washington Faction."* The question whether our Commerce is or is not to be attacked, depends intirely on the Military operations in Germany & Italy.

If you will part with the Reports of the British Comrs. of Accts.[9] I shall be glad to purchase them. The 1st Volo. is with you the 2d. & 3d. are here. I shall be glad to have the book soon with a bill including Gallatins work.[10]

Yrs. with truth   Oliv Wolcott
                                                  Decr. 8. 96

A Hamilton Esq

ALS, Hamilton Papers, Library of Congress; copy, Connecticut Historical Society, Hartford.

1. For the loan from the Bank of New York, see H to Wolcott, August 5, 1796.
2. Warrant No. 6608 for two hundred thousand dollars "For the amount of a loan, made by the Bank to the United States, on the 8th of October 1794" was issued to the Bank of New York on October 8, 1796 (D, signed by Charles Wilkes, RG 217, Miscellaneous Treasury Accounts, 1790–1894, Account No. 8300, National Archives). Warrant No. 6609 for ten thousand dollars "For interest for twelve months, from 8th Octr 1795 to 8 Octr 1796 at Five ℔ Cent ℔ Annum, on a loan of Two hundred thousand Dollars . . ." was issued to the Bank of New York on the same day (D, signed by Charles Wilkes, RG 217, Miscellaneous Treasury Accounts, 1790–1894, Account No. 8294, National Archives).
3. Charles Wilkes was cashier of the Bank of New York.
4. See H to Wolcott, August 5, 1796.
5. After paying the two hundred thousand dollars due to the Bank of New York on October 8, 1796, the United States used the remainder of the loan of three hundred and twenty thousand dollars obtained from the Bank of New York (H to Wolcott, August 5, 1796) to pay one hundred and twenty thousand dollars to the Bank of the United States. This payment represented the second installment of the principal of four hundred thousand dollars which had been borrowed from the Bank of the United States in 1792 in pursuance of Section 16 of "An Act for raising a farther sum of money for the protection of the frontiers, and for other purposes therein mentioned" (1 *Stat.* 262 [May 2, 1792]). See George Washington to H, May 7, 1792; "Agreement with the President, Directors, and Company of the Bank of the United States," May 25,

1792. See also "Report on Foreign Loans. Supplementary Statement Showing the Sums Borrowed in the United States," January 10, 1793. On January 2, 1797, Joseph Nourse, the register of the Treasury, wrote: ". . . I also Certify that there was paid on Account of said Loan the 18 August 1796 One hundred and twenty thousand Dollars being the Amount of Warrant No. 6412 . . . Leaving a Balance due to the Bank of the United States on the 31 December 1796 of One hundred and eighty thousand Dollars which Balance was discharged on the Day . . ." (D, signed by Nourse, RG 217, Miscellaneous Treasury Accounts, 1790–1894, Account No. 8508, National Archives).

6. Washington sent this material to Congress on January 19, 1797 (*Annals of Congress*, VI, 1914, 2711-69). Washington's enclosing letter and the accompanying documents are also printed in *ASP, Foreign Relations*, I, 559–776.

7. This letter, which is dated January 16, 1797, is printed in *ASP, Foreign Relations*, I, 559-776.

8. Thomas Paine, *Letter to George Washington, President of the United States of America. On Affairs Public and Private* (Philadelphia: Printed by Benjamin Franklin Bache, No. 112 Market Street, 1796).

9. *The Reports of the Commissioners for Taking, Examining and Stating the Public Accounts, With the Appendixes Complete*, Volume 1 by William Molleson, Volumes 2 and 3 by John Lane (London: T. Cadell, 1783–1787). These reports had originally been issued as four separate pamphlets published annually in London from 1711 through 1714.

10. Albert Gallatin, *A Sketch of the Finances of the United States* (New York: Printed by William A. Davis, No. 438 Pearl Street, 1796). The book was published on November 16, 1796.

From Stephen Higginson

Boston Decr 9. 1796

Dr Sir

Your Letter of 28 of last month [1] I received, & communicated its contents to some of our Electors. a majority of them were at first inclined to throw away their Votes from Mr Pinckney lest he should rise above Adams; [2] but your information as to Vermont; [3] with some observations made to them shewing the danger of so doing decided all but three, who were determined upon interested & personal motives to waste theirs. several hours were spent in discussion before they voted, the result was 16 for Adams, 13 for Pinckney, 2 for Governor Johnston [4] & 1 for Mr Elsworth.[5] Several of Adams's particular friends were very busy to induce those three to stand firm. They are extremely alarmed for his safety & not without reason. if the other NE: States have been united for Adams & P:, as I expect, the latter will probably get sufficient seperate Votes in the middle & southern States to bring him in; & if Jeffersons friends shall have despaired of his election before the day, they may give many Votes to Pinckney to exclude Adams, in which case he may have a large majority. what then is to be done? Mr Adams & many of his friends will be very clamorous, They will swear the union of Pinckney with him was a trick to prevent his election; & many of Us here shall never again be upon terms with him, he will never forgive our not being willing to hazard all to serve him. his disposition will not brooke the disappointed; & he may be hurried by his temper to break with every one who preferred the public to him.

Should he fail, which I expect, some attempts should be made to conciliate & appease him, or serious inconveniences may result. It may be well for you & Govr. Jay with the president &c to contemplate the Event & arrange for it. Your Judge Smith [6] sent Letters to some of our Electors, & I believe to Newhampshire, soliciting Votes for Burr very strongly, & rather pressing for Jefferson. Mr Holton [7] recd. one from him, & I believe Mr. Gerry [8] also; but Holton was so circumstanced he could make no attempts in favour of Burr, who will not have one Vote I presume in NE: We have yet no accounts from New hampshire, Rhode Island or Connecticut.

Should Pinckney be elected care must be taken early to guard him against Adet &c, who have strong hopes, I know, of attaching him to their Views & party. This will remain with you in the middle States to effect.

With much respect I am Sir yours &c   Stephen Higginson

ALS, Hamilton Papers, Library of Congress.
1. Letter not found, but see H to ———, November 8, 1796.
2. This is a reference to the fear among some Federalists that Thomas Pinckney might receive more electoral votes in 1796 than John Adams. See Robert G. Harper to H, November 4, 1796; Oliver Wolcott, Jr., to H, November 6, 1796; H to ———, November 8, 1796; H to Jeremiah Wadsworth, November 8, December 1, 1796.
3. See H to Wadsworth, December 1, 1796, note 4.
4. Samuel Johnston was elected governor of North Carolina in 1787 and resigned in 1789 to become a United States Senator. He served in the Senate until March 3, 1793.
5. Oliver Ellsworth of Connecticut was Chief Justice of the United States.
6. Melancton Smith.
7. In addition to being a Presidential elector, Samuel Holten had been a member of the House of Representatives from Massachusetts from 1793 to 1795 and was appointed judge of the Probate Court for Essex County in 1796.
8. Elbridge Gerry was a leading Massachusetts politician who had been a member of the House of Representatives from 1789 to 1793.

Federal Republican [1]

[New York, December 12, 1796]

FOR THE MINERVA.
TO THE CITIZENS OF NEW-YORK.

FELLOW CITIZENS,

ELECTIONS in Republics are always of importance. The approaching one may with truth be said to be peculiarly so. No one can

The [New York] *Minerva, & Mercantile Evening Advertiser,* December 12, 1796.

1. This article was designed as campaign literature for the congressional election in New York City on December 13, 14, and 15, 1796. The Republican candidate was Edward Livingston, who was serving his first term in the House of Representatives. Livingston's nomination was little more than a formality, and it was made at "a respectable meeting of a number of Citizens at Hunter's Hotel" on November 29, 1796 (*The* [New York] *Argus. Greenleaf's New Daily Advertiser,* November 30, 1796). A few days later the Federalists selected their candidate. "At a numerous and respectable meeting" on December 2, 1796, Federalist leaders "resolved with only two dissenting voices, that JAMES WATSON be supported at the ensuing election . . ." (*The* [New York] *Minerva, & Mercantile Evening Advertiser,* December 3, 1796). Watson, a New York merchant, had represented New York City in the New York Assembly in 1791, 1794, and 1795, was speaker of the Assembly in 1794, and at the time of his nomination was a member of the New York Senate.

The three-day election was accompanied by a spirited and sometimes scurrilous battle in the newspapers supporting the rival candidates. The article printed above appeared on election eve.

Not only was H the leading Federalist polemicist, but he also personally directed his party's campaign. According to one newspaper, ". . . Mr. Hamilton does not confine his attention to any ward in particular. He patroles the whole city and strains every nerve in favor of the yankey candidate, ne quid res publica detrimente capiat" (*The* [New York] *Argus. Greenleaf's New Daily Advertiser,* December 15, 1796). The numerous references to H which appeared in the city's newspapers suggest that he rather than Watson was running for office, and as Watson's prospects of election dimmed, some Federalists made a last-minute effort to drop him and to nominate H. The *Argus* reported: "At a Meeting of Citizens at A. Moore's in Chatham Street, on Tuesday evening the 13th December, 1796, for the purpose of nominating a suitable person to represent this city and county in Congress, the following resolutions were adopted:

"Resolved, as the opinion of this meeting, That the present juncture of the political and commercial affairs of this country, is the most critical of any ever experienced by the citizens of the United States; and that none but a man of *literary abilities,* deserves their suffrages as a representative in Congress.

"Resolved, therefore, That *Alexander Hamilton, Esq.* from his talents, integrity, and Republican spirit, is better calculated to represent this city and

doubt that the steady and prosperous course of our government, hitherto is very much owing to the well deserved weight and influence of the excellent and beloved patriot, who now fills the presidential chair, and is shortly to quit it. If our best hopes are realized, as to his successor, the state of parties forbids us to expect that he will possess the universal confidence which has enabled his predecessor to stem the torrent of faction, and keep the vessel of state upright. It is then, evidently, of far greater importance than it has heretofore been, that the legislative department shall be well composed, and particularly that there shall be a majority in the House of Representatives, of a character truly *American*, unequivocally attached to the constitution of our country, resolved to execute the government with fairness, and to pursue under all circumstances, a course of measures, conducive to the true interest of our nation, unbiassed and unwarped by *foreign influence* or *menace*. In this great and essential object, all lesser considerations should be lost.

Two candidates are presented to our choice, *James Watson*, and *Edward Livingston*. Let us see who of them has the best title. Mr. Watson served his country with reputation, in the army during our war with Great Britain. Mr. Livingston was too young to take any part. Mr. Watson has been repeatedly elected in our state legislature, and has conducted himself with prudence. Mr. Livingston began his public career, as a member of Congress, at its last session, and it was marked with extreme temerity and impropriety. With a total disregard of that modesty, which is one of the best criterions of merit in a young man, and even a duty in an inexperienced young man, he set out with attempting a flagrant inroad upon the constitution of his country—one which if it had not been defended by the firmness of the President and the good sense of the people, would have precipitated us into incalculable evils.[2] Every step of this extraordinary transaction was marked with impropriety. If he was

---

county in Congress, than *James Watson*, at this alarming crisis; and that it be seriously recommended to the true Federal Republicans in this city, to support him with all their interest." (*The* [New York] *Argus. Greenleaf's New Daily Advertiser*, December 14, 1796.)

H was not nominated, and Livingston was re-elected by a margin of 550 in a total vote of 4,174.

2. This is a reference to Livingston's role in the debate in the House of Representatives on the implementation of the Jay Treaty. See the introductory note to H to George Washington, March 7, 1796.

even resolved to participate in the attempt, it was arrogant and unbecoming in him to take the lead. These were plain symptoms that he had not even acted in due concert with the party, with which he had inlisted; for though they came into the measure, they pursued it on ground differently from that which he had taken.³ His manner of conducting the thing was in other respects exceptionable; characterised by virulent and disgusting exclamations against men who (if they had even erred as he pretended in the measure he combated) had acquired from the uniform tenor of their public and private life, a title to *decent treatment* at least, and by a manifest spirit of hostility to THAT MAN who has merited and has obtained the love and veneration of all good citizens. When Mr. Livingston's immediate constituents, and with unexampled unanimity by their memorial to the House of Representatives expressed their sense to him against the course he was pursuing ⁴—did he take this sense as a guide? Did he pursue the maxim which the leaders of the party have constantly in their mouth, viz. that the Representative ought to be governed by the sense of his constituents? No such thing—he superciliously persisted to the last in opposing a provision for the treaty. Thus his conduct on the opening of his political career, may justly be denominated, assuming, rash, foolish, intemperate and obstinate.

In the comparison therefore of services, Mr. *Watson* has positive merit—Mr. Livingston not only no positive merit but positive demerit.

In the comparison of other qualifications, the advantage is full on the side of Mr. *Watson*. If Mr. Livingston has some outside showey talents, they are more than counterbalanced by the good sense and discretion, knowlege of business and of commerce, maturity of years and experience of Mr. Watson.

Mr. Watson is also a man of republican principles, *manners* and *habits* Let all who have eyes judge for themselves how this description will apply to Mr. Livingston—*His democracy, if genuine, is at least more at its ease in a coach.*

If we advert to private character, that of Mr. *Watson* in a reli-

3. See the introductory note to H to Washington, March 7, 1796.
4. This is a reference to a petition adopted on April 19, 1796, by those New Yorkers who objected to the attempt by Republicans in the House of Representatives to block appropriations for the Jay Treaty. See H to Rufus King, April 20, 1796, note 3.

gious and moral sense will stand the test. I leave that of Mr. Livingston to the observation and judgment of his fellow-citizens.

One point I must however more particularly touch. To prejudice Mr. Watson it is alleged that he has made his fortune by speculation. This word speculation is of very vague and indefinite meaning. Every merchant is a *speculator* by the nature of his calling. Is he therefore a bad man? But be all that as it may, one thing is certain— that if Mr. Watson has been a speculator, Mr. Livingston has also been one, and the objection if it means any thing lies against one candidate equally with the other. Here the account is balanced.

But what turns the scale decidedly in favor of Mr. Watson, is his uniform attachment to the constitution and government of his country. Tho known to entertain sentiments friendly to the French revolution, without approving its excesses, he has never been disposed to sacrifice the peace and interest of the country to France— nor is there any danger that he will ever consent to sacrifice the rights and honor of the country to any foreign nation, whether a kingdom or a republic. It is a further consideration in his favor that he is a man free from pecuniary embarrassment and under no temptation from this cause to betray his trust. In choosing a man for an important public station, it is no objection to him that he is not rich. But if he be deeply embarrassed with debt, and withal has habits of expense, it is a very serious objection to him. It may expose his virtue to a severe trial. The example of a certain ex-*secretary* is a warning to us in this particular.[5]   FEDERAL REPUBLICAN

5. This is a reference to the charges made against Secretary of State Edmund Randolph in August, 1795. See Oliver Wolcott, Jr., to H, July 30, September 26, 1795.

[*To the Citizens of New-York*] [1]

[New York, December 13, 1796]

The [New York] *Argus. Greenleaf's New Daily Advertiser*, December 27, 1796.
1. In reprinting this handbill signed by "A True American," the *Argus* stated that on December 13, 1796, "three thousand of the following hand-bill were slily pushed under the knockers and doors of the citizens under cover of

the darkness of the night." The *Argus* suggests, but does not categorically state, that H wrote this handbill. No other evidence has been found that H was its author.

In the same issue the *Argus* reprinted a second handbill, which was signed by "A Real Whig" and was distributed on December 14, 1796, along with the suggestion that H may have been its author also.

From Luke Codwise [1]

New York, December 15, 1796. "Mr. J W Delaney [2] & myself having made a settlement of our Accounts you will please discontinue the Suit commenced against him on my Account." [3]

ALS, Hamilton Papers, Library of Congress.
1. Codwise was a New York sea captain.
2. John William Delaney was a New York merchant.
3. As captain of the brig *Glasgow*, Codwise left New York on November 25, 1795, for a voyage to the West Indies. On July 22, 1796, when he was returning to New York by way of Port-au-Prince, a French privateer captured his vessel and took it into Leogane where the cargo was confiscated and Codwise was imprisoned. On September 28, with six other American captains, he escaped from Leogane on board the ship *Union*, Samuel Davis master, which took him to Rhode Island (*The* [New York] *Minerva, & Mercantile Evening Advertiser,* November 15, 16, 1796). Part of the confiscated cargo (three hundred and ninety-nine barrels of herring and some tobacco, which Codwise had acquired in the West Indies) had belonged to Delaney, and it was apparently Delaney's refusal to make good the loss which caused Codwise to bring suit against him.

On November 4, 1796, the *Minerva* printed a list of "vessels belonging to New-York" which had been "captured and carried into Leogane." In this list was the following entry: "Brig Glasgow, Z. Godwish of New-York, detained 65 days; 1 seamen dead, 2 abandoned."

For the dispute between Codwise and Delaney, see H's Law Register, 1795–1804 (D, partially in H's handwriting, New York Law Institute, New York City).

To William Cooper [1]

[New York, December 16, 1796]

Dr. Sir

I have received your letter with a Post note of a thousand dollars on account of the Mortgage of the lands formerly *Holkers* in which Mr. Church is interested.[2] The papers respecting this affair in my possession will be looked up & sent to Mr. Laurance³ by Mondays Post. This letter will serve you as a Receipt. Yrs. truly

A Hamilton

N Y   December 16. 1796

William Cooper Esqr

ALS, from a typescript furnished by an anonymous donor.

1. Cooper, the founder of Cooperstown, New York, was appointed judge of the Court of Common Pleas for Otsego County on February 17, 1791. He served as a Federalist member of the House of Representatives from March 4, 1795, to March 3, 1797, and again from March 4, 1799, to March 3, 1801.

For background to this letter, see H to John Chaloner, June 11, 1793. See also Thomas FitzSimons to H, March 21, July 14, December 17, 1795.

2. Under the date of December 12, 1796, H made the following entry in his Cash Book, 1795–1804: "Cash Dr. to John B Church for this sum received Wm. Cooper on acct of his Mortgage on Holkers estate   1000" (AD, Hamilton Papers, Library of Congress).

3. John Laurance purchased land in partnership with Church and H. See H to Robert Troup, July 25, 1795, note 17; "John B. Church's Account with Alexander Hamilton," June 15, 1797.

To Rufus King

New York Decr. 16. 1796

I have received, my dear Sir, your several letters of the 25 of August 10 & 11th. of Septr. You know my sentiments towards you too well to ascribe my delay in answering them to any other cause than the imperiousness of avocations with which I could not dispense.

Public opinion, taking the Country at large, has continued since you left us to travel on in a right direction, and, I trust, will not easily deviate from it. You will have seen before this reaches you Mr. Adet's communications.[1] We conjecture, as to the timing of them, that they were intended to influence the election of President by the apprehension of War with France. We suppose also they are designed in the same way to give support to the partizans of France and that they have for eventual object the placing things in such a state, as will leave France at liberty to slide easily either into a renewal of cordiality or an *actual* or *virtual* war with the U States. If the war of Europe continues, the efforts of France will be likely to be levelled as a primary object against the Commerce and Credit of Great Britain and to injure these she may think is adviseable, to make war upon our Trade forgetting perhaps that the consequence may be to turn it more intirely into the channels of Great Britain. These reflections will be obvious to you. I only make them to apprize you of the view which is taken of the subject here. Thus far appearances do not indicate that the purpose of influencing this Country has been obtained. I think in the main the effect has been to impress the necessity of adhering more firmly to the Government.

You need not be told that every exertion, not degrading to us, will be made to preserve peace with France. Many of the opposite party, however they may be pleased with appearances of ill humour in France, will not wish it to go the length of War. And we shall endeavour to avoid it, in pursuance of our general plan of preserving peace with all the World. Yet you may depend that we shall not submit to be dictated to or to be forced into a departure from our plan of neutraily, unless to repel an attack upon us.

Our anxiety has been extreme on the subject of the Election for President. If we may trust our information, which there is every reason to trust, it is now decided that neither *Jefferson* nor *Burr* can be President. It must be either *Adams* or *Pinckney*, the *first most probably*. By the throwing away of votes in New England lest *Pinkney* should outrun *Adams*, it is not unlikely that Jefferson will be *Vice* President. The event will not a little mortify *Burr*. Virginia has given him only one Vote.

It was to be expected of course that the Senates answer to the Presidents speech [2] would be flattering to him. But the result in the house of representatives has been better than was expected. An address which I have not yet seen but stated by our friends to be a very good one has passed the house with only twelve dissentients consisting of the most fiery spirits.[3] The address is not only *generally complimentary* to the President but includes, it is said, an *explicit approbation of his administration*—which caused the division.[4] Edward Livingston is in the minority.

After giving you these consolatory accounts, I am now to dash the Cup a little, by telling you that *Livingston* is in all probability reelected in the City. The principal cause has been an *unacceptable* candidate on our part, *James Watson*.[5] There were four Gentlemen who would certainly have succeeded but neither of them would accept. In *Watson* we could not unite opinions. He was more *disagreeable* than I had supposed to a large body of our friends—and yet after the declining of the four persons alluded to we could not do otherwise than support him. For he had gotten a strong hold on most of the leading Mechanics who act with us.

But in the state at large we shall better our representation, and I hope for a majority in the next house of Representatives. As an omen of this, there are several *new members* in Congress from different states, who hitherto vote with our friends.

The favourable change in the conduct of Great Britain towards us strengthens the hand of the friends of Order & peace. It is much to be desired that a Treatment, in all respects unexceptionable from that quarter, should obviate all pretext to inflame the public mind.

We are labouring hard to establish in this country principles more and more *national* and free from all *foreign ingredients*—so that we may be neither "*Greeks nor Trojans*" but truly Americans. Adieu

Affectly Yrs. A Hamilton

Rufus King Esq

ALS, New-York Historical Society, New York City.

1. Pierre Auguste Adet to Timothy Pickering, October 27, November 15, 1796 (*ASP, Foreign Relations*, I, 576–77, 579–83). See also H to Oliver Wolcott, Jr., November 1, 1796; George Washington to H, November 2, 3, 21, 1796; H to Washington, November 4, 5, 11, 19, 1796; Wolcott to H, November 17, 1796.

2. H is referring to Washington's eighth annual message to Congress, which was delivered on December 7, 1796 (*Annals of Congress*, VI, 1591–97; LC, George Washington Papers, Library of Congress). For H's role in the preparation of this message, see "Draft of George Washington's Eighth Annual Address to Congress," November 10, 1796. The Senate's reply, adopted on December 10, is printed in *Annals of Congress*, VI, 1520–21.

3. The answer of the House of Representatives to Washington's annual message was approved by a vote of 67 to 12 (*Annals of Congress*, VI, 1667). The answer was presented to the President on December 16, 1796 (*Annals of Congress*, VI, 1673–74).

Attached to this letter is a clipping from *The* [New York] *Minerva, & Mercantile Evening Advertiser*, December 17, 1796, giving an account of the proceedings in the House of Representatives on December 15. The clipping reads: "On the question being about to be put on the answer as amended, Mr. [Thomas] Blount [of North Carolina] said he wished the Yeas and Nays might be again taken that posterity might see that he was not consenting to this address. The question was carried by 67 to 12. The Noes were Messrs.

Blount, [Isaac] Coles [of Virginia], [William B.] Giles [of Virginia], [Christopher] Greenup [of Kentucky], [James] Holland [of North Carolina], A[ndrew] Jackson [of Tennessee], [Edward] Livingston [of New York], [Matthew] Locke [of North Carolina], W[illiam] Lyman [of Massachusetts], [Samuel] Maclay [of Pennsylvania], [Nathaniel] Macon [of North Carolina], and [Abraham B.] Venable [of Virginia]."

4. For the debate in the House on the answer to Washington's annual message, see *Annals of Congress*, VI, 1603–07, 1611–75.

5. See "Federal Republican," December 12, 1796.

To Herman LeRoy, William Bayard, and James McEvers

New York, December 16, 1796. Discusses the Holland Land Company's interest in Robert Morris's proposed negotiations with the Seneca Indians.[1]

ALS, Gemeentearchief Amsterdam, Holland Land Company. These documents were transferred in 1964 from the Nederlandsch Economisch-Historisch Archief, Amsterdam.

1. LeRoy, Bayard, and McEvers were partners in a New York City mercantile firm which represented the Holland Land Company in the United States.

H wrote this letter in his capacity as an attorney for the six Dutch banking firms which formally organized as the Holland Land Company on February 13, 1796.

The treaty to be negotiated concerned approximately four million acres of land in New York which Morris had acquired from Massachusetts in 1791. The Massachusetts claim to these lands, which went back to the 1620 charter of the Plymouth Company, was settled in 1786 by an agreement between Massachusetts and New York. Under this agreement, Massachusetts was given the preemption rights (that is, the right to purchase the title to the land from the Indians), while New York was given all governmental rights over the lands in question (see H's "Notes on the History of North and South America," December, 1786; "Defence of the Funding System," July, 1795, note 34; H to Morris, March 18, 1795, note 29). Thus, in 1791, Morris purchased not the land but rather the right of Massachusetts to deal with the Indians for this land. Morris sold about 3.6 million acres of this tract to the Holland Land Company. The company retained £37,500 of the purchase money until Morris secured the Indian title and completed the necessary surveys.

From 1791 to 1795, warfare prevented any settlement, and in 1795, when peace was restored by the Treaty of Greenville, Morris lacked the necessary funds to treat with the Indians. Accordingly, the Holland Land Company advanced him £9,000 out of the £37,500 retained to begin the negotiations. The Holland Land Company desired the treaty, for it could not sell the lands purchased from Morris until the Indian title had been extinguished. Morris wanted the Indians to relinquish their title so that he could use his lands west of the Holland Land Company's purchase to secure or pay some of his numerous debts.

On March 2, 1797, George Washington sent the following letter to the Senate: "Application has been made to me, to permit a treaty to be held with the Seneca nation of Indians, to effect the purchase of a parcel of their land under a pre-emption right derived from the State of Massachusetts, and situated within the State of New York, and it appearing to me reasonable that such opportunity should be afforded, provided the negotiation shall be conducted at the expense of the applicant, and at the desire and with the consent of the Indians; always considering these as prerequisites, I now nominate Isaac Smith, to be a Commissioner to hold a treaty with the Seneca nation, for the aforesaid purpose" (*Executive Journal*, I, 229). On the following day the Senate approved Smith's nomination, but Smith declined the appointment, and Jeremiah Wadsworth was appointed in his place (*ASP, Indian Affairs*, 1, 626). Smith was a Federalist member of the House of Representatives from New Jersey from 1795 to 1797 and an associate justice of the New Jersey Supreme Court from 1777 to 1804.

Negotiations with the Seneca Indians began on August 28, 1797, and an agreement was signed on September 15, 1797. Morris, who did not attend the negotiations, was represented by his son Thomas. The Indians agreed to sell to Morris the lands in question (except for some reserved lands or reservations) for one hundred thousand dollars, which was to be invested in stock of the Bank of the United States. The treaty, or more accurately, the agreement, is entitled "Contract entered into, under the sanction of the United States of America, between Robert Morris and the Seneca Nations of Indians" and is printed in *ASP, Indian Affairs*, I, 627.

For background to this letter and for other relevant documents, see forthcoming Goebel, *Law Practice*, III.

To Stephen Higginson

[*New York, December 20, 1796.* On January 12, 1797, Higginson wrote to Hamilton: "Your Letter of 20 of last month I have received." *Letter not found.*]

To Oliver Wolcott, Junior

[New York, December 21, 1796]

Dr. Sir

I did not understand by your letter of the 17th. of November whether you meant or not to authorise the immediate commencement of the sale of Stock.[1] If you think this measure will become indispensable, it may be well to anticipate the execution; though indeed sales of Stock are at this juncture nearly impracticable. Yet I imagine it will be agreeable to the Bank to have permission to anticipate.

A very prudent letter has lately been written by the President of the Bank of the U States [2] to the Office of Discount here, among other things, advising a *reduction* of the ballance due from the Bank of NYork to 100000 Dollars.[3] This letter, which in my opinion leaves, as it ought to do, to the Directors of the Office here discretion to execute the idea with due regard to circumstances, has however been construed by them in too peremptory a light—and accordingly they have drawn from the Bank of New York pretty rapidly 150000 Dollars—which begets an apprehension that subsequent calls may be equally rapid, and exciting fear and jealousy is likely to produce too sudden a retrenchment of the business of the Bank of New York, and as the Office, being confined as they suppose to discounting twice their capital cannot by increased accommodations fill the void, there is danger of stagnating & convulsing the business of the City so as to give a shock to Credit. The Direction here are sensible of the danger, but several of them take the intimation from Philadelphia in too strict a sense—& cannot resolve to alleviate the apprehensions of the Bank of New York.

Though this Bank of NY has reduced and is reducing its discounts, there are circumstances of the moment which continue to incline the ballance in favour of the Office, but it is easy to see, taking in the payments of the Government in February, that there will be a natural change and consequently it is every way imprudent to force them.

If the last loan of the Bank of New York to Government had no other use than that which you hint,[4] this still was very important. And it is interesting all round that a disposition should exist to repeat similar accommodations. But you easily see how cautious & disaffected spirits are armed against it when they can say "We told you that you would embarrass yourself by your loan to Government" & in truth if this had not been made the Bank of New York would now stand on high ground.

Pray interpose with Mr. Willing to obtain an explanatory letter leaving more clearly the *time* & *manner* of accomplishing the Reduction of the present Ballance to their discretion.

I will say nothing more of any anticipated payment—but if this were practicable to the extent of 50 or 100000 Dollars it would be consolatory to the Directors & leave the residue more to your convenience.

Dont derive from this letter any source of alarm. Every thing is sound with both Banks here. I know the state of both. But there is danger that *fear* and *jealousy* in the Directors of the Bank of New York may produce evil which it is unnecessary to hazard.[5]

I shall send you the first opportunity the volume of Reports of Comrs.[6]

Yrs. truly   A Hamilton

PS Mr Caleb Brewster is a candidate for the Office of first Mate in the Revenue Cutter here. I remember he rendered very meritorious services in the War [7] & I am told has been bred a seamen. In these respects he has a good claim. His character otherwise is not known to me. But if it affords no objection I think he will be an eligible man.

It is said Walker [8] is to resign. In this case Jonathan Burrall [9] wishes to succeed. There cannot you know be a more fit man & he will be intirely acceptable here.

Ol Wolcot Junr Esq

ALS, Connecticut Historical Society, Hartford.
  1. Although Wolcott wrote to H on November 17, 1796, his letter dealt with foreign affairs rather than banking matters. On the other hand, Wolcott did write to H concerning the Bank of New York on December 8, 1796.
  2. Thomas Willing.
  3. See H to Wolcott, December 6, 1796, note 2; Wolcott to H, December 8, 1796.
  4. See Wolcott to H, December 8, 1796, notes 1 and 5.
  5. In the margin opposite this paragraph H wrote: "I wish to see your report on Direct taxes." This report, which is dated December 14, 1796, is printed in *ASP, Finance,* I, 414–41.
  6. See Wolcott to H, December 8, 1796, note 9.
  7. Brewster, an ensign in the Fourth New York Regiment at the outset of the American Revolution, was appointed a captain lieutenant in the Continental Artillery on June 23, 1780.
  8. Benjamin Walker was the naval officer for the port of New York. For additional information on Walker's activities, see Robert Morris to H, April 27, 1796.
  9. During the American Revolution, Burrall had been assistant to the paymaster general of the Continental Army, assistant paymaster general, and deputy paymaster general. From 1786 to 1789 he was commissioner for settling the accounts of the quartermaster and commissary general departments. In 1792 he became cashier of the New York Office of Discount and Deposit of the Bank of the United States.

To Oliver Wolcott, Junior

[New York, December 23, 1796]

My Dear Sir

I wrote to you two days ago on the subject of obtaining an instruction from the Bank of the U States to the Direction of the Office here to prevent a speedy repetition of their call on the Bank of New York. This Bank has so large a proportion of its whole Capital in the power of the Office that if it be not tranquillized on the subject of demands from that quarter, it will be driven to such violent operations as cannot fail to convulse Credit & among other evils prevent the collection of the Revenues. The danger is urgent & a prompt explanation is essential.

The situation of the Bank of NYork is no doubt materially owing to the prolongation of the old & the new loan to Government.[1] Its Capital is 900,000 Dollars—its discount 1600000. Here is certainly no imprudence.[2]

Many of the Merchants here are anxious for an accommodation for the duties similar to that which I upon certain trying occasions made.[3] I know not what is possible on your part.

Yrs. truly   A Hamilton
Decr. 23. 1796

O Wolcot Jun. Esq

ALS, Connecticut Historical Society, Hartford.

1. The "old" loan was one of two hundred thousand dollars which the Bank of New York made to the United States in 1794. See Wolcott to H, June 28, 1796; H to Wolcott, August 5, 1796, note 2.

For information on the "new" loan, which was for three hundred and twenty thousand dollars, see H to Wolcott, August 5, 1796; Wolcott to H, December 8, 1796, notes 2 and 5.

2. Section 9 of "An Act to Incorporate the Stockholders of the Bank of New-York," which was passed March 21, 1791, reads in part: "That the total amount of the debts which the said corporation shall, at any time owe, whether by bond, bill, note, or other contract, over and above the monies then actually deposited in the bank, shall not exceed three times the sum of the capital stock subscribed, and actually paid into the bank . . ." (*New York Laws*, 14th Sess., Ch. XXXVII).

3. One such occasion was the spring of 1792. See H to William Seton, March 19, 1792.

To Oliver Wolcott, Junior

New York December 28. 1796

Dear Sir

I received yesterday your's by Post,[1] which I communicated immediately to the Directors of both Banks, that is, so much as concerned each party. It has been very consolatory to the Bank of New York & will do good. All will be well.

Mr. Alexander McComb [2] applied, while I was in Office, respecting some land he & Edgar [3] had purchased of the Public and on which they had made a partial payment which by the terms of sale was forfieted.[4] I remember my opinion was under all the circumstances that it was proper for the government to give relief, either by a grant of a quantity of land equitably equivalent to the payment or by restitution of the Circumstances. I will thank you, as far your leisure will permit and your judgment correspond, to pay attention to the subject.

Yrs. truly   A Hamilton

Oliver Wolcott Jun Esq

ALS, Connecticut Historical Society, Hartford.

1. Letter not found. See H to Wolcott, December 6, 21, 23, 1796; Wolcott to H, December 8, 1796.
2. Macomb was a New York City merchant and land speculator.
3. William Edgar was a New York City merchant. Edgar and Macomb had settled before the American Revolution in Detroit where they became traders and land speculators. During the American Revolution they became partners with Macomb's younger brother William in the Detroit firm of Macomb, Edgar, and Macomb and conducted a lucrative business supplying the Indian department of the British army.
4. On August 5, 1790, Macomb and Edgar presented a petition to the House of Representatives "praying to be released from a contract entered into with the United States, for the purchase of a quantity of Western lands." The petition was referred to the Secretary of the Treasury (*Journal of the House*, I, 290). After keeping the petition for the rest of his term of office, H failed to report on it, and finally returned it with a number of others under a covering letter to the Speaker of the House (H to Frederick A. C. Muhlenberg, January 5, 1795), which was read and ordered to lie on the table on January 6, 1795 (*Journal of the House*, II, 284).

In a memorial which Edward Livingston presented to the House on May 13, 1796, Macomb and Edgar stated that in 1787 they had contracted with the

United States to buy eighty-nine thousand acres of land northwest of the Ohio River for $80,000, that they had paid the first installment of $29,669, and that they had defaulted on the remaining payments. They therefore asked that they be permitted "to complete the payment of the purchase money of [the] land ... on the original terms of the purchase, and to obtain a grant for the same" or that they be granted the amount of land for which they had already paid (*Journal of the House*, II, 554; *Annals of Congress*, V, 1360). On January 30, 1798, after hearing a report on Macomb and Edgar's memorial, the House rejected their request (*Journal of the House*, III, 153).

From Robert Morris

Philada. Decr. 31st. 1796

Dear Sir

You will find annexed hereto the Copy of a letter just received from Charles Bridgen [1] Esqr. and enclosed my Answer,[2] which after reading You will be kind enough to send to him. I suppose myself to be founded in saying that the suit contemplated, cannot be brought against me, otherwise no Man whose Name is on another Mans paper, can be safe, At any rate I request your Aid as a professional Man and will Chearfully pay such Compensation as you shall say is right for the Service you render me or the trouble this Application may Occasion you. I have no property in the State of New York that Mr Bridgen can come at even if his Suit could be Maintained, therefore He had better seek for payment in the regular Course against the drawer of the Bill.

I am Dr Sir   Your Obedt Servant   Robt. Morris

Alexr Hamilton Esqr

ALS, Hamilton Papers, Library of Congress; LC, Robert Morris Papers, Library of Congress.

1. Bridgen was a New York City attorney.

On December 31, 1796, Bridgen wrote from New York to Morris: "Messrs. [William] Talbot & [William] Allum of this City Merchts. have applied to me to proceed against your property in this State under our Act for relief against absconding and absent Debtors. They hold a bill endorsed by you and of which I shall have a copy made on the other side hereof ..." (copy, Hamilton Papers, Library of Congress). Bridgen is referring to "An Act for Relief against absconding and absent Debtors" (*New York Laws*, 9th Sess., Ch. XXIV [April 4, 1786]). The bill, which is dated February 4, 1796, reads: "At sixty days sight pay this second of exchange first not paid, to the order of Robert Morris Esqr. Nine hundred & seventy two pounds eight Shillings Stg value received, which place to the acct. of . . . Jno. Nicholson." The bill is endorsed by Morris, and at the bottom is written: "To John Henry Cazenove nephew &c. Merchants in London." Beneath that is written: "Pay to the order of Mr. Gilbt. Karney," and this notation is signed by Ralph Mather, a New York City merchant (copy, Hamilton Papers, Library of Congress).

2. Morris's letter to Bridgen, which is dated December 31, 1796, reads: ". . . I apprehend that no such suit . . . can lie against me. I am not an inhabitant of the State of New york, but of the City of Philada. I am here on the Spot . . . & consequently I cannot be called an absconding or absent *Debtor*. The Bill . . . is to be paid by the Drawer, and altho I am liable as endorser, yet I do not Consider it as any debt, nor shall I think of paying it as long as I can possibly avoid it for I think Application Should in the first instance be made to the Drawer" (ALS, Hamilton Papers, Library of Congress; LC, Robert Morris Papers, Library of Congress).

See also H's Law Register, 1795–1804 (D, partially in H's handwriting, New York Law Institute, New York City).

To  [1]

[1796] [2]

Dear Sir:

Poor *Duer* has now had a long & severe confinement—Such as would be adequate for no trifling crime. I am well aware of all the blame to which he is liable and do not mean to be his apologist—though I believe he has been as much the dupe of his own imagination as others have been the victims of his projects. But what then? He is a man—he is a man with whom we have both been in habits of friendly intimacy—he is a man, who with a great deal of good zeal has in critical times rendered valuable services to the Country. He is a husband, who has a most worthy & amiable wife perishing with chagrin at his situation—Your relation by blood—mine by marriage. He is a father who has a number of fine children [3] destitute of the means of education & support every way in need of his future exertions.

These are titles to sympathy, which I shall be mistaken if you do not feel. You are his creditor. Your example may influence others. He wants permission, through a letter of license to breathe the air for *five* years. Your signature to the enclosed draft of One will give me much pleasure.

Yrs. AH

JCH Transcripts.

1. This letter may have been addressed to Walter Livingston, for in the first paragraph H describes William Duer's wife, Catharine, as "Your relation by blood—mine by marriage." Livingston and Catharine Duer were cousins, as Livingston's father, Robert, and Catharine Duer's mother, Sarah, were the children of Philip and Catrina Van Brugh Livingston. H was Catharine Duer's cousin by marriage, for Elizabeth Hamilton and Livingston's wife, Cornelia Schuyler Livingston, were cousins. Elizabeth Hamilton's father, Philip Schuyler, and Cornelia Livingston's mother, Gertrude, were the children of John and Cornelia Van Cortlandt Schuyler. See Florence Van Rensselaer and William Laimbeer, *The Livingston Family in America and Its Scottish Origins* (New York, 1949), and Don R. Gerlach, *Philip Schuyler and the American Revolution in New York: 1733–1777* (Lincoln, Nebraska, 1964), 314.

2. In *JCHW*, V, 546–47, and therefore in JCH Transcripts, this letter is dated August, 1793. The text of the letter, however, suggests a later date. In *HCLW*, X, 49, this letter is also dated August, 1793, but Henry Cabot Lodge adds as a footnote: "I give this letter as dated in the edition of 1850 [*JCHW*], where it is misplaced, but its language would suggest a later period, somewhat near the end of Duer's confinement in 1797." Joseph Stancliffe Davis suggests that this letter was written in 1796 or 1797 (Davis, *Essays in the Earlier History of American Corporations* ["Harvard Economic Studies," XVI (Cambridge, 1917)], I, 330). As Duer, who had been imprisoned for debt on March 23, 1792, was released from debtors' prison for a short time in 1797 at H's intercession, H probably wrote this letter in late 1796 or early 1797.

For Walter Livingston's business relations with Duer, see Livingston to H, January 29, 1795, note 6.

3. William and Catharine Duer had eight children. See Van Rennsselaer and Laimbeer, *The Livingston Family*, 99.

From James McHenry

[*Philadelphia, 1796–January, 1797.* At this time, McHenry "suggested to Hamilton the establishment of a permanent navy yard, and enclosed a draft of his departmental report in which he tried not to censure his predecessors." [1] *Letter not found.*]

Steiner, *James McHenry*, 180, note 1.

1. Although Steiner dates this letter February 21, 1797, his description of its contents indicates that it was written earlier.

In the House of Representatives on January 19, 1797, "A Letter was received from the Secretary of the Treasury, enclosing the Report of the Secretary of War, on the subject of the Naval Establishment, and an estimate respecting the ports and harbors of the United States. What related to the Naval Establishment was referred to a committee on that subject, and what respected the ports and harbors was referred to a committee appointed to take their state into consideration" (*Annals of Congress*, VI, 1913).

In response to a letter of December 21, 1796, from Josiah Parker of Virginia, chairman of the House committee for "inquiring into the state of Naval Equipments &c &c," McHenry reported on January 11, 1797, "that, if Congress perceives advantages in the extension of their marine, or think it expedient that early precautions should be taken to secure to the United States a lasting fund of live oak for future use, it will be proper that authority should be given for the purpose, as well as to purchase a site for a navy yard" (*ASP, Naval Affairs*, I, 26–27). The committee's report, dated January 25, 1797, reads in part: "Your committee further report, as their opinion, that a sum of money would be appropriated for the purpose of purchasing and fitting up a navy yard . . ." (*ASP, Naval Affairs*, I, 26).

From Ann Mitchell [1]

[1796]

My Father—James Lytton Senr. deceased—Planter of the Island of St Croix in the year 1769—In his Will confirmed by his Majesty— he bequeathed ⅐ of his Estate to my Brother James Lytton Junr.—

AL, Hamilton Papers, Library of Congress.
1. This letter is endorsed in Elizabeth Hamilton's handwriting: "letter from Mrs Ann Mitchel to Alexr Hamilton."
Ann Mitchell, the daughter of James and Ann Lytton, was H's cousin. Her mother was the sister of H's mother, Rachel Lavien. In 1759, when she was sixteen years old, she married John Kirwan Venton. They had one child, a daughter named Ann Lytton Venton. John Venton died in 1776, and in 1780 his widow married George Mitchell, a native of Scotland who had migrated first to Virginia and then to St. Croix. Ann Mitchell died in Christiansted in 1827. See Holger Utke Ramsing, "Alexander Hamilton og hans mødrene staegt Tidsbilleder fra Dansk Vestindiens barndom," *Personalhistorisk tidsskrift*, 24 cm., 10 Raekke, 6 bd. (Copenhagen, 1939).
Although it cannot be explicitly documented, it seems certain that Ann Mitchell provided H with money from her father's estate and thus enabled him to migrate to North America and to attend college. See "Ann Lytton Venton's Order in favor of Alexander Hamilton," May 3, 1773; Broadus Mitchell, *Alexander Hamilton, Youth to Maturity, 1755–1788* (New York, 1957), 14, 18; *Alexander Hamilton, The National Adventure, 1788–1804* (New York, 1962), 549. Just before his duel with Aaron Burr, H wrote to his wife: "Mrs Mitchel is the person in the world to whom as a friend I am under the greatest Obligations. I have ⟨not⟩ hitherto done my ⟨duty⟩ to her. But ⟨resolved⟩ to repair my omission as much as ⟨possible⟩ I have encouraged her to come to ⟨this Country⟩ and intend, if it shall be ⟨in my po⟩wer to render the Evening of her days ⟨c⟩omfortable. But if it shall please God to put this out of my power and to inable you hereafter to be of ⟨s⟩ervice to her, I entreat you to d⟨o⟩ it and to treat ⟨h⟩er with the tenderness of a Sister" (H to Elizabeth Hamilton, July 10, 1804).
The following entries appear in H's Cash Book, 1795–1804: for July 11, 1796, "Account of Donations Dr to Cash for this sum paid my Cousin Mrs. Mitchells draft upon me   100"; for January 10, 1797, "Account of Donations for this sum paid my cousin Mrs Mitchells draft upon me   100"; on April 13, 1797, "Account of Donations   Dr. to Alex Robinson for Mrs. Mitchells draft on me accepted & surrendered say 19. 10/ Phil Curr   52"; on June 20, 1797,

2/7ths to his Children to be divided when the youngest was of age—
2/7th to my deceased Sisters Son John Hallwood—and in consequence of my being married to a man unfortunate in his conduct—
he nominated my daughter Anne Lytton Venton as Heir to the remaining 2/7ths—The interest only to be paid to me for our joint support during the life of her Father John Venton. But expressly ordering and willing the said 2/7ths to be paid to me upon his decease. In order to prevent my Husband from taking measures to compel me to aid him in his indeavours to disannul my fathers Will—Major John Coakley and Thomas Lillie Esqr Executors—and my brother —went with me to General Clawsen and obtained permission for me to come to America with my daughter when the said Thomas Lillie having the direction of my Fathers property remited to me such a part of the interest of the 2/7ths as was sufficient for our support. In 1775 and 1776 my husband and Thomas Lillie both died. My brother then with out informing me—or the aforesaid Legatee John Hallwood gave up my Fathers Estate and concerns to the Dealing Court. Dealing Master James Lowin immediately sold at publick sale a Sugar Plantation—the principal part of the Estate. My Brother became the purchaser at 65 000 Rld. I received letters from him informing me of it and that he would pay me 6 ₱ Ct on the 2/7th of the purchase till the payments were due according to the conditions of the sale and 8 pr Ct from then till paid. This he failed to do. In 1778 and 1779 my brother and a Mr Thomas Tucker who was appointed my Curator by Government, very urgently requested my return to St Croix to attend the close of the Dealing. Upon my arrival there with my daughter I was informed by Dealingmaster Towers my Brother and all parties concerned—that as in their opinion the expression of my Fathers Will was somewhat ambiguous they had had a meeting for the purpose of taking it in to consideration—and that they had agreed my right to demand and receive the 2/7ths was good—it appearing to be my Fathers intention by order-

---

"To Account of Donations for received of A Robinson in reimbursement of Mrs. Mi[t]chells draft 100" (AD, Hamilton Papers, Library of Congress). Shortly before his duel with Burr, H sent Mrs. Mitchell four hundred dollars. See H to Ann Mitchell, June 28–July 11, 1804.

See also "Ann Lytton Venton's Quittance with Alexander Hamilton," May 16, 23, 1772, May 26, June 3, 1773; "Endorsement by Alexander Hamilton on Note of Ann Lytton Venton," January 25, 1779; H's Cash Book, March 1, 1782–1791, note 146; and H to Sempill and Company, May 20, 1786.

ing it to be paid to me to preserve it for me and not from me. The close of the Dealing was protracted. I could not by the most earnest entreaty procure even as much of the interest as would supply my daughter and self with the common necessaries of Life—and had it not been for the humane and friendly assistance of the Revd Doctr Hugh Knox[2] I could not have supported the distress I found my self involved in. My Brother now sold the Estate to a Mr John James taking in part payment St James Island at the value of 5000 Rld—which with the interest of the 65 000 unpaid while he held the Plantation and the difference of (to the best of my knowledge 5000 Rld in the sale mentioned by taking off some Slaves and what he had before received—amounted to more than his own ⅓th. John James Purchaser—then came forward as a Curator to a Don Valesco a Mullato boy said to be a Son of my Brother Peter Lytton insane and deceased before my Father he produced a bit of paper said to be found in his house—bequeathing to said Mullato 11 000 Rld requiring a reservation to be made of that sum in the Estate for said boy. In the same year 1780 a Robert Halliday—a man with out property or Credit made a claim and commenced a suit against my Fathers estate for the sum of 28000 Rld. Dealing Master Towers made these claims a fresh pretext for not closing the Dealing and in his Regulation of it made a reservation of 36 000 Rld for them till decided.

My Brother—with David Beekman[3] Esqr Guardian to my Brothers Children and Dealingmaster Towers now declared themselves dissatisfied with their former award respecting the intention of my Fathers Will and again convened to reconsider it. They now determined that the Portion ordered to be paid to me at the death of John Venton my Husband should not be paid to me so long as my Daughter lived—nor to her so long as I lived. Neither has the interest of it been regularly paid to me—nor could I ever yet learn from them what they allowed my daughter and self a claim to—my Brothers ⅓th being paid the three remaining shares are equal. In 1781 my Nephew John Hallwood Legatee died. He made a Will

2. Knox was a Presbyterian minister who had settled in St. Croix in 1772. See H to The Royal Danish American Gazette, September 6, 1772, note 1.

3. Beekman, a merchant in St. Croix, had been Nicholas Cruger's partner. H had worked as a clerk in their firm. See Walton and Cruger to H, October 9, 1771.

bequeathing to me ¼ of what remained unpaid of his share but no part to my Brother or his Children. It was left in the hands of the Rev. Doctr. Knox Executor. In 1780 I married a Mr George Mitchel —Burger who had come to St Croix to attend the process of his Brothers Robert Mitchells Dealing—to which Dealingmaster Towers was indebted 10 000 Rix Dollars by a judgment from Copenhagen. In the course of his attendance and different contests he was obliged to contract some debts—his Creditors became urgent with him concluding that if he withdrew himself his Creditors could and would by their united power compel Dealingmaster Towers to bring forward and close our Dealings—which he found he could not—we came to America—but he has been unfortunately disappointed. In 1791 my husband George Mitchel sent me with my daughter to St Croix with a full power of Attorney. On our arrival we found Hollidays suit and Valesco's claim appeared no nearer a decision than when we left that place. We found that the Dealing Master Towers had not even obliged John James to pay the interest of the sum for which he purchased the Plantation—that he had to the injury of the Heirs died insolvent—that the said Plantation had been Sold again but no payments made—and that no progress was made in the Dealings of my Father James Lytton Senr or Robert Mitchell. I entreated my Brother and David Beekman guardian to his Children, to join me in a petition to Government they would not. I then in my own name only presented a petition to his excellency General Walterstorff [4] praing him to order the suit of Robert Holliday to be decided. The suit was ordered to be decided and the decision was in favor of my Fathers Estate. Robert Holliday was fined 3 mark danish and to pay all charges. Tho a man destitute of reputation or property he was by some means enabled to appeal to the upper court where his suit Still rests. With difficulty I prevailed with my Brother and David Beekman to attend the then Dealingmaster Mr Prom with me. He read my Fathers Will to them—he expressed with indignation his astonishment at the cruel treatment I had received and said—if there was any meaning in words—it was clear to him I ought to have received ⅔ths of what my Father died pos-

---

4. Ernst Frederich von Walterstorff was governor general of the Danish West Indies from 1787 to 1794.

sessed of—at the death of my former Husband. To this my Brother objected, that it was contrary to Mr. Tower's regulation of the Dealing—and as one of the members of the Dg court was absent—they protested against the proceedings of the day—and would never after attend with me—or join me in any measure for bringing the Dealing to a final settlement and close. Dealing Master Prom then told me he saw I should never recover my right—but by a petition to his Majesty—and that he was satisfied that would prove effectual. In despair of obtaining redress by any other means I made a formal demand of my right in the D. Ct.—and returned in 1792 with my daughter to America where we have suffered and still suffer every hardship incident to poverty [5]—without hope of redress but from the Justice and clemency of—

5. Ann Mitchell lived in Burlington, New Jersey, from 1784 until late in 1796. She made several trips during those years to St. Croix in attempts to secure her inheritance. See Ramsing, "Alexander Hamilton," *Personalhistorisk tidsskrift*.

From William M. Smith

[1796–1800] [1]

Hond Sir

Your kindness in taken me under your Paternage [2] claims my warmest returns of Gratitude. let me beg that you Receive the thanks of that sincere heart, that never has, nor I hope never will be ungratefull. I believe in the worse of Time's when Men Soul's trembled at danger, when most was Alarm'd at a for boding Storm. a few, a Virtuous few Stood. I humbly trust I am one of them. remember that Silent hour on the Battery,[3] when Nothing but Horrow was before us. the word. We dare die. But it has pleased the Almighty after much Trouble to turn the Scale and Under his protecting power in these State's Man can live as free as Liberty can desire.

I can truly say I never did deceive either in the Army or private Life. I must confess that Misfortune has a little turn'd my ⟨tem⟩per. Now let me beg continue your kind Assistance. I will be punctual in every trust, that to me may be intrusted—but if after You have done what you see right in my behalf and Unsuccessfull. Still me and mine will ever pay a Gratefull return with Mrs Smith and Little one is Compliments to Your self Lady and family

I am with true esteem   Your Obedient Servant   Wm M Smith

Col Alexander Hamilton

ALS, Hamilton Papers, Library of Congress.
 1. This letter is addressed to H at "No. 26 Broad Way," his residence in New York City from 1796 to 1800.
 2. See H to Nicholas Fish, September 16, 1794.
 3. See "Certificate of John Hanson by Anthony L. Bleeker, Peter S. Curtenius, Alexander Hamilton, John Lamb, and Hercules Mulligan," January 24, 1796, note 2.

1797

From Wade Mosby [1]

Richmond, January 1, 179[7].[2] Acknowledges message that Hamilton will serve as his attorney in the suit brought against him in New York by Leeds and Mumford.[3] States: "I am sure that when you are fully possessed of all the circumstances relative thereto you will find [it] to be one of the most Rascally proceedings you ever were witness to. . . . I wait your answer hoping that you will quickly put and end to the Suit and rid me of so disagreeable business."

ALS, Hamilton Papers, Library of Congress.
 1. Mosby was a member of the Richmond, Virginia, firm of Mosby, Smith, and Carrington.
 2. Mosby incorrectly dated this letter 1796.
 3. The suit to which this letter refers was *Wade Mosby, Josiah Smith, Paul J. Carrington, Samuel Sackett, and Samuel Watson* v *Jedediah Leeds and John Mumford*. For an account of this case with the relevant documents, see Goebel, *Law Practice*, II, 316–27.
 An entry in H's Cash Book, 1795–1804, for December 19, 1796, reads: "Cash for received in suit of Wade Mosby & others v. Leeds &c 25" (AD, Hamilton Papers, Library of Congress).

From James Ricketts [1]

[*Elizabethtown, New Jersey*] *January 1, 1797.* "I feel you will think that I have not paid proper attention to your letter.[2] Immediately on the receipt of it I wrote to Mr. Livingston[3] to send me an account of the Dividends which he had made, and the proportions which he had paid me on acct. of his Sisters Legacy, his answer I recd. the day before yesterday which is as follows: 'I have recd. your letter of the 26th. Inst. and submitted to Mr. Harrison[4] Council for the Estate, whether the Executors could with propriety comply with your request who answer'd as follows: "I think it will be right you should inform Mr. Ricketts that having instituted a

Suit at Common Law, he must proceed therein as he shall be advised, but that the Council for the Executors thinks no information should be given to enable you to prosecute any Cause except in Equity." ² I do not know that I am perfectly correct with respect to two of the four Dividends that have been made, because I was not informed of them, and Mrs. Ricketts's proportion of them was detained by the Executors on acct. of the supposed Debts but I believe them to be as follows. The First was a Dividend of 10,000 Dolls of which I recd. my proportion 1000 Dollrs, the Second & third must have been for 10,000 & about 7,000—my proportion of which is abt. 3000 Dollr. (which sum Mr. Livingston agreed to lay out in 6 pr Ct. Stock) the fourth & last Dividend was 10,000 of which I recd. my proportion 1800. I hope my account of it will enable you to proceed. . . ."

ALS, Hamilton Papers, Library of Congress.
1. For background to this letter, see Ricketts to H, June 24, 1796, notes 1 and 2.
2. Letter not found.
3. Philip Livingston was the son of Peter Van Brugh Livingston. James Ricketts had married Sarah Livingston, daughter of Peter Van Brugh Livingston and his first wife, Mary Alexander Livingston, who had died in 1769.
4. Richard Harison.

From Edward Carrington [1]

Richmond, January 3, 1797. "I have just now seen Mr Wade Mosby of my Neighbourhood in the Country, whose Agent . . . has just returned from N. York where he has employed you in a Suit to which Mr Mosby is a party. He wishes me to say to you what his Character & circumstances are. I have known him from his Childhood to this day, and can with confidence say he is a man who has supported the character of a Gentleman uniformly, and, being himself honest, is too apt to rely on others being so, as he fatally experiences, I verily believe, in the case now under your care. I am sufficiently informed of the transaction between him & Leeds here to be well satisfied that the debt due to Leeds & Mumford, has been bona fide, paid. . . ."

ALS, Hamilton Papers, Library of Congress.

1. Carrington was supervisor of the revenue for Virginia.
For an explanation of the contents of this letter, see Wade Mosby to H, January 1, 1797, and Goebel, *Law Practice*, II, 316-27.

From Robert Morris [1]

Philada. Jany. 7th. 1797

Dear Sir

I have arranged with Capt Chas Williamson for the debt Contracted with Colo Wm S. Smith in August 1791 of which fifty Thousand Dollars. in Six ₱ Ct Stock remains to be transferred and delivered & for the performance thereof I have given to Capt. Williamson Assignee of Colo Smith a satisfactory Security, in Consequence Whereof that Tract of Land in the Genesee Country for which I gave Colo Smith a Deed of Conveyance is to be reconveyed to me, and a Suit which was instituted by Colo Walker in the Court of Chancerry is to be withdrawn & rendered Null & Void, for a more full & perfect information of these matters I refer you to the enclosed Copies of the Articles of Agreement between Colo Smith and me, and of the Defeazant executed by him. The Original of the latter is with me, the Original of the former and the Deed of Conveyance were left with Colo Smith and I suppose are now in the hands of Colo. Walker who Acted as Atty to Capt Williamson, the latter will do every thing to be done for restoring to me my Title to the Tract of Land West of the Genesee River free of all incumbrance either by means of my Deed to Colo Smith or of the suit in Chancerry, but I must request your immediate care and attention as a professional Man to see this done in all due Form & without loss of time for which I will chearfully pay the Compansation you will say is right.

I am Dr Sir   Your Obed Servt   Robt Morris.

Alexr. Hamilton Esqr.

ALS, Hamilton Papers, Library of Congress; LC, Robert Morris Papers, Library of Congress.

1. This letter concerns a debt which Morris owed to William Pulteney and William Hornby and the efforts of their representatives to have Morris pay or secure this debt. For an explanation of this debt and the negotiations con-

cerning it, see the introductory note to Morris to H, April 27, 1796. See also Morris to H, May 3, 10, 17, 31, 1796; H to Charles Williamson, May 17–30, 1796.

From Stephen Higginson [1]

Boston Jany 12. 97

Dr Sir

Your Letter of 20 of last month [2] I have received. The election of Mr. Adams seems to be secured, but with an excess only of one vote,[3] which is close work indeed. This, while it avoids the point I before stated to you, will involve another, I fear, more dangerous & difficult. The blind or devoted partisans of Mr. Adams, instead of being satisfied with his being elected, seem to be alarmed at the danger he was in of failing; & they have the folly to say, that this danger was incurred wholly by the arrangement of pushing him & Pinckney together. They go farther & say, that this arrangement was intended to bring in Pinckney & exclude him. They affect to believe this to have been the intention, because the character of Adams for discernment & independence forbid all hope of influencing the decissions of the Executive, he being the president; but had Pinckney been introduced, his pliability would have continued the influence of a few over the measures of the executive, which has been too conspicuous during the present administration. At the head of this Junto, as they call it, they place you & Mr Jay; & they attribute the design to him & you of excluding Mr A: from the Chair, which the arrangement alluded to was intended to effect. They affect also to believe, that it is for the interest of the Country to have Mr. Jefferson for vice president rather than Pinckney—that he will serve readily under mr. Adams, & will be influenced by & coincide with him.

These Sentiments, however foolish & impudent They may appear, are dealt out freely by some of his particular connections, who seem to consider the Country as made for the man, & not the man for the Country; & it is believed, that mr. A: himself entertains them, perhaps has communicated them. Those who know the man, will not be much surprised if he should himself say the same things, when his feelings are up; & it may happen, that believing thus, he may be cool & distant toward those whom he ought to be intimate with & consult upon important occasions. With such impressions he may attach himself to Jefferson, if he conducts with address, & adopt a line of conduct toward his former friends, which will divide & may much weaken the federal interest.

I suggest to you this much, perhaps not new, with a view to prepare you for appearances, which might otherwise alarm some of our friends who may not expect them. Possibly you may think of some mode of preventing the inconveniences which I fear to result from what I apprehend to be Mr Adams feelings.

With due respect I am Sir yours &c

AL, Hamilton Papers, Library of Congress.
  1. For background to this letter, see Higginson to H, December 9, 1796.
  2. Letter not found.
  3. Actually, the electoral vote was John Adams, 71; Thomas Jefferson, 68; Thomas Pinckney, 59; and Aaron Burr, 30.

To Isaac Gouverneur and Peter Kemble

[*New York*] *January 19, 1797.* "You are hereby requested to produce on the Trial of this cause [1] during the present term whensoever the same shall be the letters from the Plaintiff to you whereof a list is at foot. . . ." [2]

ADfS, Free Library of Philadelphia; ADf, Hamilton Papers, Library of Congress.
  1. This is a reference to the case of *Louis Le Guen* v *Isaac Gouverneur and Peter Kemble*, which was one of a series of cases in which H served as the attorney for Le Guen. For a discussion of these cases, see Goebel, *Law Practice*, II, 48–164.
  2. Twenty-six letters are listed covering dates from August 18, 1794, through March 28, 1796.

To James McHenry

[New York, January 19, 1797]

My Dear Sir

This will probably be handed you by Mrs De Neuville widow of Mr. De Neuville of Holland a Gentleman who embarked very zealously and very early in the cause of this country—was instrumental in promoting it and as I understand an object of persecution in consequence of it, which was a link in the chain of his pecuniary ruin.[1] I think his widow has a strong claim upon the kindness of our country as far as general considerations will admit relief—and she has a particular claim upon every body's good will, that of being a distressed & amiable woman. I ask for her your patronage & good offices.[2] Adieu My Dr. Friend

Yrs. truly

A Hamilton
Jan 19 1797

J. Mc.Henry Esqr &c

ALS, New-York Historical Society, New York City.

1. Anna de Neufville, a resident of Boston, was the widow of John de Neufville of Amsterdam. The firm of John de Neufville and Son had been the Holland agents of the Continental Congress for refitting John Paul Jones's squadron in 1779 and had also attempted to help John Adams in his efforts to obtain a loan for the United States in 1780.

On February 3, 1797, the House of Representatives received a "memorial of Anna de Neufville, widow of John de Neufville, deceased, formerly a merchant in the city of Amsterdam, in behalf of herself and her infant daughter . . . , praying compensation for services rendered, and losses sustained by the deceased, in support of the American cause, during the late war" (*Journal of the House*, II, 678). On March 2, 1797, Congress passed an act authorizing the President "to cause to be paid . . . the sum of one thousand dollars to Anna de Neufville, widow of the said John de Neufville; a like sum for the use of Leonard de Neufville, his son; and a like sum for the use of Anna de Neufville, his infant daughter" (6 *Stat.* 29). The Treasury warrant to Mme Neufville was issued on March 17, 1797 (D, RG 217, Miscellaneous Treasury Accounts, 1790-1894, Account No. 8721, National Archives). Leonard, the older of the Neufville children, had been his father's partner (Tobias Lear to H, September 21, 1789) and was now insane. An order of the Court of Common Pleas of Philadelphia County, dated March 10, 1798, which placed him in the custody of Théophile Cazenove of Philadelphia, stated that he had been insane for more than two years and that he had "one Sister of the half Blood aged about twelve years resident in Boston" (D, RG 217, Miscellaneous Treasury Accounts, 1790-1894, Account No. 9658, National Archives). It appears from this order that Cazenove had attempted to have Leonard de Neufville transferred to the custody of Stephen Higginson of Boston. The warrant for Leonard de Neufville's share of the award was issued on April 11, 1798 (D, RG 217, Miscellaneous Treasury Accounts, 1790-1894, Account No. 9658, National Archives). John de Neufville's account with the United States was finally settled on March 3, 1851, when Congress passed the following joint resolution: "That the Secretary of the Treasury be, and he is hereby, directed to examine and adjust the accounts of John De Neufville and Son, merchants of Amsterdam, with the United States, and pay any balance which may be found to be due to said firm, to the party or parties legally entitled to receive the same: *Provided*, That the amount to be paid shall not exceed the sum of eight thousand seven hundred and sixty-seven dollars and sixty cents, with interest from the thirty-first day of May, seventeen hundred and eighty-two, to the first day of July, eighteen hundred and thirty-two, at the rate of five per centum per annum, deducting all payments heretofore made" (9 *Stat.* 814).

2. During her visit in Philadelphia, Anna de Neufville sought the assistance of several prominent men including George Washington and Representative Robert G. Harper of South Carolina. See Washington to H, January 22, 1797; Harper to Andrew Craigie, January 24, 1797 (ALS, New-York Historical Society, New York City).

To William Loughton Smith

[New York, January 19, 1797]

My dear Sir

Mrs. De Neufville widow of Mr. De Neufville formerly of Holland is on her way to Philadelphia to solicit the Kindness of Congress in virtue of services rendered the American cause by her husband. You probably Know their history as South Carolina was particularly concerned.[1] From what I have heard it seems to me her pretensions on the score of her husband to the Kindness of this Country are strong—as a distressed and amiable woman she has a claim to every body's Kindness.

What are you about in Congress? Our affairs seem to be at a very critical point with France. We seem to be brought to the same point with her as we were with Great Britain when Mr Jay was sent there. One last effort of negotiation to produce accommodation and redress, or measures of self defence. Have you any thoughts of an Embargo? There may be Ere long a necessity for it. Are you in earnest about additional revenue [2]—this is very necessary.

  Yours truly   Alexander Hamilton

                      Jan. 19. 1797

JCH Transcripts.

1. Early in 1781 Commodore Alexander Gillon had been authorized by the state of South Carolina to buy frigates for the state navy. When he was in Amsterdam, he ran out of money and had to give up the cargo of his one homeward-bound frigate, the *South Carolina*, to John Laurens in exchange for financial assistance. Laurens engaged the firm of John de Neufville and Son to provide and ship a new cargo under the supervision of Captain William Jackson. Jackson and John de Neufville and Son overspent, and when the frigate sailed for South Carolina in August, 1781, much of the cargo had to be left behind (D. E. Huger Smith, "Commodore Alexander Gillon and the Frigate South Carolina," *The South Carolina Historical and Genealogical Magazine*, IX [October, 1908], 189–219).

For Gillon's activities, see H to Pierce Butler, February 19, 1794, note 2. See also George Washington to John de Neufville, January 6, 1784 (LC, George Washington Papers, Library of Congress); Neufville to Washington,

February 15, August 19, 1783 (ALS, George Washington Papers, Library of Congress).

2. Smith was chairman of the House Committee of Ways and Means, which had been instructed "to consider the subject of further revenue, and the provisions for more effectually securing the internal revenues" (*Annals of Congress*, VI, 1787–88). On January 12, 1797, the Committee of Ways and Means made a report which included the following resolution: "*Resolved*, That there ought to be apportioned, according to the last census, on the several States, the sum of ———, to be raised by the following direct taxes, viz:

"'A tax ad valorem, under proper regulations and exceptions, on all lands, with their improvements, including town lots, with the buildings thereon.

"'A tax on slaves, with certain exceptions.'" (*Annals of Congress*, VI, 1843.)

This resolution was in part the result of proposals in a report on direct taxes which Oliver Wolcott, Jr., submitted to the House of Representatives on December 14, 1796 (*ASP, Finance*, I, 414–65).

To George Washington

New York Jan 19. 179[7] [1]

Sir

Mrs. De Neuville widow of Mr. De Neuville formerly of Holland lately passed through this City.[2] On her way she called upon me and announced her intention to make application to Congress on the ground of the political services rendered the UStates by her husband, as in fact a principal cause of his pecuniary misfortunes—and expressed a wish that I would bring her case under your eye. I told her that your situation did not permit you to take an agency on similar matters depending before Congress and that you was very delicate on such subjects. She replied that you might perhaps indirectly promote her cause and that from a letter from you to her husband [3] she was encouraged to think you would be disposed to befriend her. I yielded at last to female importunity & promised to mention the matter. I do not know what the case admits of, but from some papers which she shewed me it would seem that she has pretensions on the kindness of this Country.

Our Merchants here are becoming very uneasy on the subject of the French captures and seizures.[4] They are certainly very perplexing and alarming—and present an evil of a magnitude to be intolerable if not shortly remedied. My anxiety to present Peace with France is known to you—and it must be the wish of every prudent man that no honorable expedient for avoiding a Rupture be omitted.

Yet there are bounds to all things. This Country cannot see its Trade an absolute prey to France without resistance. We seem to be where we were with G Britain when Mr Jay was sent there—and I cannot discern but that the Spirit of the Policy then pursued with regard to England will be the proper one now in respect to France (viz) a solemn and final appeal to the Justice and interest of France & if this will not do, measures of self defence. Any thing is better than absolute humiliation. France has already gone much further than Great Britain ever did.

I give vent to my impressions on this subject though I am persuaded the train of your own reflections cannot materially vary.

With respectful & Affect Attachmen I have the honor to remain Sir Yr. very Obedt   A Hamilton

The President of the U States

ALS, George Washington Papers, Library of Congress; copy, Hamilton Papers, Library of Congress.

1. H mistakenly dated this letter "1796."
2. See H to James McHenry, January 19, 1797; H to William Loughton Smith, January 19, 1797.
3. Washington to John de Neufville, January 6, 1784 (LC, George Washington Papers, Library of Congress).
4. The French policy of seizing American ships was based on a resolution of the Directory on July 2, 1796. This resolution stated in part: ". . . All neutral or allied Powers shall, without delay, be notified that the flag of the French republic, will treat neutral vessels, either as to confiscation, as to searches, or captures, in the same manner as they shall suffer the English to treat them" (*ASP, Foreign Relations*, I, 577).

A second translation of this resolution reads: "It shall be notified, without delay, to all the neutral or allied Powers that the flag of the French republic shall be used against neutral vessels, be it for the purpose of confiscation, search, or detention, (*visite ou prehension*) in the same manner that they suffer the English to use theirs in regard thereto" (*ASP, Foreign Relations*, III, 287).

In a letter dated October 27, 1796, Pierre Auguste Adet, French Minister to the United States, sent a copy of the July 2, 1796, resolution to Timothy Pickering and wrote: ". . . The French Government, then, finds itself, with respect to America, at the present time, in circumstances similar to those of the year 1793; and, if it sees itself obliged to abandon, with respect to them and neutral Powers in general, the favorable line of conduct it had pursued, and to adopt different measures, the blame should fall upon the British Government. It is their conduct which the French Government has been obliged to follow.

"The undersigned minister plenipotentiary conceives it his duty to remark to the Secretary of State, that the neutral Governments, or the allies of the republic, have nothing to fear as to the treatment of their flag by the French, since, if keeping within the bounds of their neutrality, they cause the rights of that neutrality to be respected by the English, the republic will respect them. But if, through weakness, partiality, or other motives, they should suffer the English to sport with that neutrality, and turn it to their advantage, could they then complain, when France, to restore the balance of neutrality to its equilibrium, shall act in the same manner as the English? No, certainly; for the neutrality of a nation consists in granting to belligerent Powers the same advantages; and that neutrality no longer exists, when, in the course of the war, that neutral nation grants to one of the belligerent Powers advantages not stipulated by treaties anterior to the war, or suffers that Power to seize upon them. The neutral Government cannot then complain if the other belligerent Power desires to enjoy advantages which its enemy enjoys, or if it avails itself of them; otherwise, that neutral Government would deviate, with respect to it, from the line of neutrality, and would become its enemy." (*ASP, Foreign Relations*, I, 577).

For an account of French spoliations of United States commerce, including a list of 316 captured American vessels, see "Report of the Secretary of State respecting the depredations committed on the commerce of the United States, since the 1st of October, 1796," which Timothy Pickering submitted to President John Adams on June 21, 1797 (*ASP, Foreign Relations*, II, 28–65).

From Angelica Church

[London, January 20, 1797]

I would have you to understand Mon tres cher Monsieur that my eyes have recovered all their former lustre, and that they have been ineffectually employed in searching for the grace and elegance of your friend,[1] nor have I yet been able to discover that ease and je ne sais quoi by which Sterne observes *the gentleman* [2] may be so readily ascertained. As to his capacity for Bargain making that I cannot deny, as I do really beleive that he took his *Carosposa* weight and Measure. It was not so in days of chivelry, nor when you were young.

We are all going to see you, perhaps to importune you, perhaps to be happier, and it may be to repent—but I am a little sad. The accounts we hear from America are not flattering, and I dread their effect on my children.

I have this moment seen Mrs. King, they seem to be very agreeably settled, and are remarkably polite and attentive.

My love at home, I wish you joy of your president.

Farewell my dear friend, I want you to tell me that my children have a prospect of happiness and that I may be free from terrors of fevers [3] and Negro plots, the latter they say are the cause of your fires.[4]

If I consider only myself, I know your attachment and that of Elizas.

Adieu

Jan: 20. 1797

AL, Hamilton Papers, Library of Congress.
  1. This is apparently a reference to Rufus King, United States Minister Plenipotentiary to Great Britain. See H to Angelica Church, June 25, 1796.
  2. See Laurence Sterne, *The Life and Opinions of Tristram Shandy, Gentleman* (2nd ed., London: R. and J. Dodsley, 1760–1767).
  3. For the yellow fever epidemic in New York City in 1796, see H and Richard Harison to Richard Bayley, July 19, 1796, note 3.
  4. This is a reference to a number of fires which occurred in various cities in early December, 1796. On December 19, 1796, *Claypoole's* [Philadelphia] *American Daily Advertiser* carried the following report from New York City: "The minds of the citizens are in a state of agitation; and well they may be; the recent FIRES at Baltimore, Philadelphia, Savannah, Morrisville, and this city, besides various detected attempts, are sufficient to alarm all good citizens, and to rouse them to vigilance. . . ." See also *The* [New York] *Argus. Greenleaf's New Daily Advertiser*, December 12, 13, 15, 1796.

New Yorkers were particularly alarmed, and on December 9, 1796, *The Argus* wrote: "A FIRE IN THIS CITY. Broke out about One o'clock this morning, which raged tremendously, and consumed all that block of stores, at the lower end of Wall-street, comprised between Stewart and Jones and Cook's stores, in Wall-street, and Steuart and Jones and Bruce's new stores in front-street, consisting of above eighteen stores, with an immense value in goods; continuing its impetuous rage, sweeping all before it to the fish-market, about 40 buildings—where were hopes of arresting its further progress. It still raged when the paper went to the press. Particulars to-morrow." On the following day, *The Argus* wrote: "The sketch we gave in haste yesterday morning, was not incorrect so far as it went. Since then we have taken pains to ascertain a minute and we believe accurate statement, for the guidance of the public.

"The fire commenced about one o'clock yesterday morning, in the range of stores on Murray's wharf, and raged with such fury as to baffle all human skill, until all the buildings from thence to the Fly-market, on the east side of Front-street, were consumed to ashes. . . . The buildings alone are estimated at about *seventy thousand* dollars. . . ."

H did not need to be told about the fires in New York City. On January 28, 1797, Robert Troup wrote to King: "Hamilton has for some time past been laid up with a lame leg, got by watching the City. Have you heard that within two months past frequent attempts have been made to burn the City? It is the case. . . . Who are concerned in them, or what in particular has led to them we cannot discover. The consequence, however, has been a serious alarm, which produced a nightly watch consisting of about 20 in each ward . . ." (King, *The Life and Correspondence of Rufus King*, II, 136–37).

As Troup indicates, no evidence was found concerning a plot to set the fires, but on December 14, 1796, *The* [New York] *Minerva, & Mercantile Evening Advertiser* carried the following report: "*Serious Cause of Alarm!*

"Citizens of New-York, you are once more called upon to attend to your safety. It is no longer a doubt—it is a fact, that there is a combination of incendiaries in this city, aiming to wrap the whole of it in flames! The house of Mr. Lewis Ogden, in Pearl-street, has been twice set on fire—the evidence of malicious intention is indubitable—and he has sent his black man, suspected, to prison. Last night an attempt was made to set fire to Mr. Lindsay's house in Greenwich street—The combustibles left for the purpose are preserved as evidence of the fact. Another attempt, we learn, was made last night in Beekman-street. A bed was set on fire under a child, and his cries alarmed his family.

"Rouse, fellow citizens and magistrates—your lives and property are at stake. Double your night-watch—and confine your servants."

See also *The* [London] *Times*, January 17, 18, 1797.

To Theodore Sedgwick

[New York, January 20, 1797]

Dear Sir

I received your late letter[1] in due time. You seem to be of opinion to defer to a future period the commencement of direct taxation.[2] I acknowlege I am inclined to lay gently hold of it now. Leaders of the opposite party favour it now, perhaps with no good design. But it will be well to take them while in the humour and make them share the responsibility. This will be the more easy as they are inclined to take the lead. Our external affairs are so situated, that it seems to me indispensable to open new springs of revenue and press forward our little naval preparation [3] & be ready for augment-

ALS, Hamilton Papers, Library of Congress.

1. Letter not found.
2. The House of Representatives was at this time debating the desirability of raising extra revenue by direct taxes. See H to William Loughton Smith, January 19, 1797.
3. On March 27, 1794, Congress had passed "An Act to provide a Naval Armament," which provided for the construction of six frigates (1 *Stat.* 350–51). Progress was so slow that a year later only the hulls of three frigates had been completed and construction on the hulls of two other frigates had just begun. After the negotiation of a peace treaty with Algiers in 1795, work on the frigates stopped altogether. On April 20, 1796, however, a supplementary naval act authorized completion of three of the frigates, the *United States*, the *Constitution*, and the *Constellation* ("An Act supplementary to an act entitled 'An act to provide a Naval Armament' " [1 *Stat.* 453–54]).

After President Washington in his annual message of December 7, 1796, had again called the attention of Congress to the need for a strong navy (*Annals of Congress*, VI, 1592–97), the House of Representatives on December 16, 1796, appointed a committee headed by Josiah Parker of Virginia to inquire ". . . into the state of the Naval equipment, ordered by former act of Congress; and whether any, and what, other Naval force shall be necessary for the protection of the commerce of the United States, and the support of their

ing it. But on the whole I have always leaned to the opinion that *half* a *million* from direct taxes was enough to begin with—nor should I have proposed more.

What are we to do with regard to our good allies? Are we to leave our commerce a free prey to them? I hope not. It seems to me we are even beyond the point at which we were with G Britain when Mr Jay was sent thither & that something like a similar plan ought to be pursued, that is, we ought to make a final effort to accommodate & then resort to measures of defence. I believe *ere long* an embargo on *our own Vessels* will be adviseable; to last till the conduct of France changes or till it is ascertained it will not change. In the last event the following system may be adopted—to grant special letters of *mark* with authority to repel aggressions and capture *assaisants*—to equip our frigates—to arm a number of *sloops of war* of existing Vessels to convoy our merchantmen. This may be a middle term to general hostility though it may slide into the latter. Yet in this case it may be well to let France make the progress. But at all events we must protect our commerce & save our honor.

As to the ballance business the agitation of the question has been every way unfortunate.[4] There is not an *individual* in the state of

---

flag" (*Annals of Congress*, VI, 1671). On December 21, Parker, on behalf of the Naval Committee, requested Secretary of War James McHenry to submit a report on progress made toward construction of the frigates already authorized and estimates of the sum needed to complete them. McHenry's report, dated January 11, 1797, estimated that approximately $200,000 would be required to finish the three frigates (*ASP, Naval Affairs*, I, 25–28). Convinced that this sum ". . . will be insufficient under existing circumstances . . . ," the committee recommended that "the vessels should be finished as soon as possible, and that ——— dollars should be appropriated for the purpose . . ." (*Annals of Congress*, VI, 1983). On March 3, 1797, Congress appropriated $172,000 to finish the three frigates ("An Act making appropriations for the Military and Naval establishments for the year one thousand seven hundred and ninety-seven" [1 *Stat.* 508–09]). The ships were completed and launched in 1797.

4. This is a reference to the congressional debate over attempts to settle the accounts of the United States and the individual states. "An Act to provide more effectually for the settlement of the Accounts between the United States and the individual States" (1 *Stat.* 178–79 [August 5, 1790]) had provided for the establishment of a board of three commissioners. See Tobias Lear to H, August 19, 1793, note 1. On June 29, 1793, the commissioners made their final report. They found that Massachusetts, Connecticut, New Hampshire, Rhode Island, New Jersey, South Carolina, and Georgia had balances due them. The remaining states, including New York, were debtors of the United States. New York owed $2,074,846.

The question of payment of debts due the United States by the several

New York, who is not profoundly convinced that the settlement was *wholly artificial* and as it regarded the rule of quotaing manifestly unjust, and consequently that there is no justice in paying it.[5] I never saw but one mode of getting through the business which is for Congress to call for a certain sum of each debtor state annually say a *fiftieth* part declaring that if not paid each installment shall bear interest from the time it becomes due but till then the principal to carry no interest. I believe the state for harmony sake would yield to such an arrangement. It may be said this will be only a nominal payment. I answer—true—but an *artificial* ballance ought only to be *nominally* paid. The conduct of some Gentlemen in the late question has pained me much. It is inconsistent with a tacit pledge of faith. Every New Yorker who had any thing to do with our fiscal arrangements has been personally compromitted.

Yrs. truly   A Hamilton
                                                                     Jan 20.1797

Theodore Sedgwick Esqr

---

states became an issue in the second session of the Fourth Congress, which convened on December 5, 1796. On December 20, 1796, Joshua Coit, Representative from Connecticut, called "the attention of the House to a subject which he thought of some importance—it was the balances due from certain States to the United States. Three years, he said, had elapsed since the report was made by the Commissioners on that subject. He did not know what order was proper to be taken, but something ought to be done; he thought the first step would be to ask the debtor States for payment. . . ." Coit then offered a resolution directing the Committee of Ways and Means "to report whether any, and what, further measures ought to be taken relative to the balances which . . . were found due from certain States to the United States" (*Annals of Congress*, VI, 1691).

5. Congressmen from New York took the lead in opposing the resolution, arguing, as John Williams put it, that "had a just and equitable settlement been made . . . the State of New York would have been a creditor State . . ." (*Annals of Congress*, VI, 1747). For the attempts to settle this problem in the 1796–1797 session of Congress, see *Annals of Congress*, VI, 1529, 1531–32, 1538, 1540 42, 1552 53, 1563, 1565, 1569, 1691–93, 1696, 1747–62, 1783, 1785, 1789–1815, 2166–67, 2183, 2326–27, and 2335. Congress was unwilling to call on the debtor states for payment, and the balances which they owed were never collected.

To Robert Morris

[*New York, January 21, 1797.* On January 23, 1797, Morris wrote to Hamilton: "Your letter of the 21st inst. is just received." *Letter not found.*]

From George Washington

Philadelphia 22d. Jany. 1797.

My dear Sir

Your letter of the 19th. instant was received yesterday.

From the general impression on my mind, relative to Mr. De Neuvilles claim[1] on the justice of this country, a delay, or a refusal to administer it, would be hard; but I must add, that I am too little acquainted with the particulars to form a correct opinion, and were it otherwise, I do not see how I could, with propriety, appear directly or indirectly in the business, as I do not recollect having had any agency therein. The numberless applications of this sort which are made to me (often in the dernier ⟨r⟩esort) without the means of relief, are very distressing to my feelings.

The conduct of France towards the United States, is, according to my ideas of it, outrageous beyond conception: not to be warranted by her treaties with us; by the Law of Nations; by any principle of justice; or even by a regard to decent appearances. From considerations such as these something might have been expected; but on her profession of friendship and loving kindness towards us I built no hope; but rather supposed they would last as long, and no longer, than it would accord with their interest to bestow them; or found it would not divert us from the observance of that strict neutrality which we had adopted, & was persevering in.

In a few days, there will be published a statement of facts, in a letter of references, to General Pickney; containing full answers to all the charges exhibited in Mr Adets notes, against the conduct of this government.[2] After reading them with attention, I would thank you for your sentiments thereon, fully, and frankly communicated; and what you think ought further to be attempted, to preserve this country in Peace, consistently with the respect which is due to ourselves?

In some of the Gazettes, and in conversation also, it is suggested that an Envoy extraordinary ought to be sent to France; But is not General Pinckney gone there already for the express purpose of explaining matters, and removing inquietudes? With what more could another be charged? What would that Gentleman *think* of having a person treading on his heels, by ⟨the time⟩ ³ he had arrived in Paris, when ⟨the argu⟩ments used to induce him to go there ⟨are all⟩ that could be urged to influence ⟨that other⟩—and where is the character to be ⟨had, ad⟩mitting the necessity, in all respec⟨ts accep⟩table and qualified for such a tru⟨st? The⟩ sooner you can give me your sen⟨timents⟩ on these queries, the more plea⟨sing they⟩ will be to

Dear Sir   Your sincere f⟨rd. &⟩ affectionate ⟨Servant⟩

Go: W⟨ashington⟩

ALS, Hamilton Papers, Library of Congress; ADfS, George Washington Papers, Library of Congress.

1. On February 2, 1797, Anna de Neufville wrote to Washington: "When I had the honour to wait upon you Sir, you was pleased to ask me wether my husband had appleid to old Congress, which I answerd in the negative to you, owing not understand perfect by your meaning, he has So far appleid as to have Send a Copie of the list of debtors and Creditors, with a letter or petetion, to Request theire influence, in ordre to be Sooner remboursed: in particulars I do not Remember; but Should any Such papers be in Congress it might be of Some use in my favour Stating the validity of the Large advances my husband has made for this Country; your Philanthropi must plead my excuse Sir and fergive the Bolt intrution, of a unhappy widow for her orphan child, of troubling you . . ." (ALS, George Washington Papers, Library of Congress).

2. This is a reference to a letter which Timothy Pickering wrote to Charles Cotesworth Pinckney on January 16, 1797 (LC, RG 59, Diplomatic and Consular Instructions of the Department of State, 1791–1801, Vol. 3, June 5, 1795–January 21, 1797, National Archives). In this letter Pickering replied to charges by Pierre Auguste Adet that the United States had surrendered its rights as a neutral to Great Britain and had violated its treaty agreements with France. For Adet's complaints concerning United States policy, see Adet to Pickering, October 27, November 15, 1796 (*ASP, Foreign Relations*, I, 576–77, 579–83). See also Washington to H, November 2, 3, 21, 1796; H to Washington, November 4, 5, 11, 19, 1796; H to Oliver Wolcott, Jr., November 1, 1796; Wolcott to H, November 17, 1796.

3. The material within broken brackets in this letter has been taken from the draft in the George Washington Papers, Library of Congress.

From Robert Morris

A Hamilton Esqr   Philada Jany. 23d. 1797

Dr Sir

Your letter of the 21st inst.[1] is just received none of a previous date in reply to mine of 31st Ulto ever reached me, nor have I received from you any acknowledgement of the receipt of my letter to you of 7th Inst. which was sent by Captn Williamson in order to have the mortgage to Colo Smith removed & the suit in Chancery brought by Colo Walker discharged. This latter is a very important business as you know and I am anxious to know the needfull therein has been done agreably to the promise of Captn Williamson.[2] With respect to the suit meditated by Mr Bridgen[3] I wish measures to be stopped untill Mr Nicholson the drawer of the bill[4] (who is soon expected) shall return from the City of Washington where he now is when I will consult him and make in consequence such propositions as may be acceptable to the parties unless in the meantime the affair should be adjusted with Ralph Mather the last endorser who I suspect to be the real owner of the bill as I have heard of his endeavoring to make a negotiation on the first bill of the suit whilst Mr Bridgen threatens a suit on the second. I will address you again on this business soon as Mr Nicholson arrives & in the mean time I rely on your taking care of Dr Sir

Yr Obedt Servt   RM

P S I am not sure that Mr Mather offered the same bill for negotiation but I suppose it to be so.

LC, Robert Morris Papers, Library of Congress.
1. Letter not found.
2. The preceding sentences in this paragraph refer to a debt which Morris owed to William Pulteney and William Hornby and the efforts of their representatives to have Morris pay or secure this debt. For an explanation of the debt and the negotiations concerning it, see the introductory note to Morris to H, April 27, 1796. See also Morris to H, May 3, 10, 17, 31, 1796, January 7, 1797; H to Charles Williamson, May 17–30, 1796.
3. The remainder of this letter concerns a threatened suit against Morris by Charles Bridgen on behalf of William Talbot and William Allum. For this suit and the principals involved in it, see Morris to H, December 31, 1796.
4. For John Nicholson, see Morris to H, June 7, 1795, note 7.

From Timothy Pickering

[*Philadelphia, January 23, 1797.* On February 6, 1797, Hamilton wrote to Pickering: "I duly received your letter of the 23 of Jany." Letter not found.]

To Timothy Pickering

[New York, January 23, 1797]

Dear Sir

I remember that very early in the day & prior to any act of Great Britain the French passed a decree violating with regard to all the neutral powers the principle of *free ships free goods* & I think making provisions liable to seizure. This decree was afterwards rescinded as to America—then again revived & then again revoked.[1] I want copies of these decrees for a particular purpose [2] useful to the Government & presuming they must be on the files of your department, you will oblige me much by letting me have copies as speedily as may be convenient.

With respect & true esteem   I am Dr Sir   Yr Obed servt

A Hamilton
Jan 23. 1797

T Pickering Esqr

ALS, Massachusetts Historical Society, Boston.
  1. This is a reference to the decree of the National Convention of May 9, 1793, the first article of which reads: "Les bâtimens de guerre et corsaires français peuvent arrêter et amener dans les ports de la République, les navires neutres qui se trouveront chargés en tout ou en partie, soit de comestibles appartenant à des neutres et destinés pour des ports ennemis, soit de marchandises appartenant aux ennemis" (Duvergier, *Lois*, V, 345). On May 23, 1793, "conformément à l'article 16 du traité passé le 6 février 1778," the Convention issued a decree exempting United States vessels from the provisions of the decree of May 9 (Duvergier, *Lois*, V, 371). This decree was suspended on May 28, 1793 (Duvergier, *Lois*, V, 381), and was reinstated on July 1, 1793 (Duvergier, *Lois*, VI, 1). For English translations of these decrees, see *ASP, Foreign Relations*, III, 284–85.
  2. For H's use of the material he requested from Pickering, see "The Warning No. V," March 13, 1797, and "The Warning No. VI," March 27, 1797.

To George Washington

[New York, January 25–31, 1797][1]

Sir

The sitting of the Court[2] and an uncommon pressure of business have unavoidably delayed an answer to your last favour.[3] I have read with attention Mr. Pickerings letter.[4] It is in the main a substantial and satisfactory paper, will in all probability do considerable good in enlightening public opinion at home—and I do not know that it contains any thing which will do harm elsewhere. It wants however in various parts that management of expression & *suaviter in modo* which a man more used to diplomatic[5] communication could have given it and which would have been happy, if united with its other merits.

I have reflected as maturely as time has permitted on the idea of an extraordinary mission to France, and notwithstanding the objections, I rather incline to it under some shape or other. As an imitation of what was done in the case of Great Britain, it will argue to the people equal solicitude. To France it will have a similar aspect (for Pinckney will be considered there as a mere substitute in ordinary course to Mr. Monroe) and will in some degree soothe her pride. The influence on party, if a man in whom the opposition has confidence is sent, will be considerable in the event of non success. And it will be to France a bridge over which she may more easily retreat.

The best form of the thing in my view is a commission including three persons who may be called "*Commissioners* Plenipotentiary & extraordinary." Two of the three should be Mr. Madison and Mr. Pinckney.[6] A third may be taken from the Northern states and I know none better than Mr. *Cabot*[7]—who or any *two* of whom may be empowered to act.

Mr. Madison will have the confidence of the French & of the opposition. Mr. *Pinkney* will have something of the same advantage in an inferior degree. Mr. *Cabot* without being able to prevent their doing what is right will be a salutary check upon too much Gallicism, and his *real* Commercial knowlege will supply their want of it. Besides that he will enjoy the confidence of all the friends of the Administration. His disposition to preserve peace is ardent and unqualified.

This plan too, I think will consist with all reasonable attention to Mr Pinkneys feelings.

Or (which however I think less eligible) Mr. Madison & Mr. Pinkney only may be joint Commissioners—without a third person.

Mr. Cabot (if appointed without being consulted) will I think certainly go. If not the other two may act without him.

The power to the Commissioners will be to adjust amicably mutual compensations and the compensations which may be due by either party and to revise and remodify the *political* and *commercial relations* of the two Countries.

In the exercise of their power they must be restrained by *precise* instructions to do nothing inconsistent with our other existing Treaties or with the *principles* of construction of those with France adopted by our Executive Government as declared in its public acts and communications & nothing to extend our *political* relations, in respect to alliance—but to endeavour to get rid of the mutual guarantee in the Treaty [8] or if that shall be impracticable to stipulate *specific succours* in lieu of it, as so many troops, so many ships, so much money &c, strictly confining the *casus fœderis* to *future defensive Wars* after a general & complete pacification terminating the present War, and defining offensive war to be where there is either a *first* declaration of War against the ally, or *first* commission of *actual* hostility on the territory or property of the ally by invasion or capture.[9] As to Commerce with the above restrictions there may be full discretion. These are merely inaccurate outlines.

Unless Mr. *Madison* will go there is scarcely another character that will afford advantage.

Cogent motives of public utility must prevail over personal considerations. Mr. Pinckney may be told in a private letter from you that this is an unavoidable concession to the pressure of public exigency & the state of *internal parties*.

With true respect & Affect Attachm   I have the honor to be   Sir Yr. Very Obed servt.   A Hamilton

The President.

ALS, George Washington Papers, Library of Congress.

1. In *JCHW*, VI, 194, *HCLW*, X, 223, and Hamilton, *History*, VI, 573, this letter is dated January 22, 1797.
2. The January term of the New York Supreme Court began in New York City on January 17, 1797.
3. Washington to H, January 22, 1797.
4. See Washington to H, January 22, 1797, note 2.
5. In MS, "dispolatic."
6. On December 22, 1796, Charles Cotesworth Pinckney had been named United States Minister Plenipotentiary to France to succeed James Monroe (*Executive Jounral*, I, 217).
7. George Cabot was a Massachusetts merchant and Federalist politician who had been a member of the United States Senate from March 4, 1791, to June 9, 1796, when he resigned.
8. This is a reference to Article 11 of the Treaty of Alliance between France and the United States signed at Paris on February 6, 1778. In this article the United States agreed to guarantee French possessions in the New World "against all other powers," and France guaranteed the territorial integrity and the "liberty, Sovereignty, and Independence absolute, and unlimited" of the United States (Miller, *Treaties*, II, 39–40).
9. H's discussion of the *casus fœderis* refers to Article 12 of the Treaty of Alliance between France and the United States. This article stipulated that "in case of a rupture between france and England," the reciprocal guarantee of Article 11 of the treaty "shall have its full force and effect the moment such War shall break out" (Miller, *Treaties*, II, 40).

From Fisher Ames

(In confidence)   Philada Jany 26. 1797

Dr Sir

My last[1] was written hastily & under some impressions of the moment which I had not time to unfold. The close respecting your taking a seat in the next house (to be elected) would pass for an awkward compliment if you did not know me (and yourself) too well for such an interpretation.

You desire an inside view of our stage. I begin with the *outside*. Our relations with France are serious. All the french party seem to expect & desire an extra envoy,[2] which is an objection—as probably they hope thus to soothe the resentments so tardily roused against France—to exhibit a shew of supplication on our part, & to ground some new delusive connection on the adjustment of existing com-

ALS, Hamilton Papers, Library of Congress.
1. Letter not found.
2. See George Washington to H, January 22, 1797; H to Washington, January 25–31, 1797.

plaints. On the other hand, it would be a literal & exact adherence to the late precedent in regard to G. B. it might afford a pretext for the french to relax, & in case they should not, animate & unite opinions for the necessary result. But as mr Pinkney is gone instructed on this very subject,[3] the course adopted is I believe to rely on his mission & *not* to send an extra Envoy. I wish you would direct your most mature thoughts to the subject, and if you should not approve the negative, you ought, (permit me to say) chuse your own way of bringing your sentiments into consideration in the proper place. Should it not be an object to negotiate an abrogation of the clause which guarantees the W Indie possessions to France?[4] However vague it may be & valid or urgent as our excuses might seem, the clause would embarrass Govt. & furnish a text for partizans to raise clamors in case of a future war (the U. S being at peace) & our non compliance with a demand for its execution.

More taxes are necessary & when trade is so much disturbed by war & will be not much less effected by peace land taxes Seem to be the only safe resource.[5] But my creed is that three things ought first to concur. To systematize & perfect the collection of our internal revenues, to extend them to the most eligible & productive new objects—and to prepare the public mind for the tax on lands, only to the Amot of the deficiency. Neither of these has been effected. The dread of the latter is at the same time the best means of getting more indirect taxes & of conciliating the people to a land tax. It is necessity, the perception of which will produce Salutary efforts in

3. In his instructions to Pinckney, dated September 14, 1796, Timothy Pickering wrote: "Faithfully to represent the disposition of the Government and people of the United States (for their disposition is one), to remove jealousies and obviate complaints, by shewing that they are groundless; to restore that mutual confidence which has been so unfortunately and injuriously impaired; and to explain the relative interests of both countries, and the real sentiments of our own; are the immediate objects of your mission" (LC, Massachusetts Historical Society, Boston).

4. This is a reference to Article 11 of the Treaty of Alliance between the United States and France, signed on February 6, 1778. See H to Washington, January 25–31, 1797, note 8.

5. This sentence and the remainder of this paragraph can best be understood in the context of the debates in the House of Representatives on the relative merits of direct taxes (including a tax on land) and indirect taxes. The debates followed a proposal by the House Ways and Means Committee on January 12, 1797, for direct taxes on land and slaves (H to William Loughton Smith, January 19, 1797, note 2). For the House debates on direct and indirect taxes, see *Annals of Congress*, VI, 1747–62, 1767–87, 1790–1815.

the first instance & a reasonable acquiescence in the next. A tax on Salt is a good one,[6] but it would be hard to carry through, & it's foes would combine wtih some of it's advocates to refuse the draw-back on Salted Fish called a bounty [7]—which is not to be admitted. Snuff is condemn'd as vexatious & trivial,[8] that on auctions [9] as bad in principle. The licence tax [10] extended to taverns & so arranged as in part to augment with the sales of the retailer would be productive. To effect this last idea how would it answer to rate licences for 3 Gallons very low for more & under 20 still higher—if a separate licence by the same dealer for Madiera Sherry & Port still higher for each, as he must be a dealer of capital. To abolish the distinction in favor of home made spirits & to levy it on the Sales of *all* spirits & wines.[11] Equality would not be produced, but inequality as it now exists would be somewhat diminished.

The public should also see a plan or mode of levying a direct tax pass into a law—the vote for the actual levy of a tax to be suspended till the next session & then to be for the deficiency. The moderation of the tax would, on experiment, destroy & disappoint the prejudices against it, and the preparation of opinions would be the best possible. The aversion would seem to have resisted delayed & diminished the evil to the utmost.

The anti gents make their calculations no doubt that a direct tax

6. On January 17, 1797, Robert G. Harper of South Carolina proposed to the House of Representatives an increase in the tax on salt (*Annals of Congress*, VI, 1864, 1870).

7. In a letter to William Loughton Smith, chairman of the House Committee of Ways and Means, on January 19, 1797, Oliver Wolcott, Jr., stated that if the tax on salt were increased, it would be "proper to readjust the bounties on the exportation of Salted Fish & Provisions & the allowances to Vessels employed in the Cod Fisheries . . ." (ADf, Connecticut Historical Society, Hartford).

8. For the duties on snuff, see "An Act to alter and amend the act intituled 'An act laying certain duties upon Snuff and refined Sugar'" (1 *Stat.* 426-30 [March 3, 1795]). For opposition to the tax, see *Annals of Congress*, V, 1406-15. See also Tench Coxe to H, December 26, 1794 (seventh letter).

9. "An Act laying duties on property sold at Auction" (1 *Stat.* 397-400 [June 9, 1794]).

10. "An Act laying duties on licenses for selling Wines and foreign distilled spirituous liquors by retail" (1 *Stat.* 376-78 [June 5, 1794]).

11. This is a reference to the differences between the duties on imported and domestic spirits. See "An Act for raising a farther sum of money for the protection of the frontiers, and for other purposes therein mentioned" (1 *Stat.* 259-63 [May 2, 1792]) and "An Act concerning the Duties on Spirits distilled within the United States" (1 *Stat.* 267-71 [May 8, 1792]).

will sharpen popular feelings—augment clamors against the debt bank &c—enfeeble & discredit the other species of revenue, especially internal. Perhaps they expect favoritism in the assessments.

Our proceedings smell of anarchy. We rest our hopes on foolish & fanatical grounds—on the superior morals & self supporting theories of our age & country—on human nature being different from what it is & better here than any where else. We cannot think it possible our Govt. should stop or that there is the least occasion to provide the means for it to go on. Internal revenues demand system & vigor. The collection must be watched & enforced. We want officers, courts, habits of acquiescence in our country & the principles in Congress that would begin to form any of these. The western country scarcely calls itself dependent on the union. France is ready to hold Louisiana.[12] The thread of connection is slender & that event I fear would break it. Yet we disband regiments.[13]

Our trade has spoliations to endure from France & G Britain. Yet we are not willing to abandon, or protect it as others do by a naval force.[14] An European would be ready to believe we are in jest in our politics or that newspaper declamation and the frothy nonsense of town meetings speeches comprise the principles of our conduct. For I am obliged to observe even good men adopt errors or pursue truth with a spirit not much more friendly to order & stability in Govt than their adversaries! Who for instance can think without alarm on the frequency & seductive nature of the disgraceful sequestration and anti credit motions in the house.[15] Facts of this vile

12. On August 4, 1796, for example, James Monroe wrote to Pickering: "It is said, that a treaty of alliance, offensive and defensive, between France and Spain, is in great forwardness, whereby the latter cedes to the former Louisiana, and perhaps the Floridas. I have no authentic information of this; but the source from whence it came is of a nature to merit attention" (Monroe, *A View of the Conduct of the Executive*, 361). Pickering transmitted Monroe's letter to Washington on October 20, 1796 (LC, RG 59, Domestic Letters of the Department of State, Vol. 9, October 12, 1795-February 28, 1797, National Archives).

13. On January 24, 1797, the House of Representatives "*Resolved* That all such parts of the act, entitled 'An act to ascertain and fix the Military Establishment of the United States,' which relate to the light dragoons ought to be repealed, and that the four regiments of infantry be reduced to three" (*Annals of Congress*, VI, 1982). For the text of "An Act to ascertain and fix the Military Establishment of the United States," passed on May 30, 1796, see 1 *Stat.* 483-86.

14. See H to Theodore Sedgwick, January 20, 1797, note 3.

15. For "sequestration and anti credit motions," see H's "Report on a Plan for the Further Support of Public Credit," January 16, 1795.

nature do not occur in other countries, or if they do, they precede & create convulsion. Here they are received as civilly as if infamy did not form an atmosphere about them, contaminating all who breathe in it. We are formed but of late for independent sovereignty —experience has not laid on her lessons with birch, & we forgot them. Our whole system is little removed from simple democracy. What we call *the Govt.* is a phantom, as long as the Democrats prevail in the house. The heads of departments are head clerks. Instead of being the ministry the organs of the executive power and imparting a kind of momentum to the operation of the laws, they are precluded of late even from communicating with the house by reports. In other countries they may speak as well as act. We allow them to do neither.[16] We forbid even the use of a speaking trumpet, or more properly as the Constitution [17] has ordained that they shall be dumb, we forbid them to explain themselves by signs. Two evils obvious to you result from this. The efficiency of the Govt. is reduced to it's minimum. The proneness of a popular body to usurpation is already advancing to it's maximum. Committees already are

16. Ames is referring to the fact that heads of departments could not report to Congress in person and could submit written reports only upon the request of either the House or the Senate. In the bills creating the State and War departments, no provision was made for reports by either Secretary to Congress ("An Act for establishing an Executive Department, to be denominated the Department of Foreign Affairs" [1 *Stat.* 28–29 (July 27, 1789)]; "An Act to establish an Executive Department, to be denominated the Department of War" [1 *Stat.* 49–50 (August 7, 1789)]; "An Act to provide for the safe-keeping of the Acts, Records and Seal of the United States, and for other purposes" [1 *Stat.* 68–69 (September 15, 1789)]). In Section 2 of "An Act to establish the Treasury Department," however, Congress required the Secretary of the Treasury to "report, and give information to either branch of the legislature, in person or in writing (as he may be required), respecting all matters referred to him by the Senate or House of Representatives . . ." (1 *Stat.* 66 [September 2, 1789]). On January 9, 1790, the House, contrary to H's desire, voted to receive his "Report Relative to a Provision for the Support of Public Credit" in writing (*Annals of Congress*, I, 1043–45). The practice of the House in regard to oral communications by heads of departments was firmly established in November, 1792, when the House voted not to permit H and Secretary of War Henry Knox to appear in connection with the investigation of Arthur St. Clair's military defeat (*Annals of Congress*, III, 679–84). For a discussion of the marked resistance of the House to executive influence and leadership after 1794, see Leonard D. White, *The Federalists: A Study in Administrative History* (New York, 1959), 73–75.

17. Section 2 of Article II of the Constitution provided that the President "may require the Opinion, in writing, of the principal Officer in each of the executive Departments, upon any Subject relating to the Duties of their respective Offices. . . ."

the Ministers,[18] & while the house indulges a jealousy of encroachment on it's functions, which are properly deliberative, it does not perceive that these are impaired & nullified by the monopoly as well as the perversion of information by these very Committees. The silly reliance of our coffee house & congress prattlers on the responsibility of members to the people &c &c is disgraced by every page of the history of popular bodies. We expect confidently that the house of representatives will act *out* of it's proper character—for if it should act according to it, we are lost.

Our govt. will be in fact a mere democracy which has never been tolerable nor long tolerated.

Our proceedings evince the truth of these speculative opinions. No one was furnished with proper information nobody was answerable for what he presumed to give. The Committee of Ways & Means has not I am told written a page these two years. It collects the scraps & fritters of facts at the Treasury, draws crude hasty results tinctured with localities. These are not supported by any form'd plan of co operation with the members, & the report calls forth the pride of all the motion makers. Every subject is suggested in debate, every popular ground of apprehension is invaded—there is nothing to enlighten the house or to guide the public opinion. All this has happened. I am now preaching daily to those few who will hear me rail and endeavoring to form a common sentiment—that some thing must be done—that it must begin & be approved at the Treasury—that the antis will exult in our shame if we forbear to arrange an efficient plan &c. This is in train, not very far advanced, nor with good omens. It is as to our projected combination you will perceive strictly a *secret*.

My own wishes are to extend our indirect taxes and to pass a bill prescribing the Mode of levying a land tax, holding up the idea in debate at the time of a small amount only. But the apathy & inefficiency of our body is no secret to you. We are generally in a flat calm, & when we are not, we are near sinking in a tempest. When a Sovereign Convention engrosses the whole power it will do nothing or some violence that is worse. Sooner or later individuals & public

---

18. On March 26, 1794, for example, the House resolved to refer the question of additional revenue to its own committee, instead of requesting the opinion of the Secretary of the Treasury (*Annals of Congress*, IV, 531).

bodies will act out their principles. Our's are I fear essentially more democratic than republican, which latter are alone fit for our country. We think the executive power is a mere pageant of the representative body—a custos rotulorum, or master of ceremonies. We ourselves are but passive instruments whenever the Sovereign people chuse to Speak for themselves, instead of our speaking for them.

The momentum imparted to our political machine is Weak & the resistance strong. Faction appears of course in such a State of things. This I confess naturally excites a counter influence—but the power even of party seems to be dissipated. We are broken to pieces. Some able man of the first order of abilities & possessing the rare union of qualities that will fit him to lead a party is wanting. For want of such a leader, many who would do good are useless. My natural temperament unfits me for a Seat where I cannot bear to sit quite inactive although such efforts as I can make will be unavailing.

No session of Congress has exhibited such a dissipation of the party which has been arrayed in support of the Govt. Th⟨is⟩ [19] will be some excuse for my forebodings of the decline of our affair⟨s.⟩

One might have hoped that Govt would find in party all the combination & energy that is excluded from it's organisation. I see however that this auxiliary unless compacted together by the violent action of the rival party will subdivide or fall into inaction—and even when roused to the utmost, it is in need of a clear Sighted guide.

As this is the state of our politics what is to be done? The friends of the Govt. have increased within two or three Years in numbers & zeal—but few of them Know or could be made to believe that it's fair outside conceals such alarming weakness.

Your's truly   Fisher Ames

I understand Bank Shares have been lately attached by law process. This strikes my mind as a very anarchical proceeding.

Porcupine [20] is a writer of smartness & might do more good, if

---

19. Material in broken brackets taken from *JCHW*, VI, 203.
20. William Cobbett, the English author, lived in the United States from 1792 to 1800. He began his career as a political pamphleteer in 1795 in Philadelphia under the pseudonym of "Peter Porcupine" and in 1796 opened a bookshop in Philadelphia and began publication of *Porcupine's Political Censor*, a monthly journal in pamphlet form.

directed by men of sense & experience—his ideas of an *intimate* connection with G Britain justly offend correct thinkers—& still more the multitude.[21] He proposes a new daily paper,[22] a business much overdone. It's circulation out of the City will not be great. Would not a paper once or twice a week, exclusively political, answer better. Pray let Webster have the paragraph for his Minerva.[23]

21. See, for example, *Porcupine's Political Censor for November, 1796*, in which Cobbett wrote: ". . . [The French] well know, that there is but one check to their ambitious project; and that is, an alliance offensive and defensive between Great Britain and America" (Cobbett, *Porcupine's Works; containing various Writings and Selections, exhibiting a faithful picture of the United States of America; of their govenments, laws, politics and resources; of the characters of their Presidents, Governors, Legislators, Magistrates and Military Men; and of the Customs, Manners, Morals, Religion, Virtues and Vices of the People: comprising also a complete series of historical documents and remarks, from the end of the war, in 1783, to the Election of the President, in March, 1801* [London: Cobbett and Morgan, 1801], VI, 373). Again, in *Porcupine's Political Censor for December, 1796*, he wrote: "Surely no nation was ever so completely duped as America has been by the French and their partizans! By a sincere and hearty alliance with Great Britain, she would not only place herself in a situation to make a peremptory demand of indemnification from France, but, in case of a refusal, would be able to strip both France and Spain of every inch of territory they possess in this hemisphere" (*Porcupine's Works*, IV, 315).
22. *Porcupine's Gazette and Daily Advertiser* began publication in Philadelphia on March 4, 1797.
23. On January 28, 1797, the following paragraph appeared in *The* [New York] *Minerva, & Mercantile Evening Advertiser*, published by George E. Hopkins, Joseph D. Webb, and Noah Webster, Jr.: "William Cobbett of Philadelphia has issued proposals for publishing a Daily Paper in that city, under the title of 'Porcupine's Gazette.' The reason he assigns for it, is, that there are *too many papers* already—that is, so many ill conducted papers calculated to mislead the people, that another is become necessary to undeceive them—Peter will prove a terrible scourge to the 'Patriots.'"

From Gerrit Boon[1]

Oldenbarneveld [*New York*] *January 26, 1797.* Discusses the case of *Herman LeRoy, William Bayard, and Boon* v *Peter Servis and others.*[2]

ALS, Hamilton Papers, Library of Congress.
1. Boon, a native of the Netherlands, was an agent of the six Dutch banking firms which formed the Holland Land Company on February 13, 1796. H was an attorney for the company.
For background to this letter, see Théophile Cazenove to H, April 29, 1795.
2. For this case and other relevant documents, see forthcoming Goebel, *Law Practice*, III.

The Warning No. I [1]

[New York, January 27, 1797]

There are appearances too strong not to excite apprehension that the affairs of this Country are drawing fast to an eventful crisis. Various circumstances dayly unfolding themselves authorise a conclusion that France has adopted a system of conduct towards the neutral maritime nations generally which amount to little less than actual hostility. I mean the total *interruption* of their Trade with the ports of her enemies: A pretension so violent, and at the same time so oppressive humiliating and ruinous to them, that they cannot submit to it, without not only the complete sacrifice of their commerce but their absolute degradation from the rank of sovereign and independent States.

It seems to have become latterly a primary object in the policy of France to make the principal attack upon Great Britain through her Commerce, in order, by extinguishing the sources of her revenue and credit, to disable her from continuing the war and compel her to accept any conditions of peace which her antagonist may think fit to prescribe. It is to this plan, we are to attribute the unjustifiable treatment of Tuscany, in the seizure of Leghorn, and shutting her ports against the English contrary to the will of her own government.[2] The same plan has dictated the attempts, which appear to

---

ADf, Hamilton Papers, Library of Congress; *Gazette of the United States, & Philadelphia Daily Advertiser,* January 27, 1797.

1. The other issues of "The Warning" are dated February 7, 21, 27, March 13, 27, 1797.
2. On June 25, 1796, a division of the French army entered Leghorn. On June 26, Napoleon wrote to the Grand Duke of Tuscany: "The flag of the French Republic is constantly insulted in the port of Leghorn. The property of the French merchants is violated there; every day is marked by some attempt against France, as contrary to the interests of the Republic as to the law of nations. The Executive Directory have repeatedly preferred their complaints to the minister of your Royal Highness at Paris, who has been obliged to avow that it is impossible for your Royal Highness to repress the English, and to maintain a neutrality in the port of Leghorn" (Debrett, *A Collection of State Papers,* V, 39). On the same day, the Tuscan Foreign Minister, Vittorio Fossombroni, replied: ". . . A sovereign in friendship with the Republic cannot but regard, with the most extraordinary surprise, the orders given to your Excellency from the Directory. His Royal Highness will

have been made to oblige Naples to exclude Great Britain from her ports during the present war.³ And there have been indications of a design to effect a similar restraint on all the Italian states, and expel the British Trade wholly from the Mediterranean.⁴ The same object of wounding Great Britain through her commerce has been promoted by the War into which Spain has been drawn,⁵ and may be considered as the principal advantage expected from it: While it is likewise understood to be the intention to force Portugal to suspend her commercial relations with Great Britain. The late decree forbidding the importation of British manufactures into France ⁶ is a further proof of the eagerness with which the policy of destroying the British Commerce is pursued; since it is presumeable from the derangement of French manufactures by the war, that there must have been a convenience in the supply which that importation has afforded.

Tis obviously to the same origin, that we are to trace the decree lately communicated by the French Minister to our Government, with respect to the intended treatment of the Trade of neutrals,⁷ and the spoliations which ours has for some time past suffered.⁸ While

---

not resist the execution of them by force, but will preserve the good understanding with the Republic, still flattering himself with the hope that your Excellency will, on better information, revoke your present resolves" (Debrett, *A Collection of State Papers*, V, 40).

3. The third article of the treaty of peace between France and the kingdom of the Two Sicilies, concluded on October 10, 1796 (Martens, *Recûeil*, VI, 235–38), stipulated that the King of the Two Sicilies should not open his ports at any one time to more than four warships belonging to any of the belligerent powers.

4. Two instances were the Papal States and Genoa. The fourth condition of the suspension of arms between France and the Pope, June 23, 1796, reads: "Les ports des états du pape seront fermés aux bâtimens des puissances en guerre avec la république, et ouverts aux bâtimens francais" (Martens, *Recûeil*, VI, 239). Similarly, the first article of the convention between France and the republic of Genoa, October 9, 1796, reads: "Les anglois ayant insolement violé la neutralité du territoire de la république de Gênes, le décret du gouvernement, qui leur ferme ses rades et ses portes, sera maintenu jusqu'à la paix" (Martens, *Recûeil*, VI, 252).

5. On August 19, 1796, France and Spain concluded a treaty of alliance at San Ildefonso (Martens, *Recûeil*, VI, 255–62).

6. On October 31, 1796, the French legislature passed a law prohibiting the importation of British exports and manufactures (Duvergier, *Lois*, IX, 241–43).

7. For the French decree of July 2, 1796, see H to George Washington, January 19, 1797, note 4.

8. For French depredations on the commerce of the United States, see H to Washington, January 19, 1797, note 4.

neutral nations were permitted to enjoy securely their rights, besides the direct commerce between them and the British dominions, the commerce of Great Britain would be carried on in neutral bottoms, even with the countries where it was denied access in British bottoms. It follows that the abrigement of neutral rights is essential to the scheme of destroying the British Commerce: And here we find the true solution of those unfriendly proceedings, on the part of France, towards this country, which are hypocritically charged to the account of the Treaty with Great Britain and other acts of pretended infidelity in our Government.

Did we need a confirmation of this truth, we should find it in the intelligence lately received from Cadiz. We are informed through a respectable channel,* that *Danish* and *Swedish* as well as *American* Vessels, carried into that port by French Cruisers, have with their cargoes been condemned and confiscated by the French Consular Tribunal there, on the declared principle of intercepting the Trade of neutrals with the ports of the enemies of France. This indiscriminate spoliation of the commerce of neutral powers is a clear proof that France is actuated not by particular causes of discontent given by our Government but by a general plan of policy.

The practice upon the decree is a comment much broader than the text. The decree purports that France would observe towards neutrals the same conduct which they permitted her enemies to observe towards them. But the practice goes a great deal further. None of the enemies of France, even at the height of their power and presumption, ever pretended totally to cut off the Trade of neutrals, with her ports. This is a pretension reserved for her to increase the catalogue of extraordinary examples, of which her Revolution has been so fruitful.

The allegations of discontent with this Country are evidently a mere colouring to the intended vilolation of its rights by treaty as

---

* Note Mr. Iznardi our Consul at Cadiz lately arrived [9] who mentioned the fact as here stated adding without reserve that the principle abovementioned is avowed in the correspondence of the French Consul at Cadiz.

9. Joseph M. Yznardi. On January 6, 1797, the following item appeared in *The* [New York] *Argus, and Greenleaf's New Daily Advertiser:* "Mr. Isnardi, consul at Cadiz, arrived in the ship William Henry . . . informs that the French order to take Americans, is generally executed in that quarter, and that a number of American Vessels . . . have been carried in and ordered to be condemned." See also *ASP, Foreign Relations*, II, 53–54.

well as by the laws of Nations. Some pretext was necessary and this has been seized. It will probably appear hereafter that *Denmark*, and *Sweden* have been mocked with a similar tale of grievances. It is indeed already understood, that Sweden, outraged in the person of her Representative, has been obliged to go the length of withdrawing her Minister from Paris.[10]

The complaints of France may be regarded principally as weapons furnished to her adherents to defend her cause notwithstanding the blows she inflicts. Her aim has been in every instance to seduce the people from their Government, and by dividing to conquer and oppress. Hitherto happily the potent spells of this political sorcery have in most countries been counteracted and dissipated by the sacred flame of patriotism. One melancholy exception serves as a warning to the rest of mankind to shun the fatal snare. It is nevertheless humiliating that there are men among us depraved enough to make use of the arms she has furnished in her service—and to vindicate Her aggressions as the effects of a just resentment provoked by the ill conduct of our government. But the artifice will not succeed. The eyes of the people of this Country are every day more and more opened to the true character of the politics of France. And the period is fast approaching what it will be universally seen in all its intrinsic deformity.

10. Early in 1796, proposals for a marriage between King Gustavus IV Adolphus of Sweden and Alexandra, the granddaughter of Catherine II of Russia, endangered the already weak alliance between Sweden and France. On February 26, 1796, the Swedish Regent, Karl, Duke of Södermanland, recalled his ambassador to France, Erik Magnus, Baron Staël von Holstein. When Staël refused to leave Paris, the Regent on April 22, 1796, wrote him another letter of recall and also instructed him to tell the French not to send another ambassador to Sweden to replace the outgoing Louis-Grégoire Lehoc (Berndt von Schinkel, ed., *Minnen Ur Sveriges Nyare Historia* [Uppsala, 1880], I, 300–01). Shortly afterward the Regent sent Gottfried Mauritz, Baron von Rehausen, to replace Staël in the capacity of chargé d'affaires. The Directory, however, refused to receive Rehausen, since his appointment was thought to have been influenced by Russia (James Monroe to Timothy Pickering, July 24, 1796 [LC, RG 59, Despatches from United States Ministers to France, Vol. 4, August 15, 1794–October 21, 1796, National Archives). On August 2, 1796, on the Regent's instructions, Staël wrote a letter to the French Foreign Minister, Charles Delacroix, protesting that, since Rehausen had ". . . been appointed to attend ad interim to the affairs of Sweden, at a time when a rupture with Russia was every instant expected . . . His appointment could not, therefore, have been influenced by the Empress of Russia . . ." (Debrett, *A Collection of State Papers*, V, 62). Later in August the Directory expelled Rehausen and recalled the French chargé d'affaires in Sweden, Henri Perrochel.

The desire of a power at war to destroy the commerce of its enemy is a natural effect of the state of war, and while exercised within bounds consistent with the rights of Nations who are not engaged in the contest is intirely justifiable. But when it manifestly overleaps these bounds, and indulges in palpable violations of neutral rights, without even the color of justification in the usages of War, it becomes an intolerable tyranny—wounds the sovereignty of Nations and calls them to resistance by every motive of self preservation and self respect.

The conduct of France from the commencement of her successes, has by gradual developpements betrayed a spirit of universal domination; an opinion that she has a right to be the legislatrix of Nations; that they are all bound to submit to her mandates, to take from her their moral political and religious creeds; that her plastic and regenerating hand is to mould them into whatever shape she thinks fit & that her interest is to be the sole measure of the rights of the rest of the world. The specious pretence of enlightening mankind and reforming their civil institutions, is the varnish to the real design of subjugating them. The vast projects of a Louis the XIV dwindle into insignificance compared with the more gigantic schemes of his Republican successors.

Men, well informed and unprejudiced, early discovered the symptoms of this spirit. Reasoning from human nature they foresaw its growth with success; that from the love of dominion inherent in the heart of man, the Rulers of the most powerful Nation in the world, whether a monarch, a Committee of safety, or a Directory, will for ever aim at an undue empire over other nations—and that this disposition, inflamed as it was by enthusiasm, if encouraged by a continuation of success, would be apt to exhibit itself during the course of the French Revolution in excesses, of which there has been no example since the days of Roman Greatness.

Every day confirms the justice of that anticipation. It is now indispensable that the disagreeable and menacing truth should be exposed in full day to the people of America—that they should contemplate it seriously and prepare their minds for extremities which nothing short of abject submission may be able to avert. This will serve them as an armour against the machinations of traiterous men, who may wish to make them instruments of the ambition of a foreign power, to persuade them to concur in forging chains for mankind, and to accept as their reward the despicable privilege of wearing them a day later than others.

Already in certain circles is heared the debasing doctrine that France is determined to reduce us to the alternative of War with her enemies or war with herself and that it is our interest and safety to elect the former.

There was a time when it was believed that a similar alternative would be imposed by Great Britain.[11] At this crisis there was but one sentiment. The firmest friends of moderation and peace no less than the noisiest partisans of violence and war resolved to elect war with that power which should drive us to the election. This resolution was the dictate of morality & honor, of a just regard to national dignity and independence. If any consideration, in any situation, should degrade us into a different resolution, we that instant espouse crime and infamy; we descend from the high ground of an independent people and stoop to the ignominious level of Vassals. I trust there are few Americans who would not cheerfully encounter the worst evils of a Contest with any nation on earth rather than subscribe to so shameful an abdication of their rank as men and citizens.

AMERICUS

11. See the introductory note to H to Washington, March 8, 1794.

From John Dunn [1]

Dublin [*Ireland*] *January 28, 1797.* "I take the liberty of enclosing to you an account current furnished to me by Mr. John Barclay of Philadelphia relative to a fund in his hands by me anxiously desired to be entrusted to your care—A late account of some unfortunate circumstances occurring in Mr. Barclay's affairs makes me anxious in the extreme that the Property in his hands should be effectually secured—Mr. Barclay has written to Mr. Wilson the American Consul here who recommended Mr. Barclay to me *that I shall be secured to the last shilling.*[2] When I first took the Liberty of addressing you [3] I addressed you as a Gentleman whose high Honor & distinguished Character had taught me to look up to him with confidence as the Depository of a Trust—You then Sir filled a public

Station—That situation being now changed and you having returned to the Profession of the Law (to which I have the honor to belong) I do now with more earnestness and more Confidence request and entreat that you will in your professional Character use your Endeavours to have the Property in Mr. Barclays hands duly secured. Indeed Sir it is a consolation to me of peculiar Importance at this moment that I have professional assistance of such a distinguished kind to rely upon and which I do not entertain a Doubt you will speedily and effectually employ for my Protection and Safety. . . ."[4]

ALS, Hamilton Papers, Library of Congress.
  1. For an explanation of the contents of this letter, see Dunn to H, March 25, 1794.
  2. In a letter which Dunn sent to Barclay on January 28, 1797, and which he enclosed to H, he wrote: "In a letter which you lately wrote to Mr. Joseph Wilson you state a change in your Situation for which I am truly concerned, but inform Mr. Wilson that I shall be secured to the last shilling. In order that your just Intentions may be carried into effect in the most beneficial manner for me I have given authority to Mr. Hamilton to act in the business for me whose professional Skill & high Character must render it an easy matter to bring the business to a speedy and honorable conclusion" (ALS, Hamilton Papers, Library of Congress).
  3. Dunn to H, March 25, 1794.
  4. An entry in H's Cash Book, 1795–1804, under the date of August 26, 1797, reads: "Cash Dr. to Costs & Fees . . . received by Dun v Barkly 30" (AD, Hamilton Papers, Library of Congress). A similar entry was made in H's Law Register, 1795–1804 (D, partially in H's handwriting, New York Law Institute, New York City).

From Timothy Pickering

Philadelphia Jany. 30. 1797.[1]

Dear Sir,

I am sorry to have so long delayed an answer to your letter of the 23d. but we have been unusually occupied, and the decrees you referred to were not readily found: that of the 28th of May 1793 I have now discovered in a printed volume of the proceedings of the Convention for that month. So I now inclose you copies—[2]

1st of the decree of May 9th 1793, violating our treaty, by rendering neutral vessels laden with provisions liable to capture, as well as enemy's property on board neutral vessels.

2d. of the decree of 23d May, repealing the former in respect to American vessels.

3d. of the decree of the 28th of May reversing the last decree.

4th. of the decree of July 1st 1793, repealing that of the 28th of May.

These appear to be all the decrees referred to in your letter: but there must have been a subsequent one alike violating our treaty,[3] which Mr. Monroe forbore to ask the repeal of, lest, as he said, the French Government should demand a performance of the guarantee:[4] yet the very claims in behalf of American merchants whose properties had been captured, were to be made by him on the principle that the decree in question was a violation of our treaty. After this matter was pressed upon him by Randolph (as well as I recollect) he urged the repeal, which was passed Jany. 4th 1795.[5] If this decree and that which it repeals will be useful to you, copies shall be furnished.

It appears probable from the tenor of some of Gouv. Morris's letters,[6] that the decree of 9th May & 28th of the same month, were passed (at least the latter) to answer the views of the captors of certain vessels taken before the 9th of May—and that of May 28th specially to ennable the captors to hold the ship Lawrance.[7]

I am with great & sincere respect Dr. Sir, your obt. servt.

T. Pickering

Alexander Hamilton Esq.

ALS, Hamilton Papers, Library of Congress.

1. In *JCHW*, VI, 204, this letter is incorrectly dated June 30, 1797.

2. For the French decrees listed by Pickering, see H to Pickering, January 23, 1797, note 1.

3. The "subsequent" decree was dated July 27, 1793, and reinstated the decree of May 9, 1793 (Duvergier, *Lois*, VI, 71). Under its authority numerous condemnations occurred.

4. On September 15, 1794, James Monroe wrote to Secretary of State Edmund Randolph: ". . . I was not instructed to desire a repeal of the decree, and did not know but that it had been tolerated, from the soundest motives of political expedience. This Republic had declined calling on us to execute the guarantee, from a spirit of magnanimity, and a strong attachment to our welfare. This consideration entitled it to some attention in return. An attempt to press it, within the pale of the stipulation contained in the . . . articles of the treaty of Amity and commerce, might . . . create a disposition to call on us to execute that of the treaty of alliance" (LC, RG 59, Despatches from United States Ministers to France, 1789–1869, Vol. 4, August 5, 1794–October 21, 1796, National Archives).

5. This decree is dated January 3, 1795, and reads: "Considering that since, and notwithstanding the notoriety with which . . . [the British] cabinet contrives to insult and violate the rights of neutral nations by causing their vessels charged with merchandise, destined for the ports of France, to be seized, yet the National Convention has enjoined it, by the seventh article

of the law of the 13th of this month, upon all officers, civil and military, strictly to observe, in all their dispositions, the treaties which unite France with the neutral Powers of the ancient continent, as likewise with the United States of America, declaring all articles of a contrary import in any other law to be absolutely null and void.

"Fully, therefore, to carry into effect the said law, according to its true intent and meaning, it is hereby ordered:

"Art. 1. The Commission of Marine and of the Colonies shall notify, without delay, to all the commanders of armed vessels, divisions, and squadrons, the articles above mentioned of the law of the 13th of this month; and in consequence, that they are to consider the fifth article of the arrêt of the 25th Brumaire last, which authorized the seizure of merchandises belonging to an enemy, on board neutral vessels, until such enemy shall have declared French property on board such vessels free, as now null and void.

"Art. 2. The merchandises called contraband, though belonging to a neutral Power, shall continue subject to seizure.

"Art. 3. All arms, instruments, and munitions of war of every kind, horses, and their equipage, and all kind of merchandises and other effects, destined for an enemy's port, actually blockaded or beseiged, shall be deemed contraband of war." (*ASP, Foreign Relations*, III, 286.)

6. See Gouverneur Morris to Thomas Jefferson, June 25, 1793; Morris to Pierre Henri Héléne Marie LeBrun-Tondu, June 19, 1793 (*ASP, Foreign Relations*, I, 366–68).

7. Pickering was mistaken, for the ship in question was the *Laurens*. In a report to Congress dated February 27, 1797, he wrote: "... on the 28th of May, the Convention repealed their decree of the 23rd. The owners of a French privateer that had captured a very rich American ship, (the Laurens) found means to effect the repeal, to enable them to keep hold on their prize" (*ASP, Foreign Relations*, I, 748).

To George Washington

[New York, January 31, 1797]

Dr. Sir

My late situation exposes me to applications which I cannot resist without appearing unkind. It is understood that Mr. Walker [1] is about to resign the place of naval Officer. Mr. Jonathan Burrall [2] Mr. Rogers [3] (Walker's Deputy) and Col Giles [4] (the present Marshall) have all three mentioned the subject to me and requested me to express my opinion of their qualifications to you.

As to Mr. Burrall there is no doubt he will be in every sense an excellent appointment. I believe as a man of business on a large scale he may be superior to either and his character is irreproachable. He is now Cashier of the Office of Discount & Deposit is respectably connected by marriage much esteemed & has been an old servant of the public.

Every thing that I have heared of Mr. Rogers' moral character and capacity for business is intirely in his favour. I have no doubt he is fully worthy of the appointment—is a remarkably accurate accountant & has had long experience in the particular Office. The place is more necessary to him than to either of the others. His station in society generally is inferior to that of the other two.

Mr. Giles you know. I have no doubt he is intirely competent to the Office—he pleads as a merit his perseverance in his present Office though for a long time it was unproductive & he considers the continuance of the present emoluments which are now well enough, as uncertain—they arising from particular circumstances. He is however not quite decided in his wishes on the subject; by tomorrow he will decide.

I have the honor to remain   Most respectfully Sir   Very Obed serv
A Hamilton
Jany 31. 1797

The President

ALS, George Washington Papers, Library of Congress.
1. Benjamin Walker.
2. See H to Oliver Wolcott, Jr., December 21, 1796.
3. Richard Rogers was a clerk in the New York naval office. On February 20, 1797, the Senate approved his nomination as naval officer for the District of New York (*Executive Journal*, I, 226–27).
4. Aquila Giles was marshal of the District of New York.

To Theodore Sedgwick [1]

[New York, January, 1797]

Dr. Sir

I have been reading the report of the Secretary of the Treasury on the subject of direct taxes.[2] I think it does him credit. The gen-

ALS, Hamilton Papers, Library of Congress.
1. In *JCHW*, VI, 381, and in *HCLW*, X, 327, this letter is dated 1798. In Hamilton, *History*, VI, 592, and in *HCLW*, X, 227–28, the first paragraph of the letter H wrote to Sedgwick on January 20, 1797, is mistakenly printed as the first paragraph to this letter.
2. This report, which is dated December 14, 1796, is printed in *ASP, Finance*, I, 414–65. See also H to William Loughton Smith, January 19, 1797; H to Sedgwick, January 20, 1797; and Fisher Ames to H, January 26, 1797.

eral principles and objects are certainly good. Nor am I sure that any thing better can be done.

I remember, however, that I once promised you to put in writing my ideas on the subject. I intended to have done it and communicated them to the Secretary. My hurry & press of business prevented me. But I concluded lately to devote an Evening to a rude sketch & to send it to you. You may shew it to the Secretary & confer. If in the course of the thing it can be useful to the general end we all have in view it will give me pleasure—if not there will have been but little time mispent. Of course no use will be made of it in contradiction to the views of the Treasury Department.

As to the part which relates to land, I do not feel any strong preference of my plan to that in the Report;[3] for this in my opinion ought to be considered only as an auxiliary, and not as the *pith* of the tax. But I own I have a strong preference of my plan of a house tax to that in the Report.[4] These are my reasons.

3. In his report of December 14, 1796, Oliver Wolcott, Jr., recommended that "the value of lands" be considered "as the most eligible criterion of assessment" (*ASP, Finance*, I, 439).
4. In his report of December 14, 1796, Wolcott made the following recommendations for a tax on houses: ". . . Houses, therefore, being, in respect to their occupants, unproductive objects, and, in a fiscal view, mere indices of expense, the expediency of subjecting them to direct taxation is somewhat questionable.

"It is conceived that the houses and other buildings of the great body of farmers and laborers of a country ought to be regarded as objects of *necessary expense*, which are supported out of the profits of labor, or some other productive fund. Houses of this description are not, therefore, the most eligible objects of public revenue. If the tax were imposed by an uniform rule, its operation would not be materially different from an equal capitation: if imposed according to the value of the building, it would be very unequal, in respect to the revenue of individuals, and would, moreover, tend to discourage durable improvements.

"Such houses, however, as exceed in value the average of those occupied by farmers and laborers, may be regarded as among the most suitable objects of taxation. Perhaps there is no single criterion by which the comparative expenses of individuals can be so fairly estimated as by their dwellings. The assessment of a tax upon certain descriptions of houses only, unless restrained by legal provisions, might, however, be attended with difficulties arising from the danger of prejudice and partiality on a subject where no sense of a common interest would operate to prevent abuses.

"As a security against oppression, it is proposed that the law should declare, that houses, with the lots upon which they are erected, not exceeding two acres in any case, and not exceeding a certain value, to be defined in respect to each State, shall be wholly exempted.

"It is further proposed, that all houses and lots, exceeding in value the description to be exempted, should be distributed into three classes, with

It is more comprehensive, embracing all houses, and will be proportionably more productive. It is more certain, avoiding the evasions and partialities to which valuations will be forever liable—and I think it for that reason, likely to be at least as equal. I entertain no doubt that the rule of rates, adapted as they are to characteristic circumstances, will in fact be more favourable to equality than appraisements. I think the idea of taxing only houses of above a certain annual value will be dissatisfactory. The comparison of the proprietors of houses immediately above with those immediately below the line will beget discontent—and the errors of valuations will increase it.

I think, there will be a great advantage in throwing the weight of the tax *on houses,* as well because lands are more difficult to manage as because it will fall in a manner less dissatisfactory.

My plan as to houses can easily be combined with that in the Report as to land.

Some years ago I proposed a similar plan in the legislature of this state.[5] It went through three readings and had a great majority in its favour—but as it was essentially different from what had always before obtained in the state it was thought best to postpone to feel the sense of Constituents. I left the legislature. Changes in our political situation rendered the plan of state taxation less important—& the business shrunk out of sight. But there was every appearance that the plan would have been popular in this state.

You observe I confine myself to a Million. I would not bear hard in this way. I would add as aid, the taxes contemplated last session, on stamps, collateral successions, new modification of some articles of imports & let me add *saddle* horses. The idea of taxing slaves generally will not work well. If confined to all menial servants for luxury as Coachmen footmen cooks &c. it would be eligible.

Yrs. truly   A H

Mr Sedgwik

---

reference to their value, to be taxed uniformly in each class, at specific rates, to be prescribed by law." (*ASP, Finance,* I, 440.)

5. See "New York Assembly. An Act for Raising Certain Yearly Taxes Within This State," February 9, 1787.

[ENCLOSURE]⁶

A Million of Dollars per annum to be raised on buildings and lands on the following plan

I Upon inhabited dwelling houses thus— ⁷

Upon every such house of the description and denomination of a log house at the rate of 20 Cents for each room or apartment thereof exclusive of Garret & Cellar

Upon every other inhabited dwelling house of two rooms or apartments, exclusive of Halls or Entries garrets & Cellars, at the rate of 25 Cents for each room or apartment

Upon every such house of three rooms or apartments exclusive as before at the rate of 33⅓ Cents for each room or apartment

Upon every such house of four rooms exclusive as before at the rate of 40 Cents for each room or apartment

Upon every such house of five rooms exclusive as before at the rate of 60 Cents for each room or apartment

Upon every such house of six rooms exclusive as before at the rate of 75 Cents for each room or apartment thereof

Upon every such house of seven rooms & upwards exclusive &c. at the rate of 100 Cents &c

Upon every room in a garret or cellar of a House of the foregoing descriptions having a fire place and upon every kitchen whether in a cellar or adjacent building at the rate of 20 Cents for each room or kitchen

Upon each room or apartment of every such house painted inside the further sum of 25 Cents

6. ADf, Connecticut Historical Society, Hartford; copy, Hamilton Papers, Library of Congress.
The document which H sent to Sedgwick has not been found, and the enclosure printed above was sent by H to Wolcott on June 6, 1797. In his enclosing letter to Wolcott on June 6, H wrote: "Last session, I sent *Sedgwick*, with request to communicate it to you, my project of a *building* tax. Inclosed is the rough *Sketch*. I do not know whether there was any alteration in the copy sent to him."
In *HCLW*, III, 312, the enclosure is dated June 7, 1797.
7. In the margin H wrote: "*Remarks* These rates have been adjusted by applying their operation to a number of Houses from which it appears that they find a sufficiently exact proportion to the rent & they avoid the expence & uncertainty of valuation. Other circumstances of discrimination if thought adviseable may be added."

Upon each room or apartment of every such house papered inside or painted & bordered with paper the further sum of fifty Cents

Upon every chimney faced with tiles or cut stone other than marble the further sum of 50 Cents

Upon every Chimney faced with marble the further sum of 100 Cents

Upon ever stair case of Cedar or Ebony wood the further sum of 50 Cents

Upon ever stair case of Mahogany wood the further sum of 100 Cents.

Upon every room or apartment with stucco cornishes the further sum of 100 Cents

Upon every room with a stucco cieling the further sum of 200 Cents; but the same room shall not also be rated for cornishes of such work.

Upon every such house with pillars or pilasters outside in front the further sum of 100 Cents—

Upon every such house faced outside and in front in whole or in part with marble the further sum of 200 Cents—

These rates to be paid by the occupiers of the house whether Owners or tenants. When a house is let by parcels the landlord to be deemed the occupier.

Upon all store houses not being parts of dwelling houses in use at the rate of $\frac{1}{40}$ part of the yearly value to be determined by the actual rent if rented if not by an estimate or valuation thereof

Upon all grist Mills at the rate of 125 Cents for each run of stones therein

Upon all saw Mills at the rate of fifty Cents for each saw usually worked therein not exceeding three and for each saw above that number 25 Cents—

Upon all wharves in the Cities and Towns of Portsmouth Boston &c (enumerating the principal towns) at the rate of 12½ Cents for each foot in front thereof

Upon all wharves in any other City or Town at the rate of 6 Cents [8]

Upon all Lumber yards in the Cities or Towns of Boston Ports-

---

8. H bracketed this and the preceding paragraph and in the margin wrote: "Remarks Or this may be thrown into more classes."

mouth &c (enumerating the principal Towns) at the rate of 2½ Cents for each hundred square feet

Upon all lumber yards in other Cities or Towns, & at the rate of 1¼ Cent for each hundred square feet.

Cottages inhabited by paupers to [be] excepted—to be judged of and ascertained by the Assessors hereafter described.

The amount of the foregoing taxes in each state to be ascertained within a time to be limited by law for that purpose by the Assessors and a report thereof to be made to the Treasury, which shall then proceed to apportion according to the prescribed quota the sum remaining to make up the Million of Dollars to be levied. For example —Suppose there were five states & the product of the House tax of each as follows—

A	100 000
B	150 000
C	200 000
D	50.000
E	100.000
	600.000

There would then remain towards the Million to be levied on lands 400 000. Let there be then assigned to each state so much in land tax as together with its house tax will equal the [9]

9. The remainder of this document is missing.
In the margin H wrote: "Remarks The mode of ascertaining to be by an actual calling at each house & receiving of the Occupiers a list of the particulars which are criterions of the tax—the Officer to have power to administer an oath. A proper penalty to be annexed to misrepresentation & a power to be given upon cause of suspicion testified on oath to issue a warrant to inspect the House for ascertaining the fact. This will reconcile the idea of the sanctity of the *Castle* with the security of the Revenue."

From Rufus King [1]

[*London, February 4, 1797. Letter not found.*]

1. Letter listed in Rufus King's "Memorandum of private Letters, &c., dates & persons, from 1796 to Augt 1802," owned by Mr. James G. King, New York City.

To Robert Morris

[*New York, February 4, 1797.* On February 9, 1797, Morris wrote to Hamilton: "Your favour of the 4th only reached me Yesterday." Letter not found.]

From Rufus King

London. feb. 6. 1797

Dear sir

I have had the pleasure to receive your Letter of the 16. of Decr. and I need not express the Satisfaction which the information that it contained afforded me, the Probable termination of the Election of Pr. the general Temper of the Country, & the Effect likely to be produced by Mr. Adet's notes are such as I had not only hoped but expected; if by prudence & Firmness, which have hitherto kept us out of this Extraordinary and dessolating war, we shall be able to maintain the public peace and national Honor, we shall not only increase our Reputation as a wise people but we shall moreover establish a Precedent of inestimable worth for future Times of Trouble and Embarrassment. Nothing can exceed the applause that is here given to our Government, and no American who has not been in England can have a just Idea of the admiration expressed among all Parties of General Washington. It is a common observation that he is not only the most illustrious, but also the most meritorious Character that has hitherto appeared. The King is without doubt a very popular character among the People of this Nation; it would be saying very much, to affirm that next to him, General Washington is the most popular character among them, and yet I verily believe this to be the fact. I mention these Circumstances, not only because it will give you as it has afforded me much pleasure to hear them mentioned but also because they shew a more liberal

ALS, Hamilton Papers, Library of Congress; LC, New-York Historical Society, New York City.

manner of thinking and speaking respecting us, and a more rational Estimate of our Affairs than formerly existed. Much credit is due to Mr. Jay on this Score; who we thought would do honor, and be of advantage to our Country, but Who has done much more than I could have imagined, had I not seen the clearest proofs of his Success. He had great difficulties to encounter, he overcame many of them, some still exist, and when they will be surmounted I am unable to say. Time and patience are necessary to form a satisfactory opinion how far we shall finally be able to agree. In the main our affairs here are in a good train, the treaty I think will be fairly and fully executed. You remember the Opinion given by certain Gentlemen upon the construction of the 7. article of the treaty.[1] We have experienced embarrassments on this Subject—and for several weeks the business of the Commissioners[2] was entirely at a Stand, the advocate of this Government having denied their Power to examine any question that had been decided by the H. Court of Appeals.[3] The question was delicate; the pride and as it was alledged the importance of men of Rank and influence were almost enlisted against our pretensions, and a little imprudence might have thrown the Business

1. For the text of Article 7 of the Jay Treaty, see "Remarks on the Treaty . . . between the United States and Great Britain," July 9–11, 1795, note 39.

For criticisms of Article 7 by some Americans, see "The Defence No. XV," September 12 and 14, 1795, notes 4, 9, 16; "The Defence No. XVI," September 18, 1795, note 4.

2. The commission consisted of five members. The British members were John Nicoll and John Anstey. The American members were Christopher Gore and William Pinkney. John Trumbull, an American, was chosen by lot to be the fifth member.

3. In mid-December, 1796, the commissioners suspended proceedings because of disagreement over the extent of their jurisdiction in prize cases already decided by the British High Court of Appeals and High Court of Admiralty. On January 24, 1797, King met with Lord Grenville, who had instructed the British commissioners "that it was the opinion of the King's Government, that they should proceed in examining and deciding *every Question* that should be brought before them according to the conviction of their Consciences: in doing which they would examine cases already decided, and award on them and all others, according to the Provisions of the Treaty, which it would likewise be their duty to consider and interpret" (King to Timothy Pickering, February 20, 1797 [LS, RG 59, Despatches from United States Ministers to Great Britain, 1792–1870, Vol. 5, August 10, 1796–December 28, 1797, National Archives]). For King's report on the suspension of proceedings by the commissioners, see King to Pickering, February 20, 1797 (LS, RG 59, Despatches from United States Ministers to Great Britain, 1792–1870, Vol. 5, August 10, 1796–December 28, 1797, National Archives). In King, *The Life and Correspondence of Rufus King*, II, 620–34, King's letter to Pickering is dated February 26, 1797. See also Moore, *International Adjudications*, IV, 81–90.

into the worst possible situation. This did not happen; with moderation caution, and a conciliatory mode of proceeding these Difficulties have been intirely removed—and all is now proceeding in a satisfactory manner. The result of several conferences has been after the manifestation of much candor and fairness, on the part of this Government, a direction to the British Commissioners to unite with ours, and to proceed to hear and decide every Question that shall be brought before them according to the Provisions of the Treaty, which it was added it was the Duty of the Comrs. to consider and interpret. They have accordingly decided a case of considerable consequence, which is that of the Patersons of Baltimore—a Ship & Cargo belonging to them had been captured & condemned in the W. Indies.[4] This Sentence had been affirmed in the High Court of appeals, and a memorial in behalf of Patersons was preferred to the Comrs. for Compensations for their Loss & Damages. The Commissioners have pronounced (Doctor Nicholl only dissenting of a full Board) that they have Jurisdiction of the Cause, and that upon its merits the Pattersons are intitled to full & complete compensation for their Loss & Damages to be paid &c. according to the Provisions of the Treaty.

By Letters received today from Paris I learn the unpleasant information that Genl. Pinckney was on the 28 ulto. ordered by the Directory to leave Paris,[5] and that he intended to depart for Holland (where he will wait the orders of our Govt) on the 31. I can-

4. For the case of the brig *Betsey*, which was owned by William and George Patterson of Baltimore, see Oliver Wolcott, Jr., to H, October 6, 1795, note 2.

5. Charles Cotesworth Pinckney arrived in Paris on December 5, 1796. On December 11, 1796, the French Minister of Foreign Affairs, Charles Delacroix, wrote to James Monroe that the Directory would "not acknowledge nor receive another minister plenipotentiary from the United States, until after the redress of the grievances demanded of the American Government, and which the French republic has a right to expect from it" (*ASP, Foreign Relations*, II, 6). For more than a month the French government refused either to receive Pinckney or to give him written orders to leave the country. After Pinckney had made it clear that he would not depart without being expressly directed to do so, the French issued such orders, and Pinckney left Paris and arrived at Amsterdam on February 17, 1797. For Pinckney's account of his experiences in France along with enclosures of copies of the relevant documents, see Pinckney to Pickering, December 20, 1796, January 6, February 18, 1797 (LC, RG 59, Despatches from United States Ministers to France, 1789–1869, Vol. 5, November 17, 1796–September 24, 1797, National Archives). This material is printed in *ASP, Foreign Relations*, II, 5–10, where Pinckney's first letter is incorrectly dated December 10, 1796.

not fully account for this Step after the irresolution that for some time has existed; whether it is to be ascribed to information which has been thought sufficient to satisfy the Directory of the Result of the Election for Pr. or whether it is to be attributed to the late astonishing victories of Buonaparte which have litterally destroyed an Army of 40.000 Austrians,[6] I am uncertain—perhaps both have contributed to this Extraordinary Step.

Yrs very sincerely   Rufus King

Col. Hamilton

6. This is a reference to a succession of French victories in Italy in early 1797. At Rivoli on January 14, 1797, Napoleon defeated the Austrian forces, which numbered twenty-eight thousand and were under the command of General Josef Alvinczy. Two days later in the vicinity of Mantua, Napoleon captured almost all the nine thousand soldiers commanded by Marquis Giovanni de Provera. On February 2, 1797, the fortress of Mantua with eighteen thousand men surrendered to the French.

To Timothy Pickering

[New York, February 6, 1797]

Dr Sir

I duly received your letter of the 23 of Jany [1] with its inclosure,[2] for which I am much obliged to you. I have read it with great pleasure. It is a substantial satisfactory paper will do good in this Country & as to France I presume events will govern there.

Is it not proper to call upon the Merchants to furnish your Department with statements & proofs of the spoliations which we have suffered from the French as was done when the English were in their mischievous Carreer? [3]

Yrs. with true esteem   A Hamilton
                      Feby 6. 1797

I received your other letter [4] with certain enclosures.

T Pickering Esq

ALS, Massachusetts Historical Society, Boston.
1. Letter not found.
2. This enclosure was apparently a copy of Pickering to Charles Cotesworth

Pinckney, January 17, 1797. See George Washington to H, January 22, 1797; H to Washington, January 25-31, 1797.
3. See Edmund Randolph to Washington, March 2, 1794 (LC, RG 59, Domestic Letters of the Department of State, Vol. 6, January 2-June 26, 1794, National Archives).
4. Pickering to H, January 30, 1797.

The Warning No. II [1]

[New York, February 7, 1797]

Independent of the commands of honor, the coolest calculations of interest forbid our becoming the instruments of the Ambition of France, by associating with her in the War. The question is no longer the establishment of liberty on the basis of Republican Government. This point, the enemies of France have ceased to dispute. The question now is whether she shall be aggrandized by new acquisitions, and her enemies reduced by dismemberments, to a degree, which may render her the Mistress of Europe, and consequently in a great measure of America. This is truly the remaining subject of contention.

They who understood the real strength and resources of France, before the present war, knew that she was intrinsically the most powerful nation of Europe. The incidents of the War have displayed this fact in a manner which is the astonishment of the world. If France can finally realize her present plan of aggrandisement, she will attain to a degree of greatness and power, which if not counteracted by internal disorder, will tend to make her the terror and the scourge of Nations. The spirit of moderation in a State of overbearing Power is a phœnomenon, which has not yet appeared and which no wise man will expect ever to see. It is certain, that a very different spirit has hitherto marked the career of the new republic; and it is due to truth to add, that the ardent, impetuous and military genius of the French affords perhaps less prospect of such a spirit in them than in any other people.

'Twere therefore contrary to our true interest to assist in building

ADf, Hamilton Papers, Library of Congress; *Gazette of the United States, & Philadelphia Daily Advertiser*, February 7, 1797.
1. The other issues of "The Warning" are dated January 27, February 21, 27, March 13, 27, 1796.

up this Colossus to the enormous size at which she aims. 'Twere a policy as shortsighted as mean to seek safety in a subserviency to her views, as the price of her clemency. This at best would be but a temporary respite from the rod; if indeed that can be called a respite, which is of itself the sacrifice of a real to a nominal independence.

These reflections are not designed to rouse a spirit of hostility against France, or to inculcate the idea that we ought of choice to participate in the War against her. They are intended merely to fortify the motives of honor, which forbid our stooping to be *compelled*, either to submit, without resistance, to a virtual war on her part—or to avert her blows by engaging in the war on her side.

When it was the opinion, that France was defending the cause of Liberty, it was a decisive argument against embarking with her in the contest, that it would expose us to hazards and evils, infinitely disproportioned to the assistance we could render. Now that the question plainly is, whether France shall give the law to mankind, the addition of our opposition to her plan could have too little influence upon the event to justify our willingly encountering the certain dangers and mischiefs of the enterprize. 'Tis our true policy to remain at peace, if we can, to negotiate our subjects of complaint as long as they shall be at all negotiable,[2] to bear all that a free and independent people is at liberty to bear, to defer a resort to arms 'till a last effort of negotiation shall have demonstrated that there is no alternative, but the surrender of our sovereignty or the defence of it—that the only option is between infamy or war. But if unhappily this period shall ever arrive, it will impose a sacred and indispensable duty to meet the contest with firmness, and relying on a just providence confidently to commit the issue to the God of battles!

While it is a consolation to know, that our Government, on this as on other trying occasions, will act with perfect prudence, and will do every thing that honor permits to preserve peace: Yet it is not to be forgotten that there is a point at which forbearance must stop—beyond which moderation were baseness—where we must halt and make a stand for our rights or cease to pretend to any.

2. In *JCHW*, VII, 622, this sentence ends: ". . . as long as they shall be at all negotiable to defer and ———." The remainder of this paragraph and the following paragraph are omitted.

When the indiscriminate seizure of our vessels by British Cruisers under the order of [the sixth of November, 1793,] [3] had brought our affairs with Great Britain to a crisis which led to the measure of sending a special envoy to that Country, to obtain relief and reparation, it was well understood that the issue of that mission was to determine the question of peace or war between the two nations. In like manner, it is to be expected that our Executive will make a solemn and final appeal to the Justice and Interest of France, will insist in mild but explicit terms on the renunciation of the pretension to intercept the lawful commerce of neutrals with the enemies of France and the institution of some equitable mode of ascertaining and retributing the losses which the exercise of it has inflicted upon our Merchants.[4] If the experiment shall fail, there will be nothing left but to repel aggression and defend our commerce and independence. The resolution to do this will then be imposed on the Government by a painful but irresistible necessity and it were an outrage to the American name and character to doubt that the people of the United States will approve the resolution, and will support it with a constancy worthy of the justice of their cause and of the glory they have heretofore deserved and acquired.

No: let this never be doubted! The servile minions of France— those who have no sensibility to injury but when it comes from Great Britain, who are unconscious of any rights to be protected against France, who at a moment when the public safety more than ever demands a strict union between the people and their government traiterously labour to detach them from it, and to turn against the government for pretended faults, the resentment which the real oppressions of France ought to inspire—these wretched men will discover in the end, that they are as insignificant as they are unprincipled. They will find that they have vainly flattered themselves with the cooperation of the great body of those men with whom

---

3. Space left blank in MS. The bracketed material has been taken from the *Gazette of the United States, & Philadelphia Daily Advertiser*, February 7, 1797. The British order in council of November 6, 1793, instructed British naval commanders to "stop and detain all ships laden with goods the produce of any colony belonging to France, or carrying provisions or other supplies for the use of any such colony, . . . [to] bring the same, with their cargoes, to legal adjudications in our Courts of Admiralty" (*ASP, Foreign Relations*, III, 264).

4. See H to George Washington, January 25–31, 1797.

the spirit of party has hitherto associated them. In such an extremity the adventitious discriminations of party will be lost in the patriotism and pride of the American character. Good citizens of every political denomination [5] will remember that they are Americans—that when their Country is in danger, the merit or demerit of particular measures is no longer a question—that it is the duty of all to unite their efforts to guard the national rights, to avert national humiliation, and to withstand the imposition of a foreign yoke. The true and genuine spirit of 1776, not the vile counterfeits of it which so often disgust our eyes and our ears, will warn every truly American heart and light up in it a noble emulation to maintain inviolate the rights and unsullied the honor of the Nation. It will be proved to the confusion of all false patriots, that we did not break the fetters of one foreign tyranny to put on those of another. It will be again proved to the world that we understand our rights and have the courage to defend them.

But there is still ground to hope that we shall not be driven to this disagreeable extremity. The more deliberate calculations of France will probably rescue us from the present embarrassment. If she perseveres in her plan she must inevitably add all the neutral powers to the number of her enemies. How will this fulfil the purpose of destroying the commerce of Great Britain? The commerce of those powers with France will then intirely cease and be turned more extensively into the channels of Great Britain, protected by her navy with the cooperation of the maritime force of those powers. The result will be the reverse of what is projected by the measure. The commerce and revenue of Britain will in all likelihood be augmented rather than diminished; and her arms will receive an important reinforcement.

Violent and unjust measures commonly defeat their own purpose. The plan of starving France was of this description and operated against the views of its projectors. The plan now adopted by France of cutting off the trade of neutrals with her enemies, alike violent and unjust, will no doubt end in similar disappointment. Let us hope that it will be abandonned and that ultimate rupture will be avoided —but let us also contemplate the possibility of the contrary and prepare our minds seriously for the unwelcome Event. AMERICUS

5. In MS, "demonination."

From Robert Morris

Alexr Hamilton Esqr
New York

Philada Feby. 9th. 1797

Dear Sir

Your favour of the 4th[1] only reached me Yesterday. I will get Mr Tilghman[2] or Mr Lewis[3] to write to you on the point you desire.[4] In the mean time as I am anxious to have the Land business settled,[5] I think it best to have the papers assigned to Mr Garrett Cottringer in such manner as to Vest him with the right for the present and as that he may release or convey to me my or my order hereafter. The C[h]ancery suit[6] must be dismissed & I will pay your draft at a few days sight for Amot. of the Charges.

I am Dr Sir   Yours &c.   RM

LC, Robert Morris Papers, Library of Congress.
1. Letter not found.
2. William Tilghman was a Philadelphia attorney.
3. William Lewis was a Philadelphia attorney whom Morris had consulted in the past. See Lewis to H, May 4, 1796.
4. Although H's letter has not been found, the "point" on which he desired information concerned a suit which Charles Bridgen was threatening to bring against Morris on behalf of William Talbot and William Allum. See Morris to H, December 31, 1796; January 23, 1797.
Morris had endorsed a bill of exchange drawn by John Nicholson. This bill ended up in the hands of Talbot and Allum who were pressing Morris for payment (Morris to H, December 31, 1796). Morris contended that Nicholson should pay this bill, but H wanted the opinions of attorneys in Pennsylvania on that state's laws concerning this matter. Morris accordingly asked William Tilghman to write to H on this matter. See Morris to H, February 27, 1797.
5. The "Land business" refers to Morris's conveyance to Garrett Cottringer of fifty thousand acres of Genesee land to be used to pay a debt owed to William Pulteney and William Hornby. See the introductory note to Morris to H, April 27, 1796.
6. For this suit, see the introductory note to Morris to H, April 27, 1796.

To Timothy Pickering

[New York, February 10, 1797]

Dr Sir

If I recollect right, Chancellor Livingston while Secy for foreign Affairs reported a censure upon Our Commissioners who made the peace with G Britain for not obeying their instructions with regard to France.[1] Will you favour me in confidence with the real state of this business? I was at the time a member of Congress. It was immediately on the arrival of the provisional articles.[2]

I trust my Dear Sir *effectual measures* are taking to bring us to some issue with France to ascertain whether her present plan is to be persisted in or abandonned. For surely our Commerce ought not to be thus an undefended prey.

Yrs truly

A H

Feby 10. 1797

T Pickering Esq

ALS, Massachusetts Historical Society, Boston.
1. Robert R. Livingtson, Secretary of State for Foreign Affairs at the time of the conclusion of a peace treaty between the United States and Great Britain in 1783, had raised the question of whether the American commissioners had violated their instructions by negotiating a peace treaty without the knowledge and concurrence of France. See "Continental Congress. Remarks on the Provisional Peace Treaty," March 19, 1783, note 1. Livingston's opinion on the treaty is discussed at length in Pickering to H, April 5, 1797.
2. The provisional peace treaty between the United States and Great Britain, signed on November 30, 1782, reached Congress on March 12, 1783. See, for example, James Madison to Edmund Randolph, March 12, 1783 (Edmund C. Burnett, ed., *Letters of the Continental Congress* [Washington, D.C., 1921–1938], VII, 75–76).

To Hall and Stimpson [1]

New York, February 11, 1797. "The suits against Riley as a Partner of Wetmore are expected to be matured for Trial at the ensuing Circuit Court which begins the 20th of March. I should of course want the original documents to establish the Copartnership and the original notes & acknowleged accounts to establish the respective demands of the parties. As the measures preparatory to Trial are attended with considerable advances to Officers of Courts say about five pounds in each suit the Gentlemen concerned will not expect that I should make these advances. I request therefore that an adequate sum be remitted. . . ." [2]

ALS, W. W. Corcoran Papers, Library of Congress.
1. For background to this letter, see Hall and Stimpson to H, October 24, 1796.
2. Under the date of March 14, 1797, H noted in his Cash Book, 1795–1804: "To Hall & Stimpson received on account of suits against Riley 90" (AD, Hamilton Papers, Library of Congress).

To Rufus King

[New York, February 15, 1797]

My D Sir

Geave me leave to recall to your recollection and acquaintance Mr. De Talon the bearer of this, who, as he informs me, goes to Europe on private business.[1] I need not observe that he is an interesting man, as you know all his titles to the attention, which your situation will permit you to afford. You must not think, I forget you, because I do no write (for this is only my third letter).[2] I am overwhelmed in professional business and have scarcely a moment for any thing else.

You will have learnt the terrible depredations which the French have committed upon our Trade in the West-Indies on the declared principle of intercepting our whole Trade with the ports of her enemies. This conduct is making the impression which might be expected though not with that electric rapidity which would have attended similar Treatment from another power. The present session of Congress is likely to be very unproductive. That body is in the situation which we foresaw certain *anti* executive maxims would bring them to.

Mr. Adams is President, Mr. Jefferson Vice President. Our Jacobins say they are well pleased and that the *Lion* & the *Lamb* are to lie down together. Mr. Adam's PERSONAL friends talk a little in the same way. Mr. *Jefferson* is not half so ill a man as we have been accustommed to think him. There is to be a united and a vigorous administration. Sceptics like me quietly look forward to the event— willing to hope but not prepared to believe. If Mr. Adams has *Vanity* to plan a plot has been laid to take hold of it. We trust his real good sense and integrity will be a sufficient shield.

Yrs. Affectly

A Hamilton
Feby. 15. 1797

R King Esq

ALS, New-York Historical Society, New York City.
1. At the outbreak of the French Revolution, Antoine Omer Talon was civil lieutenant of the prison of the Châtelet and chief justice of the Criminal Court of France. In 1792 he was accused of plotting to smuggle the King out of France and fled to the United States. He was a founder and an agent of the Asylum Company, which established a colony for French refugees on the Susquehanna River. In 1797 he became interested in the Ceres Company, an agricultural land development to the west of the Asylum Company's property. It was in this connection that Talon was going to Europe.
2. H to King, November 30, December 16, 1796.

To Oliver Wolcott, Junior

[New York, February 17, 1797]

I groan My Dr. Sir at the disgraceful course of our affairs. I pity all those who are officially in their vortex. The behaviour of Congress in the present crisis is a new political phœnomenon. They must be severally arraigned before the Bar of the Public. How unfortunate that our friends suffer themselves by their passiveness to be confounded in the guilt.

Yrs. truly

A H
Feby. 17. 1797

ALS, Connecticut Historical Society, Hartford.

The Warning No. III [1]

[New York, February 21, 1797]

The Paris Accounts [2] inform us that France has lately exercised towards Genoa an act of atrocious oppression, which is an additional and a striking indication of the domineering and predatory Spirit by which she is governed. This little Republic, whose territory scarcely extends beyond the walls of her metropolis, has been compelled, it seems, to ransom herself from the talons of France by a contribution of nearly a million of Dollars; a large sum for her contracted resources. For this boon, "the French Government engages on its part to *renounce all claims upon Genoa, to forget* what has passed during the present war, to forbear any future demands." It would appear from this, that France to colour the odious exaction, besides the pretence of misconduct towards her in the present war has not disdained to resort to the stale and pitiful device of reviving some antiquated and derelict claim upon the Country itself. In vain did the signal hazards encountered by Genoa to preserve her neutrality in defiance of the host of enemies originally leagued against France, in vain did the character and title of Republic plead for a more generous treatment: the attractions of plunder predominated. The Spirit of Rapine callous to the touch of justice, blind to the testimony of truth, deaf to the voice of entreaty, had marked out and devoted the victim. There was no alternative but to compound or perish.

If it be even supposed, though this has never appeared, that at

ADf, Hamilton Papers, Library of Congress; *Gazette of the United States, & Philadelphia Daily Advertiser*, February 21, 1797.

1. The other issues of "The Warning" are dated January 27, February 7, 27, March 13, 27, 1797.
2. H is referring to the following item, dated "Paris, Nov. 15," which appeared in the *Gazette of the United States, & Philadelphia Daily Advertiser*, on February 8, 1797: "The Republic consents to pay four millions and a half liv[r]es Tournois to France, half of which is to be instantly paid in specie, and the rest at an appointed time. The French Government engages, on its part, to renounce all claims on Genoa, to forget what has passed during the present war, and not to trouble the Genoese with any future demands." The convention between France and Genoa is dated October 9, 1796.

some period of the war, Genoa may be chargeable with acts of questionable propriety in relation to France, it is manifest that it ought to be attributed to the necessity of a situation which must have obliged her to temporise. A very small and feeble state in the midst of so many great conflicting powers, parts of her territories occupied by armies which she was unable to oppose—it were a miracle indeed if her conduct in every particular will bear the test of a rigorous scrutiny. But if at any time the pressure of circumstances may have occasioned some slight deviation, there is nevertheless full evidence of a constant solicitude on the part of Genoa to maintain to the utmost of her ability a sincere neutrality. It is impossible to forget the glorious stand which she at one time made against the imperious efforts of Great Britain to force her from her neutral position.[3] The magnanimous and exemplary fortitude which she displayed on that occasion excited in this country universal admiration and must have made a deep impression. 'Tis only to recollect that instance to be satisfied that the treatment which she has just experienced from France merits the indignant execration of mankind. Unfortunate Genoa! how little didst thou imagine that thou wert destined so soon to be compelled to purchase thy safety from the crushing weight of that hand which ought to have been the first to rise in thy defence.

How fruitful, at the same time, of instruction to us is this painful example! The most infatuated partisans of France cannot but see in it an unequivocal proof of the rapacious and vindictive policy which dictates her measures. All men must see in it that the flagrant injuries, which we are now suffering from her, proceed from a

3. In October, 1793, a combined English and Spanish squadron entered the port of Genoa, captured three French vessels, and seized the stores of another French ship which were in the public magazines at Spezia. To a complaint from the Genoese government, the British envoy, Francis Drake, replied on October 5: ". . . In other times and in other circumstances, neutrality might be laudable, but in this moment it is not possible. . . ." He then urged the Genoese government ". . . to repel the dangers which menace it; to co-operate with the allied powers in re-establishing order, and a permanent peace in Europe; to cut all ties whatever with the present rulers of France, and to drive from its bosom all their agents and adherents" (Debrett, *A Collection of State Papers*, II, 341–43). Threatened with a declaration of war by France, the Genoese, however, refused to accept Drake's proposal. They also refused to dismiss diplomatic representatives in Genoa despite Drake's orders that they do so. A British squadron then blockaded the port of Genoa. On August 26, 1794, the British ended the blockade.

general plan of domination and plunder; from a disposition to prostrate nations at her feet, to trample upon their necks, to ravish from them whatever her avidity or convenience may think fit to dedicate to her own use.

The last intelligence from France seems to dispel the doubt whether the depredations in the West Indies may not have resulted from misapprehension or abuse of the orders of the French Government. It is now understood to be a fact that the Cruisers of France every where are authorised to capture and bring in all vessels bound to the ports of her enemies.[4]

This plan is pregnant with the worst evils which are to be dreaded from the declared and unqualified hostility of any foreign power. If France after being properly called upon to renounce it, shall persevere in the measure, there cannot be a question but that open war will be preferable to such a state. By whatever name treachery or pusyllanimity may attempt to disguise it, 'tis in fact war, war of the worst kind, WAR ON ONE SIDE. If we can be induced to submit to it longer than is necessary to ascertain that it cannot be averted by negotiation, we are undone as a people. Whether our determination shall be to lock up our Trade by embargoes, or to permit our commerce to continue to float an unprotected prey to French Cruisers, our degradation and ruin will be equally complete. The destruction of our Navigation & Trade, the annihilation of our mercantile capital, the dispersion & loss of our seamen obliged to emigrate for subsistence, the extinction of our Revenue, the fall of public credit, the stagnation of every species of industry, the general impoverishment of our citizens, these will be minor evils in the

4. In a report dated June 21, 1797, on French depredations on American commerce from October 1, 1796, to June 22, 1797, Timothy Pickering wrote: "As applicable to captures made since last October [1796], the decree of the Executive Directory of the 2d of July, 1796, merits the first attention. It announces that the conduct of France towards neutrals will be regulated by the manner in which they should suffer the English to treat them. At Malaga and Cadiz, the French consuls have interpreted this decree to authorize the capture and condemnation of American vessels for the single circumstance of their being destined to a British port. But its fullest effect has been produced in the West Indies, whose seas swarm with privateers and gun boats, which have been called forth by the latitude allowed to their depredations by the indefinite terms of that decree, and the explanatory orders of the agents of the Directory at Guadaloupe and St. Domingo . . ." (*ASP, Foreign Relations*, II, 28). For the decree of July 2, 1796, see H to George Washington, January 19, 1796, note 4.

dreadful catalogue. Some years of security and exertion would repair them. But the humiliation of the American mind would be a lasting and a mortal disease in our social habit. Mental debasement is the greatest misfortune that can befal a people. The most pernicious of conquests, which a state can experience, is a conquest over that elevated sense of its own rights which inspires a due sensibility to insult and injury, over that virtuous pride of character which prefers any peril or sacrifice to a final submission to oppression, and which regards national ignominy as the greatest of national calamities.

The records of history contain numerous proofs of this truth. But an appeal to them is unnecessary. Holland and Italy present to our immediate observation examples as decisive as deplorable. The former within the last years has undergone two revolutions by the intervention of foreign powers without even a serious struggle. Mutilated of precious portions of its territory at home, by pretended benefactors but real despoilers; its dominions abroad slide into the possession of its enemies rather as derelicts than as the acquisitions of victory. Its fleets surrender without a blow. Important only by the spoils, which it offers, no less to its friends than to its enemies— every symptom about is portentous of national annihilation.

With regard to Italy, 'tis sufficient to say, that she is debased enough not even to dare to take part in a contest on which at this moment her destiny is suspended.

Moderation in every nation is a virtue. In weak or young nations, it is often wise to take every chance by patience and address to divert hostility and in this view to *hold parley* with insult and injury —but to *capitulate* with oppression, rather to surrender at discretion to it is in any nation that has any power of resistance as foolish as it contemptible. The honor of a nation is its life. Deliberately to abandon it is to commit an act of political suicide. There is treason in the sentiment avowed in the language of some, and betrayal by the conduct of others, that we ought to bear any thing from France rather than go to war with her. The Nation which can prefer disgrace to danger is prepared for a Master and deserves one.

From Gerard Bancker and Philip Livingston [1]

New York, February 22, 1797. "In our Character of Executors, we are Trustees for a Number of persons who do not think the Claims of Mr. & Mrs. Ricketts well founded, and who would suppose us blameable, if we afforded them any Facilities, Whatever therefore may be our own inclinations, we are advised to put the Claimants to their Bill for discovery, and to submit ourselves to the Chancellor, whether in a Matter perfectly within his Jurisdiction, he will suffer his Court to be a Hand Maid for others. . . ."

LS, in the handwriting of Gerard Bancker, Hamilton Papers, Library of Congress.
1. For background to this letter, see James Ricketts to H, June 24, 1796; January 1, 1797.
Bancker was treasurer of New York State from 1778 until his death in 1798.

To Robert Morris

[*New York, February 23, 1797.* On March 3, 1797, Morris wrote to Hamilton and referred to "Yours of the 23d." *Letter not found.*]

To Theodore Sedgwick

[New York, February 26, 1797]

My dear Sir

The present inimitable course of our public affairs proves me to be a very bad politician so that I am afraid to suggest any idea that occurs to me. Yet I will give over my timidity & communicate for your consideration a reverie which has struck me.

It is a fact, that the resentment of the French Government is very much levelled at the actual President. A change of the person (however undespicable in other respects) may give a change to the passion, and may also furnish a bridge to retreat over. This is a great advantage for a new President & the most ought to be made of it. For it is much our interest to preserve peace, if we can with honor and if we cannot it will be very important to prove that no endeavour to do it has been omitted.

Were I Mr. Adams, then I believe I should begin my Presidency by naming an extraordinary Commission to the French Republic. And I think it would consist of three persons, Mr. Madison Mr. Pinkney & Mr. Cabot.[1] I would pursue this course for several reasons, because I would have a man as influential with the French as Mr. Madison yet I would not trust him alone lest his Gallicism should work amiss—because I would not wound Mr. Pinkney so recently sent in the same spirit. Thirdly I think *Cabot* would mix very useful ingredients in the Cup.

This Com~ should be charged to make explanations, to remonstrate, to ask indemnification and they should be empowered to make a new Treaty of commerce not inconsistent with our other Treaties—& perhaps to abrogate or remodify the Treaty of Alliance.

That Treaty can only be inconvenient to us in future. The Guarantee of our sovereignty & Independence henceforth is nominal. The Guarantee of the West-India Island of France as we advance in strength will be more & more real. In future & in a truly defensive war I think we shall be bound to comply efficaciously with our Guarantee. Nor have I been able to see that it means less than obligation to take part in such a war with our whole force. I have no idea of Treaties which are not executed.

Hence I want to get rid of that Treaty by mutual *consent* or to liquidate its meaning to a Treaty of *definite* succour in a clearly *defensive* war, so many men, so many ships, so much money &c to be furnished by one ally to the other.[2] This of course must be so managed as to exclude unequivocally the present War in all its possible mutations.[3]

Such objects are important enough for *three*. In executive matters, I am as little fond as most people of plurality—but I think it pedantry to admit no exceptions to any general rule. And I believe under the circumstances of the case a Commission would be adviseable. I give my dream as it has occurred. You will do with it what you please.

Yrs.

AH
Feby. 26. 179⟨7⟩

The idea here given to be useful ought to be executed at once. The Senate should not be permitted to disperse.

ALS, Hamilton Papers, Library of Congress.
1. H had made the same recommendation and suggested the same commissioners in H to George Washington, January 25-31, 1797.
2. This is a reference to the Treaty of Alliance between the United States and France signed at Paris on February 6, 1778. For information on the articles of the treaty which H wished to have modified, see H to Washington, January 25-31, 1797.
3. In the margin opposite this paragraph, H wrote: "The idea of a definite duration would also be useful."

From Robert Morris [1]

Philada. Feby 27th. 1797

Dear Sir

Mr Tilghman [2] authorizes me to tell you that our Law respecting endorsements is exactly the same as the Law of England & that 20 ℔ Ct is the Amot of Damages on protested Bills drawn here upon Europe.[3]

Mr. Nicholson is returned to this City & I think the holders of his bill should Apply to him for payment. I think he would make some arrangement with them so as to secure the payment and allow compensation for time. I wish you would mention this to them; I will aid the Negotiation if they will open one.

I am very anxious to have the affair of the Genesee Tract settled as proposed in my last,[4] that is, to have the Chancery Suit withdrawn or dismissed and the Deed or Mortgage assigned to Mr. Cottringer, or done away so that the property Revest in me, one or the other I pray to have done immediately & give preferrance to that which you may think best for me. But I pray that no longer delay may be offered as my intended operations require it & are essential. Let me hear from you & be assured of the Esteem & regard of Dr Sir

Your Obed Servt.   Robt Morris

Alexr Hamilton Esqr
New York

ALS, Hamilton Papers, Library of Congress; LC, Robert Morris Papers, Library of Congress.

1. The first two paragraphs of this letter refer to a threatened suit by William Talbot and William Allum against Morris over a bill which had been drawn by John Nicholson and which Morris had endorsed. See Morris to H, December 31, 1796; January 23, February 9, 1797, note 4.

The last paragraph concerns a debt which Morris owed to William Pulteney and William Hornby and Morris's efforts to pay or secure this debt. For this debt and the negotiations concerning it, see the introductory note to Morris to H, April 27, 1796. See also Morris to H, May 3, 10, 17, 31, 1796, January 7, 23, February 9, 1796; H to Charles Williamson, May 17–30, 1796.

2. See Morris to H, February 9, 1797.

3. For an explanation of the contents of this paragraph, see Herbert Alan Johnson, *The Law Merchant and Negotiable Instruments in Colonial New York: 1664–1730* (Chicago, 1963), 39–40.

4. Morris to H, February 9, 1797.

The Warning No. IV [1]

[New York, February 27, 1797]

The emissaries of France when driven from every other expedient for extenuating her depredations have a last refuge in the example of Great Britain. The Treatment which we receive from France (say they) is not worse than that which was received from Great Britain. If this apology were founded in fact it would still be a miserable subterfuge. For what excuse is it to France, or what consolation to us, that she, our boasted friend and benefactress, treats us only not worse, than a Power which is stigmatised as an envious rival and an implacable foe?

The conduct of Great Britain appealed to in justification of France was admitted by all to be inexcuseable. The Gallic Faction thought it so extreme as to call for immediate reprisals. The real patriots differed from them only in thinking that an armed negotiation to end in reprisals, if unattended with success was preferable to immediate hostilitity.[2] How dare the men, who at that period were

ADf, Hamilton Papers, Library of Congress; *Gazette of the United States, & Philadelphia Daily Advertiser*, February 27, 1797.

1. The other issues of "The Warning" are dated January 27, February 7, 21, March 13, 27, 1797.

2. H is referring to Britain's failure to fulfill the terms of the definitive treaty of peace of 1783 and her spoliations of United States commerce, which led in March, 1794, to a thirty-day embargo on all United States shipping. For the embargo of March 26, 1794, see the introductory note to H to George Washington, March 8, 1794; "Cabinet Meeting. Opinion on the Best Mode of Executing the Embargo," March 26, 1794. The Federalist solution to the Anglo-

the clamorous champions of our national dignity, how dare they (I ask) now to stand forth the preachers, not of moderation (for in the propriety of this all unite) but of tame submission, but of a servilitity abject enough to love and cherish the hand which despoils us, to kiss the Rod which stings us with unpro[vo]ked lashes? What logic what magic can render innocent or venial in France that which was so critical and odious in Great Britain?

The pretext (we know) of France is that we have permitted Great Britain to treat us in the same manner and that she acts on the principle of a just retaliation; and her deluded or debauched adherents are mean or prostitute enough to reecho the excuse.

Let us grant for argument sake all that can be pretended on this subject namely that through want of energy in our administration or from the opinion which it entertained of the situation of the country, there has been too much patience under the oppressions of Great Britain—is this really a justification to France? Is a defect of vigour in the Government of one country, or an under estimate of ill means for repelling injury, a sufficient cause for another Government lavish in professions of friendship, to imitate towards it the aggressions which it has suffered from another? What in private life would be said of the man, who calling himself the friend of another, because the last had too passively allowed a third, the enemy of both, to wrest from him a portion of his property, should deduce from this a pretext to strip him of the remainder? Has language epithets too severe for such a character? Is not the guilt of unjust violence, in a case like this aggravated by that of hypochrisy and perfidy?

But this is not our only reply. The truth is (and a truth we may boldly proclaim) that we never did tolerate the aggressions of Great Britain; that we have steadily resisted them and resisted with success. In the respectable attitude of an armed negotiation, seconded by the self-denying and very influential measure of an embargo—we sent to demand a revocation of the orders under which we suffered and retribution for the losses we had sustained. The orders were revoked and the retribution has been stipulated and the stipulation is in a

---

American crisis had been the appointment of John Jay as Envoy Extraordinary to Great Britain. See the introductory note to H to Washington, April 14, 1794.

course of honourable and liberal execution. The redress of ancient grievances on the ground of a reciprocity demanded by every principle of rectitude, has been superadded to that of more recent ones. Our flag at this moment proudly waves on the ramparts, which had been so long detained from us; and Indian butcheries along the whole extent of our vast frontier have been terminated. More than this: the Redress obtained from Great Britain was a principal c⟨ause⟩ of the happy accommodation of our dispute with Spain of the recognition of our right to navigate the Missi[ssi]ppi and of the establishment of a Southern boundary equal to our most sanguine wishes.* ³ These are the fruits (and immense fruits they are) of a vigorous though temperate resistance to the aggressions of Great Britain.

'Tis therefore in every sense false that our Government has *permitted* Great Britain to *do* as France is now *doing*. Except here and there, the accidental irregularity of the Command of a particular Ship—there is not one clear right which the laws of nations intitle us to cla⟨im⟩ that is not now respected by Great Britain, and to a degree unusual in the history of the treatment of neutral nations by great belligerent powers.

It follows, that the suggestion on which France bottoms her ill treatment of us is a frivolous and colourless pretext. Tis to confound all just ideas to consider a temporary forbearance as a permission or acquiescence—to pretend to retaliate upon an injured party the injury which it has endured from another, to pretend above all to

---

* *Note* This consequence was foreseen & foretold. And the prediction is confirmed by that part of the declaration of war of Spain against B which makes it a charge against the latter that in the Treaty with the U S she had "no respect or consideration for the known rights of Spain" ⁴ and in the sudden disappearance after that Treaty of the obstacles which had so long impeded our negotiations with Spain.

3. H is referring to the Treaty of Friendship, Limits, and Navigation between the United States and Spain, which was signed at San Lorenzo el Real on October 27, 1795 (Miller, *Treaties*, II, 318–38).

4. On August 19, 1796, Spain and France signed a treaty of alliance at San Ildefonso (Martens, *Recûeil*, VI, 255–62). On October 8, 1796, Spain declared war against Great Britain. The declaration was accompanied by a manifesto, issued three days earlier, in which the King of Spain accused Lord Grenville of ". . . bad faith . . . by his silence upon the subject of all his negotiations with other powers, particularly in the treaty concluded on the 19th November, 1794, with the United States of America, without any regard to my rights, which were well known to him" (Debrett, *A Collection of State Papers*, V, 115).

retaliate that injury after it is passed, has ceased, and has been redressed. We are bound to conclude that our real crime in the eye of France is that we had the temerity to think and to act for ourselves, & did not plunge headlong into War with G B that the principal streams of our commerce from the national relations of demand and supply flow through the channels of her commerce and that the booty which its offers to rapacity exceeds the organised means of protextion.

But a Country containing five millions of people, the second in the number of its Seamen that sinew of maritime power with an export of sixty millions, understanding its rights not deficient in spirit to vindicate them, if compelled against its will to exert its strength and resources, will under the guidance of patriotic and faithful councils be at no loss to convince its despoilers that there is as much folly as wickedness in such a Calculation. This reflection ought at once to console and animate us though the remembrance of former friendship & a spirit of virtuous moderation will induce us still to wish that there may [be] some error in appearances that the views of France are not as violent & as hostile as they seem to be—that an amicable explanation may still dispel the impending clouds and brighten the political horison with a happy reconciliation.

To William Beekman [1]

[*New York, March 1, 1797.*] [2] "Having reconsidered the case of your Uncle (Wm. Beekman's) Will [3] with the authorities—I advise the Devisees to claim all that by the Partition became his several property & which in my former opinion with Mr. Evertson [4] was considered as passing by his Will, not merely a *proportion* equal to his interest before Partition in the part which remained to him after partition. The principle seems to be not only that a partition simply is not a revocation of the devise but that the part acquired in severalty in lieu of the part before held in common passes wholly to the devisee. . . ." [5]

ALS, New-York Historical Society, New York City.
1. Beekman was a New York City merchant. His uncle, who was named William, had died in 1795.

2. H did not date this letter, but Beekman's endorsement reads: "Recd. 1st. March 1797."

3. H's undated notes of the facts of this will may be found in the New-York Historical Society, New York City.

An entry in H's Cash Book, 1795–1804, for December 21, 1795, reads: "for this sum of Beekman for opinion concerning Will 5" (AD, Hamilton Papers, Library of Congress).

4. The first opinion on William Beekman's will which Nicholas Evertson, also a New York City attorney, and H made is dated September 2, 1796 (Df, in the handwriting of H and Evertson, New-York Historical Society, New York City; DS, with insertions in H's handwriting, New-York Historical Society, New York City).

An entry in H's Cash Book, 1795–1802, for September 1, 1796, reads: "Devisees of Wm. Beekman for opinion on sundry questions concerning the Will of William Beekman 50" (AD, Hamilton Papers, Library of Congress).

5. On March 4, 1796, H and Evertson prepared the following opinion: "Question relative to the estate of William Beekman Decd.

"Did the writings termed compact wills restrain the parties from making another will before the death of either of them without mutual consent?

"We are of opinion that the writings termed compact wills did restrain the parties thereto from making any other will inconsistent therewith without consent of parties concerned antecedent to the death of one of them—and advise the Executors to conform to this principle in the disposition of the estate." (DS, New-York Historical Society, New York City.)

Under the date of March 7, 1797, H made the following entry in his Cash Book, 1795–1804: "Beekman for additional fee for opinion & advice concerning the estate of William Beekman senior deceased 30" (AD, Hamilton Papers, Library of Congress).

From Robert Morris

Colo Hamilton Esqr   Philada March 3d 1797
New York

Dear sir

On the day I wrote you last,[1] Mr Westerloe [2] left at my House Yours of the 23d.[3] I expect the pleasure of his company soon. I hope Mr Bridgon's Clients will as was proposed in my last letter to you come or send to Mr Nicholson who is disposed to put their demand upon the most satisfactory footing in his power,[4] & I expect the business may be so settled as that the Money will be forth coming sooner than by Legal process it can be obtained, for as I am not properly the payer, altho' responsible, I shall resist as long as I can if they pursue me instead of seeking paymt from the real debtor or principal who is willing to arrange the matter of their Content. I want sadly to have the affair of the Genesee Land finished by Colo

Walker it is become indispensible to have it done in one or other of the modes mentioned in my last letter if the Assignment of Colo Smiths Deeds or Mortgage is made to Mr Cottringer he can release such parts as I convey.[5] And the remainder will not be subject to Attachment. The President has nominated a Commr to preside at the Treaty which I intend to hold with the Indians, and I expect the senate will this day give their assent so that I hope it may not be long before I make a purchase but my wish is to have this as little known as possible.[6] I mention it to you that you may advise Mr Church to give Mr Marshall two Dollars an Acre for the 10,000 Acres mortgaged to him[7] I could now sell it for 2/ N York currency on a credit shorter than the time I am to pay Mr Church and I am confident that it will be worth four, to six or eight dolls pr Acre by that time. My wants cause me to desire a Sale and if I must sell had not Mr Church better to take the benefit than let others do it. The moment the Indian title is obtained there will be a rush of People into that Country that will raise the price of land beyond that or any other part of America, & the settlements will be made by Men of property, & respectable character who are now laying by Money, and preparing themselves for the purpose. Nothing is more certain than these things & Mr Church has the opportunity of doubling trebling or Quadrupling his money, tell him therefore to embrace it.

I am Dr Sir Yours &c. RM

LC, Robert Morris Papers, Library of Congress.
  1. Morris to H, February 27, 1797.
  2. Presumably Rensselaer Westerlo, an Albany lawyer.
  3. Letter not found.
  4. This is a reference to a threatened suit against Morris for the payment of a bill drawn by John Nicholson, Morris's partner in several enterprises, and endorsed by Morris. Charles Bridgen's clients were William Talbot and William Allum. For information concerning this matter, see Morris to H, December 31, 1796; January 23, February 9, 1797, note 4, February 27, 1797.
  5. This is a reference to a debt which Morris owed to William Pulteney and William Hornby and the efforts of Morris to pay or secure this debt. For an explanation of this debt and the negotiations concerning it, see the introductory note to Morris to H, April 27, 1796. See also Morris to H, May 3, 10, 17, 31, 1796, January 7, 23, February 9, 27, 1797; H to Charles Williamson, May 17-30, 1796.
  6. For information on Morris's negotiations with the Seneca Indians, see H, to Herman LeRoy, William Bayard, and James McEvers, December 16, 1796, note 1.
  7. James Marshall, Morris's son-in law who was in England to sell securities

and lands for Morris, was also attempting to settle the debt which Morris owed to John B. Church. To secure this debt Morris had mortgaged to H for Church one hundred thousand acres in the Genesee country, and he was now attempting to convince Church that he should purchase that land. For an account of Morris's debt to Church and for his attempts to pay it, see the introductory note to Morris to H, June 7, 1795. See also Morris to H, July 20, November 16, December 18, 1795, January 15, March 6, 12, 14, 30, April 27, May 3, 10, 17, 18, 31, 1796; William Lewis to H, May 4, 1796; H to Williamson, May 17–30, 1796.

To Herman LeRoy, William Bayard, and James McEvers [1]

[March 4–July 18, 1797] [2]

Dr. Sir

I have considered with attention the draft of instructions to Mr. Bayard, which appear to me full and judicious.

There are but two points upon which I would submit a reflection or two—

I It is prescribed that no money shall be advanced for any quantity of land purchased more than in the proportion of the intire sum to the intire quantity.

It is *possible* that this restriction may be inconvenient, as the Indians may insist upon a higher rate for their land. In such case, would it be well to lose the opportunity of the present Treaty? Is there a probability that at any future time a better bargain may be made? If not will it not be adviseable to leave a full discretion to go all reasonable length in the application of the fund?

II It is enjoined that no payment be made or engaged to be made but in exchange for titles which will assure the full property of the land.

If this means no more than *titles* from the Indians, the injunction only expresses a matter of course. If any thing more is intended embarrassment may arise, for strictly speaking no such titles can be obtained till after the ratification of the Treaty by the President & Senate & it is probable that the payments cannot wait so long—Besides it seems to me that the proper mode is to obtain a cession or release of the lands from the Indians to the UStates in trust for such persons as prior to the treaty were intitled hereto—Then the property will enure of course to the present Owners—But whatever be the mode it is necessary to avoid any restriction that may embarrass the affair—

As to a power from Mr Le Roy, it does not appear to me strictly necessary. Yet it may be well to have a letter engaging his concurrence in what may be done. Yet a more formal power can be attended with no inconvenience.

I remain D. Sir   Yr obed serv   A Hamilton

Messrs. Le Roy & Bayard [3]

ALS, Buffalo Historical Society, Buffalo, New York.
 1. For background to this letter, see H to LeRoy, Bayard, and McEvers, December 16, 1796, note 1.
 2. This letter was written after March 3, 1797, when the Senate agreed to appoint a commissioner to treat with the Indians, and before July 19, 1797, when Théophile Cazenove sent instructions to Bayard for negotiating with the Indians (Evans, *Holland Land Company*, 187, note 1). Bayard, along with John Lincklaen, Gerrit Boon, and Joseph Ellicott, represented the Holland Land Company at the meetings with the Indians.
 3. The envelope is addressed to "Messrs. Le Roy Bayard & McEvers."

From William Pattersen [1]

[Kingston] Ulster County [New York], March 5, 1797. "As you are the only persen I think I Can with Safty apply too to assist me in giting my Militerie Lot [2] as it is well known I have faithfull Served my Country it gives me the more Confidence to Crave your assistance. I must inform you that I have found my Discharge and have it Now in my Possession. I have found Blanchar the Person who took out the Patent Deed for my Lot No. 32 in Cato [3] he Lives in Cats kill town in the County of Albany. . . . I must beg the favor of you to write me a Letter of advice as Soon as you Receive this or as Soon as you think it Necessarie (which will perhaps be after you have made Some Inquiry in the business) I shall again inform you whre I Live which is in Franklin township Huntingdon County on the Little Juniata River State of Pennsylvania. . . ."

ALS, Hamilton Papers, Library of Congress.
 1. Pattersen (Patterson) served in the First New York Regiment during the American Revolution.

2. For land bounties pledged to soldiers from New York for service during the American Revolution, see "An Act for granting certain Lands promised to be given as Bounty Lands by Laws of this State, and for other Purposes therein mentioned" (*New York Laws*, 7th Sess., Ch. XLIII [May 11, 1784]).

3. On July 7, 1790, Pattersen was granted five hundred acres in Lot No. 32 in Cato, the third township in the military tract (*The Balloting Book and Other Documents relating to Military Bounty Lands in the State of New-York* [Albany, 1825], 31, 114, 117). The patent was delivered to John Blanchard (*The Balloting Book*, 173).

Bill from James Robinson [1]

[New York, March 7, 1797]

1796
Augt: 13th   Alexander Hamilton Esqr:
                To James Robinson for fence

42 boards @ 1/	£2–2.
32 half Do: @ /6d	16.
18 posts @ 2/ and 12 lb Nails @ 1/2	2–10.
7 days Labour carpenters @ 11/	3–17.
4 Loads cartage @ 2/	8.
	£9–13

Received New York March 7. 179[7] [2] of Alexander Hamilton the amount of the above account being for the use of the lot of John Barker Church in broad way.[3]   Jams. Robinson

DS, Hamilton Papers, Library of Congress.

1. Robinson was a builder who lived at 52 Greenwich Street, New York City.

2. This receipt is in H's handwriting. H incorrectly wrote "1796."

On March 7, 1797, H made the following entry in his Cash Book, 1795–1804: "John B. Church Dr. to Cash paid Robinson Carpenter for fencing his lot—Dolls. 28.63" (AD, Hamilton Papers, Library of Congress). H also noted in his "Account with John B. Church," June 15, 1797, the equivalent payment in New York currency of eleven pounds, eleven shillings (not nine pounds, thirteen shillings, as Robinson charged in his bill), on March 7, 1797, to "Robinson Carpenter for fencing your lot."

3. The lot to which H is referring is one of the lots which H had acquired for Church in 1796. See "Receipt from Morgan Lewis," March 18, 1796.

From Rufus King

London Mar 8. 1797

Dear Sir,

On the 28 ulto. the Bank of England stopped payment in Specie.[1] And since every Bank in Great Britain has followed the Example; the Directors say the Bank is more than Solvent, exclusive of their capital Stock invested in the Funds. Committees of the two House of Parliament, which have examined the affairs of the Bank, confirm by their Report the Declaration of the Directors,[2] and Associations are forming throughout The Kingdom to receive and circulate Bank notes. Many whom I meet profess to believe that the Bank will soon be able to resume their former Course of Payments. But I see so few of the causes (if they exist) which are to effect this Restoration that I am somewhat skeptical—and my want of Faith is in some measure excuesed by circumstances that I think will for the present prevent the return of the Golden Age. No nation has supported a more perfect Credit than England: none has been able to substitute in so great a degree Paper in lieu of Coin—and in no Country therefore is the quantity of Specie comparatively so small as in England. This Fact

ALS, Hamilton Papers, Library of Congress.

1. On February 25, 1797, the reserves of the Bank of England were so low that its directors asked the government to intervene. On the next day the Privy Council issued the following order: "Upon the Representation of the Chancellor of the Exchequer stating that, from the Result of the Information which he has received, and of the Enquiries which it has been his Duty to make respecting the Effect of the unusual Demands for Specie that have been made upon the Metropolis, in consequence of the ill-founded or exaggerated Alarms in different parts of the country, it appears that unless some measure is immediately taken there may be Reason to apprehend a want of a sufficient Supply of Cash to answer the Exigencies of the Public Service; it is the unanimous Opinion of the Board, that it is indispensably necessary for the Public Service that the Directors of the Bank of England should forbear issuing any Cash in Payment until the Sense of Parliament can be taken on that Subject, and the proper Measures adopted thereupon, for maintaining the means of Circulation, and supporting the Public and Commercial Credit of the Kingdom at this important Conjuncture; and it is ordered that a Copy of this Minute by transmitted to the Directors of the Bank of England, and they are hereby required, on the Grounds of the Exigency of the case, to conform thereto until the Sense of Parliament can be taken as aforesaid" (*The London Gazette*, February 25-28, 1797).

2. For the report of the committee of the House of Commons on March 3, 1797, see *Parliamentary Register*, LX, 747-48.

was not practically believed—the Bank have now proved it to the conviction and dismay of the country: Besides Parliament have authorised the Bank to issue notes under £5—and they have also repealed the Laws prohibiting individuals from making and circulating their notes payable on Demand for Sums under £5.³ The consequence is, that the Banks are throwing into Circulation 20/. & 40/. notes to Supply the Absence of Guineas; and the manufacturers and private Bankers are likewise issueing to their workmen & Customers small Bills of every Denomination, which supply the absence of Shillings and Six penny Pieces.⁴ Before the Bank stopped payment, the merchants and Bankers were for a long time unable to obtain the usual quantity of Discounts with which they had been accustomed to be accomodated; immediately after this event every body was accomodated, and no one asked and was refused a Discount; thus a very large augmentation of the Notes of the Bank had taken place, and by the continuation of the emission of these Notes, aided by the numberless species of small notes issued by private Bankers, Manufacturers, and Projectors, the Quantity of Paper now afloat, and which will increase, forbids the expectation that the Bank will be able to open their Specie Vaults. Bank notes are already at a depreceation, which is proved by the reluctance with which every one parts with a Guinea by the sudden rise of for Exchange, and by the Demand for the amer. Stocks; which have risen in the course of a week Bk stock from £103. to £117 per Share—6 pr C. from 80 pr Ct. to 90. 3 pr Cts from 49 pr Ct. to 55. while the British three per Cents vibrate between 50 and 52.

Farewell yr's very sincerely   Rufus King

P S. Since ⟨the capture of Mantua,⁵ the Austrians have notified this court of⟩ ⁶ their resolution to prosecute the war, relying on the

3. See "An Act to remove Doubts respecting Promissory Notes of the Governor and Company of the Bank of *England* for Payment of Sums of Money under Five Pounds" (37 Geo. III, C. 28 [March 3, 1797]).

4. On February 27, 1797, a meeting of merchants and bankers resolved "That We, the undersigned, being highly sensible how necessary the Preservation of Public Credit is at this time, do most readily hereby declare that we will not refuse to receive Bank Notes in Payment of any Sum of Money to be paid to us, and we will use our utmost Endeavours to make all our Payments in the same Manner" (*The* [London] *Times*, February 28, 1797).

5. See King to H, February 7, 1797, note 6.

6. The words in brackets have been taken from *JCHW*, VI, 211.

On February 6, 1797, Count Ludwig Joseph Max von Starhemberg, the

cooperation of G B. What Effect the pecuniary State of England may have upon their Disposition to persevere, I will not conjecture—without money the Emperor will not be able to go on. Thus you see a very interesting subject brought within a narrow compass. France will harass and work our commerce regardless of Justice. She makes our Treaty with Eng. the Pretence—had we made no Treaty her conduct wd. be the same. She has recently required of Hamburgh & Bremen to suspend and prohibit all commerce with Engld. As yet she has not succeeded in her views, tho she has recalled her Minister from Hamburgh.[7] The Demand has likewise been repeated at Copenhagen,[8] and a refusal to comply has produced a diplomatic

---

Austrian Ambassador to England, wrote to Lord Grenville: "Quoique le courier que j'attends de Vienne, et qui doit me rapporter les instructions nécessaires à l'égard de la convention qui concerne vos avances mensuelles, ne soit point encore arrivé, je me fais un vrai plaisir d'avoir l'honneur de vous annoncer que j'ai appris, par une voie sûre non-officielle, qu'on a accueilli vos dernières propositions avec l'amitié reconnaissante qu'elles méritaient. Cette information me rassure un peu sur le fâcheux effet que pourra produire la mauvaise nouvelle de la défaite d'Alvinzy. J'ai de nouveau la certitude que les Français veulent faire des offres avantageux à ma Cour pour la détâcher de l'Angleterre. J'aime à croire à la bonne foi; et la conduite constante de mon maître me raffermit dans cet heureux sentiment. Mais je plains l'Empereur et son ministre; ils auront des rudes attaques à soutenir. Il' s'agira, je crois, de défendre seulement le Tyrol, et de porter des plus grandes forces encore vers le Rhin. N'y aurait-il pas moyen pour nous fournir la possibilité de détacher beaucoup de troupes de l'Italie, de forcer le Roi de Naples à rentrer en jeu? Il a une armée assez considérable prête à marcher. Je ne voudrais pas qu'il vous en coutat beaucoup plus que des menaces; mais l'Amiral Jarvis venant près de Naples, comme fit Truguet au commencement de la guerre, pourrait bien produire le même effet. Ceci est peut-être un songe creux; pardonnez-le à mon zèle.

"Vous pourriez, en autre, nous prouver d'une manière bien digne de vous dans ce moment combien vous vous occupez de nos intérêts. Il était convenu entre nous que vous nous payeriez les 300,000 livres du mois de Janvier immédiatement. Cet argent a été mis à notre disposition; mais vous vous rappellerez en même temps, qu'en nous promettant de nous faire encore au mois de Février une avance semblable, vous vouliez attendre notre réponse pour mettre cette somme à notre disposition. Cette réponse ne peut plus tarder, et sera conforme à vos désirs. Ainsi si vous m'autorisiez à mander par votre courier que nous pouvons, dès à présent, tirer ces 300,000 livres, ce procédé, rempli de grace de votre part, serait apprécié comme il doit l'être dans la circonstance, et vous ne courrez aucun risque. Je me flatte que vous m'applaudirez vous-même d'avoir suggéré cette idée à votre désir constant de nous être utile, si votre bon esprit ne m'avait pas déjà prévenu." (*Dropmore Papers*, III, 297.)

7. In this and the preceding sentence, King was repeating rumors which proved to be incorrect. See Eli F. Heckscher, *The Continental System* (Oxford, 1922), 57.

8. On February 7, 1797, the following item appeared in *The* [London] *Times*, dated Copenhagen, January 21: "A report is current here, that the

Altercation as pointed perhaps as that between Col. Pickering and Mr. Adet.[9]

Our Affairs in the mediterranean are settled or nearly so. Col. Humphries [10] informs me that we stand well with Algiers. We have concluded a Treaty of Peace with Tripoli,[11] and it is probable shall soon make a similar treaty with Tunis: [12] the Dey of Algiers having invaded the Tunissean Territories principally says Col. Humphries to compel the Bey to conclude a Peace with the U States of Amer. for the accomplishment of which the Dey offers to advance the money from his own Treasury and engaged to guaranty this Treaty as he has done that with Tripoli. Strange event.

Col Hamilton

French Minister, [Philippe Antoine] *Grouville*, in concert with the Spanish Envoy, Chevalier de *Normandez*, has proposed to our Court to refuse the English for the future of a free passage through the Sound, and consequently to exclude them from the Baltic trade. But this report seems to be without foundation."

9. For the "diplomatic altercation" between Timothy Pickering and Pierre Auguste Adet, see *ASP, Foreign Relations*, I, 559–88. See also George Washington to H, November 2, 3, 21, 1796, January 22, 1797; H to Washington, November 4, 5, 11, 19, 1796, January 19, 25–31, 1797; H to Oliver Wolcott, Jr., November 1, 1796; Wolcott to H, November 17, 1796.

10. David Humphreys was appointed United States Minister Resident to Portugal in 1791, commissioner in Algerine affairs in 1793, and Minister Plenipotentiary to Spain in 1796.

11. This treaty was signed at Tripoli on November 4, 1796, and at Algiers on January 3, 1797 (Miller, *Treaties*, II, 349–85).

12. The Treaty of Peace and Friendship with Tunis was signed on August 28, 1797 (Miller, *Treaties*, II, 387–426).

From Robert Morris

Philada. March 8th. 1797

Dear Sir

You have herewith the Copy of a letter from Mr Bridgen to me & my reply [1] which you will cause to be delivered, if they will apply to Mr Nicholson the business will be accomplished with him but if they possitively will not, I must request you to adjust the matter on my behalf on the best terms & longest time you can obtain.[2] I am impatiently waiting an Answer to my last letter [3] on the

business with Colo Walker,⁴ it is of the greatest & most immediate importance to have it finished. I hope this days Mail will bring the information from you to
Dr Sir   Your Obedt hble servt   Robt Morris

Alexr Hamilton Esqr
New York.

ALS, Hamilton Papers, Library of Congress; LC, Robert Morris Papers, Library of Congress.
  1. Morris to Charles Bridgen, March 8, 1797 (LC, Robert Morris Papers, Library of Congress).
  2. For information concerning the matters discussed in this sentence, see Morris to H, December 31, 1796; January 23, February 9, 1797, note 4, February 27, 1797.
  3. Morris to H, March 3, 1797.
  4. For the "business with Colo Walker," see the introductory note to Morris to H, April 27, 1796. See also Morris to H, May 3, 10, 17, 31, 1796, January 7, 23, February 9, 27, March 3, 1797; H to Charles Williamson, May 17–30, 1796.

To Robert Morris

[*New York, March 8, 1797.* On March 9, 1797, Morris wrote to Hamilton: "I have this moment received yours of yesterday." *Letter not found.*]

From Robert Morris

Alexr Hamilton Esqr   Philadelphia March 9th 1797
New York

Dear sir
  I have this moment received yours of yesterday[1] with the deed to Mr Cottringer[2] for which accept my thanks. Mr Ralph Mather the last endorser of the bill on which Mr Bridgon threatens to bring suit, has opened a negotiation here with Mr Nicholson respecting it,[3] and as I hope an arrangement will be made so as to satisfy the owners of sd Bill you will be good enough to prevail on them to wait the issue of this negotiation before you enter into any engagement on

my part and I will inform you the result as soon as it is ascertained. I am Dr Sir

Yours &c   RM

LC, Robert Morris Papers, Library of Congress.

1. Letter not found.

2. This is a reference to a debt which Morris owed to William Pulteney and William Hornby and which Benjamin Walker was trying to collect for them. For Garrett Cottringer's part in this transaction, see Morris to H, March 3, 1797. For further information on this debt, see the introductory note to Morris to H, April 27, 1796. See also Morris to H, May 3, 10, 17, 31, 1796; January 23, February 9, 27, March 8, 1797; H to Charles Williamson, May 17–30, 1796.

3. For the suit against Morris threatened by Charles Bridgen and for John Nicholson's part in this matter, see Morris to H, December 31, 1796; January 23, February 9, 1797, note 4, February 27, March 3, 8, 1797.

From William Hamilton [1]

[*Greenock, Scotland, March 10, 1797.* On May 2, 1797, Hamilton wrote to William Hamilton: "Some days since I received with great pleasure your letter of the 10th of March." *Letter not found.*]

1. William Hamilton was H's uncle and Laird of Grange, Ayrshire, Scotland.

To William Tilghman [1]

New York, March 10, 1797. ". . . You will oblige me by letting me know what have been the laws & practice of Maryland with regard to naturalization—pointing me to the parts of its Constitution & laws which respect the subject. I have under consideration an important question of Insurance [2] in which this inquiry is necessary."

ALS, Historical Society of Pennsylvania, Philadelphia.

1. Tilghman was born in Maryland and practiced law there before moving to Philadelphia in 1793.

2. The "question" was raised in *Daniel Ludlow and Gulian Ludlow* v *John B. Coles; Same* v *Archibald Gracie* in the New York Supreme Court. See Goebel, *Law Practice*, II, 770.

From William Tilghman

Philadelphia, March 13, 1797. Replies to Hamilton's letter of March 10, 1797, and answers questions concerning provisions on naturalization in Maryland's constitution and statutes.

ALS, Hamilton Papers, Library of Congress.

The Warning No. V [1]

[New York, March 13, 1797]

I have asserted, that the conduct of Great-Britain towards us and other neutral powers has been at no period so exceptionable, as that of France at the present juncture.[2] A more distinct view of this truth may be useful, which will be assisted by a retrospect of the principal acts of violation on both sides.

Tho the circumstance was cotemporarily disclosed in all of our newspapers, yet so blind and deaf were we rendered by our partiality for France, that few among us, till very lately, have been aware, that the first of those acts is fairly chargeable upon her. Such notwithstanding is the fact. The first in order of time is a decree of the National Convention of the 9th of May, 1793,[3] which reciting that neutral flags are not respected by the enemies of France, and enumerating some instances of alledged violation, proceeds to authorize the vessels of war and cruizers of France to arrest and conduct into her ports *all neutral vessels* which are found *laden in whole* or in *part* with *provisions belonging to neutrals,* or *merchan-*

Gazette of the United States, & Philadelphia Daily Advertiser, March 13, 1797; ADf (incomplete), Hamilton Papers, Library of Congress.
 1. Although the draft is essentially the same as the newspaper version, it differs in the order of the paragraphs.
 The other issues of "The Warning" are dated January 27, February 7, 21, 27, March 27, 1797.
 2. See "The Warning No. IV," February 27, 1797.
 3. This order is printed in Duvergier, *Lois,* V, 345, and *ASP, Foreign Relations,* I, 244, 749. See also H to Timothy Pickering, January 23, 1797, note 1; Pickering to H, January 30, 1797.

dizes belonging to *the enemies* of France; the latter to be confiscated as prize for the benefit of the captors, the former to be detained, but paid for according to their value at the places for which they were destined.

The instances enumerated as the pretext for so direct and formal an attack upon the rights of neutral powers, except two, turn upon the pretension to capture the goods of an enemy in the ships of a friend. Of the remaining two, one is the case of an American vessel going from *Falmouth* to *St. Maloes* with a cargo of wheat, which the decree states was taken by an English frigate and carried into Guernsey, where the agents of the English government detained the cargo, upon a promise to pay the value, as not being for French account;[4] the other is the case of some French passengers going in a *Genoese* vessel from *Cadiz* to *Bayonne*, who were plundered on the passage by the crew of an English privateer.[5]

There is no question but that Great Britain, from the beginning of the war, has claimed and exercised the right of capturing the property of her enemies found in neutral bottoms; and it has been unanswerably demonstrated, that for this she has the sanction of the general law of nations. But France, from the exercise of that right by Great Britain, when not forbidden by any treaty, can certainly derive no justification for the imitation of the practice, in opposition to the precise and peremptory stipulations of her treaties. Every treaty which established the rule of *"free ships free goods"* must have contemplated the unequal operation of that rule to the contracting parties, when one was at peace, the other at war; looking

---

4. The preface to the decree adopted by the National Convention on May 9, 1793, states that the Committee of Marine had reported "Que le navire *le John*, capitaine Shkleley, chargé d'environ six mille quintaux de blé d'Amérique, allant de Falmouth à Saint-Malo, a été arrêté par une frégate anglaise, et conduit à Guernesey, où les agens du Gouvernement ont simplement promis de faire payer la valeur de la cargaison, parce qu'elle n'était pas pour compte français" (Duvergier, *Lois*, V, 344). A translation of this decree is printed in *ASP, Foreign Relations*, I, 749.

5. In the preface to the decree adopted by the National Convention on May 9, 1793, the Committee of Marine stated "Que cent un passagers français, de différentes professions, embarqués à Cadix par ordre du ministère espagnol, sur le navire génois *la Providence*, capitaine Ambroise Briaser, pour être amenés à Bayonne, ont été indignement pillés par L'équipage d'un corsaire anglais" (Duvergier, *Lois*, V, 344). For the translation of this decree, see *ASP, Foreign Relations*, I, 749.

for indemnification to the correspondent right of taking friends property in enemies ships, and to the reciprocal effect of the rule, when the state of peace and war should be reserved. To make its unequal operation in an existing war, an excuse for disregarding the rule is therefore a subterfuge for a breach of faith, which hardly seeks to save appearances. France, as she was once, would have blushed to use it. It is one, among many instances, of the attempts of revolutionary France to dogmatize mankind out of its reason; as if she expected to work to change in the faculties as well as in the habits and opinions of men.

The case of the American vessel carried to Guernsay is that of a clear infraction of neutral right. But standing singly, it was sufficient evidence of a plan of the British government to pursue the principle. It countenanced *suspicion* of a secret order for the purpose; but it did not amount to *proof* of such an order. There might have been misapprehension or misrepresentation; or if neither was the case the circumstance was resolveable into the mere irregularity of particular agents—it is unjustifiable to ascribe to a government, as the result of a premeditated plan, and to use as the ground of reprisals, a single case of irregularity happening in a detached portion of the dominions of that government. France was bound to have waited for more full evidence. There was no warrant in a solitary precedent for general retaliation; even if we could admit the detestable doctrine, that the injustice of one belligerent power towards neutral nations is a warrant for similar injustice in another.

The violation of the courtesy of war in the instance of the French passengers, however brutal in itself, was truly a frivolous pretext for the decree. The frequency of irregular conduct in the commanders and crews of privateers, even in contempt of the regulations of their own governments, naturally explains such a transaction into the cupidity of individuals, and forbids the imputation of it to their government. There never was a war in which similar outrages did not occur in spite of the most sincere endeavors to prevent them.

The natural and plain conclusion is, that the decree in question was a wanton proceeding in the French government, uncountenanced by the previous conduct either of its enemies, or of the neutral nations who were destined to punishment for their faults.

For, the first order of the British government authorizing the seizure of provisions is dated the 6th of June 1793,[6] nearly a month posterior to the French decrees. A[nd] there is not the least vestige of any prior order, the presumption is that none ever existed. If any had existed, the course of things has been such as to afford a moral certainty that it would have appeared. The subsequent date of the British order is a strong confirmation of the argument, that the affair of the vessel carried to Guernsey was nothing more than a particular irregularity.

The publicity of all the proceedings of the French government, and the celerity of communication between Paris and London, leave no doubt that the decree of May the 9th was known in London before the order of June the 6th.[7] It follows that France herself furnished to Great Britain the example and the pretext for the most odious of the measure with which she is chargeable; and that, so far as precedent can justify crime, Great-Britain may find in the conduct of France the vindication of her own.

An obvious reflection presents itself. How great was the infatuations of France thus to set the example of an interruption of neutral commerce in provisions, in the freedom of which she was so much more interested than her adversaries! If the detention of the cargo at Guernsey was a bait, we cannot but be astonished at the stupid levity with which it was swallowed.

We are no less struck with the eager precipitancy with which France seized the pretext for a formal and systematic invasion of the rights of neutral powers; equally regardless of the obligations of treaty and of the injunctions of the laws of nations. The presumption of the connivance of a neutral power in infractions of its rights is the only colourable ground for the French idea of retaliation on the sufferers. Here the yet early stage of the war and the recency of the facts alledged as motives to the decree preclude the supposition of connivance. The unjust violence of France, consequently, in resorting to retaliation, stands without the slightest veil. From this prominent trait we may distinguish, without possibility of mistake, the real character of her system.   AMERICUS.

6. H is referring to the British order in council of June 8, 1793 (rather than June 6), which ordered British naval commanders to detain and to bring into British ports all neutral vessels bound for French ports with cargoes of corn, flour, or meal (*ASP, Foreign Relations*, I, 240).

7. The draft ends at this point.

From William Laight [1]

[New York] March 14, 1797. "Had there not been frequent Instances in many respectable Offices in this City where Events of a similar kind have been effected, which I am now solicitous of obtaining, I should deem it presumptuous to address you on the Subject: Let this, in addition to the solicitude of a Parent for the Establishment of a Son in the line of his Profession be my Apology. Edward W. Laight, after his matriculation at Columbia College, was instructed in the Rudiments & Principles of Law by Coll: Burr.... He has been admitted to the Bar as an Attorney. Of his qualifications Professional Men are better Judges than myself. The Object I aim at is, to have him patronized by a Person of Merit & Celebrity, more for the purpose of improvement than for present Emolument.... The wish of my heart is that Coll: Hamilton should be such a Patron. If therefore it is not incompatible with Coll. Hamiltons Views to receive as an Attorney in his Office a Young Man, of, at least decent Manners & educated as above mentioned, I should be made happy by his giving me an opportunity of acceeding to such Terms as he himself would prescribe." [2]

ALS, Hamilton Papers, Library of Congress.
1. Laight was a New York City merchant.
2. No evidence has been found that Laight entered H's law office. David Longworth, *American Almanack, New-York Register, and City Directory* ... (New York, 1798), lists "Laight, Edward W. (& C. D. Colden) masters in chancery, 47 Wall." See also Goebel, *Law Practice*, II, 228, 229n, 512, 774.

From Philip Schuyler [1]

Albany March 19th 1797

My Dear Sir

I shall not fail to call the attention of the senate to the insecure state of the port of New York and to detail the distressing consequences which must result should the Metropolis be laid under contribution, be conflagreated, or possessed by a hostile foreign power:

but I apprehend nothing more will be done than Authorizing the Governor to take measures for Its security, If a war with some European power should appear to him inevitable.

It is to be lamented that the most influential characters in the representation from New York could not be prevailed on to remain here: by thus neglecting their duty they have commited the affairs of their constituents to less able hands, and painful results must be expected.

If Gentlemen of consideration in the public mind continue to refuse seats in either branch of the Legislature, It is certain that a variety of evils will result to the community, and the metropolis will be most deeply Affected. I wish therefore, that the necessity in Gentlemen to step forward and offer a consent to be candidates at the ensuing election [2] may be strongly urged. Mr. Burr, we are informed, will be a candidate for a seat in the assembly; [3] his views It is not difficult to appreciate. They alarm me, and If he prevails I apprehend a total change of politics in the next assembly—attended with other disagreable consequences.

Mr. Adams's speeches to the senate at taking leave,[4] and expressions, in that, at his Inaugeration,[5] have left very unfavorable impressions in my mind, and created alarm, but It may not be prudent to state the reasons. We are all in health, and All Join in love to you & all with you,

I am Dear Sir Most sincerely Yours   Ph: Schuyler

ALS, Hamilton Papers, Library of Congress.
1. When Schuyler wrote this letter, he was a member of the New York Senate. On January 24, 1797, the New York legislature elected him to the United States Senate to succeed Aaron Burr, whose term expired on March 3, 1797 (*Journal of the Assembly of the State of New-York; At Their Twentieth Session*, 69).
2. This is a reference to the elections which were to be held in New York in April, 1797.
3. In April, 1797, Burr was elected to the New York Assembly.
4. The second session of the Fourth Congress adjourned on March 3, 1797 (*Annals of Congress*, VI, 1580). John Adams's first speech was delivered on February 15, 1797 (*Annals of Congress*, VI, 1549–51). On February 23, 1797, Adams responded to the Senate's answer to his speech of February 15 (*Annals of Congress*, VI, 1557–58).
5. For Adams's inaugural address, see *Annals of Congress*, VI, 1582–86.

To Timothy Pickering

[New York, March 22, 1797]

Dr Sir

It is now ascertained that Mr Pinckney has been refused and with circumstances of indignity.[1] What is to be done? The share I have had in the public administration added to my interest as a Citizen make me extremely anxious that at this delicate Crisis a course of conduct exactly proper may be adopted. I offer to your consideration without ceremony what appears to me such a course.

First. I would appoint a day of humiliation and prayer. In such a crisis this appears to me proper in itself and it will be politically useful to impress our nation that there is a serious state of things—to strengthen religious ideas in a contest which in its progress may require that our people may consider themselves as the defenders of their Country against Atheism conquest & anarchy. It is far from evident to me that the progress of the war may not call on us to defend our fire sides & our altars. And any plan which does not look forward to this as possible will in my opinion be a superficial one.

Second. I would call Congress together at as *short a day* as a majority of both houses can assemble.

3 When assembled I would appoint a Commission extraordinary to consist of Mr. Jefferson, or Mr. Madison, together with Mr Cabot & Mr. Pinckney.[2] To be useful it is important that a man agreeable to the French should go. But neither *Madison* nor *Jefferson* ought to go alone. The three will give security. It will flatter the French Pride. It will engage American confidence & recommend the people to what shall be eventually necessary. The Commission should be instructed to explain, to ask a rescinding of the order under which we suffer & reparation for the past—to remodify our Treaties under proper guards. On the last idea I will trouble you hereafter.

4. The Congress should be urged to take defensive measures. These to be 1 An *Embargo* unless with convoy by special license.

Additional Revenue or additional expences.

2 The Creation of a naval force—including the prompt purchase and equipment of Sloops of War. This force to serve as Convoys to our Trade.

3. Commissions to be granted to our Merchant Vessels authorising them to arm to defend themselves to capture when attacked but not to cruise. The same instructions to our convoys.

4. The origination of a provisional army of Twenty five thousand men to be ready to serve if a War breaks out—in the mean time to receive certain compensations but not full pay. The actual increase of our establishment in Artillery & Cavalry.

The following considerations appear to me weighty. The Empress of Russia is dead. Successors are too apt to contradict predecessors. The new Emperor may join Prussia.[3] The Emperor of Germany by this mean or by the fortune of War may be compelled to make Peace.[4] England may be left alone. America may be a good outlet for trouble—some armies which the Government is at a loss to manage. The governing passion of the Rulers of France has been revenge. Their interest is not to be calculated upon. To punish and humble us—to force us into a greater dependence may be the plan of France. At any rate we shall best guarantee ourselves against calamity by preparing for the worst. In this time of general convulsion, in a state of things which threatens all civilization tis a great folly to wrap ourselves up in a cloak of security.

The Executive before Congress meet ought to have a *well digested* plan & to cooperate in getting it adopted.

Yrs. truly

A Hamilton
March 22 1797

T Pickering Esq

ALS, Massachusetts Historical Society, Boston.

1. For the refusal of the French Directory to receive Charles Cotesworth Pinckney, United States Minister Plenipotentiary to France, see Rufus King to H, February 6, 1797, note 5.

2. For H's earlier suggestion that such a mission be appointed, see H to George Washington, January 25–31, 1797; H to Theodore Sedgwick, February 26, 1797.

3. Catherine II died in November, 1796. She was succeeded by her son, Paul I, who began his reign by withdrawing Russia from the European war and informing Great Britain and Austria that he intended to send no more troops to Germany. Of Paul's predilection for Prussia, Count Simon Woronzow, the Russian Minister to Great Britain, wrote on January 9, 1797, to Lord Grenville: ". . . J'ai réçu . . . l'assurance positive . . . que l'Empereur n'est pas

pour la Cour de Berlin en fait de politique, et qu'admirateur de l'ordre et de la discipline de l'armée Prussienne qu'il vent imiter, il n'est nullement Prussien pour le reste, et qu'il est très decidé a contenir Fréderic Guillaume, s'il s'avise d'inquiéter l'Autriche" (*Dropmore Papers,* III, 292).

4. See King to H, March 8, 1797.

From Uriah Tracy [1]

Philada. 23d.[-24] March 1797

Sir

You will probably remember, I applied to you for James Johnson of Salisbury in Connecticut, for the purchase of a tract of Land lying in that Town, of which you had the care & disposal.[2] Johnson has lately written me, that the sale is not yet completed & wishes me to pursue the business, as he is still very desirous of purchasing the Land.

You will recollect how far the negociation has proceeded & whether you mean to sell to Johnson—please to let me know as I wish to inform him what he must do to finish the Contract, on his part.

I am, Sir, with respect   Your very humble sert.   Uriah Tracy

Alexr. Hamilton Esqr.

NB. I am detained here [3] by indisposition. You can, if you please direct a line to me here. I hope to be in health sufficient to go on to Connecticut soon, when I shall, on my way, see you at New York.

Since writing the within I have se⟨en⟩ the Speech of Barras to Citizen Munroe on his taking leave.[4] Pardon me, when I say—the most diabolical & at the same time vapid puffing speech that ever disgraced a Burletta like that of Tommy Thumb.[5] I foresee a struggle now in our Councils to send Maddison or Gallatin, or possibly John Swanwick [6] or Ned Livingston,[7] Envoy Extraordinary to the Cut-throat Directory. The United States, for fear of being subject to G. Britain will struggle hard, to be so to France. God in his infinite mercy grant, that we may be sunk in an Asphaltic Lake rise, where once stood the States—rather than subject ourselves to that nest of Assassins.

Yrs. U. Tracy.

Mr. Hamilton.

ALS, Hamilton Papers, Library of Congress.
1. Tracy was United States Senator from Connecticut and state's attorney for Litchfield County.
2. The land in question belonged to John Barker Church and was located in Salisbury, Litchfield County, Connecticut.
3. Congress had adjourned on March 3, 1797, but the Senate had reconvened in special session for one day on March 4, 1797 (*Annals of Congress*, VI, 1580).
4. The speech which Paul François Jean Nicolas Barras, President of the Directory, made to James Monroe on December 30, 1796, was printed in the [Philadelphia] *Aurora. General Advertiser* on March 24, 1797. It reads: "On this day presenting your letters of recall . . . you give to Europe a very strange spectacle.

"France, rich in her liberty, encompassed by her train of victories, strong in the esteem of her allies, will not abuse herself by calculating the consequences of the commission of the American government to the suggestions of its ancient masters.

"The French Republic hopes, that at least the successors of Columbus and of Penn always jealous of their liberty, will never forget what they owe to France. They will weigh in their wisdom, the magnanimous good will of the French people, with caresses of certain perfidious persons, who meditate to bring them back to their former slavery. Assure, Sir, the good American people, that, like them, we adore liberty; that they shall always have our esteem; and that they will find in the French people, that republican generosity which knows how to grant peace as it knows how to make its sovereignty respected.

"As for you, Mr. Minister Plenipotentiary you have contended for principle, you have known the true interests of your country; depart with our regret. We give up in you a representative to America, and we keep the remembrance of a citizen, whose personal qualities do honor to that title."
5. Henry Fielding, *The Tragedy of Tragedies; or the Life and Death of Tom Thumb* (London, 1730).
6. Swanwick was a Republican member of the House of Representatives from Pennsylvania.
7. Edward Livingston was a Republican member of the House of Representatives from New York.

From Timothy Pickering

Philadelphia March 26. 1797.

Dr. Sir,

On the 25th I was favoured with your letter of the 22d. The first measure of calling Congress together had been determined on by the President the preceding evening; and I had the draught of the proclamation inclosed, in my hand, to present to him, when I received your letter.[1] Some other of the measures suggested had been contemplated; and all will receive attention from me & my colleagues. I beg you to continue to communicate to me your ideas on public affairs, especially at the present interesting period.

You mention the appointing a commission extraordinary: we more than doubt the propriety of this step. The Directory have declard "qu'il ne reconnoitra, et ne recevra plus de Ministre Plenipotentiare des Etats Unis, jusqu' apres la redressement des griefs demandé au Gouvernment Americain, et que la Republique Francaise est en droit d'en attendre."[2] These "griefs" are doubtless those detailed by Citizen Adet and M. Delacroix, as exhibited in the notes of the former and the summary of the latter, and which you will see in my letter to General Pinckney,[3] which I had the pleasure to send you in print. *All the important acts of the government must therefore be* REVERSED, *before a minister can be admitted*. The former is impossible —and there seems therefore no opening at present for a new mission. This new mission is what the enemies of our government wish for; however circumstances may oppose it. In suggesting "a commission extraordinary," I presume you did not know that the refusal to receive "another minister, until" &c. had been so peremptory.

I am going to prepare a state of the information received from Mr. Pinckney for the press anonymously, yet with clear marks of authenticity; and it will, if approved by the President, be speedily published.[4] It seems highly important that the public mind should be enlightened as to *facts*.[5]

I am very sincerely & respectfully yours   T. Pickering

Alexander Hamilton Esq

ALS, Hamilton Papers, Library of Congress; ALS, letterpress copy, Massachusetts Historical Society, Boston.

1. On March 25, 1797, President John Adams issued a proclamation convening Congress on May 15 (*Annals of Congress*, VII, 29).

2. This quotation is taken from a letter from Charles Delacroix, the French Minister of Foreign Affairs, to James Monroe, stating that Monroe's recall and Charles Cotesworth Pinckney's credentials had been presented to the Directory (Delacroix to Monroe, December 11, 1796 [LC, RG 59, Despatches from United States Ministers to France, 1789–1869, Vol. 5, November 17, 1796–September 24, 1797, National Archives]). For English translations of this letter, see *ASP, Foreign Relations*, I, 746–47; II, 6.

3. Pickering to Pinckney, January 16, 1797 (LC, RG 59, Diplomatic and Consular Instructions of the Department of State, 1791–1801, Vol. 3, June 5, 1795–January 21, 1797, National Archives). This letter is printed in *ASP, Foreign Relations*, I, 559–75. See George Washington to H, January 22, 1797, note 2; H to Washington, January 25–31, 1797, note 4.

4. See the enclosure to Pickering to H, March 30, 1797.

5. Pickering endorsed the letterpress copy of this letter: "Letter to Coll Hamilton March 26, 1797. answer sent March 27th." Pickering was mistaken, for H answered this letter on March 29, 1797.

From Robert Morris

Alexander Hamilton Esqr
New York

Philada. March 27th. 1797

Dear Sir

I wrote a few lines from Mr Nicholsons house on Saturday whilst waiting to see Mr Mather; he did not come there untill I was obliged to come away, but Mr Nicholson informs me he came afterwards and that they are likely to effect an Arrangement for the Bill of Exchange and that Mr Mather has written to stay any proceedings in New York untill they hear again from him.[1] This being a debt of Mr Nicholsons I am desirous that he should settle it, but should he fail I must ultimately do it, and if in the end it falls to my lot, I now request that you will use your discretion, and make the best Arrangement you can for me. I pledge my honor that there is no other encumbrance on the 100000 Acres of Genesee land Mortgaged to Mr Church than that Mortgage and I am extreemly averse to suffering any other to go on it.[2] I want Mr Church to buy it. He may do that now, so as to double his Money on me, respecting this I wrote you some time ago [3] to which you did not reply.

I am Dr Sir   Yours &c.   RM

LC, Robert Morris Papers, Library of Congress.

1. In this and the following sentence Morris is discussing a suit which Charles Bridgen threatened to bring against him on behalf of William Talbot and William Allum. For this suit and for Ralph Mather's and John Nicholson's connection with it, see Morris to H, December 31, 1796, January 23, February 9, 1797, note 4, February 27, March 3, 8, 9, 1797.

2. This sentence concerns a debt which Morris owed to John B. Church. He had secured this debt with a mortgage on one hundred thousand acres in the Genesee country and was now endeavoring to have Church purchase these acres. See the introductory note to Morris to H, June 7, 1795. See also Morris

to H, July 20, November 16, December 18, 1795, January 15, March 6, 12, 14, 30, April 27, May 3, 10, 17, 18, 31, 1796, March 3, 1797; William Lewis to H, May 4, 1796; H to Charles Williamson, May 17–30, 1796.

This is the last mention in Morris's extant correspondence with H of the money he owed to Talbot and Allum. Meanwhile, they had instituted, with Bridgen as their attorney, legal proceedings to obtain payment from Morris. In June, 1797, H, appearing before the court as Morris's attorney, agreed that Morris owed Talbot and Allum $5,413.44. Morris was given three years to pay this money. For this case and the events leading up to it, see forthcoming Goebel, *Law Practice*, III. In 1801 in a summary statement concerning his debts and assets, Morris wrote: "The oldest Judgment against me in the State of New York was one to William Talbot and William Allum, under which, (as is said,) all my Rights and Claims in the Genesee Country have been executed and sold by the Sheriff" (Morris, *In the Account of Property*, 4).

3. Morris to H, March 3, 1797.

The Warning No. VI[1]

[New York, March 27, 1797]

It has been seen that the Governt of France has an indisputable title to the culpable preeminence of having taken the lead in the violation of neutral rights; and that the first instance on the part of the British Government is nearly a month posterior to the commencement of the evil by France.[2] But it was not only posterior—it was also less comprehensive. That of France extended to *all provisions*, that of Great Britain to certain kinds only, CORN FLOUR and MEAL.

The French decree, as to the U States, was repeatedly suspended and revived.[3] As to other neutral nations, it continued a permanent precedent, to sanction the practice of Great Britain.

This decretal versatility is alone complete evidence of want of principle. It is the more censureable, because it is ascertained that it proceeded in part at least from a corrupt source. The sacred power of law-making became the minister and the accomplice of private rapine. Decrees exacted by the solemn obligations of Treaty were

ADf, Hamilton Papers, Library of Congress; *Gazette of the United States, & Philadelphia Daily Advertiser*, March 27, 1797.

1. The other issues of "The Warning" are dated January 27, February 7, 21, 27, March 13, 1797.

2. See "The Warning No. IV," February 27, 1797; "The Warning No. V," March 13, 1797.

3. See H to Timothy Pickering, January 23, 1797, note 1; Pickering to H, January 30, 1797.

sacrificed to sea-rovers to enable them to enjoy the prey for the seizure of which they ought to have been condignly punished.*

The next and the most injurious of the acts of Great Britain is the order of the 6th. of November 1793, which instructs the Commanders of Ships of War and Privateers to stop detain and carry in *for adjudication* all Ships *laden* with the *produce* of any French Colony or carrying provisions or other *supplies* for the use of such colony.⁵ It was under the cover of this order, that were committed the numerous depredations on our commerce, which were the immediate cause of sending an envoy to Great Britain.

The terms of this order were ambiguous, warranting a suspicion that they were designed to admit of an oppressive interpretation and yet to leave room for a disavowal of it. Whether this was really the case or whether the order was in fact misconstrued by the British Officers and Tribunals in the West Indies, it is certain that the British Government almost as soon as their construction was known in England not only disclaimed it, but issued a new order dated the 8th of January 1794 ⁶ revoking that of the 6th of November, and expressly restraining the power to detain and carry in vessels for adjudication to *such* as were laden with the *produce* of a *French Island going* from a *port in the Island to a port Europe*—to *such* as were *laden with the like produce belonging to subjects of France*

---

* The Report of the Secretary of State mentions (as was known at the time) that one Repeal was effected by the influence of the Owners of a Privateer which had captured the valuable American Ship *Laurens*, to give effect to her condemnation.⁴

4. This is a reference to a report made by Pickering which was submitted to Congress on February 28, 1797. Pickering wrote: "On the appearance of the decree of 9th of May [1793], the American minister at Paris remonstrated against it, as a violation of the treaty of commerce between France and the United States. In consequence hereof, the Convention, by a decree of the 23d of the same month, declare, 'That the vessels of the United States are not comprised in the regulations of the decree of the 9th of May.' M. le Brun [Pierre Henri Hélène Marie Lebrun-Tondu], the minister for foreign affairs, on the 26th of May, communicated this second decree to our minister, accompanying it with these words: 'you will there find a new confirmation of the principles *from which the French people will never depart*, with regard to their good friends and allies, the United States of America.' Yet two days only had elapsed before those principles were departed from: on the 28th of May, the Convention repealed their decree of the 23d. The owners of a French privateer that had captured a very rich American ship, (the Laurens) found means to effect the repeal, to enable them to keep hold on their prize . . ." (*ASP, Foreign Relations*, I, 748).

5. For this order, see "The Warning No. II," February 7, 1797, note 3.
6. For this order, see *ASP, Foreign Relations*, III, 264.

whithersoever bound—to *such* as should be found *attempting to enter a blockaded port*—to *such* as were *laden* in whole or in part *with naval or military stores bound to a French Island.*

This last order obviated in a great measure the mischief of the former; and though its principles were in some respects such as we ought never to recognise; yet were they conformable with the practice of the principal maritime powers in antecedent modern wars, especially of France & Great Britain.

These acts comprise the whole of those on which the British Spoliations have been founded. Taken with all the latitude of construction adopted by the British Officers and Courts in the West Indies they amount to this and to no more—"the *seizure and appropriation of our corn flour and meal going to a French port, on the condition of paying for them—the seizure and confiscation of our vessels* with their cargoes—*when laden* with the *produce* of a *French Colony* or in act of carrying provisions or other supplies for the use of such colony." Our Trade with France herself except in corn flour & Meal and in contraband articles has in the worst of times remained unmolested, and has even been allowed to be carried on directly from British Ports.

Iniquitous and oppressive as were the acts of G B how very far short do they fall of the more iniquitous and oppressive decrees of France, as these have been construed and acted upon—not only by its Colonial Administrations but by some of its Tribunals in Europe. The decree of the 2d. of July 1796 [7] purports in substance that France will treat the neutral powers as they have permitted her enemies to treat them. But under this masked battery the whole of our trade with the enemies of France has been assailed. The two Edits of her proconsuls in the West Indies * proclaim the capture

---

* Santhonax and Co. 27 November 1796 [8] Victor Hughes 13 Pluviose 5 year of Republic.[9]

7. For this decree, see George Washington to H, January 19, 1797, note 4.

8. This edict reads: "The commission resolves that the captains of French national vessels and privateers are authorized to stop and bring into the ports of the colony American vessels bound to English ports, or coming from the said ports.

"The vessels which are already taken, or shall be hereafter, shall remain in the ports of the colony until it shall be otherwise ordered." (*ASP, Foreign Relations*, I, 752–53.)

9. This edict, dated February 1, 1797, reads in part: ". . . considering that, in virtue of the 2d article of the treaty of alliance, concluded at Paris on the

of all neutral vessels bound to or coming from English Ports and the uniform consequence is confiscation of vessel and cargo. We are now likewise officially informed that a French consular Tribunal at Cadiz has condemned neutral vessels carried in there on the same broad principles.[10] The evil to us has been magnified by various aggravations. Our vessels going from one neutral port to another, even our vessels going to and returning from French ports have been the victims of the piratical spirit which dictated those Edicts. Outrage imprisonment fetters disease and death inflicted or brought upon the Commanders and crews of our vessels cause the bitter cup of our sufferings to overflow and leave the imagination at a loss for a parallel without seeking for it in the ferocious regions of Barbary.

The ambiguity of the British order of November was a just subject of reproach to its authors. What shall we say of the perfidious ambiguity of the French decree of the 2d. of July 1796? When retaliation of the partial injuries which neutral nations had suffered from the enemies of France were denounced—who could have dreamt that a universal war on their Trade was meditated? Who that has a spark of the American in his soul can refuse his utmost indignation as well at the manner as at the *matter of this atrocious proceed-*

6th of February, 1778, between the United States and France, the former Power engaged to defend the American possessions in case of war, and that the Government and the commerce of the United States have strangely abused the forbearance of the republic of France, in turning to its injury the favors granted to them of trading in all the ports of the French colonies.

"That, by permitting neutral vessels any longer to carry provisions of war and of subsistence to men, evidently in state of rebellion, would be to prolong civil war, and the calamities and crimes flowing therefrom—decree as follows:

"Article 1. The ships of the republic and French privateers are authorized to capture and conduct into the ports of the republic neutral vessels destined for the Windward and Leeward Islands of America, delivered up to the English, and occupied and defended by the emigrants. These ports are, Martinico, St. Lucie, Tobago, Demarara, Berbice, Essequibo;

"And at the Leeward, Port au Prince, St. Mark's, l'Archaye, and Jeremie.

"Art. 2. Every armed vessel, having a commission from either of the said ports, shall be reputed a pirate, and the crews adjudged and punished as such.

"Art. 3. The vessels and cargoes described in the 1st and 2d articles are declared good prize, and shall be sold for the benefit of the captors.

"Art. 4. Every captured vessel, which shall have cleared out under the vague denomination of *West Indies*, is comprehended in the 1st and 2d articles.

"Art. 5. The decree of the 4th of last Nivose, in pursuance of the resolution of the executive directory, of the 14th Messidor, 4th year, shall be executed till further orders, as far as shall not be contravened by the present decree. . . ." (*ASP, Foreign Relations*, I, 759–60.)

10. See "The Warning No. I," January 27, 1797, note 9.

ing? Not only the partisans of France, the advocates for the honor of Republican Government, but the friends of human nature must desire that the final explanation may reject as a criminal abuse the practice upon that decree and repair as far as possible the mischief which it ha⟨s⟩ occasioned.

But the Treaty with Great Britain, (still exclaim the dupes or hirelings of France) that abominable instrument is the Pandora's box from which all our misfortunes issue—when that instrument was confirmed who could have expected any thing better?

Peace ye seduced or seducing babblers! Had Denmark or Sweden any share in making that reprobated Treaty? Besides the refutation of your flimsey pretence by the ill treatment in other shapes of several of the neutral powers in Europe—by the information from Cadiz of the indiscriminate seizure and condemnation of neutral vessels going to or coming from English ports—[11] Do ye not read in the recent accounts from St. Bartholomews a *Swedish* Island that not Americans only, that Danes, that Swedes, that all the neutral nations partake in the common calamity—alike the prey of a devouring rapacity? [12] Will ye still persist then in the barefaced imposture of ascribing to the treaty grievances which are the mere effects of a spirit of Oppression & Rapine?

Read the letter of Mr Skipwith to Mr Monroe dated at Paris the 3d of October 1794 [13] *prior* to the signature of the Treaty by Mr. Jay. Remember that he is an American Agent, acting under the eye of an American Minister, and that both the Minister and the Agent are distinguished by a partiality for France which exempt them from the suspicion of exaggerating her misdeeds. What does that letter tell us? Why in express terms, that *"innumerable embarrassments* and difficulties had *for a long time* oppressed our commerce in *different Ports* of the *Republic*—that if the French Government did

11. See "The Warning No. I," January 27, 1797, note 9.
12. St. Bartholomew, one of the Leeward Islands, was ceded to Sweden by France in 1784 in return for certain trading privileges in the Swedish port of Goteborg and for maintaining the friendly alliance with France. See Reinhard H. Luthin, "St. Bartholomew: Sweden's Colonial and Diplomatic Adventure in the Caribbean," *The Hispanic American Historical Review*, XIV, No. 3 (August, 1934), 307–24.
13. The letter from Fulwar Skipwith to James Monroe, along with a list of American vessels captured by the French, is printed in *ASP, Foreign Relations*, I, 749–52.

not soon remedy, the *incessant abuses* and *vexations* practiced *dayly* upon our Merchants *the trade of the U States with France* must cease."

Hence may ye learn that long before our Treaty with Great Britain the vexations of our Trade in the ports of France were so extreme as to have become intolerable; that "the *indiscriminate capture of our vessels at sea by the vessels of War of the Republic*" * formed only one class of the injuries which our Commerce had sustained—in a word that the predatory system of France existed before the Treaty and has only of late acquired greater activity from the cravings of an exhausted Treasury.

The man who after this mass of evidence shall be the apologist of France and the calamniator of his own Government is not an American. The choice for him lies between being deemed a fool a madman or a Traitor. AMERICUS

Note * This also is a passage verbatim from Mr. Skipwiths letter. And he produces a long [14] list of cases to support his assertions.
14. In MS, "lost."

To Timothy Pickering

New York March 29. 1797

Dear Sir

The post of yesterday brought me your letter of the day before.[1]

I regret that the idea of a Commission extraordinary appears of doubtful propriety. For after very mature reflection I am intirely convinced of its expediency. I do not understand the passage you cite as excluding the reception of a *special extraordinary Minister* but of an ordinary resident Minister. It seems impossible that the Directory can mean to say that they will shut the door to all explanation even as to the *nature* and *measure* of the redress of grievances which they require. They speak too hastily not to authorise large interpretation of what they say.

But if I were certain they would not hear the Commission, it would not prevent my having recourse to it. It would be my policy, if such a temper exists in them to accumulate the proofs of it with a view to Union at home.

This Union (I do not expect to proselite all the leaders of faction) appears to me a predominant consideration—& with regard to France more than ordinary pains are requisite to attain it.

That the enemies of the Government desire the measure is a cogent reason with me for adopting it—because I would meet them on their own ground & disarm them of the Argument that all has not been done which might have been done towards preserving peace.

The *estimation* of the merit of all our past measures depends on the final preservation of Peace. This, besides the interest of the Country in peace, is a very powerful reason for attempting every thing. The best friend of the Government will expect it—& if this expedient be not adopted it seems to me Rupture will inevitably follow.

There is an opinion industriously inculcated (which nobody better than myself knows to be false) that the *actual* administration are endeavouring to *provoke* a war. It is all important, by the last possible sacrifice, to confound this charge. I cannot but add that I have not only a strong wish but an *extreme anxiety* that the measure in question may be adopted.

To attain the end of it however it is very material to engage in the errand a man who will have the full confidence of the adverse party & who will be agreeable to France. This cannot be done without coupling others with him. Hence the idea of a Commission which to me appears capable of attaining every advantage & obviating every danger.

I am also desirous of impressing the public Mind strongly by a Religious Solemnity—to take place about the Meeting of Congress. I also think the Step intrinsically proper.

Affecly I am Dr Sir   Yr. Obed serv   A Hamilton
                                                              March 29, 1797

T Pickering Esq

ALS, Massachusetts Historical Society, Boston.
1. Pickering to H, March 26, 1797.

From Timothy Pickering

Philadelphia March 30. 1797.

Dear Sir,

I believe I mentioned in my last,[1] that I was going to sketch a state of facts relative to Mr. Pinckney's mission for publication. I now inclose it. That the facts should be known to our citizens was deemed important. I thought it highly important that the Representatives should come together [2] impressed with the sentiments of their constituents on the reprehensible conduct of the French Government, which made loud complaints of wrongs, but refused to hear our answer, or to enter on any discussion of the subjects of complaint, by refusing to acknowledge a special minister, sent from the U.S. for the direct purpose of making explanations; and that demanded of conscious innocence a confession of offences and redress of injuries never committed, as the preliminary of receiving our minister. The abominable depredations on our commerce—their unfounded complaints—their preposterous refusal to hear our answer—and the indignities offered to our ambassador, combined, and fully known to the people of the U.S. it might be fairly hoped would so powerfully operate in removing their ill founded and ill requited attachments to France, and even excite such a spirit of just resentment & pride, as would effectually controul certain men who have seemed willing to chain us to that republic & make us lick the feet of her violent and unprincipled rulers.

The statement of facts being prepared, I expected to hand it yesterday to Mr. Fenno [3] for publication: but some scruples arose about its expediency. The facts are carefully extracted from General Pinckney's letters of December 20,[4] & January 6.[5] The objections were, that, it might be deemed *irritating*—that it would be deemed an *official* publication, tho' anonymous—that such manifestly official

ALS, Hamilton Papers, Library of Congress.

1. Pickering to H, March 26, 1797.
2. On March 25, 1797, President John Adams issued a proclamation convening Congress on May 15 (*Annals of Congress*, VII, 49).
3. John Fenno was editor of the *Gazette of the United States, & Philadelphia Daily Advertiser*.
4. LC, RG 59, Despatches from United States Ministers to France, 1789–1869, Vol. 5, November 17, 1796–September 24, 1797, National Archives. This

publications have not heretofore been made, except to Congress, and that at their approaching session the letters themselves will be laid before both Houses. That America will expect the Executive to use every means of cultivating peace, and to hazard nothing which can be construed into a tendency to provoke a war. But the same objections, substantially, were made by our French-American patriots to my letter to General Pinckney,⁶ tho' written with extreme moderation, & containing answers and explanations to complaints which the French minister himself had the impudence to address to the Citizens of the U.S.⁷ whom those patriots would gladly continue to keep in the dark; and in short, prostrate by an unconditional submission at the feet of the most ambitious and horrible tyrants that ever cursed the earth.

The publication being thus suspended, I inclose the statement for your information. You need not return it, as I have a fair copy. I need not have been so minute in the detail: but the substance of the facts I still think ought to be published, and without delay; and in such form as to bear evident marks of authenticity, without which they will not gain universal belief, & therefore fail of the impression which I wished to have had produced by the publication. If you can drop me a line expressing your opinion on the matter, I shall be much obliged.

I am with sincere respect   Dr Sir Your obt. servt   T. Pickering

Alexr. Hamilton Esq

---

letter is printed in *ASP, Foreign Relations*, II, 5–8, where it is mistakenly dated December 10, 1796.

5. LC, RG 59, Despatches from United States Ministers to France, 1789–1869, Vol. 5, November 17, 1796–September 24, 1797, National Archives. An extract of this letter is printed in *ASP, Foreign Relations*, II, 9–10.

6. Pickering to Charles Cotesworth Pinckney, January 16, 1797 (LC, RG 59, Diplomatic and Consular Instructions of the Department of State, 1791–1801, Vol. 3, June 5, 1795–January 21, 1797, National Archives). See also George Washington to H, January 22, 1797; H to Washington, January 19, 25–31, 1797; H to Pickering, February 6, 1797; Rufus King to H, March 8, 1797, note 9.

7. This is a reference to letters of protest which Pierre Auguste Adet sent to Pickering on October 27 and November 15, 1796 (*ASP, Foreign Relations*, I, 576–77, 579–83). These letters were then printed in several newspapers. See, for example, *Claypoole's* [Philadelphia] *American Daily Advertiser*, November 1, 28, 1796. See also Washington to H, November 2, 3, 21, 1796, January 22, 1797; H to Washington, November 4, 5, 11, 19, 1796, January 19, 25–31, 1797; H to Oliver Wolcott, Jr., November 1, 1796; Wolcott to H, November 17, 1796.

[ENCLOSURE]

A Statement of Facts relative to General Pinckney's mission to France.[8]

General Pinckney, appointed minister plenipotentiary from the United States to the French Republic, left Philadelphia near the end of September, and arrived at Paris the 5th of December last, in the evening. On the 6th, he sent, by his secretary, to Mr. Monroe his letters of recall; and immediately afterwards waited on Mr. Monroe, who shewed him a letter from M. Delacroix,[9] the French Minister for foreign affairs, dated December 2. 1796, in which M. Delacroix, remarked, that Mr. Pinckney's arrival appearing to be at hand, if it had not already taken place, he thought it his duty to inform Mr. Monroe of the formalities to be observed on that occasion; & then tells him, the usage is, that the minister recalled and his successor send to the Minister for foreign affairs, the copy of their letters of recall and of credence.

Genl. Pinckney deeming it more respectful to the Minister to acquaint him with his arrival, & to inform him that they would wait upon him at any hour he would appoint, with their letters of credence and recall, Mr. Monroe on the same day (Decr. 6th) wrote to M. Delacroix accordingly, and requested he would appoint a time when Mr. Pinckney & himself should have the honor of attending him, for the purpose of presenting to him copies of those documents.

On the 9th of December Genl. Pinckney received from Mr. Monroe a letter imforming him that M. Delacroix had appointed that day, between one and four o'clock, to receive them. M. Delacroix letter is dated that day, in answer to Mr. Monroe's of the 6th; and

---

8. ADf, Hamilton Papers, Library of Congress. The information in this enclosure is based on Pinckney's dispatches to Pickering along with various documents which Pinckney enclosed. See Pinckney to Pickering, December 20, 1796, January 6, February 18, 1797 (LC, RG 59, Despatches from United States Ministers to France, 1789–1869, Vol. 5, November 17, 1796–September 24, 1797, National Archives). This material also constituted a part of the report which Pickering submitted to the House of Representatives on May 17, 1797 (*ASP, Foreign Relations*, II, 5–10). See also King to H, February 6, 1797.
9. Charles Delacroix.

after reciting the object of the interview, M. Delacroix said, he should be eager to receive him that day, at any hour from one to four o'clock, afternoon, if that would be convenient to him; & prayed him to propose it to General Pinckney. Accordingly Mr. Monroe, & General Pinckney with his Secretary Major Henry Rutledge, about two o'clock, waited on M. Delacroix; and Genl. Pi[n]ckney was introduced to him by Mr. Monroe as his successor. On receiving their letters of credence and recall, M. Delacroix said he would deliver them without delay to the Directory. He desired Major Rutledge to let him have the names of baptism, & ages of himself & Genl Pinckney, that cards of hospitality might be made out, which he said was necessary to reside there unmolested. Their names & ages were immediately given; and M. Delacroix promised to send the cards the next morning.

When this interview was known, the reports which had been spread abroad, before Genl. Pinckney's arrival, that he would not be received by the Directory, vanished. However, on Monday Decr. 12th, Mr. Monroe's secertary (Mr. Prevost) [10] called on Genl. Pinckney, and told him that Mr. Monroe had just received a letter from M. Delacroix; & desired to know if Genl. Pinckney had received one: The latter answered that he had not. Mr. Prevost then shewed Genl. Pinckney M. Delacroix' letter to Mr. Monroe. It is dated the 11th of December; and after mentioning that he had laid before the Executive Directory the copy of Mr. Monroe's letter of recall, & Genl. Pinckney's letters of credence, M. Delacroix says the Directory had charged him to inform Mr. Monroe, *that they would not acknowledge nor receive another minister plenipotentiary from the United States, until the injuries stated to the American Government had been redressed.*

Genl. Pinckney waited till the next day, Decr. 13th, expecting to receive a like notification from M. Delacroix; when, not hearing from him, Genl. Pinckney wrote him a letter, in which after reciting the substance of that which M. Delacroix had written on the 11th to Mr. Monroe, he expressed his regret at the determination of the Directory, and that he was not permitted even to attempt to explain the sentiments of America and its government, or in the terms

10. John B. Prevost.

of his letters of credence, to endeavour *to efface unfavourable impressions, to banish suspicions, and to restore that cordiality which was at once the evidence and pledge of a friendly union.* Genl. Pinckney then suggested, that as official copies of his letters of credence and of Mr. Monroe's letters of recall had been delivered to M. Delacroix, the determination of the Directory should have been communicated immediately to him (Genl. Pinckney) that he might, without delay, transmit the same as from the Executive of the French Republic to the Government of the U. States. He also desired to be informed whether it was the intention of the Directory that he should immediately quit the territories of the French Republic; or whether he & his family might stay until he heard from his government.

This letter Genl. Pinckney sent by his Secretary to M. Delacroix, who opened and read it in Major Rutledge's presence. When he had finished, he desired Major Rutledge to return to Genl. Pinckney as his answer, *That the Executive Directory knew of no minister plenipotentiary from the United States, since the presentation of Mr. Monroe's letters of recall;* and that the Executive Directory had charged him to notify to Mr. Monroe, *that they would not acknowledge nor receive another minister plenipotentiary from the United States, until the injuries stated to the American Government had been redressed:* which notification the Directory relied on Mr. Monroe's imparting to his own government, as well as communicating to Genl. Pinckney. As to the second subject of Genl. Pinckney's letter, (whether the Directory intended that he should quit the territories of the Republic, or stay till he heard from his government) M. Delacroix said he could return no answer until he had laid it before the Executive Directory. Major Rutledge asked if Genl. Pinckney should expect an answer. M. Delacroix replied, that the intentions of the Directory should be signified either to him or to Mr. Monroe.

On the 15th of December, M. Giraudet [11] called upon Genl. Pinckney, & said he was chief secretary in the department of foreign affairs: that he came on the part of the Minister of foreign affairs, to signify to him, that with respect to his letter to M. Delacroix, he could not directly communicate with Genl. Pinckney, but only with

11. Charles-Philippe-Toussaint Guiraudet.

Mr. Monroe, as such direct communication would be acknowledging Genl. P. as Minister, when the Directory had determined not to receive him: that as to the other part of his letter, relative to his remaining there, he supposed Genl. P. was acquainted with the local laws of France relating to strangers. Genl. Pinckney answered that he was not. M. Giraudet then said there was a decree forbidding all strangers to remain in Paris without particular permission, which as the Directory did not grant to General Pinckney, the general law would of course operate. To this Genl. P. answered, that he could not conceive that the having of a direct communication with him would involve the consequence that had been mentioned. Had Mr. Monroe died before his arrival, the information that they would not acknowledge him must have been communicated to Genl. P. himself; and that Mr. Monroe having received his letters of recall, could not now act officially, any more than if he had ceased to exist. That with regard to the law of France relating to strangers, it did not apply to the requisition in his letter, which was to be informed whether it was the intention of the Directory that he should quit France, or be allowed to stay till he heard from his government.

Mr. Giraudet said he rather imagined it was the intention of the Directory that Genl. Pinckney should quit the territories of the Republic; but as it admitted of a doubt, he would mention it to the minister, and communicate the result in the evening. Genl. Pinckney then further desired to be informed, if obliged to quit the Republic, in what time he must depart, as his baggage had not yet arrived from Bourdeaux: adding, that he meant not to ask any personal favour, but to have the intention of the Directory clearly expressed, in relation to him in the public character in which he came to France. M. Giraudet said he would do what he desired; and departed. In the evening he returned, and said, That in answer to the doubt entertained at the former meeting, the Minister (Delacroix) could only answer, that he had understood the Directory to mean, that Genl. Pi[n]ckney was to quit, not Paris only, but the territories of the French Republic. That as to the time in which it was necessary to depart, the Minister would not designate it; but he would have another communication with the Directory; and that their intentions should be made known in a more explicit manner on both points. M. Giraudet then said he must inform Mr. Pinckney, that in all probability M. Delacroix would not be the organ thro' which he would receive the answer, as *the Minister of police* was the officer under whose department his case would come. To this Genl. Pinckney replied, That M. Delacroix & the Directory had received the official copy of his letter of credence: That it was in the power of the Directory to receive him or not; but they could not divest themselves of their knowledge of the public character in which he came to France: That in that character he was entitled to the protection of the law of nations, whether the Directory received him or not. That if they permitted him to stay till he heard from his government, he was under the protection of that law: and if they ordered him to quit the territories of the Republic, still he was entitled to letters of safe-conduct and passports for his journey. Genl. Pinckney closed this conversation with M. Giraudet, with desiring him to inform M. Delacroix, that he requested that whatever further passed might be in writing, that no mistakes might happen by verbal communications, and that he might know explicitly the intentions of the Directory.

After this, ten days having elapsed without any communication from M. Delacroix, and complaints having been received by Genl. Pinckney of inconveniences to which american citizens in France were subjected, for want of passports signed by their minister: he thought it his duty, tho' not acknowledged by the French Government, to endeavour to remedy this grievance. For americans coming from the territories of a power at war with the Republic, on arriving in its ports, were thrown into confinement, unless they could give security for their good behaviour, until they could obtain passports from our minister at Paris—after being countersigned by the minister of foreign affairs. Genl. Pinckney therefore directed his secretary, Major Rutledge, to wait upon M. Delacroix, to represent this subject, and to obtain from him, unofficially, the determination of the Directory concerning his residence or departure from the territory of the Republic. Accordingly, on the 26th of December, Major Rutledge waited on M. Delacroix, and mentioned the situation of the American citizens lately arrived in France, who had been thrown into prison; where they remained, for want of passports, which could not now be obtained, there being no acknowledged minister from the U. States. General Pinckney therefore wished to be informed to what authority he should refer them for relief. M. Delacroix answered, that an order had been made on this subject; and that in future all petitions on behalf of American Citizens, for passports, should be addressed to the Minister of the General Police: That however, he would charge himself with any which Genl. Pinckney might then have by him, if he preferred the channel of his department. Major Rutledge then asked M. Delacroix if he had heard any thing further from the Directory as to their intentions respecting General Pinckney's remaining where he was. M. Delacroix answered with marks of great surprize—That he thought he had already explained himself with sufficient clearness on the subject: that he had long since signified to General Pinckney, the impossibility of his staying: that he thought he had exercised much *condescension* in having been so long silent, which he had been induced to do, by Genl. Pinckney's having complained of the delay of his baggage, which he supposed must by this time have arrived from Bourdeaux: that, in short, *he should be sorry if his further stay should compel him to give information to the minister of the Police.!!!* Major Rutledge answered, that if permitted, he would call to M. Delacroix recollection the communication he had made to General Pinckney, thro' his secretary M. Giraudet. That gentleman had indeed told Genl. Pinckney, that he must consider himself in the light of any common stranger, to whom a card of hospitality was denied, and who was compelled, by the laws respecting foreigners, to withdraw from the territories of the Republic: but General Pinckney had refused to regard himself in any other situation than that in which he had entered France; which was not in a private capacity, but in a public character, which had been officially announced to the Directory: that he was not subject to the law respecting strangers, but was under protection of the law of nations: M. Giraudet then took leave, with a promise to communicate to the Minister of foreign affairs the ground which Mr. Pinckney had taken. In the evening he returned, and said that the Minister would again lay Genl. Pinckney's letter before the Directory, & that their intentions should be made known to him as soon as possible. Major Rutledge then remarked, that he supposed all this had been faithfully related to him by his Secretary. M. Delacroix answered, That Genl. Pinckney must have mistaken M. Giraudet, as to his intention of again laying Genl. Pinckney's letter before the Directory. Major

Rutledge replied, That this was impossible; for he had been present at both conversations, in which the material parts had passed in English, and been repeated in French. M. Delacroix then said that M. Giraudet had acted without his authority. Major Rutledge answered, That Genl. Pinckney had nevertheless waited until that moment in expectation of hearing from him, agreeably to M. Giraudet's promise: that the General was very far from intending to dispute the will of the Directory; what he wanted was a communication of that will in *writing*. M. Delacroix said it had already been given. Major Rutledge desired to know when. M. Delacroix answered, in the notification which he had made, by order of the Directory, to Mr. Monroe: that this contained their sentiments on the point of Mr. Pinckney's staying; in as much as that his not being received, implied that he should depart. Major Rutledge denied that this was a fair deduction. M. Delacroix insisted that it was. Major Rutledge said it had not so struck Genl. Pinckney, nor any person with whom he had conversed: but however, if such was the construction to be put upon it, he flattered himself that M. Delacroix could have no objection to expressing it upon paper, in order that Genl. Pinckney might have something more substantial than the authority of the *word* of his secretary, to justify himself to his own government, for quitting a spot to which he had come in obedience to their orders. Here M. Delacroix turned away, with some warmth, and said he should do no such thing: *that Genl. Pinckney might make his own deductions—he desired to have no more communications with him.* Major Rutledge withdrew.

This behaviour of M. Delacroix did not discompose Genl. Pinckney. He considered that he was at the post where his duty required him to remain, until he received orders from his own government how to conduct himself, or until the French government should give him a written order to depart; or send him passports as a minister of his country whom they would not suffer to remain within their territory; or do some other unequivocal act that would justify his going.

Such appears to have been the conduct of the French Government; and such the situation of Genl. Pinckney, until some time in January last. If they finally order him to quit France, it will surprize no one. The Directory, it is said, have already sent away *thirteen* foreign ministers; and a late Emigrant, now in Paris,¹² has assured them, *that the United States are not of greater consequence, nor ought to be treated with more respect than Genoa or Geneva.* (Genoa is a little bigger than the state of Delaware; and Geneva, almost of as great extent as the little *county* of Delaware in the state of Pennsylvania; that is, about *thirteen* miles long and *eleven* broad.)

12. For the identification of Charles Maurice de Talleyrand-Périgord as the "late Emigrant," see Pickering to H, April 5, 1797.

To Oliver Wolcott, Junior

[New York, March 30, 1797]

My Dear Sir

Every one who can properly appreciate the situation of our Affairs at this moment, in all the extent of possible circumstances, must be extremely anxious for such a course of conduct in our Government which will unite the utmost prudence with energy. It has been a considerable time my wish that a Commission extraordinary * should be constituted to go to France to *explain demand negotiate* &c.¹ I was particularly desirous that the first measure of the present President's Administration should have been that. But it has not happened. I now continue to wish earnestly that the same measure may go into effect & that the meeting of the Senate may be accelerated for the purpose. Without *opening* a new channel of negotiation, it seems to me the door to accommodation is shut—& rupture will follow if not prevented by a general peace. Who indeed can be certain that a general pacification of Europe may not leave us alone to receive the law from France? Will it be wise to omit any thing to parry if possible these great risks?

Perhaps the Directory have declared they will not receive a Minister till their grievances shall have been redressed? ²

This can hardly mean more than that they will not receive a residing Minister. It cannot mean that they will not hear an extraordinary Messenger, who may even be sent to know what will satisfy?

* Madison   Pinkney   Cabot

Suppose they do. It will still be well to convince the people that the Governt has done all in its power and that the Directory are unreasonable.

But the enemies of the Government call for the measure. To me this is a very strong reason for pursuing it. It will meet them on their own ground & disarm them of the plea that something has been omitted.

I ought (My good friend) to apprize you, for you may learn it from no other—that a suspicion begins to *dawn* among the friends of the Government that the *actual* administration [3] is not much averse from War with France. How very important to obviate this!

The Accounts just received offer a great danger that the Emperor may be compelled to make peace.[4] *Paul* of Russia is evidently lukewarm in the cause of the allies.[5] From lukewarmness to enmity, where fortune takes the other side, is but a step.

If England is left to bear the Burthen alone, Who can say that France may not venture to sport an army to this Country. It may get rid of troublesome spirits.

As in the case of England, so now, My Opinion is to exhaust the expedients of Negotiation & at the same time to prepare *vigorously* for the Worst. This is sound policy. Any omission or deficiency either way will be a great error. God bless you.   A Hamilton

March 30. 1797

O W Jun Esq

ALS, Connecticut Historical Society, Hartford; copy, Hamilton Papers, Library of Congress.

1. H had recommended such a policy as early as January, 1797 (H to George Washington, January 25–31, 1797), and had continued to suggest it during the succeeding two months (H to Theodore Sedgwick, February 26, 1797; H to Timothy Pickering, March 22, 1797).
2. See Pickering to H, March 26, 30, 1797.
3. Above this word H wrote: "*Ministers.*"
4. See Rufus King to H, March 8, 1797.
5. See H to Pickering, March 22, 1797, note 3.

From Oliver Wolcott, Junior

Philadelphia Mar. 31. 1797

Dear Sir,

I have recd. your Letter of March 30th. and I consider it as a great acquisition. It developes the origin of a circumstance which came to my knowledge at the close of the last session which filled my mind with inexpressible surprize. To you I will say but in the most perfect confidence that the President had determined on instituting a Commission, but *it would not have been composed as you now propose*.[1] I believe no one of the heads of Departments knows of the

ALS, Hamilton Papers, Library of Congress; ADf, Connecticut Historical Society, Hartford; copy, Connecticut Historical Society, Hartford; LC, Connecticut Historical Society, Hartford.

1. Wolcott is referring to John Adams's proposal to appoint a mission to France which would include prominent Republicans. On March 5, 1797, Adams discussed Franco-American relations with Thomas Jefferson and one member of his cabinet, presumably Wolcott. In 1809 Adams wrote the following account of these meetings: ". . . I asked Mr. Jefferson what he thought of another trip to Paris, and whether he thought the constitution and the people would be willing to spare him for a short time? Yes. That is right, said Mr. Jefferson; but without considering whether the constitution will allow it or not, I am so sick of residing in Europe, that I believe I shall never go there again. I replied, I own I have strong doubts whether it would be legal to appoint you; but I believe no man could do the business so well. What do you think of sending Mr. Madison? Do you think he would accept of an appointment? I do not know, said Mr. Jefferson. Washington wanted to appoint him some time ago, and kept the place open for him a long time; but he never could get him to say that he would go. Other characters were considered, and other conversations ensued. . . .

"From Mr. Jefferson I went to one of the heads of departments, whom Mr. Washington had appointed, and I had no thoughts of removing. Indeed I had then no objection to any of the Secretaries. I asked him what he thought of sending Mr. Madison to France, with or without others? Is it determined to send to France at all? Determined? Nothing is determined till it is executed, smiling. But why not? I thought it deserved consideration. So it does; but suppose it determined, what do you think of sending Mr. Madison? Is it determined to send Mr. Madison? No; but it deserves consideration. Sending Mr. Madison will make dire work among the passions of our parties in Congress, and out of doors, through the states! Are we forever to be overawed and directed by party passions? All this conversation on my part was with the most perfect civility, good humor, and indeed familiarity: but I found it excited a profound gloom and solemn countenance in my companion, which after some time broke out in 'Mr. President, we are willing to resign.' Nothing could have been more unexpected to me than this observation—Nothing was farther from my thoughts than to give any pain or uneasiness. I had said nothing that could possibly displease, except pronouncing the name of Madi-

decision except myself, I had attributed it to Mr. Ames[2] from a casual expression, & I own that by means of my most sincere & urgent expostulations nay supplications, it was postponed.

I am far from believing, that considering General Pinckneys *diplomatic rank,* his personal character, & the *special* objects of his mission, which were *specified in his Letters of Credences* and *communicated to the Directory* that there is any just or even specious pretext for his rejection. On the contrary it appears to me that France has insolently rejected a fair & *suitable* proposition for a discussion and adjustment of the existing disputes—That the national indignity is such, that it *must be noticed.* There is a point, but where I allow to be uncertain, below which the Government cannot stop without loosing the confidence of the people and producing that despondency, loss of Credit & want of public concert, which would ruin our affairs. I wish we may find that our apathy has not been already carried to a fatal extreme.

The plan of measures I would propose is as follows.

1st. That the President should in his speech to Congress take a view of the complaints of France & of the measures adopted by his predecessor, particularly in the mission of Mr. Pinckney & should give them his decided approbation. That he should intimate but in delicate terms that France has rejected a suitable opportunity for discussion, but that this would not prevent him from persevering in the line of Negociation. That measures would be accordingly

---

son. I restrained my surprise, however, and only said, I hope nobody will resign; I am satisfied with all the public officers." (*Correspondence of the Late President Adams. Originally Published in the Boston Patriot. In a Series of Letters* [Boston: Everett and Munroe, 1809], 63–64.)

2. On March 3, 1797, Fisher Ames had completed his fourth and final term as a Federalist member of the House of Representatives and had returned to Dedham, Massachusetts, to practice law. In 1809 Adams recalled his conversation with Ames on March 5, 1797: "The morning after my inauguration, Mr. Fisher Ames made me a visit, to take leave. His period in Congress had expired. . . . Mr. Ames, with much gravity and solemnity, advised me to institute a new mission to France. Our affairs with that republic were in an unpleasant and dangerous situation, and the people, in a long recess of congress must have some object on which to fix their contemplation and their hopes. And he recommended Mr. George Cabot, for the northern states to be one of the three, if a commission was to be sent, or alone, if but one was to go.

"I answered Mr. Ames, that the subject had almost engrossed my attention for a long time. That I should take every thing into serious consideration. . . ." (*Correspondence of the Late President Adams,* 61.)

pursued for renewing proposals to & entering upon negociations with the Government of France whenever its consent can be obtained.

2nd. That the President should recommend, and in more than usual terms of confidence, the adoption of the following measures. 1st. an increase of Revenue 2nd. The arming our Vessells for defence with the right of capturing the attacking force. 3d. The equipment of a number of stout merchant Ships & Gallies to defend our Coasts. 4th. The fortification of our Ports. 5th. The enrollment of a Land force, (principally with a view of preventing insurrections of Slaves in the Southern States,) 6th. A power in the Executive to arrest Vessells & persons suspected of intending to cruize against our Trade, or Nations with whom we are at peace.

3d. A serious and firm call upon Congress for their united and vigorous support of the Executive, with an appeal to the honour generosity & patriotism of the people, in the present critical State of Affairs. My own ideas of the system & intentions of France lead me further in *defensive* & *cautionary* measures, that I have proposed but I am sensible of the impolicy of anticipating public opinion.

On the subject of negociation, I would ever be ready to meet France & would keep an Agent, or if you please Agents, in Europe ready for that purpose; but I am not willing to admit that the Government has already done *less* than the occasion required, or that France is *justifiable* in refusing to recognize Mr. Pinckney. I am also free to declare that I conceive the claims of France to be in any other than the last & most extreme necessity, utterly inadmissible. They in fact require a surrender of National Independence. I would propose to *retract* nothing.*

The idea of a Commission consisting of Mr. M.[3] or any man like him, I must own to you is one which I can never adopt without the utmost reluctance. I have no confidence in Mr. M—he has been a frequenter of Mr. Adets political meetings.[4] I have been just in-

---

* Note I would not refuse a remodification of Treatles If desired.

3. James Madison. See H to George Washington, January 22, 1797; H to Theodore Sedgwick, February 26, 1797; H to Timothy Pickering, March 22, 29, 1797; H to Wolcott, March 30, 1797.

4. Pierre Auguste Adet announced the suspension of his functions as French Minister to the United States on November 15, 1796. See H to Washington, November 19, 1796, note 8. He remained in the United States to work for a Republican victory in the election of 1796, and he did not leave the United States until May, 1797. For a discussion of Adet's political activities in the

formed that Mr. Adet has suggested the idea of sending this Gentleman. We know that the French count upon the support of a party in this Country, and so shameless is the faction grown, that positive proof of a devotion to French views, is with many no injury to a mans popularity. If the government suffers France to dictate what description of men shall be appointed to public trusts, our Country is undone—from that moment, the confidence of all the old fashioned, honourable & virtuous men of the interior Country is irrecoverably lost.

Another consequence of not rejecting the interference of France is, that it will encourage other Nations to interfere especially G. Britain, & will moreover countenance the calumny, that a British faction exists. The french say, that Mr. Jay & his friends were in the British interest, & that *therefore* he was appointed. Will it be safe or proper to appoint a Man known to be of the French party, & thus give to a falshood, the force of argument? If I know any thing of human nature, this will be the effect on the minds of Thousands.

I have no objection to sendg a man of neutral politicks, at least on party questions, if he be a man of sense, firmness & integrity. General Pinckney is of this description. If a Commission of three is generally prefered, it is a point perhaps not to be contested, though I own it does not strike me agreably. Yet how is the Commission to be composed, must all concur, or will the concurrence of two suffice? In either case mutual confidence will be essential to success. From what was on the point of being done, I presume Mr. C—— to be out of the question.[5] If a man of his principles were to be associated with Mr. M. either nothing would be done or something worse than nothing. Mr. M—— would insist on a submission to France, or would obstruct a settlement & throw the disgrace on the friends of Government. Either result would deliver the Country bound hand & foot to French influence. If nothing was done the obstinacy of the federalists would be complained of, if something was done however humiliating, the responsibility would be divided & all the mischiefs would be attributed to the despera⟨te⟩ state of affairs induced by the *fatal Treaty* with G.B.

---

election of 1796, see Adet to Charles Delacroix, Minister of Foreign Relations, September 24, 1796 (Turner, "Correspondence of French Ministers," 947-49).

5. George Cabot. See Washington to H, January 25-31, 1797; H to Sedgwick, February 26, 1797; H to Pickering, March 22, 29, 1797; H to Wolcott, March 30, 1797.

You known that I am accustomed to respect your opinions, & I am not so ignorant of the extent of your influence upon the friends of Government as not to be sensible, that if you are known to favour the sending of a Commission, so the thing must & will be. When the body of both parties concur in a measure individual opinions stand for nothing. In this case what would be the objection against sending Mr. Ingersoll [6] of this City or som⟨e⟩ such character, to be united with J. Q. Adams [7] or Mr. Murray,[8] & Genl. Pinckney to rendezvous at Amsterdam, until the consent of France to negociate can be obtained. Is it necessary that the mission should procede directly to France, & *must* Mr. M―― be a member?

I should be sorry if the friends of the Governt. were to consider me or any of the public officers as desirous of producing a War with France because I should consider this as evidence that our Affairs are desperate. If the public pulse does not beat higher than that of the Government all is over. There ought ⟨to⟩ be a Zeal for strenuous measures, & this Ze⟨al⟩ ought to be an Engine in the hands of Gov⟨ern⟩ment for preserving peace. I think I can assure you, that the motion of our Ship cannot be adjusted to a minute Scale, if the present course is attempted to be varied, it will in future be nearly opposite to the present.

The present is a moment of apparent tranquillit⟨y⟩ but I conjecture that it is a Calm which forebodes a hurricane; the Executive will either fin⟨d a⟩ violent & steady Gale from one point, or be assailed with a Tornado, which will throw every thing into confusion. I predict that no treaty, no compromise, no concession will afford security.

Revenue is essential, & there will I fear be insuperable objections started by the friends & enemies of Government. Credit has been abused has been exhausted, in senseless speculations.

Having no ambition to gratify, no theory or project to support, I

---

6. Jared Ingersoll was a Philadelphia attorney and attorney general of Pennsylvania from 1790 to 1799. He had served in the Continental Congress in 1780 and 1781 and was a delegate to the Constitutional Convention.

7. John Quincy Adams, the son of John Adams, was Minister Resident at The Hague from 1794 to 1796. On May 30, 1796, the Senate confirmed his appointment as Minister Plenipotentiary at Lisbon (*Executive Journal*, I, 213).

8. William Vans Murray, a Maryland Federalist, had served as a member of the House of Representatives from March 4, 1791, to March 3, 1797. On March 2, 1797, the Senate confirmed his appointment as United States Minister Resident to the Netherlands (*Executive Journal*, I, 228).

shall be ready to aid my Country with my best exertions & shall be happy to receive your opinions, and to know the state of public opinion. No person can exceed me in sincere wishes that what is proper may be done.

 Yrs assuredly   Oliv Wolcott Jr.

A Hamilton Esq.

To James McHenry

[New York, March, 1797] [1]

My Dear Friend

Take my ideas and weigh them of a proper course of conduct for our administration in the present juncture.

You have called Congress—tis well.[2]

When the Senate meets (which I should be glad to see anticipated) send a Commission extraordinary to France. Let it consist of *Jefferson* or *Madison* Pinckney & a third very safe man, say *Cabot*.

Proclaim a Religious solemnity to take place at the Meeting of Congress.

When Congress meet, get them to lay an Embargo with liberty to the executive to grant licenses to depart to Vessels *armed* or sailing with *Convoys*.

Increase the Revenue vigorously—& provide naval force for *Convoys*. Purchase a number of Vessels now built the most fit for Sloops of War & Cutters and arm & commission them to serve as Convoys. Grant Qualified letters of marck to your Merchantmen to arm defend themselves & capture those who attack but not to cruise—or attack.

Form a provisional army of 25000 men. To be engaged eventually & have certain Emoluments. Increase your Cavalry & Artillery in immediate service.

Or do as much of all this as you can. Make a last effort for peace but be prepared for the worst.

The Emperor Paul is at best Equivocal. A successor is apt to differ from a predecessor. He seems to be a *Reformer* too. Who can say into what scale his weight may be finally thrown? [3]

If things shall so turn that Austria is driven to make peace & England left to contend alone—who can guarantee us that France may not *sport* in this country a *proseliting* army? Even to get rid of the troops, if it fails, may be no bad thing to the Government of that Country. There is a *possible* course of things which may subject us even to an internal invasion by France. Our calculations to be solid should contemplate this possibility.

I know in your administration there is a doubt about a *Commission* or Envoy extraordinary.[4] I am very sorry for it, because I am sure it is an expedient measure. But perhaps France has said she will receive no Minister till her grievances shall be redressed. Tis hardly possible this can refer to any but a *Minister who is to reside*. A *special extraordinary* mission cannot be intended to be excluded—because it is at least necessary to know what measure of redress will satisfy if any is due. But grant she will refuse to hear. Still the great advantage results of shewing in the most glaring light to our people her unreasonableness—of disarming a party of the plea that all has not been done which might be done—of refuting completely the charge that the *actual* administration desires War with France.

But the enemies of the Government desire the measure. Tis the strongest reason for adopting it. This will meet them on their own ground & shut their mouths.

But to answer the end a man who will have their confidence must be sent—Jefferson or Madison. To do this & to be safe others must be united, say Pinkney & Cabot. Hence the idea of a Commission.

I am really my friend anxious that this should be your plan. Depend on it it will unite the double advantage of silencing enemies & satisfying friends.

I write you this letter on your fidelity. No *mortal* must see it or know its Contents. Yrs.   A Hamilton

J Mc.Henry Esq

ALS, Hamilton Papers, Library of Congress.
1. In *HCLW*, X, 241, this letter is dated March 22, 1797.
2. On March 25, 1797, President John Adams issued a proclamation convening Congress on May 15 (*Annals of Congress*, VII, 49).
3. See H to Timothy Pickering, March 22, 1797, note 3.
4. See Pickering to H, March 26, 1797; Oliver Wolcott, Jr., to H, March 31, 1797.

INDEX

COMPILED BY JEAN G. COOKE

"An Act concerning the Duties on Spirits distilled within the United States" (May 8, 1792), 484

"An Act for establishing an Executive Department, to be denominated the Department of Foreign Affairs" (July 27, 1789), 486

"An Act for raising a farther sum of money for the protection of the frontiers, and for the purposes therein mentioned" (May 2, 1792), 484

"An Act for the relief and protection of American Seamen" (May 28, 1796), 234

"An Act in addition to an act intituled 'An act supplementary to the act, intituled An act to provide more effectually for the Collection of the Duties on Goods, Wares and Merchandise imported into the United States, and on the Tonnage of Ships or Vessels'" (May 26, 1796), 1-2

"An Act laying duties on licenses for selling Wines and foreign distilled spirituous liquors by retail" (June 5, 1794), 484

"An Act laying duties on property sold at Auction" (June 9, 1794), 484

"An Act making appropriations for the Military and Naval establishments for the year one thousand seven hundred and ninety-seven" (March 3, 1797), 474

"An Act making Appropriations for the Support of Government for the year one thousand seven hundred and ninety-two" (December 23, 1791), 57

"An Act making further provision for the expenses attending the intercourse of the United States with foreign nations; and further to continue in force the act intituled 'An Act providing the means of intercourse between the United States and foreign nations'" (March 20, 1794), 244

"An Act making further provision for the expenses attending the intercourse of the United States with foreign nations; and to continue in force the act, intituled 'An act providing the means of intercourse between the United States and foreign nations'" (May 30, 1796), 233, 290-91

"An Act making further provision for the support of Public Credit, and for the redemption of the Public Debt" (March 3, 1795), 214-15

"An Act making provision for the payment of certain Debts of the United States" (May 31, 1796), 204-5, 214-15, 244, 289-90, 291

"An Act providing for the Sale of the Lands of the United States, in the territory northwest of the river Ohio, and above the mouth of Kentucky river" (May 18, 1796), 222

"An Act supplementary to an act entitled 'An act to provide a Naval Armament'" (April 20, 1796), 228, 473

"An Act supplementary to the act, intituled 'An act to provide more effectually for the collection of the Duties on goods, wares and merchandise imported into the United States, and on the tonnage of ships or vessels'" (February 26, 1795), 1-2

"An Act supplementary to the act

"Act supplementary to act" (*Cont.*) making provision for the Debt of the United States" (May 8, 1792), 204
"An Act to alter and amend the act intituled 'An act laying certain duties upon Snuff and refined Sugar'" (March 3, 1795), 484
"An Act to ascertain and fix the Military Establishment of the United States" (May 30, 1796), 485
"An Act to establish an Executive Department, to be denominated the Department of War" (August 7, 1789), 486
"An Act to establish an uniform rule of Naturalization; and to repeal the act heretofore passed on that subject" (January 29, 1795), 120
"An Act to establish an uniform System of Bankruptcy throughout the United States" (April 4, 1800), 199
"An Act to establish the Treasury Department" (September 2, 1789), 486
"An Act to provide a Naval Armament" (March 27, 1794), 228, 473
"An Act to provide for the safekeeping of the Acts, Records and Seal of the United States, and for other purposes" (September 15, 1789), 486
"An Act to provide more effectually for the collection of the duties imposed by law on goods, wares and merchandise imported into the United States, and on the tonnage of ships or vessels" (August 4, 1790), 350-51
"An Act to provide more effectually for the settlement of the Accounts between the United States and the individual States" (August 5, 1790), 474
Adams, John, 141, 184, 396, 398, 467; and France, 522, 567, 569-70; presidential candidate, 371-72, 375, 376, 377-78, 403-6, 418-19, 437-38, 445, 465-66; President of U.S., 471, 515-16, 544, 548-59, 558, 570, 575; and Seneca Indians, 529, 530-31
Adams, John Quincy, 243-44, 573
Addison, Joseph, and Richard Steele: *The Spectator*, 341-42
Adet, Pierre Auguste, 307; and Franco-American relations, 223-24, 226-27, 361-67, 374, 376, 380, 398-400, 408-9, 410-11, 411-14, 421-22, 423, 427, 444, 446, 476-77, 491, 505, 549, 559, 571-72; functions suspended, 408, 412, 571-72; Hamilton on, 372-73, 389-90; *letter from*, 304-5; *letters from* Timothy Pickering, 213, 221, 241, 390; *letter from* George Washington, 60-61; *letters to* Timothy Pickering, 212-13, 232, 240-41, 361-62, 363, 399-400, 409, 470-71; and the *Mount Vernon*, 221-22, 238; and Timothy Pickering, 373, 374, 412, 436-37, 536
Agriculture, board of: George Washington on, 364-65, 381, 382-84
Albany, N.Y.: and Jay Treaty, 138-39; petition of merchants of, 1-2
Alexandra (of Russia), 493
Algiers, 33, 227-28, 536; U.S. treaty with, 34, 114, 121-22, 125-26, **136**, 148, 228, 473
Aliens: and Jay Treaty, 14; and landownership, 18, 45-47, 51, **84**; naturalization of, 120
Alliance, 37
Allum, William, 453, 478, 513, 524, 529, 550-51
Alvinczy, Josef, baron von Barberek, 416, 508, **535**
American Iron Co., 237, **342**
American Revolution, 12, 355-61
"Americanus," 421-34
"Americus," 490-95, 509-12, 517-20, 524-27, 539-42, 551-56
Ames, Fisher, 112, 369, 570; *letters from*, 110, 482-89; *letter to*, 135
Amsterdam, 262
Annapolis, Md., 121, **136**
The Annual Register, 429
Anstey, John, 306, **506**
"The Answer," 421-34
Anthony, Joseph, 122
Arcambal, Louis, 417
Arcola, Battle of, 416
Armand, Charles Tuffin, 203
Articles of Confederation: and treaties, 5, 24, 25-31, 32, 33, 93
Articles of war, 252
Ash, John: *Grammatical Institutes*, 340, 342
Ashfield, Richard, 317
Asia, 50
Asylum Co., 516
Attorney General, *see* Lee, Charles

INDEX 579

Auctions: tax on, 484
Austria, 43; relations with France, 415-16, 422-23, 508, 534, 535, 546, 568, 575

Bache, Benjamin Franklin, 65, 172, 221-22, 231-32, 238, 410-11
Bailey, Theodorus, 118
Baldwin, Abraham, 22-23
Ball, Joseph, 122
Baltimore, Md., 121, 125-26, 136
Bancker, Gerard: *letters from*, 252, 521
Bank of New York, 50-51, 326, 347; and Bank of the U.S., 251, 448-50, 451, 452; loans by, 243-44, 250, 254-55, 263, 288, 289-91, 420-21, 435-37, 449, 451; president of, *see* Verplanck, Gulian
Bank of Pennsylvania, 243-44
Bank of the U.S., 343, 485; and Bank of New York, 251, 448-50, 451, 452; directors of, 52-53, 200; Hamilton's draft on, 55; loan by, 436-37; New York branch, 35, 50-51, 52-53, 254, 347, 420, 435, 448-50, 451, 452, 498; sale of stock of, 205, 214-15, 243, 251, 448
Barclay, John, 124-25, 495-96; *letter from* John Dunn, 496
Barclay, Thomas, 255-57, 260-61, 310-11
Barney, Joshua, 325-27, 337
Barras, Paul François Jean Nicolas, 547-58
Barthélemy, François, 321-22, 323; *letter from* Charles Delacroix, 322
Bassano, 416
Batavian Republic, 309
Bavaria, 416
Bayard, William, 52-53, 142, 198, 489; *letters to*, 447-48, 530-31
Bayley, Richard, 374-75, 393, 395; *letter from* Hamilton and Richard Harison, 258-60
Beaulieu, Louis Joseph de, 203
Beaumarchais, Amelie Eugénie, 358
Beaumarchais, Pierre August Caron de, 391-93; *letter from*, 355-61
Beaumetz, Bon-Albert Briois, chevalier de, 69-70
Bedloe's Island, 289
Bedlow, Catharine (Mrs. William): *letter from*, 289
Bedlow, Isaac, 289

Bedlow, William, 289
William Bedlow adsm. *Medcaff Eden*, 289
Beekman, David, 458, 459
Beekman, William: *letter to*, 527-28
Belknap, Jeremy: *The History of New-Hampshire*, 12-13
Benson, Egbert, 47, 80-81, 310-11
Berlin, 111, 535
Bermuda Hundred, Va.: collector of customs at, *see* Heth, William
Bernstorff, Andreas Peter, count von, 111
Bernstorff, Christian Günther, count von, 111
Bernstorff, Joachim Frederik, count von, 111
Betsey, 507
Bicknell, Robert, 55
Binney, Horace, 173
Blackstone, Sir William: *Commentaries on the Laws of England*, 16
Blanchard, ——— (Mr.), 184
Blanchard, John, 531-32
Bleecker, Anthony L., 49
Bleecker, Barent: *letter to*, 79-80
Blount, Thomas, 66-67, 113, 123, 446-47
Bollman, Justus Erich, 42-43, 165-67; *letters from*, 109-10, 110-11; *letter to* Timothy Pickering, 111
Bond, Phineas, 131, 146-48, 337; *letter to*, 325-27; *letters to* Timothy Pickering, 113, 128-30, 147
Boon, Gerrit, 531; *letter from*, 489
Boudinot, Elias: *letter to*, 248-49
Boudinot, Elisha, 248; *letter from*, 195-99
Bouvier, Julian, 184, 189
Bowman, John, 324
Bowman, Sarah Lynch (Mrs. John), 324
Bradford, Richard H., 116, 117, 119
Brandywine, Battle of, 203
Breck, Samuel, 122
Brewster, Caleb, 450
Briaser, Ambroise, 540
Bridgen, Charles, 478, 513, 528-29, 536-37, 537-38, 550-51; *letter from* Robert Morris, 454; *letter to* Robert Morris, 453
Bronson, Ann (Mrs. Isaac), 78
Bronson, Isaac, 78
Brooke, Robert: *letter from* George Washington, 312-13

INDEX

Brown, Andrew, 411
Burgoyne, John, 432, 433
Burk, Thomas, 35, 36, 158-59
Burlington, N. J., 460
Burr, Aaron, 51, 543, 544; and election of 1796, 403-4, 407, 418-19, 438, 445, 466
Burrall, Jonathan, 450, 498-99; *letter from*, 50-51
Butler, John, 329

Cabot, George, 22, 480-82, 545, 567, 570, 572, 574, 575
Cadiz, 154, 519
Calogan, John, and Sons, 70
"Camillus," *see* "The Defence"
Campbell, William, 396-97
Canada, 133, 147, 155
Carleton, Guy, *see* Dorchester, Lord
Carleton, Thomas, 256
Carriage tax case, 40-41, 54, 63, 66, 169, 206
Carrington, Edward, 156; *letter from*, 463-64
Carrington, Paul J., 462
Carter, John, *see* Church, John B.
Catherine II, 493, 546
Cattell, Sarah Lynch (Mrs. William), 324
Cattell, William, 324
Cazenove, John Henry, 454
Cazenove, Théophile, 345, 356, 467, 531; *letter from*, 51; *letters to*, 45-47, 346
Ceres Co., 516
Charles, archduke of Austria, 415-16
Charles IV, 156
Charleston, S.C., 411
Chase, Samuel, 245
Chemung, N.Y., 75
Chemung County, N.Y., 75
Chenango country, 344
Cherokee Indians: treaty with, 31
Chevallié, John A., 359, 361; *letter from* Oliver Wolcott, Jr., 357
Chevallié, Pierre François, 357
Church, Angelica (Mrs. John B.), 69-70, 78-79, 141, 188, 322-23; *letters from*, 56, 471-73; *letters to*, 38, 233-34, 235-36, 333-34; *letters to* Elizabeth Hamilton, 43, 334
Church, Catherine, 334
Church, John B., 38, 43, 200, 215-16, 324, 443-44, 547-48; and Tench Coxe, 205-6, 258, 391; house and land for, 56, 78-79, 236, 250, 532; *letter from* Robert Morris, 186-88; Robert Morris's debt to, 40, 63-64, 74-76, 103, 141, 143, 144, 145, 157, 159-60, 166-67, 184-90, 207-8, 529-30, 550; return to the U.S., 233, 334
"A Citizen," 227
Clason, Isaac, 127
Clavigero, Abbé D. Francesco Saverio: *The History of Mexico*, 12-13
Clawsen, —— (Gen.), 457
Claypoole, David C., 170-71, 173, 318
Claypoole, Septimus, 318
Cliland, George, 317
Clinton, George: *letter from* James Monroe, 220; *letter to*, 71
Coakley, John, 457
Cobbett, William ["Peter Porcupine"]: *Porcupine's Works*, 488-89
Cochrane, Alexander F., 325, 327, 337-38
Codwise, Luke: *letter from*, 443
Coe, Amanda: *letter from*, 315-16
Coit, Joshua, 475
Colden, Alexander, 58-59, 71
Colden, Cadwallader, 59
Colden, David, 59
Coleman, William: *letter to* Timothy Pickering, 343-44
Coles, Henry, 229
Coles, Isaac, 447
Coles, John B., 127, 229, 538
Collectors of customs: at Bermuda Hundred, Va., *see* Heth, William; at Boston, Mass., *see* Lincoln, Benjamin; and prizeships, 240-41, 348-51, 378, 380
Cologon, Bernard, 70
Cologon, Thomas, 70
Colquhoun, Patrick, 141-42
Colt, Peter, 135
Columbia College, 543
Columbus, Christopher, 548
Commerce: regulation by Congress, 7, 8-10, 14, 17, 20, 21; by treaties, 8-10, 17, 20, 21, 24, 27-28, 30, 34, 90-92. *See also* Jay Treaty; Spoliations
Congress of the U.S.: acts of, *see under* Act; adjournment of, 548; and commerce, regulation by, 7, 8-10 14, 17, 20, 21; and Constitution, 5; convening of, 293, 558, 574-75; and election of 1796, 439-42; and Jay Treaty, 13-22; and naturalization,

INDEX 581

14, 18, 20; petition to, 1-2; and piracies, 14; and public debt, 22; and reports by department heads, 486; and taxes and duties, 13-14; and treaties, 13, 18-19, 91-100; and war power, 17. *See also* House of Representatives; Senate
Connecticut: accounts, 474; and election of 1796, 403, 438; and Jay Treaty, 151; New York border dispute, 336; U.S. Representatives from, *see* Coit, Joshua, *and* Hillhouse, James, *and* Wadsworth, Jeremiah; U.S. Senator from, *see* Tracy, Uriah
"Connecticut Gore," 336
Constable, William, 210, 211
Constellation, 228
Constitution (U.S.), 12; and alliances, 7; amendments proposed by Virginia, 52-53; Article I, 5, 52; Article II, 5-6, 67, 486; Article III, 5; Article IV, 5; Article V, 5; Article VI, 4, 5-6; and declaration of war, 17; defense of, 24; and delegated powers, 87; and executive power, 9; and Jay Treaty, 3-10; 14-22, 29, 31-34, 64, 131-32, 134, 138; and legislative power, 9, 91-98; objections to, 23-25; opposition to, 25; and reports of heads of departments, 486; and treaties, 6-7, 9, 10, 15-19, 22-34, 72-73, 76, 77, 89-100, 105
Constitution, 228
Constitutional Convention, 5, 22-24, 25, 33, 100
Continental Navy, 402
Contraband, 429-30, 431, 498
Cooper, William, 114; letter to, 443-44
Cooperstown, N.Y., 114, 444
Copenhagen, 111, 535-36
Cornwell (Cornwall), Lewis, 58-59
Cornwell (Cornwall), William, 59
Corp, Samuel, 78
Corsange and Co., 220
Cosby's Manor, 79-80
Cottringer, Garrett, 144, 207, 434, 513, 523, 529, 537-38
Cowper, Robert, 149; *letter from*, 115-19
Coxe, Tench, 258; *letters from*, 184, 205-6, 390-91
Crabb, Jeremiah, 398
Crady, Timothy, 35, 36, 158-59
Craigie, Andrew, 142

Craik, George W.: *letter from* Timothy Pickering, 411
Craik, William, 397-98
Creek Indians, 31
Culbertson, James, 35
Cunningham, Joseph, 426-27
Curtenius, Peter S., 49
Cutting, John Browne: *letter from*, 183-84

Dallarde and Swan, 220
Dallas, Alexander J., 13
Danforth, Asa, 143, 144, 167
Danish West Indies, 459
Davidovich, Paul, baron, 416
Davis, Samuel, 443
Dawson, Joshua, 221-22
Dayton, Elias, 39
Dayton, Jonathan, 150, 151, 248-49, 407; *letter from*, 39; *letter from* Theodore Sedgwick, 404-7; *letter to*, 11; *letters to* Theodore Sedgwick, 403-4, 404
Deane, Silas, 432; *letter to* Robert Morris, 426-27
Dearborn, Henry, 67, 151
Deas, William Allen: *letter from* Timothy Pickering, 39
Debaques, ―― (Messrs.), 326
Decker, Isaac, 119
Decrosses, Germain Pierre: *letter from*, 119-21
"The Defence": No. I, 3, 13, 22; No. XVII, 3, 85; No. XXVII, 27; No. XXXVI, 3-10, 15, 16; No. XXXVII, 13-22; No. XXXVIII, 22-34
De Haert, Balthazar, 303
Delabigarre, Peter, 225-26, 417
Delacroix, Charles, 321-22, 493, 549, 560-66; *letter to* François Barthélemy, 322
Delaney, John William, 443
Delarue, André-Toussaint, 358
Delaware, 151, 567
Delaware, 232. See also *Mount Vernon*
Denmark, 430, 492-93, 555
De Saussure, Henry William, 223-24
Detroit, 307, 452
DeWitt, Simeon, 75-76
Dexter, Samuel, 211
Dickson, David, 200-1
Distilled spirits: tax on, 484
Dominick, ―― (Capt.), 232
Dorchester, Lord, 147, 307

Dover, 426
Drake, Francis, 518
Drummond, Archibald: account with, 340-42
Duane, James, 328-29
Maria Duane, v. John Voght, 328
Ducher, Gaspard Joseph Armand, 324-25
Duer, Catharine Livingston (Mrs. William), 454-55
Duer, John, 172
Duer, William, 120, 140, 195-99, 217-18, 221-22, 343, 396-97, 454-55; *letter from*, 10
Duncanson, William M., 230-32
Dunkerque, 426-27
Dunlap, John, 318
Dunn, John: *letter from*, 495-96; *letter to* John Barclay, 496
Du Ponceau, Peter Stephen, 108
Duties: and Jay Treaty, 13-14; and sale of prizes, 348-49, 350-51

Eden, Medcaff, 289
Edgar, William, 218, 452-53
Education: Hamilton's views on, 456; George Washington's views on, 311-13, 319
Election of 1796, 239, 247, 248-49, 265-66, 371-72, 395-98, 403-7, 416, 422, 437-38, 465-66, 505, 521-22, 571-72; Hamilton's views on, 376, 377-78, 418-19, 439-42, 445, 515-16
Electoral College, 377
Eliza: capture of, 325-27, 337-39
Ellicott, Joseph, 531
Ellsworth, Oliver, 437-38
Embargo: Hamilton on, 468, 474, 545, 574; of 1794, 525-26
Enos, Roger, 51
Espinasse, Isaac: *Cases, Argued and Ruled at Nisi Prius . . .* , 340-42
Europe: war in, 132, 154-55, 182-83, 191-92, 286-87, 306, 339-40, 433-34
Evertson, Nicholas, 140, 527-28
Executive Department, 5-6, 9, 19

Faipoult de Maisoncelle, Guillaume Charles, 219
Fairfax, Denny, 249
Fauchet, Jean Antoine Joseph, 226, 417
"Features of Jay's Treaty," 13
"The Federalist": No. XLII, 24; No. LXIV, 24

"Federal Republican," 439-42
Fenno, John, 171, 558; *letter to*, 227
Fielding Henry: *The Tragedy of Tragedies . . .* , 547-48
Filson, John: *The Discovery, Settlement And present state of Kentucke . . .* , 12-13
Fish, Nicholas, 172
FitzSimons, Thomas, 81, 122; *letter to*, 54
Fleury, François Louis Teisseydre, marquis de, 314-15, 324-25; *letter from*, 201-4
Flying Fish, 221, 231-32, 323
Foreign officers: debt to, 202, 203, 204, 220
Fort Miami, 307
Fort Schuyler, 236, 252
Fossombroni, Vittorio, 490-91
France, 70; and Austria, 415-16, 422-23, 508, 534, 568, 575; and Canada, 155; consuls to U.S., 374-75, 417; decrees of, 479, 496-98; and Denmark, 430, 492-93, 535-36, 555; Directory, 209, 322; and Genoa, 491, 517-18, 567; and Germany, 339-40, 415-17, 436, 546; and Great Britain, 155, 192, 225, 227, 230, 241, 361-62, 363, 400, 445, 490-92, 497, 512, 535, 540-42, 552, 568; and Italy, 339, 399, 415-17, 436, 491, 508, 520; and Jay Treaty, 222, 367, 399, 400, 409, 429, 431, 535, 555, 556, 572; king of, 61, 146, 516; and Louisiana, 485; marine laws of, 424-26, 428, 429-30; Minister to U.S., *see* Adet, Pierre Auguste, *and* Fauchet, Jean Antoine Joseph, *and* Genet, Edmond Charles, *and* Ternant, Jean Baptiste de; and Naples, 491, 535; and neutrals, policy toward, 231-32, 321-22, 323, 361-62, 366-67, 412, 470-71, 479, 490, 491-93, 496-98, 511, 539-42, 551, 553-55; and Charles Cotesworth Pinckney, 545, 546, 558-67; situation in, 59-62, 162-64; and Spain, 192, 485, 491, 526; and Sweden, 492-93; and Treaty of 1783, 514; and United Netherlands, 192, 520; U.S. consul general in, 335; U.S. conventions with, 28, 30, 32, 359-60; U.S. debt to, 192; U.S. Minister to, *see* Monroe, James, *and* Morris, Gouverneur, *and* Pinckney, Charles Cotesworth; U.S., proposed treaty with,

413, 522; U.S. relations with, 59-62, 162-64, 190-94, 212-13, 223-27, 230-32, 237-38, 246-47, 253, 265, 361-67, 371-75, 378-80, 389-90, 398-400, 408-14, 421-34, 436-37, 444-45, 468-71, 474, 476-77, 479-83, 489, 490-95, 496-98, 507-12, 518-22, 524-27, 535, 539-42, 545-50, 551-75; U.S. special envoy or commission to, 243-44, 246-47, 477, 480-93, 522, 545, 549, 556-57, 567-75. *See also* Privateers, French; Prizes, and France; Spoliations, of commerce, by France; Treaties, with France (1778)
Francis II, 165
Francis, Tench, 231-32
Franklin, Benjamin, 218, 432; *Two Tracts: Information to those who would remove to America. And, Remarks concerning the Savages of North America*, 12-13
Franklin, Jesse, 370
Franklin, William Temple, 141
Frederick II, 111
Frederick County, Md., 397
Freeman, Nathaniel, 150-51
"Free ships, free goods," 193, 479, 540
French West Indies, 60, 163, 194, 231, 241, 483, 519, 522, 553-54
Frestel, Felix, 55, 68, 107, 109, 165
Frigates (U.S.): construction of, 227-28, 243-44, 473-74
Friuli, 416
Furman, Gabriel, 35

Gallatin, Albert, 67, 105, 112, 149, 547; *A Sketch of the Finances of the United States*, 436-37
Gaspée, 402
Genesee country, 142, 145, 157, 189, 190, 344, 464, 513, 523, 528, 530, 550
Genesee River, 464
Genet, Edmond Charles, 192, 363, 398, 421, 436
Genoa, 491, 517-18, 567
George I, 422-23
Georgia, 151, 372, 418-19, 474; land speculation in, 211-12; U.S. Representative from, *see* Baldwin, Abraham
Georgia Mississippi Co., 211
Georgia Yazoo land companies, 211
Gérard, Conrad-Aléxandre, 432
Germany, 339-40, 399, 415-17, 436, 546

Gerry, Elbridge, 23, 438
Gibbs, Laura Wolcott, 212
Gibraltar, 155, 422-23
Giles, Aquila, 498-99
Giles, William B., 447
Gillon, Alexander, 468
Girard, Stephen, 125
Glasgow, 443
Glover, John C.: *letter from*, 395
Goelet, Peter: *letter from*, 237, 241; *receipt from*, 342
Goold, Edward, 124
Gore, Christopher, 306, 506
Goteborg, 555
Gouverneur, Isaac: *letter to*, 466
Gracie, Archibald, 538
Graham, Stephen, 116, 117, 118, 119, 149
Grattan, ——— (Mrs.), 334
Great Britain, 146-48, 422-23, 505, 518, 533-34, 546; and Canada, 155; chargé d'affaires of, to U.S., *see* Bond, Phineas; and *Eliza*, 325-27, 337-39; and France, 155, 192, 225, 227, 230, 241, 361-62, 363, 400, 445, 490-92, 497, 512, 535-36, 540-42, 552, 568; and impressment of seamen, 130, 184, 389-90, 412; and Jay Treaty, 5, 7, commission under, (Article 5) 14, 64, 81, 255-57, 260-61, 310-11, (Article 6) 64, 67-68, 311, (Article 7) 64, 67-68, 305-7, 596-7; Minister to U.S., *see* Hammond, George, *and* Liston, Robert; and neutrals, policy toward, 321-23, 540-42, 551-54; and "Peter Porcupine," 489; and privateers, 398, 427-28, 540; and prizes, 355, 375-76, 378, 379-80, 398, 427, 429, 506-7; Russian Minister to, 546-47; and ships of war, 375, 378-79; spoliations by, 128, 224, 485, 524-25, 540-42, 552-53; and Treaty of 1783, 17, 29, 514, 524; U.S. Minister to, *see* King, Rufus, *and* Pinckney, Thomas; U.S. relations with, 29, 60, 61-62, 128-30, 194, 247, 321-22, 323, 363, 413, 446, 470, 174, 477, 479, 480, 483, 489, 495, 505-6, 511, 524-27, 539-42, 551-54; and western posts, 14, 147-48, 306-7, 526
Greene, Nathanael, 419
Greene, William: *letter from*, 70-71
Greenleaf, James, 63-64, 142; *letters from*, 261-63, 263-64; *letter to*, 264
Greenup, Christopher, 447

Greenville, Treaty of, 31, 113, 128-30, 147
Grenville, Lord, 416, 506, 526, 535, 546-47
Grouville, Philippe, 536
Guadaloupe, 519
Guernsey, Nathan, 217
Guiraudet, Charles-Philippe-Toussaint, 562-65
Gurney, Francis, 122
Gustavus IV Adolphus, 493

The Hague, 244, 573
Hall, ——— (Capt.), 427
Hall, James, 329
Hall and Stimpson: *letters from,* 329, 352; *letters to,* 374, 514-15
Hall and Stimpson v *Riley and Wetmore,* 352
Halliday, Robert, 458, 459
Hallwood, John, 457, 458
Hamburg, 212-14, 535
Hamilton, Alexander: on Pierre Auguste Adet, 380, 389-90; admitted to N.Y. Circuit Court, 108; and carriage tax case, 40-41, 54, 63, 66, 169, 206; and John B. Church, attorney for, 38, 40, 56, 63-64, 74-76, 78-79, 103, 141, 143, 144, 145, 157, 159-60, 166-67, 184-90, 205-6, 207-8, 215-16, 233, 236, 250, 258, 324, 334, 391, 443-44, 529-30, 532, 547-48, 550; defense of, 37-38; on direct taxes, 473-74, 500-4; and Archibald Drummond, 340-42; duel, 456; on William Duer, 454-55; and Dutch banking firms, 45-47, 51; on education, 456; and election of 1796, 376, 377-78, 418-19, 439-42, 445, 515-16; on embargo, 468, 474, 545, 574; and forged letters, 115-19, 149; on France, U.S. envoy or commission to, 480-82, 567-68, 573, 574-75, U.S. relations with, 191-94, 494, 521-23, 545-46, 557 (*see also* "The Answer"; "The Warning"); on Georgia claim, 211-12; health of, 318, 472; and Holland Land Co., attorney for, 346, 447-48; on Jay Treaty, 64-69, 85-103, 107, 108-9, 112-15, 129-31, 136-37, 158, 193-94, 327, 354, 361, 367-68, 379-80, 398-99, 413, 429, 431, 441, 555, 556 (*see also* "The Defence"); on Thomas Jefferson, 376-77; on Rufus King, 174; land purchased by, 250; law clerks of, 38, 172, 230, 303; and Robert Lenox, 34-36; and Maturin Livingston, 41-42, 44-45; loans by, to William Duer, 10, to Robert Morris, 229-30, 242, 400-1, 434, to Isaac Sherman, 320; and John F. Mercer, 396-98; and Ann Mitchell, 456-57; and monarchy, 396; on a navy, 546; and N.Y. Supreme Court, 352, 354, 480, 482; and James Nicholson, 42, 44; and Ohio Co., 401-2; on a provisional army, 546; on public credit and debt, 204-5, 214-15; "Report on Manufactures," 12; and seal for U.S., 208-9; on sinking fund, 214-15; and Society for Establishing Useful Manufactures, 201; on Robert Troup, 381; and George Washington, advice requested by, 66, 103, 175-78, 238-40, 293, 308-9, 314, 319, 362, 365, 367, 394, 462-77, eighth annual address, 319, 320, 364, 373-74, 381-88, 393-95, 408-10, 446, Farewell Address, 169-83, 214, 239-40, 247-48, 264-88, 292-303, 307-9, 311-14, 316, 317-19, 320-21. *See also* "Americanus"; "Americus"; "The Answer"; "Federal Republican"; "A Real Whig"; "To the Citizens of New-York"; "To the Citizens Who Shall be Convened This Day in the Fields in the City of New York"; "A True American"; "The War in Europe"
Hamilton, Elizabeth, 37, 38, 56, 141, 162, 172-73, 216, 233, 235-36, 392, 419, 455, 456, 461, 472; *letter from,* 352; *letters from* Angelica Church, 43, 334; *letters to,* 353, 353-54
Hamilton, James A., 172, 173
Hamilton, John Church, 172, 173, 248, 392-93
Hamilton, Philip, 392-93
Hamilton, William: *letter from,* 538
Hammond, Abijah, 392-93
Hammond, George, 174
Hanson (Hansen), John W.: certificate on, 49-50
Hanson (Hansen), Mary (Mrs. John W.), 49-50
Harison, Richard, 140, 381-82, 462-63; *letters to,* 184, 189; *letter to* Richard Bayley, 258-60
Harper, Robert G., 211, 468, 484; *letter from,* 369-72

INDEX 585

Harris, James, *see* Malmesbury, Earl of
Harrison, George, 393
Harrison, Richard, 359
Hartshorne and Lindley, 242
Haskins, Caleb, 115, 116, 117, 119
Hatfield, Richard: *letter to*, 292
Havana, Cuba, 57
Henry, prince of Prussia, 111
Henry, John, 395
Henry, Patrick, 138, 151-53, 158-59, 372
Heth, William: *letters from*, 36-38, 347
Hicks, John, 35
Higbee, Joseph, 242, 434
Higginson, Stephen, 467; *letters from*, 437-38, 465-67; *letters to*, 414-15, 448
Hillhouse, James, 67, 137-38
Hobart, John Sloss, 36
Hodge, William, 426
Hoffman, Josiah Ogden, 42, 49-50, 108, 336
Holker, John, 443-44
Holland, James, 447
Holland Land Co., 45, 51, 70, 346, 393, 489; and Seneca Indians, 447-48, 530-31
Holten, Samuel, 438
Hopkins, George E., 489
Hornby, William, 141-42, 144, 188, 208, 343-44, 345, 348, 464, 478, 513, 524, 529, 538
House of Representatives, 5; and election of 1796, 439-44, 446; and Jay Treaty, 64-69, 72-74, 76-77, 81-105, 106-7, 108-9, 112-15, 121-23, 124-28, 131-34, 136-40, 147-48, 149-51, 153, 306, 363-64, 369-70, 440-41; petitions to, 57, 452-53, 467, 468-69; and reports by department heads, 486; and revenue, 469; and Secretary of Treasury, 487; and sequestration, 485; Speaker of, *see* Dayton, Jonathan; and taxes, 483-84; and treaties, 52; and George Washington's eighth annual address, 445-47
Houses: tax on, 500-3
Howell, David, 255-57; *letter from*, 310-11
Hudson, N.Y., 1-2
Hudson's Bay Co., 129
Huger, Benjamin (father), 42-43, 215-16
Huger, Benjamin (son), 215-16, 251-52
Huger, Francis Kinloch, 42-43, 215-16
Hugues (Hughes), Victor, 553
Humphreys, David, 536
Hunter, David: *letter from*, 249
Hunter's Hotel, 439
Hunter v Fairfax Devisee, 249
Hussey, George G., 325-26, 337-38
Hylton v United States, 40-41. *See also* Carriage tax case

Imlay, Gilbert: *A Topographical description of the Western Territory of North America* . . . , 12-13
Impeachment, 25
Impressment of seamen, 130, 184, 389-90, 412
Indians, 526; and Great Britain, 128-30, 146-48; and Jay Treaty, 128-30, 146-48; trade with, 128-30, 146-48, 218; treaties with, 29, 31, 113, 121-22, 126, 128-30, 146-48. *See also* Cherokee Indians; Creek Indians; Iroquois League; Seneca Indians; Six Nations
Ingersoll, Jared, 573
Innes, James, 81
Ireland: immigrants from, 259
Iroquois League: treaty with, 31
Italy, 339, 399, 415-17, 436, 508, 520

Jackson, Andrew, 447
James Jackson ex dem. William H. Ludlow and Mary, his wife v Nathan Guernsey, 217
Jackson, John 234-35
Jackson, William, 468
James, John, 458, 459
James River Co., 312-13
Jarvis, Charles, 53
Jay, John, 37, 120-21, 152, 158, 160-61, 164, 166, 170, 175, 217, 255, 257, 260-61, 311, 368, 468, 470, 474, 506, 552, 572; and election of 1796, 438, 465; and France, 246, 373, 399-400; and Jay Treaty, 64-65, 81-82, 83-84, 103, 132, 136-37, 525; *letter from*, 58-59; *letter to*, 71; and George Washington, 164, 166, 214-15, 239, 365, 372-73. *See also* Jay Treaty
Jay Treaty, 56, 526; and aliens, 14; appropriations for, 151, 158; Article 1, 15; Article 2, 29, 306; Article 3, 130, 147; Article 5, 64, 67, 81, 255, 310, commission under, 14, 64, 81, 255-57, 260-61, 310-11; Article 6, 64, 67, 80-81, 257, 311, commission

Jay Treaty (*Continued*)
under, 64, 67-68, 311; Article 7, 64, 67, 80-81, 257, 306, 506, commission under, 64, 67-68, 305-7, 506-7; Article 8, 64, 80-81; Article 9, 29, 85; Article 10, 15; Article 12, 194; Article 17, 15; Article 18, 15, 431; Article 19, 15; Article 20, 15; Article 21, 327; Article 22, 15, 17; Article 23, 15, 163, 195; Article 24, 15, 241, 355, 367-68, 375, 379-80; Article 25, 355, 367-68, 375, 379-80; Article 28, 193, 224; and congressional power, 13-22; and Constitution, 3-10, 14-22, 29, 31-34, 64, 131-32, 134, 138; Jonathan Dayton on, 39; defense of, 131-34 (*see also* "The Defence"); and duties, 13-14; and earlier treaties, 413; and *Eliza*, 338; and France, 60, 163-64, 193, 222, 238, 240, 367, 399, 409, 429, 431, 535, 555, 556, 572; and Great Britain, 5, 7, 13-14, 19, 39, 64, 83-85, 89, 300, 306, 506; and House of Representatives, 64-69, 72-74, 76-77, 85-103, 103-5, 106-7, 108-9, 112-15, 121-23, 124-28, 131-34, 136-40, 147-48, 149-51, 153, 306, 363-64, 369-70, 440-41; and Indians, 128-30, 146-48; and Judiciary Department, 15; and law of nations, 14; objections to, 13-15, 17-18, 33, 249, 398 (*see also* "Features of Jay's Treaty"); and piracy, 14, 28, 327; and privateers, 84, 240-41, 327, 367-68; and prizes, 354-55, 361-62, 367-68, 375-76, 379-80; ratification of, 39, 64, 233-34; reception of, in Albany, N.Y., 138-39, in Annapolis, Md., 121, 136, in Baltimore, Md., 121, 125-26, 136, in Lansingburgh, N.Y., 140, in New York City, 44, 123, 126-28, 130-34, 135-37, 138-39, in Philadelphia, 123, 124-26, 136, in Richmond, Va., 137-38; resolution for implementing, 149-51; and Senate, 39, 64, 81, 132, 138, 148; and state laws, 17; and trade, 14; and Treaty of Greenville, 146-48; and U.S. boundaries, 14, St. Croix, 14, 81, 255-57, 260-61, 310-11; and "Virginia Faction," 133; and George Washington, 39, 64-69, 76-77, 80-81, 85-103, 103-5, 106-7, 112-15, 121-23, 132, 136, 138, 148, 364, 370; and western posts, 14, 147-48, 306-7

Jefferson, Thomas, 118, 149, 176, 190, 421; and commission to France, 545, 569, 574, 575; and election of 1796, 369, 371-72, 376, 397, 403-5, 418-19, 437-38, 445, 465-66; *letters from* James Madison, 65, 66; *letter from* James Monroe, 220; *Notes on the State of Virginia*, 12-13; Vice President, 515-16
Johnson, Horace, 324
Johnson, Horace and Seth, and Co., 324
Johnson, James, 547-48
Johnson, Seth, 324
Johnston, Samuel, 437-38
Jones, John Paul, 467
Jones, Samuel, 47, 48, 135
Jourdan, Jean Baptiste, 339-40, 415-16
Judiciary Department, 15
Julian Alps, 416

Karl, duke of Södermanland, 493
Karney, Gilbert, 454
Kemble, Peter, 466
Kent, James, 235; *letter from* Jedidiah Morse, 11-13
Kentucky, 151; U.S. Representative from, *see* Greenup, Christopher
Kercado, Lawrence: *letter from*, 216-17
Keteltas, Walter, 35-36
King, Mary Alsop (Mrs. Rufus), 236, 461
King, Rufus, 42, 86, 168, 172, 174, 178, 183-84, 194-95, 214-15, 223-24, 234, 236, 366, 470-71; *letters from*, 105, 121-23, 124-26, 149-51, 151-53, 291, 305-7, 321-23, 323, 415-17, 504, 505-8, 533-36; *letters from* John Marshall, 152-53, 153; *letter from* James Monroe, 321; *letter from* William Tatham, 155-56; *letter from* Robert Troup, 472; *letters to*, 52-53, 76-77, 106, 112-15, 123, 126-28, 135-36, 136-37, 158-59, 160-61, 444-47, 515-16; *letter to* James Monroe, 322
King's College, 162
Kinloch, Cleland, 216
Kinloch, Francis, 216, 324
Kinloch, Mary, 216
Kitt (Kitts), Frederick, 318-19
Knox, Henry, 146, 201, 486
Knox, Hugh, 458, 459
Kyd, Stewart: *A Treatise on the Law of Bills of Exchange*, 341-42

INDEX

Lafayette, George Washington Motier, 55, 68, 106-7, 109, 164-66
Lafayette, Marie Joseph du Motier, marquis de, 42-43, 107, 110-11, 164-66, 175, 215, 358
Laight, Edward W., 543
Laight, William: *letter from*, 543
Lake George, 307
Lake Ontario, 188
Lamb, John, 49
Land: alien ownership of, 45-47, 51, 84; speculation in, 40, 45-47, 70, 120, 124, 135, 141-45, 157, 159-60, 205-6, 211-12, 218, 258, 262-63, 343-44, 346, 400-2, 452-53, 513; tax on, 469, 483, 487, 500. *See also* Asylum Co.; Ceres Co.; Genesee country; Georgia Mississippi Co.; Holland Land Co.; North American Land Co.; Ohio Co.; Pulteney Associates; Washington, D.C.; Yazoo Co.
Lane, George, 211
Lane, John, *see* Molleson, William
Langdon, John, 124
Langdon, Woodbury: *letter from*, 124
Lansingburgh, N.Y., 140
La Providence, 540
Lasher, John, 79
Latimer, George, 122
Laurance, John, 52-53, 381-82, 444
Laurens, John, 468
Laurens, 498, 552
Lavien, Rachel, 456
Law of nations, 14, 20, 62, 413, 430, 431, 476, 493, 540
Lear, Tobias, 170, 171, 309, 318
Leary, John, Jr., 201
Lebrun-Tondu, Pierre Henri Hélène Marie, 552
Lee, Arthur, 432
Lee, Charles, 40-41, 55, 66, 85, 105, 211, 221, 245, 249, 397
Lee, Henry, 152-53
Leeds, Jedediah, 462
Leeds and Mumford, 462, 463
Leghorn, 490-91
Le Grand, Ferdinand, 102-3, 104, 432
Le Guen, Louis, 225-26
Louis Le Guen, v Isaac Gouverneur and Peter Kemble, 466
Lehoc, Louis-Grégoire, 493
Le John, 540
Lenox, James, 173
Lenox, Robert, 159; certificate on, 34-36

Léogane, 443
LeRoy, Herman, 142, 198; *letters to*, 447-48, 530-31
Herman LeRoy, William Bayard, and Gerrit Boon v Peter Servis and others, 489
LeRoy, Bayard, and McEvers, 210
Lewis, Francis, 51
Lewis, Gertrude, 78
Lewis, Morgan, 42; *receipt from*, 78-79
Lewis, William, 54, 103, 144-45, 159-60, 338, 513; *letter from*, 141
Lewis v Burr, 51
Licenses: tax on, 484
Lille, 416
Lillie, Thomas, 457
Lincklaen, John, 531
Lincoln, Benjamin, 203, 240-41
Lindsay, ——— (Mr.), 473
Liston, Robert, 174; *letter from*, 337-39
Livingston, Brockholst, 44, 108, 140
Livingston, Catharine, 38
Livingston, Catrina Van Brugh (Mrs. Philip), 455
Livingston, Cornelia Schuyler (Mrs. Walter), 455
Livingston, Edward, 44, 107, 439-42, 445, 447, 452-53, 547-48; and Jay Treaty, 64-65, 68, 69-70, 73-74, 77, 85, 105, 108, 123, 134, 363-64, 440-41; *letter to* Margaret Beekman Livingston, 42
Livingston, Henry (Hendrick), 229; *letter to* Walter Livingston, 229
Livingston, John: *letter to* Walter Livingston, 229
Livingston, John R., 135, 201
Livingston, Margaret Beekman: *letter from* Edward Livingston, 42
Livingston, Margaret Lewis (Mrs. Maturin), 42
Livingston, Mary Alexander (Mrs. Peter), 463
Livingston, Maturin: *letter from*, 44; *letters to*, 41-42, 44-45
Livingston, Peter R., 42
Livingston, Peter Van Brugh, 234-35, 463
Livingston, Philip, 235, 252, 455, 462-63, 521
Livingston, Robert (third lord of the Manor), 38, 135, 228-29, 455
Livingston, Robert Cambridge, 135, 229

Livingston, Robert James, 42
Livingston, Robert R., 42, 44, 78, 143, 144, 226, 407, 514; *letter to* James Monroe, 120
Livingston, Sarah, 234, 455
Livingston, Walter, 455; *letters from,* 134-35, 228-29; *letter from* Henry Livingston, 229; *letter from* John Livingston, 229
Livingston, William, 44
Loans: by Bank of the U.S., 436-37. See also Bank of New York, loans by
Locke, Matthew, 447
Lockey, George, 215-16
Lombardy, 416
London: panorama of, 48
London Associates, *see* Pulteney Associates
London Association, *see* Pulteney Associates
"Lost million," 355-61
Louis XIV, 428, 494
Louis XVI, 146
Louisiana, 485
Low, Nicholas, 392-93; *letter to,* 347
Lowell, John, 222
Lowell, John, Jr.: *letter from,* 222
Lowin, James, 457
Daniel Ludlow, and Gulian Ludlow v John B. Coles, 538
Daniel Ludlow, and Gulian Ludlow v Archibald Gracie, 538
Ludlow, Gulian, 538
Ludlow, William H., 217
Lyman, William, 447
Lynch, Sabina, 324
Lynch, Thomas, 324
Lyon, Daniel, 292
Lyon, Joseph, 292
Lytton, Ann (Mrs. James), 456
Lytton, James, Sr., 456, 459
Lytton, James, Jr., 456, 457, 459-60
Lytton, Peter, 458

McCormick, Daniel, 263, 288, 329-30
McEvers, James: *letters to,* 447-48, 530-31
McHenry, James, 168-69, 223-24, 393-94, 395, 409, 474; *letters from,* 245, 455-56; *letter from* George Washington, 245; *letters to,* 212-14, 252-53, 466-68, 574-75

McIntosh, William, 201
Maclay, Samuel, 134, 447
Macomb, Alexander, 210, 217-18, 304, 452-53
Macomb, William, 218, 452
Macomb, Edgar, and Macomb, 218
Macon, Nathaniel, 447
Madison, James, 149, 369, 522; as commissioner to France, 480-81, 545, 547, 567, 569-75; and Jay Treaty, 22-23, 72-74; *letters to* Thomas Jefferson, 65, 66; *letter to* James Monroe, 66; and George Washington's Farewell Address, 169-70, 175-76, 295
Maitland, David, 157
Malaga, 519
Malmesbury, Earl of, 415, 416-17
Manning, F. E., 360
Mantua, 416, 508, 534
Manufactures, 381, 384, 387-88
Marshall, Hetty Morris (Mrs. James), 56, 188
Marshall, James, 56, 187-88, 529-30
Marshall, John, 40, 56, 223, 249; *letter from,* 137-38; *letter to,* 112; *letters to* Rufus King, 152-53, 153
Marshall, Thomas: and the Society for Establishing Useful Manufactures, 200-1
Marshall, Thomas (seaman), 325, 337
Mary, 395
Maryland, 121, 151, 538, 539; U.S. Representatives from, *see* Crabb, Jeremiah, *and* Craik, William, *and* Mercer, John F., *and* Murray, William Vans, *and* Smith, Samuel, *and* Sterett, Samuel
Mason, George: "Objections to This Constitution of Government," 23
Mason, Stevens Thomson, 397-98
Massachusetts, 52-53, 150, 403, 407, 447, 474; U.S. judge for the District of, *see* Lowell, John; U.S. Representatives from, *see* Ames, Fisher, *and* Dearborn, Henry, *and* Freeman, Nathaniel, *and* Gerry, Elbridge, *and* Holten, Samuel, *and* Lyman, William, *and* Sedgwick, Theodore; U.S. Senators from, *see* Cabot, George, *and* Sedgwick, Theodore, *and* Strong, Caleb
Mather, Ralph, 478, 537, 550
Mercer, John F., 396-98
Mersereau, Joshua, 303
Michilimakinac, 307

INDEX 589

Military academy: proposed by George Washington, 316, 317, 381-84, 385
Miller, Catharine (Mrs. Phineas): *letter from*, 419
Miller, Joseph I., 206
Miller, Phineas, 419
Mississippi River, 14, 25, 274, 300, 526
Mississippi Territory, 156
Mitchell, Ann (Mrs. George): *letter from*, 456-60
Mitchell, George, 456, 459
Mitchell, Robert, 459
Molleson, William, and John Lane: *The Reports of the Commissioners . . .*, 436-37, 450
Monroe, James: and France, 48, 59-61, 162-63, 213, 239, 314-15, 326, 365-66, 371, 407, 480, 482, 507, 548, 555; *letter from* Rufus King, 322; *letter from* Robert R. Livingston, 120; *letter from* James Madison, 66; *letter from* Jacob Van Staphorst, 200; *letter from* Willink, Van Staphorst, and Hubbard, 219-20; *letter to* George Clinton, 220; *letter to* Thomas Jefferson, 220; *letter to* Rufus King, 321; *letters to* Timothy Pickering, 212, 323, 485; *letters to* Edmund Randolph, 330, 497; recall of, 220, 221-22, 223, 231-32, 246-47, 309, 560-63
Moore, A., 439
Moreau, Jean Victor, 415-16
Morocco: treaty with, 28-29, 30, 34
Morris, Gouverneur, 65, 161, 162-64, 174-75, 209, 407, 497; *letter from*, 59-62; *letter to* George Washington, 59
Morris, Mary (Mrs. Robert), 145, 185, 188, 190, 254
Morris, Richard, 317
Morris, Robert, 56, 135, 203, 252, 254, 262-63, 447-48; debts of, to John B. Church, 63-64, 74-76, 103, 141, 143-45, 157, 159-60, 166-67, 184-88, 188-89, 190, 207-8, 529-30, 550, to Hamilton, 229-30, 242, 400-1, 434, to Benjamin Walker, 141-45; *letters from*, 40, 54, 63-64, 74, 74-76, 103, 141-45, 157, 166-67, 184-88, 190, 207-8, 229-30, 242, 400-1, 434, 453-54, 464-65, 478, 513, 523-24, 528-30, 536-37, 537-38, 550-51; *letter from* Charles Bridgen, 453; *letter from* Silas Deane, 426-27; *letters to*, 47, 63, 70, 71, 166, 199, 218, 234, 380, 476, 505, 521, 537; *letter to* Charles Bridgen, 454; *letter to* John B. Church, 186-88; *letter to* Robert Morris, Jr., 186
Morris, Robert, Jr., 187; *letter from* Robert Morris, 186
Morris, Thomas, 207-8, 448
Morris Reserve, 142, 143, 144, 208
Morse, Jedidiah: *The American Geography . . .*, 11-13; *letter to*, 11-13
Mosby, Wade, 463; *letter from*, 462
Wade Mosby, Josiah Smith, Paul J. Carrington, Samuel Sackett, and Samuel Watson v *Jedediah Leeds and John Mumford*, 462
Mosby, Smith, and Carrington, 462
Mount Vernon: capture of, 221-22, 230-32, 238, 243-44, 246-47, 321-23
Muhlenberg, Frederick A. C., 67, 149
Mulligan, Hercules, 49
Mumford, John, 462
Murgatroyd, Thomas, 221, 230-32
Murray, William Vans, 245, 573
Muskingum River, 401
Myers, Helen, 140
Myers, John R., 140

Nancy, 259
Naples, 491, 535
Napoleon, 415-16, 490, 508
National university: proposed by George Washington, 311-14, 316, 317-18, 319, 320, 381, 384-85
Naturalization, 14, 18, 20, 538, 539
Naval officer for the port: of New York City, *see* Walker, Benjamin
Navy: proposals for a, 381, 385-86, 394, 408, 455-56, 473-74, 546
Negroes: suspected of arson, 472-73
Nelson, William, 127
Neufville, Anna de (Mrs. John), 466-68, 469; *letter to* George Washington, 477
Neufville, John de, 466-68, 469, 476-77
Neufville, Leonard de, 467
Neutrality: advantages of, 191-93; and prizes, 379; of U.S., 421, 423, 427, 433-34, 477
Neutrality, proclamation of (1793), 182-83, 192, 286-87, 398

Neutral nations: British policy toward, 321-23, 540-42, 551-54; French policy toward, 231-32, 321-22, 323, 361-62, 366-67, 412, 470-71, 479, 490, 491-93, 496-98, 511, 539-42
Neutral rights, 551-55
Neutral ships: and France, 231-32, 321-22, 323, 361-62, 366-67, 412, 470-71, 479, 496-98, 511, 539-42; and prize goods, 350; rules for, 222
New Brunswick, 256
New England, 377
New Hampshire, 150, 438, 474; governor of, see Wentworth, Benning; U.S. Representative from, see Smith, Jeremiah
New Jersey, 11, 39, 151, 248, 474; U.S. Representatives from, see Boudinot, Elias, and Dayton, Jonathan, and Smith, Isaac
New Orleans, 57
The [New York] Argus. Greenleaf's New Daily Advertiser, 442-43
New York City, 35, 49, 211-12, 216, 258-60, 289; 328, 472-73; elections in, 158-59, 439-42; Metropolitan Fair, 211; port of, 1-2, 543-44; reactions to Jay Treaty in, 123, 126-28, 130-34, 135-37, 138-39
New-York Evening Post, 343
New York State, 52-53, 75-76, 151, 252, 258-60, 474-75, 501; acts of, 45-47, 58-59, 303-4, 316, 451, 453, 532; alien ownership of land in, 45-47, 51; Connecticut border dispute, 336; elections in, 377, 446, 544; governor of, see Clinton, George, and Jay, John; legislature, 35-36, 49-50, 58-59, 543-44; Massachusetts land controversy, 447; Supreme Court, 36, 38, 51, 70, 109, 124, 140, 217, 235, 315-16, 352, 354, 480, 482; U.S. attorney for the District of, see Harison, Richard; U.S. judge for the District of, see Duane, James, and Laurance, John, and Troup, Robert; U.S. marshal for the District of, see Giles, Aquila; U.S. Representatives from, see Bailey, Theodorus, and Benson, Egbert, and Cooper, William, and Laurance, John, and Livingston, Edward, and Van Allen, John Evert, and Van Cortlandt, Philip, and Williams, John; U.S. Senators from, see Burr, Aaron, and King, Rufus, and Laurance, John, and Schuyler, Philip
Niagara, 307
Nicholson, James, 42, 44
Nicholson, John, 63-64, 262-63, 454, 478, 513, 523-24, 528-29, 536, 537-38, 550
Nicoll, John, 306, 506-7
Nixon, John, 122
Noble, Arthur, 235-36
"No Jacobin No. IV," 423
Normandez, Chevalier de, 536
North, Lord, 432-33
North, William, 36
North American Land Co., 185, 187, 188, 263
North Carolina, 151, 331-33, 370-71, 438; U.S. judge for the District of, see Sitgreaves, John; U.S. Representatives from, see Blount, Thomas, and Franklin, Jesse, and Holland, James, and Locke, Matthew, and Macon, Nathaniel, and Tatum, Absalom; U.S. Senator from, see Johnston, Samuel
Northwest Territory, 222
Nourse, Joseph, 202, 437
Nova Scotia, 256

Ogden, Lewis, 473
Ogden, Samuel, 143, 144, 145, 157, 166, 207
Ohio Co., 401-2
Ohio River, 401, 453
Old Jersey, 35
Olmütz, 43
Ostend, 422-23
Oswego, 307
Otsego County, N.Y., 303, 444

"Pacificus No. IV," 371
Paine, Thomas: letter to George Washington, 436-37
Palm, Karl Joseph von, 422-23
Papal States, 491
Paris, 330
Paris, Treaty of (1763), 155
Parish, John, 212-14; letter from Timothy Pickering, 213
Parker, Josiah, 455, 473-74
Party spirit: dangers of, 19, 272, 273-86, 296-300, 488
Patterson, Alexander, 206, 391
Patterson, Catherine Livingston (Mrs. John), 38

INDEX

Patterson, George, 507
Patterson, John: *letter from,* 38
Patterson, John W., 38
Patterson, Robert, 38
Patterson, William, 507; *letter from,* 531-32
Patton, Robert, 115, 116, 149
Paul I, 546, 568, 574
Pearsall, Thomas, 127
Pendleton, Nathaniel, 172
Penn, William, 548
Pennsylvania, 24-25, 151, 332, 336, 567; and election of 1796, 372, 376, 378, 403, 405; U.S. attorney for the District of, *see* Rawle, William; U.S. judge for the District of, *see* Lewis, William, *and* Peters, Richard; U.S. Representatives from, *see* Fitz-Simons, Thomas, *and* Gallatin, Albert, *and* Maclay, Samuel, *and* Swanwick, John
Perignon, Dominique-Catherine, marquis de, 154
Perregaux, Jean Frédéric, 220
Perrochel, Henri, 493
Peters, Richard, 223-24
Petition: of merchants of Albany, N.Y., 1-2
Pettit, Charles, 125-26
Philadelphia: reaction to Jay Treaty in, 121-22, 123, 124-26, 136
[Philadelphia] *Aurora. General Advertiser,* 65, 238
[Philadelphia] *Claypoole's American Daily Advertiser,* 318
[Philadelphia] *Dunlap and Claypoole's American Daily Advertiser,* 318
"Philo-Jay," 37
Pickering, Timothy, 110-11, 146, 172, 329, 337-38; and Pierre Auguste Adet, 366-67, 373, 374, 389-90, 410-11, 412, 436-37, 536; and Franco-American relations, 223-24, 231, 238, 362, 471, 477, 480, 508-9, 519, 552; Hamilton on, 412; and Jay Treaty, 66, 82, 105, 148; *letters from,* 80-81, 255-57, 335-36, 479, 496-98, 548-50, 558-67; *letters from* Pierre Auguste Adet, 212-13, 232, 240-41, 361-62, 363, 399-400, 409, 470-71; *letter from* Justus Erich Bollman, 111; *letters from* Phineas Bond, 113, 128-30, 147; *letter from* William Coleman, 343-44; *letters from* James Monroe, 212, 323, 485; *letter from* William Rawle, 338;

letter from George Washington, 395; *letter from* Oliver Wolcott, Jr., 357; *letters to,* 167-68, 260-61, 329-30, 479, 508-9, 514, 545-47, 556-57; *letters to* Pierre Auguste Adet, 213, 221, 241, 390; *letter to* George W. Craik, 411; *letter to* William Allen Deas, 39; *letter to* John Parish, 213; *letters to* Charles Cotesworth Pinckney, 336, 483; *letter to* William Rawle, 338; *letter to* George Washington, 170; *letter to* Joseph M. Yznardi, 157; and George Washington's eighth annual address, 395, 409
Pinckney, Charles Cotesworth: and Pierre Auguste Adet, 408, 436-37; and France, 223-24, 246-47, 308-9, 314-15, 319, 335-36, 371, 373, 412, 476-77, 480-82, 483, 507-8, 508-9, 545-46, 549-50, 558-67, 570, commission to, 480-82, 545, 567, 572, 574, 575; *letters from,* 58, 215-16; *letters from* Timothy Pickering, 336, 483; *letters to,* 48, 251-52, 324-25
Pinckney, Mary Stead (Mrs. Charles Cotesworth), 216
Pinckney, Thomas, 42-43, 165, 166; and election of 1796, 158-59, 372, 376, 377-78, 403-4, 406, 418, 437-38, 445, 465-66; Minister to Great Britain, 151-53, 168, 174, 178, 194, 224, 322-23
Pinkney, William, 306, 506
Pintard, John, 195-99
Pintard, Lewis, 196, 197
Piracy, 14, 20, 28, 327
Pinckney Treaty, *see* Treaty of Friendship, Limits, and Navigation between the United States and Spain
Pitcairn, Joseph, 329-30, 334-35
Pitt, William, 364, 396, 415, 417
Platt, Richard: *letter from,* 140
Plymouth Co., 447
Poland, 422
Pollock, Carlisle, 78
Pollock, Oliver, 57
Ponthière, Louis de, 203
"Porcupine, Peter," 488-89
Porcupine's [Philadelphia] *Gazette and Daily Advertiser,* 489
Porcupine's Political Censor, 489
Port-au-Prince, 443
Portugal, 243-44

INDEX

Potomac Co., 312-13
Powell, John Joseph: *An Essay upon the Learning of Devices* . . . , 341-42
President (U.S.), 5-6, 176; and reports of department heads, 486; and treaties, 6, 9-10, 18-19, 22-23, 25, 31, 32, 52, 72-73, 76, 77, 89, 90, 93, 94, 95, 98, 100-1. *See also* Adams, John; Election of 1796; Washington, George
Prevost, John B., 561
Price, John, and Co., 215
Prime, Nathaniel, 211
Privateers, 228; British, 398, 427-28, 540; French, 231-32, 240-41, 242-44, 322-23, 325-26, 348, 421, 423-28, 443, 498, 552; and Jay Treaty, 84, 240-41, 327, 367-68; and prizes, 242-44, 348, 354-55, 375-76, 378
Prize goods, 429-30
Prizes: and collectors of customs, 348-51; and France, 348-50, 354-55, 367-68, 375-76, 378-80, 398, 411, 412, 423-29, 498; and Great Britain, 354-55, 375-76, 378, 379-80, 398, 427, 429, 506-7; and Jay Treaty, 354-55, 361-62, 367-68, 375-76, 378-80; and privateers, 242-44, 348, 354-55, 375-76, 378; sale of, 348-50, 354-55, 367-68, 375-76, 378-80, 412, 423-24
Prom, ―――― (Mr.), 459, 460
Provera, Giovanni, marquis de, 508
Prussia, 27-28, 30, 43, 546, 547
Public credit, 243-44; Hamilton on, 204-5, 214-15
Public debt, 22, 192, 214-15, 219-20, 381, 388, 474-75, 485; to foreign officers, 202, 203, 204, 220
Public officers: compensation of, 381, 386-87
Pufendorf, Samuel von: *Of the Law of Nature and Nations* . . . , 425
Pulaski, Casimir, 203
Pulteney, William, 141-42, 144, 166-67, 188, 189, 208, 343-44, 345, 348, 464, 478, 513, 524, 529, 538
Pulteney Associates, 120, 141-42, 343
Pulteney Association, *see* Pulteney Associates
Putnam, Rufus: *letter from*, 401-2

Rainetaux, Anthony, 357
Ramsay, David: *The History of the American Revolution*, 12-13
Randall, Thomas, 71
Randolph, Edmund, 23, 82, 85, 407, 442; *letters from* James Monroe, 330, 497; *letter from* George Washington, 245
Rawle, William, 234; *letter from* Timothy Pickering, 338; *letter to* Timothy Pickering, 338
Ray, Cornelius, 127
Ray, James, 232
"A Real Whig," 443
Rees, David, 395, 398
Rehausen, Gottfried Mauritz, baron von, 493
Republican party, 397
Revenue, 483-84, 485, 571, 574
Rhode Island, 150, 438, 474
Richery, Joseph de, 225-26
Richmond, Va., 137-38
Ricketts, James, 521; *letters from*, 234-35, 462-63
Ricketts, Sarah (Mrs. James), 252, 463, 521
Riley, Hannah (Mrs. Isaac), 250
Riley, Isaac, 250, 352, 514-15
Ringwood Iron Co., 79-80
Rivoli, 508
Robertson, William: *The History of America*, 12-13
Robinson, Alex, 456-57
Robinson, James, 532
Robinson and Hartshorne, 434
Rochefontaine, Etienne Nicolas Marie Bechet, Sieur, *see* Rochefontaine, Stephen
Rochefontaine, Stephen, 168-69; *letter from*, 146
Rogers, Moses, 127
Rogers, Richard, 498-99
Rogers, William, 78
Ross, David: *letter from*, 395-98
Rou, Baron de: *letter from*, 330
Rozier, Jean Antoine Bernard, 374-75
Russia, 546-47, 568, 574
Rutgers, Hendrick, 289
Rutledge, Charles, 154-57
Rutledge, Henry, 561, 562, 564, 565, 566

Sackett, Samuel, 462
Sadler, Henry, and Co.: *letter from*, 417-18
St. Bartholomew, 555
St. Clair, Arthur, 65, 486

St. Croix, 456
St. James Island, 458
Salt: tax on, 484
Salted fish: drawback on, 484
Sands, Comfort, 215, 252
San Ildefonso, Treaty of, 491, 526
San Lorenzo el Real, 114, 153, 181, 526
Santo Domingo, 62, 120, 192, 216, 226, 231, 232, 375, 519; French commissioners in, *see* Hugues, Victor, *and* Sonthonnax, Léger-Félicité
Saratoga, Battle of, 432
Sargent, Winthrop: *letter from* Oliver Wolcott, Jr., 222
Sawyer, Helena, 289
Schenectady, N.Y., 328
Schimmelpennick, Rutger Jan, 45, 46
Schuyler, Cornelia Van Cortlandt (Mrs. John), 455
Schuyler, Gertrude, 455
Schuyler, John, 455
Schuyler, Philip, 236, 354, 455; *letters from,* 138-40, 252, 543-44
Seaman, Edmond, 127
Secretary of State, 48. See also Pickering, Timothy; Randolph, Edmund
Secretary of the Treasury, *see* Hamilton, Alexander; Wolcott, Oliver, Jr.
Secretary of War, 48, 203. See also Knox, Henry, *and* McHenry, James
Sedgwick, Theodore, 67, 114; *letter from,* 402-7; *letters from* Jonathan Dayton, 403-4; 404; *letters to,* 473-75, 499-504, 521-23; *letter to* Jonathan Dayton, 404-7
Segonde, James, 203
Senate, 5; and Jay Treaty, 39, 64, 81, 132, 138, 148; and treaties, 6, 9-10, 18-19, 22-23, 25, 31, 32, 72-73, 76, 77, 89, 90, 93, 94, 95, 100-1; and Virginia's proposed changes in, 52-53; and George Washington's eighth annual address, 445-46
Seneca Indians, 447-48, 529, 530-31
Sequestration, 485
Servis, Peter, 489
Seton, William, 157, 392-93
Sewall, Samuel, 211
Shaw, Samuel, 71
Shaw and Randall, 70-71
Sherman, ——— (Mrs. Isaac), 317
Sherman, Isaac: *letters from,* 317, 320
Ships: merchant, arming of, 546, 571, 574
Shkleley, ——— (Capt.), 540

Sinclair, Sir John: *letter to* George Washington, 364, 366
Sinking fund, 204-5, 214-15
Sitgreaves, John: *letter to* John Steele, 331
Six Nations: treaty with, 31
Skipworth, Fulwar, 219-20, 335-36, 555, 556
Slaves, 571; tax on, proposed, 469, 483
Smith, ——— (Mrs. William M.), 460
Smith, Isaac, 448
Smith, Jeremiah, 370
Smith, Josiah, 462
Smith, Melancton, 438
Smith, Samuel, 121-22, 125-26, 136, 151
Smith, Thomas, 140
Smith, William Loughton, 243-44; *letter from* Oliver Wolcott, Jr., 484; *letters to,* 72-74, 468-69
Smith, William M., 460-61
Smith, William S., 141-43, 144, 157, 166, 185, 188, 207-8, 343-44, 345, 348, 464, 478, 529
"Smith Folly," 344
Snuff: tax on, 484
Society for Establishing Useful Manufactures, 10, 120, 197, 200-1, 234, 347
Sonthonnax, Léger-Félicité, 225-26, 553
South Carolina, 48, 151, 370, 371, 404, 406, 468, 474; U.S. Representatives from, *see* Harper, Robert G., *and* Huger, Benjamin (son), *and* Smith, William Loughton
South Carolina, 468
Soyer, Helena, 289
Spain, 432, 489; and France, 192, 485, 491, 526; and Jay Treaty, 526; king of, 422, 428; minister to U.S., 308-9; Treaty of Friendship, Limits, and Navigation with U.S. (1795), 114, 121-22, 125-26, 136, 148, 152-53, 181, 274, 300, 526; U.S. envoy to, *see* Pinckney, Thomas
Sparks, Jared: on George Washington's Farewell Address, 171, 173
Speculation: in land, *see* Land, speculation in; in securities, 45, 141-45, 262-63, 343-44; in Washington, D.C., 63-64, 232, 263, 400-1
Spoliations: of commerce, by France, 221-22, 223, 225-27, 230-32, 237-38, 321-22, 323, 359, 469-71, 485, 491-92, 498, 508, 511, 515, 519, 535, 555-56,

Spoliations *(Continued)*
  by Great Britain, 128, 224, 485, 524-27, 540-42, 552-53
Stadnitski, Peter, and Son, 45, 46
Staël von Holstein, Erik Magnus, baron, 493
Starhemberg, Ludwig Joseph Max, count von, 534-35
State Department: reports to Congress, 486
States: and Jay Treaty, 17; U.S. accounts with, 474-75
Steele, John (N.C.): *letter from,* 331-33; *letter from* John Sitgreaves, 331; *letter to,* 329
Steele, John (Va.), 156
Steele, Richard, *see* Addison, Joseph
Sterett, Samuel, 122, 392-93
Sterne, Laurence: *The Life and Opinions of Tristram Shandy,* 471-72
Steuben, Frederick William Augustus Henry Ferdinand, baron von, 120, 203
Stevens, ——— (Mrs. Edward), 162
Stevens, Edward: *letter from,* 161-62
Stevens, John, Sr., 39
Stewart, Walter, 122
Stimpson, Charles, 329
Stockholm, Andrew, 201
Stockholm, 111
Stratton, Henry, 37, 347
Strong, Caleb, 402
Strong, Joseph: *letter from,* 303-4
Sullivan, James, 255-57
Superintendent of Finance, 40
Supervisor of the revenue: for Virginia, *see* Carrington, Edward
Supreme Court of the U.S., 80, 112, 249; associate justice, *see* Wilson, James; and carriage tax case, 40-41, 54, 63, 66, 169, 206; Chief Justice, *see* Ellsworth, Oliver
Susquehanna River, 303-4, 516
Swabey, Maurice, 305-6
Swan, James, 219-20
Swanwick, John, 547-48
Sweden, 27-28, 30, 492-93, 555

Talbot, William, 453, 478, 513, 524, 529, 550-51
Talleyrand-Périgord, Charles Maurice de, 69-70, 355-56, 357, 567; *letter from,* 391-93
Talon, Antoine Omer, 515-16
Tatham, William: *letter from,* 154-57; *letter to* Rufus King, 155-56
Tatum, Absalom, 370
Taxes: direct, 469, 473-74, 483-84, 499-500; indirect, 487; proposed, 469, 483-84, 487
Taylor, Othniel, 143, 144, 167
Ten Cate, Isaac, 45
Ten Cate, Isaac, and Hendrick Vollenhoven, 45
Tennessee: admitted to Union, 209
Ternant, Jean Baptiste de, 192
Thetis, 325
Thurston, John, 127
Tichenor, Isaac, 418-19
Tilghman, William, 513, 523-24, 539; *letters from,* 258, 261; *letters to,* 254, 258, 538
Tioga County, N.Y., 75, 303
"To the Citizens of New-York," 442-43
"To the Citizens Who Shall be Convened This Day in the Fields in the City of New York," 131-34
Towers, ——— (Mr.), 457, 458, 459-60
Townsend and Franklin, 417
Tracy, Uriah: *letter from,* 547-48
Treasury Department: Assistant Secretary of, *see* Coxe, Tench, *and* Duer, William; auditor of, *see* Harrison, Richard; commissioner of the revenue, *see* Coxe, Tench; comptroller of, *see* Steele, John; register of, *see* Nourse, Joseph; reports to Congress, 486; Secretary of, *see* Hamilton, Alexander, *and* Wolcott, Oliver, Jr.
Treaties: of alliance, 17, 22, 90-91, 92; under Articles of Confederation, 5, 24, 25-31, 32, 33, 93; and boundaries, 31; classes of, 17; of commerce, 17, 22, 90-91, 92; and Congress, 13, 18-19, 91-100; and Constitution, 6-7, 9, 15-19, 22-34, 72-73, 76, 77, 89-100, 102, 105; and Constitutional Convention, 22-24, 33; as contracts, 8; defined, 8, 10, 73, 76, 77, 89, 90-96; and House of Representatives, 52; with Indians, 29, 31, 121-22, 126, 148; and legislative power, 91-100; and naturalization, 20; of peace, 17-18, 90-91, 92; powers under, 20; power to make, 6, 10, 369-70; and President, 6, 9-10, 18-19, 22-23, 25, 31, 32, 52, 72-73, 76, 77, 89, 90, 93, 94, 95, 98, 100-1; and regulation of commerce, 8-10, 17, 20, 21, 24, 27-28, 30,

INDEX 595

34, 90-92; and Senate, 6, 9-10, 18-19, 22-23, 25, 31, 32, 72-73, 76, 77, 89, 90, 93, 94, 95, 98, 100-1; as "supreme law of the land," 6, 15-16, 24; and Virginia amendments, 52
Treaties of peace and amity with: Algiers, 114, 121-22, 125-26, 136, 148, 228, 473; Morocco, 28; Tripoli, 536; Tunis, 536
Treaties with France (1778), 27-28, 30, 62, 163, 191-93, 231, 243, 367-68, 375-76, 378-80, 399-400, 409, 412, 413, 432, 433, 476, 477, 481-82, 483, 496, 497, 522-23, 545, 552, 553-54; infractions of, 421, 423-24, 427-28, 429
Treaty of Amity, Commerce, and Navigation between the United States and Great Britain, *see* Jay Treaty
Treaty of Friendship, Limits, and Navigation between the United States and Spain, 114, 121-22, 125-26, 152-53, 181, 274, 300, 526
Treaty of 1783, 17, 29, 514, 524
"Triangular Tract," 142
Tribotet, —— (Mrs.), 156
Trieste, 416
Tripoli, 536
Troup, Robert, 140, 259-60, 343, 348; Hamilton on, 381-82; *letter to* Rufus King, 472
"A True American," 442-43
Trumbull, John, 305-6, 506
Trusty, 427
Tucker, Thomas, 457
Tunis, 536
Tuscany, 490-91
Two Sicilies, the, 491

Union, 443
United Netherlands, 27-28, 30, 192, 219-20, 308-9, 416, 520; U.S. Minister to, *see* Murray, William Vans
United States: accounts with states, 474-75; Army, 245, Provisional, 546, 571, 574, reduction of, 485; boundaries, 14, 29, 31, 81, 255-57, 260-61, 310-11; frigates, construction of, 227-28, 243-44, 473-74; independence of, 432-33; jurisdiction over the sea, 424; Mint, 224, 248-49; Navy, 227-28; neutrality, 421, 423, 427, 433-34, 477; ports of, 571; seal of, 208-9; surveyor general of, *see* Putnam, Rufus
United States, 228

United States attorney for the District of: New York, *see* Harison, Richard; Pennsylvania, *see* Rawle, William
United States judge for the District of: Massachusetts, *see* Lowell, John; New York, *see* Duane, James, *and* Laurance, John, *and* Troup, Robert; North Carolina, *see* Sitgreaves, John; Pennsylvania, *see* Lewis, William, *and* Peters, Richard
United States marshal for the District of: New York. *see* Giles, Aquila
United States Sanitary Commission, 211-12
Utrecht, Treaty of, 428-29

Valesco, Don, 458, 459
Valin, René-Josué: *Nouveau Commentaire Sur L'Ordonnance de La Marine . . . ,* 424-26, 428-29, 431
Van Allen, John Evert, 116, 118, 149
Van Allen, "William" E., 116
Van Cortlandt, Philip, 121-23
Van Cortlandt, Pierre, 230
Van Cortlandt, Pierre, Jr.: *receipt to*, 230
Van Eeghen, P. and C., 45, 46
Van Polanen, Roger Gerard, 308-9
Van Rensselaer, Margaret (Mrs. Stephen), 307, 354
Van Rensselaer, Stephen, 353-54; *letter to*, 307
Van Staphorst, Jacob: *letter to* James Monroe, 220
Van Staphorst, Nicholaas, 46
Van Staphorst, Nicholaas and Jacob, 45
Van Vechten, Abraham: *letters from*, 217, 328-29
Varick, Richard, 35, 259
Vattel, Emeric de: *Law of Nations*, 7, 430
Venable, Abraham B., 447
Veneto, 416
Venton, Ann Lytton (Mrs. John Kirwan), 456
Venton, Ann Lytton (daughter), 456, 457, 458, 459, 460
Venton, John Kirwan, 456, 457, 458, 459
Vergennes, Charles Gravier, comte de, 432
Vermont, 151, 418-19; U.S. Senator from, *see* Tichenor, Isaac

Verona, 416
Verplanck, Gulian, 127, 254-55, 263, 288, 420-21, 435
Vicenza, 416
Vice President, *see* Election of 1796
Virginia, 25, 151, 313, 357; amendments to Constitution (U.S.), 52-53; and election of 1796, 372, 406; supervisor of the revenue for, *see* Carrington, Edward; U.S. Representatives from, *see* Coles, Isaac, *and* Giles, William B., *and* Madison, James, *and* Parker, Josiah, *and* Venable, Abraham B.; U.S. Senator from, *see* Mason, Stevens Thomson
Voght, John, 328-29
Vollenhoven, Hendrick, 45, 46

Wadsworth, Jeremiah, 200, 448; *letters to,* 336, 377-78, 418-19
Walker, Benjamin, 120, 141-45, 157, 166-67, 207-8, 450, 464, 478, 498-99, 529, 537, 538; *letters from,* 343-44, 345; *letter to,* 348
Walker v Morris, 142, 143
Waln, Robert, 122
Walterstorff, Ernst Frederich von, 459
War: power to declare, 17
War Department: reports to Congress, 486; Secretary of, *see* Knox, Henry, *and* McHenry, James; and Wayne-Wilkinson dispute, 252-53
Warder, John, and Co., 187
Ware v Hylton, 112
"The War in Europe," 339-40
"The Warning": No. I, 490-95, No. II, 509-12; No. III, 517-20; No. IV, 524-27; No. V, 539-42; No. VI, 551-56
Washington, Bushrod, 223-24
Washington, George, 48, 110, 118, 156, 194-95, 213-14, 216, 252-53, 505, 521; addresses of, eighth annual, 316, 317, 319, 364, 373-74, 381-88, 393-95, 408-9, 409-10, 445-46, 473, first annual, 319, first inaugural, 319 (*see also* Washington's Farewell Address); and Pierre Auguste Adet, 363, 366-71, 372-74, 399-400, 408, 410; on agriculture, 364-65, 381, 382-84; criticism of, 308, 399-400, 410, 436-37; on education and a national university, 311-14, 316, 317-18, 319, 320, 381, 384-85; and France, 224; envoy to, 238-40, 246-47, 477, Minister to, 407; Hamilton's advice requested, 66, 163, 175-78, 238-40, 293, 308-9, 314, 319, 362, 365, 367, 394, 462-77; and John Jay, 164, 166, 214-15, 239, 365, 372-73; and Jay Treaty, 39, 64-69, 76-77, 80-81, 81-103, 103-5, 106-7, 112-15, 121-23, 132, 136, 138, 148, 364, 370; and Marquis de Lafayette, 55, 110-11, 164-66; *letters from,* 55, 66, 81, 103-5, 162-66, 174-78, 204, 237-40, 292-93, 307-9, 311-14, 318-20, 320, 362-66, 366-67, 388, 393-95, 409-11, 476-77; *letter from* Gouverneur Morris, 59; *letter from* Anna de Neufville, 477; *letter from* Timothy Pickering, 170; *letters from* John Sinclair, 364, 366; *letters to,* 42-43, 64-69, 81-82, 82-83, 83-85, 85-103, 106-8, 108-9, 109, 161, 169-74, 190-95, 214-15, 225-27, 246-48, 264-88, 293-303, 316, 317-18, 320-21, 372-74, 374-75, 381-82, 389-90, 408-9, 469-71, 480-82, 498-99; *letter to* Pierre Auguste Adet, 60-61; *letter to* Robert Brooke, 312-13; *letter to* James McHenry, 245; *letter to* Timothy Pickering, 395; *letter to* Edmund Randolph, 245; *letters to* Oliver Wolcott, Jr., 65-66, 233; and James Madison, 169-70, 175-76, 295, 569; and military academy, 316, 317, 381-84, 385; on Navy, 473; and Anna de Neufville, 468, 476-77; and Charles Cotesworth Pinckney, 48, 246-47, 308-9, 319, 476-77, 480-82; and power to borrow, 231, 233, 291; praise of, 370-71; proclamation of neutrality, 182, 192, 286, 398; on Republican party, 176, 239; retirement of, 239, 247, 294, 305, 364, 371, 376-77; seeks advice of cabinet, 104-5, 170, 245; and Seneca Indians, 447-48; and Fulwar Skipworth, 335-36; and Treaty of Greenville, 128-30
Washington, D.C., 48, 313-14; land speculation in, 63-64, 232, 263, 400-1
Washington's Farewell Address: address of 1792, 169, 175-76, 294-95; advice to country, 269, 295-303; authorship of, controversy over, 172-73; on central government, 181, 277; on commerce, 181, 182, 285-86; on Constitution (U.S.), 275-76, 279, 295-96, 297, 301; and education, 311-14, 316, 317-18, 318-19; on entangling

alliances, 180, 181-82, 271, 272, 282-85; 302-3; on existing alliances, 285; first draft, 169-70, 173, 175-78, 214-15; on foreign influence, 181, 272, 284, 286, 298; and Hamilton, 168-83, 214, 239-40, 264-88, 292-303, 307-9, 311-14, 317-19, 320-21; on his administration, 286-87; on internal alliances, 275-76, 295-97; on Jay Treaty, 300; and James Madison, 169-70, 176, 295; on morality, 181, 280-81, 282, 302; on national unity, 180-81, 270-74, 295-303; and neutrality proclamation, 182, 286-87; on party spirit, dangers of, 272, 273-86, 296-300; on peace, 180, 181, 272, 281-82, 302; on presidency, 176; publication of, 170-71, 308-9, 318, 377; on public credit, 281, 302; on religion, 181, 280-81, 282, 302; on retirement, reasons for, 266-69; second term, reasons for accepting, 266-67, 294-95; on sectionalism, dangers of, 271, 273-75, 299-300; on separation of powers, 279-80, 301; on standing armies, danger of, 272; on war in Europe, 182-83

Watauga Association, 154
Watson, James, 127, 142, 262; and election of 1796, 439-42, 445-46; *letter from*, 199-200; *letter to*, 210-11
Watson, Samuel, 462
Watson and Greenleaf, 262
Wayne, Anthony, 31, 245, 252-53
Webb, Joseph D., 489
Webster, Noah, Jr., 489
Wentworth, Benning, 124
Wentworth, Sir John, 256
Wentworth, Michael, 124
Westerlo, Rensselaer, 528-29
Western lands: and establishment of a national university, 313-14
Western posts, 14, 133; evacuation of, 146, 147-48, 306-7, 526
West Point, 146
Wetmore, Seth, 352, 514-15
Wharton, Isaac, 52-53
Whelen, Israel, 122, 205-6, 390
Whipple, Abraham, 401-2
Whiskey Insurrection, 332, 396
Wigram, John, 229
Wilkes, Charles, 326, 435-36; *letter from*, 51
Wilkes, John, 432-33
Wilkinson, James, 245, 252-53

William Henry, 492
Williams, John, 475
Williams, Jonathan: *letters from*, 217-18, 304
Williams, Samuel, 214
Williamson, Charles, 144, 210, 344, 464, 478; *letter to*, 188-89
Willing, Thomas, 231-32, 248-50
Willing, Morris, and Co., 40
Willink, Wilhem, 46
Willink, Wilhem and Jan, 45
Willink, Van Staphorst, and Hubbard: *letter to* James Monroe, 219-20
Wilmington, N.C., 411
Wilson, David, 325, 337
Wilson, James, 190, 346; *letter from*, 345
Wilson, Joseph, 495-96
Wilson, William, 146, 168
Winstanley, William, 48
Winterbotham, William: *An Historical, Geographical, Commercial and Philosophical View of the United States of America* . . . , 11-13
Wolcott, Oliver, Jr., 234, 359, 393, 395, 455; and direct taxes, 469, 499-500; *letters from*, 40-41, 124, 146-49, 220-22, 230-33, 240-41, 242-44, 248, 261, 289, 292, 314-15, 348-51, 375-76, 398-400, 435-37, 569-74; *letter from* William L. Smith, 484; *letters from* George Washington, 65-66, 233; *letters to*, 69-70, 128-31, 200-1, 204-5, 211-12, 219-20, 223-24, 227-28, 250, 251, 254-55, 263, 288, 289-90, 290-91, 354-55, 361-62, 367-68, 378-80, 411-14, 420-21, 448-50, 451, 452-53, 516, 567-68; *letter to* John A. Chevallié, 357; *letter to* Timothy Pickering, 357; *letter to* Winthrop Sargent, 222; and power to borrow, 231, 233
Woronzow, Count Simon, 546-47
Wurmser, Dagobert Siegmund, count von, 416

Yazoo Co., 211
Yellow fever, 258-60, 471-72
Yrujo, Carlos Martinez, marquis de Casa, 308-9
Yznardi, Joseph M., 154, 156, 492; *letter to* Timothy Pickering, 157

Zinzendorf, Ludwig Philipp, graf von, 423